Urbanization in the Americas

World Anthropology

General Editor

SOL TAX

Patrons

CLAUDE LÉVI-STRAUSS
MARGARET MEAD
LAILA SHUKRY EL HAMAMSY
M. N. SRINIVAS

MOUTON PUBLISHERS · THE HAGUE · PARIS
DISTRIBUTED IN THE USA AND CANADA BY ALDINE, CHICAGO

Urbanization in the Americas from its Beginnings to the Present

Editors

RICHARD P. SCHAEDEL
JORGE E. HARDOY
NORA SCOTT KINZER

MOUTON PUBLISHERS · THE HAGUE · PARIS

DISTRIBUTED IN THE USA AND CANADA BY ALDINE, CHICAGO

General Editor's Preface

Urban anthropology – the study of modern cities and their problems – is a relatively new and rapidly growing specialty. But it has deep roots in the discovery of "lost" cities of antiquity, including the excavation of cities which flourished in the western hemisphere long before the European era. This book brings into a single frame pictures of the old, the newer, and the newest. And it turns out that at least in the Americas the problems of cities have not changed. The book not only carries through in time but is fully interdisciplinary and international. It owes its origin to a series of brilliant symposia at successive meetings of the International Congress of Americanists, followed by a conference in Oshkosh, Wisconsin, which was part of the worldwide Congress which accounts for the emergence of this series of books.

Like most contemporary sciences, anthropology is a product of the European tradition. Some argue that it is a product of colonialism, with one small and self-interested part of the species dominating the study of the whole. If we are to understand the species, our science needs substantial input from scholars who represent a variety of the world's cultures. It was a deliberate purpose of the IXth International Congress of Anthropological and Ethnological Sciences to provide impetus in this direction. The *World Anthropology* volumes, therefore, offer a first glimpse of a human science in which members from all societies have played an active role. Each of the books is designed to be self-contained; each is an attempt to update its particular sector of scientific knowledge and is written by specialists from all parts of the world. Each volume should be read and reviewed individually as a separate volume on its own given subject. The set as a whole will indicate what changes are in store for anthropology as scholars from the developing countries join in studying the species of which we are all a part.

The IXth Congress was planned from the beginning not only to include as many of the scholars from every part of the world as possible, but also with a view toward the eventual publication of the papers in high-quality volumes. At previous Congresses scholars were invited to bring papers which were then read out loud. They were necessarily limited in length; many were only summarized; there was little time for discussion; and the sparse discussion could only be in one language. The IXth Congress was an experiment aimed at changing this. Papers were written with the intention of exchanging them before the Congress, particularly in extensive pre-Congress sessions; they were not intended to be read aloud at the Congress, that time being devoted to discussions – discussions which were simultaneously and professionally translated into five languages. The method for eliciting the papers was structured to make as representative a sample as was allowable when scholarly creativity – hence self-selection – was critically important. Scholars were asked both to propose papers of their own and to suggest topics for sessions of the Congress which they might edit into volumes. All were then informed of the suggestions and encouraged to rethink their own papers and the topics. The process, therefore, was a continuous one of feedback and exchange and it has continued to be so even after the Congress. The some two thousand papers comprising *World Anthropology* certainly then offer a substantial sample of world anthropology. It has been said that anthropology is at a turning point; if this is so, these volumes will be the historical direction markers.

As might have been foreseen in the first post-colonial generation, the large majority of the Congress papers (82 percent) are the work of scholars identified with the industrialized world which fathered our traditional discipline and the institution of the Congress itself: Eastern Europe (15 percent); Western Europe (16 percent); North America (47 percent); Japan, South Africa, Australia, and New Zealand (4 percent). Only 18 percent of the papers are from developing areas: Africa (4 percent); Asia-Oceania (9 percent); Latin America (5 percent). Aside from the substantial representation from the U.S.S.R. and the nations of Eastern Europe, a significant difference between this corpus of written material and that of other Congresses is the addition of the large proportion of contributions from Africa, Asia, and Latin America. "Only 18 percent" is two to four times as great a proportion as that of other Congresses; moreover, 18 percent of 2,000 papers is 360 papers, 10 times the number of "Third World" papers presented at previous Congresses. In fact, these 360 papers are more than the total of *all* papers published after the last International

Congress of Anthropological and Ethnological Sciences which was held in the United States (Philadelphia, 1956).

The significance of the increase is not simply quantitative. The input of scholars from areas which have until recently been no more than subject matter for anthropology represents both feedback and also long-awaited theoretical contributions from the perspectives of very different cultural, social, and historical traditions. Many who attended the IXth Congress were convinced that anthropology would not be the same in the future. The fact that the next Congress (India, 1978) will be our first in the "Third World" may be symbolic of the change. Meanwhile, sober consideration of the present set of books will show how much, and just where and how, our discipline is being revolutionized.

Closely related to the subject matter of this book are others in the series on the Americas, ancient and modern; on urbanism, population, ethnicity, migration; politics and development; economic and social problems, including conflict; and on architecture, art, archaeology, and folklore in many parts of the world.

Chicago, Illinois SOL TAX
September 10, 1976

Table of Contents

Introduction: Two Thousand Years of Urbanization in the Americas

RICHARD P. SCHAEDEL, JORGE E. HARDOY, and
NORA SCOTT KINZER

THEMES, APPROACHES, AND THE SEARCH FOR COMMONALITIES

This volume provides a sampling of papers presented at the series of symposia on Urbanization Processes in America held since 1966. These symposia provided a forum with an immense scope, in terms of time and space, and covered a wide variety of topics, ranging from humanistic philosophy to scientific theory. The editors have selected the papers appearing in Section I from the first four symposia, which were held in conjunction with the Americanist Congresses. Section II contains papers presented at a fifth, extraordinary symposium organized as part of the International Congress of Anthropological and Ethnological Sciences in Chicago, which represented an effort to broaden the basis of discussion even farther.

Seen as a whole, the symposia touched upon virtually every imaginable aspect of the urbanization process. Case histories of almost every Latin American country were reviewed in terms of three broad time parameters (prehistoric, colonial, and republican-contemporary). Comparative macrostructural studies involving North, Central, and South America were synthesized. The dawn of urbanism in all three regions was examined and its culmination in metropolises of 10,000,000 diagnosed. Cholula, Ciudad Guayana, Chanchán, and Pernambuco competed for attention with Potosí, Taxco, Antigua, and La Serena as exemplars of various hypotheses of urbanization along with the more familiar pristine or contemporary urban giants such as Buenos Aires, Mexico City, Cuzco, or São Paulo. Architects discussed town planning with archaeologists, investment strategies and urban land speculation with economists, and decision making on squatters settlements with anthropologists and political scientists. Art historians and historians, along with geographers, sociologists, and ethnohistorians, examined theses on shifting roles, over a two-thousand-year time span and within a myriad of culturally contrasting conditions, of shrine, palace, and market place and changing world views.

Argentines, Germans, Peruvians, Brazilians, Mexicans, Belgians, and many others joined in as the seat of the symposia moved from Mar del Plata to Stuttgart to Lima to Rome and finally to Chicago. Despite the varied interests that the wide variety of themes stimulated among such a broad spectrum of scholars, the outstanding quality that sustained these convocations was a shared concern to determine the commonality of urban processes. From the start of the symposia, the consensus of the coordinators was that these commonalities did indeed exist, but that there was no way of knowing how time-specific or area-specific they would be.

For this reason, no general theme was proposed for the first two symposia. Papers were invited and programmed primarily with major epochs in mind, so that certain disciplines or subdisciplines tended to cluster in those sessions where their expertise was traditionally relevant. By the third symposium in Lima, a bold experiment was launched, and themes were proposed which were broad enough to be treated in all three time frames. While not spectacularly successful in eliciting non-time-specific commonalities, the experiment produced a spate of theoretically significant papers (this partly accounts for the predominance of the papers selected from this symposium). In the fourth symposium, coordinators retrenched somewhat. A general theme of the city and its area of influence was chosen, and half the symposium was dedicated to treating this theme in paired sessions, using macrostructural and microstructural formats. For the first time there was an interface between adherents of the two approaches. The themata proved more congenial to human geographers, sociologists, and social anthropologists, who heretofore had been rather scantily represented and who were to make substantial contributions in the next gatherings. The fifth symposium, the extraordinary session at the International Congress of Anthropological and Ethnological Sciences, provided the opportunity of testing the relevancy of the premises in the larger scope of urbanization processes in other parts of the world. Unlike the last two preceding symposia, no theme or temporal parameter was specified, with the objective of observing whether themes or parameters would emerge of their own accord.

A short history of the dynamics of the five symposia will help place the present volume in its proper perspective. (See the Appendix for a complete listing of papers and participants for the first four symposia.)

A DIGEST OF SYMPOSIA I, II, III, AND IV

Mar del Plata (1966)

The first symposium on urbanization was permeated by an atmosphere of inquiry into what the different disciplines focusing on the urbanization process might have in common and what techniques and information might be profitably exchanged. The large component of archaeologists within the symposium tended to shift the thrust of the papers and discussions in the direction of defining, if possible, the general characteristics and variations in the urbanization process. A certain consensus emerged that autogenous urbanization (the specific domain of the archaeologists) represented a relatively rare constellation of three simultaneous subprocesses (nucleation, population growth, differentiation *cum* specialization), whereas derived urbanization (whether imposed or indirect, via stimulus diffusion) was by far the more common process. In the first case ecological factors seem to represent the crucial determinants, while in the second the significant variable would be the mix of sociopolitical and economic functions performed in established urban hierarchies.

Viewed in this light, the examples of colonial urbanization represent studies of derived – and specifically of imposed – urbanization. Several foci for research emerged. Most important and general, perhaps, was the focus on identifying different patterns in colonial America, particularly in Brazil and Hispanic America but also regarding French, Dutch, and Anglo-American urbanization. Of almost equal importance was the identification of "stages " within the colonial period which might in a general way serve to operationalize certain overall trends hypothesized by Morse, from centrifugality in the sixteenth and seventeenth centuries to centripetality in the late eighteenth and much more markedly in the late nineteenth century. Another seminal focus was introduced by Hardoy, who set up a preliminary scheme for ranking colonial cities in the late sixteenth and seventeenth centuries and established a methodology for determining the basic functions of cities.

In concentrating on the primary function of cities, much of the disparity between disciplinary approaches could be resolved. Many papers on colonial urbanization focused on the administrative, religious, or defensive functions. As studies by Kubler and Guarda illustrated, by analyzing the cities in terms of their primary functions, pre-Hispanic and colonial continuities emerge which point to certain commonalities in the spatial concentration of the population which have been hitherto ignored.

Morse and Mann introduced other central foci that bore fruit in the later symposia. Morse drew attention to the need for explaining Latin

American urbanization as a recent (nineteenth/twentieth-century) special variant of world urbanization trends, insisting on both a structural and ideological orientation. Mann stressed the need for utilizing density-intensity indices, not only in contemporary cities, but as universal criteria for measuring thresholds of qualitative and quantitative human productivity.

Stuttgart (1968)

The next symposium tended to "flesh out" problems within the three broad time periods by developing possibilities of explicating crucial variables, contrasting variant urbanization patterns, and putting them in comparative focus. Some progress was achieved along these lines for the prehistoric time period in contrasting overall urbanization trends between highlands and lowlands. This was accomplished by operationalizing Inca and Chimú urban hierarchies (Thompson, Rodríguez Suy Suy) according to community patterns along lines suggested by Price, utilizing an implicit criterion of site stratification.

The papers on colonial urbanization explored one of the main research directions called for in the first symposium, defining and debating the relevance of the complex ingredients of the imposed urbanization during the sixteenth century ("the key to the American urban spatial structure"); this was well exemplified in the presentations of Kubler, Hardoy, and Palm, and Gasparini and Bonet added valuable case histories. Another sequel was the much-needed documentation on the economic function of colonial cities (in presentations by participants Pohl, Tschuhl, Hartung) and further explanation of how the administrative function was implemented in theory and practice (by Markman, Robertson, Verlinden, and Liehr).

The nineteenth/twentieth-century phase was better represented this time, presenting diverse views on the significance of current urban trends and emphasizing the probable distortions of population concentration diagnosed as tertiarization and primacy (by Matos Mar, Iutaka, and King).

The underdocumented nineteenth-century antecedents for these phenomena were dealt with in papers on Argentina (by Cortés Conde) and Peru (by Morse).

Lima (1970)

By the end of the second symposium enough research foci had been identified to invoke what had been a latent potential of these sessions from the beginning, the treatment of a single phenomenon or set of phenomena in three different time periods. The themes selected revolved around the general theme of "urban transformation" in three parameters: transformation of people (class stratification and realignments of the differentiated components of the social system); urban density transformation (envelopment or segregation); and regional or areal (macrospatial) transformation (the structural realignment of axial networks of cities or of urban hierarchies). Six specific topics were chosen that could be dealt with through the tripartite temporal prisms:

1. High primacy. This was identified as a prevailing though not universal characteristic of recent Latin American urbanization (e.g. Browning and Davis' early publications). In a processual context it was seen as a problem of determining under what conditions the type of population consolidation represented by the capital of the nation-state (or major subdivisions of an empire) is determinant in the origin and growth of the primate city.

2. Urbanization and natural resource transformation. This theme was directed at the identification of the ecological determinants of urbanization that emerged in previous symposia at all three time levels. The contrast between the urban system/resource base "counterpoint" of pre-Hispanic, colonial and pre- or proto-industrial independent Latin American economies and societies was brought out in clear relief by the papers of Bonavía, Mauro, and Cortés Conde. (In the fourth symposium Morse deepened this analysis within the nineteenth century by including areas of the United States with many contrapuntal regions of Latin America.)

3. The determinants of urban hierarchies. This theme, like the first two, is derived from spatial transformation, but is specifically concerned with the systems or networks of cities. It was closely related to the next topic.

4. Foreign influences in the formation of urban hierarchies. The actual sessions, judging from the contributions in the prehistoric and colonial periods, did not produce the desired concentration of focus, but the overall impact of these themes was to enunciate the thesis, first expounded by Quijano (1968), that urbanization in Latin America was essentially the spatial manifestation of external and internal dependency or colonialism. This was explicated in paradigmatic form by Rofman and Kaplan with more emphasis on the sociocultural concomitants of modernization, a processual construct that is frequently confused with recent Latin American urbanization. As a consequence of this emphasis on dependency and its relationship to tertiarization, many of the sessions in the fourth symposium had these processes as their explicanda.

5.   Sectoral transformations. This topic derives from the main theme of "people transformation," i.e. the change in occupational categories from primary to secondary and tertiary sectors. Mamalakis presented a much needed graphic compilation of sectoral trends providing a macroframework for further research on tertiarization/urbanization correlation for all Latin American countries (1950–1965). Price attempted to apply a kind of sectoral breakdown of the population to pre-Hispanic cities of Mesoamerica, a point tangentially referred to in Schaedel's paper for the Andean littoral urban centers.

6.   Related to the sectoral transformation of people by occupational categories was the topic on the internal structure of cities, which had to do with the human realignments in density transformations, either in an agglutinative or isolating format. Scobie treated the phenomenon in Buenos Aires when the immigration impact was most noticeable (1875–1914). His suggested proposition indicates that the Latin American *conventillo* [slum] and *barriada* [squatment] patterns (successive types of settlement manifestations of accelerated internal migration to the large cities) had an earlier counterpart in accelerated immigration; and that the effect of rapid population increase on sectoral transformation was probably more delayed in the earlier Argentine case in reducing the marginality of immigrants than has been true for contemporary *barriada* dwellers (internal migrants). Calnek compared the process of population absorption in pre-Hispanic Teotihuacán and Tenochtitlán, indicating that the latter had a more agglutinative structure than the former.

Rome (1972)

The first session was on the general topic of how urban systems were conditioned or determined by sociopolitical systems. Hardoy's paper, which dealt with all three major time periods (pre-Hispanic, colonial, and nineteenth-century-to-modern) in terms of case histories, proposed the thesis that Latin American urbanization has been a process imposed from without by conquering or dominating groups throughout its two-thousand-year history. The position was also taken that sociopolitical systems determine the productive system, which in turn determines the spatial structure (urbanization pattern). The cases of the Inca empire, the early colonial town foundings by Ovando and Pedrarias, and urbanization in Castro's Cuba were used to illustrate the prevailing role of the sociopolitical system.

Katz's paper reinforced the example of the Inca sociopolitical system cited by Hardoy, while contrasting the sociocultural and demographic composition of Tenochtitlán and Cuzco.

Morse, departing sharply from Hardoy's position that external dependency was the major cause for the Latin American urbanization process, directed himself to sweeping analogies and contrasts between the urbanization process in the United States and Latin America. He took care to separate the sociopolitical (but more clearly the cultural) factors from the economic and ecological variables, and in so doing attempted to explain the different patterns of urbanization in the two areas, at least since the end of the eighteenth century, as a consequence of different hierarchies of values. Yet one may note that the "elitism" which dominates "privatism" in Morse's Latin American scale of values is not unlike Hardoy's conceptualization of the political and economic power-holding groups that he sees as ordaining the spatial structure over time to best fulfill their own requirements.

The emphasis in the second session was on microstructural phenomena involved in the urban systems, specifically on the mechanisms of articulation (economic, sociopolitical, religious, cultural) between the lowest rungs of urban hierarchy and the rural microsocieties (hamlets or villages). Schaedel briefly defined the linkage mechanisms through which the rural settlements articulate with the macrostructure of the nation-state as reflected in the urban system. He then analyzed the changes in these linkage mechanisms in the past few decades under the impact of agrarian reform programs, particularly in Venezuela, Mexico, Peru, and Bolivia. He stressed that the rural community has its own dynamics, the principal function of which is the renewability of its resources; that the urban hierarchies have consistently ignored or exploited the rural hinterland, thereby disadvantaging themselves as ultimate consumers of resources and forcing the rural communities to adopt the unwanted path of migration to hyperurbanized centers, causing a minimal man/land ratio within an ever-shrinking ecological potential. He suggests a restructuring of the urban-rural linkages to provide a two-way flow of information, resource renewability, and reciprocal terms of trade between the urban hierarchies and the rural communities. Such restructuring of the traditional unidirectional, urban-dominated pattern could resolve both the rural-urban imbalance and the threat to shrinking national ecological potential.

Torres Rivas presented case histories of urban-rural imbalances in the Central American countries. He detailed the different tendencies in the growing pauperization and proletarianization of rural manpower, leading to high degrees of precarious temporary migrant labor and seasonal immigrant labor, as well as spontaneous colonization of doubtful permanence, and urbanization. Whether the prevailing situation is one (as in Salvador) of a basically impoverished ladino but still non-proletarianized peasantry (with an excess labor force ratio of 40:1), or a basically indigenous one (as in Guatemala) operating within the constraints of the "internal colonialism" syndrome, the imbalance in terms of un- and underemployed rural population and a minimally industrialized, export-oriented urban sector has grown within the past twenty-five years to critical proportions. Furthermore, the migration to the capital city is predominantly from the smaller urban centers, and the processes of rural-rural migration and immigration represent only palliative solutions, increasing the insecurity of the rural population.

Clearly this is a situation where traditional, unidirectional linkage mechanisms (political and economic) continue to operate to the detriment of the microsociety, despite the one abortive effort to restructure them "from the top down" in Guatemala's agrarian reform. The Central American situation (with the possible exception of Costa Rica) resembles Cuba prior to Castro, except for a lesser degree of unionization of the salaried work force and less absorptive capacity of the capital cities for rural migrants. Whether the linkages, particularly political and economic ones, may be restructured by altering the cultural and religious linkages (as Torres suggests in a single example in Guatemala), or whether the structural bases for these linkages are transformed by force (as the traditional ones have been maintained by force), the existing pattern of excessive horizontal mobility in the rural areas (already characterized by high indices of violence) can be expected to trigger pressures to reorder urban-rural relations.

Preston's paper on rural-urban transformation documented a significant type of microsocietal response to restructuring linkage mechanism with the macrosociety (mentioned in Schaedel's paper) when dominant political and economic constraints were removed with agrarian reform. This type of response was the creation of "new towns" or the introduction of a "new stratum" into the Bolivian urban hierarchy.

The contrast between the case histories of restructured urban-rural linkages in countries with effective agrarian reform (referred to by Schaedel and Preston) and those without it (described by Torres) points to an important variable between the macrosocieties involved. Both Bolivia and Central American countries represent outstanding examples of the "dependency syndrome," but the economic raw materials base in Bolivia was minerals, while in Central America it was export agriculture. The dominant unidirectional pattern of urban-rural linkages in the Central American countries was therefore reinforced by foreign influences (through the support of conservative elites) upon which the nation's export earnings and economic elite depended. In Bolivia, with the collapse of the mining economy and its subsequent nationalization, the climate for restructuring land-tenure patterns was favorable, and such restructuring eliminated the traditional economic restraint. In Bolivia no reinforcement from foreign sources interfered with the restructuring process since agricultural exports were not the basis for the dependency, however much foreign influence was a determinant in reestablishing it in the mining and petroleum sector.

The third session was devoted to regional case studies of the relations between urban and sociopolitical systems. Viotti discussed the nineteenth-century situation in Brazil, describing the transformation in power and investment directed by oligarchic mercantile groups from one strongly based on export of raw materials and ports to one dynamizing both the internal and external markets. Kemper's paper, essentially a microcosmic view of one source of migration to cities, showed how in the microsociety (Tzinztunzan, Mexico) the independent variable of demographic growth (lower mortality since 1940) has been the primary source of (1) seasonal outmigration and slow urbanization and (2) urbanization primarily to Ciudad Mexico so that the village, even while doubling its population in thirty years, maintained its equilibrium. He also illustrated the secondary effects of unequal terms of trade as hampering thrusts toward higher productive potential within the microsociety, which was further exacerbated by derived consumption "needs" diffused through "modernization affects" of seasonal outmigration. The "urbanization" of the village (which is incidentally a *municipio* capital and hence formally if not demographically "urban") is described in cultural terms that could be denominated "modernization" (e.g. more consumer goods, more literacy, more information flow). Structural differences are reflected in what appears to be a trend toward unequal redistribution of the surplus (referred to in Schaedel's paper) from a preexistent pattern of reciprocal redistribution, presumably maintained through leveling mechanisms. This is reflected in the stratification pattern, the growth of "laborers" and "miscellaneous services" *vis-à-vis* farmers, even though the village remains essentially a craft-specialized village (47 percent in pottery making). The transformation of the labor force into pottery retailers and new occupations may ultimately generate enough income to maintain the urban patterns of differential redistribution. The rate of population growth in the next decade should indicate whether the villagers stabilize in the lower rungs of the urban hierarchy or revert to a rural structure.

The fourth session was originally planned to focus on the "upper levels" of rural (or micro-) society and to examine the relationships that define structural differences (if they indeed exist) between the rural and the urban (macro-) systems. Price's paper was directed at identifying the juncture diachronically, i.e. that point in time when the largest of the species of microsociety (which anthropologists generally classify as chiefdoms or *señorios*) develop into a state (the pristine form of macrosociety). The main conclusion from her analysis of the pre-Columbian transitions in Mesoamerica and the Andes was that states can exist without a city community pattern, but that the state-type polity is a necessary requisite for the city community pattern. Considerable debate ensued as to whether the Mochica and Tikal polities as inferred from their respective archaeological settlement patterns could be considered nonurban states, or represented nonegalitarian paramount chiefdoms that illustrated the inherent incapacity of microsocietal institutions to integrate widespread but densely clustered populations.

Markman presented the case history of the microsociety during colonial times, using the experience of the Dominican order in colonial Chiapas and Guatemala. Although the Dominicans identified their town planning as an instrument of urbanization, the end products – as Markman penetratingly points out – were in many cases "essentially Christian ceremonial centers." Thus the Dominicans, by replacing the old ceremonial focus, reified one of the necessary conditions for urbanism without effecting it. The cases in which the Dominican experiment succeeded represent imposed urbanization in which the introduction of the political and economic institutions of the macrosociety provided the sufficient conditions for urbanism. The significance of Markman's contribution was to show the persistence and perhaps revitalization of the proto-urban settlement type of ceremonial center, adapted to a new religion during the colonial period. This phenomenon had been previously suggested by Kubler (for Cholula) and by Schaedel (for the Peruvian altiplano).

Buechler dealt with the main theme synchronically, using Bolivian case histories. He showed that "traditional" patterns of culture at the village level do not necessarily vanish with urbanization and "modernization" but on the contrary are invigorated by these transformations. The conventional dichotomy between "traditional" and "modern" structures is thus rendered questionable. Each may sustain the other when urbanization leads to higher levels of macrosocietal integration: the countryside becomes "urbanized" and the cities continue to receive sociocultural inputs from the villages. Singelmann's commentary was directed to Buechler's presentation, and a debate ensued, largely stimulated by the chairman's proposal of discarding the urban-rural dichotomy as a heuristic device. His point was further elaborated in the paper that he presented in the final session.

The fifth session was focused on the theme of "supplying the city." Calnek concerned himself with the growth of a supply system for

Tenochtitlán during the fifteenth and early sixteenth century. His use of ethnohistorical data demonstrated the intricate and necessary relationship that existed between the coordination of the lacrustine resources (upon which Tenochtitlán depended for food supply) and the primary growth of Tenochtitlán.

De Solano, recognizing that the theme was being treated for the first time for colonial cities, proposed a methodology for attacking the problem. His suggestions for short-term analysis concentrated on sociocultural variables, and for long-term studies on ecological factors. The interaction of the two might well be illustrated by a case study of the supply of colonial Mexico City, as contrasted with Tenochtitlán.

Mamalakis developed the supply theme by an analysis of recent urban-rural allocations of services (both by product and persons employed). He showed empirically what has often been suggested, that services have catered principally to cities not only to the detriment of the hinterland but to the country's overall welfare as well. This finding based upon macrostructural analysis was in substantial agreement with Schaedel's postulation regarding the overall disequilibrium produced by depleting the microsocietal (rural village) resource base.

The sixth session was devoted to analyzing the city as a center of transformation in three distinct time periods. Millon used the example of America's earliest city, Teotihuacán, to show how the transformational function (principally manufacture of cutting tools, but also involving construction materials) came to absorb up to one fourth of the resident population. The intense elaboration of its ceremonial function, together with marketing, provided the dynamics for urbanizing ever-increasing rural migrants until an estimated peak total of 160,000 had been reached by the eighth century.

In dealing with the transformational process in the nineteenth-century Latin American city, Singer emphasized the essentially exploitative role of cities in extracting resources and manpower from their hinterlands, deriving this process from the colonial model of the conquest city. Throughout subsequent phases of commercialization and import-substitutive industrialization, the kinds of transformations of products and people only benefited the urban areas.

The disequilibrium in spatial structure that Singer outlined for the nineteenth and early twentieth century was developed for the contemporary Latin American city by Rofman. He analyzed the current situation as a metropolitanization process, in which the crucial determinants of spatial structure rest increasingly with multinational corporations and other corporate investment strategies which, when not external to the countries concerned, are beneficial to a small internal elite. This only exacerbates the disequilibrium. These new metropolitan conglomerates have developed and continue to expand under principles that are in strong opposition to optimum national spatial concentration of population *vis-à-vis* resource potential. This process is viewed as counterproductive in terms of urban planning criteria and of the economic cost to the total society.

In session seven, devoted to migration, the emphasis switched from the transformation of products to that of people. Borah and Cook, dealing with some of the scarce colonial data, produced evidence to show that, contrary to what has often been assumed, Mexican cities actually "maintained themselves through their own live births and even gained some increase." Although rural-urban migration occurred, it was sharply limited by the rule of inverse distance.

Browning analyzed the "tertiarization" problem, calling for a more sophisticated disaggregation of "sectors," particularly the tertiary, in order to determine the real absorptive capacity of the occupational structure of Latin American cities. Browning's own data from Monterrey tends to show that for this industrial city there was no noticeable trend for persons with low socioeconomic antecedents to concentrate in the service sectors. He suggested that more careful analysis is needed from economists and sociologists to reevaluate and perhaps upgrade the developmental role of the services.

Leeds proposed a series of tentative propositions about urbanization that would encompass and subordinate, if not eliminate, polar axes such as rural and urban. These propositions would ultimately depend upon a general theory of "the evolution of specialization," with concomitant coordination systems and subsystems.

Summation of the First Four Symposia

One of the main accomplishments of the symposia was the identification of the major problems and alternate diagnoses at the macrostructural level. The symposia have also served to delineate research directions and to see that these directions were pursued. By initially establishing and more or less consistently utilizing functional definitions of urban types and urban systems (Schaedel, Hardoy, and Morse), the symposia have contributed to explicating the shift in predominance within cities and urban systems of the political, economic-ecological, or ideological (cultural, religious) functions over time. The relevance of the dynamics of the changing prevailing functions of cities was evident in the synchronic studies of Mamalakis and Browning in the third and fourth symposia on growth of the service sector, hinting at what appears to be a new, predominantly service function of cities (interstitial to political and economic functions).

The interdependence of distinct sets of urban and rural phenomena in explicating urban trends and their consequences was another problem area identified and diagnosed. The two-way nature of the urbanization feedback as seen from the rural community was stressed, and the various mechanisms of rural or rural-urban juncture points were elucidated. With these sets in analytical balance the important question was raised of the desirability of "hypercephalization" trends in terms of their repercussions on total resource renewability and national ecological balance. Consensus between the positions reached by macrostructural analysis and those attained through summaries of microstructural research was achieved. Discussions brought out the point that current decision-making policy (or lack of same) on urbanization in Latin American countries should be directed at refocusing investment in intermediate regional levels and microstructural rural economies in order to guide a more balanced distribution of population and at obtaining a more functional relationship between space-intensive clusters and underutilized resource bases. This implies the reorientation or creation of a viable urban policy and is what Hardoy refers to as "urban reform."

The main directions for future research appear to have been two: (1) research of an applied character, having to do with urban reform (whether from the human/spatial engineering-ecology-resource base orientation, or from devising transformational allocations of manpower which are more harmonious [but still productive] than those generated by the counterproductive supply-and-demand process manipulated by private enterprise); and (2) research with a more theoretical focus, which will identify and weigh the variables determining thresholds of urbanization on micro- or macrostructural levels. These two directions are clearly complementary. Given the climate of awareness in both Latin America and the United States regarding the need for urban reform and the current experimentation (e.g. Cuba, Chile, Venezuela, and Peru), and the role of these symposia in encouraging constant, up-to-date feedback between theoretical and applied research, it was felt that all should benefit from the microstructural/macrostructural, synchronic/diachronic interplay of these symposia.

The Extraordinary Session in Chicago

At the suggestion of Sol Tax, an extraordinary symposium was organized as part of the International Congress of Anthropological and Ethnological Sciences in Chicago. The purpose of this special symposium was twofold. First, the Urbanization in the Americas "serial" would be given a broader exposure, particularly to test whether some of the commonalities which had emerged might be relevant to urbanization processes in Africa, Asia, and other continents. It was hoped that there would be a forum of urbanists from these areas that would stimulate discussion on the issues. The second objective was frankly experimental. It consisted in not specifying a theme (as we had done in the last two previous symposia) or even a temporal parameter (urbanization in the western hemisphere was our only topical requirement). We hoped by this approach to objectively test "where the action was" in terms of current urbanization research both (1) to act as a control on our organizational perspicacity in the future, and (2) to see if there was any prevailing centripetality of focus in the studies volunteered. Although an effort was made to encourage Latin American and European participation to redress what we considered to be a certain imbalance in the high proportion of North American contributions, due to budgetary difficulties this idea had to be scrapped.

The results can be seen in the papers presented in Section II of the present volume, with a commentary by Nora Kinzer. They could also be observed in the discussion at the general meeting in Chicago and in the interface among participants at the workshop meetings held a week before the general sessions. Regarding the workshop, the most singular innovation was the significant participation of women, which might have been due, at least in part, to the coordinators' original decision to delegate primary responsibility for the organization and focus of this extraordinary session to Nora Kinzer. This new source may account for the interest in contemporary ethnic, occupational, and sex groups and in network analysis, which was manifest for the first time in the history of the symposia. Previously, the sociological and anthropological focus had been almost exclusively on macro-structural groupings.

Yet another new direction was the thrust toward situational case analysis. This package of contributions seems to represent a kind of centrifugal direction, characteristic of the "fact-gathering" stage in any science, which has apparently evolved out of a refinement or even a dissatisfaction with the hypotheses on urban change in precolonial and colonial historical periods.

In the general session, the coordinators presented a synthesis of the workshop session and a brief exposition of the nature of the symposia, including some of the more general conclusions that had emerged regarding primacy, tertiarization, and urban reform in Latin America that might be area-specific or comparable to urban trends in other broad areas, particularly of the Third World.

In approximately an hour of discussion at Chicago, representatives from other meetings on urbanization and urbanism – particularly those from the Near East and Africa – contributed valuable commentaries and questions; this suggested the desirability of establishing a mechanism for periodically assembling and discussing data on comparative urbanization in world-wide (or at least Third-World-wide) perspective. Some progress along these lines has been made, but this ambitious hope can only be realized when urbanists from other broad regions have established some group similar to the core group of the Latin American urbanists in order to synthesize the consensus of their findings.

Aftermath

The regular biennial pattern of the Urbanization in the Americas symposia was resumed in the Forty-first International Congress of Americanists in Mexico City in 1974. The influence of the extraordinary session was felt with the incorporation of a strong contingent of social anthropologists presenting microstructural analyses of contemporary urban living and migratory behavior. The proportion of women participating was also high. There was some debate as to whether the symposia should continue to blend the urban-historical approach with a contemporary social-science approach. Since then a new journal has come into being (*Journal of Urban History*) which may represent a gravitational point for the more historically minded urbanists. The evaluation sessions of the Mexico City symposium, however, produced consensus that the symposia should persevere in their holistic quest. The sixth regular biennial session in Paris in 1976 will be focused on a review of accomplishments and a definition of the commonalities so far perceived.

APPENDIX: PAPERS AND PARTICIPANTS IN THE SYMPOSIA ON URBANIZATION IN AMERICA

FIRST SYMPOSIUM (37TH CONGRESS OF AMERICANISTS, MAR DEL PLATA, 1966)

Pre-Hispanic Period (Coordinator, Richard P. Schaedel)

SESSION I – Terminology, Methodology, and Definition of Concepts
Chairman: Ralph L. Beals (University of California, Los Angeles)
Discussants: Pedro Armillas (University of Southern Illinois)
                   John Murra (Institute of Andean Investigations, New York and Lima)
                   William T. Sanders (Pennsylvania State University)

Papers presented:
1. Richard P. Schaedel (University of Texas): "On the definition of civilization, urban, city and town in prehistoric America"
2. William A. Longacre (University of Arizona): "Urbanization in pre-Columbian America: some methodological suggestions from non-urban research in the southwestern United States"
3. William J. Mayer-Oakes (University of Manitoba): "A model for the study of pre-Spanish urbanization in the Valley of Mexico"
4. R. T. Zuidema (Holland; Universidad de Huamanga, Peru): "The relation between the pre-Hispanic settlement patterns and the principles derived from the Inca social structure"
5. Lawrence Mann: "Activity density-intensity analysis – a research framework for ancient settlements and modern cities"

SESSION II – Incipient and Peripheral Forms of Urbanization
Chairman: Gordon R. Willey (Harvard University)
Discussants: William T. Sanders (Pennsylvania State University)
              William A. Longacre (University of Arizona)
Papers presented:
1. Melvin L. Fowler (University of Wisconsin, Milwaukee): "The temple town community: Cahokia and Amalucan compared"
2. Donald E. Thompson (University of Wisconsin, Madison): "Provincial Incaic installations in the Huanuco area"
3. Duccio Bonavía (Museo Nacional de Antropología y Arqueología, Lima): "Population centers on the *montaña* frontier of Ayacucho"
4. Marta Ottonello de García Reynoso and Guillermo Madrazo (Museo Etnográfico, Buenos Aires): "Types of pre-Hispanic centers on the Argentine *puna* and its borders"

SESSION III – Planned Urban Centers in Central and South America
Chairman: Jorge E. Hardoy (Consejo Nacional de Investigaciones, Argentina)
Discussants: William J. Mayer-Oakes (University of Manitoba)
              Pedro Armillas (University of Southern Illinois)
Papers presented:
1. William T. Sanders (Pennsylvania State University): "Growth and subsequent course of urbanization in the Valley of Teotihuacán"
2. René Millon (University of Rochester): "Latest conclusions on America's earliest city"
3. Horst Hartung (Universidad de Guadalajara): "Urban interpretations of Tikal, Copan, Uxmal and Chichén Itzá"
4. Erwin Walter Palm (University of Heidelberg): "Observations regarding the plan of Tenochtitlán"
5. Antonio Rodríguez Suy Suy (Universidad Nacional de Trujillo): "Chan Chán: an adobe metropolis, its ecological base"

SESSION IV
Chairman: Richard P. Schaedel (University of Texas)
Discussants: Donald E. Thompson (University of Wisconsin, Madison)
              Melvin L. Fowler (University of Wisconsin, Milwaukee)
Papers presented:
1. Pedro Armillas (University of Southern Illinois): "Ecological factors in the development of the advanced civilizations of the Valley of Mexico"
2. Duccio Bonavía (Museo Nacional de Antropología y Arqueología, Lima): "Towns of the Late Horizon on the jungle fringe of Peru: some observations"

3. Emilio Harth-Terré (Lima, Peru): "The plaza and its socio-religious function in the Incaic centers"

Colonial Period (Coordinator, Ralph A. Gakenheimer)

SESSION V – Elements of the Colonial City Within Geographic, Economic, and Social Contexts
Chairman: Ralph A. Gakenheimer (University of North Carolina)
Discussants: Woodrow Borah (University of California, Berkeley)
              Charles Gibson (University of Michigan)
              Richard P. Schaedel (University of Texas)
Papers presented:
1. Agustín Zapata Gollan (Museo Etnográfico, Santa Fe, Argentina): "Urbanization of Old Santa Fe"
2. Federico G. Cervera (Santa Fe): "A sanitary and demographic study of the city of Old Santa Fe, Argentina – 1573–1660"
3. Victor F. Nícoli (Museo Etnográfico, Santa Fe, Argentina): "Observations regarding the magnetic deviations of the plans of Santa Fé and Buenos Aires"
4. Jorge E. Hardoy (Consejo Nacional de Investigaciones, Argentina) in collaboration with Carmen Aranovich: "Urban gradations and functions in Hispanic America *circa* 1600 – the first results"
SESSION VI – Colonial Institutions and Their Influence on the Process of Urbanization
Chairman: Jorge E. Hardoy (Consejo Nacional de Investigaciones, Argentina)
Discussants: Horst Hartung (Universidad de Guadalajara)
              Richard M. Morse (Yale University)
Papers presented:
1. Charles Gibson (University of Michigan): "Spanish-Indian institutions and colonial urbanism in New Spain"
2. Ralph A. Gakenheimer (University of North Carolina): "Effects of the municipality on the growth and pattern of the XVIth-century Peruvian city"
3. Gabriel Guarda (Universidad Católica, Chile): "Military Influence on the cities under Chilean rule" (a summary of this paper was read by the Chairman)
4. George Kubler (Yale University): "The colonial plan of Cholula"

The Nineteenth and Twentieth Centuries (Coordinator, Richard M. Morse)

SESSION VII – Formation of the Contemporary City
Chairman: Jorge E. Hardoy (Consejo Nacional de Investigaciones, Argentina)
Discussants: Roberto Cortés Conde
              Tulio Halperin
              Nicolás Sánchez Alborñoz
Papers presented:
1. Richard M. Morse (Yale University): "Cities and society in XIXth-century Latin America: the illustrative case of Brazil"
2. Patricio Randle (Consejo Nacional de Investigaciones, Argentina): "Cities

and frontiers (1779–1879): a century of urbanizing the desert of Buenos Aires"

3. James R. Scobie (Indiana University): "Changing urban patterns: the *Porteño* case, 1880–1910" (a summary of this work was read by the Chairman)
4. Adolfo Critto (Instituto de Sociología, Córdoba, Argentina): "Analysis of the country and of the city after the migration from the country to the city of Córdoba"

Although the authors were not present, the following papers were received:

1. T. Lynn Smith (University of Florida): "The changing functions of Latin American cities"
2. Lázaro Devoto (Córdoba): "Communication and creation of the city"
3. Michael M. Kane (United States): "The role of the participants of the 37th International Congress of Americanists in the development of urban planning and architecture of today and tomorrow"

General Conclusions of the Symposium

SESSION VIII
Chairman: Jorge E. Hardoy
During this session a report on the Symposium was presented and the conclusions generally discussed.

SECOND SYMPOSIUM (38TH CONGRESS OF AMERICANISTS, STUTTGART, 1968)

Pre-Hispanic Urbanization (*Coordinator, Richard P. Schaedel, U.S.A.*)

SESSION I – Variations in Urbanization Trends in Middle America – Highlands and Lowlands
Chairman: Charles DiPeso (U.S.A.)
Discussant: Stephan F. Borhegyi (U.S.A.)
Papers presented:

1. Gordon R. Willey (U.S.A.): "Urban trends in the lowland Maya area and the Mesoamerican highland contrasts"
2. Alfonso Caso (Mexico): "Los barrios de Tenochtitlán: algunas observaciones por agregar"
3. Horst Hartung (Mexico): "Observaciones sobre los trazos de centros ceremoniales Mayas"
4. Angela Müller Dango (Germany): "Comienzos de la urbanización en Michoacán"

SESSION II – Planning Concepts in Pre-Hispanic Urbanization
Chairman: Richard P. Schaedel (U.S.A.)
Discussant: Duccio Bonavía (Peru)
Papers presented:

1. Hermann Trimborn (Germany): "Las ruinas de Macas"
2. Antonio Rodríguez Suy Suy (Peru): "Urban characteristics of Chan Chán manifested in other North Coast centers"
3. Donald E. Thompson (U.S.A.): "Peasant Inca villages in the Huanaco region"
4. R. T. Zuidema (Holland): "The Inca cosmological model applied to temple and city building"

Colonial Period (Coordinator, Erwin Walter Palm, Germany)

SESSION III – Fundamentos históricos y sociales
Chairman: Richard Konetzke (Germany)
Discussant: Sidney D. Markman (U.S.A.)
Papers presented:
1. Charles Verlinden (Belgium): "Structure sociale et administration à Mexico au début de l'époque coloniale comme bases de l'urbanisation"
2. Lewis Hanke (U.S.A.): "What needs to be done now on the history of the Villa Imperial de Potosí"
3. Reinhard Liehr (Germany): "Die Zusammensetzung der *ayuntamientos* in Neuspanien nach den bourbonischen Reformen"
4. Hans Pohl (Germany): "Lateinamerikanische Städte als Gewerbezentren in der Kolonialzeit"
SESSION IV – Mexico
Chairman: Carlos D. Bayon (France)
Discussant: Graziano Gasparini (Venezuela)
Papers presented:
1. George Kubler (U.S.A.): "Open-grid town plans in Europe and America, 1500–1520"
2. Donald Robertson (U.S.A.): "Provincial town plans from late 16th century Mexico"
3. Erwin Walter Palm (Germany): "La aportación de las órdenes mendicantes al urbanismo en el virreinato de la Nueva España"
4. Peter Tschuhl (Germany): "Über die vorspanische Anlage von Cholula"
SESSION V – México, América Central, y Sudamérica
Chairman: Erwin Walter Palm (Germany)
Discussant: Antonio Bonet Correa (Spain)
Papers presented:
1. Jorge E. Hardoy (Argentina): "El modelo clásico de la ciudad colonial"
2. Horst Hartung (Mexico): "Ciudades mineras de México: Taxco, Guanajuato, Zacatecas"
3. Sidney D. Markman (U.S.A.): "*Pueblos de españoles* and *pueblos de indios* in colonial Central America"
SESSION VI
Chairman: Charles Verlinden (Belgium)
Discussant: Donald Robertson (U.S.A.)
Papers presented:
1. Jorge Luján Muñoz (Guatemala): "El edificio circular en el Convento de Capuchinas, Antigua"
2. Antonio Bonet Correa (Spain): "Las ciudades antiguas de Nicaragua"
3. Graziano Gasparini (Venezuela): "Formación de la ciudad en Venezuela, siglo XVI"
4. Carlos D. Bayon (France): "Las antiguas vistas del Cuzco de la Biblioteca Nacional de Paris"

The Nineteenth and Twentieth Centuries (Coordinators, Richard M. Morse, U.S.A., and Hanns-Albert Steger, Germany)

SESSION VII
Chairman: Hanns-Albert Steger (Germany)
Discussant: Jorge E. Hardoy (Argentina)

Papers presented:
1. Richard M. Morse (U.S.A.): "The Lima of Joaquín Capelo"
2. Roberto Cortés Conde (U.S.A.): "Aspectos económicas en las tendencias de urbanización en la Argentina en la segunda mitad del siglo XIX"
3. Sugiyama Iutaka (U.S.A.): "Regional urbanization and primacy in Brazil"
4. Elke Möller (Germany), "Ciudad y administración pública (investigación empírica en Córdoba, Argentina)"
5. José Matos Mar (Peru): "Urbanización, migración y desarrollo en el Perú"
SESSION VIII
Chairman: Herbert Harvey (U.S.A.)
Discussant: Sugiyama Iutaka (U.S.A.)
Papers presented:
1. Arden King (U.S.A.): "Some social implications of urbanism"
2. Hanns-Albert Steger (Germany): "Stadt und Universität"
3. Barbara J. Price (U.S.A.): "Cause, effect and the anthropological study of urbanism"
SESSION IX – Evaluation of the Symposium.

THIRD SYMPOSIUM (39TH CONGRESS OF
AMERICANISTS, LIMA, 1970)

General Theme: Urban Transformations

SESSION I – Urbanization and Governmental Systems: City and State
1. Richard P. Schaedel (University of Texas): "The city and the origin of the state in America"
2. Woodrow Borah (University of California, Berkeley): "European cultural influence in the formation of the first plan for urban centers that has lasted to our time"
3. Harley Browning (University of Texas): "Primacy variations in Latin America during the 20th century"
SESSION II – Urbanization and Natural Resources
1. Duccio Bonavía (Museo Nacional de Antropología y Arqueología, Lima): "Factores ecológicos que han intervenido en la transformación urbana a través de los últimos siglos de la época precolombina"
2. Roberto Cortés Conde and Nancy López de Nisnovich (Centro de Investigaciones Económicas, Instituto Torcuato Di Tella, Buenos Aires): "El desarrollo agrícola en el proceso de urbanización (funciones de producción, patrones de poblamiento y urbanización)"
3. Alejandro B. Rofman (Centro de Estudios Urbanos y Regionales, Buenos Aires): "La influencia del proceso histórico en la dependencia externa y en la estructuración de las redes regionales y urbanas actuales"
SESSION III – Spatial Characteristics of Urbanization
1. John Murra (Cornell University): "The formation of the Incan 'tribute' network reflected in urbanization"
2. Frédéric Mauro (Université de Paris, Nanterre): "Prééminence urbaine et réseau urbaine dans l'Amérique coloniale"
3. Alejandra Moreno Toscano (El Colegio de México): "Economía regional y urbanización: tres ejemplos de relación entre ciudades y regiones en Nueva España a finales del siglo XVIII"
SESSION IV – External Influences on the Formation of Urban Networks and on the Characteristics of Cities

1. Jorge Enrique Hardoy (CEUR, Buenos Aires): "Las formas urbanas europeas durante los siglos XV al XVII y su utilización en América Latina. Nota sobre el transplante de la teoría y práctica urbanística de españoles, portugueses, holandeses, ingleses y franceses"
2. Marcos Kaplan (Instituto Torcuato Di Tella, Buenos Aires): "La ciudad latinoamericana como factor de transmisión de poder socioeconómico y político hacia el exterior durante el período contemporáneo"

SESSION V – Sectoral Transformation and Urban Growth

1. Barbara J. Price (Temple University): "Population composition in pre-Hispanic Mesoamerican urban settlements. A problem in archaeological inference"
2. James R. Scobie (Indiana University): "El impacto de las migraciones en la estructura urbana"
3. Markos Mamalakis (University of Wisconsin, Milwaukee): "Urbanization and sectorial transformation in Latin America, 1950–1965"

SESSION VI – The Internal Structure of Cities

1. René Millon (University of Rochester): "The case of Teotihuacán"
2. Ralph Gakenheimer (Massachusetts Institute of Technology): "The early colonial mining town. Some special opportunities for the study of urban structure"
3. Anthony Leeds (University of Texas, Austin): "The cases of Rio de Janiero and Lima"

SESSION VII – The Cultural Role of Cities

1. Edward Calnek (University of Rochester): "Pre-Columbian cities: the case of Tenochtitlán"
2. Graziano Gasparini (Universidad Central de Venezuela): "La ciudad colonial como centro de irradiación de las escuelas arquitectónicas y pictoricas"
   Discussant: Erwin Walter Palm (Heidelberg, West Germany)
3. Richard M. Morse (Yale University): "The limits of metropolitan dominance in contemporary Latin America"

FOURTH SYMPOSIUM (40TH CONGRESS OF AMERICANISTS, ROME, 1972)

General Theme: The City and Its Hinterland

SESSION I – Sociopolitical Systems and Urban Systems. Comparative Macro-structural Analyses (nation-state)
Chairman: Richard P. Schaedel

1. Jorge E. Hardoy (Centro de Estudios Urbanos y Regionales, Buenos Aires): "Instruction – Socio-political systems and spatial structures in Latin America. A selection of historical and contemporary cases"
2. Richard M. Morse (Department of History, Yale University): "The development of Latin American urban systems in the 19th century"
3. Friedrich Katz (Department of History, University of Chicago): "The Inca and Aztec urban systems and their socio-political systems"

SESSION II – Sociopolitical Systems and Urban systems. Urban-rural (Micro-structural) Systemic and Transformational Linkages
Chairman: Jorge E. Hardoy

1. Richard Schaedel (Department of Anthropology, University of Texas): "Variations in the patterns of contemporary and recent urban-rural (macro/microsocietal) linkages in Latin America"

2. Edelberto Torres Rivas (Programa de desarrollo centroamericano en las ciencias sociales, San José, Costa Rica): "Restructuring the urban-rural linkages in Central America"
3. David Preston (Department of Geography, University of Leeds): "Rural-urban transformation in Bolivia"

SESSION III – Sociopolitical Systems and Urban Systems. Regional case studies
Chairman: Markos Mamalakis

1. Roberto Cortés Conde (Director, Instituto Torcuato Di Tella, Buenos Aires): "The antecedents of the Argentine urban system"
2. Emilia Viotti (Rio de Janeiro): "The formation of the Brazilian urban system in the 19th century"
3. Robert V. Kemper (Department of Anthropology, University of California, Berkeley): "The case of contemporary Mexico"

SESSION IV – Sociopolitical Systems and Urban Systems. The Culmination of the Urbanization Process in Microsocieties (chiefdoms, señoríos, cacicazgos, and Their Subsequent Forms (unidades étnicas)
Chairman: Anthony Leeds
Discussant: Peter Singelmann (University of Missouri)

1. Barbara J. Price (Department of Anthropology, Temple University): "Prehispanic chiefdoms"
2. S. D. Markman (Department of Art, Duke University): "The Dominican townscape for 'pueblos de indios' in colonial Chiapas"
3. Hans Buechler (Department of Anthropology, Syracuse University, Syracuse): "Fiesta cycles and urban-rural communications systems in Bolivia"

SESSION V – The Supplying of the City
Chairman: Harley L. Browning

1. Edward E. Calnek (University of Rochester): "The organization of urban food supply systems: the case of Tenochtitlán"
2. Francisco Solano (Instituto Gonzalo Fernández de Oviedo, Madrid): The provisioning of the colonial city"
3. Markos Mamalakis (Center of Latin American Studies, University of Wisconsin, Milwaukee): "Services in the contemporary Latin American city: the case of Chile"

SESSION VI – The City as a Center of Transformation
Chairman: Harold Blakemore

1. René Millon (Department of Anthropology, University of Rochester): "Teotihuacán and the transformational processes"
2. Paul Singer (CEBRAP, São Paulo): "The transformational process in the 19th-century Latin American city"
3. Alejandro Rofman (Centro de Estudios Urbanos y Regionales, Buenos Aires): "The contemporary Latin American city"

SESSION VII – The City as Center for Migrations
Chairman: Richard M. Morse

1. Woodrow Borah and Sherburne F. Cook (University of California, Berkeley): "17th- and 18th-century cities in Latin America"
2. Harley L. Browning (Department of Sociology, University of Texas, Austin): "Cityward migration, tertiarization and other alarums in contemporary Latin America"
3. Anthony Leeds (University of Texas, Austin): "Latin American hierarchies and socio-political systems – a synthetic overview"

SESSION VIII – Evaluation. Plans for publication and future meetings

REFERENCES

ANONYMOUS
  1967 Conclusions and evaluation of the symposium on "The process of urbanization in America since its origins to the present time." *Latin American Research Review* 2 (2): 76–90.
  1969 Simposio sobre "El proceso de urbanización en América." *Boletín del Centro de Investigaciones Históricas y Estéticas* 11: 138–154. Caracas.
COWELL, BAINBRIDGE
  1976 The Fifth Symposium on Urbanization in America: a report on the proceedings. *Latin American Research Review* 11 (1): 187–194.
HARDOY, JORGE E., RICHARD P. SCHAEDEL, *compilers*
  1975 *Las ciudades de América Latina y sus áreas de influencia a través de la historia.* Buenos Aires: SIAP.
HARDOY, JORGE E., RICHARD P. SCHAEDEL, *editors*
  1969 *El proceso de urbanización en América desde sus orígenes hasta nuestros días.* [The urbanization process in America from its origins to the present day]. Buenos Aires: Instituto Torcuato Di Tella.
HARDOY, JORGE E., ERWIN WALTER PALM, RICHARD P. SCHAEDEL
  1972 "The process of urbanization in America since its origins to the present time," in *Verhandlungen des XXXVIII. Internationalen Amerikanistenkongresses*, Stuttgart-München, August 1968, volume four, pp. 9–318.
QUIJANO, ANIBAL
  1968 Dependencia, cambio social y urbanizacion en Latinoamérica. *Revista Mexicana de Sociología* 30 (3): 525–570.
SCHAEDEL, RICHARD P. *et al.*
  1972 *Urbanización y proceso social en América.* Lima: Instituto de Estudios Peruanos.

PART ONE

Congress of Americanists Papers

The Selected Papers: An Overview

RICHARD P. SCHAEDEL

The following articles were chosen from almost 100 presentations and over 1,500 printed pages. Categories for the papers were established on the basis of whether their content was predominantly (1) theoretical or methodological, (2) comparative, or (3) case (study) specific. Within these broad categories, works were selected which reflected – where possible – the broad temporal divisions used throughout the symposia: prehistoric, colonial, and nineteenth century to the present. Bearing in mind that no author should be represented by more than one presentation, the only other criterion used was the judgment as to which papers were the best for each category.

The nineteen pieces selected, offer a reasonably good sampling of the kinds of problems posed, hypotheses introduced and tested, and new directions for research followed (some of which are summarized in the foregoing Introduction). The comparative studies show the real potential of this type of symposium, which provided its contributors with an ideal forum for their imaginative propositions. The reader can perceive that the archaeologists took the initiative in this category, the historians followed, and lately the other social scientists have joined in.

The case study was by far the largest category at the beginning and represented the area with the narrowest problem focus. Those papers selected represent the clearest expressions of a well-defined problem, the applicability of which transcends their time and space parameters.

Without any deliberate intent of the editors, the selection happens to represent proportionately the disciplinary spread of the symposia. The initial imbalance through the high proportion of archaeologists and historians was adjusted after the second symposium. The selected papers (eight by North Americans, eight by Latin Americans, and three by Europeans) also reflect the proportion of nationalities involved.

The editors deeply regret that they could not include a larger selection, for many excellent studies had to be passed over. Our hope is that the reader will be sufficiently stimulated by the papers we chose to review the published version of the symposia in which they were given.

One final note of acknowledgement should be added, both to the participants who presented papers in the four symposia and to the "unsung heroes" of these gatherings who participated as chairmen, discussants, rapporteurs, and co-coordinators. In the first two symposia, results of the evaluation session (which always follows the regular sessions) were published (Anonymous 1967, 1969). In the third and fourth symposia these were not published, but in a way the extraordinary meeting in Chicago served this purpose. It also represented a bench mark and climax of four biennial gatherings, from which a new cycle – beginning in Mexico City and continuing in Paris – is now under way.

REFERENCES

ANONYMOUS
   1967   Conclusions and evaluation of the symposium on "The process of urbanization in America since its origins to the present time." *Latin American Research Review* 2 (2): 76–90.
   1969   Simposio sobre "El proceso de urbanización en América." *Boletín del Centro de Investigaciones Históricas y Estéticas* 11: 138–154. Caracas.

SECTION ONE

Method and Theory

The City and the Origin of the State in America

RICHARD P. SCHAEDEL

The main theoretical points of this article are: (1) the development of the city in the urbanization process largely parallels the centralization of the higher levels of political integration represented by the secular state, and (2) the forms of the town and city are preconditions for the permanent consolidation of the state. The theocratic "states," of which the lowland Maya of the Classic Period are an example, were able to evolve an incipient urban form manifested spatially in the diversified ceremonial center, within which only limited state functions were carried out. The so-called states of aboriginal North America represent the same kind of limitations and are considered chiefdoms (following Sanders and Marino [1970] as opposed to Sears [1968]).

Implicit in the archaeological analysis is that we are operating with uniform aggregates, composed of a hierarchy of settlements, indicating a supracommunity settlement pattern that reflects cultural (artifact) homogeneity and a commonly shared government. This hierarchy may be one of *primus inter pares*, as conceivably would be the case with protohistoric Colombian chiefdoms (Steward and Faron 1959: 212–231; Reichel-Dolmatoff 1965; Trimborn 1968), and archaeologically may correspond to the Gallinazo Period polity of the Virú Valley or the Huancho settlement of the Rimac during the later phases of the Middle Horizon (Tiahuanacoid Period) (Stumer 1954a); or it may constitute a clearly defined capital and categories of satellite provincial headquarters, characteristic of the Chimú kingdom (Rodríguez Suy Suy 1972).

The sequence that will be briefly presented here refers to the evolution of the state and city on the North Coast, Peru, but I shall include parallel developments in the rest of the Central Andes and shall offer broad comparisons with Mesoamerica and North America. The city has been defined previously (Schaedel 1969) and I shall have occasion to emphasize the systemic definition, as opposed to definitions based exclusively upon cultural criteria, in order to indicate that aspect of the urbanization process which is conducive to the multifunctional centralization phenomenon[1] which is crucial to state formation.

Crudely put, the growth of the social functions of a complex society as reflected in developing settlement patterns can be seen by analogy with building blocks. The first public architecture is represented by the religious shrine, usually an isolate, surrounded by the village of undifferentiated habitations.[2] Shortly thereafter the defensive building appears (Collier 1961: 105) in the form of a hill redoubt or walled area for retreat; it is also an isolate. Somewhat later, public buildings having other functions are noted. These may be: administrative-hydraulic outposts where canal intakes (and presumably gates) were located; entry and exit houses or buildings near the access to settlements, a pass, or a narrows; or large courtyard areas for marshaling people (possibly with marketing, military, or tribute-gathering functions). The fusing of these functions as reflected in their juxtaposition within a single settlement only became a reality during the Post-Classic Period in Peru and the Classic in Teotihuacán. Furthermore, the change (or a recombination of the building blocks) took place rather abruptly on the Peruvian North Coast, simultaneously with a drastic change in ekistics (Schaedel 1966b), or what the geographers call "environmental perception."

Urbanization trends in Peru were proceeding within a theocratically-militarily controlled society along lines similar to those in the Maya lowlands during Classic times, with some accommodation in housing for religious elites and artisans, leading gradually to the incorporation

[1]   To clarify at least one of the many terminological problems raised by this topic, I should like to indicate that by "multifunctional centralization" I refer to a phenomenon similar to what Sanders and Price (1968: 201) call "nucleation" in the following context: "Nucleation in a civilized society can therefore be considered as a social invention with the primary function of socio-economic integration and control."

[2]   This sequence can be extrapolated from Willey's summaries of building types for the Virú Valley by period (Willey 1953). Since his study, the pattern of Pre-ceramic settlements reported by Engel, Lanning, and others and the work on Chavinoid sites reported by Wallace (1962), Strong (1957), and Tello (1956) lend support to this formulation. Although the complexity and volume of the religious shrine in the Early Horizon as well as the qualitative excellence of the artifacts emphasize the predominance (if not the monopoly) of the religious function during this period, they should not blind us to the fact that the communities were small and dependent largely upon floodwater irrigation supplemented by marine resources. As Collier (1961: 105) cautiously infers, "these communities were integrated by priestly leadership." The shift from Middle to Late Formative reflects a change of emphasis from religious to political functions in a status-based society. This point is made by Adams (1956: 228–231) for New and Old World civilizations.

of marshaling areas for military purposes. These settlement patterns reflect a group of expanding theocratic polities bent upon extending hegemony over weaker and smaller societies. In the process of the expansion, the conquering group established a "capital" or main ceremonial center and subsequently smaller satellite units from which the dominance over the local society was effected. Neither their size nor their differentiation reflects much diversification of function, and as seats of states, they could have housed a tiny population, poorly equipped to control the people they "dominated." They showed little awareness of resource control by their location and represented at best a dispersed kind of polity.

The nature of the Huari expansion remains to be elucidated in detail for much of the Central Andes, but from the evidence so far at hand none of the Tiahuanacoid A (Early Middle Horizon) coastal or highland sites reflects a different settlement pattern. Like that of the Mochica, the Huari conquest appears to have been directed to the "capitals" of the theocratic polities, aiming at their defeat and re-orientation. Yet sometime during this phase of conquest the Huari expansion must have confronted the inefficiency of the expansion *qua* problem of control in a strictly territorial sense, and developing as a result a bold solution for restructuring the principal settlements in order to encompass the functions, not only of military and religious control but of economic or resource control as well.

This solution was largely instrumental in breaking away from the traditional sociopolitical trend, reflected in the growing ceremonial center pattern, to provide a truly urban environmental concept for the capital of the regional units. In the coastal valleys, this involved the integration of the various types of buildings already accumulating at the valley necks into a single large religio-military-hydraulic settlement. In Mexico, the units developed gradually around the earlier religious center (at least in the first appearance of a polyfunctional urban center at Teotihuacán [Sanders and Price 1968: 141]).

The Early Horizon: What are Tribes and Chiefdoms?

In the theocratic chiefdom, we may have the transition between the status-based "rank-societies" and the strata-based "stratified societies" which led to the pristine state that Fried (1967) was so preoccupied in finding. In order to determine what the pre-state "stratified societies" might be in the evolutionary sequence of coastal Peru, it will be necessary to clear up some of the terminological confusion concerning the uses of *chiefdom* and *state*.

Sanders and Price (1968) and Sanders and Marino (1970) have

defined the "civilizations" of the Classic Period in both Mesoamerica and Peru as states in contrast to the Formative chiefdoms and "farming tribes." In this they are opposed by Coe (1965), Flannery et al. (1967), and Lanning (1967), who ascribe statehood to the Olmec and Chavin.[3] Sears (1968) has carried this notion of "precocious statehood" to North America, attributing two sequential statehood patterns to (1) Etowah and (2) Cahokia as equivalent to a typical Middle Mississippi polity. While the introduction to the Sanders and Marino work promises to provide much-needed operational definitions of bands, tribes, chiefdoms, and ancient states (divided into urban and nonurban), their inability to apply the scheme in concrete cases is manifest throughout the book. The utility of their definitions, moreover, is vitiated by the introduction of a series of undefined "states" (which appear as legends in the synthetic charts), such as farming chiefdom, farming tribe (as contrasted with what other types of tribe or chiefdom?), probably farming state, empire, complex tribal confederation, and incipient chiefdom.

The argument of Sanders and Price has the merit of introducing some structural definitions into the characteristics of statehood. I suggest that such criteria as capital size (1,000 to 10,000 for polities ranging in population from 5,000 to 100,000) and degree of centralization, differentiation, and specialization be employed to separate chiefdoms from the larger category of supracommunity polity – the urban or nonurban state. In the Peruvian sequence, whether one uses village form or ceremonial center or both, any multivalley settlement hierarchy that one attempts to construct prior to Gallinazo (or Late Formative) fails to provide evidence for a unified polity of any duration (e.g. compare Huaca Prieta, Punkuri, los Cerrillos, and Guañape for common sociocultural denominators). Even within one valley during Chavinoid times, shrines show considerable formal diversity. At most, the type of social organization that might be inferred for a given region in the Early Horizon would be a chiefdom of limited population.[4]

The beginnings of what might be called the nonurban ancient state emerge with the ceremonial centers of Mochica and perhaps the somewhat earlier versions of Gallinazo and Gallinazo-like manifesta-

[3] Steward and Faron (1959) also classify the Chavin and other Formative cultures of Peru as "theocratic states" (with no antecedent chiefdom phase) as they jump from the era of incipient farming and "folk society" to theocratic states. When they deal with chiefdoms outside the Central Andes (1959: 174ff.), they classify them into militaristic and theocratic, and include class stratification and statehood as prerequisites.

[4] Recent undocumented claims for a supracommunity hegemony during the Early Horizon (Sanders and Marino 1970: 71–72; Fung de Lanning, personal communication) may ultimately be proven, although there is little likelihood that the reconstructed polity would surpass the capabilities of an Olmec chiefdom (Sanders and Price 1968: 126–127).

tions in other valleys.[5] This prototype is defined by Sanders and Marino, but it is not identified with specific manifestations. Heuristically speaking, this is regrettable, because (1) the urban ancient state would seem to follow, although it might have coexisted for a time with the nonurban ancient state; and (2) the small and the large urban state can be correlated with the town and the city, respectively.

The Early Intermediate Period: Chiefdoms and Extended Chiefdoms or the Nonurban State

In the Virú Valley, where the evidence is most detailed, sufficient data are available to demonstrate cultural homogeneity during most of the Post-Chavin Formative. The diversity of social integration (reflected in the coexistence of the *castillo*-fortification complexes with the multiroomed dwelling complexes) may indicate that the communal structures were integral parts of the supracommunity hegemony. If the interpretations of Willey (1953) and Strong and Evans (1952) are correct, i.e. that the valley was unified, then the type of polity could conform to a nonurban ancient state with the pattern indicated in Table 1.[6]

Table 1

Major population clusters	Estimated population
Capital-major population center (11.5 hectares of the Gallinazo group). House mounds and religious structures	2,500
Surrounding rural area	1,000
Four *castillo*-fortification complexes on both sides of the valley narrowing	2,500
Five clusters of minor ceremonial centers	5,000
Total	11,000

On the basis of the probable destruction of structural remains since Conquest times, particularly in the area of the present village of Virú around Cerro Santa Clara, one may estimate an additional 5,000 inhabitants. This analysis would yield a population for the polity of 16,000 rather than the 25,000 that Willey estimated on the basis of maximum ecological potential.

[5] The degree of differentiation of settlements in Gallinazo argues for a relatively small polity, but the cultural evidence indicates status rather than class stratification. The hypothesis can be advanced for a multivalley polity based upon Gallinazo-like sites in the Moche, Chicama, Jequetepeque, Lambayeque, Leche, and including Vicus.
[6] The reasoning for this and subsequent calculations on persons per acre and urban density is given in the appendix.

In any case, this political configuration suggests a total and capital population well within the chiefdom average and indicates differentiation of functions (albeit in distinct settlement units), including hydraulic control, valley and regional defense, and religious hierarchy (in the principal and satellite pyramid sites). The dense agglomeration of dwellings at the Gallinazo group suggests that most of the artisans of the polity may have been concentrated there. The cultural inventory and cemetery content indicate status differentiation but not enough segregation by groups to suggest marked class stratification. If we estimate that 25 percent of the urban concentration at the Gallinazo group were artisans and nonagricultural workers, and if we add about 600 administrative specialists, chiefs, and attendants for the remaining population clusters, we could calculate that 1,200 people, or 7.5 percent of the polity, were engaged in secondary or tertiary activities.

Let me emphasize that the specifications for *urban* are only partially met at the Gallinazo center. Very similar to this type of architectural differentiation is the site of Cerro Culebras, an early Maranga Period settlement in the Chillón Valley (Stumer 1954b). Until there is a better definition of the ancient nonurban state, I consider that both the Gallinazo and Cerro Culebras sites correspond to the capitals of chiefdoms.

Moving to the Mochica Period, the unitary basis is enlarged from a single valley to many. The demographic parameters increase accordingly, but there is not a corresponding extension of settlement pattern differentiation. Size is the major change. In terms of the societal evidence (based upon the Virú Valley data) as reflected in the settlement patterns, the same forms are continued from the Gallinazo Period. The basic innovation is a certain planning or regularity of structure.[7]

The Mochica polity at its maximum expansion would have had a capital in the Moche; complete occupation of the Chicama, Virú, and Santa valleys; strategically located centers in the Nepeña, Jequetepeque, and Lambayeque (with no trace as yet in the intervening valley of Zaña); and possible outlying centers in the Leche. The potential maximum cultivable area for this polity would be about 250,000 acres. Assuming a conservative one-person-per-irrigated-acre ratio, the supporting population would be 260,000. The capital could have encompassed residences of differing quality to accommodate 10,000 persons. The other valley capitals were supported by populations of between 1,000 and 8,000; the evidence of elite housing for a permanent

[7] Isolated large houses and regular agglutinated villages increase in number; community buildings appear; but the isolated pyramid increases at the expense of the pyramid-dwelling construction, indicating a retreat from urbanism (Willey 1953: 177, 233, 397).

specialized group would not exceed 5 percent of that of the supporting population.[8]

Except for the several types of ceremonial centers, the Mochica settlements consisted of isolated buildings (Willey 1953: 233), large vacuous compounds, annexes that could have served as marshaling areas, and defensive constructions in the form of *castillos* or buttressed hillside redoubts. The interconnecting threads or networks of communication and transportation for the polity appear to be cumbersome at best (when considering the control of the entire area by force). Although the growing strategic importance of the valley necks appears to be reflected in the location of the secondary centers at or near those points, only the hypothesized provincial capital of Pampa Grande would be a primary center (and may have been the latest).

The uniformity of Mochica artifacts, construction techniques, and forms argues against the possible contention that the polity was divided into several states. The overall multivalley settlement hierarchy consisted of (1) one outstanding center (with an enclosed area of dispersed buildings large enough to encompass the capital population of the nascent state or super-chiefdom); (2) key ceremonial centers which served as subcapitals (either one to a valley or one each for the north and south banks); (3) tertiary satellite defensive centers in locations at the valley narrows; (4) tertiary satellite ceremonial centers; and (5) miscellaneous isolated buildings and pyramids.

By rearranging Willey's population clusters for the Virú Valley during the Huancaco (Mochica) period, we have the general configuration and population estimate indicated in Table 2.

Table 2

Population clusters	Estimated population
(2) Key ceremonial center-subcapital (Huancaco)	7,770
(4) Tertiary satellite ceremonial center (Huaca Verde)	4,340
(3) Tertiary satellite defensive center (El Gallo)	1,050
(3) Tertiary satellite defensive center (San Juan)	1,190
(5) Isolated structures (Huaca Carranza, Santa Clara-buttressed hill)	*
	14,350

* Included in the Huancaco cluster.

[8]   This is an average for the secondary or subcapitals. Evidence for housing is almost entirely absent at Pañamarca, most of the hypothesized ceremonial centers in Chicama (Rosario-Ongollape, Paz de Azucar), and Huacas de Chimbote. Some housing area is present in Huancaco and Incapampa. There is considerable evidence in Pampa Grande, comparable in size to the zone Uhle labeled "town" between the Huaca del Sol and Huaca de la Luna.

Allowing for the destruction of buildings (as we did for the Gallinazo Period projection), we may add 5,000 to the total, making the estimated population for Virú during the Mochica occupation 19,350.

A similar projection for the Moche Valley is presented in Table 3.

Table 3

Population clusters	Estimated population
1. Main capital of polity (Huaca del Sol – de la Luna)	10,000
2. Tertiary defensive center (Galindo)	1,500
3. Tertiary defensive center (Katuay – Kumbray)	1,500
4. Tertiary defensive center (Santo Domingo)	1,500
5. Tertiary ceremonial center (Cerro de la Virgen)	1,500
6. Tertiary ceremonial center (Huaca de los Chinos – Quirihuac)	3,000
7. Isolated structures – pyramids (e.g. Quevedo); buttressed outcrop (Pesqueda); administrative buildings	2,000
(Galindo)	21,000

To this estimate we may add the usual compensating factor for population of destroyed buildings, bringing the total to 26,000.

Calculating the total area of the Mochica polity, using total current cultivable hectarage and a ratio of one person per acre (1 hectare = approximately 2,5 acres), and comparing these figures with those derived above, we arrive at the figures given in Table 4.

Table 4

Valleys	Hectares cultivated	Estimated population:		Ratio
		agricultural	by building	
Leche (15 percent)	10,000	25,000		
Lambayeque				
Jequetepeque(33¹/₃percent	14,000	35,000		
Chicama	35,000	87,500		
Moche	12,000	30,000	26,000	1.15
Virú-Chao	10,000	25,000	19,350	1.29
Santa	15,000	37,500		
Nepeña	8,000	20,000		
	104,000	260,000		

From this comparison, we note that population estimates based upon agricultural potential exceed those based upon extant public buildings (which in some of the valleys is all we can use). Nevertheless, as Kosok (1959: 51, 56) and Rodríguez Suy Suy (i.p.) have shown, the actual area under cultivation is well below the maximum figure that should be utilized to derive prehistoric agricultural (and population) potential (because of the change in crop pattern and consequent abandonment of the "overflow" water which was utilized in prehistoric times). Until the extension of the various prehistoric canal networks can be more precisely dated, we prefer to opt for the maximum area irrigated by "overflow" water as dating from Middle Horizon and later in most of the valleys (Rodríguez Suy Suy i.p.). With regard to calculations for the Early Intermediate (Mochica) Period, the conservative estimates are therefore retained.

The interpretation that suggests itself in terms of social organization and particularly political organization is that of a fairly disarticulated and undifferentiated polity. Sanders and Price (1968: 201) would probably diagnose the polity as deficient in nucleation. Cultural evidence from grave lots and mural iconography indicates that warriors and priests were the upper class, artisans were in a lower category, and probably attendants and commoner-farmers were in the lowest stratum. There is no differentiation so far detectable in the settlement pattern to indicate that nonagricultural specialists were permanently concentrated in great numbers in any one center except the capital in Moche. The capitals seem to reflect a society not unlike that described in the historical accounts of the Chorotegan and Nicarao chiefdoms, whose more elaborate capitals correspond to the domains of the paramount chiefs (with maximum populations of 10,000), where religious rites were performed and jural rights were mediated, and whose smaller village centers (1,000 population) correspond to the domains of the subject chiefs (Lothrop 1926). The major capital of the Mochica polity, although it apparently enjoyed hegemony over most of the seven valleys, was simply larger but not more differentiated than the ceremonial centers in the individual valleys.

The Middle Horizon Polities – Stratified Societies Going Toward Pristine States: the State and the Town

It is interesting to speculate on the relationship and precedence of city to state in the prehistoric record, and we are now proposing their contemporaneity. The Mexican evidence indicates that the theocratic-mercantile Teotihuacán grew out of a combination of ceremonial centers with gradually merging hinterlands, and that from this urban nucleus grew a kind of city-state, which extended or imposed its trading influence upon other centers. In the Peruvian case, the evidence points so far to the preexistence of a nonmercantile, fairly mobile, predatory inchoate state (or interregional chiefdom) with a massive ceremonial center at Huari, related to another at Tiahuanaco, which imposed itself on similar but more stationary polities. Only after this fusion or conquest did the secular trend toward cities emerge, presumably as a consequence of occupation and control techniques called into being by conquest.

The Middle Horizon settlement patterns introduce the type of differentiated settlement that could contain the multiple functions of the state hierarchy (Schaedel 1966a). Previously, the functions of defense and religion were discharged by disparate settlements. Defense and religion were sometimes combined, but only to service a small area, and they were seldom if ever related to the controlling economic function of water supply and distribution. In Middle Horizon settlements the combination and integration of the three functions are reflected in the type of *quebrada* or hillside town. There is a corresponding increase in the area encompassed by the principal settlement and a diminution in the distribution of minor settlement foci (Strong 1957; Thompson 1964; Stumer 1954a). It is the concentration of multiple functions that characterizes the state, signifying the effective control and presumed unequal distribution of the resources of the polity, which I am stressing.

In the Peruvian coastal sequence, this seems to have come about through conquest as a response to the hyperextension of an undifferentiated, loosely federated polity. The development may have been autogenous among the north coast people (research on such sites as Pampa Grande and Incapampa can resolve this question). The pattern may have already been developed in Huari (the presumed homeland for the militaristic-religious expansion). At any rate, the problem of territoriality was resolved in the period between A.D. 750 and 1200 and resulted in the formation of what I would call the true state and true urban living.

The Middle Horizon polities over most of coastal Peru are reflected in the town settlement pattern, whereas the Early Intermediate was characterized by a spreading hierarchy of two or three levels of ceremonial centers and satellite villages. There are usually only two or three major town sites in any valley in the Middle Horizon, and, except in valleys where old religious sites were reoccupied and remodeled (e.g. Pacatnamu, Huaca del Sol, and Pañamarca), the concentration was usually up-valley, near the neck.

While there may have been a short-lived pan-Peruvian "empire" at this time, maintained through occupied ceremonial centers and *castillos*, the evidence so far accumulated indicates a rapid disaggregation into what I would call semiautonomous states ("semi" because of a presumptive religious bond), consisting of two or more

contiguous coastal valleys with possible proximal highland relationships. Their cultural homogeneity, on the basis of limited studies now
available, rests upon similarity of pottery types. The list gives some
idea of the hypothesized Middle Horizon states with population
projections based upon currently cultivable land at the ratio of one
person per acre (see Table 5).

Table 5

Possible state	Potential population
1. Chillón, Chancay, Huaura, Supe, Fortaleza, and Pativilca	160,000
2. Casma, Nepeña and Santa, Huarmey (Callejon de Huaylas)	75,000
3. Virú, Moche, and Chicama (Huamachuco)	140,000
4. Jequetepeque, Zaña, Lambayeque, Leche (Cajamarca)	*

* No figures for this state are given, because the degree of occupation in all valleys
was partial.

Most of the towns have similar characteristics, and it would be
premature, on the basis of the scant research done so far, to propose
a hierarchy of capitals. In this period of state formation the coexistence of chiefdoms based upon ceremonial centers is to be expected
(and is implicit in Kosok's study [1959] of the Lambayeque).[9] I
believe that these galaxies of towns in the coastal valleys represent
the establishment of small (Huari or Huari-affiliated) elites who were
detached from their base of support and who tried to control, by the
concentration of valley resources, the potential of their specific
domains. The elites of the contiguous valleys probably supported one
another without necessarily forming a hierarchy.

The argument for a pre-Chimú, Lambayeque-Leche-Zaña, intervalley polity at the end of the Middle Horizon has been presented by
Kosok (1959: 68), and it is probable that Purgatorio in Tucumé became
a later capital. This hegemony, as Kosok pointed out, by no means
indicates that the Lambayeque was entirely unified, but it does show
rather graphically the concentration of towns at the valley necks and
the probable unification of several valleys under one state prior to the
Chimús. It also begs the question of whether Purgatorio might not
correspond to the first true city.

[9] Kosok (1959: 68) posits a center for the middle-lower Lambayeque in Middle
Horizon in Chotuna, where the settlement pattern of ceremonial centers was maintained, while a multivalley polity developed at the valley necks of the Leche, Lambayeque, and Zaña with town settlements in Cipán, Patapo, and Pampa Grande. The
most highly urbanized center corresponding to this epoch is Purgatorio in the Leche
Valley.

Leaving for a moment the process of developing statehood to return to the urban factor, we may postulate that during Middle Horizon times the percentage of the population concentrated in towns (hence technically urban) was higher than in any other period. The larger towns would average 10,000 persons (Patapo, Talambo, and Cipán-Collique), and the smaller ones about 2,000 (Agua de Onda and Pueblo Moxeque).[10] Judged in terms of medium population capacity, most valleys would have exceeded the 1:10 urban-rural ratio.

The Pristine State Achieved: Chimor and Other "Kingdoms"

The consolidation of stratification as reflected in the differential segmentation of the coastal towns was achieved on a multivalley scale on the coast during the Late Intermediate Period. The city of Chanchán with its provincial elite centers clearly reflects a heightened differentiation between classes of society. It also implicitly reflects the proliferation of specialization of managerial and service occupations. Rowe's (1948) excellent summary of the historical sources amply confirms the evidence of the settlement hierarchy that Chimor was indeed a full-blown state. With the growth and expansion of the Chimú state, a major drive at further intervalley consolidation took place, in which the urban population and presumably the managerial skills of all the subject valleys were drawn to the capital. The replication of minor capitals (Rodríguez Suy Suy 1972) based upon the Chanchán model (protected strong points at the valley neck, frequently united by roads and intervalley irrigation) clearly indicates a firm, systematized state organization with a differentiated hierarchy of officialdom (not to say bureaucracy). An intricate centrifugal and centripetal dialectic was evolving in consonance with coastal ecology. Chimor's inner and outer defense works were probably considered the Maginot Line of their day.

The demographic hinterland of Chimor could have contained between 500,000 and a reasonable but not absolute maximum of 750,000 people. Its urban population ranged from an estimated minimum of 70,000 (with 50,000 in Chanchán) to 105,000 (with 75,000 in Chanchán).[11] Compared with European cities and polities of the same time period, this ratio of 14 percent urban is extraordinarily high. Chanchán was certainly a case of primacy, though not as extreme as

[10]   Using a ratio of 100 persons per hectare for the area of uninterrupted building (expanded core area).
[11]   The considerable urban depopulation in the other North Coast valleys with the growth of Chanchán is impossible to fix with any precision (as only the Casma and Virú valleys have been studied in detail). See Appendix 2, Table 2A, for probable minimum estimates based on reconnaissance and architectural evidence.

Teotihuacán. This ratio may well indicate a pristine example of concentration of services, public enterprise, and cumulative investment in the capital at the expense of regional balance, a situation which the more geopolitically oriented Inca exploited effectively.[12] In the case of Teotihuacán, the sectoral imbalance may have reached the point where, according to Mamalakis's theory (1969), its demise could be explained on grounds of acute sectoral conflict.

It would be worth investigating the extent to which subsequent Mesoamerican capital cities altered these self-destructive excesses of high primacy. It is impressive that once the town with multifunctional differentiation and centralization had become established, it became the eminently propitious vehicle for the propagation of the state (macro or micro) which preserved the core of specialized managerial talent needed for its maintenance.[13]

Fried (1967) emphasizes the tenuous nature of the form of political society which bridged the gap between the stratified society (post-chiefdom) torn by conflict and the state. The explanation of how this hiatus was effected is to be found in the development of the city. The solution of the problems of dense urban living, developed independently in Peru and Mesoamerica, prevented the stratification pattern from collapsing into chiefdoms and consolidated the differentiation of social strata in densely structured and integrated urban conglomerates.

The highland pattern in Peru, on the other hand, if it ever was consolidated,[14] quickly disintegrated in the Post-Huari Period and

---

[12] The fragmentation of the kingdom of Chimor by the Incas is still imperfectly understood, but some indication of the size of the units into which it was subdivided can be inferred from documents cited by Espinoza Soriano (1969–1970: 11).

[13] The other regions of coastal Peru parallel to a large extent the North Coast through the extended chiefdom period, comparable to the Mochica on the North Coast (e.g. the ceremonial center at Cahuachi for several South Coast valleys). The sequence during and after Middle Horizon, however, while indicating strong and weak Huari-Tiahuanacoid impulses depending on individual valleys, would seem to show state consolidation on a one – or two – valley basis (Rostworoski de Diez Canseco 1970; Menzel and Rowe 1966; Stumer 1954a; Means 1931). In order to determine whether there was a political disaggregation process after a presumed pan-Peruvian Huari "empire," as Sanders and Price postulate for Post-Classic Mesoamerica (1968: 207–209), the settlement evidence for both areas needs to be documented.

[14] Ground plans for highland centers of the Middle Horizon are notorious by their absence. The calculated density for "urban" Tiahuanaco (Parsons 1968: 244–245) is unfortunately based upon densities derived from Sanders' study of Mexico. Densities for compact villages of the altiplano that would be more relevant run somewhat lower (Schaedel 1960). Sanders has allowed me to study his plan of Piquillacta. This settlement would compare favorably with coastal towns in terms of differentiation and systemic features, but calculations of density would not be possible unless the functions of many quadrangles could be established as residences and not exclusively storage rooms (contradictory personal communications from Sanders and Luis Barrera).

Despite Menzel's affirmation (1968: 94) of the amazing uniformity of the Tiahuanacoid religious pantheon, the documented establishment of a settlement hierarchy for this lapsed into one of loosely federated chiefdoms. Polities of the size and extent of the Chimú state arose but failed to maintain themselves at the statehood level without the development of the city in the southern altiplano. Such was the "kingdom" of Chucuito, which (according to Murra's ethnohistorical research [1969]) corresponds to the stratified society without an established state. The southern altiplano "urban" sites that might correspond to capitals of Chucuito-like kingdoms (Schaedel 1969) all lack the degree of differentiation in form of the hypothesized coastal capitals of the Middle Horizon and reinforce the notion advanced here that these polities had not yet outgrown the kinship-based form of social organization in which political hierarchy depended upon moiety and ayllu divisions.

Thus I conclude that while statehood may temporarily emerge without the crystallization of its functions in a differentiated but integrated settlement, only a truly urban format that consolidates, if not intensifies, the stratification pattern can guarantee its continuance.

APPENDIX 1

In an attempt to arrive at a ratio for computing demographic densities for prehistoric Peru, the figures given for Moche by Gillin (1947) were analyzed:

Area	Population	Density
Total 976 hectares	3,773	3.86 persons per hectare
Urban 19 hectares	2,148	113.05 persons per hectare
Rural 957 hectares	1,625	1.69 persons per hectare

In order to obtain a more plausible figure for the overall prehistoric density, the urban components (*forasteros* [outsiders] and *Mocheros* [i.e. the locals] working outside Moche) who would not have inhabited the prehistoric center were eliminated.

Total population 3,773 less 500 *forasteros* equals 3,273. Of the native population of 3,273, 21 percent of the total between the ages of twenty and fifty-nine, or the economically active males, equals 687. From the economically active males, 100 were subtracted as working outside Moche, leaving 587 economically active males deriving income from the Moche area. Their holdings in hectares averaged 1.66. Assuming three dependents per adult male, the prehistoric population would be 2,348, yielding a density of 0.41 persons per hectare, or 1.09 persons per acre. Because no deduction was made for

alleged "empire" in the entire central and southern region of Peru is still in the desideratum stage. See Appendix 1, Table 1A, for a highly hypothetical projection of the indices derived for each valley.

house lots of the urban components, the estimated density would be closer to one person per acre, if not somewhat less.

Bennett's calculation (1950) of 5,000 people for the Gallinazo group made no allowances for temples and plaza areas. A revision of Bennett's plans indicates that approximately 25 percent of the 115,000 square meters of building mounds were probably devoted to courts and pyramidal structures, leaving 86,250 square meters for habitation. Following Bennett's assumption that seven generations were represented in Gallinazo 3 and that the average room space was 4.1 meters, there would have been 3,005.22 persons in any one generation. Thus the magnitude of the population would be closer to 3,000 than to the 5,000 Bennett suggested.

This revised figure yields a high density for the 11.5 hectares of what would correspond to the "urban core" of the Gallinazo group of 273 persons per hectare. If, however, we include the additional mound area that Bennett did not utilize in his projections but which forms part of the total Gallinazo group area of 1,050 hectares, the total "urban" sector of Gallinazo would include an area of 20 hectares (although, for these additional 8.5 hectares, there is no indication of use). With this extended urban area, the density per hectare would be reduced to 157, which is high but not unreasonable.

In order to balance Bennett's "room count" technique against other calculations, the urban density figures obtained from Moche were applied to the Gallinazo group. Using the maximum of twenty hectares for the urban sector yields a population of 3,926 for the entire group. The minimum calculation would be 2,338. Combining the results of the two techniques, I consider 3,500 a reasonable estimate for the entire group, with 2,500 "urban" and 1,000 rural.

Another and more hazardous index is the ratio of public buildings to population. Using the same Gallinazo group figures (considered as 1,000-hectare model unit), we can project an index of 600 to 800 persons to each hectare of public building (nonresidential) in order to calculate the supporting population. To derive most of the estimates in this study, a ratio of 700:1 was used.

This index is suggested only where the remains of residential buildings have disappeared (which is frequently the case). It should also only be used where the overall pattern of building types and settlements is worked out and where the estimates of population by agricultural potential can be used as a control.

Table 1A represents a highly hypothetical projection of the indices arrived at for each valley.

Table 1 A. Scheme of urban and political growth on the north coast of Peru

Period	Culture name	Settlement pattern	Polity	Hectarage	Population
100–250	Gallinazo 3	Ceremonial-dwelling complex (capital of 11.5 hect.)+ fortification complexes	Centralized multi-community hegemony (chiefdom)	8–12,000	20,000
250–500	Mochica 3	Ceremonial center+ village+segments of elite housing			
250–500	Mochica 4	Ceremonial center+ castillo+regular village+elite housing	2–3-valley Hegemony (extended chiefdom	15–40,000	30–75,000
500–750	Mochica 5	As above+annex compounds (capital encloses 100 hect.)	Multi-valley (super chiefdom)	100,000	250,000
750–800	Tiahuanacoid A (M.H I)	Remodeled ceremonial centers, circular castillos	Inter-regional chiefdom	150,000*	375,000
800–1200	Tiahuanacoid B–C (M.H II)	Hillside towns, administrative-civil architecture, palaces	Semi-autonomous states	30–65,000*	75–160,000
	(Casma-Chicama)	a) Ceremonial centers+dwelling mound clusters	Chiefdoms	5–15,000	20–40,000
	Middle Lambayeque	b) Apartment house clusters+annexes – Purgatorio	Autonomous state	50,000	123,000
1200–1480	Chimú	City+provincial capitals+towns	State	200,000	600,000
1480–1530	Inca/Chimú	Towns, garrisons, palaces, depots	Provinces of empire	10–50,000	25–125,000

* Includes calculations of central polities as far as the Chillón.

APPENDIX 2

Table 2A. The Chimú polity heartland: estimated irrigated area (in hectares) and population in prehistoric times

Valley	Area irrigated today	Area maximally irrigated	Total population estimate[a]	Mean urban population estimates
Motupe	5,000		12,300	500
Leche	15,000		36,900	2,000
Lambayeque	50,000	75,000	123,000	5,000
Zaña	15,000		36,900	2,000
Jequetepeque	42,000		79,680	4,500
Chicama	35,000		86,100	1,500
Moche	12,000	29,500	29,520	50,000 (max. 75,000)
Virú-Chao	10,000		24,600	500
Santa	15,000	.	36,000	1,000
Nepeña	8,000		19,680	1,500
Casma	9,000		22,740	1,500
Totals	216,000	324,400[b]	531,360	70,000 (max. 95,000)

Source: Kosok's unpublished statistics for cultivable areas of the north coast, gathered from various government ministries and private sources and from the author's survey of North Coast valleys (1952–1955).

[a] Based on the ratio of one person per acre.

[b] If the projected maximum cultivated area in prehistoric times, based upon the studies of Kosok and Rodríguez Suy Suy for the Lambayeque and Moche, can be applied to the entire North Coast in the same ratio to currently irrigated land, then the total potentially cultivable area would be of this magnitude, and the total population could be 750,000. This would allow the revised urban estimates.

REFERENCES

ADAMS, ROBERT M. C.
1956 Some hypotheses on the development of early civilizations. *American Antiquity* 21(3): 227–232.

BENNETT, WENDELL C.
1950 *The Gallinazo group, Virú Valley, Peru*. Yale University Publications in Anthropology 43. New Haven, Conn.: Yale University Press.

COE, MICHAEL D.
1965 *The jaguar's children: pre-Classic Central Mexico*. New York: Museum of Primitive Art.

COLLIER, DONALD
1961 "Agriculture and civilization on the Coast of Peru," in *The evolution of horticultural systems in native South America: causes and consequences*, 101–109. *Anthropologica*, supplement 2.

ENGEL, FRÉDÉRIC
1957b Sites et établissements sans céramique de la côte péruvienne. *Journal de la Société des Américanistes* 46: 67–155. Paris.

ESPINOZA SORIANO, WALDEMAR
1969–1970   Los mitmas yungas de Collique en Cajamarca, siglos XV, XVI,
XVII. *Revista del Museo Nacional* 26: 9–57.

FLANNERY, KENT V., ANN V. KIRKBY, MICHAEL J. KIRKBY, AUBREY
WILLIAMS, JR.
1967   Farming systems and political growth in ancient Oaxaca. *Science:*
158: 445–454.

FRIED, MORTON H.
1967   *The evolution of political society: an essay in political anthropology.*
New York: Random House.

KOSOK, PAUL
1959   "El valle de Lambayeque," in *Actas del II Congreso Nacional de
Historia del Peru:* 1 (49–67).
1965   *Life, land and water in ancient Peru.* New York: Long Island University Press.

LANNING, EDWARD P.
1967   *Peru before the Incas.* Englewood Cliffs, New Jersey: Prentice-Hall.

LOTHROP, SAMUEL K.
1926   *The pottery of Costa Rica.* New York: Museum of the American
Indian.

MAMALAKIS, MARKOS
1969   The theory of sectoral clashes. *LARR* 4(3): 9–46.

MEANS, PHILLIP AINSWORTH
1931   *Ancient civilizations of the Andes.* New York: Charles Scribner's
Sons.

MENZEL, DOROTHY
1968   New data on the Huari empire in Middle Horizon Epoch 2A. *Ñawpa
Pacha* 6: 47–114.

MENZEL, DOROTHY, JOHN HOWLAND ROWE
1966   The role of Chincha in late pre-Spanish Peru. *Ñawpa Pacha* 4: 63–76.

MURRA, JOHN
1969   An Aymara kingdom in 1567. *Ethnohistory* 15: 115–151.

PARSONS, JEFFREY R.
1968   An estimate of size and population for Middle Horizon Tiahuanaco,
Bolivia. *American Antiquity* 33(2): 243–245.

REICHEL-DOLMATOFF, G.
1965   *Colombia.* New York: Praeger.

RODRÍGUEZ SUY SUY, VICTOR ANTONIO
1972   "Characteristicas urbanas de Chan Chán manifestadas en otros
centros de la costa norte del Perú," in *Verhandlungen des 38. Internationalen Amerikanisten-kongresses,* volume four. München.
i.p.   "Irrigación prehistória en el valle de Moche y su posible rehabili-
tación," in *Actas y Memorias de 29° Congreso de Americanistas.*
Lima.

ROSTWOROSKI DE DIEZ CANSECO, MÁRIA
1970   *Etnohistoria de un valle costeño duranté el Tahuantinsuyu.* Lima.

ROWE, JOHN HOWLAND
1948   The Kingdom of Chimor. *Acta Americana* 6(1–2): 26–59.

SANDERS, WILLIAM T.
1965   *The cultural ecology of the Teotihuacán Valley. A preliminary report
of the results of the Teotihuacán Valley Project.* Department of
Sociology and Anthropology, Pennsylvania State University.

SANDERS, WILLIAM T., JOSEPH MARINO
1970   *New World prehistory: archaeology of the American Indian.* Englewood Cliffs, New Jersey: Prentice-Hall.
SANDERS, WILLIAM T., BARBARA J. PRICE
1968   *Mesoamerica. The evolution of a civilization.* New York: Random
House.
SCHAEDEL, RICHARD P.
1960   *Recursos humanos del Departamento de Puno. Plan regional para
el desarrollo del sur del Perú,* volume five (PS/B9). Lima.
1966a Incipient urbanization and secularization in Tiahuanacoid Peru.
American Antiquity 31(3) 1: 338–344.
1966b "Urban growth and ekistics on the Peruvian coast," in *Actas y
Memorias del 36° Congreso Internacional de Americanistas* 1: 3–11.
1969   "On the definition of civilization, urban, city and town in prehistoric
American," in *Actas y Memorias del 37° Congreso Internacional de
Americanistas.* Buenos Aires.
SEARS, WILLIAM
1968   "The state and settlement patterns in the New World," in *Settlement
archeology.* Edited by K. C. Chang. Palo Alto: National Press Books.
STEWARD, JULIAN H., LOUIS C. FARON
1959   *Native peoples of South America.* New York: McGraw-Hill.
STRONG, WILLIAM DUNCAN
1957   *Paracas, Nazca and Tiahuanacoid cultural relationships in south
coastal Peru.* Memoir 13. Society for American Archaeology, Salt
Lake City.
STRONG, WILLIAM DUNCAN, CLIFFORD EVANS
1952   *Cultural stratigraphy in the Virú Valley, northern Peru.* New York:
Columbia University Press.
STUMER, LOUIS
1954a Population centers in the Rimac Valley, Peru. *American Antiquity*
20: 130–148.
1954b The Chillón Valley of Peru: excavations and reconnaissance
1952–1953. *Archaeology* 7: 171–178.
TELLO, JULIO C.
1956   *Arqueología del Valle de Casma: culturas Chavin, Santa o Huaylas
Yunga y Sub-Chimú.* Lima.
THOMPSON, DONALD E.
1964   Post-Classic innovations in architecture and settlement patterns in
the Casma Valley, Peru. *Southwestern Journal of Anthropology* 20:
1: 91–105.
TRIMBORN, HERMANN
1968   "South Central America" and "The Andean civilizations," in *Pre-
Columbian American religions.* Edited by W. Krickeberg et al.
83–146. New York: Holt, Rinehart and Winston.
UHLE, MAX
1913   Die Ruinen von Moche. *Journal de la Société des Américanistes* 10:
95–112. Paris.
WALLACE, D. T.
1962   Cerrillos, an early Paracas site in Ica, Peru. *American Antiquity* 27:
3: 303–314.
WILLEY, GORDON R.
1953   Prehistoric settlement patterns in the Virú Valley, Peru. *Bureau of
American Ethnology Bulletin* 155. Washington, D.C.

PREHISTORIC

Cause, Effect, and the Anthropological Study of Urbanism

BARBARA J. PRICE

Assuming that urbanism is a nomothetic process, i.e. that its occurrence in time and space is regular and subject to law, I shall examine briefly some of these regularities and their implications for anthropological method and research strategy. It cannot be assumed that theory is merely a supplement to empirical study, or that there can be no valid theory until "all the facts are in," or even that theory will eventually emerge from collections of fact alone. Rather, without the guidance of theory, whether explicitly stated or not, there can be no valid empirical research: facts themselves are only as useful as the framework into which they are fitted. A theoretical framework provides the initial statement of problem, determines what indeed constitutes evidence, and suggests the most productive means of recovering and interpreting such evidence.

Because the present aim is synthesis, I feel that the most productive theoretical framework is that of evolution, in this case the evolution of social systems in general and the evolution of a recurrent and evidently highly adaptive kind of settlement pattern called urbanism in particular. Although much of the following discussion is based on archaeological evidence of preindustrial cities, it is clear that the theoretical position developed is also capable of dealing with contemporary examples. Indeed, consideration of both the past and the present is essential. Archaeological evidence is the raw material for any conclusions about cultural evolution; by its nature, evolutionary theory is diachronic, and the basic evolutionary principles of variation, adaptation, and selection cannot be documented except by reference to the longest possible time span. Similarly, if we rely on the principle of uniformitarianism – i.e. that processes observed to operate in given ways in the present can be assumed to have operated in similar ways in the past – then contemporary evidence can be judiciously used to interpret the archaeologically known remains of past societies.

It must be remembered that these regularities are viewed as similarity of process rather than of form. Specific formal features may vary widely from one example to another, in that different kinds of structure may perform similar functions. On the other hand, as total functional contexts differ, superficially similar forms or structures may differ quite sharply in their functional implications. It is essential to set forth initially the criteria by which an urban community may be recognized – to define such communities irrespective of time, space, or specific cultural-historical traditions. Although some will doubtless regard definitional problems as overly scholastic, let me point out that without some, albeit heuristic, way of stating the similarities and differences on which definitions and classifications are based, the logical result is either the treatment of each instance as unique or the reduction of all instances of the phenomenon to a single instance. In neither case would any statement of regularities of cause and effect be possible. As Willey and Phillips (1958) observe, a typology is not an explanation, but without one we have no means for providing explanations. Because the dimensions of similarity and difference are selected by the investigator for their relevance to a particular problem, no one classification of settlement types is inherent in the data. The diversity of definitions in the sociological and anthropological literature on urbanism reflects the multiplicity of problems in the study of so complex a phenomenon.

Urbanism must be viewed as an ecological and demographic process. Whatever else the term may mean, it refers to a particular kind of settlement pattern, a reflection of the adaptation of a human population to its environment. More specifically, urbanism results from a combination of three subprocesses, each of which may in certain circumstances occur independently of the others. Only when they occur together, intensifying and reinforcing each other, however, does the formation of an urban community result (Sanders and Price 1968). The first of these processes is population growth: urban communities are by definition large ones, with population ranges usually in the thousands for towns and in the tens of thousands for cities. The second process is nucleation, or the growth of internal population density within a single settlement relative to its sustaining area. Population differentiation is the third condition of urbanization. Two factors are at work in this differentiation: (1) social stratification, characteristic of all civilizations regardless of urbanism, and (2) socioeconomic differentiation and specialization of production, with a sizable proportion of the population freed from full-time food production and thus dependent on the surplus produced by others.

This process view of urbanism has certain implications for analysis. Demographic growth is the basic evolutionary index of adaptive success. It is the result, first, of differential reproduction, and second, of the expansion of a range of the population possessing a given trait at the expense of competing populations lacking such. Either the latter are destroyed or absorbed, or they acquire the adaptive trait in question – this is one aspect of what anthropologists call diffusion. An adaptive trait, in evolutionary terms, is one which spreads in time and space; for this reason, a strictly synchronic analysis of sociocultural processes is inadequate. Urbanism, as I have said, is "evidently highly adaptive," a conclusion based on the enormous, explosive increase in its geographical range from 4000 B.C. to the present. An increasing percentage of the world's population is coming to live in urban communities, a situation which demands explanation from a comparative cross-cultural and diachronic perspective.

In no case can the evolution of urbanism be considered apart from the relation between city and sustaining area: as an adaptive feature, urbanism must be viewed as one among many possible arrangements of people in a landscape. Why, then, has this particular pattern been selected *for* at certain times and in certain places, and why, on the contrary, does it appear elsewhere to have been selected *against*? It seems highly probable that certain characteristics of the total environment, both physical and social, may be regarded as permissive, limiting, or even forcing conditions in the development of urbanism. Conversely, urban communities must be regarded as inevitably modifying, in turn, the total ecosystems that produced them.

Populations may increase in size and density on a regional basis without the resultant or concomitant formation of urban communities; the lowland Maya of Late Classic time seem to constitute a striking, if controversial, example. Nucleation of settlements, Rowe (1963) to the contrary, may occur even in rural villages for various reasons: among the Pueblo Indians, highly localized distribution of limited water supplies restricts settlement; in parts of the Amazon Basin, endemic warfare places a premium on tight clustering of population for offensive and defensive purposes. In these latter instances, the population clusters themselves remain individually quite small and undifferentiated, both internally and with respect to one another.

Even population differentiation may assume a nonurban form. Two types of such differentiation have been noted. The first is social stratification, or differential access to strategic resources (Fried 1960, 1967). This type of differentiation is characteristic of the state or civilization: a large social system based upon relationships of institutionalized power among the component groups (Service 1962). Some civilizations appear to have lacked settlements which in demographic terms may be called truly urban (Coe 1961), but all societies at this level of development manifest what Sanders and Price (1968) have called site stratification. Site stratification is present when, within a given area, contemporaneous settlements differing in size, structure, and function exist within a social network that includes them all. This is simply the material counterpart of social stratification. None of the settlements which comprise the network need be urban, although where urban settlements exist, they are inevitably part of a larger pattern of site stratification. If the village/town/city distinction is a pattern typical of some civilizations, then that of hamlet/minor cere-monial/elite residence center/major center is another. In the case of the latter (nonurban) civilization pattern the comparatively small elite groups and their immediate retainers reside in ceremonial centers of various sizes and types, centers which otherwise lack permanent residents, although they act as foci for a dispersed regional population of rural producers. Because such centers usually contain elaborate monumental construction, they may at first glance appear to be urban, and may indeed be termed urban-like.

The second type of population differentiation, while more closely linked with true urbanism (see below), may yet occur in its absence, again on an essentially acephalous, decentralized regional basis. This is the socioeconomic specialization of production, not only in food-stuffs, but in craft products and in services. Such a pattern means that no group in the society as a whole is entirely self-sufficient and that each group must produce a surplus of some commodity to exchange for what it does not itself produce. The result of this is what Durkheim calls "organic solidarity." We may also call it symbiosis (Sanders 1956). Inevitably, trade accompanies symbiosis.

An example of regional symbiosis between often highly differen-tiated rural localities is found in contemporary highland Guatemala. Agricultural and craft specializations are well developed (Tax 1937; McBryde 1947), but nearly all the resulting commerce takes place in an essentially rural context. Peasant communities are integrated into a far-flung regional market system – but the markets meet in regular cycles in rural settlements. No significant nucleation of population has occurred in many areas; in even the most noted market centers, the market meets only weekly, and many such settlements are largely empty on nonmarket days (cf. Bunzel 1959). There are relatively few true urban centers in highland Guatemala, except for Guatemala City, Antigua, and Quezaltenango, and much of the market system of the region appears to operate in comparative independence of such centers. In Wolf's terms (1966), the symbiotic pattern is held together on a basis of essentially horizontal coalitions between specialized rural groups in a basically nonhierarchical structure.

The nonurban civilized pattern of symbiosis seems to be rather a parasitic one, where a small elite group of non-food-producers exacts necessary goods and services from a tributary peasant population. Such a population tends to be composed of generalized and relatively unspecialized producers; full-time professional specialists are usually few in number and attached directly to the elite group in one way or another. This is symbiosis insofar as differentiated parts of an overall site stratification pattern coexist within a single social system; it approaches parasitism in that it is force, overt or veiled, which channels peasant surpluses into the center. In Wolf's terms, the coalitions involved are almost entirely vertical ones.

The urban symbiotic pattern combines both of the above extremes in the relationship between sustaining area and city; in addition, the entire regional socioeconomic system becomes quantitatively larger and qualitatively more complex. As in the case of the nonurban ceremonial center pattern, the city exists as part of a more widespread system of site stratification. The city can be viewed as the top of a pyramidal model. It therefore represents the locus of political and economic power in its region, as does the ceremonial center, and is capable of using force to ensure the channeling of rural surplus to its residents. Like the residents of the ceremonial centers, urban dwellers are not themselves primary producers and thus depend upon a sustaining population for their food supplies. But unlike the nonurban center, the city contains large numbers of permanent residents, a situation which drastically alters the economics of distribution of goods and services.

Urban residents are specialists in a great variety of non-food-producing activities. While rural dwellers may also have such specialties, as in highland Guatemala, such specialization is by locality and by community: the rural pattern in Mesoamerica tends to be that anyone in a community with a nonsubsistence specialty will have the same one as his neighbors. Specialization at the rural level tends, therefore, to be part-time and, more significantly, rural communities lack internal symbiosis. Only where economic symbiosis occurs within the confines of a single settlement can the economic pattern be termed truly urban. This explains the nucleated settlement pattern of cities: professional specializations in government, religion, exchange, crafts, etc., are considerably more remunerative than is food production, and the clustering of population reflects the comparative economics of land use.

But full-time specialization on such a comparatively broad scale implies a market sufficiently large to support these specialized producers. Craftsmen and middlemen deal not merely in luxury goods for the consumption of a small elite, as in the ceremonial center pattern, but rather in basic staples, catering to a mass market and involving a total regional population. Overall patterns of economic specialization, both part- and full-time, are thus governed by positive feedback and self-reinforcing: the larger the population served by the market, the larger the market and the more frequently it meets. The more specialized such a population, the greater its dependence on the market for basic subsistence needs and thus the larger the market becomes. Consequently, more specialization becomes possible and necessary, and the need for centralized direction and control increases. The hierarchical pattern of the city becomes an efficient solution to problems of social control, of production, and especially of distribution – problems resulting from increased size and volume.

The vertical coalitions expressed in the nonurban pattern of site stratification thus become functionally more significant in the overall socioeconomic structure – they have more work to do. Besides directing surpluses to a comparatively small elite group, they must service an entire regional populace. The concentration of specialists in the city and the concomitant growth of rural specialization suggest that many of the needs of even the peasant population are manufactured in or distributed through the urban center. As in the nonurban situation, force – taxation, tribute, tithes, corvée labor – is still significant. But exchange of the surplus produce of diverse specialists acts as an additional impetus to assure that urban residents will be fed: fair exchange is no robbery. And the centralized regulation of the system from which all derive benefit (albeit differentially) becomes not only more essential but, paradoxically, less overtly exploitative.

Economically, therefore, the base of the city rests on three major types of symbiosis: rural-rural, rural-urban, and intra-urban – and on a complex mesh of both horizontal and vertical social coalitions. It remains to consider the evolutionary implications of these patterns and their relationship to archaeological and ethnographic research strategies. The preceding discussion strongly implies that it is impossible to explain the structure or function of any single part of the immensely complex network without reference to the relationship of that part to the whole. Wolf (1956) has made this point concerning ethnographic community studies of peasant groups in a complex society. It is equally relevant to the study of urban groups themselves, past or present. Cities exist as parts of wider ecosystems and represent responses to certain kinds of ecological and demographic processes, responses which in turn set up further adaptive challenges.

In the evolution of cities, the first prerequisite would appear to be a sizable rural population base. Just as absolute size alone does not define an urban community, the exact size of the demographic base in each instance is a matter for empirical investigation. The "critical mass" would depend upon, among other considerations, the total geographical and ecological setting; it must be regarded as a variable, not a constant. An essential permissive factor is, however, agricultural productivity, which would limit the total population potential of the area.

A second prerequisite would seem to be the diversity of the rural population of the sustaining area. The kind of intrasettlement symbiosis characteristic of urban communities may be viewed as, in a sense, an intensification and centralization of the symbiotic patterns of the hinterland and those between the city and the hinterland. A permissive and stimulating factor in the development of such a rural base would appear to be microgeographical variation of the environment: its presence would increase the probability of specialization of production as a response to demographic growth, and its absence, all other factors being equal, would tend to inhibit such a response. Specialization on a local basis as a solution to problems of population pressure can work only if there is guaranteed access to the surpluses produced in other localities, and the differential land use inherent in such a strategy represents a technological phenomenon in the broadest sense, an overall intensification of production. Microgeographical variation is a permissive, not a forcing, condition: essentially similar environments may nonetheless be differentially utilized or zoned, as is often the case with industrial societies. And ecological variation may, indeed must, be analyzed as much in sociological as in geographical terms – the socioeconomic specializations practiced by neighboring communities are as important as the amount and quality of agricultural land or other resources available. Furthermore, analysis must include the technology not only of production but of transport and communication as well.

Yet, on the basis of present evidence, the evolution of urbanism seems to be associated with environments that are ecologically diverse (Coe 1961; Sanders and Price 1968). This suggests a relationship between geographical diversity and the development of broad regional symbiotic patterns. The theory linking the existence of such patterns with the evolution of cities seems to account successfully for the distribution in pre-Columbian Mesoamerica of urban and nonurban civilizations in central Mexico and the Maya area respectively. On the basis of the rather meager comparative data available, this is consonant with what is known of the development of the Mesopotamian city-states (Frankfort 1951; Adams 1966) and accounts for the absence of urbanism in pre-New Kingdom Egypt (assuming that further research sustains the still tenuous conclusion that this civilization was in fact nonurban). It seems also to explain with some success the ruralization of Western Europe after the seventh century

A.D. (Pirenne 1956). If one test of a theory is its explanatory power, then the theory presented here would seem to have some merit. It has also suggested directions for further empirical research, essential to its own ultimate modification and refinement.

The overall methodological implications of the nature of the urbanism process for anthropological research strategy are considerable. The very physical and sociological prominence of urban communities has distinctly affected the course of research history. Their dominant position as the peaks of regional site stratification pyramids has been a double edged sword and, paradoxically, has not favored the holistic view advocated above. In archaeology, with its historical roots firmly planted in a tradition of classical studies which emphasize the particular, work has often concentrated on urban or urban-like sites, first, because of their striking visibility as ruins, and, second, because they are the settlements most likely to yield the remains of the kind of elite culture so favored by art historians and museums. Not only have explanatory problems and nomothetic questions of cause and effect been neglected until recently, but the traditional archaeological approach to urban research has tended to lack even a functional concept of the city as a whole. If the sustaining areas have been scanted, so, too, has most of the city itself, with the exception of the most elaborate tombs, temples, and elite residences. Since World War II, however, the emphasis of archaeology, and especially of New World archaeology, has shifted to a more integrated nomothetic approach (Harris 1968; Adams 1968). Indeed, the considerable work accomplished and in progress stimulated this paper (cf. especially Sanders 1965; Millon 1964, 1967).

The impact of urban dominance has been very different in ethnology. As in archaeology, the traditional approach has been one-sided, but it has come from the opposite side. Traditional ethnographic community studies have tended to emphasize the most primitive, isolated, "exotic" groups in any area. Once again, only since World War II have cultural anthropologists become interested in complex societies. The effect, until recently, has therefore been to ignore urban communities as too progressive, too innovative, not sufficiently "ethnic." When urban studies have been undertaken, they have tended to focus on the poorest, most disadvantaged urban dwellers. As in archaeological work, parts are intensively studied without relating them to the whole. If any statement of the evolution of elite groups is incomplete without reference to their relationships with subordinate groups, then the subordinate groups cannot be fully described, much less explained, except by reference to the elite groups. This is, after all, why such segments, rural or urban, are indeed disadvantaged: they stand in a subordinate relationship to a politically dominant group.

This is not to imply that in every instance the nature or patterning of the symbiotic relationships discussed will be the same. As overall ecological and demographic factors vary from one case to another, so, too, does the relationship between the city and its hinterland and so, too, do the specific parameters responsible. In some cases, the presence of the city may stimulate increased size and differentiation of the rural communities near it and may foster the growth of secondary urban communities in its vicinity; in other cases, it may inhibit such growth. All that can definitely be said now is that the presence of an urban community will invariably modify the total ecosystem of which it is a part; the direction of such modification in any given instance is a matter of empirical investigation. Industrial systems vary among themselves and differ in their characteristics from pre- or nonindustrial systems, but the same kinds of analytical principles will be applicable to all instances, even when the particulars vary. If industrialization, from the perspective of the evolution of urban life, is new, and if in many parts of the world it is newer still, it nonetheless remains true that such new resource bases, new means of exploitation of these resources, and concomitant new social arrangements require no changes of principles of analysis. Changes of this sort will inevitably affect, in measurable ways, the size, distribution, and composition of population, and the interrelationships of groups within a large, complex, stratified social network. It is these processes which have been stressed here.

The approach advised in this paper has been process-oriented rather than cultural-historical, insofar as this kind of analysis is more likely to reveal the regularities of cultural evolution. Superficial differences between distinctive historical sequences become less obtrusive, while comparative treatment of underlying similarities becomes both possible and productive. The object has been to provide a conceptual framework which will have the broadest possible diachronic and comparative applicability. The recognition of similarities is the first step toward explaining them. In an attempt at explanation, I have presented a functional system which is regarded as an evolutionary regularity, with certain consequences whenever and wherever it appears. When the processes outlined here (population growth, nucleation, differentiation) occur, in response to whatever specific conditions, as parts of an interrelated functional system, they appear to constitute such a regularity.

REFERENCES

ADAMS, ROBERT McC
  1966   *The evolution of urban society: early Mesopotamia and pre-Hispanic Mexico.* Chicago: Aldine.
  1968   Archaeological research strategies: past and present. *Science* 160 (3833): 1187–1192.
BUNZEL, RUTH
  1959   *Chichicastenango: a Guatemalan village.* Seattle: University of Washington Press.
COE, MICHAEL D.
  1961   Social typology and tropical forest civilizations. *Comparative Studies in Society and History* 4 (1): 65–85.
FRANKFORT, HENRI
  1951   *The birth of civilization in the Near East.* Bloomington: Indiana University Press.
FRIED, MORTON H.
  1960   "On the evolution of social stratification and the state," in *Culture in history: essays in honor of Paul Radin.* Edited by Stanley Diamond. New York: Columbia University Press.
  1967   *The evolution of political society: an essay in political anthropology.* New York: Random House.
HARRIS, MARVIN
  1968   *The rise of anthropological theory.* New York: Thomas Crowell.
McBRYDE, FELIX W.
  1947   *Cultural and historical geography of southwest Guatemala.* Institute of Social Anthropology Publication 4. Smithsonian Institute, Washington, D.C.
MILLON, RENÉ
  1964   Teotihuacán mapping project. *American Antiquity* 29 (3): 345–352.
  1967   Teotihuacán. *Scientific American* 216 (6): 38–48.
PIRENNE, HENRI
  1956   *Medieval cities.* Garden City, N.Y.: Doubleday Anchor.
ROWE, JOHN H.
  1963   Urban settlement in ancient Peru. *Ñawpa Pacha.* Berkeley: Institute of Andean Studies.
SANDERS, WILLIAM T.
  1956   "The central Mexican symbiotic region," in *Prehistoric settlement patterns in the New World.* Edited by Gordon R. Willey. Viking Fund Publications in Anthropology 23. New York.
  1965   "Cultural ecology of the Teotihuacán Valley" (multilith). Pennsylvania State University, Department of Sociology and Anthropology.
SANDERS, WILLIAM T., BARBARA J. PRICE
  1968   *Mesoamerica: the evolution of a civilization.* New York: Random House.
SERVICE, ELMAN R.
  1962   *Primitive social organization: an evolutionary perspective.* New York: Random House.
TAX, SOL
  1937   The municipios of the midwestern highlands of Guatemala. *American Anthropologist* 39: 423–444.

WILLEY, GORDON R., PHILIP PHILLIPS
  1958   *Method and theory in American archaeology.* Chicago: University of Chicago Press.
WOLF, ERIC R.
  1956   Aspects of group relations in a complex society: Mexico. *American Anthropologist* 58: 1065–1078.
  1966   *Peasants.* Englewood Cliffs, N.J.: Prentice-Hall.

COLONIAL

The Scale and Functions of Spanish American Cities Around 1600: An Essay on Methodology

JORGE E. HARDOY, *with the collaboration of*
CARMEN ARANOVICH

The greatest difficulty encountered by the investigator of the urbanization process in periods prior to census taking is the lack of information permitting comparisons and determination of trends. As a result, it becomes more convenient either to focus the problem at an exclusively local level, utilizing cases which are particularly well documented in existing publications and archives, or else to concentrate on very specific aspects or sectors of urbanization. Despite the obvious limitations of such focuses, historians have paid little attention to the comparative study of processes in several regions. Perhaps the reason lies in the scant use historians have made of strict methods of analysis and projection, such as those used by sociologists, economists, and planners interested in contemporary urbanization. Also of significance is the lack of interest which historians have shown for interdisciplinary methods in approaching the subject (Glaab 1965).

In an effort to approach closer to the reality of the urbanization process in a specific historical period, we decided to utilize the methodology which is applied to the contemporary analysis of relationships between the scale of a city and its functions, and which is also applied to the determination of plans for human groupings. The purpose of this article is to explain that methodology. The first conclusions of a more extensive study on urbanization in the Spanish colonies of America around 1600 derived from the use of this methodology were published in 1968 (Hardoy 1968).

We wish to express our appreciation to Matilde Milesi de Marequi, Licentiate, for her statistical advice, and to Oscar Yujnovsky, Architect, to Dr. Alejandro Rofman, and to Nélida Lugo, Licentiate, for ideas which contributed to the development of our methodology. (A summary of this article was read at the Conferences on social and economic history organized by the Asociación de Historia Económica y Social in Buenos Aires, 24–26 August 1966.)

Our methodology permits the inclusion of other elements of appraisal to the extent that these are detected and analyzed. In addition to its application to other stages of the historical process of urbanization in one or several regions, it also permits a comparative tracing of the evolution of cities for an extended period. Moreover, it can help ascertain the causes which determined this evolution and the trends followed, as well as detect particular characteristics of the process.

THE PERIOD ANALYZED

The methodology was applied to the determination of characteristics of urbanization and correlations between scales of Spanish cities in America around the year 1600 and the functions fulfilled in these cities. Besides the availability of information, there were a number of other reasons for choosing a period of approximately fifty years of American urban history, i.e. the period between the eighth decade of the sixteenth century and the third decade of the seventeenth century.

In the first place, the process of exploration and colonization initiated by the Spanish immediately after the Conquest had, by the end of the sixteenth century, reached a level of expansion which already included the principal territories of the colony, in terms of population and natural resources; this expansion was scarcely extended at all during the two following centuries. In the second place, within the inexact boundaries of those territories the principal cities of the colony had been founded by this time. These cities were, or in time became, the capitals of the viceroyalties and, with a few exceptions, the seats of the *audiencias*, the main ports, and the most prosperous mining centers. In the third place, during the period analyzed there occurred a reorganization of the functions fulfilled by some centers, with the result that their ranks in the hierarchy also changed. These changes were the consequence of many factors, including the final restructuring of the merchant fleet system, and a reorganization in the administration of justice and religious matters. In this process Santiago lost its status to Havana, Coro to Caracas, Santa Marta to Cartagena, Concepción to Santiago in Chile – to cite only a few examples. Furthermore, a number of cities were abandoned for economic reasons, specifically in those territories which had been conquered in the first stage of colonial expansion. In the fourth place, the general characteristics of the regional economies in each viceroyalty had been determined with sufficient accuracy during the period under analysis. And although these economies experienced variations in the volume of their production during the following two hundred years, changes with regard to their classification were relatively few in number. Lastly, by the decade of 1530–1540 the model of the Spanish American colonial city had attained its final physical characteristics, which were repeated without major changes until long after the end of the colonial period, except in mining centers, a few ports, and other special cases.

AREA OF STUDY

The methodology was applied to the study of urbanization throughout the territory conquered and controlled by Spain until the end of the sixteenth century, with two exceptions: Florida, which was of little importance in the continental urban system at that time, and Brazil. Brazil was under the control of the Spanish Crown between 1580 and 1640, but owing to the manner in which it was colonized it offered a completely different pattern of urban groupings; Portuguese American cities, moreover, differed in their internal structure from Spanish American ones. The cities of the Philippine Islands have also been excluded, for obvious geographic reasons.

USE OF SOURCES

The Spanish Crown produced an enormous, varied body of information on its American colonies which in large part has been lost or has not yet been made available. On the basis of official data and first- or second-hand travel experiences, the sixteenth, seventeenth, and eighteenth centuries produced a variety of works related to the geography and history, as well as to the economic, political, and at times even social situation of the American colonies. Many of those works were published considerably after the deaths of their authors, and from time to time new editions of recently discovered archival materials appear.

A systematic analysis of information gathered in a number of general works corresponding to successive periods of the colonial period, we felt, would significantly increase our knowledge of the Spanish colonies. However, it was necessary to use a methodology which – in addition to permitting the arranging of this information – would at the same time permit the introduction of materials from private works, unpublished manuscripts and materials in local archives which are less accessible to the researcher. Such an overall plan permitted an orderly introduction, for each period and region, of the most relevant material available for an analysis of the urbanization process, thereby facilitating multiple correlations among a variety of indicators.

There are a number of works which provide a synthesis of material on a continental basis starting from the second half of the sixteenth century. These permit a continual analysis with intervals no greater than a few decades. Having decided to utilize the methodology in a well-defined period of colonial history, we initiated our analysis with sources from the libraries of Buenos Aires, plus the ordering of what Hardoy had gathered in previous research outside the country.

Two authors, López de Velazco (1894) and Vázquez de Espinosa (1948), define the limits of the period analyzed and provide the most important sources of our study of development. This is because of the variety and quantity of their information and its suitability for our framework. In spite of errors of information and interpretation, López and Vázquez present two of the most complete syntheses of our period for analyzing the process of colonial urbanization. We accepted the information which was detailed by these authors as valid and did not introduce corrections for known errors.[1] We made extensive use of other primary sources[2] to offset, as far as possible, significant gaps in our information in order to fill in the framework, but not in order to correct errors. We also had recourse to contemporary general and special studies[3] for the same purpose. It would have been a very complex task to correct in detail the information provided by our two principal sources and would, moreover, have diverted us from our goals. It is our belief that in general works on urbanization (such as the present one), the ordering of data which are varied, if not necessarily accurate, is of greater importance than the use of exact but scarce statistics, the search for which would require considerable effort. Furthermore, we doubt that such statistics would substantially change the overall view which we seek to present through the application of this methodology.

[1] For example, the omission of several universities founded before López de Velazco and Vázquez de Espinosa completed the editing of their respective works; the setting up of the Tribunal of the Holy Office (the Inquisition) in Cartagena in Vázquez de Espinosa's work; or the estimate of the number of inhabitants, etc.
[2] Among the primary sources of regional interest consulted are (including modern compendiums): Aldrete (1674), García Icazbalceta (1904), de Herrera (1945–1947), de Salinas (1957), del Paso y Troncoso (1905–1906), de Acosta (1792 [1608]), de Vargas Machuca (1892 [1599]), de la Mota y Escobar (1940), Matienzo (1910), Anonymous Chronicler (1958), de Encinas (1945–1946 [1596]), Jiménez de la Espada (1881–1897), Cervantes de Salazar (1971), Latorre (1916), de Carcenas (1945 [1591]), Instituto Histórico de Marina (1943), de Lizárraga (1909: 485–660), Vargas Ugarte (1947), and Fernández Piedrahita (1942). Among the sources of local interest are: Antonelli (1901: 136–156), Capoche (1959), de Mogaburu and de Mogaburu (1935), Suardo (1935), and Cobo (1956).
[3] Among other contemporary works consulted, the following were especially useful: Borah (1943, 1954), Marco Dorta (1960), Riva Palacio (1887–1889), Vicuña Mackenna (1869–1870, 1924), Wright (1916), Bessio Moreno (1939), Múñoz Camargo (1892), Bromley and Barbagelata (1940), Toussaint et al. (1938), Hanke (1956), Haring (1939), Lafuente Machain (1942, 1944), Kubler (1948), Menéndez Pidal (1944), and Cook and Simpson (1948).

DEFINITIONS

At the time they were written, both of our principal sources considered citizens (*vecinos*) to be male adults and did not distinguish occupations. A *vecino* had to have "a position such as would permit him to be elected as a *ciudadano* [townsman] in a Spanish city, since many Spanish settled in native towns and villages where they were not able to have citizenship" (Borah 1951: 6).

We shall regard as cities all the Spanish settlements mentioned by López de Velazco and Vázquez de Espinosa which had ten or more *vecinos*. We did not take into account those centers described as having a smaller number of *vecinos* or those in which the number is not mentioned. We also excluded "Indian pueblos or farms (*estancias*)" where the Spanish population was generally limited to one or two clergy in charge of the evangelization of the native population.

HYPOTHESES

The objective for which we prepared this methodology was the analysis of the characteristics and trends of the urbanization process in a particular time of the colonial period in Spanish America. Although the object of the present article is to explain the methodology, we regard it as fundamental to explain the principal hypotheses presented which, when tested, would clarify the causes and trends of urbanization in Spanish America around 1600.

1. We considered that given the precarious state of interior transport routes along which products and persons were moved and given that there were very few cases of urban industries (with the exception of mining) having regional influence, the regional plan of human groupings should not be distorted. In addition to the topography, which is so varied in Peru, Bolivia, Mexico, and Colombia (possibly the four most important countries of the colony), the factors capable of distorting the outline, as in fact they did, were: the location of mining resources; the location of ports necessary for maintaining contacts with Spain and among the colonies themselves; and the productive potential of the various agricultural areas, represented by different degrees in the density of the native population for pre-Conquest times.

2. A second hypothesis revolved around the scale of each city. We assumed that the scale of each city would depend on the productive strength of its sphere of influence. In areas of little productive force, the cities would be small with a high degree of self-sufficiency and spatially more dispersed; in areas with greatest economic strength,

they would be larger, dependent to a certain degree on production outside their immediate sphere of influence, and adjusted within these rather well-interrelated systems. We know that when the Conquest took place, the siting of the first cities was determined principally by two factors: (a) the existence of native cities and the concentration of a dense native rural population (Hardoy 1965), and – as soon as ports appeared and as the exploration and incorporation of the new territories advanced – (b) the existence of mining centers, agricultural centers, Indian towns, etc.

3.   Our third hypothesis was that the scale and the continuing occupation of the centers founded on the basis of the above two factors would depend on the productive strength of their respective spheres of influence. And this production would be indicated (except for the main administrative centers) by the number of tribute payers and by the attitude assumed by native groups with respect to colonization, considering that the Spanish population (and the white race in general) were not directly affected by production in the primary sector. On the other hand, the factors which determined the location of regional and local ports and mining centers were in force throughout the colony as a whole.

4.   We assumed, in the fourth place, that the distribution of government activies during the period under study would already have conformed to the productive and strategic advantages of certain areas within the most accessible regions; and that by the end of the sixteenth century it would reflect a policy of domination and consolidation on a continental scale and not, as during the first years of the Conquest, the need to face and solve *de facto* situations as a matter of urgency.

5.   A fifth hypothesis was related to the location of religious functions and the centers for administering them. Considering that religion was at all times a weapon of Spain's conquest policy, it was logical to assume a close correlation between the seats of administration of the state and of religion, as well as the principal institutions of education and inquisition which they used.

6.   Finally, we assumed that, considering the precarious nature of regional infrastructures, the services concentrated in each city would be directed almost exclusively to the population of that city and would be maintained by it, and would therefore give us a measure of the scale of same.

EXPLANATION OF THE METHODOLOGY

Two elements of appraisal were necessary to test the accuracy of the hypotheses: (1) the scale of the cities, as expressed by their actual population or by some index of their relative size; and (2) a listing of basic functions presented in such a manner as to permit the inclusion of other indicators (whenever they were found to be sufficiently representative) permitting a separate analysis, by one or several functions of specific cities or classes of cities, or even of correlations between functions. The framework which was to permit the classifying of the most important sources of information for this study (as well as the different types of supplementary information, whether from primary or secondary sources) had to give a fundamental importance to these two elements of appraisal.

The work was arranged in the following manner (see Table 1). First, the information provided by López de Velazco and Vázquez de Espinosa was listed in the order presented by each writer. Next the information was arranged according to a continent-wide hierarchy of cities in terms of scale. Then the hierarchies were redistributed with respect to the territories belonging to each viceroyalty and, within these, to each *audiencia*. A parallel task was that of compiling in a second table any information which completed, corrected, or corroborated, as the case might be, that presented by López de Velazco and Vázquez de Espinosa. Utilizing the framework developed from López de Velazco, we made a series of correlations between the cities previously classified according to five ranks and the functions carried out in each one. A similar procedure was followed with the information supplied by Vázquez de Espinosa.

With these elements of appraisal it was possible to compare the continental and regional course of the urbanization process and its principal characteristics during the period between the decades of the 1570's and the 1620's, approximately.

The arrangement of these data allowed us to develop a series of conclusions which we regard as being of great value for explaining a particular stage of the colonial period. It also provides a basis for realizing projections and, once the limitations of the methodology used are established, will signal other possible courses in the analysis of the urbanization process of the past.

ANTECEDENTS OF FOUNDING

Included in the format were five columns, to be filled in with data on the founding of each city. In one column the name of the founder is recorded. The other four permit a systemized presentation of information which may be correlated with the functions presented below (for example, the age of the settlement or the existence of a native city on the site, correlated with the scale of a center, or with the

Table 1. Scale and functions of cities

Bibliographical source	No.	City name	Distance from principal center	Characteristics of countryside	Antecedents of founding					Population of cities					Administrative functions					Religious administrative functions		Religious functions							Services								Inquisition	
					Year of founding	Did a native settlement exist?	Dates of prior Spanish founding(s)	Name of founder	Determinants of founding	White	Mestizo	Indian	Mulatto	Negro	Viceregal seat	Audiencia seat	Gobernación	Office of Corregidor	Office of Alcalde Mayor	Archbishopric	Bishopric	Monastery	Convent	Cathedral	Parish	Hermitage	Hospital	Press	Theater	University	Academy	Primary School	What is taught?	Other services	Tribunal of the Holy Office	Delegation of the Tribunal

Table 1. (cont'd)

	Economic functions													Financial functions					Defense		
	Regional								**Urban**												
		Number of tribute payers		Primary sector			Secondary sector		Tertiary sector	Primary sector	Secondary sector		Tertiary sector									
									Port					Markets								
Number of *encomenderos*	Private	Crown	Agriculture	Livestock	Mining	Export industries	Exclusively local industries	Regional	Local		Export industr.	Exclusively local industries	Number	Frequency	Others	Labor composition	Accounts Tribunal	*Caja Real*	Officials of the *Real Hacienda*	Foundry Office	*Casa de Moneda*	Professional army	City defenses	*Presidio*

regional precedence which that center may have acquired, or with its specialization in specific functions; the successive changes of a city's location correlated with its index of growth or decrease and the factors which caused it; the causes which determined the founding of a city correlated with the functions which that city later fulfilled and its scale; etc.).

CRITERIA FOR THE DETERMINATION OF POPULATION

Various methods were tested to obtain an approximation of the figures most accurately representing the total population of the cities during the period analyzed. This was done because we felt that the number of citizens did not constitute a representative gauge. The methods tested and the limitations of each are explained below.

Censuses

If urban censuses had existed for a representative number of cities and with the necessary frequency, our work would have gained in accuracy and diversity. The few censuses which we found for the period between the 1570's and the 1620's present figures either in totals or broken down by sex or ethnic groups. Undoubtedly other censuses exist to which we did not have access, but we believe that they would not have changed the situation described. Furthermore, even among the few censuses analyzed there is no unifying system with regard to date of execution or criteria for the classification of data. This is because they almost always resulted from viceregal or local initiative and were not a product of a general questionnaire. Detailed general questionnaires did circulate through America during the five decades analyzed; their object was to systemize information on the Indies for the determination of Crown policy. However, none of these inquiries required accurate information on urban population. The *Padrón de Lima* commissioned by the viceroy of Montesclaros in 1614 is one of the most detailed. The total population of Lima in that year was 25,434 inhabitants; the census divides them by sex into Spaniards, Christian Negroes, Mulattoes, Indians, and Mestizos (de Salinas 1957: 245). Several censuses of Lima were made during the colonial period, at least one of which took place during the years of our study: the census of 1599, which recorded a population of 14,262 inhabitants (Bromley and Barbagelata 1940).

Lacking such precision, but ordered in accordance with a similar procedure, is the information provided on Panama City in 1610. At this time the city had a total population of 4,831 inhabitants, among whom are included (vaguely estimated) 3,500 Negro male and female slaves (*Colección de documentos* 1879a). The same occurs with Santiago, Chile, in 1613, when among its 10,617 inhabitants were counted 1,717 Spanish, 8,600 Indians, and 300 Negroes (Vicuña Mackenna 1924). At times the figures only include white population in any detailed manner, such as in El Villar Don Pardo (present-day Río Bamba) which, in spite of being described as a *villa* [chartered town] with 314 Spaniards, must have had a native and mestizo population (*Colección de documentos* 1879b). In other cases the information is adjusted to tens or hundreds, as in an account of Zacatecas of 1608, when the city had 1,200 Creoles, 300 Spaniards, about 10 foreigners, and about 3,000 Indians and Negroes, including mestizos and mulattoes (*Colección de documentos* 1879f). There are also many cases of total figures: Buenos Aires in 1622, according to the census of Góngora, had 1,203 inhabitants (Bessio 1939: 421–431); around 1599, some 50,000 inhabitants lived in Mexico City and its environs, among whom 7,000 were Spaniards (Vargas Ugarte 1947: 141–186). It is evident that the use of censuses presents limitations such as those mentioned; but even so, their compilation would be of great use.[4]

Number of Dwellings

Another customary manner of indicating the scale of a city was by means of the number of dwellings or houses, and occasionally the number of families (de Salinas 1957: 246). For example, in 1610 Tunja had 313 tile- and straw-roofed houses, of which 88 were high, 163 low, and 62 covered with straw (*Colección de doocumentos* 1879c); in 1609 Portobelo had 50 houses excluding suburbs (*Colección de documentos* 1879d); in 1610 Santa María de Leiva had 80 houses (*Colección de documentos* 1879e); in 1629 Lima had 4,000 houses in the city alone (Cobo 1956: Chapter IX); Santa Marta had 30 dwellings and Nombre de Dios again as many when the engineer Antonelli visited them around 1587 in order to plan their fortifications (Antonelli 1901); and Quito had 600 houses belonging to Spaniards in 1582 (Jiménez de la Espada 1885–1895: vol. 3, pp. 24 ff.), and 2,500 houses in 1650 (Jiménez de la Espada 1885–1895: vol. 3, Appendix I, 14 ff.).

Some scholars, such as de Herrera (1945–1947), use mixed formulas when they refer to the size of some cities: Mexico City, for example, in the last decade of the sixteenth century, had "four thousand

[4] One of the most detailed compendiums is that of Rosenblatt (1954), especially Appendices II and IV of volume one.

Castilian citizens and thirty thousand or more Indian houses, in the four ancient *Barrios* into which the City had been divided in its heathen days...''; Lima "has more than three thousand citizens" in the same decade, and "many assert that there are in this City twelve thousand Women from all Nations, and twenty thousand Negroes"; Potosí "must have 500 houses belonging to Castilians who attend to the Mines and to traders, and up to fifty thousand Indians" (de Herrera 1945–1947). On the other hand, de Herrera limits himself to stating the number of citizens in the smaller cities.

The number of dwellings, houses, or hearths provides us with a scale of size which is very far from representing the total population. In this respect, if there had been a simultaneous valuation for a significant number of cities, the application of this method would have a value similar to that of the number of citizens. Since we have not found a single work with such a range, any evaluation based on this system would be incomplete.

For the purpose of achieving a magnitude which would approximate the actual population and which at the same time would serve to compare with that achieved through other methods, we endeavored to multiply the number of dwellings by a representative index of the number of persons per dwelling, excluding religious orders and the military who in general lived in residences pertaining to their status.

Some estimates indicate that an index somewhat higher than six would be the most accurate. An index of 6.3 results from a comparison between the 25,452 inhabitants which Lima had in 1614 and the 4,000 houses which Cobo estimated fifteen years later. An index of 6.6 appears in 1569 in the parish of the Mexico City cathedral, when there were 1,169 houses occupied by 7,825 persons of their "confession (del Paso y Troncoso 1905–1906: vol. 3, p. 3). On the other hand, when Panama City had 4,831 inhabitants in 1610, there were 484 dwellings in the city, including tile-roofed town houses, shacks, and Indian huts, which produces an index of 10.

The definition of house or dwelling is not very clear. It is evident that the high index which is seen in Panama City includes people of every race and condition, and one can assume that the majority of the 3,500 Negro male and female slaves lived in the shacks and Indian huts. But who lived in the 4,000 houses which according to Cobo existed in Lima in 1629? Does he include in that figure the dwellings of the Negroes and Indians who, taken as a whole, represented the majority of the population? Adopting an index of 6.3 persons per dwelling, Quito in 1582 must have had 3,780 persons living in Spanish houses (which in general would mean the same as houses of white people), although, of course, not all were Spanish. And in 1650 the total population must be been 15,750 persons. At first sight these figures appear to be logical, since at that time Quito was the fourth city of the viceroyalty of Peru in terms of population, inferior to Lima, Potosí and Cuzco.

The number of dwellings related quite closely to the number of citizens since in 1580 Quito had 400 citizens (according to López de Velazco), and around 1630 there were 3,000 citizens (according to Vázquez de Espinosa). However, information on the number of dwellings in the various cities is not only scarce but also very scattered for periods of many years, a situation which prevents comparisons.

Relationship Between Extension of Physical Area and Density

We have explored the possibility of determining the approximate population of a city by estimating the density of occupation of its physical area. Given a collection of urban plans representative of a certain period, we thought we would be able to approximate the total population by assigning a density per hectare to the occupied urban area. Regrettably, however, the known cartography was neither accurate nor representative, as would be necessary. Furthermore, there are few reconstructions of the layout of populated areas of colonial cities.

During the sixteenth and the beginning of the seventeenth centuries, numerous atlases were published which included urban plans of Spanish America. Starting with Bordone's, which dates from 1528, the following (among many others) appeared: the atlas of Ramusio (1563–1565 [1556]), the atlas of du Pinet (1564), the atlas of Braun and Hogenberg (1576), that of Bigges (1589), that of de Champlain (1602–1603), etc. These works usually included plans and views of some Spanish-American cities, but they frequently lacked accuracy or were simply idealized reconstructions of cities with which the authors were not familiar. Moreover, few examples of urban plans prior to 1630 are included in contemporary collections, in spite of the fact that collections were made in the most specialized archives.[5] This would indicate that few urban maps were produced until well into the seventeenth century (apart from a few exceptional cases which were generally centers of strategic value or very important cities). We made some attempt to use this system. In 1609 the area of Panama City laid out in streets was approximately 1600 by 700 steps of two feet per step, that is, 960 by 520 meters, and a total of approximately 50

---

[5] We refer especially to the following collections: Carrera Stampa (1949), Latorre (1916), Chueca Goitía and Torres Balbas (1951), Outes (1930), Torres Lanza (1921), Taullard (1940), Angulo Iníguez (1933–1939), Bromley and Barbagelata (1940), Toussaint et al. (1938), Municipalidad de Buenos Aires (1910), and others.

hectares.[6] We estimated that 40 percent of the area was occupied by the Casas Reales, the principal church, the three plaza's, the monasteries and convents of San Francisco, La Merced, las Monjas, the Jesuits and the Dominicans, the Bishop's residence, the Hospital of San Juan de Dios, the jail, the kitchens, and other outbuildings and unconstructed areas near the coast. The housing of the populace must have been located in the remaining 60 percent, some thirty hectares. If this were the case, since Panama City in 1610 had 4,831 inhabitants, we would have a high, and very improbable, net residential density of 161 inhabitants per hectare, and a gross density of 97.6. However, it may be expected that a good number of the 3,500 Negro slaves, freedmen, and mulattoes which constituted the population lived scattered outside the boundaries indicated on the plan.

A plan of Portobelo around 1600 represents the city as being formed by six blocks of houses with a maximum of 134 lots (Chueca Goitía and Torres Balbas 1951: 270, Plate 2). Nothing in the plan allows one to assume the use to which those lots were assigned or which ones were developed, although considering Portobelo's commercial (as well as seasonal) function, we assume that many structures would remain unoccupied for the major part of the year.

One frequently finds reproductions of designs which served as a basis for the distribution of lots in a new settlement.[7] However, they do not in themselves permit an estimate of the number of inhabitants, since the lots which are occupied are usually not indicated. Thus, without having other information it is impossible to estimate the number of persons accompanying the individual to whom each site was awarded. Thus, the fact that 65 lots (out of a maximum of 96) may appear as intended for houses in the original plan of Caracas, which dates from 1567, does not mean that there were already 65 houses or huts.

Another procedure, also based on the cartographic documentation of the period, would be to estimate the boundaries of the city, superimposing them to a more accurate later plan or even to a contemporary plan, assigning a density to the occupied area and thus obtaining an estimate of the population. We applied this procedure to the city of Quito in 1582, when the built-up zone (with varying intensity) covered an area of approximately 1,100 meters per side, or about 120 hectares in all. From this area it was necessary to subtract 25 percent, which was occupied by the many convents or by lands which could not be used owing to the existence of the deep vales

[6]   Estimated by Chritóbal de Roda, engineer, on the basis of the plan drawn in 1609.
[7]   Examples of this type can be found in Chueca Goitía and Torres Balbas (1951); see Plates 1, 17, 19, 24, and 349, all of the sixteenth century. This collection also contains reproductions of plans from the following centuries.

crossing the city from north to south.[8] If we attributed to the 120 hectares a gross density similar to that of Lima in 1599,[9] the population of Quito would have been 5,448 inhabitants. This is a figure which bears a relation to the number of citizens in both cities, 2,000 in Lima and 600 in Quito in 1580 (according to López de Velazco), and does not differ much from that obtained through the application of an index figure to the number of dwellings.

A variant of the above system would have been possible if more detailed plans had existed indicating the number of dwellings per block of houses, at least in some districts of certain cities. Once the density of one or several blocks had been obtained, the previous procedure could have been followed. A number of examples of this type of plan do exist, both general and of districts of a city. However, the majority of them belong to the second half of the seventeenth century and to the eighteenth century, when the population density of the principal cities appears to have been considerably higher. Among the general plans (although somewhat prior to the period under study) is that of Mexico City, attributed to Santa Cruz.[10] Even assuming that López de Velazco's estimate of 30,000 or more houses is exaggerated, it turns out in any case to be out of proportion to the limited number of five or six hundred scattered shanties which Santa Cruz depicts. In addition, the relation seems high between the 4,000 Spanish citizens and the possible dwellings which might be contained in the (probably) eighty blocks, some incomplete, which are roughly indicated on the plan.

A reduced sector of Cartagena was reproduced on a plan of 1571 (Chueca Goitía and Torres Balbas 1951: II, 32, Plate 38). It shows several incomplete blocks of houses surrounding the Plaza Real near the new wharf. The only complete block reproduced must have had a density of 126 inhabitants, assuming that the twenty-one doors drawn represent a business or warehouse (a possibility because of the location in a commercial area) and assuming that the owners' homes were above.

A plan which reproduces a central sector of Cholula provides us with another measure of density. Assuming that each door with direct access to the street represents one living unit, we would have an average of between thirteen and fourteen dwellings per block, or seventy-eight to eighty-four persons. This smaller net residential

---

[8]   In order to carry out this calculation, an estimate of the area of Quito in 1582 was superimposed on the plan of Tomás López, printed in Madrid in 1786.
[9]   See note 12.
[10]   The plan attributed to Santa Cruz probably represents Mexico City between 1556 and 1562. See the historical, urban, and bibliographical study of Toussaint et al. (1938: 133–168).

density in comparison with that of Cartagena would be justified by the latter's being surrounded with walls.[11]

Some scattered data plus a study of successive plans (over a number of years) would indicate that cities, at least the main ones, were gradually becoming more heavily densified within the boundaries of the initial design. As a result, it is necessary to have accurate data in order to use this system of estimating total population, owing to changes of density.[12]

Because of the lack of sufficient plans, it does not appear to us that this system is either trustworthy or representative.

Number of Citizens

The number of citizens (*vecinos*), like the number of dwellings, houses or hearths, only gives us a scale of size. Therefore it cannot be taken as representative of the actual population of a city, since there was no standard relationship between number of citizens and total population for cities of different rank or even of the same rank. The importance of using the number of citizens as a measure of the scale of one city with respect to another lies in the frequency with which this fact is used by the authors of various compendiums during the colonial period. Furthermore, this system allows us to determine (for different periods) the development of centers with specified ranks and functions in relation to one another, and it even permits an index of urbanization for each of the viceroyalties or *audiencias*.

By multiplying the number of citizens by a representative index of the average number of members in a family, we would be able in the majority of cases to estimate the total white population in a city. This would include certain groups of families which had already inter-married with people of native blood who fulfilled the conditions indicated in the definition of citizen. It is reasonable to assume that the index adopted would provide us with the size of the social family and not of the natural family, since it is logical that relatives, servants, and even employees would be grouped around each resident. This is the criterion used by Borah, who estimates that an index figure of six,

[11]   The city of Trujillo, on the northern coast of Peru, occupied an area of approximately 100 hectares, excluding the bulwarks and ramparts. In 1701 it had a population of 9,286 inhabitants, with a gross density of 92.8 inhabitants per hectare; to reach the net residential density, this figure can easily be raised by 25 percent, to 126 inhabitants per hectare, if we subtract the area occupied by the plaza, numerous convents, the hospital, reservoirs, etc.

[12]   In 1599 Lima had 14,262 inhabitants and occupied 314 hectares with a density of 45.4 inhabitants per hectare. In 1614 it had 25,434 inhabitants and occupied 316 hectares with a density of 80.4 inhabitants per hectare. Let us recall that Lima's fortifications were only started in 1684 (Bromley and Barbagelata 1940).

although conservative, is closer to reality than a figure of five, which was frequently used during the colonial period as a measure of the size of a Spanish family. Borah regards the latter figure as too low to allow for natural increases in population (Borah 1951: 9). Members of the clergy would not be included in this estimate of the white population.

Of the 25,434 persons registered in Lima in 1614 in the census ordered by the viceroy of Montesclaros, there were 5,257 Spanish men and 4,359 Spanish women, or 37.8 percent of the total population.[13] The census indicates that "three thousand citizens were taken from these numbers" in Lima, meaning those corresponding to the Spanish group (de Salinas 1957: 245). The relation between the Spanish population and the number of citizens would have been 3:2.

Among the 4,831 inhabitants of Panama City in 1610, the white population was 1,027, that is, 21.2 percent of the total, among whom 548 were citizens, 403 women, and 146 children (*Colección de documentos* 1879f). The number of citizens in this example comprised more than half of the white population. In 1613, when Santiago in Chile had 1,717 Spaniards who constituted 16.2 percent of the total, the number of citizens must have been somewhere between the 350–400 which López de Velazco mentions in the decade from 1570 to 1580 and the 536 citizens (306 married and 230 bachelors) indicated by Vázquez de Espinosa some fifty years later (Vicuña Mackenna 1924). Estimating the number of citizens in 1613 at 472, their relation to the Spanish population would have been 1:4. In 1608 Zacatecas had a white population of 1,500 persons, which represented 33 percent of the total; the number of citizens must have been between the 300 mentioned by López de Velazco and the 1,000 indicated by Vázquez de Espinosa (*Colección de documentos* 1879f). Estimating the number of citizens in 1608 at 692, the relation to the Spanish population would be 1:2. On the other hand, in Jaén, a small center in Quito province with 144 whites and 25 *vecinos* in 1606, the relation would have been 1:6 (*Colección de documentos* 1879g).

The above estimates would indicate that the index figure of six used by Borah, although correct in terms of its relation to the demographic growth necessary in connection with the Spanish population, would not agree with the facts. What is most probable is that a high percentage of citizens remained legally bachelors, as indicated by the data on Panama City and Santiago in Chile; also that the growth of the Spanish urban population (which constituted the great majority of the total white population in Spanish America) occurred through the

---

[13] In 1614, colored people constituted 52.3 percent. Negroes alone represented 40.8 percent of the total population. See de Salinas (1957: 245).

continual influx of immigrants coming directly from the Iberian peninsula.

All in all, the use of an index number such as that analyzed above would only serve to establish the white urban population with certain additions, which constituted a very variable percentage of the total population of the city.[14]

Conclusions

The use of number of citizens for the proposed study may be made bearing in mind the following considerations:

1.   We are dealing with a measurement of scales useful for purposes of comparison but completely irrelevant for calculating the total population of the city.

2.   Since the measurement of scale is the one used most frequently in relation to other types of data during the colonial period, it is the one which permits the most detailed comparative studies.

3   Such a basis permits a simple arrangement by scale of classifications which represent the relative importance of the functions fulfilled in the various groups of cities.

DETERMINATION OF RANKS

Ranks were established by relating the four types of functions chosen: *administrative*, *religious-administrative*, *religious*, and *services*. The number of citizens was regarded as an independent variable.

For the purpose of determining the importance of each function, a weighting was made for the final year of the period studied (see Table 2).

Determination of Values for Functions

The steps taken to arrive at the relative importance of the functions analyzed were the following:

1.   Calculation of the median for each function.

2.   Choosing the median which registered the smallest value.

3.   Calculation of the ratio (or quotient) between the value of the median of each function and the median of smallest value.

4.   Employment of this procedure for the two end dates of the study, 1580 and 1630.

[14]   According to estimates based on primary sources, the white population was probably 14 percent of Mexico City in 1599 and 5 percent of Potosí in 1603.

Table 2. Weighting index according to functions for 1580 and 1630

Functions		*López de Velazco* *1580*	*Vázquez de Espinosa* *1630*
Administrative	Viceregal capital	33.66	36.25
	Audiencia seat	6.00	5.25
	Government offices	1.20	1.50
	Alcaldía Mayor	1.00	1.25
Religious-Administrative	Archbishopric	7.33	10.00
	Bishopric	2.46	2.00
Religious	Monasteries	1.67	1.00
	Convents	6.66	2.50
Services	Hospitals	4.00	2.00
	University	33.66	36.25
	Academies	6.00	4.12
	Inquisition	33.66	36.25

5. Computation of the values thus obtained for each city, finding in this manner the total value of functions for each center considered.

Mexico City, with 133.62, proved to be the case of maximum concentration. On the other hand, we found a number of cases with a function value of 0 (zero), that is to say, cities having no function which could be classified by this method.

The absence of discontinuities in the weighting value of functions with respect to sudden changes in the number of citizens allowed us to establish five ranks of hierarchy. Independent of the number of functions concentrated in each city, rank I was established for cities with the highest weighting index and rank V for those which had the smallest index. In making the study we noticed that some cities were not located within the rank established for that number of residents. This occurred, for example, with some mining centers and ports of cities which, having lost population because of identifiable circumstances, still retained functions established prior to the causes which determined the decrease of their population. Consequently five ranks resulted between the scales presented in Table 3. Once the ranks had been established and for the purpose of determing whether any urban centralization had occurred and to what degree, we determined the number of citizens according to each rank and the corresponding percentage (see Table 4). It must be borne in mind that Vázquez de Espinosa cites ninety-four cities mentioned by López de Velazco and sixty-nine cities which the latter did not cite. Furthermore, Vázquez de Espinosa does not record population data for cities of lesser importance, although he mentions their names; this affects the general percentages.

Table 3. Determination of scale for the ranks

Rank	Number of citizens López de Velazco (1580)	Number of citizens Vázquez de Espinosa (1630)
I	2,000	9,500
II	500	500 to 4,000
III	90	250 to 400
IV	25 to 90	60 to 250
V	10 to 25	10 to 60

Table 4. Total number of cities and citizens according to rank

	1580			1630		
Rank	Total no. of citizens	Percentage of total citizens	No. of cities	Total no. of citizens	Percentage of total citizens	Total no. of cities
I	5,000	22	20	24,000	32	2
II	3,500	15	6	32,500	42	29
III	9,730	42	50	10,200	13	31
IV	4,030	18	85	8,556	12	79
V	756	3	46	692	1	24
	23,016	100	207	75,948	100	165

DETERMINATION OF FUNCTIONS

The perusal of López de Velazco and Vázquez de Espinosa gave us a preliminary idea of the type of information available for comparative purposes; we were later able to complement and verify their data with that provided by other authors.[15] The information provided by López de Velazco and Vázquez de Espinosa has much in common. This allowed us to make a preliminary listing of functions which needed very little alteration.

Administrative Functions

Three scales are distinguishable in the administration of government and justice in the colonial period (see Table 1). Government at a local scale was in the hands of the *cabildos*, or municipal councils; the level which we might call provincial or departmental was entrusted to the governors, *corregidores*, and *alcaldes mayores*; and finally there was

---

[15]   See notes 2, 3, and 5 for a bibliographical sampling.

a regional or almost continental scale which encompassed a much larger territory and depended on the viceroys. With respect to law and order, the local judges represented the courts of first instance; the governors, *corregidores*, and *alcaldes mayores* had provincial jurisdiction; and the *audiencias* were the supreme court of the colonies with a regional sphere of influence.

A number of functions fulfilled by official respresentatives on all levels (including those mentioned by López de Velazco and Vázquez de Espinosa), though not sufficiently important for inclusion in our framework, should nonetheless be dealt with at this point. The following is a brief explanation of the functional and dependence relationships of the most representative colonial institutions:

VICEROYALTIES. Two viceroyalties existed in 1600: that of New Spain, with jurisdiction over New Spain, New Galicia, Central America, the Antilles, and the Philippine Islands; and that of Peru, with jurisdiction over all the Spanish possessions of South America. The viceroy was the highest authority in the territory of his jurisdiction and the direct representative of the king. There were a number of captaincies-general under the viceroyalties which possessed very broad civil and military powers. The captain-general presided over the *audiencia* corresponding to the territory under his control.

AUDIENCIAS. Ten *audiencias* existed in America in 1600: Santo Domingo (1526), Mexico City (1527), Panama City (1535), Lima (1542), Santiago de los Caballeros de Guatemala (1543), Guadalajara or New Galicia (1548), Santa Fe de Bogotá (1549), Charcas or La Plata (1559), San Francisco de Quito (1536), and Santiago de Chile (1609), which replaced that of Concepción. Althought established as courts of justice, with the passage of time they acquired other functions. The *audiencias* of Lima and Mexico City were the most important ones and their presidents, who at the same time were the viceroys, issued orders to the rest.[16] The boundaries of the *audiencias* usually coincided with those of the captaincies-general. In very important cases, decisions of the *audiencias* could be appealed in the Council of the Indies.

GOVERNORS, CORREGIDORES, AND ALCALDES MAYORES. These coexisted in the same viceroyalty and in practice had quite similar functions, although in theory the *alcalde mayor* governed a subdivision of the *audiencia* while the *corregidor* (of Spanish cities) presided over meetings of the *cabildos* and supervised or promoted

[16] Pierson and Gil (1957). See Chapter two for a synthesis of Spain's colonial institutions.

activities within his jurisdiction. Apparently governors were responsible for larger territories called provinces. "These representatives exercised, within their jurisdiction, a broad judicial and political authority, generally combined with broad military powers" (Pierson and Gil 1957: 42).

CABILDO. This body had local jurisdiction and existed in every city with the title of same, that is to say, in practice in every place where a concentrated Spanish group resided. The *cabildo* was made up of *regidores* and *alcaldes* who were responsible for matters which affected the city, including the collection of local taxes. At the local level they functioned as courts of first instance. The *cabildos* legislated at the local level, though they were subject to the approval of higher authorities. Native villages were governed at the local level in a different manner. Owing to the fact that *cabildos* existed in all Spanish cities, regardless of size, we decided not to include them among the administrative functions in our framework.

Moreover, special tribunals existed in the complicated colonial bureaucracy, as well as other institutions which were in charge of specific tasks with respect to the control of institutions already mentioned. López de Velazco and Vázquez de Espinosa mention the administrative functions which each city fulfilled during the period of their respective analyses. Thus it was relatively simple to establish three decreasing values for the seats of the viceroyalties, *audiencias*, governors, *corregidores*, and *alcaldías mayores* [jurisdictions of *alcaldes mayores*]. A clarification of the different values we give to viceroyalties and *audiencias* is necessary, since in theory the courts fulfilled a judicial function whereas the viceroyalties fulfilled administrative, political, and legislative functions. Considering that in practice the *audiencias* of Lima and Mexico City possessed a higher status than the others and were at the same time seats of the viceroyalties, it seemed logical to us to establish a hierarchical differentiation. One alternative might have been to establish separately an administrative hierarchy: (I) viceroyalty, (II) governorships, *corregimientos*, and *alcaldías mayores*, (III) *cabildos*; and a judicial hierarchy: (I) *audiencias*; (II) and (III) the same. However, it seemed simpler to us to omit the *cabildos*, for the reasons already explained, and to adopt the procedure used.

By determining the number of judges of an *audiencia* or the number of *regidores* of a city, we would have had another index of the importance of some centers with respect to others. For example, in the period we studied, the number of judges in the *audiencias* of

[17]   In 1580 there were four archbishoprics and twenty-two bishoprics; in 1630 there were five archbishoprics and twenty-nine bishoprics.

Panama City, Quito, Charcas, and Santo Domingo was four, while in Lima and Mexico City there were eight. It is clear that this numerical difference of official or local representatives fulfilling similar tasks would reflect the greater activity concentrated in a particular locality. However, we did not find sufficient information to establish correlations with the scale of cities and other functions.

Religious-Administrative Functions

By papal concession the Kings of Spain had the power to suggest to the Pope candidates for important Church positions in America. In practice the candidate often took over his office without awaiting the papal decision. In this manner the Church (and within it, mainly the secular clergy) became an effective instrument of colonial policy.

The Church organization established two hierarchies, represented by the archbishoprics and bishoprics. Their number grew constantly during the sixteenth century and throughout the fifty years of our study.[17] A number of reasons accounts for this growth. At the beginning of the seventeenth century, as the colonial administrative organization progressively stabilized itself and as the territorial limits of Spanish expansion and the characteristics of regional economies became defined, the hierarchical system of centers in Spanish America was becoming consolidated. Parallel to this, the instability which was noted at the beginning of the colonial period in some religious-administrative localities was gradually disappearing. Undoubtedly the decrease of native population in some areas and the appearance of new centers in the recently incorporated territories weighed heavily in these changes of locality. The seats of the archbishoprics and bishoprics were thus determined by a clear hierarchical concept which corresponded to the relative importance of the political and commercial functions of various cities.

Religious Functions

In planning a new city, a number of sites were set aside for monasteries and convents of religious orders, whose representatives frequently accompanied the founder. Socially and economically the Church constituted a force of enormous power. The various orders had control of education and the responsibility of keeping the hospitals functioning. In addition, the Church exercized an unquestionable political pressure through the Inquisition, as well as economic pressure through the possession of valuable properties and the granting of loans. In other words, many of the services which are normally rendered in a modern city were administered in the Spanish American colonial city by the religious orders. Thus we cannot be surprised by the number of clergy who were living in the principal cities[18] and by the fact that the convents and churches were the most representative works of colonial urban architecture.

In time virtually every city of Spaniards of rank IV or higher and even some of rank V had a religious community. Of course, in a city of twenty-five *vecinos*, such as Jaén, 160 leagues from Quito, there was a single monastery with one monk, contrasting with the numerous religious communities located in Lima, Mexico City, and, to a lesser degree, in the cities which were the seats of the bishoprics. Due to lack of data, we were not able to award different values to religious communities in accordance with their order of importance (for example, according to the number of clergy living in each or according to the activities they promoted). Nor were we able to determine the number of religious communities opened in each city, a fact which would have allowed us to work out an index of the importance of concentration of this function in each center. Therefore, we simply decided to determine in which cities there were religious communities and in which there were none.

Services

Among the innumerable services which a city offers (primarily to its inhabitants, and – to much smaller degree – to the settlers of its area of immediate influence), we were only able to gather information suitable for comparison for those analyzed below.

HOSPITALS. The oldest Spanish hospital in America was that of San Nicolás de Bari, which was founded by Nicolás de Ovando in 1503 in the city of Santo Domingo. Following royal instructions, Ovando ordered the construction of other hospitals in the interior of Santo Domingo Island (Palm 1946). The instructions of the Catholic Monarchs to Ovando clearly established the general policy in this respect: "...have them built in towns where you see the most obvious need for hospitals where the poor may be taken in and cured, Christians as well as Indians...." And nine years later Diego Colón was

---

[18]   In 1614 the clergy had 2,016 members and constituted 7.9 percent of Lima's population, which can be raised to 10 percent if we include those employed by the convents. In Quito, a city of 3,500 *vecinos* according to a description of 1650, there were 258 nuns, 105 lay sisters, 20 noviciates, a number of poor young girls and others who were cared for by the sisters, and no less than 108 female servants in the three convents; and 340 friars lived in three of the five monasteries.

ordered to find out "whether it is necessary for one or more hospitals to be built...."[19]

Beginning with this period, it became common to designate the sites necessary for the construction of a hospital in the founding plans of the majority of the New Spanish cities. But the term "hospital" should not confuse us. In the majority of cases a number of years and even decades passed before the royal instructions were manifested in a permanent construction. In 1550 in Santo Domingo, the hospital which was to replace the precarious temporary building of the San Nicolás de Bari Hospital was still under construction (Palm 1946). And there are references to the fact that in 1568 the *cabildo* of Cartagena requested funds for the San Sebastián Hospital, which had possibly been founded as an institution at almost the same time as the city, in 1533 (Marco Dorta 1960: 37).

The colonial period had already considerably advanced before a hospital (and even several in one city) existed in almost all the cities of a certain category. There exists, however, quite a contrast between the hospitals of Tunja and Lima. In the former, a city of rank II, there was a single, four-bed infirmary for Spaniards (where Indians were also cared for); its income was insufficient to care for the large number of patients. This situation greatly contrasts with the numerous institutions which existed in Lima. In 1630 Lima had eight hospitals, each designated for a specific group: Indians, Spaniards, lepers, clergy, naval personnel, orphans, women, and convalescents.

The number and quality of the hospitals depended on the wealth and scale of the city. This was because the hospital was an essentially urban service and almost entirely maintained by donations, aside from the revenue which had been assigned to it. As it was a service to which the entire population was entitled, it is very important to determine its relation to the size of the city and to analyze this over a period of years. Regrettably, for our correlation the same value is held by the Tunja Hospital of four beds of 1610 and the Indian Hospital in Mexico City, in which between 220 and 300 sick were attended to simultaneously in eight rooms, by two doctors, two surgeons, five chaplains, and assistant staff, and the expenditures of which were paid for by the proceeds of a theater. In order to establish a differentiation of the importance of each, it would have been desirable to have other information, such as the number of hospital beds or the number of doctors, surgeons, and staff. However, we only found isolated references to this type of information, which represents appraisal elements of great significance when one is able to classify them accurately.

[19] Both instructions are found in *Colección de documentos* 1879h).

EDUCATION. In colonial society, education was an urban activity and restricted to the upper classes (primarily to men, and to a lesser degree to women). The great mass of the population, including the urban population, was illiterate. The education imparted by the religious orders to the native population was essentially of an evangelizing nature. Colonial education, at the level of academies (*colegios*) or universities, was virtually a monopoly of the Church; and even those universities which had been set up by the Crown were directed and under the direct influence of one of the orders, especially the Jesuits, Dominicans, and Franciscans.

In our work we have used the existence of academies and universities as an index of educational services in a city. López de Velazco and Vázquez de Espinosa give incorrect figures for the number of universities existing in America at the time their works were written. Both authors mention only two universities, those of Lima (1551) and Mexico City (1551), when in fact five had been established in the time of López de Velazco and ten when Vázquez de Espinosa was writing.[20] It may have happened that some of the universities were not operating at that particular time or that both authors applied a different criterion than that used now for defining a university, or that many of them were only academies or seminaries. It is known that a clear distinction was made between major and minor universities, the former being academies with authorization to grant university diplomas; however, the authors of the period make no reference to this distinction.

We do not have a clear idea of what courses were prescribed in academies and at what level they were prescribed. The public schools for children appear to have constituted a different level than the colleges, in spite of the fact that the primary sources which were consulted do not indicate this. Undoubtedly the number of colleges varied with the scale of the city, but both authors are imprecise. In some cases the number of colleges is given; in others (Mexico City for example) they simply mention that colleges existed. References to the number of children's schools are made by a large number of authors. We have not taken into consideration religious schools devoted to converting the Indians. In any case, in spite of the inaccuracies indicated, the presence of both universities and academies on one hand as opposed to academies alone on another is a clear index of the respective importance of cities.

[20]   Besides the University of Lima and that of Mexico, the following universities had been authorized: Santo Tomás de Aquino in Santo Domingo (1538); Santiago de la Paz in Santo Domingo (1558); and Bogotá in 1563. Between 1580 and 1630 the following were authorized: San Fulgencio in Quito (1586); Córdoba (1613); Javeriana in Bogotá (1622); San Gregorio Magno in Quito (1622); and San Francisco Javier, in Chuquisaca (1624).

The existence and characteristics of educational services could be established more precisely with additional elements of appraisal. Higher education constituted one of the services located in the principal cities which attracted a select minority from other cities lacking colleges and universities.

CULTURAL ACTIVITIES. Customs and activities which were characteristic of Spanish and European educated society were gradually introduced into the colonial cities. Theatrical plays and poetry contests, the reading of imported books and the printing of books locally, the publication of information sheets and later of periodicals and newspapers – all these constituted cultural manifestations of colonial society. Some, such as the theater, were popular, while others, such as the possession of a library, were more select, but in any case they were practically the only cultural activities during the seventeenth and eighteenth centuries.

It is possible to intercalate inauguration dates of theaters in American cities and dates when printing presses were established. Both factors reaffirm the high concentration of functions operating in the principal cities. The publication of information sheets and later of daily newspapers was possible, but it would only have validity for later decades of the colonial period.

THE INQUISITION

In 1478 the Catholic Monarchs obtained papal authorization to appoint inquisitors, thus obtaining total control over one of the principal instruments of political and religious unity within the peninsula and in the colonies. From the earliest days of the colonies, the bishops of the Indies possessed powers of inquisition, but only in 1569 was the first Tribunal of the Holy Office set up by Philip II; it began to function a year later in Lima. In 1571 a second tribunal was established in Mexico City, and in 1610 a third in Cartagena with jurisdiction over the New Kingdom of Granada, Venezuela, the islands of Santo Domingo and Barlovento, and Central America as far as Nicaragua (Marco Dorta 1960: 124).

These tribunals of the Inquisition were few in number and were located in the main cities. These were delegates to centers of secondary importance. For economic reasons, the proposal to create another tribunal in South America was not favored, nor was the idea for one in Santo Domingo (Turberville 1948: 162–168).

The location of the tribunals gives us a measure of the importance of cities. There were a number of logical reasons why the two capitals of the viceroyalties became the tribunal seats. The most obvious is the concentration of complementary institutions in political and religious aspects, in whose unity the Crown was always concerned. A second reason was the existence of special counsel (*consultores*) only in the large cities. De Salinas says in this respect: "The Consultant Jurists and Professors of Canon Law (of the Tribunal of the Inquisition) are the Judges who select the Holy Tribunal from the body of this Royal *Audiencia*. The Censors are learned and great Theologians, who because of their great erudition, virtue, and purity are chosen by the Holy Tribunal" (1957: 148). Furthermore, "the great public event which demonstrated the power of the Inquisition was the *auto de fé*" (Turberville 1948: 94); and if we listen to the authors of the period, the dignity of their execution produced an impressive public spectacle of supreme transcendence. De Salinas says that at the end of December 1625 an *auto de fé* was held in Lima, where a stage was set up "which was so large that it had room for more than twelve thousand persons" (1957: 149), and he adds: "the *Auto* ended, spreading radiance, after great labors, for the great increase of our Catholic Faith, and for the greater authority of the Holy Tribunal" (1957: 151).

The location of a third tribunal in Cartagena, with an area of influence over the islands and the northern part of South America, corresponded to its status as a port with easy access to a wide maritime area and to its intermediate geographical position with respect to the ports of Lima and Mexico City.

ECONOMIC FUNCTIONS

Studies on the economic structure of Spanish American cities are few in number and incomplete; we soon reached the conclusion that we would not have enough information for a comparative analysis.

For example, de Salinas provides valuable information for the city of Lima (ca. 1630) which permits one to deduce, on the basis of the number of businesses of each type, the number of employees in each. Furthermore, since he supplied the number of artisans in detail, it is possible to approximate a valid figure for the commercial and industrial sector. De Salinas also details the number of employees in the vice-regal and local administrations, the university, and the number of clergy for 1614, when the city had slightly over 25,000 inhabitants. That is to say, it would be possible to estimate the composition of labor in Lima for the government, industrial, and commercial sectors, and possibly for some services (de Salinas 1957).

Data which are less precise but equally valuable appear in a report of 1603 on Potosí, to which could be added the number of natives employed in extractive activities (Jiménez de la Espada 1885–1895: I, 123). In a 1610 description of Tunja, details are quoted of the number of officials of every kind (*Colección de documentos* 1879c). Possibly mention is made of the number of textile or hat workshops existing in a city, or the number of ships built in a specific port, or the number of skilled people in a mining center.

On the basis of the general information assembled, we may assume that a city's economy was based in large part on the "basic" activities, including the services. It was these which determined the scale of commercial and industrial activity and, therefore, to a certain degree constituted a measure of the total population. Unfortunately we do not have quantitative data to measure this. It is almost certain that in every city of the upper two and possibly three ranks there were industries whose production was "exported" to its area of immediate commercial influence, and – in cases of very special articles – across the boundaries of the *audiencias* and even to Spain or Asia. Nevertheless, we cannot expect that this type of enterprise had very great significance in the colonial urban economy, except for manufacturers of products with a large and constant market, located in centers with very special advantages and generally for not very long periods. In other words, the "export" industries (such as the cannon industry in Lima, bells in Arequipa, ship construction in Guayaquil or Havana, or hats in Mexico City, to quote a few examples) did not, in terms of percentage, employ a large number of workers. A different case is that of the silk industry during its brief period of prosperity in the middle and at the end of the sixteenth century, when it ultimately employed 14,000 workers (mainly Indians and Negroes) in the provinces of Mexico, Puebla, and Oaxaca (Borah 1943). One may also mention the porcelain, glass, and ceramics industries in Puebla, and gold and silver works and the manufacture of furniture in Mexico City. It turned out to be impossible for us to determine, even with the roughest approximation, the distribution of employment in any significant series of examples of different ranks.

It would have been interesting to examine the role of cities, at least those of the upper ranks, with respect to the market formed by their area of "regional" influence and the way this demand influenced the scale of the industrial and commercial sector over and above that determined by "local" demand. Since we did not see any possibility of finding any record of transactions we speculated on the number and frequency of market days, hoping this might give us an idea of the size of a center and the regional attraction it exerted.[21] However, we

---

[21]   Lima, a city of Rank I, had a number of daily markets. Leiva, a city of Rank III, had a market every four days. The use of this type of information could be of great value in determing the commercial value of a city.

found only scattered pieces of information, which were not suitable for comparison.

To sum up, if we exclude the extractive industries (such as industries derived from mining, which had to be concentrated near the sources of raw materials and which determined the formation of some of the large-scale cities of the colonial period, in regard to population), we see that urban industries were almost always on a small scale, generally composed of workshops of the family type. We believe it would be possible to ascertain the location of a given type of industry if we had access to the necessary records. This has been partially attempted for manufactured goods in Peru (Silva Santisteban 1964).

We only found one comparable measure of the economic potential concentrated in cities, namely, the number of taxpayers. López de Velazco presents a list which includes the taxpayers corresponding to 89 of the 189 centers which he mentions, that is, 47 percent of the total. Nevertheless, we wish to state that the correlation between the scale of cities and the number of taxpayers served to confirm that the latter factor could not be used as an index of the respective economic strength of cities. It could only be used as an additional element of appraisal (not one of the most important), owing to the imprecise nature of the information provided by the sources.

FINANCIAL FUNCTIONS

The Crown established a bureaucracy in America designed to collect revenues from various sources. The *Caja Real* was in charge of collecting at the local level, and the officials of the Royal Exchequer (the *Real Hacienda*) were its administrators. The number of officials varied according to the importance of the city and to the prevailing economic conditions in each city. Accounts tribunals were set up in the principal cities to control regions, to which the officials of the Royal Exchequer rendered accounts.

In the mining regions (or, more precisely, in the capitals of regions rich in mining resources), *casas de moneda* were established to coin gold and silver. In general, the money coined facilitated trade by enormously increasing the availability of circulating currency. The first *casa de moneda* was established in Mexico City. As regional production developed, however, these minting houses were established in the capitals of the viceroyalties or *gobernaciones* [jurisdictions of governors] with mining wealth and in the principal mining centers. Foundry offices were established, especially in mining regions, in order to levy duty (the royal "fifth") on the extracted metal.

CONCLUSIONS

As our work progressed, we noted the possibility of introducing the use of other sources of appraisal which, while incomplete, would serve to establish certain defining characteristics between cities of different rank. They are the following:

WAGES. For example, salaries differ enormously for officials fulfilling similar tasks in cities of different rank. These discrepancies are observed between the same officials of cities of the same scale in viceroyalties or different *audiencias*.

PRICES. Obviously the cost of products varied between cities of the same rank within the same *audiencia*, depending (among other factors) on the cost of transport. But even the cost of certain identical products produced near cities of equal rank varied. It is possible (although with a large margin of error) to determine the number of certain professional groups in certain cities. Though it would be very improbable that one would achieve an extended series, we believe that it would clarify a problem of great interest, i.e. the correlation between professional people, by number and discipline, and the scale of the centers.

REFERENCES

ALDRETE, BERNARDO
  1674 *Del origen y principio de la lengua castellana*. Madrid. Written c. 1600.
ANGULO IÑÍGUEZ, DIEGO
  1933–1939 *Planos de monumentos arquitectónicos de América y Filipinas existentes en el Archivo General de Indias*. Universidad de Sevilla.
ANONYMOUS CHRONICLER
  1958 *Descripción del virreinato del Perú. Crónica inédita de comienzos del siglo XVII*. Rosario.
ANTONELLI, JUAN B.
  1901 "A relation of ports," in *Principal navigations*, volume ten. Edited by Richard Hakluyt, 135–156. Glasgow.
BESSIO MORENO, NICOLÁS
  1939 *Buenos Aires, estudio crítico de su población*. Buenos Aires.
BIGGES, WALTER
  1589 *A summary and true discourse of Sir Francis Drake's West Indian voyage*. London.
BORAH, WOODROW
  1943 *Silk raising in colonial Mexico*. Ibero-Americana. Berkeley: University of California Press.
  1951 *New Spain's century of depression*. Ibero-Americana 35. Berkeley: University of California Press.

1954   *Early colonial trade and navigation between Mexico and Peru.* Ibero-Americana 38. Berkeley: University of California Press.

BORDONE, BENEDETTO
1528   *Libro di Benedetto Bordone.* Venice.

BRAUN, G., F. HOGENBERG
1576   *Civitatis orbis terrarum.*

BROMLEY, JUAN, JOSÉ BARBAGELATA
1940   *Evolución urbana de la ciudad de Lima.* Lima.

CAPOCHE, LUÍS
1959   *Relaciones del asiento y villa imperial de Potosí.* Biblioteca de Autores Españoles. Ediciones Atlas, Madrid. Written c. 1585.

CARRERA STAMPA, MANUEL
1949   Planos de la ciudad de Mexico. *Boletín de la Sociedad Mexicana de Geografía y Estatística* 67 (2/3); 265–427. Mexico City.

CERVANTES DE SALAZAR, FRANCISCO
1971   *Crónica de la Nueva España.* Biblioteca de Autores Españoles. Ediciones Atlas. Madrid. Written c. 1554.

CHEVALIER, FRANÇOIS
n.d.   Signification sociale de la fondation de Puebla de los Angeles. *Revista de Historia de América* 23: 105–130.

CHUECA GOITÍA, F., L. TORRES BALBAS
1951   *Planos de ciudades iberoamericanas y filipinas.* Madrid.

Colección de documentos inéditos relativos al descubrimiento, conquista y organizaciones de las antiguas posesiones españolas de América y Oceania sacados de los Archivos del Reino, y muy especialmente del de Indias (CDIAPE)
1879a   "Descripción de la ciudad de Panama (1610)," in *CDIAPE,* volume nine, 79–108. Madrid.
1879b   "Descripción de la villa El Villar Don Pardo, sacade de las relaciones hechas en el año 1605 por mandato de su majestad," in *CDIAPE,* volume nine. Madrid.
1879c   "Descripción de la ciudad de Tunja, sacada de las informaciones hechas por la justicia de aquella ciudad el 30 de mayo de 1610 años," in *CDIAPE,* volume nine, 393–448. Madrid.
1879d   "Descripción de Puertovelo (1610)," in *CDIAPE,* volume nine, 108–120. Madrid.
1879e   "Relación de Santa María de Leiva (1610)," in *CDIAPE,* volume nine, 448–451. Madrid.
1879f   "Relación de Nuestra Señora de Zacatecas (1608)," in *CDIAPE,* volume nine. Madrid.
1879g   "Descripción de la ciudad de Jaén y su distrito en la provincia de Quito, sacada de las relaciones hechas el año 1606 por Guillermo de Martos, corregidor," in *CDIAPE,* volume nine, 347–358. Madrid.
1879h   "Instrucción al Comendador de Lares Fray Nicolas de Ovando de la Orden de Alcantara sobre lo que había de hacer en las Islas e Tierra Firme de Mar Océano como governador de ellas (1501)," and "instrucción que se envió al Almirante Don Diego Colón (1509)," in *CDIAPE,* volume thirty-one. Madrid.

COBO, PADRE BERNABÉ
1956   *Historia de la fundación de Lima.* Biblioteca de Autores Españoles. Ediciones Atlas. Completed c. 1639.

COOK, SHERBURNE, LESLEY SIMPSON
    1948   *The population of central Mexico in the sixteenth century.* Ibero-
    Americana 37. Berkeley: University of California Press.
DE ACOSTA, JOSÉ
    1792   [1608]   *Historia natural y moral de las Indias.* Madrid.
DE CARCENAS, JUAN
    1945   [1591]   *Problemas y secretos maravillosos de la Indias* (facsimile
    edition). Madrid: Instituto de Cultura Hispánica.
DE CHAMPLAIN, SAMUEL
    1602–1603   *Bref discours des choses plus remarquables que Samuel Cham-
    plain de Brovage a reconnues aux Indes Occidentales.*
DE ENCINAS, DIEGO
    1945–1946   *Cedulario indiano* (reproduction of the 1596 edition). Madrid.
DE HERRERA, ANTONIO
    1945–1947   *Historia de las Indias.* Buenos Aires: Guarania.
DE LA MOTA Y ESCOBAR, ALONSO
    1940   *Descripción geográfica de los reinos de Nueva Galicia, Nueva Vis-
    caya y Neuva León.* Madrid. Written c. 1600–1610.
DE LIZÁRRAGA, FRAY REGINALDO
    1909   *Descripción brede de toda la tierra del Perú, Tucumán, Río de la Plata
    y Chile.* Nueva Bibioteca de Autores Españoles. Madrid. Written
    c. 1610.
DEL PASO Y TRONCOSO, FRANCISCO
    1905–1906   *Papeles de Neuva España,* volumes one to eight. Madrid.
DE MOGABURU, J., F. DE MOGABURU
    1935   *Diario de Lima (1640–1694).* Lima.
DE SALINAS, FRAY BUENAVENTURA
    1957   *Memorial de las historias del Neuvo Mundo. Perú.* Lima. Written c.
    1630.
DE VARGAS MACHUCA, BERNARDO
    1892   *Milicia y descripción de las Indias.* Madrid. Written c. 1599.
DU PINET, ANTOINE
    1564   *Plantz, pourtraitz et descriptions de plusieurs villes et forteresses tant
    de l'Europe, Asie et Afrique, que des Indes et terres neuves.* Lyon.
FERNÁNDEZ PIEDRAHITA, L.
    1942   *Historia de la conquista del Nuevo Reino de Granada,* volumes
    twelve to fifteen. Biblioteca Popular de Colombia. Bogotá.
GARCÍA ICAZBALCETA, JOAQUÍN
    1904   *Relación de los obispos de Tlaxcala, Michoacán, Oaxaca y otros
    lugares en el siglo XVI.* Mexico City.
GLAAB, CHARLES
    1965   "The historian and the American city: a bibliographical survey,"
    in *The study of urbanization.* Edited by P. Hauser and L. Schnore.
    New York: John Wiley and Sons.
HANKE, LEWIS
    1946   *The imperial city of Potosí.* The Hague: Martinus Nijhoff.
HARDOY, JORGE E.
    1965   La influencia del urbanismo indígena en la localización y trazado
    de las ciudades coloniales. *Ciencia e Investigación* 21(9) September:
    386–405.
    1968   "Escalas y funciones urbanas en América Hispánica hacia 1600.

Primeras conclusiones," in *Actas y Memorias del 37° Congreso de Americanistas, Mar del Plata, 1966*, volume two, 171–208. Buenos Aires.

HARING, C. H.
1939   *El comercio y la navegación entre España y las Indias en la época de los Habsburgo*. Paris.

INSTITUTO HISTÓRICO DE MARINA
1943   *Colección de diarios y relaciones para la historia de los viajes y descubrimientos*, four volumes. Madrid.

JIMÉNEZ DE LA ESPADA, MARCOS
1885–1895   *Relaciones geográficas de Indias*, four volumes. Madrid.

KUBLER, GEORGE
1948   *Mexican architecture of the sixteenth century*, two volumes. New Haven, Conn.: Yale University Press.

LAFUENTE MACHAIN, RICARDO
1942   *La Asunción de Antaño*. Buenos Aires.
1944   *Buenos Aires en el siglo XVII*. Buenos Aires.
1946   *Buenos Aires en el siglo XVIII*. Buenos Aires.

LATORRE, GERMÁN
1910   *Relaciones geográficas de Indias*. Seville.
1916   *La cartografía colonial americana*. Seville.

LÓPEZ DE VELAZCO, JUAN
1894   *Geografía y descripcíon universal de las Indias*. Edited by Justo Zaragoza. Madrid.

MARCO DORTA, ENRIQUE
1960   *Cartagena de Indias*. Cartagena.

MATIENZO, JUAN
1910   *Gobierno del Perú*. Buenos Aires. Written before 1573.

MENÉNDEZ PIDAL, GONZALO
1944   *Imágen del mundo hacia 1570*. Madrid.

MUNICIPALIDAD DE BUENOS AIRES
1910   *Documentos y planos relativos al período edilicio colonial de la ciudad de Buenos Aires*. Buenos Aires.

MÚÑOZ CAMARGO, DIEGO
1892   *Historia de Tlaxcala*. Mexico City.

OUTES, FELIX F.
1930   *Cartas y planos inéditos de los siglos XVII y XVIII y primer decenio del XIX*. Buenos Aires.

PALM, ERWIN
1946   Hospitales antiguos de la Española. *Multa Pancis Medica* (September–October).

PIERSON, W. W., FEDERICO G. GIL
1957   *Governments of Latin America*. New York: McGraw-Hill.

RAMUSIO, GIO BATTISTA
1563–1565   [1556]   *Delle navigationi et viaggi* (third edition). Venice.

RIVA PALACIO, VICENTE, *editor*
1887–1889   *México a través de los siglos*. Mexico City.

ROSENBLATT, ÁNGEL
1954   *La población indígena y el mestizaje en América*. Buenos Aires: Nova.

SILVA SANTISTEBAN, FERNANDO
1964   *Los obrajes en el virreynato del Perú*. Lima: Museo Nacional de Historia.

SUARDO, JUAN A.
1935   *Diario de Lima (1629–1634)*. Lima.
TAULLARD, A.
1940   *Los planos más antiguos de Buenos Aires (1580–1880)*. Buenos Aires: Peuser.
TORRES LANZA, PEDRO
1921   *Relación descriptiva de los mapas, planos, etc. del virreinato de Buenos Aires existentes en el Archivo General de Indias*. Buenos Aires.
TOUSSAINT, M., F. GÓMEZ DE OROZCO, J. FERNÁNDEZ
1938   *Planos de la ciudad de México, siglos XVI y XVII*. Mexico City: Instituto de Investigaciones Estéticas, Universidad Autónoma de México.
TURBERVILLE, A. S.
1948   *La inquisición española*. Mexico City: Fondo de Cultura Económica.
VARGAS UGARTE, P. RUBEN
1947   *Relaciones de viajes (siglos XVI, XVII, XVIII)*. Lima: Compañía de Impresiones y Publicidad.
VÁZQUEZ DE ESPINOSA, ANTONIO
1948   *Compendio y descripción universal de las Indias Occidentales*. Smithsonian Miscellaneous Collection 108. Washington, D.C.: Smithsonian Institution.
VICUÑA MACKENNA, BENJAMÍN
1869–1870   *Historia de Valparaíso*, two volumes. Valparaíso.
1924   *Historia crítica y social de Santiago*. Santiago, Chile.
WRIGHT, I. A.
1916   *The early history of Cuba, 1492–1586*. New York.

COLONIAL

An Introduction to the Study of Provisioning in the Colonial City

FRANCISCO DE SOLANO

Provisioning in general has always aroused the interest of the specialist, even though his attention has been focused primarily on projecting his particular administrative, social, and/or religious orientation. For this reason, there are few studies in modern historiography where the nature, importance, fluctuations, and implications of provisioning are viewed in depth. The bibliography is largely based on official documentation, namely:

1. The legal dispositions emanating from the highest State organ of Spanish American affairs (the Council of the Indies), as a rule dictated *a posteriori*. Some of these were collected during the Spanish period (see Appendix, Section 1), while some have been classified just recently (see Appendix, Section 2).

2. The dispositions, ordinances, agreements, and edicts of Indian authorities (viceroys, *audiencias* [courts], governors) (see Appendix, Section 3).

3. The documentary collections embracing the correspondence of minor authorities (royal officials, cities, ecclesiastics, private persons), geographical descriptions, reports, etc. (see Appendix, Section 4). But in all these documentary collections, the theme of provisioning – however basic – is present only indirectly, the vital atmosphere of the city eludes the reader, an atmosphere that is still preserved in the municipal archives and notarial records. This can be found amply in the *actas de los cabildos* [municipal records], though only a few of the *actas* of the numerous urban centers of the Spanish Indies have been published (see Appendix, Section 5). Nonetheless, they reflect municipal preoccupations and concerns exclusively: prices in time of scarcity; deprivation of certain groups for lack of provisioning; problems created by the scarcity of grain, foods of animal origin, or water; the insufficiency of municipal lands; etc.

It is only recently that alimentation (Philipe 1961; Hemardiquer 1970) and provisioning of cities have been considered as subjects of ordinary historical analysis, resolved into chronological stages of greater or lesser density. Braudel emphasizes the existence of short- and long-term trends (1970: 15–22). These are short trends with respect to the reflections of contemporaries; by taking into consideration the social climate, political and economic circumstances, basic causes of upheaval, tensions and provocative acts, etc., one can make extra-ordinary deductions. In the same way, long-term junctures can be evaluated: demographic phenomena, urban and rural dominion, the distribution of property, agricultural cycles and meteorology, the achievements of the *cabildos* [municipal councils] in the face of the ambitions of individuals and/or the centralization of the State – these are good examples of the long- or very long-term trend.

The provisioning of the Ibero-American cities during the Spanish period depended on many factors, but what differentiates the city from the noncity is an economic factor: consumption on the one hand, and production, exchange, and the processing of goods with incidental (secondary) industries on the other. The pattern of consumption is determined by cultural and ecological factors and import distributing systems. The complex implications involved, together with the hyp-notism exercised up till now by political, diplomatic, and ideological history, have reduced the bibliography of this theme (where it is of any use at all) to meager proportions.

Colonization in the Spanish Indies was essentially urban. The Ibero-American city offered a high degree of integration and cohesion. Colonization, carried out with scanty technical, financial, and human resources, was affected by fusing distant products and men into a single heritage in the cities. This fusion was enlarged by the more or less extensive and effective incorporation of the aboriginal populations (with all the biological consequences of the resulting interracial con-tact). Dense land settlement made possible the organization of a "region" around a city, with subsistence farming maintaining the density of population: thus an economic unit was formed which lasted for centuries (Ramos 1970). To analyze the conditions and types of collective structuration in urban centers is a task of great importance and consequence. Such analysis must naturally be accompanied by the examination of methods, causes, and effects in the organization of urban space.

But the city, as a human and spatial unit engendering stimuli and behavior patterns, cannot originate or be sustained without an agrarian base. Every urban agglomeration in the Spanish Indies – from the first designs to the studied structuration of the New Ordinances for the Philippines of 1573 – relies on a suitable rural area, which speaks well for the intentions of the founders; and if this site happens to coincide later with important routes and commerce, the prestige and success of the city is assured. The prosperity, as well as the decline and death of a city, has many causes; one of the most important is the manner in which the problems of provisioning are solved. A permanent solution of this problem involves four factors:

1. demography
2. facility of communications
3. regional ecology
4. meteorology and agricultural cycles.

If geography plays an important role in all aspects of history, in the matter of provisioning that role is fundamental. But provisioning is also associated with the structuration or ideology of the society, its tastes and eating habits, religious norms and inclinations. All of these topics must be seriously considered when one is engaged with the urban problem, in general or in particular, and above all when establishing its links with the hinterland. The city gains or loses the hinterland in proportion to the increased or decreased necessity of the latter.

A full understanding of our topic, calls for the direct investigation of municipal documents, notarial registers, hospital accounts, administrative ledgers of ecclesiastical centers, etc. as well as of the documentation in the national archives. At the same time, attention must be given to certain factors which we consider to be indicators for an in-depth analysis, for short- as well as for long-term trends.[1]

METHODOLOGICAL CONSIDERATIONS

A study of urban provisioning – its dynamics and the heritage of the hinterland – should stand out clearly from the typological categories of cities (e.g. coastal or interior, located in fertile or arid zones, political/administrative nature), and it should include an examination

---

[1] The *encomenderos* [commissioners] settled in the city contributed, in a very significant fashion, to the development of the hinterland. For within the orbit of the city, not only physically but also juridically, were the allotments and Indian *encomiendas* whose proprietors lived in the urban nucleus. Thus the perimeter of Cuzco stretched for 300 kilometers (Moore 1954: 146). But with the creation of new urban nuclei, the original jurisdictional limits of the municipality were not strictly enforced, although the city repeatedly claimed villages that should be cut off from their municipal termini. Trujillo did this in 1583, asking for Cajamarca, Saña, and Santa (Archivo General de Indias 1583), and Piura did so in 1627, requesting Olmos, Motupe, Salas, Penachi, and Copis (Archivo General de Indias 1627).

These examples show the difference between municipal termini and hinterland, between municipal jurisdiction and economic influence and dependence.

of alimentary habits in the light of ethnic differentiation, structural factors, municipal resources, and sociopolitical attitudes.

DYNAMICS OF SHORT PERIODS

1. THE TYPOLOGY OF CITIES. If we distinguish between alimentation and consumption on the one hand and the processing of goods on the other, we see that Spanish American cities display certain peculiarities that give them a special character.

1a. To physical and ecological characteristics are added alimentary ones, arising from the geographical conditioning to which the eating habits of the European must submit. But his resistance to the native diet, which was completely successful only in certain cases, brought about one of the most marked transformations in native landscape and society.

In the Spanish Indies, the European's alimentary typology (Mediterranean foods: bread-making cereals, garden produce, dried vegetables, oil, wine, and mutton; Atlantic foods: beef, animal fats, milk and its derivatives, non-bread-making cereals, and fruits) was combined with the food that sustained and would continue to sustain the native population. These superimposed elements introduced greater complexity into the provisioning of cities, the adequacy of the solution depending on the following factors: the category of city and number of European inhabitants, the capacity for the organization of arable and pastoral land, and the transformation wrought in the landscape and in native societies.

Geographical situation causes the nature of alimentation to vary. Natural resources have determined the nature of labor in urban societies, the craft guilds attaining size and importance in accordance with the economic and administrative rank of the city.

Inland cities are great consumers of meat and have difficulty in providing themselves with fish, while coastal and near-coastal cities can profit from both elements. Supply of fish is essential to a Christian population, since on certain days of the year it constitutes the staple food – in spite of the Papal dispensation conferred on Spain. Fish can be provided to inland cities by rivers, ponds, and neighboring lakes, but always inadequately due to the distaste of the inhabitants or to insufficient supply; this source is supplemented by dried and smoked salt-water fish. Fish of the Atlantic and the Pacific even reaches cities far inland, such as Mexico and Potosí.

The tone of a city is defined by the wood, stone, or limestone available for basements, frameworks, structures, and platforms; these materials reveal its situation in an arid or tropical region, in one near or far from quarries. The need for wood as one of the few sources of power of the epoch was one of the causes of deforestation and soil erosion. In the same way, the expansion of certain types of cultivation, such as that of the vine, caused wheat and maize fields to recede to terrains either unfavorable in themselves or lacking in manure. The advantages of cattle raising for the supply to cities of meat, leather, milk, and wool resulted in the expulsion of the native from lands traditionally devoted to agriculture. The need for wood, leading to tree cultivation, reduced areas in which agriculture could have expanded. These factors produced regional subdivision at a time when demographic density was beginning to rise, mediocre soils came under cultivation and were soon exhausted, and a less flexible system of crop rotation was adopted. Conditions less prejudicial to the productivity of agriculture and the necessities of the city were to come about during the long history of Spanish America, or – as regards the short historical unit – when the rural population growth subsided and when changes of habitat and reclassification of the soil took place, brought about by intense mobility and the raising of the standard of living in one part of urban society.

To products must be added water, which is indispensable for population, cattle, agriculture, and sanitation, and which provides power for driving the water mills.

1b.   As to the founding of cities, the European created urban centers in the following ways:

1. on preexisting urban centers or near regions that can expect a growing demographic density;

2. spontaneously or accidentally, impelled by discoveries of precious metals;

3. deliberately, in order to maintain a land or sea route of economic importance, or the possession and control of a certain region, or the defense of frontiers or areas subject to native attack.

In the first case, the problem of provisioning was in large measure resolved by the pre-Hispanic systems, which the European used and improved, though this procedure occasioned radical transformations of the aboriginal population. In the other two instances, the European had to secure a base for the maintenance of ports, towns in the vicinity of silver mines, and garrisoned fortresses, almost all situated in areas of low productivity. The majority of these centers – although juridically some do not qualify as cities – might be termed "artificial," having no proper agricultural basis; as a result, the viceregal administration tended to achieve provisioning by granting special allowances for the supply of certain goods, especially in those cities where the population was considerably increased at different times of the year. This procedure was indispensable in the economic zone of the Route of the Indies (Havana, Portobelo, and Panama, for example). Provisioning was also achieved by means of a very elaborate structuring as in Potosí, whose hinterland extends nearly to the Pacific and the Atlantic (Cobb 1949; Helmer 1950).

1c.   Commercial relations, marketing, and processing inherent in the urban economy and its needs in Spanish America were rigidly determined by social structure and racial differences.

Guild activities of the Europeans drew on the native population according to its cultural level, the attitudes and pressures of the white laboring classes, and the degree of participation or passivity of the Indian (Gibson 1964: ch. 9).

One of the chief concerns of the European was to incorporate the native world. But in spite of the efforts of the State in the egalitarian spirit of Christianity, the Indian found himself occupying the lowest rung in a society under the orders of a white minority. Numerically the Indian represented a powerful element which might have lent quite another color to social reality and which was capable of producing class consciousness. But a series of factors prevented the awakening of this consciousness. The standard of living and education of the Indian rose in the urban centers in accordance with the degree of his absorption of the cultural advances initiated and maintained by the European, and was connected to the receptivity and responses offered by the Indians.

2.   URBAN NECESSITIES AND DEMOGRAPHY. The relationship between population level, the consumption of goods and urban needs varies in Spanish American cities because every urban nucleus in the Spanish Indies consisted of a population of three different racial elements – white, Indian, and Negro in varying proportions, with such biological results as were occasioned by their contact – and each element had its own social and nutritional habits. As a result, there were constant difficulties in provisioning, which was frequently disrupted by destructurizing factors (climatic, physical, or sociological). Municipal concern was constantly directed towards supplying this entire population, and for our purposes it is necessary to establish the exact proportion between need, consumption, and number of inhabitants in the urban center (citizens, permanent residents, lodgers, temporary residents, floating population). These facts are to be determined by the censuses, tax rolls, lists of travelers, military, civil service, and ecclesiastical endowments, etc.; and also by cycle of

births, marriages, and deaths traced through parish records, property of the deceased, etc. (for which the suggestions of Rosenblatt [1954, 1967] are of great assistance, and especially the brilliant school of historical demography of Berkeley under the inspiring direction of Cook and Borah). Thus by determining as exactly as possible the numbers of inhabitants, and comparing them with the subsistence records of food and goods, we can answer the question of whether the colonial city was adequately provisioned, how it was provisioned, and the fluctuations to which the provisioning was subject. The different urban necessities may be detected in various sources:

2a. *Alimentary Necessities.* The white population and its satellites (servants, Negroes, and *mestizos*) accusomed to wheat, wine, and fats, and the Indian population with its associated groups (the poor and the "mixed castes" who have adopted their diet) faithful to maize and to the fermented liquors (*pulque* and *chicha*), can be determined by analyzing the following:

1. Municipal accounts, reflected in the registers and journals of the granaries and wheat exchanges, in which are entered income and expenditures; tolls, which give the exact figure of the various products brought into the city, as do other taxes on consumption, such as excise.

2. Accounts of hospitals, ecclesiastical centers, etc. which reflect on the one hand the state of health of the city and on the other hand an important section of the population which supplied itself from its own vegetable gardens and properties and which therefore is not reflected in the municipal registers.

3. Industries related to alimentation: for instance, wind and water mills, horizontal and vertical types, the number of which shows the level of sustenance and the possibilities of supply for the urban center. As generators of power, mills are an unusually rewarding subject of investigation due to their close connection with population growth (Calvento 1966).

Within this area of alimentary necessities should be included: fodder, hay, stalks of maize, straw, and oats, all of which are indispensable for the feeding of cattle which are kept in the city or which are destined for the slaughterhouse or for transport.

2b. *Social Necessities.* Differences in social necessities between the classes were quite marked, and "necessities" were conditioned by mentality, behavior, and sociological exigencies and climate. Even esthetic tastes and norms were important. "Baroque" is by rights the style of Spanish America, although the city did not benefit directly. Its splendors were reserved for private and ecclesiastical buildings; the city itself was not beautified. Indian baroque, apart from the external richness of certain façades, is an intimate art, intended to be seen and experienced in interiors (of temples and houses) and to be embodied personally in the external luxury of clothing and in the magnificent display of private or public celebrations, such as royal births and marriages, accession of monarch, arrivals of viceroys and archbishops, etc. Exterior manifestations were also in baroque fashion: carriages, pomp, cavalcading, etc., signaling a life-style which was imitated by the native aristocracy (López Sarrelangue 1965).

All of this was a spur to social mobility, generated by the social whitening of *mestizo* and the mulatto; for the creole – of middle or lower rank – the accoutrements of acquiring nobility and a high life-style were directly connected with the property and land system because of the seignorial power they conferred ("land is not riches, but rather lordship," as the proverb goes). This mobility produced the social tensions, exploitation, usurpation, and confrontations which are more acute in and around the cities because there the organization of competitive groups is easier and more effective.

The necessities of the different social classes may be recognized from the descriptions, reports, and accounts in the works of writers and chroniclers of the Spanish Indies (Esteva Barba 1964), as well as in the documentary sources previously indicated, which depict clothing (shirts, gorgets, hats, skirts, footwear, etc.) and textiles (cotton, wool, silk, shirting, cantala, etc.); housing (dwellings, furniture, kitchen utensils, spoons, nails, pottery, etc.); lighting (wax and tallow candles, oil); ornaments (goldsmith's work, jewels, cabinetwork, paintings, carpets); religious beliefs (aids to devotion: books, crosses, medals, rosaries, candles, ex-votos) and cultural appurtenances (sacred vessels, ornaments, images, paintings, bells, incense, etc.) and amusements (cards, books, saddles, stirrups, etc.).

2c. *Power Requirements.* Fuels and power mills play a fundamental part in the structure of preindustrial society, not only by virtue of their use in the textile, mineral, and metallurgical industries, which saves muscular energy – but also by virtue of their connection with the possibilities of supply for urban nuclei. The diffusion of water and wind mills for grain, oil, flour, etc., as well as the exploitation of woods as a source of fuel (houses, furnaces, etc.), are phenomena which are strictly related to population increase. Makkai (1971) analyzed the possibility of arriving at the supply capacity of cities through the study of the volume of the various types of hydraulic wheels and their rate of output; for example, the output per hour of a mill is five times the output of two men working a hand mill, and at least double that of a mill worked by animal traction.

3. WORK, PRODUCTIVITY, AND PROCESSING TECHNIQUES. Agricultural and technological productivity in the countryside has been defined as the measure of the efficiency with which available resources are converted into goods and desired services (Cipolla 1971); this statistic is arrived at by a combination of the totality of production factors (in real terms) with the product (also in real terms). In the economic system of the sixteenth through the nineteenth centuries, one observes definite technological progress, improvements in economic scale, and division of labor, not to mention the increase in work force accompanying the phenomenon of urbanization and the formation of communities and guild corporations.[2]

This climate of productivity is linked both the macro- and microeconomics. In microeconomics, work and the natural riches of production dominate. Consequently the effects of productivity are to be sought in the combination of these two factors. But before the industrial revolution, labor was exploited as much as natural wealth. Slicher van Bath (1965) and van der Wee (1971) call attention to the fact that the benefits of productivity in the strict sense are only realized slowly and with difficulty. Conditions favoring increasing demand might considerably augment physical production per enterprise unit in a given economy without necessarily resulting in important disbursements of capital or massive importation of raw materials. On the other hand, subsequent to the Spanish Conquest the utilization of factors of production is in abeyance, simulated or real, in that the augmentation of productivity is derived from the exploitation of natural reserves. During the seventeenth and eighteenth centuries, the absorption of labor was speeded up, while physical productivity gave way to economic productivity under the influence of increasing urbanization.

In macroeconomics, capital as a factor of production played a fundamental part in the preindustrial period. But this capital was closely linked to interprovincial trade. It circulated and its role was vital, above all through its impact on the commercial and urban substructure, which was in turn influenced by an eagerness to increase the volume of goods. And the importance of this interprovincial trade made possible the creation of dynamic models of economic growth.

4. CORRESPONDENCE BETWEEN SOCIAL CLASS AND PROVISIONING. Provisioning, inevitably, is intimately linked with social mentality and social action. When provisioning is defective, the pro-

---

[2] The best study of guild organization, although it concentrates on the viceroyalty of New Spain, is that of Carrera Stampa (1954). Barrio Lorenzot (1921), Muro Arias (1956), Chinchilla Aguilar (1956), Samayoa Guevara (1956, 1960), and Landazuri Soto (1959), among others, have also worked in this field.

blems created by scarcities, periodical food crises, endemic famine, and/or conditions of alimentary deficiency result in social malaise, which manifests itself in riots, demonstrations, and popular uprisings.[3] The history of our daily bread, of our daily maize, brings together the great social history of the well-to-do and the deprived, the rich and the poor. A great number of the undernourished are not included in statistics – the old, the infirm, the insane, orphans, the unemployed, those evicted from their holdings, ruined country folk, the victims of circumstance, etc. All these people, in years of adversity, aggravate the problems of cities, in which scarcity is inevitably accompanied by a rise in the price of food (Florescano 1965, 1969) producing social conflict or rendering it more acute. Marginal (though reflecting the state of this problem) is the consideration of popular entertainments – bullfights, theatres – and public demonstrations against heretics, which served as a safety valve to popular anger, channeling it against the enemies of religion instead of against civil power at those junctures when the city suffered the greatest dearth of provisions.

Social classes also determine food habits, not only with regard to diet but to provisioning as well. A large section of the city – including the nobility and religious orders – evaded the municipal tax on meat, and statistical accounts and controls do not register this section, which, for whatever reason, had special avenues of supply. The white man's eagerness to attain the status of gentleman, whether right or wrong, does not proceed from an exclusively social interest. Nobles did not pay taxes and had the right to secure victuals in times of scarcity and to enjoy discounts at other times. Religious orders were free of sales tax and their provisioning is also not entered in municipal account books because they had their own butchers and granaries, eluding municipal controls. Of course charity and the feeding of the poor fell to these religious institutions. But in studying this subject, we should not forget the extent to which bakeries and butcheries and stores of flour and maize were in the hands of the ecclesiastical class.

Nutrition, Diets, and Tastes. The population of Spanish America had an ill-regulated diet. It is only recently that alimentary regimes have begun to be studied, with calculations of calories and vitamins (Spooner 1961, 1962; Lisanti 1963). And when we compare the nutritive value of different foods (cereals, meat and fish, milk foods and fats, beverages, etc.) we see that calories were ill-balanced, which indicates that the alimentary sensitivity of Spanish Americans changed

[3] Génaro García (1907), Querol Roso (1935), Feijoo (1964, 1965), and Guthrie (1945) analyze events in the city of Mexico. Felice Cardot (1961) does the same for the Venezuelan area.

very slowly. To the alimentary tastes of the Spanish peninsula, Indian products were introduced tardily. The Castilian stew, made of chick-peas, meat, and bacon, becomes the creole stew, in which chick-peas (an expensive item) are replaced by meal, *arracache* [an herb similar to the carrot], sweet manioc, maize, and the Andes potato. The eighteenth century also witnessed a change in taste, with the adoption of sweetened dishes in preference to sharp-flavored ones, of cocoa and other genuinely American fruits.

A monotonous diet, rather than a frugal one, was becoming ever more irregular and deficient as one descended the social scale. Quantity made up for quality. Culinary technique was rudimentary, acquisitions from Roman and Arab cooking had been forgotten, and Renaissance and/or Oriental refinements came late or were reserved for select tables. Pre-Hispanic cuisine had few attractions for the European, who could not habituate his palate to certain ingredients such as the *axayacatl*, insects of the valley of Mexico which delighted the Nahua. On the other hand, condiments were adopted fairly quickly: the *chili* with its rich vitamin content made up for dishes based on cereals, fish, and wine. In general, there was a great deficiency of vitamin D and a considerable deficiency of vitamins A and C. The result was poor resistance to infection and the rapid progress of epidemics.

Sparse and deficient food justified abundance during the festivals, whether religious, civil, private, official, or municipal: they compensated by the luxury of abundance. Fiestas and holidays were the occasions of a good table in the cities with a return to monotony and routine for the rest of the year. A disruptive element, however, was provided by ecclesiastical events. The Catholic calendar, developed in the Mediterranean world, was out of step with the American world. The arrival of Christmas in summer may have merely trivial consequences, but this cannot be said of the traditional slaughtering months, especially for the pig, arriving at the time when the Church was celebrating Lent. This meant that the population had to maintain permanent abstinence if it wished to be strictly observant of the commands of the Church. In Guatemala, for example, the parish priest of the Indian pueblos and tableland *villas* solicited dispensations from the Archbishop in 1772 so that the populace might be able to eat meat at this time in general contravention of those commands.

Alimentary consumption comprised two large categories: (1) Food of animal origin, the highest rated being beef, which was out of reach of the purse of the poor, who had to content themselves with pork. The figure for meat consumption per day was about 250 grams and may also correspond to the quantity of fish, which replaced it on days of abstinence. Bacon, lard, eggs, and beverages: milk (food for invalids), beer, chocolate, and wine (indispensable in Catholic countries for the celebration of the Mass). (2) Food of vegetable origin, obviously cereals, vegetable garden products, and fruits. A third group – of complementary products – consisted of spices and condiments (sometimes local, sometimes imported) and salt, as indispensable to human beings as to cattle and irreplaceable in food conservation.

Urban groups are differentiated through their alimentary tastes, which influence demand, but it is not by their acquisitive power alone that they differentiate themselves: manual workers preserve certain traditional rural habits evidenced by the monotony of their diet. This produces a mentality resistant to innovations. "Alimentary customs do not develop in line with the economy" (Sorre 1952: 184) and are only modified under the persistent stress of economic crisis. Oats, for example, came into use by the populace in Mexico during the economic crisis of 1784; up till then they had been given only to animals (Chávez Orozco 1953a).

5. TRANSPORT AND COMMUNICATIONS, ROADS AND HIGH-WAYS. It is the fertile rural region together with roads, highways, and trade that gives birth and growth to a city. A city is inconceivable without roads, and the more important these are, the more the importance of the city will grow, provincial and regional characteristics becoming recessive. The economic function of communication routes, whether by land or sea, is of capital importance, for in the majority of cases it means the circulation of goods, their transport from the place of production to that of consumption. A good transport network presupposes deregionalization and the effective transition from an urbanized economy to a provincial and/or national one, from a local and domestic economy to one of a much more national scope.

The European encountered regions where a pre-Hispanic culture had developed a superb network of roads, but the large part of the American continent completely lacked a transport network. This meant that during the greater part of the sixteenth century people relied on the existing network, that of the sea and rivers (Borah 1954; Chaunu and Chaunu 1955–1959). Efforts were also made to open roads in the regions which lacked them (Jara 1969) and to improve existing ones, as in 1555, with the widening to thirty-six feet of the Chapultepec-Cuyuacán road and the roads of the *ejido* [public lands] from Mexico to Tacuba in order to permit the passage of carts. The growing political life in the seventeenth and eighteenth centuries intensified communications by the rivers (Acevedo 1949; Ybot León 1958; Lobo 1957, 1959–1960; Batista Ballesteros 1959; Molina 1960) and seaways (Chaunu 1960; Chaunu and Chaunu 1955–1959; Covington 1958; Schurz 1939; Santiago Cruz 1962). Ports in suitable places were selected and permanent defenses were maintained – the Armada de Indias, ramparts, forts, citadels (Rodríguez Casado 1949; Calderón Quijano 1942, 1953). Land routes were also promoted (Céspedes del Castillo 1946; Zúñiga 1948; Moorehead 1958; Hussey 1960).

The need for roads became ever more pressing, new ones being constructed so that local economy and production might play their part in the conveyance of products to dense population centers where consumption was on the increase. When vast areas were organized and fresh territory occupied, the structuration and continuity of communications was prepared beforehand, through and across communication routes. How these developments were tied to "territorial expansion and occupation of the soil" has been analyzed at the Third International Congress of Economic History, Bloomington (Jara 1969).

Dirt roads, following the contour of the terrain, are slow and lazy routes; mountains in the winter and marshlands in the summer obstruct them. Nonetheless, in spite of geographical and technical obstacles, they are indispensable arteries connecting the great trunk roads (the royal highways) with the local roads and distant centers of production. Maritime communications supplement the land network. Oceans are decidedly effective in speeding up communications, in spite of the everlasting conflicts in the Atlantic (international wars and the organized presence of other European nations). The Pacific, rarely frequented by other than Spanish ships (Navarro García 1965; Ramos 1970; Brand 1958) represented an extraordinary degree of intercommunication.

Intercommunication and interrelation of the various Indian territories established itself from the first moment of the Spanish presence in America. So much so that Ramos (1970) does not hesitate to divide it into three specific periods:

1. The first served as background to the trade of the age of discovery, exploration, and conquest. The bases of supply, functioning as nurturing centers, were the urban nuclei of the West Indies where European men, animals, and plants became acclimatized. For each conquest there was a center of this type, right from the time of the first expeditionary force. Success and failure, rapidity or difficulty of conquest, all depended on the link between the armies and their source of supply. It was a hasty trade, one of high prices and basic products (victuals and other items necessary for the army, though luxury foods and clothing articles are not lacking).

2. The centuries of Austrian rule are characterized by a policy of integration. In accordance with the mercantilist and protectionist orientation of the Council of the Indies and of the House of Trade, the government concerned itself mainly with protecting, promoting,

and guiding the Indies domain in such a way as to integrate all its elements. Regions of limited resources were protected by a trade in the products that were the backbone of their economy (cocoa for Venezuela for example, to the detriment of Guatemala or Guayaquil cocoa, as these two regions could reckon on other products for the maintenance of their internal economy).

3. The liberalizing currents released by the eighteenth century were to throw this system completely out of gear and were one of the main sources of competition among its different parts, which by this time operated with the same exportable products. A veritable breeding ground of tension and eventual disaffection began to develop.

In land and/or sea communications, which had to reckon with their difficulties (banditry and native attacks in the first instance, pirates and international wars in the second), we can distinguish what Braudel points out as maximum and minimum velocities, bearing in mind that maximum velocity can be as much a matter of slowness as of speed. The news, precious metals, luxury articles of clothing and food, spices, and books traveled faster than wood, salt, wheat, or flour. In spite of everything, progress brought about considerably greater speed on the land routes, which had more often caused delays. Conditions improved for reasons of strategy, finance, and supply so as to solve the problems of the urban and mining centers, to collect taxes, and to give free passage to precious metals.

But what made possible the domination of these extensive territories, especially as the seventeenth century advanced, was the increase in horses and mules. Transport by mule was an important phenomenon which has been very little studied and which deserves more attention. Transported on the backs of mules, merchandise did not require roads, but only byways and footpaths which sufficed for everything from mail service to the regular traffic of merchandise and travelers. Mules eliminated the need for human transport (the *tameme*, or native carrier) and improved the condition of the *chasqui*, or postboy. But the necessities of mineral transport and the provisioning of silver-mining towns brought about the use of teams of draught animals of truly gigantic proportions.

In spite of these facilities, however, communications as well as transport suffered from inefficiency, obstructed as they were by a combination of circumstances – bureaucratic gigantism and monopolies – to the considerable detriment of urban supplies in particular, the lowest classes suffering most.

6. DESTRUCTURIZING ELEMENTS. In spite of the ills that decimated the autochthonous population (the classic study is the work of Cook and Borah [1971]), it was in the Spanish American cities that

population multiplied in the Spanish Indies, almost from the moment of their foundation, occasioning and expanding the problem of provisioning. Hunger impelled the rural population to seek the cities in times of economic crisis, and to (and due to) the problem of scarce and poor food other problems were added and/or aggravated, producing disaffection. Such was the problem of the shantytowns; the derelict suburbs, the poverty-striken villages, the *favelas* of today must have existed without a doubt during the Spanish centuries, although we hear little of them and from very few sources.[4]

These problems with their capacity for destructurization may be occasioned by:

6a.   *Extra-Economic Agents Producing Unforeseeable Effects.*

1. Climatic vagaries: droughts, irregular harvests, maize frosts, etc., together with disease and epidemics in wheat and maize, made themselves felt in the irregularities, the deterioration, and the pressures of years of scarcity; these phenomena were necessarily reflected in movements of prices and in speculation. The corporations endeavored to find solutions in the *cómputo* [literally, "computation"], a system which maintained the price of bread at a constant level, although its weight diminished.

2. Catastrophes and wars: all the consequences occasioned by the dramatic episodes of floods, volcanic eruptions, and earthquakes, with their destruction of hydraulic installations resulting in the sterility of the soil and epidemics. The annihilation in 1687 and 1719 of the *haciendas* in the Lima Valley and its environs, which provisioned the capital of the viceroy of Peru, for example, not only led to the transformation of the landscape through the exploitation of the mountain slopes in view of pressing necessities, but was further compensated for by the importation of Chilean wheat, thus enlarging the city's hinterland to hitherto unsuspected frontiers (Ramos 1967).

6b.   *Economic Causes*

1. Diminution of purchasing power owing to the scantiness and irregularity of provisioning, which prevented the utilization of the productive capacity of the craft guilds.

2. Disorganization of economic life by factors of strife and conflict, produced or augmented by social and/or physical pressures and crises caused by defective communications, etc.

6c.   *Social and Political Causes*

It would be advisable, before indicating these, to establish a

[4]   A. von Humboldt (1822: vol. 1, 235) calculated that some 15,000 inhabitants of the city of Mexico had no home of their own at the beginning of the nineteenth century.

typology of the traditional Spanish American structures and their subdivisions in order to bring out the true meaning of the social mentalities occurring in each one of these divisions and their mutual connections and tensions, with specific characteristics for each region, territory, and administrative-political division. Such a typology would involve the following: agricultural societies; pastoral societies; the role of the native within each of these two types of society, and the effect of that role on the urban centers; the role of white minorities and of the rest of the white population; the role of the "mixed castes"; the guilds; the role of power groups: (a) the role of the aristocracy, both blood aristocracy (nobles, conquistadores and their sons, gentry), and money aristocracy (landowners and mine-owning traders); (b) officials; (c) clergy.

As divisive, destructurizing process may be noted:

1. The struggle for land. The formation of big properties (Chevalier 1952; Simpson 1952; Romero de Terreros 1956; Lockhart 1965; Martínez Ríos 1970).

2. The monopolization and usurpation of land (Gibson 1964; de Solano 1971).

3. *Mayorazgos* (entails) (Fernández de Recas 1965).

4. The struggle for water (Ruggeroni 1964).

5. The sale of offices (Parry 1963).

6. Native absenteeism.

7. The *Mesta* (sheep and cattle owners' guild) (Chávez Orozco 1956; Dusenberry 1963).

And, operating directly in and through urban centers, are:

8. The corporation monopolies.

9. The power of the big agriculturists and cattle breeders, *vis-à-vis* the small proprietor and/or trader of white and/or other races.

10. The excise of power by the State granaries and the guilds.

In the eighteenth century, difficulties arose in still another quarter, adding complications to urban problems: the municipality became politicized, with overtones of vindication produced by the clash of interests, which are extremely interesting and have not been sufficiently studied:

1. The clash between reformism and the "consolidation of properties" and "reservations of the Indian."

2. The spread of *mayorazgos*.

3. The spread of large property holdings, and the tendency towards large agrarian-commercial-industrial enterprises.

4. The new societies of cattle breeders (for instance, the gaucho societies).

5. The new economic societies: Amigos del País, Compañías Económicas (Moreyra Paz-Soldán 1956; Morales Padrón 1955; Hussey 1962).

The play of these rival interests took place in the framework of the objectives and intentions of the political economy and the overall activity of the *intendencias* (Navarro García 1959; Acevedo 1965; Deustua Pimentel 1965; Morazzani 1966).

7. THE ROLE OF THE MUNICIPALITY. Local Indian government was formed in the image of the Castilian municipality of the fifteenth and sixteenth centuries (Ots Capdequi 1958; Muro Orejón 1960), in which the urban authorities (magistrates, corregidors, and aldermen) were charged with the provisioning with food and articles of prime necessity. As to sustenance, all the urban centers (of Spaniards, of *mestizos*, and of natives) had at their disposal certain elements which had been established and defined from the moment of foundation, increasing or diminishing in accordance with the evolution and needs of the city (and coincidental in certain regions with pre-Hispanic precedents). These elements were private and communal land and included the *ejidos* (Bayle 1952; Chevalier 1952), woods, waters (Martínez Ríos 1961; Chinchilla Aguilar 1970), pastures, and uncultivated lands. The status of these resources was ratified by an increasing number of legal enactments (some of them included in the *Recopilación de Indias* of 1680[5] as well as by certain privileges: the possibility of leasing supplies to individuals, or *obligados*, who were then "obligated" to provide meat (Dusenberry 1948), fish, salt, candles, groceries (spices, oil). All supplies were channeled through two agencies:

1. The Tribunal of Exact Executorship, which controlled provisioning of food and articles of prime necessity, and had furthermore the duty of inspecting all crafts organized as guilds.

2. State granaries, which were the granaries of the city, charged with the storing of wheat and maize, the regulation of prices, and the maintenance of reserves for times of scarcity, as well as reserves of seeds for the poor farmers of the city and its environs (Rubio Coloma 1935; Guthrie 1941; Lee 1949; Fernández Xocolotzi 1949; Chávez Orozco 1954–1957; Florescano 1965).

The administration of the municipality, which had been democratically regulated by legal ordinance, theoretically elected by vote from persons living in the vicinity (Bayle 1952), lost this character from the moment state power began to grow and as soon as municipal offices could be bought. This situation developed under the pressures of the state's economic difficulties, and the offices were acquired by the most powerful who oriented the necessities of the city in terms of personal considerations. The alderman's attitude, then, ceased to possess the ideal character of attention to the problems of the community. This

---

[5] Book II, title 14, law 41; Book IV, title 13, law 6; book IV, title 14, laws 3 and 4.

explains, among many other things, the difficulty encountered in eradicating the middlemen – the bargainers – who raised prices of products in times of economic crisis and were one of the direct causes of social malaise.

Municipal economic policy constitutes an important element of the urban context (Pike 1960; Mauro 1962). The *cabildos* tended to restrain the level of expenditure, which is borne by the local consumer, without taking into account production revenues. As a result, when the city grew demographically, there was an increase in local consumption (Ramos 1967), in which case the *cabildo* must suppress the rise in prices by opposing the export of products – especially agricultural ones – in order to avoid inflation. This climate existed throughout the sixteenth and seventeenth centuries (Chávez Orozco 1953b). During the eighteenth century, these communal attitudes of the corporation were to conflict with liberalizing ideas and the development of certain regions (Martínez Ríos 1961a) to the detriment of others.

The dynamics of the provisioning of the Spanish American city can be determined for short periods if we attend to these and other data in the national and Spanish archives (Archivo General de Indias, Archivo Histórico Nacional, etc.), and above all in the municipal archives. It is in this latter remarkable source that we find the notarial material which has been so scarcely used.

DYNAMICS OF LONG PERIODS

No general study exists of the problem of the long-term provisioning of the colonial Spanish city. A study of this kind would require that the phenomena met with in shorter periods be fully defined and meshed with the series of variables that can be observed and measured over long periods. These may be listed as follows:

1. Demographic variations. The relation between population and sustenance, if we are to be guided by the celebrated binomial theorem of Malthus, is essentially determined by the number of inhabitants, the use of the soil, economic life, and social relationships, all of which contribute to its specific character. Among these variables, demography is the one that has the richest bibliography, of great assistance to the inquirer. Cook and Borah are especially outstanding in the scientific rigor of their researches (see the introductory chapters of *Essays in population history* [1971] for their considerations on methodology). For the calculation of population and its difficulties, see de Solano (1972).

2. Variations in production techniques and, consequently, in output.

3. Salaries and wages.

4. Prices of: foods, manufactured products, manual labor, building (stone, unfired brick, wood), housing, clothing (finery and work clothes), cycles of importation and exploration, etc. Price variables are much more easily regulated than others and have therefore commanded the interest of a great number of specialists; among whom the following are deserving of special mention for methodology and bibliography: Labrousse (1933, 1938), Hamilton (1934, 1936, 1947), Schaap (1945), Romano (1965a, 1965b), Vilar (1964), Frêche and Frêche (1967).

5. The distribution and fluctuation of urban and rural property: the economy of the soil (Ots Capdequi 1946; Chevalier 1952; Martínez Ríos 1970).

6. Fluctuation of income.

7. Agricultural cycles (Slicher van Bath 1965).

8. Meteorology and its connection with history. Since human history is so closely dependent on climatic history, and since the city is always dependent on cultivation and the work of the countryman, who is stimulated or set back by climatic changes, it is absolutely essential to pay attention to the climatic tone of the cycles of cold and heat, dryness and humidity, and to their fluctuations as they affect each product (Klatzmann 1961), for on them depend the provisioning, storage, health, nutrition, and disposition of the city. LeRoy Ladurie (1965a, 1965b, 1966) establishes methodologies and Florescano (1969) furnishes examples from eighteenth-century New Spain.

9. Included also are external religious demonstrations: alms, gifts to the Church, chaplaincies, the properties of confraternities, sodalities, ecclesiastical institutions, processions, masses as a subject of testamentary dispositions, etc.

There is no doubt that an investigation of this caliber entails great difficulties, especially due to the uncertainty and variety of the available statistics, requiring the utmost care in regard to establishing figures.

CONCLUSIONS

Such an attempt at the study in depth of urban provisioning in relation to the short term as well as to long periods, taking into consideration all possible implications and peculiarities, would make manifest the role of the city, its necessities and dependencies. The value of urban dynamics is best to be demonstrated by a study concentrating on the municipal archives, the notarial registries, the parish records, the account books of hospitals and religious centers, the testimony of contemporaries, and Indian historiography. The development of the hinterland will thus emerge in all its reality.

APPENDIX

Section 1

1. Vasco de Puga. *Provisiones, cédulas, instrucciones de Su Majestad* (reprint). Mexico City. 1943 [1563].
2. Diego de Encinas. *Cedulario indiano* (reprint). 1945–1946 [1597].
3. Rodrigo de Aguiar y Acuña. *Sumarios de la recopilación de las leyes, ordenanzas para las Indias Occidentales*. Madrid. 1628.
4. Juan de Solórzano y Pereira. *Política indiana* (second edition enlarged and updated by Ramiro de Valenzuela). Madrid. 1776 [1647].
5. Juan de Solórzano y Pereira. *Libro primero de la recopilación de cédulas, cartas, provisiones y ordenanzas reales*. Madrid. 1650.
6. Antonio de Léon Pinelo. *Autos, acuerdos y decretos de gobierno del real y supremo Consejo de las Indias*. Madrid. 1658.
7. *Recopilación de las leyes de los reinos de Indias* (reprint). Madrid. 1943 [1680] (other editions in 1756, 1774, 1791).
8. Antonio Javier Pérez López. *Teatro de la legislación universal de España e Indias*, ten volumes. Madrid. 1791–1794.

Section 2

1. *Reales cédulas y provisiones*, 1517–1622. Buenos Aires: Archivo General de la Nación. 1911.
2. *Cedulario de las gobernaciones de Santa Marta y Cartagena de Indias, siglo XVI*. Edited by E. Serrano Sanz. Madrid. 1905.
3. "Gobernación espiritual y temporal de las Indias," in *Colección de documentos inéditos relativos. . . antiguas posessiones de ultramar*, volumes 22–25. Edited by E. Altolaguirre Duvale. Madrid. 1927–1932.
4. *Selección de las leyes de Indias referentes a descubrimientos, colonización, incremento de la riqueza, de la beneficiencia y de la cultura en los países de ultramar*. Madrid. 1929.
5. *Cedulario de la real audencia de Buenos Aires*. La Plata. 1929.
6. *Inventario general de registros cedularios referentes a Indias*. Edited by L. Rubio. Madrid. 1929.
7. *Cedulario de la real audiencia de Buenos Aires*. Edited by R. Levene. Madrid.
8. *Cedulario cubano. Los orígenes de la colonización, 1493–1512*. Edited by J. M. Chacón. Madrid. 1930.
9. *Disposiciones complementarias de las leyes de Indias*. Madrid: Ministerio de Trabajo. 1930.
10. *Colección de cédulas reales dirigidas a la audiencia de Quito, 1601–1660*. Edited by J. A. Garcés. Quito. 1935, 1946.
11. *Prontuario de reales cédulas dirigidas a la audiencia de Guatemala, 1529–1599*. Edited by J. J. Pardo. Guatemala City.

12. *Cedulario del Perú, siglos XVI, XVII y XVIII.* Edited by R. Porras. Lima. 1944.
13. *Reales cédulas, reales órdenes, decretos, autos y bandos que se guardan en el Archivo Histórico de Lima.* Edited by J. F. Muro. Lima. 1947.
14. *Cedulario americano del siglo XVIII.* Edited by A. Muro. Seville. 1956, 1967.
15. *Reales cédulas y correspondencia de gobernadores de Santo Domingo. De la regencia del Cardenal Cisneros en adelante,* five volumes. Edited by J. Marino Inchaustegui. Madrid. 1958.
16. *Cedulario de la monarquía española relativo a la provincia de Venezuela (1509–1522).* Edited by E. Otte. Caracas. 1959.
17. *Cedulario de la monarquía española relativo a la provincia de Venezuela (1523–1550).* Edited by E. Otte. Caracas. 1961.
18. *Cédulas reales relativas a Venezuela, 1500–1550.* Edited by E. Otte. Caracas. 1963.
19. *Cédulas reales de la monarquía española relativas a la parte oriental de Venezuela, 1520–1561.* Edited by E. Otte. Caracas. 1965.
20. *Cedularios de la monarquía española de Margarita, Nueva Andalucía y Caracas, 1553–1604.* Edited by E. Otte. Caracas. 1967.

Section 3

The following are examples of the published documentation (the unpublished documents, however, remain as important as they are numerous):

1. *Memoria de los virreyes que han governado el Perú durante el tiempo del coloniaje español,* six volumes. Lima. 1859–1860.
2. *Instrucciones que los virreyes de Nueva España dejaron a sus sucesores.* Mexico City. 1867.
3. *Relaciones de los virreyes y audiencias que han gobernado el Perú,* three volumes. Lima and Madrid. 1867–1871.
4. *Relaciones de los virreyes del Nuevo Reino de Granada.* Edited by J. A. García. New York. 1869.
5. *Relaciones de los virreyes del Perú, Marqués de Mancera y Conde de Salvatierra.* Edited by J. F. Polo. Lima. 1899.
6. Libro de provisiones reales de los virreyes don Francisco de Toledo y D. Martín Henríquez de Almansa. *Revista de Archivos y Bibliotecas Nacionales.* Lima. 1899.
7. Francisco Javier de Caro. *Diario de la secretaría del virreinato de Santa Fe de Bogotá en 1783.* Edited by F. Viñals. Madrid. 1904.
8. Documentos del virrey Toledo. *Revista Histórica* 3: 314–317. Lima.
9. *Relaciones de mando. Memorias presentadas por los gobernadores del Nuevo Reino de Granada.* Edited by E. Posada. Bogotá. 1910.
10. Audiencia de Charcas. *Correspondencia de presidentes y oidores. Documentos del Archivo General de Indias,* three volumes. Edited by R. Levillier. Madrid. 1918–1922.
11. *Gobernación del Tucumán. Papeles de gobernaciones en el siglo XVI. Documentos del Archivo General de Indias.* Edited by R. Levillier. Madrid. 1920.
12. *Gobernadores del Perú. Cartas y papeles, siglo XVI. Documentos del Archivo General de Indias,* fourteen volumes. Madrid. 1921–1926.
13. Audiencia de Lima. *Correspondencia de presidentes y oidores. Documentos del Archivo General de Indias.* Edited by R. Levillier. Madrid. 1922.

14. *Libro de informes de la real audiencia de Buenos Aires (1785–1810).* La Plata. 1929.
15. *Ordenanzas del virrey D. Francisco de Toledo.* Edited by R. Levillier. Madrid. 1929.
16. *Colección de las memorias o relaciones que escribieron los virreyes del Perú acerca del estado en que dejaban las cosas generales del reino,* two volumes. Madrid. 1867–1871.
17. *Instrucción reservada que el conde de Revilla Gigedo dió a su sucesor en el mando Marqués de Branciforte.* Madrid. 1931.
18. Documentos relativos al virrey don Luís de Velasco. *Boletín del Archivo General de la Nación* 6: 191–202. Mexico City. 1935.
19. The ordinances of the audiencia of Nueva Galicia. *Hispanic American Historical Review* 18: 364–373. Edited by J. H. Parry. Durham. 1939.
20. Mandamientos del virrey don Antonio de Mendoza. *Boletín del Archivo General de la Nación* 10: 213–273. Edited by E. O'Gormann. Mexico City. 1939.
21. *Memorias de los virreyes del Río de la Plata.* Buenos Aires. 1945.
22. *Acuerdos de la real audiencia del Nuevo Reino de Granada,* two volumes. Bogotá. 1947.

Section 4

The following are a representative sample of the growing collection of documentation:

A. GENERAL

1. *Colección de documentos inéditos para la historia de España,* 112 volumes. Madrid. 1844–1895. (The index, "América en la colección de documentos inéditos para la historia de España," was compiled by M. L. Díaz-Trechuelo.) Seville. 1970.
2. *Colección de documentos inéditos relativos al descubrimiento, conquista y organización de las antiguas posesiones de América y Oceanía,* forty-two volumes. Madrid. 1864–1884. (The index for this and the following [3] publications, "Indice de la colección de documentos inéditos de Indias," was compiled by E. Schaeffer.) Madrid: Instituto Fernández de Oviedo. 1946–1947.
3. *Colección de documentos inéditos relativos al descubrimiento, conquista y organización de las antiguas posesiones españolas de ultramar,* twenty-five volumes. Madrid. 1885–1932.
4. *Cartas de Indias.* Madrid: Ministerio de Fomento. 1877.
5. *Relaciones geográficas de Indias,* four volumes. Edited by M. Jiménez de la Espada. Madrid. (Second edition, three volumes, Madrid: BAE.) 1965.
6. *Colección de libros y documentos referentes a la historia de América,* twenty-five volumes. Edited by V. Saenz. Madrid. 1904–1929.
7. *Relaciones geográficas de Indias.* Edited by Germán Latorre. Seville. 1920.
8. *Colección de documentos inéditos para la historia de Hispanoamérica,* fourteen volumes. Edited by R. Altamira. Madrid and Barcelona. 1925–1932.
9. *Papeles de Indias.* Edited by the Duque de Alba. Madrid. 1947.
10. *Documentos para la historia social de Hispanoamérica,* four volumes. Edited by R. Konetzke CSIC. Madrid. 1958–1962.

B. SPECIFIC

I. *By country*

11. *Colección de documentos para la historia de México*, two volumes. Edited by J. García Icazbalceta. Mexico City. 1858–1866.
12. *Documentos históricos del Perú, en las épocas del coloniaje y de la independencia hasta el presente*, ten volumes. Edited by M. Oriozola. Lima. 1863–1879.
13. *Colección de documentos para la historia de Costa Rica*, ten volumes. Edited by L. Fernández. Barcelona. 1886–1907.
14. *Nueva colección de documentos inéditos para la historia de México*, five volumes. Edited by J. García Icazbalceta. Mexico City. 1886–1892.
15. *Archivo Boliviano. Colección de documentos relativos a la historia de Bolivia durante la época colonial.* Edited by V. Ballivian. Paris. 1873.
16. *Colección de documentos inéditos para la historia de Chile, desde el viaje de Magallanes hasta la batalla de Maipu*, thirty volumes. Edited by J. T. Medina. Santiago. 1888–1902.
17. *Colección de documentos sobre la geografía e historia de Colombia*, four volumes. Edited by A. B. Cuervo. Bogotá. 1891–1894.
18. *Papeles de Nueva España*, nine volumes. Edited by F. del Paso y Troncoso. Madrid and Mexico City. 1905.
19. *Documentos inéditos o muy raros para la historia de México*, thirty-seven volumes. Edited by G. García and C. Pereyra. Mexico City. 1905.
20. *Documentos inéditos del siglo XVI para la historia de México.* Edited by M. Cuevas. Mexico City. 1914.
21. *Antecedentes de política económica en el Río de la Plata. Documentos de los siglos XVI al XIX.* Edited by R. Levillier. Madrid. 1915.
22. *Documentos para la historia del Ecuador.* Quito. 1922.
23. *Documentos de Nueva España, 1536–1550.* Edited by S. Montoto. Madrid. 1927.
24. *Documentos para la historia de Yucatán, 1550–1776*, three volumes. Edited by F. Scholes. Mérida.
25. *Espistolario de Nueva España*, sixteen volumes. Edited by F. del Paso y Troncoso. Mexico City. 1938–1942.
26. *Correspondencia de los oficiales reales de hacienda del Río de la Plata con Reyes de España, 1540–1596.* Edited by R. Levillier. Buenos Aires. 1911.
27. *Documentos para la historia económica y social de Cuba.* Havana. 1956.
28. *Legislación real sobre hacienda para las provincias venezolanas.* Caracas.
29. *La iglesia de España en el Perú. Colección de documentos inéditos para la historia de la iglesia en el Perú.* Edited by C. Lissón. Seville. 1943–1945.
30. *Colección de documentos para la historia de Nicaragua*, nine volumes. Colección Somoza. 1955–1958. Madrid.
31. *Virreinato peruano. Documentos para su historia.* Edited by M. Moreyra. Seville. 1951.
32. *Documentos inéditos para la historia de Colombia*, ten volumes. Edited by J. Friede. Bogotá. 1955–1962.
33. *Documentos para la historia colonial de los Andes venezolanos, siglos XVI–XVIII.* Caracas. 1957.
34. *Documentos para la historia económica de Venezuela.* Edited by A. Arellano. Caracas. 1961.

II. *By city*

35. *Colección de documentos para la historia de San Luis Potosí*, four volumes. Edited by P. F. Velázquez. 1897–1899.
36. *Correspondencia de la ciudad de Buenos Aires con los Reyes de España*, three volumes. Edited by R. Levillier. Madrid. 1915–1918.
37. *Gobernación del Tucumán. Correspondencia de los cabildos del siglo XVI. Documentos del Archivo General de Indias*. Edited by R. Levillier. Madrid. 1918.
38. Algunos documentos del Archivo de Indias sobre ciudades chilenas. *Boletín del Centro de Estudios Americanistas* 8: 1–34. Edited by J. Pabón and L. Jiménez. Seville. 1921.
39. *Fundación española del Cuzco y ordenanzas para su gobierno*. Edited by H. H. Urteaga and C. A. Romero. Lima. 1926.
40. *Oficios o cartas al cabildo de Quito por el rey de España o el Consejo de Indias, 1552–1568*. Edited by J. Garcés. Quito. 1934.
41. *Colección de documentos inéditos para la historia de Tampico, siglos XVI y XVII*. Edited by J. Meade. Mexico City. 1935.
42. *Libro de los provehimientos de tierras, cuadras, solares, aguas, etc. por los cabildos de la ciudad de Quito, 1583–1594*. Quito. 1941.

Section 5

1. *Documentos concernientes a la fundación de Montevideo y actas de su cabildo*, five volumes. Montevideo. 1885.
2. *Acuerdos del extinguido cabildo de Montevideo*, eighteen volumes. Montevideo. 1885–1943.
3. *Actas del cabildo de la ciudad de México, 1524–1816*, fifty volumes. Mexico City. 1889–1916.
4. *Libro primero de los cabildos de Lima*, three volumes. Paris: E. Torres. 1900.
5. *Acuerdos del extinguido cabildo de Buenos Aires* (fourth series), forty-seven volumes. Buenos Aires. 1907–1934.
6. *Archivo capitular de Jujuy*, four volumes. Buenos Aires. 1913–1945.
7. "Actas del cabildo de Santiago," in *Colección de historiadores de Chile*, volumes 1, 17–21, 24, 25, 28, 30–44, 46, 47. Santiago. 1913.
8. *Libro de cabildos de la ciudad de Quito*, twenty-one volumes. Quito. 1934–1958.
9. *Libro primero de cabildos de la villa de San Miguel de Ibarra, 1606–1617*. Quito. 1937.
10. *Actas capitulares del ayuntamiento de la ciudad de La Habana*, two volumes. Edited by E. Roig. Havana. 1937.
11. *Libro primero del cabildo de la ciudad de Cuenca, 1557–1563*. Quito. 1938.
12. *Actas del cabildo de Tucumán*. Tucumán: M. Lizondo. 1939–1940.
13. *Actas capitulares de Corrientes*. Buenos Aires. 1941–1946.
14. *Actas capitulares de Santiago del Estero*, six volumes. Buenos Aires. 1941.
15. *Actas del cabildo de Caracas*, six volumes. Caracas. 1943–1959.
16. *Actas del cabildo de San Juan de Puerto Rico, 1730–1750*. San Juan. 1949.
17. *Libro primero de actas de la ciudad de Pamplona en el Nuevo Reino de Granada, 1552–1561*. Bogotá. 1950.
18. *Actas del cabildo de San Juan de Pasto*. Buenos Aires. 1959.

The merit of these sources is indisputable. Until now they have been utilized only indirectly and consequently their extraordinary fruits have not been reaped. In 1962, E. Poulain set himself the task of demonstrating this in a model work, with long-term perspectives, utilizing as his source the *Actas del cabildo de México, 1524–1816.*

REFERENCES

ACEVEDO, EDGARDO OSCAR
  1949   El primer proyecto de navegación del Bermejo. *Anuario de Estudios Americanistas* 9: 371–388. Seville.
  1965   *La intendencia de Salta de Tucumán.* Mendoza.
ARCHIVO GENERAL DE INDIAS
  1583   Audiencia de Lima, legajo 126.
  1627   Audiencia de Lima, legajo 159.
BARRIO LORENZOT, FRANCISCO
  1921   *El trabajo en México durante la época colonial. Ordenanzas de gremios de la Nueva España.* Mexico City.
BATISTA BALLESTEROS, ISAÍAS
  1959   Proyectos de canales interoceánicos en América. *Revista de la Universidad de Madrid* 7 (28): 482–490.
BAYLE, CONSTANTINO
  1949   Las elecciones en los cabildos de Indias. *Revista de Indias* 9: 597–643. Madrid.
  1952   *Los cabildos seculares en la América española.* Madrid.
BORAH, WOODROW
  1954   *Early colonial trade and navigation between Mexico and Peru.* Berkeley and Los Angeles: University of California Press.
BRAND, DONALD D.
  1958   *The development of the Pacific coast during the Spanish colonial period in Mexico.* Berkeley: University of California Press.
BRAUDEL, FERNAND
  1970   "Alimentation et categories de l'histoire," in *Pour une histoire de l'alimentation.* Edited by J. J. Hermardiquer, 15–22. Cahiers des Annales E.S.C. 28. Paris.
CALDERÓN QUIJANO, JOSÉ ANTONIO
  1942   El fuerte de San Fernando de Omoa. Su historia e importancia que tuvo en la defensa del golfo de Honduras. *Revista de Indias* 3 (9): 515–548 and 3(11): 127–163. Madrid.
  1953   *Historia de las fortificaciones en Nueva España.* Seville.
CALVENTO MARTÍNEZ, MARÍA DEL CARMEN
  1966   "El abastecimiento de pan en la ciudad de México, 1700–1800," in *Actas y Memorias del 36° Congreso Internacional de Americanistas* (Seville 1964) 4: 351–364. Seville.
CARRERA STAMPA, MANUEL
  1939   "Los obrajes de indígenas en el virreinato de la Nueva España," in *Actas del 27° Congreso Internacional de Americanistas* 2: 555–562. Mexico City.
  1952–1953   Las ferias novohispanas. *Historia Mexicana* 2: 319–342. Mexico City.

1954 *Los gremios mexicanos. La organización gremial en Nueva España, 1521–1861.* Mexico City.

CÉSPEDES DEL CASTILLO, GUILLERMO
1946 *Lima y Buenos Aires. Repercusiones económicas y políticas del virreinato del Río de la Plata.* Seville.

CHAUNU, PIERRE
1960 *Les Philippines et le Pacifique des Ibériques (XVIᵉ, XVIIᵉ et XVIIIᵉ).* Paris.

CHAUNU, PIERRE, HUGUETTE CHAUNU
1955–1959 *Seville et l'Atlantique,* nine volumes. Paris.

CHÁVEZ OROZCO, LUÍS
1953a *La crisis agrícola novohispana de 1784–1785.* Mexico City.
1953b *El control de precios en la Nueva España.* Mexico City.
1954–1957 *Documentos sobre alhóndigas y pósitos novohispanos,* ten volumes. Mexico City.
1956 "Prólogo" and "Recopilación," in *Papeles sobre la mesta. La organización de los ganaderos del siglo XVI.* Mexico City.

CHEVALIER, FRANÇOIS
1952 *La formation des grandes domaines au Méxique. Terre et société aux XVIᵉ et XVIIᵉ siècles.* Paris.

CHINCHILLA AGUILAR, E.
1956 *Ordenanzas de escultores, carpinteros, entalladores, ensambladores y violeros de la ciudad de México.* Mexico City.
1970 *El ramo de aguas de la ciudad de Guatemala en la época colonial.* Guatemala City.

CIPOLLA, CARLO
1971 "Per una storia della produttivitá nei secoli del Medioevo e del Rinascimento," in *Produttivitá e tecnologie nei secoli XII–XVIII.* Prato.

COBB, GWENDOLINE B.
1949 Supply and transportation for Potosí mines, 1545–1640. *Hispanic American Historical Review* 24. Durham.

COVINGTON, J.
1958 Trade relations between Florida and Cuba, 1600–1840. *Florida Historical Quarterly* 38 (2): 114–128. San Agustin.

COOK, SHERBURNE F., WOODROW BORAH
1971 *Essays in population history,* volume one. *Mexico and Caribbean.* Berkeley and Los Angeles: University of California Press.

DE SOLANO, FRANCISCO
1971 Tierra, comercio y sociedad. Un análisis de la estructura agraria centroamericana durante el siglo XVIII. *Revista de Indias.* Madrid.
1972 Algunas consideraciones sobre demografía histórica: problems en el cálculo de la población en la América Hispana (1492–1800). *Revista de la Universidad de Madrid* 20: 79, 185–218.

DEUSTUA PIMENTEL, CARLOS
1965 *Las intendencias en el Perú (1790–1796).* Seville.

DUSENBERRY, WILLIAM H.
1948 The regulation on meat supply in the sixteenth century. *Hispanic American Historical Review* 28. Durham.
1963 *The Mexican mesta. The administration of ranching in colonial Mexico.* Urbana: University of Illinois Press.

ESTEVA BARBA, FRANCISCO
1964   *Historiografía indiana*. Madrid.
FEIJOO, ROSA
1964   El tumulto de 1692. *Historia Mexicana* 14 (1): 42–70. Mexico City.
1965   El tulmulto de 1624. *Historia Mexicana* 14 (1): 42–70. Mexico City.
FELICE CARDOT, CARLOS
1961   *Rebeliones, motines y movimientos de masas en el siglo XVIII vene-zolano*. Madrid.
FERNÁNDEZ DE RECAS, GUILLERMO
1965   *Mayorazgos de la Nueva España*. Mexico City.
FERNÁNDEZ XOCOLOTZI, EFRAÍM
1949   Maize graineries in Mexico. *Botanical Museum Leaflets* 13 (7): 153–192. Harvard University.
FLORESCANO, ENRIQUE
1965   El abasto y la legislación de granos en el siglo XVI. *Historia Mexicana* 14: 567–630. Mexico City.
1969   *Precios del maíz y crisis agrícolas en México (1708–1810)*. Mexico City: El Colegio de México.
FRÊCHE, GEORGES, GENEVIÈVE FRÊCHE
1967   *Les prix des grains, des vins et des légumes à Toulouse (1486–1868). Extrait des mercuriales suivi d'une bibliographie d'histoire des prix*. Paris.
GARCÍA, GÉNARO
1907   *Tumultos y rebeliones acaecidos en México*. Mexico City.
GIBSON, CHARLES
1964   *The Aztecs under Spanish rule*. Stanford: Stanford University Press.
GUTHRIE, CHESTER L.
1939   Colonial economy: trade, industry and labor in seventeenth-century Mexico City. *Revista de Historia de América*. Mexico City.
1941   A seventeenth-century "ever normal granary": the alhóndiga of colonial Mexico City. *Agricultural History* 45: 37–43.
1945   "Riots in seventeenth-century Mexico City: a study of social and economic conditions," in *Greater America: Essays in honor of Herbert Eugene Bolton*. Berkeley: University of California Press.
HAMILTON, EARL J.
1934   *American treasure and the price revolution in Spain, 1501–1650*. Cambridge, Mass.
1936   *Money, prices and wages in Valencia, Aragon and Navarra, 1500*. Cambridge, Mass.
1947   *War and prices in Spain, 1651–1800*. Cambridge, Mass.
HARTENDROP, A. V.
1958   *History of industry and trade of the Philippines*. Manila.
HELMER, MARIE
1950   Commerce et industrie au Pérou à la fin du XVIIᵉ siècle. *Revista de Indias* 11 (41): 519–526. Madrid.
HEMARDIQUER, J. J., *editor*
1970   Pour une histoire de l'alimentation. *Annales E.S.C.* 28. Paris: Centre d'Études. Scientifiques.
HUSSEY, ROLAND H.
1960   Caminos coloniales en Panamá. *Lotería* 60: 105–128. Panama City.
1962   *La Compañía de Caracas, 1782–1784*. Caracas.

126   FRANCISCO DE SOLANO

JARA, ÁLVARO, *editor*
1969   *Expansión territorial y ocupación del suelo.* Mexico City: El Colegio de México.

KLATZMANN, J.
1961   Les limites du calcul économique en agriculture. *Études Rurales* 1: 50–60. Paris.

LABROUSSE, ERNEST
1933   *Esquisse du mouvement des prix et des revenues en France au XVIIIe siècle.* Paris.
1938   Observations complémentaires sur les sources et la méthodologie de l'histoire des prix des salaires au XVIIIe siécle. *Revue de l'Histoire Économique et Sociale* 24: 289–308. Paris.

LANDAZURI SOTO, ARTURO
1959   *El regímen laboral indígena en la real audiencia de Quito.* Quito.

LEE, RAYMOND L.
1949   Grain legislation in colonial Mexico, 1575–1585. *Hispanic American Historical Review* 27: 647–660. Durham.

LE ROY LADURIE, EMMANUEL
1965a Histoire et climat. *Annales E.S.C.* Paris: Centre d'Études Scientifiques.
1965b Le climat des XIe et XVIe siècles: séries comparées. *Annales E.S.C.* Paris: Centre d'Études Scientifiques.
1966   *Les paysans du Languedoc.* Paris.

Legislación
1938   *Legislación del trabajo en los siglos XVI, XVII, XVIII. Relación entre la economía, las artes y los oficios en la Nueva España.* Mexico City.

LIEHR, REINHARD
1970   "Ayuntamiento y oligarquía de la ciudad de Puebla a fines de la colonia, 1781–1800," in *Jahrbuch für Geschichte, Wirtschaft und Gesellschaft Lateinamerikas (Colonia)* 7: 401–447.

LISANTI, L.
1963   Sur la nourriture des "paulistes" entre le XVIIIe et XIXe siècles. *Annales E.S.C.* Paris: Centre d'Études Scientifiques.

LOBO, EULÁLIA M. LAHMEYER
1957   *Caminho de Chiquitos ás missões guaranies, 1680–1780. Ensaio interpretativo.* São Paulo.
1959–1960   Caminho de Chiquitos ás missoes guaranies. *Revista de Historia* 40: 353–384; 41: 85–90; 42: 413–443. São Paulo.

LOCKHART, JAMES
1965   *Encomienda and hacienda: the evolution of the great state in the Spanish Indies.* Durham.

LÓPEZ SARRELANGUE, DELFINA E.
1965   *La nobleza indígena de Patzcuaro en la época virreinal.* Mexico City.

MAKKAI, LASZLO
1971   "Productivité et exploitation des sources d'énergie (XII–XVIIe siècle)," in *Produttivitá e tecnologie nei secoli XII–XVIII.* Prato.

MALCO OLGUÍN, OSCAR
1959   El gremio de petateros en la ciudad de los reyes, 1772–1779. *Revista del Archivo Nacional del Perú* 32 (2): 263–291. Lima.

MARTÍNEZ, PEDRO SANTOS
1961a *Historia económica de Mendoza durante el virreinato, 1776–1880.* Madrid: Instituto Fernández de Oviedo.

1961b Regímen jurídico de las aguas en Mendoza durante el virreinato (1776–1810). *Revista del Instituto de Historia del Derecho* 12: 13–16. Buenos Aires.

MARTÍNEZ RÍOS, JORGE
1970 *Tenencia de la tierra y desarrollo agrario en México. Bibliografía selectiva y comentada: 1522–1968.* Mexico City.

MAURO, FRÉDÉRIC
1962 Concepts économiques et économie à l'époque du capitalisme commercial, 1500–1800. *Congrès International de l'Histoire Économique.* Aix-en-Provence.

MOLINA, RAÚL A.
1960 *Las primeras navigaciones del Río de la Plata después de la fundación de Juan de Garay.* Buenos Aires.

MOORE, JOHN PRESTON
1954 *The cabildo in Peru under the Hapsburgs. A study of origins and powers of the town council in the viceroyalty of Peru 1530–1700.* Durham.
1966 *The cabildo in Peru under the Bourbons.* Durham.

MOOREHEAD, MAX L.
1958 *New Mexico's royal road. Trade and travel on the Chihuahua trail.* Norman: University Press.

MORALES PADRÓN, FRANCISCO
1955 *Rebelión contra la Compañía de Caracas.* Seville.

MORAZZANI, GISELE
1966 *La intendencia en España y en América.* Caracas.

MOREYRA PAZ-SOLDÁN, MANUEL
1956 *El tribunal del consulado de Lima.* Lima.

MURO ARIAS, LUÍS
1956 *Herreros y cerrajeros en la Nueva España.* Mexico City.

MURO OREJÓN, ANTONIO
1960 El ayuntamiento de Sevilla, modelo de los municipios americanos. *Anuario de Estudios Americanos* 19: 699–742. Seville.

NAVARRO GARCÍA, LUÍS
1959 *La intendencia de Indias.* Seville.
1965 El comercio interamericano por la Mar del Sur en la edad moderna. *Revista de Historia* 23: 11–55. Caracas.

OTS CAPDEQUI, JOSÉ MARÍA
1946 *El régimen de la tierra en la América Española durante el régimen colonial.* Santo Domingo.
1958 *Instituciones. Colección de historia de América y de los pueblos americanos,* volume 14. Barcelona.

PARRY, JOHN H.
1963 *The sale of public office in the Spanish Indies under the Hapsburgs.* Berkeley.

PHILIPE, R.
1961 Commençons par l'histoire de l'alimentation. *Annales E.S.C.* Paris: Centre d'Études Scientifiques.

PIKE, FREDERICK
1960 Aspects of cabildo regulations in Spanish America under the Hapsburgs. *Interamerican Economic Affairs* 23–24: 67–86. Washington, D.C.

PORRAS BARRANECHEA, RAÚL
1956 *El Callao en la historia peruana.* Lima.

POULAIN, EDITH
   1962   *Vie économique et sociale à Mexico d'après les Actas del Cabildo de la ciudad de México: 1524–1816*, Caen.
QUEROL ROSO, LUÍS
   1936   Negros y mulatos de Nueva España. Historia de su alzamiento en Méjico en 1612. *Anales de la Universidad de Valencia* 12: 121–165.
RAMOS, DEMETRIC
   1967   *Trigo chileno, navieros del Callao y hacendados limeños.* Madrid: Instituto Fernández de Oviedo.
   1970   *Minería y comercio interprovincial en Hispanoamérica. Siglos XVI, XVII, XVIII.* Valladolid.
RODRÍGUEZ CASADO, VICENTE
   1949   *Construcciones militares del virrey Amat.* Seville: Escuela de Estudios Hispanoamericanos.
ROMANO, RUGGIERO
   1965a   "Historia colonial hispanoamericana e historia de los precios," in *Temas de historica económica hispanoamericana*, volume two, 11–21. Paris and The Hague.
   1965b   "Mouvement des prix et développement économique: le cas de l'Amérique du Sud au XVIIIᵉ siècle," in *Actes de la IIᵉ Conférence Internationale de l'Histoire Économique* 2: 141–152. Aix-en-Provence.
ROMERO DE TERREROS, MANUEL
   1956   *Antiguas haciendas de México.* Mexico City.
ROSENBLATT, ÁNGEL
   1954   *La población indígena y mestizaje en América.* Buenos Aires.
   1967   *La población de América en 1492. Viejos y nuevos cálculos.* Mexico City.
RUBIO COLOMA, JESÚS
   1935   Sobre los pósitos agrícolas. *El Trimestre Económico* 6. Mexico City.
RUGGERONI, DANTE
   1964   Un siglo de luchas por la tierra y por el agua. Santa Maria (Catamarca). 1771–1781. *Anuario del Instituto de Investigaciones Históricas* 7: 13–30. Rosario.
SAMAYOA GUEVARA, HUMBERTO
   1956   *Los gremios de artesanos en la ciudad de Guatemala, 1524–1821.* Guatemala City.
   1960   "La reorganización gremial guatemalense en la segunda mitad del siglo XVIII. *Antropología e Historia de Guatemala.* 1: 63–106. Guatemala City.
SANTIAGO CRUZ, F.
   1962   *La nao de China.* Mexico City.
SCHURZ, WILLIAM LYTLE
   1939   *The Manila galleon.* New York.
SCHAAP, W. E.
   1945   *Étude du mouvement des prix des céréales dans quelques villes de Champagne pendant les années qui précèdent la Révolution.* Paris.
SILVA SANTISTEBAN, FERNANDO
   1964   *Los obrajes en el virreinato del Perú.* Lima.
SIMPSON, LESLEY BIRD
   1952   *Exploitation of land in central Mexico in the sixteenth century.* Berkeley and Los Angeles.

SLICHER VAN BATH, B. H.
1965   Les problèmes fondamentaux de la société préindustrielle en Europe Occidentale. Une orientation et une programme. *A.A.G. Bijdragen* 12: 5–46. The Hague.

SORRE, MAX
1952   "Géographie de l'alimentation," in *Annales de géographie*. Paris.

SPOONER, F.
1961   Régimes alimentaires d'autrefois: proportions et calculs en calories. *Annales E.S.C.* Paris: Centre d'Études Scientifiques.
1962   Régimes alimentaires d'autrefois: deux nouveaux cas espagnols. *Annales E.S.C.* Paris: Centre d'Études Scientifiques.

VAN DER WEE, HERMANN
1971   "Productivité et croissance: la notion de la productivité et son application à l'histoire économique du XIIᵉ au XVIIIᵉ siècle," in *Produttivitá e tecnologie nei secoli XII–XVIII*. Prato.

VILAR, PIERRE
1964   *Crecimiento y desarrollo. Economía e historia. Reflexiones sobre el caso español.* Madrid.

VON HUMBOLDT, A.
1822   *Political essay on the kingdom of New Spain.* London.

YBOT LEÓN, ANTONIO
1958   *La arteria histórica del Nuevo Reino de Granada.* Madrid.

ZAVALA, SILVIO
1947   *Ordenanzas del trabajo. Siglos XVI y XVII.* Mexico City.

ZÚÑIGA, NESTOR
1948   El camino de Quito a Tierra Firme. *Revista de Indias* 33–34: 891–948. Madrid.

The Influence of the Historical Process on External Dependency in the Restructuring of Present-Day Regional and Urban Networks

ALEJANDRO ROFMAN

1. THE THEORETICAL FRAMEWORK

1.1. *Introduction*

The objective of this article is to present a pattern of spatial structuration which is applicable to a dependent society throughout its historical development.

The pattern to be explained is an attempt to undertake a study of the formation of regional and urban networks. First an integral theoretical framework will be provided to explain the behavior of world society in its different historical stages. The definition of a theoretical pattern requires an identification of the dimensions of analysis of which it is comprised. These are:

1. *The international system*, which links the various national systems and discloses interrelationships among the units of which it is composed.

2. *The national system*, which consists of one of the elements making up the previous system. This includes economic, political, social, cultural, geographic, and other subsystems.

3. *Power structures*, which define degrees of dominance within each of the above systems and subsystems, corresponding to the form and characteristics of the respective modes of production relationships.

4. *Decision-making systems*, constituted by the "decision makers," whose function is to channel or execute power relationships existing in the respective systems.

5. *The system of urban-regional networks*, whose structure is based on the functioning of ranks (hierarchies) of urban centers.

6. *The historical stages in the evolution of international, national, and network systems.* These are identified in the respective analysis as periods delimited by substantial transformations in the internal relationships of each system.

The theoretical framework to which these dimensions of analysis correspond begins with the study of the international system.

1.2. *The International System*

The international system is usually presented as a functional structure which relates independent units to each other and whose power of negotiation is homogeneous. That is to say, the traditional approach asserts the independence of each national system in its relationships with the rest of the world.[1] This is as it is visualized through its juridical-institutional status and its full capability of negotiating on a world scale with a few, many, or all other national systems.

The value of this formal view of the *modus operandi* of the international system is diminished when the latter is analyzed in greater depth. The relative power of each national system cannot be measured by its "legal capacity to contract" (which is not debated), but by its freedom of action and benefits obtained in the historical process of interrelationships.

The juridical equality already mentioned is not substantiated at the levels of economic and social development. The existence of sharp disparities between the economic potentialities of each national system is a statistically proven fact. One empirical study reports that the process of great inequality between the levels of highest and lowest socioeconomic development has remained stable for the last fifty years (Lasuen, Wassernogel, and Montserrat 1968). This statistical verification is the first sign of the fact that processes underlying the simple formal relationships of international equilibrium cause and maintain a situation of imbalance persisting in time.

This inequality[2] has its roots in factors existing within the context of the international system of economic, social, and political relationships. Such factors may be classified into primary and derived, among which the following are of great importance:

[1]   The term "rest of the world" is understood as including all national units except the one under study.

[2]   Analyses of the process of international inequality have been attempted by contemporary economists, who invariably acknowledge fundamental works carried out in the nineteenth and early twentieth centuries. Among these economists, mention may be made of Gunnar Myrdal, Raúl Prebisch, and Osvald Sunkel.

1. The first primary factor is linked to the influence exerted by the adoption of capitalist means of production in the early days of modern industrial development.

The greatest economic potential of a group of national systems springs from the rapid accumulation of capital by the nations which are today the most developed. This has been rendered possible by the capitalist system of production relationships.

Such a process took place at the beginning of the period of the Industrial Revolution. At that time, the mechanism for the distribution of income was strongly dominated by the control exercised by the owner classes over the labor market and its corresponding level of recompense. The capability to appropriate the surplus generated allowed a group of privileged economic systems to dominate the framework of newly institutionalized economic relationships. When the production and distribution market of the capitalist system finally became internationalized imbalance among national systems was already structured into it. Those who, in increasing numbers, joined the internationalized framework of the economy faced a crystallized structure. As a result, they were only able to act as lesser members.

2. The second factor, derived from the first, is related to the unequal distribution of advantages derived from the process of commercial exchange among the components of the international system. A mechanism for an international division of labor was set up. It assigned to certain systems the function of being suppliers of primary products, in exchange for assumed comparable advantages. This mechanism was instituted as a collateral process of the phenomenon of appropriation of economic surplus, characteristic of the newly formalized capitalist production relationships.

Specialization in goods of primary origin from the productive structure of national systems with limited participation in the benefits of world trade, which was established from the second half of the nineteenth century, caused a gradual reduction of income in these economies. This was due to the inability of those countries to obtain remunerative prices in transactions at a world level – a process which has manifested itself without interruption since the period mentioned above. This inability also had its origin in factors of a structural nature (trade monopolization, a differentiated demand for products, production of substitutes, etc.).[3]

3. The third factor, also derived from the first, is based on the unequal rate of accumulation of economic and technical resources by each national system. This phenomenon possesses the distinctive feature of feeding on itself. The circular and accumulative quality of

---

[3]   Staffen Linder's work (1968) amply illustrates this process.

this process separates the more developed systems from the less-developed ones through a mechanism of cause and effect: an efficient productive structure for competing internationally acquires an increasing proportion of the resources generated on an international scale. The latter, upon being accumulated in ever-increasing amounts in the more developed nations, increase their competitive capacity, and so on successively.

An unequal international dispersion of the fruits of technological progress is produced. This manifests itself in the emergence in less-developed countries of "enclaves" or sectors which are highly developed in their technical efficiency. These originated in investments from countries with a very high level of development, and have little or no opportunity of spreading the profits they generate to the rest of the system.

The countries which export technology in this way "branch" their development, to use a felicitous term employed by Sunkel. They expand their national "space" to areas or sectors of countries providing primary resources. The latter do not participate in the fruits of this technical progress because they are not the effective owners of the activities established within their borders.

The analysis of these three factors allows one to reach this conclusion: the international system, as seen through an economic prism, is an interdependent system. But it is one with a varying level of participation in the nations which make it up. The more privileged nations of the system are the so-called "centric" countries; the others, those with increasingly more limited participation in earnings on the scale of the capitalist area, are called the "peripheral" countries.

Nevertheless, behind this phenomenon of international inequality, other categories of analysis operate which transcend the purely economic sectorial approach. Their importance is based not only on the fact that they explain the economic phenomenon described, but that in turn they permit a studying of the behavior of the whole social system. There are two variables to be introduced: (1) the power system and (2) the decision-making system.

The Power System.   The inclusion of power structures in the foregoing analysis results from the presence of two salient processes. One is that of the subordination which appears as a logical corollary of a system of production relationships requiring subordination in order to ensure its continuity. The other, a basic condition of survival of the socioeconomic system, was and is the generating of suitable control machinery to permit a favorable regulation of the process of uninterrupted appropriation of resources by the most-favored nations system.

It is in the analysis of the power structure on an international scale that one can recognize the method to its full extent, as the hierarchical ordering occurs between national systems. For this it is necessary to study how power is exercised, through what structures, and what decision-making system implements this exercising.

The concept of hierarchical subordination on an international scale is usually called a relationship of external dependency. In Quijano's version (1967: 1), this dependency is a peculiar system of inter-dependence in the capitalist world, within which one sector is dominant over the others. This relationship, bipolar in nature (according to Adams [1966]), is established between one source which is autonomous and another which is derived from power.

For the dependency between the different strata of power to be effective, there must necessarily and concurrently be agreement in each structure which is dominated. This agreement, which is consistent with the bipolar nature of the dependency process, is signaled through the identity of objectives between the different autonomous levels and those derived from power.

The system of stratification in which power relationships are defined operates at the level of each country, and its international links are those which identify the phenomena of hierarchical domination which has been described. In the centric country, the dominant social class has interests in common with those of the dominant social class of the peripheral country.

This machinery of interaction, which may be translated in a descending form of national subareas, however small they may be (in which the dominant groups of strata acknowledge an identity of goals with those of the upper scale in the hierarchy), does not assume a fluid process in any permanent form.

On the contrary, it acknowledges conflicts and contradictions between the dominant strata which, once dissolved, lead to new forms of hierarchical structuration of power. Changes in the demand for export products, technological innovations, struggles between external dominant groups in coalition with similar national sectors, etc., are possible grounds for these conflicts in dependent societies.

The relationship of external dependency thus defined requires implementation mechanisms which are compatible with the objectives of the dominant power structures. This applies both to autonomous structures in centric countries as well as to derived structures in peripheral countries. This machinery is represented by the decision-making system.

The Decision-making System. In the capitalist system (on which the hierarchical links between national systems are based), the most important decision-making agent is the entrepreneurial center. The State acts in the role of protagonist or in a supplementary capacity. In the end, the family group acts as the supplier of manpower and consumer of the goods which are ultimately produced.

The reigning system of production relationships establishes the permissive limits within which the decision maker operates (type of access to property, prices of goods and production factors, machinery for participation in the political system, etc.).

Decisions related to the spatial structuration of the national system (a subgrouping of those adopted for the functioning of the whole) depend on the character adopted by the political system. This occurs with consideration of the distinct form the latter may adopt and the function it exercises over the freedom of action of the system's decision-making agents. Having identified the system's decision-making agents, one must now ask how they operate when the whole society is a peripheral system, dependent on superior systems of power and hierarchy.

At the level of centric countries, the decision makers are not only the entrepreneurial centers and the political power. Two other specific types must also be recognized:

1. Associations or enterprises of a nonnational type, such as large oil and automotive companies, news agencies, etc.

2. Associations of a supranational type, i.e. intermediate associations (coffee and oil organization, etc.) and international organizations whose members are nations (for example, OAS, GATT, NATO, Common Markets, the World Bank, IMF, etc.).

At the peripheral level, those decisions are incorporated which are of very different origin, though linked to the geographic headquarters which house the real power structures which create, support, or protect them.

1.3. *National System and Dependence*

A new concept is introduced to evaluate the effect of the dependence relationship at the level of the national system: the imaginary existence of a "frontier" or boundary of the dependent society, which separates the internal power structure from the external. This boundary will be more or less penetrable for decisions which originated in the power structures of the dominant nations, depending on the capacity of the power system of the dependent society to channel or obstruct, respectively, such decisions. Thus, for example, a completely impenetrable frontier of the national system will speak of a complete rupture of the process of external dependency (see Figure 1). This analysis assumes the existence of two processes which are to be examined:

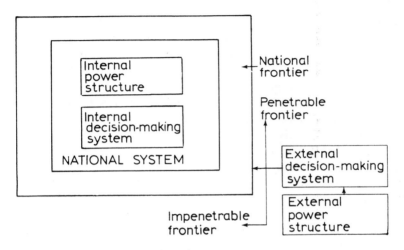

Figure 1.   National system and dependency

1.   The variation, in different historical stages, of the degree of capability and response of internal power structures. The unequal capacity for response corresponds to a categorizing of structural forms in which the dependency relationship is manifested:

a.   Between the autonomous center and the dependent national system with a certain degree of internal development. In this case, there is a greater potential capability of response; that is, the frontier is strengthened.

b.   Between the autonomous center and an enclave structure. In this situation, the inability of response is obvious. The relationship is practically colonial.

2.   Characteristics do exist in the dependent society which, without breaking the dependency relationship, render it possible or difficult for the prevailing power structure to strengthen the system's frontier. Such a variation is based on the greater or lesser level of development of the productive forces, with the corresponding degree of distribution of the benefits of this development (distribution of property and income, increase of purchasing capacity, degree of political participation, etc.). This would be positive in the first case and negative in the second.

Both processes are taken into account in the historical analysis below.

1.4. The Decision-Making System in a Dependent Society

Within the theoretical pattern which explains the investors' attitude in the capitalist system of production relationships, the decision-making agents choose that activity which, in their economic horizon, will obtain the maximum rate of return per unit of capital invested. However, in our analysis, decisions concerning investment will not enjoy the same level of freedom of selection of alternatives, either in the sectorial or spatial aspect. In this respect, decision makers may be divided into two main groups:

1.   Those linked directly to the power structures described.
2.   Those who see their economic horizon and alternatives restricted to the operative limits opened by the first.

That is to say, we accept that not all investors (at times only a few) act consciously in accordance with the process of dominance which has been analyzed. The rest, at times the majority, make decisions motivated by incentives opened by those who carry out the initial act, or with the greatest multiplier power to invest.

My hypothesis is that the urban-regional structure resulting from the cumulative investment process responds in time (in dependent societies) to the selection of alternatives made by investors belonging to the dominant power structures.

In other words, there is a spatial structure for investments, carried out by both conscious and unconscious performers of the process which has guided them to these investments. This is one more characteristic of the effect produced by the hierarchical system of scale relationships of the capitalistic world.

With the continuance of such investments, processes of agglomeration are unchained and generate external economies, which in turn increase the agglomeration phenomenon. Thus a system of points in space is set up which, in time, accumulates the benefits of the above mentioned economies. The network of centers thus depends on the multiplier effect of investments.[4] Since such an investment process chooses specific points in space, there will have to be some regional subsystems which are favored and others which receive no benefits. This will depend on the relative ability of each regional subsystem to offer location advantages which are compatible with the objectives of the decision-making system and the dominant power system.[5]

[4]   For the theory of centric towns or centric networks, we refer the reader to the works of Losch and Christaller.
[5]   Nevertheless, the action of investors does not have a similar effect on all geographic areas, when one takes into account the degree of occupation of the territory. In areas which are still uncolonized, the explicit objectives of those who make decisions at an entrepreneurial level result in the structuration of a network of centers directly influenced by those participating in the investment process. The impact is different if

The following are the location factors existing in each regional subsystem to be evaluated:

1. Its endowment with natural resources.
2. The level of the labor supply.
3. The existence of a supply of capital and the possible return on it.
4. The costs of transference necessary to link up sources of inputs, centers of production or intermediary centers, and location of the demand.

One comment is necessary. Investors characterized by belonging to dominant power structures (both autonomous and derived) usually operate in a capitalist pattern of economy as monopolistic or oligopolistic units. That is, the domination and multiplier effect of such investments is not disputed (on a spatial scale) by other competitive investments in the region selected. This is true inasmuch as these decision makers control markets, fix prices, and obtain monopolistic income through the pressure they exercise over the production conditions of the system and over the political structures permitting such domination. Political conditioning thus plays an essential role through groups "bound" to the dominant economic sector.

Furthermore, the decision-making units so described may make the effects of concentration in certain points of the national area felt, in spite of the fact that investments which were previously described as multipliers of urban-regional growth have not been specifically located in such centers.

This is true inasmuch as spatial transfers of goods and financial resources constantly take place from one urban-regional subsystem to another. In this manner other centers of the same or different urban-regional subsystems, where the receivers of these transfers reside, are favored.

This "secondary" effect acquires distinct characteristics according to who the intervening decision makers are and according to the sector of activity in which they operate. They may be divided into three large groupings:

1. Decision makers of external origin who possess investments linked to natural resources in specific localities but who centralize their administrative, marketing, financial intermediary, and other activities in groupings of different spatial (i.e. geographic) location.[6]

2. External decision makers who reserve to themselves only a part of the sequential process of "producing-marketing-exporting" of the

---

the changes emerging on the spatial plane (resulting from the investment process already described) are carried out over urban-regional systems which are already established. Superpositions from the process of spatial formation are thus produced and have the characteristic of lasting a very long time.

[6] A lucid description of this phenomenon may be read in Quijano (1968).

corresponding activity. This phenomenon is closely linked to productive processes of agricultural origin destined eventually for export.

The external dominant sector is installed in key positions within the decision-making structure of the above sequence, freeing itself from primarily productive functions. These are usually assigned to national producers, both independent and contracted labor.

Since marketing financing, transport network, and exporting are directly or indirectly in the hands of decision makers belonging to the dominant power structure, the favored centers of the urban network enjoy the external economies which those activities generate.

3.   Decision makers generate fiscal revenue which is forwarded to administrative centers of a higher rank in the urban network. In this case, the location of the productive activity which provides resources to the fiscal apparatus does not coincide with the location of investments financed by such resources. In this mechanism of the relocation between origin and destination of part of the profits obtained by external investors (or by those directly linked to the latter), the following factors have an important influence: the dominant type of activity, the existing tax system, and the goals of the public sector as an integral subsystem of the derived power structure.

The preceding description would have to be modified (at least in part) if the study were to include periods prior to the appearance of capitalist production relationships and the international division of labor at the beginning of the nineteenth century. Above all, it would be necessary to incorporate decisions adopted by participants of the political system as the most effective strategy for geographically mobilizing the flow of natural resources destined for the mother country, for (administratively) controlling the colonized territory, and for occupying it for reasons of armed defense.

Decisions adopted by power structures endogenous to the national system include those of the political subsystem, which assists and accomodates to the investment process already described.

The political decision-making system may act through: (a) the legal and administrative order which facilitates and does not impede the external decision-making process; or (b) the resolution of emerging "bottlenecks," by means of investment transactions accompanying the one carried out by external or internal agents.

Throughout the preceding analysis, special mention has been made of decision makers linked to power structures. It is now appropriate to refer to investors who do not necessarily act in harmony with the process of internal and external domination.

Their decisions, though theoretically independent, cannot contradict those acting at a higher decision-making level. The mechanism for influencing the market is already predetermined for the "independent" investor. This happens because of the type and size of investments which are carried out by the decision makers of the two power structures of superior rank in the relationship of dominance; also because of the sum total of norms and political-administrative orders which aid and condition this decision-making process.

The decision maker who is not bound to the power structures then remains identified with the objective of these structures, even when he is not part of them. That, characteristically, is the medium or small producer and intermediary of urban centers in the dependent society.

1.5. The Historical Analysis

In mechanistic historical patterns, the identification of stages of development is made by completely omitting structures of domination – by which the level of development of each national system is conditioned.

As Cardoso contends (1968), these patterns, in simplifying social processes, omitted not only the *why* but also the *nature* of social processes in order to maintain only the *how* of the possible combinations among abstract variables.

A structural approach to historical analysis is one which would permit the observation of agreements and disagreements which have come about in relationships between national systems and in the corresponding responses of each power structure and internal decision-making system. The historical stages will be determined in accordance with changes observable in the relationship of external dependency.

This analysis will establish: (a) the behavior of the dominant and dominated power structures; (b) the forms of political conditioning; and (c) the degree of response of the dependent society in its historical development, which is seen in the weakening or hardening of the "frontier" of the national system.

Therefore, only one step remains for the purposes of the spatial process, that of evaluating the impact of decisions adopted at each historical stage on the shaping of urban-regional networks.

The dynamic study will have to incorporate all the variables and parameters described above in order to illustrate the phenomenon of the structuration of systems of centers in a dependent society.

2. LATIN AMERICA AS A DEPENDENT SOCIETY

It is not necessary to enter into an analysis of Latin America's historical development or its qualification as a dependent society, since the existing literature on this subject[7] obviates the need for any special contribution. For purposes of our special approach, we will only say that the case of Latin America requires a clarification.

The period of colonial domination, from discovery to independence in the nineteenth century, does not present all the characteristics of the behavior described in Section 1. The fact is – as has been made clear – that the capitalist system had not been definitively imposed upon the structures of production and distribution of the dominant societies. This assumes that the theoretical elements to be used for this period omit a large proportion of those used to define the conceptual framework of the preceding chapter. Thus it will be necessary to work with the more specific pattern which was explained in very general terms in Section 1.5.

On the other hand, the definition and analysis of the functioning of the dependent society in the following periods will be made by using all the considerations of the theoretical pattern presented.

3. THE URBAN-REGIONAL SYSTEM IN LATIN AMERICA

An integral approach to urban-regional development in Latin America cannot be included in this work due to the wide scope of the subject. Consequently, my intention has to be to present a general summary through the critical evaluation of a selected collection of works carried out for similar purposes. I am in the process of preparing a long report, a synthesis of which appears below.

Two of the studies may be considered representative of the description of urban networks at the beginning and end of the period under analysis. Thus the initial focus refers to the situation existing at the beginning of the seventeenth century. This was the period of the final structuration of urban settlements in the area by the *conquistadores* from the Peninsula. The final focus is linked to the present state of the urban-regional system.

Hardoy and Aranovich, in their well-documented work (1969), refer to the system of urban centers of the colonies, excluding the area controlled by Portugal. Table 1 of their article permits one to infer the character of the principal groupings around 1630. It includes a list of centers classified according to the population estimated for that year. The first ten ranking cities are: Mexico City, Lima, Potosí, Cuzco, Quito, Puebla, Bogotá, Cartagena, Havana, and La Plata (Charcas). Two conclusions may be drawn from this listing:

---

[7]   A basic work with regard to this subject is that of Cardoso and Faletto (1969).

1. The basic function of each of these centers corresponded to those cited as characteristic of the colonial period.

Thus we find the existence of administrative centers situated in order to exercise political control of regions newly opened to Spanish control. This was the case of Bogotá, Mexico City, Quito, and Lima. In this respect it is interesting to point out the location of such urban centers in relation to natural maritime outlets. That is to say, while these localities did not have the attribute of being linked to the colonial power by a direct route, they were nonetheless linked by means of important ports in the respective regions of influence.

This phenomenon of bipolar relationship (administrative center-port) was to be repeated in many areas during the three centuries of colonial dependency. For example, this was true of Santiago-Valparaiso.

Similarly, also included in the listing are maritime ports which had the mission of connecting the monopolist import and export trade of the colonies. If the analysis were also to cover Portuguese dominions, five such centers would be deserving of mention: Lima (already mentioned; in practice Lima united both functions, through the port of El Callao), Havana, Cartagena, Recife, and Rio de Janeiro. Each was a port of egress for the production of the respective areas of influence. In the Spanish colonies, for example, Lima exported minerals and Cartagena and Havana were the principal ports of transhipment for the Caribbean area and the northern region of South America.

In the Portuguese colonies, Recife was the exporting center for sugar and Rio de Janeiro acquired functions similar to the previous ones mentioned, with its role as the main political-administrative center (see Singer 1968).

Finally, there were the producing centers, the bases for the concentration and subsequent distribution to ports of goods which were to be sent to Spain. Potosí, Cuzco and La Plata belong in the above list. These centers, while serving functions in addition to the one stated, may be described as settlements closely linked to the mining of *Alto Perú*.

2. The various urban centers did not function properly as a network or system on a continental scale. There were certain communication difficulties due to geographic accidents and to the low technological development of the transport system. Nevertheless, and however odd it may be, one should point out that these centers had closer links with Spain and Portugal than with each other. This process of compartmentalization was distinctive of the whole process of establishing urban centers in the area. This was true to the extent that the principal economic function of the colonies was that of providing the mother

countries with raw materials, in exchange receiving manufactured goods from them. Therefore, the only type of functioning to be expected of the incipient group of urban centers was that of directing all flows of communication outside the continent. This phenomenon, on the other hand, is to be reanalyzed in later stages.

One last comment. Given the dominant economic activities and the absence of internal trade at the level of the newly colonized area, a look at the map of urban centers in 1630 permits one to observe a very peculiar structure. There is a strong predominance of centers on the maritime coasts (which is also verified in the area of Portuguese control); exceptions are a limited number of centers in the *Cono Sur* which function as military posts or transport posts.

If we move the analysis to almost four hundred years later, the best source of information is a map and table in a work by Peter Odell which evaluates the economic activity of urban agglomerates in Latin America on the basis of the energy capacity generated in each of them (Odell 1968: 276–277). The following comments are suggested by Odell's data:

1. The first ten urban agglomerates with their respective ranking are: Buenos Aires, São Paulo, Mexico City, Rio de Janeiro, Santiago, Havana, Caracas, Lima, Rosario, and Montevideo. If one compares this list with the first one, it may be seen that the centers of Mexico City, Lima, and Havana are repeated. If Hardoy and Aranovich's study (1969) had covered the Portuguese area, it is likely that it would have included Rio de Janeiro among the first ten centers.

That is to say, there were significant variations in the long period which has passed, even though three or four centers managed to retain their position among the ten privileged centers despite obvious social, political, and economic transformations.

However, these modifications do not suppose that the other important centers of the mid-twentieth century do not show antecedents from four centuries earlier. Buenos Aires and Santiago already appeared as centers in 1630, and Montevideo and Caracas were founded shortly thereafter. That is, there is a strong element of continuity in the picture, since only São Paulo and Rosario are centers of more contemporary origin. This "inertia-effect" is a very significant feature in the evolution of the urban network in any national or international integrated system.

2. A quick glance at the form of present-day urban location in Latin America (see Odell's map) confirms the assertion I have made for the year 1630. The principal urban centers were located on the maritime coasts or on river outlets to ocean ports. The exceptions once again were centers located towards the interior of the continent which had a very close link with a maritime port. The example quoted for the colonial period could be repeated for this contemporary period. Even

urban agglomerates which are typically inland assumed relatively less importance than on the map of the colonial period. That is to say, there had been an increase in the phenomenon of urban concentration on the periphery of the continent.

The phenomenon has also been studied by Stohr and Pedersen (1969) in their analysis of Latin American transport and its effects on the spatial pattern of the area. They confirm the strong link of urban centers with centers belonging to the centric nations of the international capitalist system and the very weak interrelationships of the same centers in Latin America.

This permits the conclusion that the process of urban expansion on the Latin American continent, from its first manifestations to the present day, has maintained the same structure: a system which is poorly integrated, located with its back to the region, and with very limited success in managing to penetrate inland areas. Stohr and Pedersen compare this pattern of the almost nonexistent urban network at the Latin American level with that exhibited by both the United States and Europe. In these last two cases, they assert, the axis of the urban growth process has been moving increasingly towards the geographic interior of the respective systems. This is contrary to the process in Latin America, which has shown a reverse movement.

The explanation of the generating causes of these phenomena, as well as the processes of change which have affected urban centers, emerges from the application of the theoretical pattern included in Section 1.

In the first place, due to its extraordinary similarity to the urban network outlined for the period of the Conquest (with its objectives of military and economic domination), the contemporary Latin American urban network is an indication of the persistently weak "frontiers" of the respective national systems. This is the result of decisions made by the successive corresponding "centric" nations.

This statement finds its justification in a more detailed analysis of the different periods, in which the relationship of external dependency has been manifested throughout the almost four centuries of its existence. In this respect, three main periods may be distinguished. The first covers the disappearance of the two colonial powers as systems of direct political and economic domination up to the crisis of 1930. This was the great cycle of the incorporation of national economic structures into the phenomenon of the international division of labor. During this period, the exploitation of primary resources for shipment to the markets of the most industrialized countries was the distinctive trait of each national economy. Freedom of trade replaced trade monopoly. Political independence replaced colonial power.

The relationship of dependency was structured (with regard to the subgrouping of decisions linked to the spatial sphere) in the valorization of collecting or distributing centers of production for markets outside the continent. Each center received heavy investments, especially in basic capital stock, in order to fulfill its role efficiently. The railway network for internal communication was built by foreign capital, primarily of English origin. This was the case for Argentina, Brazil, Chile and Uruguay, to mention the most important ones.

The financing and marketing structure also depended on foreign investors. One may mention the examples of São Paulo in Brazil, Rosario in Argentina, and Valparaiso in Chile.

In some cases, the respective investment decisions selected the preexisting urban scheme and on other occasions they very rapidly developed towns which were quite small at the beginning of the period. During this stage arose those centers which (on the first list analyzed) did not exist in 1630.

The most strongly favored centers for investment were the exporting ports, the terminals of their respective productive areas of influence. In these areas, the investor from the external decision-making structure either was involved in the whole process (as in the case of Chile and Brazil) or limited himself to the final stages, leaving the area of production to national investors (as in Uruguay and Argentina).

The basic function of the national economies which had been most successfully integrated into international trade was that of producing and exporting primary goods. As this was the case, it was inevitable that productive sites with the greatest capacity for expanding over the area, and which had monopolistic or oligopolistic structures, were located at the points of transhipment abroad.

In this stage, this characteristic did not appear with similar intensity in all national systems: it depended, rather, on the relative ability of each to serve the economic power structures of the industrialized nations. This applies especially to the primary goods they were able to offer to the most developed markets. This was the case for Venezuela, which only became integrated at the beginning of this century, when oil came to form part of the intermediate products for the industrial development of the United States of America.

In this stage, the internal power structures of the national systems made external investment processes feasible through special exemptions, concessions without conditions, legislation on land ownership without restrictions, systems for contracting labor which were favorable to the contractor, development laws for foreign immigration to encourage the supply of production, etc. Likewise, to the extent that internal entrepreneurial groups were coparticipants in the decision-making system based on the capitalist structure, favorable basic legislation and common objectives with the external power structure made the "frontier" weaker and strengthened the link between the external and internal power systems.

The second stage marks a process which tried to reverse the previous trend. This stage began in national economies with a greater development of productive forces, when the 1930 crisis upset the type of commercial and financial relationships belonging to the international capitalist system. The start of World War II provided a new impetus for this weakening of the external impact on dependent national systems. The process of import substitution which arises in national economies with the largest market areas (and which is made effective through the industrialization of consumer goods) is well known.

The first effect of this phenomenon was the hardening of the "frontier" of dependent Latin American systems. The second effect, a consequence of the first, was based on the moving of fundamental decisions concerning investments from outside to inside national systems.

The strengthening of the "frontier," a product of the international conjuncture, was also accompanied by a change in the role of the State. Until that time it had been a principal promoter of the continuity of the system of external dependency. Argentina, Brazil, Chile, Bolivia, and Mexico are the outstanding examples of the period.

The impact of this new method in the progress of relationships between power structures at a different level within the same political-economic structure on the subgroup of spatial decisions was only marginal. The limited effect of the change as it operated on the level of the whole system on decisions relating to the shaping of urban-regional networks was due to two basic causes:

1. The mode of relationships of capitalist production continued in force in the respective national economies. This assumes that market incentives guided the decisions of investors and that these, whatever their origin, would be orientated by selecting the points or areas which assured maximum return for capital.

2. Having accepted the first principle, and considering that no fundamental transformations were made in systems of land ownership, the design of transport networks and the composition of investments from the public sector, etc., there were not many possibilities for significant substitutions of location.

The fact is that cost structures which rest on the existence of specific economic structures, infrastructures, etc., did not alter their relative levels with respect to the previous period.

Those experiments which sought to modify the effect of the market had little success. They were more than surpassed by agglomerative trends inherited from the previous process, and they did not disturb the balance of the basically coastal urban network in each national system. The experiments mentioned (Concepción in Chile, Brasilia in Brazil, Córdoba in Argentina, etc.) did not show the strong tendency towards agglomeration of the already developed centers.

The primacy of centers of higher rank increased in the principal countries which participated in the phenomenon of light industrialization. The main factors which stimulated investors to strengthen the generation of agglomerative economies in the largest urban centers were the following: the demand market of the large urban concentrations, the elastic supply of labor through growing internal migration, and the basic social infrastructure inherited from the previous period.

This stage did not occur with similar intensity in every country either. But in spite of this, and although those of lesser relative size and more limited development level of their productive forces were incorporated at a later date (or only in this last decade), the phenomenon of concentration occurred with an intensity similar to that in the leading countries of the continent. Structural aspects, all too well known, have accelerated this process. Of course, as in the other cases, the already developed coastal centers which are strongly supported by investments from the public sector, were chosen as administrative-industrial-commercial centers.

The third stage, that of the development of heavy and semiheavy industry, only reinforced the previous structures. This appeared in those national systems which required the respective inputs to integrate their productive processes.

This new stage manifested itself from the start of the 1950's with greater emphasis in Argentina, Brazil, Chile, Mexico, and Venezuela. Later Peru and Colombia were included.

It is very interesting to note once again the fact that in both Venezuela and Peru the process took place simultaneously with that of import substitution and not in a sequential manner, as in the largest countries of the area.

This period was characterized by a strengthening of the relationship of external dependency. The external power structures, reconstituted after the effects of the War, modified their previous behavior. With regard to the origin of decisions, this was based essentially on North American capital rather than English, as was the case before the crisis of 1930.

The difficulties of the war period had now been overcome, and the experiments which had strengthened national frontiers to a large degree had disappeared. As a result, the objectives of external investors were now to intervene directly in productive processes. The relative importance of investments in extractive activities thus decreased.

Productive investments linked to the production of intermediate inputs or capital goods were assisted by laws passed by the political powers which responded to the internal power structures of the dependent countries.

Since capitalist structures continued to prevail, the rules for locating such investments were guided by market incentives. Weak attempts to modify the spatial structure of the preceding period were nullified in the face of decisions made by the external market.

The large agglomerates offered external economies of urbanization and localization necessary to attract such activities. An efficient, supporting infrastructure, a nearby market for the processes of industrial integration, abundant manpower, high accessibility for the receipt of inputs from abroad, etc. – these are all generating factors for a new impulse to concentration in already developed centers. These have now lost their original character of ports or administrative centers in order to become the large, multifunctional metropolitan areas they now are.

The following axes are the most outstanding examples of this phenomenon: Mexico City-Veracruz, Bogotá-Cali, Caracas-Maracaibo, Lima-Callao, Rosario-Buenos Aires-La Plata, São Paulo-Santos, and Santiago-Valparaiso.

There are many national economies of Latin America which, due to the low relative development of their productive forces, have not generated the conditions for being incorporated into the last or penultimate stage. Nevertheless, the phenomenon of "coastal" concentration (in one or two centers) has also had an effect as a reflection of internal structural factors and of a reinforcement of intermediate activities, national administration, or light industrialization. In this respect, let us recall the axes of Quito-Guayaquil, Asunción, Guatemala, and Montevideo, among the most prominent examples.

This condensed description between the beginning and end of the two initial observations of this section confirms the hypotheses stated above.

The type of dependent capitalist development of Latin American economies which has been observed through the centuries has provided a geographically decentralized urban-regional system. This tends to strengthen larger concentrations, and it has not yet attained any significant internal levels of spatial integration. To speak of an "urban-regional network" in contemporary Latin America is, in practice, to refer to one or two concentrations operating as dominant centers of attraction, without the corresponding participation of the rest of the centers, which are in general expellers'of population and productive activities.

A not unrealistic hypothesis would indicate that if the present socioeconomic structure (as analyzed above) were to persist, the phenomena of concentration, interregional imbalance, and absence of integration would be accentuated in the near future in national societies in the Latin American area.

REFERENCES

ADAMS, RICHARD
1966   *Power and power domains.* Institute of Latin American Studies, Bulletin 33. University of Texas.

ALTIMIR, OSCAR, HORACIO SANTAMARINA, JUAN SOURROVILLE
1967   Los instrumentos de promoción industrial en la post-guerra, parte 1. *Revista de Desarrollo Económico* 27 (October–December). Buenos Aires.

ARIAS, JORGE
1965   Á La concentración urbana y las migraciones internas," in *Problemas de la urbanización en Guatemala.* Guatemala City.

BACIGALUPO, JOSÉ LUÍS
1969   "El proceso de urbanización en la Argentina," in *La urbanización en América Latina.* Edited by J. E. Hardoy and C. Tobar. Buenos Aires.

BRODERSOHN, MARIO
1966   *Regional development and industrial location policy in Argentina.* Buenos Aires: Instituto Torcuato Di Tella.

CARDOSO, FERNANDO
1968   "Análisis sociológico del desarrollo económico," in *Cuestiones de sociología del desarrollo económico.* Santiago.

CARDOSO, FERNANDO, ENZO FALETTO
1969   *Dependencia y desarrollo en América Latina.* Santiago.

DOS SANTOS, THEOTONIO
1969   *La crisis del desarrollismo y la nueva dependencia.* Lima.

FRIEDMANN, JOHN
1966   *Regional development policy.* Cambridge, Mass.: Harvard University Press.

FURTADO, CELSO
1969   *La concentración del poder económico en los Estados Unidos y sus proyecciones en América Latina.* Buenos Aires.

GEIGER, PEDRO
1963   *Evolução de rede urbana brasileira.* Rio de Janeiro.

GEISSE, GUILLERMO
1967   *Requerimientos de información de una política de desarrollo urbano y regional.* Santiago.

HARDOY, JORGE ENRIQUE, CARMEN ARANOVICH
1969   Urbanización en América Hispánica entre 1580 y 1630. *Boletín del Centro de Investigaciones Históricas y Estéticas* 11. Caracas.

HOOVER, EDGARD
1937   *Location theory and the shoe and leather industries.* Cambridge, Mass.

HURTADO, CARLOS
1966   *Concentración de población y desarrollo económico. El caso chileno.* Santiago.

LASUEN, J., F. WASSERNOGEL, A. MONTSERRAT
1968   La dependencia a nivel mundial. *Cuadernos de la Sociedad Venezolana de Planificación* 54–55. Caracas.

LINDER, STAFFEN
1968   *Teoría del comercio y política comercial para el desarrollo.* Mexico City.

MARTORELLI, GUILLERMO
1969   *Las inversiones extranjeras en la Argentina.* Buenos Aires.

MYRDAL, GUNNAR
1959   *Teoría económica y regiones subdesarrolladas.* Mexico City.

NORIEGA MORALES, MANUEL
1965   "El desarrollo económico y el crecimiento urbano en Guatemala," in *Problemas de la urbanización en Guatemala.* Guatemala City.

ODELL, PETER
1968   Economic integration and spatial patterns of economic development in Latin America. *Journal of Common Market Studies* 6 (3).

PREBISCH, RAÚL
1965   *Hacia una dinámica del desarrollo latinoamericano.* Mexico City.

QUIJANO, ANIBAL
1966   "El proceso de urbanización en Latinoamérica." (Mimeograph.) Santiago.
1967   Dependencia, cambio social y urbanización en Latinoamérica. *Revista Mexicana de Sociología* 30 (3). Santiago.
1968   "La urbanización de la sociedad en Latinoamérica." (Mimeographed.) Santiago.

RATINOFF, LUÍS
1966   *La urbanización en el Paraguay.* Asunción.

ROBIROSA, MARIO
1967   "Sistema nacional, sistema internacional y los modelos de dependencia-no dependencia." (Mimeographed.) Buenos Aires: CEUR.

ROFMAN, ALEJANDRO
i.p.   "Efectos de la integración latinoamericana en el esquema de localización industrial," in *Actas del 6° Congreso Interamericano de Planificación.* Lima.
1963   "Evaluación de los factores determinantes de la formación económica de Rosario y su zona de influencia." (Mimeographed.) Rosario.

SINGER, PAUL
1968   *Desenvolvimiento económico e evolução, urbana.* São Paulo.

SMITH, LYNN
1966   "The changing functions of Latin American cities." (Mimeographed.)

STOHR, WALTER, PAUL PEDERSEN
1969   Integración espacial multinacional. *Cuadernos de la Sociedad Venezolana de Planificación* 60–61 (March). Caracas.

URIBE ORTEGA, GRACIELA
1967   *La localización de la actividad manufacturera en Chile.* Santiago.

VAPÑARSKY, CÉSAR
1966   *Rank-size distribution of cities in Argentina.* Buenos Aires: CUER.

Some Problematics of the Tertiarization Process in Latin America

HARLEY L. BROWNING

Since little escapes his observant eye, Richard Morse, that peerless overviewer of the urbanization process in Latin America, recently summarized the tertiarization argument as follows (1971: 19):

It has for years been accepted that as Latin American countries urbanize and industrialize the proportion of people employed in tertiary ("service") categories relative to those in secondary (manufacturing, construction) increases more swiftly than in the nineteenth-century industrial countries. This is usually taken to mean that urbanization here "outruns" industrialization, that people are released from precarious rural occupations faster than stable secondary sector jobs are created for them.

Underlying the various discussions of the tertiarization process is an attempt to come to grips with a fundamental problem of Latin American development: the imbalance between supply and demand in the labor force of rural and urban areas. The rate of population growth, conditions of employment in rural areas, the industrialization process within a capitalist context, modernization, rural-urban migration, urbanization, and the formation of the labor markets in cities – all these are linked together in the interpretation of tertiarization.

The argument is by now a familiar one and goes something like this. Most countries in Latin America have experienced rapid population growth in recent decades because of a pronounced decline in the death rate and the maintenance of high birth rates. As the much larger groups of young people enter the age of full labor participation, they have difficulty in finding suitable work. This is particularly true in rural areas, where shortages of arable land, restrictive land tenure patterns,

I wish to thank Humberto Muñoz and Orlandina de Oliveira for suggestions, and Waltraut Feindt and Joachim Singelmann for their assistance.

and anachronistic cultivation practices make the absorption of man-power difficult.

At the same time, most of these countries have had a steady increase in the forces of modernization that are now penetrating to virtually all parts, a process which is conceptually distinct from economic growth. In my conception one aspect of modernization is the increasing awareness of life beyond the boundaries of one's original community. The national governments in the last three decades have enlarged the transportation networks of their countries in order to bring many formerly isolated areas into contact with the rest of the country. They have improved, even if only to a limited extent, the school systems so that there is increased educational attainment, even in the rural areas. The mass media provide for a greater dissemination of information, and the greater geographical mobility of the population increases the personal contacts that people have with those living in other places. But for thousands of rural or small-town communities, the agents of modernization – the hardtop road, the new school, the provision of electricity and potable water – have not been accompanied by improvements in the local economies, which often remain weak and static. Because modernization helps to make individuals aware of conditions elsewhere, it stimulates out-migration to areas of relatively greater economic opportunity, especially metropolitan areas. But relatively greater economic opportunity does not mean that the industrialization process is adequate to provide good jobs for the "floods of migrants who crowd into the mushrooming large cities," to use the imagery often used to describe this process.

In contrast to the historical instances of industrialization that took place in Western Europe and North America, the secondary (manufacturing) sector is incapable of absorbing many migrants. In part this is due to the disappointing performance of the national economies as such; and a host of factors – ranging from cultural characteristics which inhibit the emergence of entrepreneurs to dependency and imperialism – have been summoned to account for the failure to mount and sustain economic growth. In the case of manufacturing, it can be argued that advanced technology is imported directly from industrial countries. This technology tends to be capital intensive, meaning that considerable increments of output can be achieved with little addition to the labor force. And the characteristics of the migrants themselves militate against ready absorption into the secondary sector. Largely of rural origin, they are poorly educated and have few skills suitable for work in the secondary sector.

The result is that the great bulk of the migrants, if they are to find any sort of work at all, have no recourse but to go into the tertiary or services sector. In the secondary sector a growing "credentialism"

(Balán 1969), that is, a generalized requirement that applicants for all positions must have a credential, usually in the form of a certificate stating that the individual has completed the first stage of the schooling cycle (*primaria*), which is six years, effectively screens out many migrants. In the tertiary sector, there are fewer such requirements, and there is a greater elasticity of absorption. Because entering domestic service or setting oneself up as a street vendor requires little experience or capital, we find migrants concentrated in such activities.

It is evident from the above that the concept of tertiarization, as it has developed in Latin America, carries negative connotations. It can readily be linked to such other negative concepts as "over-urbanization," "hyperurbanization," and the "primate city," all signifying basic structural deficiencies of the urbanization process and the developmental process as a whole in Latin America.

CRITIQUE OF TERTIARIZATION AS A CONCEPT

Beyond the fact that one's tongue stumbles all too easily over the word, there are so many difficulties with the concept of tertiarization that it is of doubtful value in understanding the developmental process in Latin America.

The very term *tertiary* has long had a rather disreputable connotation in economics. The physiocrats of the eighteenth century believed that the source of all wealth ultimately lay in the primary sector – agriculture and minerals. Adam Smith believed that only the primary and secondary sectors were really "productive" and that the activities subsumed under the tertiary sector were "parasitic" to one degree or another. Marx seems to have followed much the same thinking although this judgment of his can be challenged. It seems fair to say that despite his great concern with the conditions of employment and of the division of labor, Marx paid very little attention to the tertiary or services sector. For example, only once in *Das Kapital* are services mentioned, and then very much in passing. This omission on his part as well as on the part of the eighteenth-century writers, is perhaps understandable, for in their times the tertiary or service category was dominated by domestic servants who, after agriculturalists, probably comprised the single largest category of employment. It is easy to see how they could be termed socially parasitic. The heritage of Marx's relative neglect of the tertiary sector has come down to us to the present day, for only recently have Eastern European communist economists been willing to concede that services can be productive. This tradition perhaps also makes more understandable the penchant

for Marxist-oriented writers in Latin America to appraise the tertiary
sector in unfavorable terms.

But the concept of the tertiary has always been handicapped for
another reason: it has no core meaning. When we think of primary,
agriculture immediately comes to mind; secondary brings forth manufacturing. Tertiary has no central connotation because it has always
been treated as a residual – that which is not in the primary and
secondary sectors. The result has been such a degree of heterogeneity
that it is difficult to talk about the "tertiary" or "service" sector in
any meaningful way. Included in the tertiary are such disparate
activities as public utilities (although these are sometimes included in
the secondary sector), transportation, communication, wholesale and
retail trade, finance, insurance and other business services, education,
health, charity, religious and voluntary organizations, government,
hotels and recreational activities, laundry and dry cleaning, various
repair services, and domestic services. Also included in the assemblage are the "free" professionals (doctors, lawyers, architects, and
engineers) who are self-employed. Given such heterogeneity, virtually
any statement regarding the tertiary as a whole is likely to be seriously
misleading when applied to a number of the above activities. The
various attempts to identify the common features of these industries
(e.g. Fuchs's statement [1968: 16] that " most of the industries in it
are manned by white-collar workers, . . . most of the industries are
labour intensive, . . . most deal with the consumer, and. . . nearly all
of them produce an intangible product ") are not very convincing.

I have come to the conclusion that tertiary will always lack conceptual precision and power. As we shall see later, any attempt to
divide the old tertiary into more homogeneous and analytically useful
categories brings its own set of problems. First, however, we need
to examine the suitability of the tertiary for an understanding of the
developmental process as it has occurred in Latin America.

TERTIARIZATION AS A DEVELOPMENTAL PROCESS

The tripartite division of the labor force has been made by a number
of scholars and can be traced back to the Swiss census of 1888. But
it was the Fisher-Clark formulation that won the day because the two
men not only established a classification scheme but went on to
suggest its use for a sequence of development. Fisher (1935) called
attention to the tripartite division, and Clark (1940) provided it with
statistical documentation, mainly from the experience of Western
Europe and the United States. As Postan puts it (1971: 87):

In Clark's formulation the tripartite order of sectors was transformed from a mere classification into an itinerary of economic progress. The lesson he taught was that economic progress had been achieved in the past and was to be achieved in the future by transferring resources first from primary occupations to secondary ones and, finally, from secondary to tertiary ones.

For Clark, the theoretical basis for the change was to be found in the income-elasticities of demand. They are, for example, lower for food than for health services. In addition, differential productivity trends favor industries in the primary and secondary sectors. Clark (1940: 7) says that "high average income per head compels a large proportion of producers to engage in tertiary production."

The Fisher-Clark thesis has not lacked criticism. Bauer and Yamey (1951) challenged the formulation on empirical grounds, maintaining that there were many exceptions, even in developed countries, to the sequence of development posited. They also questioned on several points the theoretical bases for the sequence. This is not the place for a discussion of the merits of the debate. Suffice to say that although some of the criticisms were quite telling (including the point of the heterogeneity of the tertiary sector), and although nowadays few economists would hold to the original formulation, the three-sector division of the labor force continues to be used by many economists (e.g. Kuznets 1966; Bairoch and Limbur 1968; Sabolo 1969); the various empirical and theoretical problems that have always plagued the tertiary or service sector have by no means been resolved.

In the event, whatever the applicability of the Fisher-Clark scheme to the developed countries, it is clearly inadequate to account for what is now going on in the Third World, especially Latin America. The movement out of agriculture has been a truly universal experience, but the shift of the labor force has been mainly into the tertiary sector, largely bypassing the secondary sector. It is only relatively recently that this tertiarization has not been seen in negative terms, as a sort of "wrong" sequence of development.

There are a number of reasons for reexamining the nature of sector development in the developing countries. As a host of Latin American writers have convincingly argued, the appropriateness of Western European and North American countries as guidelines for the future course of development of Third World countries is questionable. Furtado (1965) has shown that the very conditions of developing countries today are in fundamental respects not comparable to the conditions of the Western countries at the initial stages of their industrializing process. The "underdevelopment" of Third World countries is itself a historical product of the expansion of European capitalism into preindustrial countries. That heritage still is observable in the international division of labor and the distribution of the labor force in Western European countries as compared with Latin American ones. Thus, to present a table showing much higher ratios of tertiary-to-secondary employment for Latin American countries as compared to the European countries, as Browning (1958) did some years ago, and then to cite approvingly an Economic Commission for Latin America (ECLA) report (1957) that speaks of the "excessive" development of the service or tertiary sector in Latin America is misleading in at least two respects.

First, the low ratios for some European countries, such as the United Kingdom, West Germany, Sweden, and Belgium, where employment in the secondary sector is nearly as large as that in the tertiary sector, cannot be viewed as models of development to which Latin American countries should aspire, precisely because the international division of labor permits these countries to export manufactured goods to Latin American. Seen in this perspective, perhaps the European countries have had an "excessive" development of their secondary sectors.

The second reason why such comparisons are not valid has to do with the historical circumstances attending the efforts of Latin American countries to industrialize. Most of them are in what Hirschman (1968) calls the late, late industrializing group, and their secondary sectors reflect a wide range of technologies. Many enterprises, often foreign owned or controlled, import advanced labor-intensive technologies that can greatly increase output without materially increasing employment.

Taking into account the impact of the international division of labor and the impact of capital-intensive technologies, we cannot expect that employment in the secondary sector of Latin American countries *ever* will approach the 50 percent or higher level attained by some European countries, no matter how successful the economic development.

NOTEWORTHY RECENT STUDIES DEALING WITH THE TERTIARY SECTOR

Fortunately, in recent years there has been a quickening of interest in the tertiary or service sector in Latin America, primarily by economists, but also by sociologists. I will comment briefly on five studies that go beyond stereotypical characterization of the sectoral transformation of the labor force.

For a long time, the Economic Commission for Latin America (ECLA), under the leadership of Raúl Prebisch, provided what is extremely rare among the international agencies, a kind of moral leadership in analyzing and publicizing the economic or, better said, the sociopolitical economic problems of Latin America. During its period of peak influence ECLA was more than a compiler of economic facts (although it did an invaluable job in this respect). More important, it formulated and disseminated a point of view and a philosophy of the developmental process, one essentially created by Latin Americans themselves and not imported from outside.

In ECLA's presentation of data on the labor force of Latin America, two long articles are of special significance. The first (ECLA 1957) was a pioneering attempt to present comparable and comprehensive data for the postwar period for Latin America as a whole and for individual countries and to relate them to data from developed countries. The second (ECLA 1965, prepared by Zygmundt Slawinski) considered the period between 1925 and 1960 with projections to 1975, this time only for Latin America as a whole but again compared with other, mostly developed, countries. (No matter that in both articles the methodology for deriving the estimates from fragmentary and often suspect data was never made explicit; at least the data appeared consistent and reasonable.)

Of particular value was the breakdown in both articles of manufacturing into two categories, labeled "industry proper" and "handicrafts and homecrafts" in the first article and "factory sector" and "artisan sector" in the second. For 1950 it was estimated that slightly more than one-half (52 percent) of manufacturing was allocated to "handicrafts and homecrafts," with a range from 36 percent for Venezuela to 85 percent for Ecuador. The 1965 article provided Latin American employment distributions for ten industry sectors from 1925 to 1960 and then projections to 1975 (see Table 1). Note that in 1925 the factory component of manufacturing was only 26 percent. Fifty years later it will have risen to an estimated 61 percent. The percentage of the total labor force in manufacturing shows little variation throughout the period, 13.7 percent being the figure for both 1925 and 1975.

Not all artisan employment is of low productivity – some persons are highly skilled and well paid – but overall it is considerably lower than the factory portion. Construction, also a part of the secondary sector and one of the big relative gainers over the fifty-year period, is made up largely of low-paid workers. Construction provides one of the principal entry jobs for migrants to the city. In most countries it is not highly unionized, there are large fluctuations in demand and little job security, and it generally operates with a rather simple technology requiring skills familiar to men with rural and small-town backgrounds. Contrary to the impression often given in the literature on tertiarization, the service or tertiary sector has no monopoly on "marginal" labor.

Table 1. Distribution of the economically active population by branch of activity:
Latin America, 1925–1975

	1925	1950	1955	1960	1965	1970	1975
Total	100.0	100.0	100.0	100.0	100.0	100.0	100.0
A. Agricultural sector	61.3	53.1	50.0	47.3	44.9	43.1	41.4
B. Nonagricultural sector:	38.7	46.9	50.0	52.7	55.1	56.9	58.6
1. Production	16.3	19.2	19.9	20.2	19.4	21.3	21.5
a) Mining	1.0	1.1	1.1	1.0	0.9	0.9	0.8
b) Manufacturing	13.7	14.5	14.3	13.4	13.7	13.7	13.7
(i) Industrial sector	3.5	6.9	7.1	7.5	7.4	7.9	8.3
(ii) Artisan sector	10.2	7.5	7.2	6.8	6.3	5.8	5.4
c) Construction	1.6	3.7	4.5	4.9	4.8	6.7	6.9
2. Services	22.4	27.7	30.1	32.5	35.7	35.6	37.1
a) Basic services	3.2	4.2	4.7	5.2	5.6	5.8	6.0
b) Commerce and finance	6.7	7.9	8.6	9.2	9.6	10.1	10.7
c) Government	2.2	3.3	3.5	3.7	3.9	4.0	4.2
d) Other services	7.9	9.9	11.0	12.1	13.1	13.0	12.7
e) Unspecified activities	2.4	2.4	2.3	2.3	3.5	2.7	3.5

Source: Data adapted from ECLA Publication 1965, Tables 13 and 16. Data for 1955,
1970, and 1975 are projections. Projected data exclude Peru.

The ECLA breakdown of services into four classes plus unspecified
activities (assigned arbitrarily to services on the basis, probably correct, that most of the activities included in it are related to services)
is not a very helpful classification. Basic services are made up mainly
of public utilities and transportation. Unfortunately, "other services,"
the largest single category, includes both professional and domestic
services. We know that professional employment has been rising while
domestic service has been declining, so that combining them renders
the category virtually meaningless, especially for trend comparisons.

We can raise questions about the ECLA figures, but they are about
as good as we can expect to have at this time. More important,
perhaps, are the interpretations that the ECLA staff, particularly
Prebisch himself, has made of the figures and their trends. In contrast,
Ramos (1970) is a good deal more positive than most writers in his
interpretation of changes in the Latin American labor force in recent
decades, arguing that there has been a qualitative upgrading which has
been insufficiently appreciated. In his chapter "Sectorial distribution
of the labor force," he examines the determinants of sectoral employment. He also reviews the various attempts to relate sectoral change
and economic development: "The most common one, and certainly
the prevalent one in Latin American circles, is the demand-centered
theory associated with Colin Clark and A. G. B. Fisher" (Ramos 1970:
132). In a broader context, he summarizes the differences between his
own approach and that of ECLA in the evaluation of the role of labor
in the process of economic development:

Thus where ECLA sees the divergence of recent Latin American and historical United States employment trends to be a sign of imbalance and, so, undesirable, I see it as healthy – revealing the introduction of a new technology. Where ECLA focuses on capital accumulation as the principal determinant of growth via the assimilation of modern technology, I focus on skills. Where ECLA sees the excessive growth of tertiary employment, I also see the slow growth of skills. Where ECLA sees a too rapid migration to the cities, unwarranted by the limited secondary sector employment opportunities, I see a growth-fostering migration attracted by the possibilities for human capital investment. In effect, where ECLA considers these divergences from historical patterns as suspect, I consider such divergences as expected and desirable, indicating a growth process which is profiting from the Western experience, not simply repeating it (Ramos 1970: 233).

Ramos himself has cast the situation more optimistically than is warranted, but his assertion is a useful corrective to ECLA statements. Unfortunately, to a great extent he limits his analysis to a three-sector breakdown and does not confront the problems of decomposing the tertiary sector.

Two other economists, Markos Mamalakis and Paulo Singer, recently have directed their attention to problems of the sectoral transformation of the labor force. The Mamalakis approach (1970; this volume) is noteworthy for its careful attention to the interrelationship of sectoral income and sectoral employment and how they in turn relate to another fundamental structural variable, urbanization. Mamalakis (1970) also breaks down the tertiary sector into several categories. Of particular significance are the eleven "functions" he attributes to the various sectors, eight of which he links to the service sectors. The eight "functions" are listed in Table 2.

Questions can be raised about the meaning of some of the functions, e.g. whether quality maintenance and quality improvement are really distinct (and why government is in the latter but not the former), and whether the list of functions and sectors is inclusive. What is not in question is the desirability of relating the service sectors to societal functions, for this is one way to appraise the adequacy of the within-service sectoral breakdown.

Singer's study of Brazil (1971) has provided a framework for sectoral analysis that has a utility beyond the case of that country. He stresses the necessity for a broad institutional approach to the interpretation of structural change in the labor force seen over a period of years. Recognizing the need to deal with the heterogeneity of the tertiary sector, he divides it into three parts:

1. Production services (commerce, transportation, communication, warehousing).
2. Collective consumption services (government, education, health, and other social services).

Table 2. Functions linked to the service sector

Function	Sector
1. Time transformation ("action that transforms the time dimension of the stock and flow of goods and services").	Storage, trade, banking, transport.
2. Location transformation ("set of actions that transforms the locational dimensions of goods and service flows").	Trade, transport, gas, water, electricity.
3. Quantity transformation ("set of actions that transforms the quantity dimension of goods and services").	Trade, banking.
4. Quality maintenance ("set of actions that aims to maintain the quality of the human, physical, institutional, political and social capital stocks").	Health, education, repair, personal services.
5. Quality improvement ("set of actions, that improves the quality of the stock of physical, human, institutional, social and political capital").	Education, health, government, personal services.
6. Information transmission ("set of actions required to transmit information concerning economic and noneconomic events").	Communications and transportation.
7. Money ("complex of functions performed by the banking and financial intermediary system in an exchange economy").	Trade and banking.
8. Cultural and religious enrichment ("all the actions required to keep in balance and enrich the soul and spirit of society members").	Personal services.

3. Individual consumption services (liberal professions, domestic service, repairs, and other personal services).

In his longitudinal analysis of Brazil from 1920 to 1969, Singer shows that each of these sectors had periods of relative strength, and indicates their linear relationship.

In an unpublished project proposal for a large-scale survey of the tertiary sector of São Paulo, Singer establishes the following ten sectors, which he proposes to study individually:

1. Intermediary services (*comercio por atacado e varejo*).
2. Transportation services.
3. Educational, scientific, and cultural services.
4. Health services.
5. Religious and voluntary associations.
6. Public administration.
7. Recreational and entertainment services.
8. Liberal professions (including writers, architects).
9. Domestic services.
10. Services legally and morally nonsanctioned (i.e. prostitutes, beggars, criminals).

It is a commentary on the condition of studies of the tertiary sector in Latin America that Singer's proposed investigation of São Paulo would be the first *field* study of this vital part of the economy.

An article by Cardoso and Reyna (1968) remains the best short statement available on the linkage between industrialization, occupational structure, and social stratification in Latin America. Although the authors persistently mislabel as "occupational" the industry structure of the labor force, they present a sound and balanced analysis of the situation of Latin American countries *vis-à-vis* the developed countries, including sensible interpretations of what they call the "overloaded tertiary." Cardoso and Reyna summarize their argument as follows:

Although the overloaded tertiary and the presence of marginal groups testify to the social consequences of industrialization and the economic system's inability to absorb the excess of labor generated by its operations . . . , it would be premature to state that there is a complete rupture between the relatively more integrated core of the social system and the periphery, which many assume to be anomic and "available." In fact, the estimates presented in this paper and some trends in the expansion of the economic system point toward more cautious conclusions, emphasizing that the system in formulation has a certain absorption capability and, at any rate, still has many resources to expand the channels of social control, and that the patterns of deferred upward social mobility, even though somewhat mythical, are nonetheless effective (1968: 51).

Studies recently carried out in Monterrey, Mexico (Balán, Browning, and Jelin 1973), and in Mexico City (Muñoz and de Oliveira, i.p.) support this judgment. The analysis of Cardoso and Reyna needs to be deepened and extended as new evidence becomes available.

By now the reader may be growing impatient with the meandering course of this discussion. Granted that the sectoral transformation of the labor force is worth studying in its own right; that reliance upon gross sectoral categories, especially of the tertiary sector, is at best a first step in understanding the role of industries in economic development; that it is important to chart industry changes over extended periods of time; and that there are significant differences by countries – why, then, does not the author get on with it, by presenting a master table detailing industry breakdowns for each country of Latin America, for time periods going back at least to the beginning of this century. In addition, we would want to know *who* occupies *which* industry positions, and this would require an additional set of tables with cross-classifications by sex, age, occupation, class of worker, education, income, ethnic and migratory status, etc.

Lamentably, such figures are not available for Latin America. For that matter, they are not available for *any* country in the world, developed or not, in the required detail. Census bureaus only recently have developed data on the labor force and, having lacked a clear conception of what was needed, they have made many changes, particularly in their industry and occupational detailed categories, which makes the construction of a consistent set of detailed figures over time a truly frustrating enterprise. Perhaps ultimately the reason for the rather late appreciation of the importance of "human resources" for development and the significance of the role of sectoral transformation, specifically of services, in that development, is simply that the data never have been available.

ASPECTS OF THE MEXICAN EXPERIENCE

Because of the current impossibility of making a satisfactory, in-depth comparison of sectoral transformation of Latin American countries, I shall now consider some aspects of Mexican development, but not in any systematic fashion. Mexico has had sustained development over the past three decades, and as one of the larger countries of Latin America, it merits attention.

Particularly instructive, in light of the above discussion of data limitations, is an article by Keesing (1969). He makes vividly clear how difficult it is to penetrate the tangled thickets of Mexican labor force census data. It requires a heroic effort involving hundreds of man-hours of work, and is a job that cannot be turned over to a corps of clerical and research assistants because at every step difficult decisions must be made if comparability is to be achieved. Only by dominating all sources of data can the researcher arrive at the knowledgeable judgments needed to advance work in this area and provide a valid time series. Even so, Keesing provides comparable data only for 1895, 1930, and 1950, because the censuses for 1900, 1910, 1921, and 1940 were not suitable for one reason or another. The labor force data for the 1960 census have come under a cloud – it appears that a good deal of unexplained "adjusting" went on – so that only when the 1970 figures become available can we have a satisfactory record of sectoral transformation during Mexico's most intense period of economic development.

It is difficult to summarize the findings of Keesing, because his tables must be appraised in terms of the adjustments he made and the justifications he introduced for doing so. He did find, consistent with Ramos's emphasis on the upgrading of the labor force, important changes between 1930 and 1950 in the services sector (excluding utilities, transportation, communications, and commerce). It is worth citing his conclusions in full:

The other important implication of the evidence of this article is that much more attention needs to be paid, in the empirical analysis of development, to structural changes outside manufacturing, and particularly in the services sector. In industrial countries, services, when defined to exclude transportation and commerce, constitute an extremely skill-intensive sector. In the United States in 1960, for example, 30.2 percent of the labor force in this sector consisted of professional and technical workers, and another 17.9 percent were clerical workers, compared to 7.6 and 12.0 percent, respectively, in manufacturing. In Mexico domestic and laundry services constituted three-fourths of this services sector in 1895 but less than one-third by 1950. By that year, professional and technical workers made up 19.1 percent of the sector's labor force and clerical workers another 15.9 percent.

Often services seem to be regarded as a catch-all sector that plays a rather passive role in development. By concentrating empirical attention elsewhere and neglecting services, economists may have overlooked some important features of the development process (Keesing 1969: 738).

Two recent books (Solís 1970; Reynolds 1970) do much to enlarge our understanding of Mexican economic development. Reynolds notes that "if the statistics are to be believed," the tertiary sector outgained both the primary and secondary sectors in output per employed worker for the 1940–1960 period, with the tertiary going from 7,542 to 11,793 (1950 pesos), the secondary sector from 9,011 to 11,491, and the primary from 1,375 to 2,303 (Reynolds 1970: Table 2.4). Reynolds is somewhat puzzled by this trend:

The services sector remains something of an enigma... So many levels of productivity are lumped together under services, and such different capital and labor requirements are implicit in each, that generalization about the development of this sector is impossible. Since it is not customary among Latin American countries for services as a whole to achieve major productivity gains, an in-depth analysis of this sector is a priority item for future scholars despite the scanty and somewhat tenuous nature of the data available on service output, employment, and investment. The analytical difficulties are further complicated by a paucity of economic theory that relates the growth of specific services to the expansion of other key factors of the economy, including agriculture and manufacturing (1970: 301).

He attributes the Mexican trend to several factors, among them the growth of internal trade, the growth of Mexican tourism, and the "high-income elasticity of demand for services on the part of the middle classes." Reynolds sees many service activities as playing a vital role in the developmental and urbanization process. Petty commerce, construction, and domestic services are ways for rural-origin migrants to cities to find employment. They provide the worker with "a chance to acculturate, to familiarize himself with new habits of working and living which will equip him for higher skilled employment later on." Based on the Monterrey study this statement can be amended as "equip him or his offspring," for it is often the children of migrants who make the move upward.

The Monterrey study provides us with information on the socio-economic characteristics of pesons in different sectors and industries. But before presenting these data, we must address that perennial problem of how best to break down the tertiary sector into meaningful components. Katouzian (1970) offers some suggestions. Finding the Fisher-Clark dichotomy unsatisfactory, he proposes to divide the service sector into three categories: (1) complementary services; (2) new services; and (3) old services. He maintains that the new classification helps in understanding the developmental process. The "complementary services" include banking, finance, transportation, and wholesale and retail trade. They are called complementary because they accompany a rise in manufacturing production and they help in the transformation of local markets into a national market with increased foreign trade. The growth rate of employment in this sector may be expected to be more rapid in the earlier period of industrialization than the growth rate of manufacturing, but after this initial spurt it may lag during later stages.

The "new services" respond most readily to the rise in per capita incomes and the higher consumption of manufactured products, a feature of the rationale of the Fisher-Clark thesis. The category includes education, health, and entertainment. Its growth is a function of rising per capita incomes and rising per capita leisure time.

The "old services" are those that "flourished" before industrialization but have declined, in contrast to the expansion of the new services, with economic development. Included specifically are domestic services, but Katouzian is notably vague about what other industries fall within this category. This, indeed, is one of the difficulties of his scheme, for he makes no attempt to assign, systematically all service industries to his three categories. He notes, for example, that government is a "particularly heterogeneous bundle of services." Some aspects, such as education and health, increase with rising per capita incomes and therefore should be put in the new services category, while law enforcement and "bureaucratic activities" (whatever they might be) should go in the complementary services category.

Joachim Singelmann and I have made our own contribution to the sector classification problem (see Tables 3 and 4): we have allocated *all* industries to six sectors (omitting the "industry not specified" category). What we term the *extractive* sector is the same as the primary sector, except that we have moved mining to the second sector because we believe that the conditions of work, capital investment, etc., are more akin to manufacturing than to agriculture. Aside from this change, the transformative sector is the same as the secondary sector.

The tertiary sector is divided into four categories: the distributive (devoted essentially to the distribution of goods generated by the extractive and transformative sectors), producer, social, and personal

Table 3. Sector classification for male population employed in New York, Caracas, and Monterrey

Sectors	New York	Caracas	Monterrey
Extractive:			
Agricultural, forestry, fishery	0.6	1.9	1.4
Transformative:			
Manufacturing	31.4	21.6	47.1
Mining	0.1	1.2	0.7
Construction	7.1	10.0	9.8
Total	38.6	33.7	59.0
Distributive:			
Transport	7.6	7.1	6.1
Communications	1.4	1.3	0.7
Public-services enterprises	1.9	2.6	2.0
Large-scale commerce	5.8	3.8	10.0
Small-scale commerce	11.0	10.1	—
Total	27.7	24.9	18.8
Producer services:			
Finance, insurance	6.7	4.1	1.1
Publicity	0.6	—	—
Administration	2.5	1.7	2.3
Juridical (engineering and other)	1.9	—	—
Total	11.7	5.8	3.4
Social services:			
Health	2.5	1.7	2.7
Education	2.6	2.0	2.1
Charity and religious	1.1	0.8	—
Governmental	5.7	16.8	3.6
Total	11.9	21.3	8.4
Personal services:			
Restaurants, bars, etc.	3.3	5.0	5.3
Auto repair	0.9	—	—
Other repair	0.7	—	—
Domestic	0.4	1.1	4.7
Hotels, etc.	0.8	—	—
Dry cleaners, washerettes, etc.	1.1	—	—
Other	1.1	5.3	0.3
Recreation and amusement	1.1	—	—
Total	9.4	13.2	10.3
Total	99.9	99.9	99.9

Source: Census reports for the metropolitan areas of New York and Caracas; Monterrey Survey, 1965. (See Balán, Browning, and Jelin [1973].)

sectors. As far as I am aware, the allocations by Singer, Katouzian, Browning and Singelmann, and Mamalakis (whose scheme should be considered also in terms of the functions of his industry sectors) were made completely independent of one another, so that it is rather striking to find a general similarity in approach, however much the

Table 4. Sector classification for male population employed in Monterrey

	Trans-formative	Dis-tributive	Producer services	Social services	Personal services
Weekly income (pesos) Family income					
0–174	12.4	11.6	1.6	12.3	12.8
175–289	20.0	17.5	12.9	18.8	17.0
290–434	18.2	18.0	9.7	14.9	13.8
435–869	26.3	24.4	11.3	20.8	35.1
870+	17.0	18.8	59.7	29.9	11.7
Not recorded	6.1	9.7	4.8	3.3	9.6
	100.0	100.0	100.0	100.0	100.0
Number of people	Size of the work location				
1–5	16.3	48.9	35.5	8.4	59.6
6–50	21.0	18.3	32.3	21.4	26.6
51–200	13.8	7.4	21.0	17.5	2.1
201+	39.5	15.3	3.2	35.7	3.2
Not recorded	9.4	10.1	8.0	17.0	8.5
	100.0	100.0	100.0	100.0	100.0

Source: Monterrey Survey, 1965.

variation in detail. The labels may differ, but the following listing shows the convergence:

Browning and Singlemann	Singer	Katouzian
1. Distributive services Producer services	Production services	Complementary services
2. Social services	Collective consumption services	New services
3. Personal services	Individual consumption services	Old services

While Mamalakis stays closer to the individual industries themselves, his functions are comparable to the sectors of the other three (i.e. time, location, and quantity transformations correspond to distributive and producer services, and quality maintenance and improvement to social services.)

Tables 3 and 4 provide industry and sector figures for three large metropolitan areas: New York City, United States; Caracas, Venezuela; and Monterrey, Mexico. Not all individual industries could be identified for Caracas and Monterrey, but the figures for the six sectors should be reliable enough for comparative purposes. Caracas and Monterrey provide an interesting comparison. Caracas is a capital city, whereas Monterrey is a major regional center (ranking third in

Table 5. Socioeconomic characteristics of the male population of Monterrey, by activity sectors (in percentages)

	Trans- formative	Dis- tributive	Producer services	Social services	Personal services
Length of residence in Monterrey					
0–10 years	19.8	15.3	14.5	16.9	17.0
10–19 years	20.4	22.7	8.1	18.8	19.1
20 years or more	16.5	19.5	12.9	14.9	19.1
Naturalized citizens	14.4	13.1	17.7	15.6	11.7
First-generation citizens	14.6	15.3	17.7	14.3	18.1
Second-generation citizens	13.1	12.6	27.4	18.2	14.9
	100.0	100.0	100.0	100.0	100.0
N =	(825)	(366)	(59)	(149)	(85)
Educational level					
No schooling	13.9	9.6	0.0	9.7	11.7
1–5 years	38.4	35.6	14.5	26.0	42.6
6 years (primary)	21.3	30.9	4.8	21.4	27.7
Secondary	14.8	15.8	35.5	15.3	16.0
University	11.6	8.1	45.2	27.6	2.0
	100.0	100.0	100.0	100.0	100.0
Occupational level					
I (lowest)	33.6	26.7	12.9	27.3	40.4
II	27.6	26.4	3.2	25.3	21.3
III	14.2	18.8	3.2	1.3	20.2
IV	10.4	17.0	19.3	18.2	12.8
V	5.6	5.2	16.1	7.8	3.2
VI (highest)	8.7	5.9	45.2	20.1	2.1
	100.0	100.0	100.0	100.0	100.0

city size in Mexico and specializing in manufacturing). These different functions are very much apparent in the table. Nearly one-half (47.1 percent) of the men of Monterrey are employed in manufacturing, while the comparable percentage for Caracas is much lower. On the other hand, nearly one of every five men in Caracas is employed by the government, compared with one of every twenty-five in Monterrey. However, for a number of industries (construction, transportation, trade, and eating and drinking places) the percentages are quite similar. Overall, Caracas and New York are more similar to each other in sectoral distributions than is Monterrey to either of them. Caracas is very much a tertiary city, with about two-thirds of its male labor force in these activities. Monterrey is equally a secondary city. The great majority of large Latin American cities doubtless are closer in structure to Caracas than to Monterrey.

However representative Monterrey may be for Latin American cities, there are data, not otherwise generally available for Latin

American cities, which can be brought to bear on the fundamental question: are there any differences in the socioeconomic backgrounds of the men according to industry sectors? Recall that the tertiarization thesis posits the concentration of men of low socioeconomic background in the tertiary sector. In part this is because migrants to the cities, who are largely of rural background, find employment in low-paying service industries.

A thorough analysis of this matter is not possible here, but the distributions in Table 5 provide little support for the tertiarization thesis. There is considerable heterogeneity among the four sectors constituting the old tertiary. The producer services category differs most from the others, followed by social services, both including men of rather high socioeconomic status. The personal services sector, presumed to have concentrated within it men of very low socioeconomic status, does not compare unfavorably with the distributive or transformative sectors, although overall it is somewhat lower. The major conclusion to be derived from this table is that low-status or marginal men are to be found in *all* five sectors, and if we are interested in locating them, we are ill-advised to limit our search to the old tertiary or to the personal services sectors.

A CLOSING COMMENT

This review of the current state of knowledge about the tertiary sector in Latin America should make it all too evident that we are scarcely beginning to understand how the sectoral transformation actually works. We lack adequate data, without which there can be little hope for advancing the field. We also lack theories to interpret the data, theories which must be integral to the process of economic development. Such theories must not restrict themselves to a single discipline such as an economic, ecological, or demographic theory, but should take concepts and ideas from a number of sources.

What has become incontestable, to me at least, is the necessity to abandon the tertiary as a unit of analysis. It simply is too heterogeneous and its continued use will seriously block our understanding of the sectoral transformation process. Whether we decide to divide the tertiary into three or four or more categories is not as important as the initial decision to divide it. The recent work cited in this paper shows a basic agreement as to the direction in which we must move. Tertiarization as a concept and description of a process may have had some purpose initially, but that time is now past. We can safely abandon it without regret.

REFERENCES

BAIROCH, PAUL, J. M. LIMBUR
1968 Changes in the industrial distribution of the world labor force by region, 1880–1960. *International Labor Review* 98 (September): 311–336.

BALÁN, JORGE
1969 Migrant-native socioeconomic differences in Latin American cities: a structural analysis. *Latin American Research Review* (Spring): 3–29.

BALÁN, JORGE, HARLEY L. BROWNING, ELIZABETH JELIN
1973 *Men in a developing society: geographic and social mobility in Monterrey, Mexico.* Austin, Texas: University of Texas Press.

BAUER, P. T., B. S. YAMEY
1951 Economic progress and occupational distribution. *Economic Journal* 61: 741–755.

BROWNING, HARLEY L.
1958 Recent trends in Latin American urbanization. *Annals of the American Academy of Political and Social Science* 316 (March): 111–120.

CARDOSO, FERNANDO H., JOSÉ LUIS REYNA
1968 "Industrialization, occupational structure, and social stratification in Latin America," in *Constructive change in Latin America.* Edited by Cole Blasier. Pittsburgh: University of Pittsburgh Press.

CLARK, COLIN
1940 *The conditions of economic progress.* London: Macmillan.

ECLA (ECONOMIC COMMISSION FOR LATIN AMERICA)
1957 Changes in employment structure in Latin America, 1945–1955. *Economic Bulletin for Latin America* 2 (February): 15–42.
1965 Structural changes in employment within the context of Latin America's economic development. Prepared by Zygmundt Slawinski. *Economic Bulletin for Latin America* 10 (October): 163–187.

FISHER, A. G. B.
1935 *The clash of progress and security.* London: Macmillan.

FUCHS, VICTOR R.
1968 *The service economy.* New York: National Bureau of Economic Research.

FURTADO, CELSO
1965 *Development and underdevelopment.* Berkeley: University of California Press.

HIRSCHMAN, ALBERT O.
1968 The political economy of import-substitution industrialization in Latin America. *Quarterly Journal of Economics* 82: 2–32.

KATOUZIAN, M. A.
1970 The development of the service sector: a new approach. *Oxford Economic Papers* 22: 362–382.

KEESING, DONALD B.
1969 Structural change early in development: Mexico's changing industrial and occupational structure from 1895 to 1950. *Journal of Economic History* (December): 716–738.

KUZNETS, SIMON
1966 *Modern economic growth.* New Haven, Conn.: Yale University Press.

MAMALAKIS, MARKOS J.
1970   "Urbanization and sectoral transformation in Latin America, 1950–1965," in *Actas y Memorias del 37° Congreso de Americanistas.* Lima.

MORSE, RICHARD M.
1965   Recent research in Latin American urbanization: a selective survey with commentary. *Latin American Research Review* 6: 19–75.
1971   Trends and issues in Latin American urban research, 1965–1970 (Part II). *Latin American Research Review* 6 (2).

MUÑOZ, HUMBERTO, ORLANDINA DE OLIVEIRA
i.p.   Migración interna y mobilidad ocupacional en la cuidad de México. *Demografía y economía.*

POSTAN, M. M.
1971   *Fact and relevance: essays on historical method.* Cambridge: Cambridge University Press.

RAMOS, JOSEPH
1970   *Labor and development in Latin America.* New York: Columbia University Press.

REYNOLDS, CLARK W.
1970   *The Mexican economy: twentieth-century structure and growth.* New Haven, Conn.: Yale University Press.

SABOLO, Y.
1969   Sectoral employment growth: the outlook for 1980. *International Labour Review* 100: 445–474.

SINGER, PAULO
1971   *Força de trabalho e emprego no Brasil 1920–1969.* São Paulo: CEBRAP.

SOLÍS, LEOPOLDO
1970   *La realidad económica mexicana: retrovisión y perspectivas.* Mexico City: Siglo XXI.

SECTION TWO

Comparative Studies

PREHISTORIC

The Temple Town Community:
Cahokia and Amalucan Compared

MELVIN L. FOWLER

It is a common weakness among archaeologists to use the term *village* interchangeably with the term *site*, that is, locality where archaeological materials are found. This usage overlooks the sociological implications which terms such as village or town can have. The sociological implications of terminology are, in fact, quite important and need to be well developed.

For the concept of village, I prefer a combination of two definitions extant in the literature. Haury (1962: 118), first of all, has provided the following explanation:

I see [villages]...as distinct from the earlier long occupied camps... whether in caves or in the open, because of formalized architecture perhaps a closer clustering of houses, usually the presence of a larger apparently non-domestic structure, and a greater complexity of the material possessions .... The house pits...reflect a solidity of construction and an investment of labor that would arise only from need for prolonged residence.

Haury has stressed the physical aspects, such as clustering of houses, a specialized structure, and the relative permanence of occupation. On the other hand, Mumford (1961: 18) adds a social dimension to the definition when he states:

Everywhere, the village is a small cluster of families, from half a dozen to three score perhaps, each with its own hearth, its own household gods, its own shrine, its own burial plot within the house or in some common burial ground...[E]ach family follows the same way of life and participates in the same labors.

Mumford's stress is on the commonality of life in a village and the lack of specialization.

Other dimensions to the definition of village would depend upon the context in which it is found. It is possible for villages of the type outlined above to be at the peak of sociopolitical organization and territorial dominance in an area, or for such villages to be satellites to larger, more complex communities. In the latter case, a village may be a specialized craft center participating in the great tradition of the larger centers. In the former context, the village represents a point of sociopolitical development made possible by agriculture or some other stable food supply.

An even more distressing misapplication of the term village is when it is applied to large and complex archaeological sites. These are sites that show evidence of functionally distinct precincts within their boundaries, a large hinterland which they seem to dominate, and related and smaller satellite communities. One of the details that puts these large communities apart from their satellites is a central precinct set aside for religious and political purposes and manifested in specialized architecture. Among other characteristics, there is probably craft specialization within the community so that segments of the population are participating in only part of the total life as compared to the commonality Mumford specified for the village. There may also be centers and mechanisms for redistribution of goods and services both for the community itself and for the hinterland. For these types of communities I prefer the term *town*. Such towns could have arisen as a manifestation of the growing need for social and political control of increasing populations resulting from effective agricultural subsistence. Agriculture is not necessary for village life but it is a prerequisite for town life and its sociological implications.

In North America, archaeological sites that can be classed as towns are found in three different cultural settings. In one context, they are found as satellites to urban centers. This will not be discussed in this paper. In a second context towns, especially in central Mexico, can be found preceding the period when urbanism appears as a facet of developing territorial control. In this context are sites of the late Pre-Classic or Formative Period. Braidwood and Willey (1962: 350 ff.) refer to these as "temple centers" and a "kind of incipience to urbanization" which is present in the New World but which is not clear from the archaeological record of the Old World. Willey (1960) in another article used the term "temple town" to refer to this type of development. I accept this term and will use it henceforth in this paper, attributing to it the characteristics I have briefly outlined above.

The third context for such towns in North America is in areas peripheral to nuclear America where they appear as the pinnacle of the sociopolitical development. This appears to be especially true of the Mississippi Valley and southeastern areas of the United States. In this area the chroniclers of the De Soto expeditions described many such communities and their hinterlands. These men were conscious of moving from one political province to another and of going to each principal town. They met merchants who were traveling from community to community with goods to trade. They marveled at the towns with their walls and moats, dug to bring water from the river around the town. They saw the mounds upon which the temples and houses of the notables were constructed. Archaeological research has confirmed much of what was reported by these men.

In a move to contribute to our understanding of urbanism and its development, this article presents an examination of two archaeo-logical sites comparing them in terms of the concept of the temple town outlined above. One of these communities is the Cahokia site near East St. Louis, Illinois, which has long been known as the largest, and perhaps the earliest, of this type of site in eastern North America. The other site is Amalucan near the city of Puebla in the central highlands of Mexico. This site is of the Middle to Late Pre-Classic Period. More detailed descriptions of these sites will follow. The main purposes of this comparison can be stated as follows:

1. Can superficially similar sites such as Amalucan in Mexico and Cahokia in Illinois be meaningfully compared?

2. In what ways, if any, is it illuminating to consider these two communities to be "temple towns"?

3. Does such a grouping elucidate the concept of "temple town," bound it, and specify more clearly the area of its possible usefulness?

A subsidiary question is:

1. What is the effect of cultural-historical (for example, marginality) and ecological (dry highland versus humid lowland) factors on the nature of communities which have been provisionally called "temple towns"?

The following comparison will not provide definitive answers to these questions since the kinds of data available are not yet sufficiently inclusive. The comparison will, however, yield suggestions and a programmatic definition of goals for developing research.

CAHOKIA

The first site to be considered in this comparison is Cahokia, near East St. Louis, Illinois. The central feature of this locality is a large, terraced mound covering sixteen acres and rising to a height of over one hundred feet above the surrounding valley floor. Grouped around this large mound in a series of avenues and plazas are over eighty other mounds of varying sizes and shapes.

This group of mounds and related occupation covers an area of about fifteen square kilometers (about five square miles). The total area thought to have been utilized is bounded in two ways. First, there are outlying mounds which are suggestive of limits to the major site area. At least two of these mounds, Rattlesnake and Powell, were of essentially the same shape, a long rectangular mound with a ridge-like top. There are no other mounds of this shape within the limits we have suggested. These are two mounds of the southernmost and westernmost areas included within the site limits. At roughly corresponding points on the north and east are other mounds.

A second factor suggesting limits to the site are certain lines which appear on old aerial photographs suggestive of palisade and ditch lines surrounding the area. One of these lines has been tested and proven to be such a palisade. These lines converge at points on the main north-south axis of the site.

Within these limits are several areas of apparent functional difference. There are materials now coming out of the ground which suggest that the main mound and the mounds immediately around it were walled off from other parts of the town, thus setting them apart. This is doubly interesting, if further excavation confirms this, since the big mound is the only mound with four terraces; it is thus possible that it represents a structure of special importance not only for the town itself but for the surrounding areas. At one time there was a conical eminence on the third terrace of this mound. This is suggestive in light of the data we have on the Natchez that the Sun or major leader of a Natchez territory would ascend an eminence near his house every morning to greet the sun at dawn. Perhaps the big mound and its enclosed compound represents the residence and precinct of the chief political leader of the area.

Other functional areas are suggested by the different shapes of mounds within the site area. There is only one other multiple-stage or terraced mound and that is just west of the big mound, outside of the proposed enclosed compound. Besides these, there are several rectangular and square flat-topped mounds which are obviously platforms. Another form of mound is a conical and round-topped type. There is some suggestion that these may be burial mounds, although this possibility has not been thoroughly investigated. A study is currently underway classifying the types of mounds at the Cahokia site in order to determine the distribution of the types and the possible functional significance of the differing types and their distributions.

Besides the mound types mentioned above, recent excavations have demonstrated that there are other functional areas within the site. Some of these excavations have shown the residential areas to be quite intense with rebuilding of houses on the same locality several different times. In some cases these houses are well aligned with each other and form sections with street-like areas between the houses. Other areas have yielded data on what were probably plazas and ceremonial and communal structures. In some cases residential areas were built over what had earlier been public plazas.

Of particular interest is one area where a large circle of posts had been placed in the ground. This circle of evenly spaced posts had at its center another large post. Dr. Warren Wittry (1964) who excavated this structure has carried out studies indicating that this circle of posts, called Woodhenge by him, may well have been an observatory for noting both the rising and setting of the sun and moon to determine critical days for measuring the year. In line with this kind of data suggesting a concern for things astronomical is the fact that the site seems to be aligned on an axis about three degrees east of true north. The main axes of the site, the big mound, and the other larger mounds seem to follow this alignment. Currently a precise map of the entire site is being made which will give us data enabling a more precise definition of this orientation.

The question of craft specialization within Cahokia has not been studied as yet. At the present time, surface distribution studies of materials are being undertaken by investigators from two institutions. Hopefully these studies will give us data on this and other problems. There is some suggestion of such specialized areas in the finding of artifacts called microdrills in a rather limited area of the site. Gregory Perino suggests that these might have been used to drill shells in the process of bead manufacture, implying that this was a craft specialized area.

Petrographic thin section studies of ceramics from the Cahokia site and surrounding area have been carried out in the past several years. Suggestions from these studies are that there were several local areas of pottery manufacture using clays locally available. Perhaps more detailed studies of this type will make it possible to trace an interchange of such local ceramic wares.

That Cahokia participated in a larger interchange of goods with not only the surrounding area but with other regions as well is an accepted but poorly documented hypothesis. There are certain exotic materials such as galena and conch shells which suggest this. That trade routes were established and goods interchanged in the southeastern United States as early as three thousand B.C. has recently been demonstrated.

How the goods were distributed within Cahokia is another unanswered question. A structure very suggestive of a market area was excavated about 250 meters west of the big mound. This apparently was a large square enclosure of upright log construction. Spaced at regular intervals along the walls of this enclosure were circular rooms opening toward the center of the area. Only the size and shape of this suggest a market, since no data exist to confirm this idea. Another such enclosure is indicated on the early aerial photographs of the site about 500 meters to the east of the big mound.

Several other sites exist in the area surrounding Cohakia suggesting a series of smaller towns, villages, and farmsteads related to the larger center. Among these are Pulcher about ten miles to the south and Mitchell about seven miles to the north. Although these sites are rather large in themselves, none are as large and complex as Cahokia and none have terraced mounds. It is my hypothesis that these are satellite communities dominated by the larger town. It may well be that there was a well-defined political territory which was immediately controlled by Cahokia.

In this territory there were probably two distinct ethnic groups as is suggested by ceramic and other data. These ethnic groups lived at the same time within the confines of Cahokia and in separated communities outside as well.

Cahokia exerted an influence over a much larger area, in fact most of the Mississippi Valley, but this is a problem beyond that which we have chosen to discuss.

As a final note on this discussion of Cahokia, some mention should be made of the time of its occupation. Radiocarbon dates suggest that human habitation of the site area began as early as 800 A.D. and continued until at least 1500 A.D. However, it is my opinion that it reached its peak and functioned as a temple town between about 900 and 1200 A.D. After that time, it was a different type of community and had a qualitatively different relationship to the surrounding area.

AMALUCAN

The description of the Amalucan site will be much shorter since much less archaeological research has been conducted at that site. Some investigations were carried out by Linné (1942) and Noguera (1940) as well as Krieger and Sanders (1951).

Amalucan is the name of a large *hacienda* located just to the east of the city of Puebla and south of the volcanic peak of Malinche. Most of the archaeological site is now in the *ejido* lands of the village of Chachapa. The natural features dominating the landscape in this immediate area are two conical hills rising abruptly from the valley floor. The largest of these, Cerro Amalucan, has a large mound group and plaza area on its peak and the slopes of the hill were terraced. The smaller hill, Amaluquillo, apparently was not utilized.

The main cultural feature of the site is a large mound group to the east of Cerro Amalucan. This group is made up of one large multiple-stage mound, a long rectangular platform mound, and some smaller mounds forming a plaza area. Besides this main group there are several smaller groups of mounds.

Since the whole valley floor seems to have been occupied in Pre-Classic times, it is difficult to delimit the site. Using data such as continuity of surface distribution and natural features such as *barrancas*, I estimate that the site covers an area of ten square kilometers (three square miles). The surface material scattered over this area is uniformly Middle to Late Pre-Classic.

Similar Late Pre-Classic sites literally surround Amalucan. To the east is a site at Chachapa. To the north is a site of similar nature and mound types near Parecio. To the south is the site of Totimehuacan recently excavated by Dr. Bodo Spranz of the Freiburg Ethnographic Museum. In terms of site distribution and density, one might say that one of the major features of the distribution of archaeological sites in the Puebla Valley is that some 90 percent of them are Pre-Classic. The settlement pattern of that period seems to have been of a series of towns and their supporting lands almost cheek by jowl with each other. This pattern of settlement seems to have changed in Classic times with the domination of Cholula over this entire area.

Returning to the site of Amalucan itself, there seem to have been functionally distinct areas within the site. The major precinct seems to have been that of the main mound group and plaza. Only one mound at the site is multiple stage, suggesting some special function for it. This mound is nearly identical in shape to Mound 1 of Totimehuacan (Spranz 1966). This includes a similar depression on one side of the upper terrace which Spranz found at Totimehuacan to be a room that had been filled in.

Excavations in three different areas of the site have suggested other specialized areas. One of these excavations was carried out in the wall of a *barranca* to the south of the main pyramid group. Refuse pits and possibly house floors were noted in this *barranca*. Excavation demonstrated that there had been a series of refuse pits here and that there were several levels of occupation. Nearby were large, flat-bottomed pits suggesting houses. Since these types of features were not found in other sections of the site which were excavated, it is suggested that this was an area of habitation throughout the history of the site.

Another specialized area was discovered through the study of aerial photographs. On the photos, a straight dark line was noted extending in a northeasterly direction from near the central part of the large mound of the major group to an old stream channel. Further study of the photo indicated that there were similar lines nearly perpendicular to the first at regularly spaced intervals. A trench was put across the main line of this series. The excavations demonstrated that these lines were the remains of an ancient series of canals. These canals were utilized over a long period and, as they silted in, were reexcavated to clear the channel. This happened on at least five different occasions. Finally it appears that the canals were filled in and the ground leveled, probably in preparation for the building of the big pyramid. Indications are that these lines continue under the main pyramid. Thus there is evidence not only of a water distribution system but of a changed function for this section of Amalucan through time.

There is no evidence as yet to suggest the actual use to which the canals were put other than the distribution of water. One good possibility of course is irrigation. Another possibility is that they were used to distribute water to the residents of the town.

In the northwestern portion of the site, at the foot of Cerro Amalucan are other markings of the aerial photos of the same dark discoloration of the soil. These have not yet been investigated by excavation but undoubtedly represent a major aboriginal feature of the site.

The time when Amalucan was occupied can be defined by three lines of evidence. One is that the bulk of material found on the surface and in the excavations to date is Pre-Classic. The one exception to this is the southeastern portion of the site where some Classic material has been found. By far the most common form of figurine found to date is one similar to Vaillant's type E-2 This suggests a Zacatenco-Ticomán affiliation for the site.

In the stratigraphy of the site, there is a dark, black zone found in all excavations which caps all other strata below. This was found over the canal area as well as over the area of refuse pits. It appears that this is an old humus line and apparently represents a time when the site was abandoned. The material below this line is all Pre-Classic. This suggests that before Classic times the site was completely abandoned and not utilized intensively again until colonial times.

The third line of evidence is a radiocarbon date from Totimehuacan Mound 2 (Spranz, personal communication). While appraisal of this date must await Dr. Spranz's detailed analysis, it suggests an age of ca. 100–300 B.C. for some of the activity of that group.

CONCLUSION

Superficially, both Amalucan and Cahokia seem to have been the same *type* of community. Both contained a central precinct which probably represents a center of social, religious, and political control. Both had other public works of community importance. There is some evidence of craft specialization at Cahokia, but this type of data has not yet been collected at Amalucan. Both seem to be involved in a relationship with their own hinterlands and with a broader network. In this aspect, there appear to be differences in their individual relationships with the total settlement pattern. Amalucan seems to have participated in a more densely settled area with other similar communities close at hand. Cahokia was a larger community but with a much less densely settled hinterland and with more space between communities. These conclusions are speculative, since very little study or thought has been given to this type of problem. In neither of the communities are we able to make estimates of population, since sufficient control over occupation unit data has not been achieved. In both cases, however, we would surmise that population was in the order of thousands rather than hundreds.

Further studies need to be made in order to accurately define temple town communities and to adequately compare or contrast these two. These types of studies need to take lines suggested by Schaedel (1969), Mann (1969), and Longacre (1969). Particularly important to arriving at the kinds of data needed for such studies and conclusions is an application of the methods outlined in Crawford's *Archaeology in the field* (1953). Attention in this type of approach should be given to delineation of site area, collecting distributional data from the surface, defining specific features on the basis of aerial photos, distribution data, and excavation, and a reconstruction of the history of the site area. From this should develop a description of the community through time with special emphasis on functional divisions within the community and population growth. Developed along with this would be a concern for understanding the setting, both cultural and ecological, in which the community is found. Interpretation of the above types of data will be of necessity based upon ethnographic data on communities of types comparable to that thought to be represented by the archaeological sites being investigated.

When these studies have been carried out, we will be able to go somewhat beyond the hypotheses and descriptions presented above.

REFERENCES

BRAIDWOOD, ROBERT J., GORDON R. WILLEY, *editors*
   1962   *Courses toward urban life.* Viking Fund Publications in Anthropology
          32. Chicago: Aldine.
CRAWFORD, O. G. S.
   1953   *Archaeology in the field.* London: Phoenix House.
HAURY, EMIL W.
   1962   "The greater American southwest," in *Courses toward urban life.*
          Edited by Robert J. Braidwood and Gordon R. Willey, 106–131.
          Chicago: Aldine.

KRIEGER, ALEX, WILLIAM SANDERS
1951   "Map of Amalucan," in *Anales de INAH*, volume four: 1923–1953, *Estados de Nayarit, Nuevo León, Oaxaca, Puebla, etc.* Varios, Sección 8. Mexico City: Instituto Nacional de Antropología e Historia.

LINNÉ, S.
1942   *Mexican highland cultures: archaeological researches at Teotihuacán, Calpulalpan and Chalchicomula in 1934–1935.* Ethnographical Museum Publications 7. Sweden.

LONGACRE, WILLIAM A.
1969   "Urbanization in pre-Columbian America," in *The urbanization process in America from its origins to the present day.* Edited by R. P. Schaedel and J. E. Hardoy, 15–32. Buenos Aires: Instituto Torcuato Di Tella.

MANN, LAWRENCE
1969   "Activity density-intensity analysis: a research framework of ancient settlements and modern cities," in *The urbanization process in America from its origins to the present day.* Edited by R. P. Schaedel and J. E. Hardoy, 159–170. Buenos Aires: Instituto Torcuato Di Tella.

MASON, RONALD J., GREGORY PERINO
1961   Microblades at Cahokia, Illinois. *American Antiquity* 26 (4): 553–557.

MUMFORD, LEWIS
1961   *The city in history.* New York: Harcourt, Brace, Jovanovich.

NOGUERA, F.
1940   "Excavations at Tehuacan," in *The Maya and their neighbors*, 306–319.

SCHAEDEL, RICHARD P.
1969   "On the definition of civilization, urban, city and town in prehistoric America," in *The Urbanization process in America from its origins to the present day.* Edited by R. P. Schaedel and J. E. Hardoy, 5–13. Buenos Aires: Instituto Torcuato Di Tella.

SPRANZ, BODO
1966   *Las Piramides de Totimehuacan*, volume one. Puebla: Instituto Poblano de Antropología e Historia.

WILLEY, GORDON R.
1960   New World prehistory. *Science 131*, Washington, D.C. (Reprinted in *Annual report of the Smithsonian Institution, 1960*).

WITTRY, WARREN L.
1964   An American Woodhenge. *Cranbrook Institute of Science News Letter*, 33 (9): 102–107. Bloomfield Hills, Michigan.

Ecological Factors Affecting the Urban Transformation in the Last Centuries of the Pre-Columbian Era

DUCCIO BONAVÍA

It is true that Andean archaeology possesses a general theoretical picture of development which is probably the most complete of the continent: this idea has been insisted upon quite persistently. But it is also true that many casual assertions have, through constant repetition, been accepted as facts without ascertaining the extent of their validity. This is probably especially true for the Inca area. In recent years, however, many archaeologists have devoted themselves to detailed works and to the solution of small problems. On the basis of these investigations we are now able to see our initial errors with greater clarity. Above all we are able to appreciate more fully that there are still many partial or complete gaps in our knowledge. One may say that this is true of the town-planning aspect. Only Willey (1953) has studied the phenomenon in depth (in Virú), but strictly from the archaeological point of view. Thus it is a great pity that the architectural expressions of the latest periods in this valley are not the most significant ones. As a result, there is a clear need for another similar study in some coastal valley (preferably on the central coast) and in a mountain area, to provide more comparative material.

Contrary to generally accepted opinion, we now know that the Incas were not builders of cities. The type of urban concentration they knew was far from our Western understanding of the phenomenon. Rowe (1946: 229; 1963), among others, has persuasively shown this, and Bennett and Bird (1949–1960) let us suspect it, though today we know that the antecedents of the phenomenon are earlier than the North American archaeologists thought. However, this does not mean that no urban centers were built during the Tahuantinsuyo. Lanning (1967) asserts this too simplistically when he declares: "It is doubtful whether the Incas built any settlement larger than a small town" (1967: 163), or when, in questioning the urban character of Cuzco, he says that, if one regards it as a city, "It was the only one the Incas built " (1967: 67). In fact, the evidence disproves this. It is true (as will be seen later) that many of the urban centers of the Late Horizon have their roots in earlier periods; but it is also true that many of them are typically Inca and built under the Cuzco reign (Hardoy 1968: 46).

One of the greatest difficulties of this kind of study is unquestionably the lack of plans of pre-Columbian town centers. Those which do exist are, with very few exceptions, rough sketches, and very often contain serious errors. To mention only a few, we have no plans of Cajamarquilla, Marca Huamachuco, or Pacatnamú. Nor is there any overall detailed plan of Chanchán. And even in the study of samples of what existed in the Virú area, only the rough sketch (rather than the plan) was used. It is true that in many cases aerial photography has been of invaluable assistance; however, I would venture to assert that it is also responsible for many errors. Aerial photographs lack the detail which can only be known by direct cleaning of structures and by methodical excavation. This is the only way of deducing the functional nature of the structure under study and of arriving at inferences of an interpretative nature.

If one were to analyze the planimetry of the urban aggregates of the Late Horizon on the basis of the small amount of existing material, one would conclude that no basic design in Indian town planning was regularly used. I have been able to prove this personally, and Hardoy has already stated this fact (1964). What is indeed clear is that some elements (e.g. the square, principal palace, temple of the sun, home of the chosen ones, stores) are almost always found in typically Inca centers. They may be found together or separately, but always with a different layout. In other words, it appears that there were elements representing basic features of Inca social and political organization which were used by indigenous architects. However, there was no guiding plan or specific location for these elements within it.

Perhaps one of the basic reasons for this was the short duration of the period of Inca expansion. It did not allow them to exercise true planning in this field; it forced them to improvise instead. Possibly the many other problems they had to resolve during their conquest of the Andean area required preferential attention. But over and above this, technical limitations (which undoubtedly they had) and the topography in which they moved must have played an important role.

One common feature is seen in all Inca and pre-Inca centers of population: i.e. their complete adaptation to topography and the maximum use of natural features in their building of these centers. This results from the imposing geomorphological conditions which they had to master. This was undoubtedly a determining factor preventing (in many cases) any regularity of urban design, as Rowe (1946: 228) has observed. The Andean man in fact made relatively few changes in his natural environment when setting up his home. Major changes were directed towards problems of much greater importance such as the obtaining of arable lands and the carrying out of engineering works to preserve them permanently.

The Incas preferred to occupy the living sites of the groups they annexed. They only built cities or other kinds of settlements when obliged to do so, particularly to obtain some form of control in strategic places. These new centers were built by the government under the guidance of imperial architects (Rowe 1946: 228). Such is the case of the groups forming the limits or boundaries (*limes*) of the empire in the eastern area, or in Huanuco and Pumpu in the central sierra (see Thompson 1969), Cajamarca in the north, or Cochabamba in the southern area. In coastal areas we have the example of Tambo Colorado, which was built to control the Pisco Valley and surrounding areas, and Incahuasi, which was ordered built in the campaign against Chuquimanco. Paramonga, though it has been said that it is Chimú (Hardoy 1968: 43), is in fact basically Inca. We do not know for certain whether it was a temple or fortress or both (as Tello maintained). In any case, it was a place where Inca control was exercised. However, it must have been abandoned in later periods, for according to the chroniclers the site had already been deserted at the time of the Conquest. The Inca samples in Virú do not show any change or construction of new buildings with respect to earlier periods. In the Estero Period the people continued to live exactly where they had lived in the Tomaval or La Plata Period (Willey 1953). Thompson (1964) has shown a similar phenomenon in the Casma Valley. This is the fruition of a wise policy imposed by the Incas. When they were able to, they exercised their control through traditional centers of prestige. Thus they camouflaged the fact that Cuzco control had been imposed (for example, Menzel 1959). Furthermore, this is the explanation for the lack of typically Inca sites which has been noted by the archaeologists working on the coast.

It is interesting to see how the expert on the urban phenomenon (Hardoy 1964: 471) regards the sites of Piquillacta, Viracochapampa, Incahuasi, Tambo Colorado, and Ollantaytambo as typical examples of town planning among the Incas. With the evidence available to us today, we know that some of these centers are much earlier than the Late Horizon. This same reasoning helps us to understand the antecedents of the urban phenomenon in the Andean area, as well as to locate them more accurately in time. In fact, the evidence proves that the planning phenomenon is prior to the Late Intermediate Period (Chimú), and certainly goes back to the Middle Horizon (Schaedel

1966a, 1966b). Through Rowe's investigations (1963) we know one of the fundamental characteristics of this period: very large complexes of buildings with squares, corridors, and rectangular rooms, designed with a formal plan with very high walls with doors and windows. This is seen very clearly particularly in the valleys of the north coast and center. Willey (1953) has proven that in Virú planned cities are much older than the Late Horizon. They appear in the Tomaval Period and later are reinhabited in the La Plata and Estero Periods.

Apart from the classic site of Huari (specifically in its Capilla Pata sector) in the Ayacucho sierra, Marca Huamachuco in the northern sierra, Cajamarquilla on the central coast, and a site in Pampa de las Llamas in the Casma Valley, the following are now considered as sites of the Middle Horizon: Piquillacta and Virachochapampa. These centers are traditionally classified as Inca (Hardoy 1964; Harth-Terré 1959). Thus, the close similarity noted by Hardoy (from the town-planning point of view) between these two places and the others (which are indeed truly Inca), proves to us that the Incas had a formal copy of this planimetry, with very slight variations. One of these may have been the introduction of the trapezoidal or triangular shape on the design of the squares (though the latter does not appear to be an original idea of the Cuzcans either). This is in contrast to the precise quadrangular layout of the designs of Piquillacta and Viracocha-pampa. What is more, McCown himself (1945) called attention to the great similarity between the designs of Piquillacta and Viracocha-pampa. He even suggested that it involved the copying of one from the other – at least in part, if not completely. For his part, Harth-Terré (1959) had observed that the *colcahuasi* of Lunahuaná contained the complete layout of Piquillacta's public granaries and storehouses, except that this author was also convinced that Piquillacta was Inca.

We have very little information on Viracochapampa, which Belaunde (1961) defined as an example of "a rationalist architecture of a planned city." However, Rowe (1963), Menzel (1968), and Lanning (1967) declare that there is no doubt about its being located in the Middle Horizon. For Piquillacta we have the evidence published by Valcárcel (1933), Rowe (1963), Lanning (1967), and Menzel (1968), plus the unpublished investigations of Sanders. However, it is fair to say that Rowe (1946: 225) had made it clear that it was not an Inca site; and Hardoy in his second book (1968: 48) now accepts this.

If any city should be considered as the "ideal" Inca model, it is unquestionably Cuzco (Hardoy 1968). (It should be noted that Rowe [1946: 228–229] suggested that "the best example of a planned Inca settlement is the town in the Ollantaytambo Valley where the blocks of houses were accommodated in a trapezoidal-shaped area with two large squares at the edge of the area of the houses.") Since much has been written on this subject (Rowe's 1967 work is the last), it is not necessary to return to the matter. One should only note here that the plan of Cuzco is not repeated in any of the other Inca cities; also, the form of puma seen there is unique. However, I would like to call attention to one small detail. I recently had the occasion to visit Trujillo and to see the investigations being carried out by the Harvard University team. Kent Day, who is studying one of the Chanchán citadels, was kind enough to show me some of the results in advance, and I am taking the liberty of referring to one of them here. I refer to the evidence that the citadel was designed in such a manner that access to it was strictly controlled. In most cases this had to be single file, because of the narrowness of the passageways. This control was exercised from special sentry boxes, probably occupied by expert trusted staff. If we add this to what we already know about Chanchán, and read the descriptions made of pre-Columbian Cuzco, we seem in fact to be face to face with the same phenomenon – the same concept. Valcárcel (1924: 21) tells us that "each family or lineage occupied an enclosure apart " in the Inca capital. "These large separate enclosures had an original arrangement: a single door gave access to the inside: the latter was a labyrinth of narrow passages (*killas*) and rooms which opened upon large or small areas, similar to Spanish patios. Each of the royalty's enclosures had orchards, gardens, baths, large sitting rooms, water-closets, halls, courtyards, etc." And would not the same idea be applicable to the area "of the temple" of Potrero de Santa Lucía (Cieneguilla) in the Lurín Valley (Bonavía 1965), which belongs to the Inca Period?

Incahuasi is a good example to show that the "ideal" plan of Cuzco was not applied to the building of other Inca centers. The chroniclers tell us that when the Incas wanted to conquer the lands of Guarco, they encountered such resistance that they decided to build "another new city, which they named Cuzco, the same as the principal site. They likewise report that they ordered that the districts and hills should have the same names as those of Cuzco " (de Cieza de León 1941: 226–227). If the plans of the two cities are compared, the first impression is that there is no similarity between them (see the plan of Incahuasi in Harth-Terré 1933). However, if one were to analyze the city's component parts, one by one (forgetting their location within the general layout), it would be found that in fact they do coincide. The same phenomenon is noted in Huanuco Viejo (Harth-Terré 1964), where the urban layout is *sui generis*, as all the parts are grouped around a large central square. Strictly speaking, we would find a remote resemblance in Tambo Colorado (though I refrain from cataloguing this small entity as a city, even if it unquestionably had very specific control functions within the valley). However, it does not have all the elements necessary to be considered as a city – using, for example, the concepts noted by Hardoy (1964: 23).

Cajamarca is a planned garrison city, or rather, remodeled on the basis of the old northern town. The Incas built the Oshno, Acllahuasi, and Temple of the Sun next to the buildings of Caxamarca del Adoratorio de la Serpiente. They surrounded them with a rampart and introduced a triangular square "larger than any in Spain " (de Jerez 1938), "completely enclosed with two doorways which led to the town's streets" (Ruíz de Arce 1953).

It is also interesting to note that the regularity of town designs of the Middle Horizon was lost or considerably altered with the passage of time, until the peak period of the Incas. Although a detailed analysis has never been made, it would appear that Late Intermediate cities retained this regular design to a greater degree, while it tends to be lost in the Late Horizon. Even the trapezoidal shape of Inca town planning (which apparently does not exist in the Middle Horizon and which predominated over the square or rectangle in the Late Horizon) undoubtedly has its antecedents in the walled retreats of the north coast of the Late Intermediate Period – and was probably copied by the Incas.

The problem of peasant villages reveals another aspect. From an architectural point of view, the Inca organization does not appear to have left any traces in these villages. Investigations carried out in the Huanuco area show that all the communities studied have a local rural architectural style; generally speaking, there is no evidence of any expressions of the imperial Inca style (Thompson 1968: 117).

Some archaeologists have recently been studying the problem of the Middle Horizon (especially its provincial and rural aspects) in areas previously unstudied, all in the central sierra. They are increasingly reaching the conclusion that many cultural elements traditionally considered as Inca are in fact not so. They have their antecedents in this first pan-Peruvian period of conquest (Rogger Ravines and William Isbell, personal communications). This appears to be very clear particularly in ceramics. The urban phenomenon appears to provide us with the same evidence. The detailed study of population centers will be able to resolve this question for us.

I have already treated the whole problem of Inca colonization of high mountain forests, with incursions to the low forests (Bonavía and Ravines 1967, 1968; Bonavía 1968b, 1969, 1970). There is no longer any doubt on this subject (Lathrap 1970a: 176), and I shall not return to it. But it is clear that this process with its antecedents in the Early Horizon, became (even before A.D. 600) a population movement to the east, related to Quechua-speaking groups (Lathrap 1970a: 173–175).

Naturally this was not a directed and planned phenomenon, but rather a spontaneous one, with movements taking place in both directions, that is, from east to west and vice versa (Lathrap 1970b). In the Late Horizon this movement acquired features of planned colonization, though we are still not very familiar with its true mechanics. Lanning (1967) has suggested that one of the basic reasons for the collapse of the first Andean imperial organization of the Middle Horizon was the following: lack of experience in organizing an area with such great ecological differences and one which was broken up by natural barriers of formidable dimensions (1967: 140). There is no doubt that the Incas capitalized on this experience of many centuries in the conquest of new territories.

What is unquestionable is that the difficulties they faced in the process, and which the mountaineer groups in large part overcame, were of a truly enormous magnitude: this involved the domestication of an area which even today is still in a 70 percent virgin state. It has been calculated that this area covers 28,146 kilometers of Peruvian territory. This formation, which we know as "high mountain forest" (*ceja de selva*), corresponds to Tosi's (1960) "very himid mountain woods" (*bosque muy húmido montaño*). It is easily distinguished from the punas and prairies by its luxuriant vegetation, which is always green. It is characterized by relatively low temperatures, a high incidence of mist, and especially by an excess of humidity. The result is that the atmosphere, vegetation, and soil are saturated with water for the whole year. The annual precipitation varies between 1,000 and 2,000 millimeters, and the major part is of strictly orographic origin. The formation is located on the eastern watersheds of the Andes and many eastern mountain ridges, from Bolivia to Ecuador. The lower altimetric limits vary from 2,500 meters (where the formation is more humid) to 2,800 meters (where it is drier); the upper limits vary between 3,500 and 3,800 meters. Generally speaking the unpleasantness of the atmosphere in this formation results from two factors: the excessive humidity and the abrupt topography and pronounced relief. Due to a combination of very unusual causes, only twenty-five to fifty percent of the total annual precipitation is eliminated directly into the atmosphere as evaporated transpiration. The rest does so as dripping or percolated water. This has had an influence on the formation of very abrupt slopes with narrow mountain ridges of land at their summits. There is very little level or moderately sloped land. Since the dry season only lasts one month a year, the water currents are of great volume and force. As a result, the land is physically unstable, of very bad quality and highly subject to erosion; farming thus becomes extremely difficult (Tosi 1960: 148–155). These difficulties have curbed the enthusiasm of modern man, with all his technology. But they have filled the archaeologist with amazement when discovering population centers of the pre-Columbian era in these lands. Fejos (1944: 17) wrote that it was difficult for him to believe there was any human occupation of this region. Today we know that it was carried out for the whole length of the high mountain forest, from Puno Department as far as the Amazon. But, contrary to what Fejos maintains, there were no cities in the high mountain forest. No grouping known to this day (with the sole and debatable exception of Machu Picchu and perhaps some other center whose name escapes me). unites even eight of the ten criteria which Hardoy properly establishes for one to be able to speak of a "city" in the true sense of the word. As to the Cuzco groupings, Hardoy had already declared this to be so (1964: 473); now we extend it to the areas of the central and northern high mountain forest.

In the first place, none of the centers has a large area and population for their time. We do not have exact demographic calculations, nor can we have them in present conditions. However, we are able to consider some very tentative estimates. I agree with Hardoy (1964: 473) that each group discovered by Wenner-Gren's expedition must have provided dwellings for approximately a dozen families; adopting a number of five members for each family (see Bonavía 1970: 255), we would have approximately sixty people. In the central high mountain forest, Caballoyuq alone would exceed 1,500 persons. This would mean a considerable number of people, but still without meeting the other requirements to be called a city. Meanwhile, Matukalli and Raqaraqay would have little more than 250 and Condoruchco and Uchuihuamanga between 500 and 600 persons (Bonavía 1968b: 81). Estimating is very risky for Yaro (or perhaps what I tentatively called "ruins of Abiseo" [Bonavía 1968a]; see also Waldemar Espinoza Soriano's study [1967]), but I suppose it would not be more than 250 to 500 persons maximum. As we see, it is generally a matter of very low figures, if we compare them with the sierra and coastal centers of the Late Horizon. Even though Machu Picchu has been considered as a city, I believe that from every point of view it does not escape the considerations I have just mentioned. Its population (as in fact Hardoy says [1964: 477]) must not have exceeded 1,000 to 1,200.

It is true that they were permanent settlements; but they all had a minimum density below the norm for their period. In no case did they have a town plan, properly speaking, nor recognizable urban areas. In each case the problem was solved by the demands of the local topography and by a strict adherence to its needs; only the Wenner-Gren group has constructions with a definable function. For the rest, this is very hypothetical and debatable. Nor is it possible to establish differences in the social structure by means of samples from the sites.

There is an absolute homogeneity, particularly in the center and north. Furthermore, it is almost certain that all the inhabitants devoted themselves to agricultural occupations (and probably pastoral ones in some cases); but at the same time they depended on the Inca central authority for their survival. However, they supplied the latter with specific products which were grown in their ecological area and not in the rest of the territory. Very possibly they offered some services to neighboring localities, and were centers for the spread of their culture in areas in which the Incas had not yet penetrated. However, knowledge of a technological nature which they were able to bring to these areas was used more for survival than as instruction, since they were able to find very few settlements; and all of these had cultural patterns which were so different that it would have been very difficult for them to assimilate this new culture. All these groupings were basically rural.

So it is that on the breaking up of the Inca empire, a collapse of organized agriculture and a change in their patterns occurred, in passing from a planned system with state control to a kind of individualist subsistence (Grobman, Salhuana, and Sevilla 1961). This collapse became more evident in those settlements where only a highly organized and planned agriculture was able to survive. Accordingly, when central control disappeared, these settlements were abandoned and no traces of traditional remains were left in the regions in which they had been established. According to Lathrap's work (1970a: 175), this sample of association of "unpolished ceramics" tradition with heavily fortified sites (see below) situated at high altitudes, dominating expanses of terraced or semiterraced agricultural fields, suggests the following: that it was the development of an agricultural system to efficiently exploit the high eastern slopes of the Andes which permitted and brought about Quechuan expansion.

As to farming, it was probably maize (*Zea mays*) which was the most important crop in the development, colonization, and extension of other ecological regions. Some features of its cultivation allow us to see some requirements of the ecological process of Andean civilization in its advance and domestication of other regions. It is well known that maize has a great degree of adaptability to the most varied conditions; in addition, it has a high yield per hectare. For these reasons, it fits well in the primitive migratory agriculture of the tropical lowlands, as well as in the sedentary agriculture of the tablelands and highlands of the tropics (Jones and Darkenwald 1944: 362).

Today maize is cultivated both in temperate climates and in the tropics as well as in cold regions. Besides, the average annual precipitation in regions in which it is grown varies from only 234 millimeters in arid zones under irrigation to more than 5,000 millimeters in tropical regions. In Peru maize is grown not only in all departments, but also in all regions, in spite of the fact that 60 percent of the country consists of humid tropical forests, very humid tropical forests, and dry subtropical forests; thirty percent is in the mountain and alpine category, and ten percent belongs to the arid coastal region (Holdridge, 1967; Alexander Grobman, personal communication). It is considered that maize can be grown in places where the average temperature in summer is not below 19 °C or where the average temperature at night during the three summer months is not below 13 °C.

The Andean region with highest production has a monthly average temperature in summer which varies between 21 °C and 27 °C, an average nighttime temperature not below 14 °C and a season without frost of over 140 days (Jenkins 1941: 357–358). In order to obtain an optimum development of production of the grain, maize requires abundant water well distributed during the growth period of the plant. At the same time maize requires abundant sunlight in order to attain a maximum yield; it grows slowly in the shade and during periods of cloudy weather. Water is most essential during the period of greatest growth; at that time water requirements are greater in proportion than for any other cultivated plant. The plant is also sensitive to conditions created by deficiencies in the aeration of the soil; it is more sensitive in soils with an excessive amount of water, with little vegetation, or with waterproof subsoils. In general terms, maize is grown with the best results in soils in which alluvium is limited and consequently the natural vegetation is basically that of pasture land, that is, where herbaceous associations predominate.

This feature of farming seems to represent basic aspects which it is necessary to bear in mind in trying to understand the ecological process constituted by the colonization of the high mountain forests and the structuring of some of the large urban complexes. The study of agricultural terraces is of fundamental importance, since terracing probably represents the only possibility of domesticating an area so hostile to man.

According to Tosi (1960: 155), after the first exploitation of the virgin high mountain forests, many years pass, probably a hundred or more, before vegetation is restored naturally. If erosion is not controlled during this period, the destruction created would be irreparable, In fact, almost all the urban centers located in the "very humid mountain forest" (bosque montaño) have some form of terrace; nevertheless, almost nothing has been studied regarding this.

In the south in Puno Department, Isbell (1968) has reported summarily on the existence of a large number of terraces. They also abound in the Department of Cuzco, where they are very elaborate and irrigated in the complex system of canals (Fejos 1944). In the Mantaro area, agricultural terraces are simple, adapted to areas which are very craggy and to unirrigated land, and with an ingenious system of counter-erosion in the high parts (Bonavía 1970). In the environs of La Merced (Department of Junín), Lathrap (1970a: 177) has reported, without further details, on agricultural terraces in the locality known as Chacra de Giacometti. We know nothing about the northern zone. The existence of terraces has been reported, but nothing more (Bonavía 1968a).

In synthesis, all these centers follow a similar design, but the design has still not been well defined. Hardoy (1964: 473) has used the term of village (*aldea*) for them; I prefer to continue using that of town (*villa*) (Bonavía and Ravines 1968: 54), although originally it is a Spanish term.

The patterns of occupation of the three areas which have been mentioned are completely different. In the southern high mountain forest they indicate features which approach the Inca pattern. That is, according to Hardoy (1964: 478), constructions on

... stepping-stone terraces on the slopes of the mountains, apparently seeking the proximity of some quebrada through which water may run, since in the majority of the sites there was an adequate system for the supplying of water used for domestic purposes and also for irrigating crops, and suitable outlets by means of canals. The houses were generally rectangular and were grouped forming aggregates around an open space or adopting an arrangement in rows, which was the one which adapted best to the narrow terraces.

The frontier area with Bolivia has recently been studied, although we do not have a detailed report available. The town (*villa*) of Colo-Colo (in the region of the Alto Inambari) corresponds in time to the end of the Late Horizon, and to judge by a photograph (Isbell 1968: 112) it would approach, typologically speaking, the constructions of the Cuzco area; but it is impossible to infer more.

In the center we have constructions of circular shape on the summits of hills, with narrow passages. They are very often on mounds in order to achieve a horizontal position and to avoid erosion. In the surrounding areas there are agricultural terraces. There are no fields in the true meaning of the word, and one observes a complete adaptation to the medium (Bonavía 1968b).

We also have circular constructions in the north, but these are different from the ones in the center, at least from the structural point of view (Bonavía 1968a); they are decorated with a series of mosaics which are still unique today. These constructions are located on artificial plots supported by terraces; they have systems of stairways, narrow passages, and lanes, as well as a special type of terraced plazas (if the term applies). Furthermore, neither the central or northern areas have systems for providing water as exist in the south.

Not without reason, Fejos (1944) observed that none of the places he studied in the south had any form of defense; and if we exclude Matukalli in the center, this is true of all the other population centers. (It is not out of place here to recall that, generally speaking, Inca cities were not fortified. See, for example, Hardoy [1968: 48]). However, one cannot fail to observe that each and every one of these sites was located in a strategic place. It was easily defendable and almost invariably one or more sectors of the whole faced on precipices which were practically inaccessible; and the slopes of the hills on the remaining sides were very steep. Thus, in spite of everything, there was always an element of defense: created by nature, it is true, but taken advantage of by man.

It is of interest to note that Isbell (1968) and Lathrap (1970a) have indicated the existence of evidence of a settlement pattern somewhat different from what has already been described, with defensive wall systems, located in the area of the high Inambari (Puno Department) near Tarma (Department of Junín); these are pre-Inca. There are large clusters of constructions on hill summits, surrounded by a double rampart. Lathrap also includes the Chupachu de Huanuco sites in this sample, but to judge by Thompson's reports they do not have these features (and, in addition, are very late). Lathrap (1970a: 179) indicates that "the position of all these compact and defendable communities and their ingenious defence system suggest that war-like actions were very common in the late periods; and it can be assumed that these struggles were an expression of competition for agricultural lands." More investigations should be made about this, as it is natural to wonder why the use of defenses was abandoned in the Inca Period in these eastern urban centers. As already indicated, the fortified system which existed in the high Inambari in the pre-Inca Period disappeared on the same sites in the Inca Period. It appears that traces of this system tend to survive more in what is today Bolivia where (as will be seen later) there are a number of fortified Inca centers. The same happens in Ecuador: undoubtedly these are two boundaries of the Inca Empire where domination was not easy.

As I have already indicated, we did not find the typical elements of Inca urban centers in these colonized groups. Although it is true that some vestiges remain in the southern area, there is no trace in the center or north. Thus, one cannot help wondering whether this is not clear evidence that the southern builders were the same mountain people as those of the Cuzco area. Perhaps local laborers or even *mitimaes* [colonists sent by the Incas to conquered lands] were used (for the case of Huanuco, see Thompson 1968: 111–112); but at the same time they may have been allowed to apply their own town-planning and architectural concepts, with the Inca influence used only in the imposition of political and economic ideas. This falls within the Inca way of operating.

Nevertheless, there are many other centers of the Tahuantinsuyo, outside the boundaries of present-day Peru, which should be taken into account. In most cases, however, we lack documentation on them, or else they simply have not been studied. Because of lack of information they have not been included here. I will only add some very general ideas.

Of all these outside centers, we probably have the largest number of studies on northwestern Argentina. These appear to corroborate what I have already said. In fact, sites of purely Inca occupation in this region are very limited (Madrazo and Ottonello de García Reinoso 1966: 61). And as Rex González shows (1967: 24), it is "ecology in its broadest sense – the environmental and cultural medium – which guided adaptation to a more useful and advantageous procedure, which helped to consolidate the empire rapidly.... The continuity of the Inca cultural movement was maintained by adapting it to the various regions." Furthermore, it would appear that the copying of old models from the Middle Horizon becomes evident in this area, which is so far removed from the Inca center. This is so because the most significant vestige of the Inca occupation of northwest Argentina appears to be the occurrence of the "compound perimeter rectangle"; this would be nothing more than a simplified manifestation of the "rectangular enclosure compound" pointed out by Willey in Virú (Willey 1953) for the Tomaval Period. "The inscription of the rectangular enclosure compound includes a series of subtypes both from the form and functional points of view; but over and above the variations, the fundamental idea of planning by means of the perimeter enclosure still persisted. This concept acquired greater simplicity and dispersion on being retaken by the Incas, who were its introducers in northwest Argentina in the final moment of the Late Period." The places which have been studied (ten of them) are not of Inca execution; but they present isolated Inca elements which have become impoverished because of their distance from their place of origin, mixed up with local features. In some of these centers, one sees clearly the coexistence of local and Inca groups (Madrazo and Ottonello de García Reinoso 1966: 61–62).

Rex González (1967: 24) arrives at similar conclusions in his work on San Juan Province, where, from the architectural point of view, the Inca occupation is not very clear; it appears that this is basically because its characteristics varied "according to the different regions which they occupied, the existing material, skill and awareness of the manpower available."

In Bolivia there are also some interesting Inca centers, although I have little information about them. The most important ones appear to be Incallajta and Incarajay (Nordenskiöld 1956–1957; Lara 1967; de Mesa and Gisbert 1969), although the information is too incomplete for the purpose of this study. The plans are very schematic and the descriptions cursory. Both sites are located in the department of Cochabamba.

According to Nordenskiöld (1956–1957), Incallajta, a fortified city, is typically Inca, although to judge by Lara's illustrations (1967), it appears to involve more of a regional architectural manifestation. Even the few ceramics illustrated by the author appear to be regional Inca. According to de Meṣa and Gisbert (1969), "the ruins are, both because of their location and their planning, similar to Machupicchu, although considerably more reduced." They indicate further on, however, that "unlike the Cuzco examples, the buildings of Incallajta do not have polished walls, as all the structures are of rough stone mixed with cement" (1969: 88). The city is located in a very strategic place and "to the north, in the only accessible part, there is a large rampart designed in the form of a saw, like that of Sacsahuamán, but built with rough stone" (de Mesa and Gisbert 1969: 88). Incarajay (Lara 1967) unites features which are typically Inca. Ponce Sanginés (in a supplementary note to Nordenskiöld's article, 1956–1957) quotes Bennett, mentioning two "fortresses" more in the Mizque region: Batanes and Pulquina, both of the Inca Period. De Mesa and Gisbert (1969) mention the citadels of Incahuasi (in the province of Azero), Iscanhuaya (located in the boundary region of the provinces of Muñecas and Larecaja of the department of La Paz), which "is of the same type as Machupicchu" (1969: 88) and the fortress of Samaipata.

It appears that in Bolivia, Inca centers are found not on the tableland but in the valleys, forming an arc which leaves the Collas and Aymaras areas free. Almost all of these centers would be military and with an architecture of a regional nature (José de Mesa, personal communication). It should be added that the network of Inca roads in Bolivia is very extensive; and these generally "were planned in the hot valleys marking the last spurs of the cordillera; only in exceptional cases did they take the level and cold route of the puna. They did this in order to reach the regions populated by the *collas*, *charcas*, and other peoples whom they had to govern" (de Mesa and Gisbert 1969: 90).

On the other hand, when the Inca conquest of the extreme north took place (i.e. the territories of present Ecuador), it appears that the construction of urban centers such as Tomebamba, Liribamba, and Quito was encouraged. These became important centers of the empire. At the same time many fortresses were built in the highlands, in some cases near urban centers and in others occupying strategic places (Murra 1946: 811; Bedoya Maruri 1969: Oberem et al. 1969).

According to what we know, therefore, one may infer that, although the city phenomenon may have had its initial roots in the Early Intermediate Period, its extension did not come until the Middle Horizon. This has been intuitively perceived by several authors (and very properly so), especially Rowe, Schaedel, and recently Hardoy (1968). It would appear that starting from this moment in time there is a continuity in references made to areas of urban occupation; also that the town planning of the Late Intermediate and Late Horizon Periods respectively was either influenced by or copied from these original primary samples of the Middle Horizon Period. The only changes which occurred were those of form, and these were a consequence of the sociopolitical evolution which characterized those periods.

Apparently Inca town planning, when restricted to an easily accessible geographic region or regions (such as the coast), maintained certain easily recognizable norms, in spite of not having fixed norms in the design of their cities. I have already mentioned these recognizable norms. However, it was a different matter when they had to systematically seek the exploitation of natural resources in ecological areas as dissimilar and hostile as those of the high forests. Not only could they not maintain the basic features, but they were obliged to make substantial changes in form to the point of creating new urban plans. These were completely unlike those of the rest of their organization. In fact, they were so dissimilar that at first they were regarded as a phenomenon apart, having nothing to do with the Incas. Only recently have we been able to distinguish and understand them, at least in part.

In conclusion, one should note that the above is in good part theoretical and remains in the area of a working hypothesis. It is subject to studies and verifications based on systematic investigations which have not yet been carried out.

REFERENCES

BEDOYA MARURI, ÁNGEL N.
  1969 *Bicentenario del nacimiento de Federico Enrique Alejandro, Baron de Humboldt.* Quito: Casa de la Cultura Ecuatoriana.
BELAUNDE TERRY, FERNANDO
  1961 Huamachuco: doble mensaje de pasada grandeza. *El Arquitecto Peruano* 282–284 (January–February). Lima.
BENNETT, WENDELL C., JUNIUS B. BIRD
  1949–1960 *Andean culture history.* New York: American Museum of Natural History.
BONAVÍA, DUCCIO
  1965 *Arqueologia de Lurín. Seis sitios de ocupación en la parte inferior del valle.* Lima: Museo Nacional de la Cultura Peruana, and Departmento de Antropología de la UNMSM.

1968a   *Las ruinas del Abiseo.* Lima: Universidad Peruana de Ciencias y Tecnología.
1968b   "Núcleos de problación en la ceja de selva de Ayacucho (Perú)," in *Actas y Memorias del 37° Congreso Internacional de Americanistas* 1: 75–83. Buenos Aires.
1969   Die Ruinen von Abiseo. *Bild der Wissenschaft* (Heft 10, 6. Jahrgang, October): 930–939. Stuttgart.
1970   Investigaciones arqueológicas en el Mantaro medio. *Revista del Museo Nacional* 35: 211–294. Lima.

BONAVÍA, DUCCIO, ROGGER RAVINES
1967   Las fronteras ecológicas de la civilización andina. *Amaru* 2: 61–69.
1968   "Villas del Horizonte Tardío en la ceja de selva del Perú: algunas consideraciones," in *Actas y Memorias del 37° Congresso Internacional de Americanistas* 1: 153–158. Buenos Aires.

DE CIEZA DE LEON, PEDRO
1941   *La crónica del Perú.* Madrid: Espasa Calpe.

DE JEREZ, FRANCISCO
1938   *Verdadera relación de la conquista del Perú y provincia del Cuzco.* Biblioteca de Cultura Peruana, first series, 2. Paris.

DE MESA, J., T. GISBERT
1969   "Reseña de la historia del arte en Bolivia," in *La iglesia y el patrimonio cultural de Bolivia,* 70–144. La Paz, Bolivia: Comisión Nacional de Arte Sacro.

ESPINOZA SORIANO, WALDEMAR
1967   Los señoríos étnicos de Chachapoyas. *Revista Histórica* 30: 224–332. Lima.

FEJOS, PAUL
1944   *Archaeological explorations in the Cordillera Vilcabamba, southeastern Peru.* Viking Fund Publications in Anthropology 3. New York.

GONZÁLEZ, ALBERTO REX
1967   Una excepcional pieza de mosaico del N.O. argentino. Consideraciones sobre el primer fechado del C 14 y la secuencia arqueológica de la Prov. de San Juan. *Etnia* 8 (July to December). Olavarria, Province of Buenos Aires. Museo Etnográfico Municipal "Dámaso Arce."

GROBMAN, ALEXANDER, WILFREDO SALHUANA, RICARDO SEVILLA
1961   *Races of maize in Peru.* Nacional Research Council Publications 915. Washington, D.C.: National Academy of Sciences.

HARDOY, JORGE E.
1964   *Ciudades precolombinas.* Buenos Aires: Infinito.
1968   *Urban planning in pre-Columbian America.* New York: George Braziller.

HARTH-TERRÉ, EMILIO
1933   Incahuasi. *Revista del Museo Nacional* 2(2): 101–125. Lima.
1959   *Piki-Llacta. Cuidad de pósitos y bastimentos del Imperio Incaico.* Offprint of the *Revista del Museo e Instituto Arqueológico.* Universidad del Cuzco.
1964   *El pueblo de Huanuco Viejo.* Offprint of *El Arquitecto Peruano* 320–321.

HOLDRIDGE, L. R.
1967   *Life zone ecology.* San José, Costa Rica: Tropical Science Center.

ISBELL, WILLIAM H.
1968　New discoveries in the Montaña, southeastern Peru. *Archaeology*
21 (2): 108–114.
JENKINS, MERLE T.
1941　"Influence of climate and weather on growth of corn: climate and
man," in *Yearbook of agriculture*. Washington, D.C.
JONES, CLARENCE FIELDEN, GORDEN GERALD DARKENWALD
1944　*Geografía económica*. Mexico City: Fondo de Cultura Económica.
LANNING, EDWARD P.
1967　*Peru before the Incas*. Englewood Cliffs, N.J.: Prentice-Hall.
LARA, JESÚS
1967　*Inkallajta, Inkaraqay*. La Paz, Cochabamba: Los Amigos del Libro.
LATHRAP, DONALD W.
1970a　*The Upper Amazon*. London: Thames and Hudson.
1970b　"La foresta tropical y el contexto cultural de Chavín," in *100 años
de arqueología en el Perú*. Introduction, selection, comments, and
notes by Rogger Ravines. *Fuentes e investigaciones para la historia
del Perú* 3: 235–261. Edición de Petróleos del Perú. Instituto de
Estudios Peruanos.
MADRAZO, GUILLERMO B., MARTA OTTONELLO DE GARCÍA REINOSO
1966　*Tipos de instalación prehispánica en la región de la puna y su borde*.
Museo Etnográfico Municipal "Dámaso Arce" Monografía 1.
MC COWN, THEODORE
1945　*Pre-Incaic Huamachuco: survey and excavations in the northern
sierra of Peru*. Publications in American Archaeology 39 (4). Berkeley
and Los Angeles: University of California Press.
MENZEL, DOROTHY
1959　The Inca occupation of the South Coast of Peru. *Southwestern
Journal of Anthropology* 15 (2): 125–142.
1968　"*La cultura Huari*," in *Las grandes civilizaciones del antiguo Perú*,
volume six. Lima: Compañía de Seguros y Reaseguros Peruano-Suiza.
MURRA, JOHN V.
1946　"The historic tribes of Ecuador," in *Handbook of South American
Indians*, volume two. Edited by Julian H. Steward, 785–821. Smithsonian Institution Bulletin 143. Washington, D.C.
NORDENSKIÖLD, ERLAND
1956–1957　Incallajta, ciudad fortificada fundada por el Inca Tupac
Yupanqui. (Includes "Nota complementaria acerca de Incallajta"
by Carlos Ponce Sanginés). *Khana: Revista Municipal de Arte y
Letras* fourth year 4 (21–22, December); fifth year, 1 (23–24, March):
6–22.
OBEREM, UDO, W. WURSTER, R. HARTMANN, J. WENTSCHER
1969　La fortaleza de montaña de Quitoloma en la sierra septentrional del
Ecuador. *Boletín de la Academia Nacional de Historia* 52 (114,
July–December): 196–205. Quito.
ROWE, JOHN HOWLAND
1946　"Inca culture at the time of the Spanish Conquest," in *Handbook
of South American Indians*, volume two. Edited by Julian H.
Steward, 183–330. Smithsonian Institution Bulletin 143. Washington,
D.C.
1963　Urban settlements in ancient Peru. *Ñawpa Pacha* 1: 1–27. Berkeley.
1967　What kind of a settlement was Inca Cuzco? *Ñawpa Pacha* 5: 59–76.
Berkeley.

RUÍZ DE ARCE, JUAN
1953 *Advertencia a sus sucesores.* Colección Austral 1168. Buenos Aires: Espasa Calpe Argentina.

SCHAEDEL, RICHARD P.
1966a Incipient urbanization and secularization in Tiahuanacoid Peru. *American Antiquity* 31 (3), part 1 January): 338–344. Salt Lake City: University of Utah.
1966b "Urban growth and ekistics on the Peruvian Coast," in *Actas y Memorias del 36° Congreso Internacional de Americanistas* 1: 531–539. Seville.

THOMPSON, DONALD E.
1964 Postclassic innovations in architecture and settlement patterns in the Casma Valley, Peru. *Southwestern Journal of Anthropology* 20(1): 91–105. Alburquerque: University of New Mexico.
1968 "An archaeological evaluation of ethnohistoric evidence on Inca culture," in *Anthropological archaeology in the Americas*, 108–120. Washington, D.C.: Anthropological Society of Washington.
1969 "Incaic installations at Huanuco and Pumpu," in *The process of urbanization in America from its origins until our day.* Edited by Jorge Enrique Hardoy and Richard P. Schaedel, 67–74. Editorial del Instituto Torcuato Di Tella. Buenos Aires.

TOSI, JOSEPH A., JR.
1960 *Zonas de vida natural en el Perú: memoria explicativa sobre el mapa ecológica del Perú.* With an appendix by L. R. Holdridge. Instituto Interamericano de Ciencias Agrícolas Boletín Técnico 5. OAS, Zona Andina. Proyecto 39.

VALCÁRCEL, LUIS E.
1924 El Cuzco precolombino. *Revista Universitaria* 8 (44–45): 16–29. Cuzco.
1933 Esculturas de Pikillacta. *Revista del Museo Nacional* 2 (1): 19–35. Lima.

WILLEY, GORDON R.
1953 *Prehistoric settlement patterns in the Virú Valley, Peru.* Smithsonian Institution Bulletin 155. Washington, D.C.

A Comparison of Some Aspects of the Evolution of Cuzco and Tenochtitlán

FRIEDRICH KATZ

When the Spanish conquerors reached America, they encountered two large metropolitan centers: Tenochtitlán and Cuzco, capitals of the two large empires which existed on the American continent on the eve of the Europeans' arrival.

The two cities profoundly impressed the conquerors by their size, splendor, and clearly urban character. In the words of Pedro de Cieza de León:

And in no part of this kingdom of Peru was such a nobly embellished place to be found, if not Cuzco, which (as I have said many times) was the capital of the Empire of the Incas and their royal seat.... Cuzco had a great manner and quality; it must have been founded by people of great substance. There were large streets, except that they were narrow; and the houses were of pure stone, with such beautiful seams, which illustrates the antiquity of the building, since they were very large and very well hewn (de Cieza de León 1971: 330).

The impressions which Bernal Díaz del Castillo had of Tenochtitlán were even more enthusiastic:

And after having looked around well and considered all that we had seen, we turned to see the large square and the multitude of people in it, some buying and others selling; where just the noise and humming of the voices and words heard out there sounded like more than a legion; and among us there were soldiers who had been in many parts of the world: in Constantinople and all of Italy and Rome; and they said that they had never seen a square which was so well balanced and of such good layout and size, and filled with so many people.

In their development, Tenochtitlán and Cuzco displayed many similarities. In the middle of the fifteenth century they were both cities of small tribes and were without great influence in the Andean region and Mesoamerica respectively. In the course of less than a century, these tribes conquered the major part of the Andean region and Mesoamerica; and Tenochtitlán and Cuzco were converted into capitals of empires. In both cases this growth was combined with great public and urban works. Great palaces, the sumptuous Temple of the Sun, Coricancha, the fortress of Sacsahuaymán were built in Cuzco and, around the city, a large system of terraces for agriculture. While enormous palaces and temples were being built in Tenochtitlán, a complex system of dykes was erected to control the waters of the lakes among which the Aztec capital was located.[1]

The urban growth of both Cuzco and Tenochtitlán was combined with a very significant demographic increase. On the eve of the Conquest, these two cities constituted the most important administrative, political, religious, and economic centers of their respective regions. The kings, their court, and a large part of the aristocracy and bureaucracy resided there.

In spite of these resemblances in the historical evolution of the two cities, there were very important differences, related to the manner of their growth as well as to their administrative, economic, political, and religious functions.

The growth of Cuzco was essentially organized and supervised by the state.[2] Three very different forms of demographic increase took place:

1. Measures to spur the demographic growth of the original Quechua-speaking population of the city.

2. The setting up in Cuzco and its environs of important centers of development from conquered peoples.

3. The imposed obligation of members of the subjugated peoples to work in Cuzco for a certain time.

The first form of growth (that of the original population) was achieved in two ways. Shortly after the beginning of the Inca conquests, the population of Cuzco was raised to the status of nobility. This transformation included not only the population of Cuzco but also all the Quechua-speaking neighboring regions. With this massive increase of the aristocracy came the extension of polygamy, one of the privileges of the nobility. In addition, women were imported from all over the empire to Cuzco as wives and concubines of the Inca inhabitants of the city. These measures must have brought a very large increase in the Inca population of Cuzco.

Another factor which certainly contributed to the increase of the original Cuzco population was its better nutrition; this was due to the large amount of revenue which the conquests brought to the city.

---

[1] The extent and boundaries of the city of Tenochtitlán have been analyzed by Calnek (1971).

[2] For the social and economic organization of Cuzco and the Inca empire, see Métraux (1961), Moore (1958), Murra (n.d.), Rowe (1957), and Trimborn (1923–1924).

All these measures contributed to a very rapid increase of the "Inca" population of the city. Both the inhabitants of the regions near Cuzco and the women were absorbed by the original population of the city.

At the same time there was another type of demographic increase of a very different kind. Large population groups from all parts of the Inca empire, comprising very different types of settlers, were brought to Cuzco as permanent and temporary residents.

Among the permanent residents were found first of all the *colonos* [small plot holders] which were comprised of *mitimaes*, conquered peoples from far regions of the empire who could never return to their homes. The same status of permanent residents applied to artisans selected in all parts of the empire and to the Yanaconas, or semislaves, originating from all parts of the empire, who worked both for the state and the Inca nobility.

Alongside these permanent residents there was a temporary population of considerable importance in Cuzco. Thousands of taxpayers came to help build works (the *mita*, or enforced service of Indians) and to work for the Inca aristocracy.

At the same time, the nobles of the conquered regions, the *caciques*, were required to send their sons to Cuzco, on the one hand in order to assimilate the Quechua language and the Inca culture and religion, and on the other hand to serve as hostages.

All these measures contributed significantly to increasing the population of Cuzco. Nevertheless, there were also tendencies in the opposite direction, trends of emigration away from the Inca capital. When *colonos* from the remote regions of the empire settled in Cuzco or its surrounding areas, inhabitants from the Cuzcan region were sent as *colonos* to the recently conquered regions. Were they equivalent in number to the *colonos* ordered to Cuzco? It is difficult to answer this question definitively. At the same time, a quite significant number of inhabitants were sent as administrators, bureaucrats, and soldiers to the farthest parts of the empire. The fundamental characteristic of all these movements of population was the rigid control which the Inca state exercised or at least tried to exercise over them.

In Tenochtitlán there were somewhat similar efforts to increase the population, but with much less intervention on the part of the state.[3] As in Cuzco, there was an attempt to increase the population of Tenochtitlán by absorbing other groups and importing women. However, the absorption of other peoples was much more limited in the case of Tenochtitlán. In Cuzco the whole Quechua-speaking population living in the area was included in the population of the city and raised to the status of nobles. The situation was very different in the

[3] For the social organization of the Aztecs see Bandelier (1880), Carrasco (n.d.), Katz (1966, 1972), Monzón (1949), and Soustelle (1955).

Tenochcan case. Only the population of one city, Tlatelolco, close to Tenochtitlán, was absorbed by the Aztecs. The Valley of Mexico was more densely populated than the Cuzcan region and it would have been impossible for Tenochtitlán to absorb the whole population of the valley.

The elevation of a large part of the population to the status of nobles gave them, as in the Peruvian case, the right to polygamy. In contrast with the Incas, the Aztec state only intervened partially to provide the aristocracy with women. In a number of cases, the state obliged kings of subjugated states to send members of their families as wives or concubines of Aztec nobles in Tenochtitlán. In many cases the subjugated states hoped in this manner to improve their relations with the Aztecs. There were also cases in which the inhabitants of the dominated states had to send women as a contribution (tax). But in large part, the importation of women to Tenochtitlán was carried out by slave traders who had bought or carried them off by force in remote regions and sold them on the slave markets in the Valley of Mexico.[4] As in the case of Cuzco, many inhabitants of the conquered regions were obliged to work temporarily in Tenochtitlán. Nevertheless, in this sense a very important difference existed between the Peruvian and Mexican situations.

The Peruvian *mitayos* [those serving their enforced service] who came to work in Cuzco generally lived in regions far from the capital and had to reside in the city or its environs during their time of work.

In contrast with this situation, many of the taxpayers of Tenochtitlán originated from towns and cities near the capital, working there by day and returning to their homes at night.

The most essential difference between the population of Cuzco and Tenochtitlán was in regard to the role of the immigrants. In Cuzco, after the original population was raised to the status of nobles, the "plebeian" population was made up of persons brought from other parts of the empire. The division of classes there was thus matched by a national division in the Inca capital. In the Tenochtitlán case there was no such division. While some of the Aztecs had been raised to the rank of nobles, the majority continued to be "plebeians," the national and class divisions not coinciding as in Cuzco. There were also permanent immigrants in Tenochtitlán, but their role was different than in Cuzco. They constituted a much smaller part of the population than in the Peruvian case and were essentially traders, artisans and slaves.

In Cuzco the whole non-Inca population constituted a subordinate

---

[4] The largest slave market in the center of Mexico was found in Atzcopotzalco, a city conquered and dominated by the Triple Alliance. See Duran (1951: 218) and Bosch García (1944).

group which was not absorbed by the Quechua-speaking aristocracy. In Tenochtitlán the artisans and traders, in spite of their foreign origin, soon managed to become privileged groups in the city.

In contrast with the situation in Cuzco, there was very little emigration from Tenochtitlán. Some bureaucrats (essentially tax collectors), troops, and Tenochtitlán *colonos* were sent to different parts of the empire; but their number was very small, reflecting the very limited integration of the Tenochtitlán empire. Tenochtitlán did not need bureaucrats to administer the conquered territories, only tax collectors (*calpixque*). The few troops and *colonos* sent to the conquered provinces were restricted to guarding the Tarascan frontier and the trade routes to Tabasco and Yucatán.

Nevertheless, another type of population loss was greater than in Cuzco. As will be shown, the Inca armies were mainly composed of soldiers from the conquered peoples. In Mexico, the majority of military men originated from the cities of the Triple Alliance. If one adds to this the fact that in Mexico, in contrast with the Andean region, all prisoners were sacrificed, one sees that Tenochtitlán lost proportionally many more inhabitants due to wars than Cuzco.

The fact that the original population of Cuzco had been raised collectively to the status of nobility, and the fact that class differences coincided with national differences, had very profound consequences for the social organization of Cuzco. Since the whole original population changed status, it had no difficulty in maintaining its collectivist organization.[5]

As the "plebeian" population of Cuzco was of foreign origin and was completely dominated by the Inca state, it did not participate in the political life of the city. The social conflicts of which we are aware took place among the Inca elite. The coincidence of national and class differences in Cuzco meant that the dominant and dominated groups were socially isolated from each other. It also meant that it was extremely difficult to pass from the dominated class to the Inca aristocracy.

The situation was very different in Tenochtitlán: here only a part of the Aztec population was able to join the nobility, the majority remaining as *Macehuales* [plebeian Indians]. As a result there was a partial break-up of communal organizations (the *calpullis*). There are indications that the nobles tended to abandon the *calpullis* and enter into a very different type of organization, that of the military societies (Katz 1966: 163–168).

The fact that in Tenochtitlán the aristocracy and "plebeians" had a similar national origin made the passing from one social category

[5] This aspect of Inca social organization has been studied particularly by Cunow (1896).

to another much easier. Until the end of the fifteenth century, soldiers who had taken a certain number of prisoners were able to ascend to the status of nobles. This national identity of nobles and "plebeians" meant that in Tenochtitlán the latter participated in the administration of the city on a greater scale than in Cuzco.

The greater degree of integration and state control in Peru, mentioned above, also affected the economic role of Cuzco. While both the Inca and Tenochtitlán empires had enormous revenues coming from the conquered regions, in Peru only a limited part of this revenue reached the capital, where it was used to uphold the Sapay Inca, court, bureaucracy, and the nobility of Inca origin. The enormous amount of labor available to the Inca empire was also used to construct the city of Cuzco and to carry out extensive public works.

Most of the revenue, though, remained in the rest of the empire. Roads were constructed throughout, and enormous deposits of weapons and provisions were stored along them. These were primarily for the soldiers, the majority of whom were recruited in the subjugated regions.

Another portion of the revenue was used to maintain Inca garrisons, bureaucrats, and laborers in the subjugated territories. And other revenues were redistributed. As John Murra describes it:

After having monopolized the forced labor of the peasant class and controled the productive effort of servants for the service of the state, and after having abolished trade, the crown had large stores at its disposal, only a small part of which was used to maintain the court. The major part was distributed where it was believed to be most useful. In this sense the Inca state functioned as a market: it absorbed the excess production of a self-sufficient population and "interchanged" it; at the same time it maintained the king, the army, and the workers, and also distributed a large part of it as gifts and benefactions (Murra n.d.: 204).

In this manner, trade activity was limited both in Cuzco and throughout the Inca empire. In Cuzco itself, there was a small market limited to an exchange of local and regional products. This limited development of trade was not only due to the fact that the state was trying to monopolize the distribution of goods originating from other regions of the empire and goods made by artisans: it was also due to what Murra called vertical integration. This was a tendency very much older than the Inca empire. It applied to groups living in a particular ecological region who gained control of lands in another ecological region, frequently very far from their region of residence and separated from it by territories which they did not control. In this manner they achieved a certain degree of self-sufficiency and obtained (without recourse to trade) raw materials which they did not produce in their own region. Thus many inhabitants of the altiplano who grew potatoes and bred llamas obtained maize or cotton originating from the coastal regions.

Cuzco was of greater importance from the manufacturing point of view, than as a trade center. A significant part of the empire's best artisans and Acllahuasí weavers had been concentrated in Cuzco. Their products were essentially for luxury consumption and ceremonial distribution to loyal subjects of the empire.

Tenochtitlán's role was extremely different in its economic and social functions. Most of the revenue of the conquered provinces, for example, was brought to the Valley of Mexico. Only a minimal part remained in the subjugated regions to maintain the small Aztec garrisons and tribute collectors. The tributes reaching the Valley of Mexico were divided among the three cities which formed the Triple Alliance: two-fifths for Tenochtitlán, two-fifths for Texcoco, and one-fifth for Tlacopán. At the beginning of the sixteenth century a still larger percentage reached Tenochtitlán. A large part of this revenue was used to maintain the king and the Aztec bureaucracy and aristocracy, as well as a large part of the "plebeian" population. Another part was reexported from Tenochtitlán, partially in the form of raw materials and mainly in the form of products manufactured and completed by Tenochtitlán artisans.

In contrast to the situation in the Inca empire, they were not redistributed to other parts of the empire. They were sold on the markets of the altiplano or taken by traders to distant regions within and without the region of Aztec domination. For this reason, Tenochtitlán had become an enormous trade center. No one has described the trade activity of Tenochtitlán more clearly than Hernán Cortés:

This city has many squares, where there is continual marketing and trade, buying and selling. It has another square twice the size of the city of Salamanca, it is all enclosed by porticos, where each day there are over sixty thousand souls buying and selling; where there are all kinds of goods found in all lands, as well necessities such as food, jewels of gold and silver, lead, brass, copper, tin, stones, bones, shells, snails, and feathers....Finally, everything is found in these markets which is found anywhere in the world; besides those goods I have mentioned, there are so many kinds and so many qualities that because of their very number and because I cannot retain so many in my memory, and even because I am not able to put a name to them, I do not mention them. Each type of merchandise is sold on its own street, without any other merchandise being found there, and they do it properly. Everything is sold by count and measure, except that up to now nothing seems to be sold by weight (Cortés 1763: 72).

Differences in the degree of imperial integration which are seen so clearly in the demographic composition of the two cities, as well as in their administrative and trade role, were also reflected in their military role. The Inca army was in essence a pan-Andean army, recruited from all parts of the empire. The officers and some shock units were of Inca origin, but the soldiers came from the conquered territories.

The armies of the Triple Alliance were made up in essence of soldiers coming from Tenochtitlán, Texcoco, and Tlacopán. There were also some allies from the Valley of Mexico, and a very limited number of allies from other parts of the empire. The result was that Tenochtitlán, where frequently all the men went out to fight, was much more affected by wars than Cuzco. In times of major wars, few men were seen in the city, many activities ceased, and Tenochtitlán suffered proportionally more losses than Cuzco. Furthermore, war supplies, military reserves, and revenue from the soldiers remained in the cities of the Triple Alliance.

To sum up and point out the similarities and differences between Cuzco and Tenochtitlán, one could say in essence:

1. In the very short time of about a century, both Cuzco and Tenochtitlán were transformed from obscure towns into empire capitals.

2. As to their population, Tenochtitlán appears to have been much larger than Cuzco. The population of the former has been estimated between 300,000 and 1,000,000. (See Borah and Cook 1963; Rosenblatt 1954; and Dobyns 1966.) Estimates for the population of Cuzco vary between 100,000 and 200,000 (Hardoy 1968, 1972). These differences of size were accentuated by the fact that, in contrast with Cuzco, Tenochtitlán was situated in the middle of a densely urbanized region with a large number of cities.

3. Cuzco was the capital of an empire which was much more integrated than the Tenochtitlán empire and the character of the city reflected this integration. Its administrative role was much more important: its population had a pan-Andean character, reflecting in large part the social composition of the Inca empire.

Until the end of the fifteenth century, in contrast with Cuzco, Tenochtitlán had to share many attributes of a capital with its two allied cities: Texcoco and Tlacopán. At the beginning of the sixteenth century, inverse tendencies took place in the two empires. In the Inca empire, Huayna Capac created a second capital in Tomebamba in Ecuador, while Tenochtitlán was acquiring an increasingly greater predominance over its two allied cities in the Valley of Mexico.

In contrast with Cuzco, the social composition of Tenochtitlán was more homogeneous with a much smaller percentage of inhabitants from other parts of the empire.

4. In Mexico, in contrast with Peru, almost all the revenue of the empire was destined for the capitals. This resulted in much greater growth and development of these cities in contrast with the rest of the country, at least compared with the Andean region. This tendency, which had old traditions in Mesoamerica since the time of Teoti-huacán, was strongly accentuated in the Aztec period. The conse-

quence was a demographic development and relative population concentration in the Valley of Mexico much greater than in the Valley of Cuzco. There are indications that at the beginning of the sixteenth century the population had grown to such an extent that the food supply presented many serious problems. This was shown by the fact that in the great famine of 1505 the Aztec empire was not able to feed the people of its capital (de Toquemada 1723: 565). Crises of this kind do not appear to have existed in Cuzco.

5. Cuzco was in essence an administrative and religious center and, on a lesser scale, a manufacturing center. Tenochtitlán, besides having all these functions was a trade center of the first order. This fact, together with the proportionally greater revenue which came to the Aztec capital, contributed to its metropolitan and urbanized character, which Cuzco never had. This contrast was reinforced by the fact that Cuzco was a city with limited access. Guards controlled the city's entrances and exits, and there are indications that all trips required special permits. Tenochtitlán was an open city in a densely populated and highly urbanized area. Thousands of persons came to the Aztec capital each day without being subjected to controls.

6. The social struggles in the two metropolises were very different. In Cuzco they involved interaristocratic struggles for the imperial succession. The "plebeian" population of a different nationality had no rights in Cuzco; it was so firmly controlled that until the Conquest no cases have been registered of struggles between the "plebeian" population and the Inca aristocracy.

The social struggles in Tenochtitlán were of another nature, since the "plebeian" population was of the same national origin as the aristocracy. Traditionally the plebeians had enjoyed a whole series of political rights, including participation in the election of the Huey Tlatoani and the right of ascent to the noble class through distinguished feats in war. The "plebeians" appear to have struggled fiercely to maintain these rights; when at the beginning of the sixteenth century Moctezuma Xocoyotzin decided to restrict possibilities for the social ascent of the plebeians, he seems to have encountered very strong opposition, whose supporters he ordered killed.

7. The differences between the two empires and the two capitals were seen very clearly at the time of the Conquest. The Inca empire displayed much greater cohesion than the Aztec empire. When Manco Inca called for a general struggle against the Spanish, thousands of soldiers from all parts of the empire enlisted in his ranks.

When the Spanish began to besiege Tenochtitlán, many of their allies abandoned the Aztecs, and many subjugated peoples rose against them. With few exceptions, the Tenochtitláns resisted alone.

Such divergent reactions reflect the extremely different character of the two empires. Not only did profound differences exist between the two as to the degree of integration, but also to what one may call the relations between giving and taking. In exchange for the domination it exercised and the labor and lands it took, the Inca empire offered some compensations: protection for the subjugated peoples (*Pax Incaica*), redistribution of goods coming from other ecological regions, assistance in case of famine, construction of new and large public works throughout the empire, participation in victorious military campaigns.

In contrast, the Aztec empire was much more exploiting. In compensation for the enormous taxes it demanded, it offered very little to regions outside the Valley of Mexico – very limited protection in case of attack, no redistribution of goods, no help in case of famine. The Aztecs built nothing in the subjugated territories outside the Valley of Mexico and did not implant new techniques. Very few conquered peoples outside the altiplano participated in the military campaigns of the Tenochtitláns. Therefore it is not surprising that many subjugated peoples took advantage of the Spanish invasion to rise against a domination which they saw as purely of an exploiting nature.

If within their empire the Incas had more support than the Aztecs in theirs, the situation was exactly the reverse in the reaction of the two respective capitals to the Conquest. When Cuzco was besieged by the forces of Manco Inca, part of the non-Inca population and Cañari and Yanacona troops joined the Spanish. In Tenochtitlán the whole population continued fighting until the surrender of Cuauhtemoc. Such divergent reactions reflected the much more homogeneous ethnic character of the Tenochtitlán population in contrast with the multiethnic character of the Cuzcans.

A last contrast between the two cities may be demonstrated in the military aspect.

In offensive military operations in the period of the Inca conquests, the Inca empire was very superior to the Tenochcan; Inca roads, provisions stored along the highways, and the mobilization of troops from regions adjacent to the regions they wished to conquer contributed to a decisive Tahuantinsuyu offensive force. The Aztecs had to send almost all their troops from the Valley of Mexico; they had neither highways nor stores of the Inca type. Because of this, it is not surprising that the Tenochtitláns found it much more difficult to conquer distant territories.

The situation was quite different concerning battles within or around the two capitals. The majority of the inhabitants of Tenochtitlán were elite professional soldiers with great military experience. A large part of the Cuzcan population was made up of bureaucrats and servants. During the siege of Cuzco, tens of thousands of Inca soldiers were not able to dislodge some hundreds of Spanish with a very limited number of Indian allies. In contrast, the Tenochtitláns succeeded in expelling a much larger number of Spanish from their capital. In spite of their numerical and technical inferiority and in spite of a smallpox epidemic, they managed to resist for many months.

Nevertheless, when Tenochtitlán fell, the Aztec empire crumbled, both physically and psychologically. The Inca empire continued to exist for many years, until 1572; and psychologically it continued to constitute a potent force in the minds of thousands of inhabitants of the Andean region.

REFERENCES

BANDELIER, ADOLF F.
1880   "On the social organization and mode of government of the ancient Mexicans," in *Twelfth Annual Report of the Peabody Museum of American Archaeology and Ethnology* Cambridge, Mass.: Harvard University Press.

BORAH, WOODROW, SHERBURNE F. COOK
1963   *The aboriginal population of central Mexico on the eve of the Spanish Conquest.* Ibero-Americana 45. Berkeley and Los Angeles: University of California Press.

BOSCH GARCÍA, CARLOS
1944   *La esclavitud prehispánica entre los aztecas.* Mexico City.

CALNEK, EDWARD
1971   Settlement patterns and Chinampa agriculture at Tenochtitlán. *American Antiquity* 37 (1): 104–115.

CARRASCO, PEDRO
1961   The civil-religious heirarchy in Mesoamerican communities; pre-Spanish background and colonial development. *American Anthropologist* 63 (3): 483–497.

CORTÉS, HERNÁN
1763   *Cartas y documentos.* Mexico City.

CUNOW, HEINRICH
1896   *Die soziale Verfassung des Inkareiches.* Stuttgart.

DE CIEZA DE LEÓN PEDRO
1971   *La crónica del Perú.* Lima.

DE TORQUEMADA, JUAN
1723   *Monarquía indiana.* Madrid.

DÍAZ DEL CASTILLO, BERNAL
1944   *Historia verdadera de la conquista de la Nueva España*, three volumes. Mexico: Ramirez Cobañas.

DOBYNS, HENRY F.
1966   Estimating American population. *Current Anthropology* (October) 7 (4): 395–416.

DURON, DIEGO
1951   [1867–1880]   *Historia de las Indias de Nueva España y Islas de Tierra Firme*, volume two. Mexico City.

HARDOY, JORGE E.
1968 *Urban planning in pre-Columbian America*. New York: Braziller.
1972 *Pre-Columbian cities*. Translated by Judith Thorne. New York: Walker.

KATZ, FRIEDRICH
1966 *Situación social y económica de los aztecas*. Mexico City.
1972 *Ancient American civilizations*. London: Praeger.

MÉTRAUX, ALFRED
1961 *Les Incas*. Paris.

MONZÓN, ARTURO
1949 *El calpulli en la organización social de los tenochca*. Mexico City.

MOORE, SALLY FALK
1958 *Power and property in Inca Peru*. New York.

MURRA, JOHN V.
n.d. "The economic organization of the Inca state." Unpublished Ph.D. dissertation. Chicago.

ROSENBLATT, ÁNGEL
1954 *La población indígena y el mestizaje en América*. Buenos Aires: Nova.

ROWE, JOHN H.
1957 "Inca culture at the time of the Spanish Conquest," in *Handbook of South American Indians*. Edited by Julian Steward. New York: Cooper Square.

SOUSTELLE, JACQUES
1955 *La vie quotidienne des Aztèques à la veille de la conquête espagnole*. Paris.

TRIMBORN, HERMANN
1923–1924 Der Kollektivismus der Inkas in Peru. *Anthropos* 18.

COLONIAL

European Urban Forms in the Fifteenth to Seventeenth Centuries and Their Utilization in Latin America

JORGE E. HARDOY

In 1880, Latin America was a rural continent with scarcely 10 percent of the total population living in urban centers of five thousand or more inhabitants. According to the estimates of Carr-Saunders (1939), the total population must have been around 18.9 million inhabitants. The growth of the principal cities of the continent, especially the ports, was comparatively rapid between the last decades of the eighteenth century and during the time when most of the Latin American countries gained their independence. On the other hand, the elements of the urban network of 1810 or 1820 were practically the same as those of the seventeenth and eighteenth centuries. Furthermore, few changes occurred during those centuries in the relative importance of various urban centers in the territories occupied by Spain and Portugal. The most important changes were the decline of Potosí, which in the middle of the seventeenth century had been the most important city of Latin America; the replacement at the end of the eighteenth century of Bahia by Rio de Janeiro as the most important city of Brazil; and the urbanization of Minas Gerais during the first years of the eighteenth century, as the consequence of the *bandeirante* expansion and the discovery of mining resources in Brazil.

During the last two centuries of the colony, very few cities were established which were to acquire national importance after independence. Medellín, Montevideo, Pôrto Alegre, and Rosario were the most notable exceptions. Moreover, during those centuries there were few changes in the interior boundaries of the continent. It would seem that with the above exceptions and apart from some unrelated regional experiments, the city map of Spanish and Portuguese America in 1820 was approximately the same as in 1630 and 1650.[1] As we shall see,

[1] On Brazil, see de Azevedo (1956) and Goulart Reis Filho (1968); on Spanish America, Jara (1969).

there was also no change in standard regarding the type of city to be constructed. The model city built by the Spanish at the end of the eighteenth century (in Orán and in some agricultural towns of Mexico, for example) was not very different from that of 1650 or 1550. Of course, there were the differences imposed by topography, climate, and the functions each city fulfilled; but in essence these were variations of a model which had been consolidated centuries before (Hardoy 1968). Some different ideas on urban architecture were also incorporated over the years.

Without achieving the same degree of standardization, the Portuguese in Brazil also maintained town-planning standards which did not change substantially for centuries. We find the greatest innovations during the seventeenth and eighteenth centuries in territories not previously occupied, or sparsely occupied, by Europeans, such as Guiana and some smaller Caribbean islands; or else in territories where Spanish or Portuguese control was totally or temporarily replaced by another European power, as in Jamaica and northwest Brazil.

Five European powers directly influenced the urban forms of Latin America between the beginning of the sixteenth century and the end of the eighteenth century. Their impact and legacies varied greatly, just as the territorial areas directly influenced by them were very diverse. The present article is based on two theses, the first of which is that the interests of Spain, Portugal, England, Holland, and France in Latin America were linked with internal events of extraordinary political and socioeconomic impact, which engendered a great deal of confidence; the second thesis is that each country brought its distinctive cultural heritage to the areas it conquered. The internal situations of these countries on the eve of their intervention in America will be examined individually in this article. It is essential to understand that psychologically, militarily, and culturally the appearance of those five European countries in America coincided with a very special stage in their history, a stage in which, for the individual and the ruling class alike, any enterprise was possible, because a fundamental phase in the evolution of the nation had taken place. Each nation possessed firm leadership and a positive national attitude with respect to the international role which it could fulfill.

There is no great similarity in the objectives, capacity, or methods of the imperial enterprises of those five European countries in America. In each case they were ill prepared for enterprises of the magnitude undertaken. For Spain and Portugal, their presence in America was apparently accidental. The initial indecisions of their colonial policy reflected geographic unawareness of the continent which was opening up before their eyes. The confidence in or tacit acceptance of private initiatives indeed may indicate recognition (on the part of the Spanish and Portuguese Crowns) of the risks involved in colonial enterprise in what is now Latin America. Holland and France trusted in the experience of others. They did not colonize lands which had not previously been recognized or occupied by the Spanish or Portuguese. Nor did they risk comparable resources on those enterprises. England, on the other hand, advanced steadily in the Caribbean after a century of undeclared wars against Spain. During this period, English navigators carefully noted and mapped out the resources and geography of the area. The presence of these three countries in Latin America responded first to commercial interests. They only sought – or managed – to affirm their presence when they were also able to play a political role.

All the European powers brought their cultures to America, reflected in the language, religion, and customs they practiced and in the institutions and social organization they knew. The cities they founded in America, therefore, were bound to reflect the most accepted town-planning practices of the various intervening countries. This, the second thesis of the present essay, has a corollary: as the conquest and colonization of Latin America was an eminently practical undertaking for the European countries involved, the cities fulfilled purely functional requirements. With regard to location, design, and use of the ground, the European city in the Latin America of the sixteenth to the eighteenth centuries was not regarded as a work of art. It did not respond to the theoretical (urban and esthetic) concepts which were most advanced in Europe at the time. Instead, it was seen as a "large *factoría*" [trading center]. The market city of the interior, the port city, and the mining city were mere links in the fundamental cycle: from the colony (the producer of natural resources) to the mother country (the consumer, processor, and redistributor of those resources), then back to the colony (the consumer of the products manufactured in the mother country). In that vicious circle of colonialism, the market and port cities constituted the pivots around which the whole economy and colonial administration revolved.

As a result, the cities of Europe in America were intended, above all, to fulfill the administrative and trade functions assigned to them. Only occasionally was an attempt made to introduce an overall urban plan into a city of any importance. There were no more than 3 or 4 cities in the mid-eighteenth century with any significant cultural activities. However some architectural works of value (generally palaces, churches, and monasteries) were built. It is also true that there were some artistic movements of originality and quality, as in Quito in the seventeenth century and Minas Gerais in the eighteenth century. But these were isolated movements which were geographically circumscribed. Furthermore, an analysis of colonial urban cartography indicates the unchanging position of colonial cities in the seventeenth and eighteenth centuries. The reports of some objective travelers also confirm the lack of new urban works: scarcely a single public walk in the great capitals of the viceroys, or any monument, or civil engineering work such as a bridge or aqueduct. On the other hand, during the seventeenth and eighteenth centuries almost every port and interior city had its defense works, ranging from a simple fortified platform to a complex system of defenses which walled in an entire city.

TOWN-PLANNING THEORY AND PRACTICE IN ITALY: 1400–1600

Italy led Europe in the fifteenth and sixteenth centuries both in the theory of the city and in the execution of practical solutions to problems of urban growth. In the theoretical field, Italy was the center of thinking which revolved around the concept of the ideal city. In numerous treatises written and published during these centuries, one notes a gradual separation between an architectural/esthetic emphasis and a concern with purely defensive and military themes.

It could be interpreted that the need to solve concrete problems deriving from a different military technology caused the adoption of new defensive measures, which in turn affected urban forms and designs starting around 1500.

This separation is related to a clear professional division between architects and military engineers originating in the middle of the sixteenth century (de la Croix 1960; Argan 1969). The first group of authors included Alberti and Filarete; the transition was marked by the "Treatise" of Francisco di Giorgio Martini, whose influence on Pietro Cataneo, Antonio de Sangallo the Younger, and Michele Sanmichele was well known. Di Giorgio Martini "had to make a radical departure from the classic or Vitruvian town planning which demanded a square and rectangular blocks of buildings. He took the decisive step of adapting the form of his central square to the radial system of streets and, indirectly, to the circumference of the city. With this new concept, he was able to design a new type of urban plan which was to be converted into the model for later radial plans (de la Croix 1960: 270–271). Cataneo and Scamozzi were the last theoreticians of the sixteenth century who still concerned themselves equally with esthetic and military problems.[2]

De Sangallo the Younger and Sanmichele were the last architects and military engineers whose work was principally in Italy. This was

[2]   Cataneo (1572) lived between 1500 and 1572. *L'architettura de Pietro Cataneo* was published in Venice in 1572. See especially Chapter 13.

not true of Girolamo Marini, the builder of Villefranche sur Meuse: or of Jacomo Castriotto, who became superintendent of fortresses of the French Kingdom; or of Francesco de Marchi, who worked for several years in the Netherlands, or of Alghisi. All of these men, responding to a European demand for their services, worked equally in various countries of the continent. The activities of this group of brilliant engineers, who were to revolutionize military defense systems, were concentrated entirely on military problems. They were not concerned about problems of civilian towns. In their plans they limited themselves to the adoption of designs which allowed movement of cannons and troops from one point of the city to another, specifically between the central square and the bulwarks. This was the origin of their interest in radial-concentric designs and in the adoption of polygonal external forms, most appropriate for the defensive-offensive systems of bulwarks which they devised.

During the sixteenth and seventeenth centuries, the theoreticians of the ideal city of the Italian Renaissance favored a predominant form: the polygon of five to sixteen sides, with a preference for six, eight, and twelve sides. Only occasionally did they adopt a square or other form. The logical outcome was to adopt a design which would correspond to the outer form: the radial system, with the possibility of including concentric rings.[3]

The theories of the Renaissance had little influence on the designing of the new cities, in spite of the fact that some of them, mainly outside Italy, were constructed in accordance with the principles indicated.[4] However, their influence on the new defensive systems of existing cities was enormous, as is indicated by the demand for military engineers in the courts of Europe during the sixteenth and seventeenth centuries. Nor did the treatise writers of the fifteenth to seventeenth centuries have any influence on the remodeling of existing cities, whatever the architectural or military emphasis of their writings may have been. This fact has special importance, because during these years the major cities of Italy (and Europe as well) were expanded and remodeled according to completely new town-planning principles.

During the second half of the fifteenth century, the cities of Italy underwent considerable demographic growth. It was undoubtedly due to the expansion of trade, facilitated by a money economy. After the plague of 1348, which killed a third of Italy's population, the cities of the peninsula recovered slowly. Parallel to this, a glorification of the individual replaced the collective spirit of the medieval centuries.

All of Italy was already covered with cities. Until the fourteenth

[3] This was the design adopted by Fiarete and Martini, and after them by Fra Giocondo, Lorini, Maggi y Castriotto, de Marchi, and appearing implicitly in Campanella's text and others.
[4] Antonelli, the most famous military engineer employed by Phillip II in the fortification of the cities of America, was Italian.

century, except in the principal trade centers, the cities (with their rural areas of immediate influence) formed self-sufficient units. But starting from the fifteenth century, a different spirit appeared, though the cities had not yet recovered the prosperity of the twelfth and thirteenth centuries, much less that achieved around the year 1300. This new spirit was reflected in the arts and sciences and in a general attitude of greater optimism. The need to enlarge and remodel existing cities at this time resulted in the development of partial urban aggregates and in the adoption of complete town-planning schemes.

Dealing with the ordered growth of existing cities did not require an elaborate, preexistent body of laws. All the principal cities of Italy, and throughout Europe, faced practical problems. The most notorious ones were: (a) the hygiene of the cities and the supplying of water; (b) a system of streets better suited to heavier traffic (which entailed straightening out and levelling, and solving problems of crossroads); and (c) the protection of some areas from flooding by nearby rivers. These requirements were clear in the fifteenth century, before the development of artillery called attention to the weakness of medieval principles and defensive techniques.

During the fifteenth century, a number of Italian cities carried out remodelling works with the objectives indicated. In Rome, Sixtus IV issued a papal bull in 1480 establishing the concept of expropriation of urban property for the public good and formed a commission entrusted with the various problems (Lavedan 1959: 38). In Milan, Ludovico el Moro planned to reconstruct the *barrios* of the poor, providing them with facilities for improved hygiene and sanitation (Lavedan 1959: 119). But it was in Ferrara where, on the initiative of Duke Hércules I de Este, Biagio Rossetti designed a total plan of the city in 1492; this included the remodeling of the old medieval city and its expansion to several times its size, in accordance with the two principal and perpendicular axes (Lavedan 1959: 120–121; Giovanni 1931). Zevi, who devoted an important study to Rossetti, calls him the first modern European town planner. Zevi says:

The masterwork, the supreme poem of Rossetti, is not the Palace of Segismundo, nor San Cristóbal, nor the court of Ludovico el Moro: it is Ferrara in its entirety, in its living concreteness, the regulating plan, the belt of wall, the architectural integration of the old city and its extension in the indissoluble bond which unites them (1960: 511).

In Ferrara, Rossetti incorporated some truly revolutionary practical solutions for a city which in its design was still medieval: two straight axes, sixteen and eighteen meters wide, link three gates of the city with an overall area formed by four palaces. In relation to these axes was formed a more or less regular gridiron pattern of streets, which do not always meet at a right angle but which maintain a severe, unified, and appropriate design of architectural works in brick. An almost regular square – the new square – was incorporated in the new sector of the city. With reason Zevi pointed out that Rossetti's plan, as an abstract, was less attractive than that of the ideal cities of the Renaissance, since his individual architectural works cannot be compared with those of his contemporaries. But "it must be understood, on the other hand, that he [Rossetti] has carried out a different task: that of constructing a living city" (Zevi 1960: 511).[5]

I am not aware of the influence Rossetti may have had on the town planning of the sixteenth century in Italy and Europe at a time when Europe, rather than creating new cities, was thinking in terms of the expansion of existing ones with preconceived plans; that is, through the adoption of standards signifying a radical change from the medieval way of thinking (i.e. enlarging the walled area and permitting growth to continue its previous spontaneous tendencies within). Rossetti introduced a total and functional concept of the city which was to be expanded by a different standard of esthetics and system of roads in the Rome of Sixtus V and Fontana: by means of planned units with a baroque town planning concept which would use existing or intentionally incorporated churches and monuments, linked with each other by a network of streets. Rome was thus to be transformed into the largest agglomeration of processional roads ever conceived.

Various authors have pointed out that one of the principal contributions of the Italian Renaissance to the history of town planning was the designing of squares conceived as a planned architectural whole. The square of La Annunziata, in Florence, is considered one of its most representative examples. The square, like medieval squares, is still an enclosed space; but it is built as an orderly area and in accordance with a symmetry and axiality not present in its predecessors. Renaissance perspectives had to be limited by a building. The principal access to the square was through the middle of one side. Gradually, the Renaissance square gave way to an empty area, of closed angles, accessible by the intermediate points of its four sides, with a monument indicating the conjunction of the two axes. This symmetry, irreplaceable in any architectural design of the sixteenth century, was translated to the urban design, the most significant examples being the squares of Rome (Piazza del Acropoli, delle Nazione, and San Pietro) and urban projects planned with the palaces of Versailles and Karlsruhe in mind.

Italy offered the Europe of the sixteenth and seventeenth centuries much more than an aggregate of urban theories or a new urban esthetic concept. Ultimately both had limited application, especially

---

[5] See the excellent collection of plans, engravings, and photographs Zevi includes in his work, and especially the plan of Ferrara in 1597 (1960: 216–217).

the first. They did not radically change the characteristics of existing cities or their extensions. I believe that Ferrara (at the end of the fifteenth century) and Rome (before Sixtus V, during his papacy, and after it) are simply examples of how urban growth was faced in Italy. Naples, Turin, Milan, and Florence are equally significant examples. During the seventeenth century, for example, three extensions of Turin were carried out: to the south, to the southeast, and to the northwest. The model of the original checkerboard pattern was followed in all three, except that the blocks (rectangular in shape) were two to four times larger than those of the gridiron pattern of the original Roman city. Furthermore, in its expansion to the southeast, three squares were incorporated, two with central accesses corresponding to the classic model and one original one (Rasmussen 1951).

One of the less studied themes is, in fact, the criteria governing the expansion of existing cities in Europe between the fifteenth and seventeenth centuries. Undoubtedly it is a less resplendent theme than others generally favored by historians of cities. But it would furnish very valuable information on how urban growth was faced during those three centuries of rapid demographic and urban growth. It was also during this period that the bases for the industrial revolution of the eighteenth century were established.

The sixteenth century saw the spread in Europe of designs of straight streets crossing at right or almost right angles, with orderly squares and complete plans for sufficient space to absorb population growth. During this period, basic regulatory measures were also passed. Rossetti was possibly the first town planner to integrate the old part of a city with its extension. But undoubtedly during the fourteenth century there were already partial additions to existing cities which are still to be analyzed. The influence of such places on European colonial foundations in America (especially those of Spain or Portugal) is very dubious. Spain and Portugal reacted slowly and late to the cultural innovations of the Italian Renaissance. When the latter reached the peninsular courts, the conquest of America was almost complete, and the colonization of the new territories was already marked by hundreds of new cities.

TOWN-PLANNING THEORY AND PRACTICE IN SPAIN BEFORE 1520

The vast majority of the urban population of the Latin American countries colonized by Spain in the sixteenth century lived in cities whose basic design was that of the gridiron. As the Spanish American colonial gridiron was not a form used by the pre-Columbian native cultures, the only possible explanation is that it was a form imported from Spain.[6]

In a previous work (Hardoy 1968), I maintained that (a) "at the beginning of the decade of 1530 in Mexico, and in the middle of the same decade in Peru, a standard city acquired its virtually final shape, and a city model was adopted which from that time on was repeated in all Spain's colonies in America" and (b) that model "was not an integral idea transplanted from Spain to America and endorsed by suitable and simultaneous legislation; rather it was the result of a more general idea, brought from Spain, which in America underwent a progressive and spontaneous process of improvement in urban physical principles later confirmed by laws." In order to understand this process of cultural transmission, one must realize that in the first decades Spain founded three types of human settlements in America:

1. The fortified *factoría* or "fortress," as Columbus had called it.[7] It was a type of settlement which responded to the stage of the reconnaissance of a new coast and the start of efforts to trade with the local population.

2. Centers of conquest, such as Isabela, Nueva Sevilla, Santa María la Antigua del Darién, Santa Marta, and others. Without a solid economic basis, the majority disappeared. The selection of the site was almost always hasty. Its maintenance depended on the dispersal of the Indians, which was not always possible.[8]

3. Cities, properly speaking. With few exceptions, all Spanish American cities were founded after the beginning of the 1520's, when it was possible for the inhabitants of most cities to learn to exploit the natural and human resources of their region.

The first two types were temporary and therefore completely improvized, especially the *factorías*. It is doubtful, therefore, that the elements which were later to conform to the model of the Spanish American city would appear. On the other hand, the cities responded to the need felt by each conqueror to provide his enterprise with a permanent base. The city, as a permanent agglomeration, exemplified the transition from conquest to colonization; while the "fortress" and centers of conquest responded to the stage of submission and penetration.

The Spanish American city, as an expression of a colonial urban model, was tried out on the islands of the Caribbean and the coasts

[6]   The designs most resembling those of a gridiron founded by the Spanish in America were Ollantaytambo, to the north of Cuzco, and the Aztec cities. In the latter, two perpendicular axes were incorporated into cities already inhabited and, through them, a gradual regulating was introduced. In Teotihuacán, more than a thousand years before the Conquest, this concept was applied in a much more systematic manner.

[7]   Mentioned by Columbus in his diary, on 14 October 1492.

[8]   Mario Góngora (1962) calls them places of departure for "forays."

of Tierra Firme before 1520, but possibly attained its final characteristics in Tierra Firme in the middle of that decade. The fortified
factorías and centers of conquest were also used for a number of
decades afterwards in other regions of America. During this period,
discoverers or conquerors faced situations similar to those which
motivated the use of these types in the Caribbean during the last
decade of the fifteenth century and the first and second decades of
the sixteenth century. For example, the first founding of Buenos Aires
(in 1536) had the features of a fortified *factoría*.

In June 1519 at the age of nineteen, Charles, the son of Philip of
Hapsburg and Joanna the Mad, was elected Emperor. Through the
paternal line he inherited Burgundy, which extended across Flanders
as far as Holland; through the maternal line he inherited a Spain unified
by his grandparents, the Catholic Kings, and their overseas territories.
At the time of his coronation in October of that year in Aquisgrán,
his dominions already constituted a world empire.

When in the summer of 1522 Charles began one of his rare residences in Spain, "the gigantic territories of America and their ancient
riches were beginning to emerge on the consciousness of Europeans"
(Brandi 1967: 171). The year 1519 acquired for Spain a double significance similar to that of 1492, when Granada was occupied (completing the Reconquest) and America was discovered. In 1519 the
Spanish dynasty secured the Austrian dynasty, which was initiated
in 1504 when Charles's father occupied the throne for two years; and
Hernán Cortés entered into contact with one of the two great native
civilizations existing at that time in America.

Culturally speaking, Spain was opened up to the Renaissance at the
beginning of the sixteenth century. The reign of the Catholic Kings,
and especially the regencies of Fernando of Aragón and Cardinal
Cisneros, were decisive for the promotion of higher education in
Spain. The linking of Spain with the Austrian house, the Hapsburgs,
meant contact with the culture of the court of Burgundy, which was
still medieval in its wood painting, literature, tapestry, and use of
orders of chivalry at the end of the fifteenth century. In the field of
town planning, Spain in 1520 was a medieval country and remained
so until well into the second half of the sixteenth century.

Spain's basic *urban network* was established by the Romans, who
took advantage, in many regions, of the foundations of the Celts and
Iberians. They were responsible for the founding of Cartagena, Cádiz,
Córboda, Sevilla, Tarragona, Zaragoza, León, Lugo, Mérida, and
other cities which are still important today. That basic network was
supplemented centuries later by the foundations of the towns which
were successively occupied in Spain by the Christian Visigoths and
Arabs. Many cities of Roman origin were also occupied by the Visi-

goths and Arabs, resulting in the modification of the original design to such an extent that it is practically unrecognizable.

In the eighth century, Christians lived a rural and miserable existence in the northwest of the peninsula. León was the seat of the principal Christian court in the tenth century; Oviedo and Santiago were other cities of evident importance. In the rest of Spain, the Arabs promoted a flourishing civilization based on agricultural production and quality handicraft which they sold by means of a well-organized trade. In those centuries Córdoba was the principal cultural center of Western Europe. Two types of cities, one medieval and Christian, the other Arab, existed in Spain simultaneously; they were separated territorially in the peninsula.

Ricard wrote that the Moslem cities grew through private initiative, since Islam was a civilization without municipal institutions (Ricard 1950: 321–327). Winding streets, which ended in cul-de-sacs, blocks of houses which were irregular in their shape and length, and the absence of defined squares were features of the walled-in central nucleus – the "medina" – of any Moslem city. Toledo and Ecija are excellent examples (Torres Balbas 1954). Possibly there were political, economic, and technical disadvantages facing the Christian feudal lords at the start of the Reconquest which spurred them to seek the support of social groups whom they had traditionally neglected. Land concessions, privileges, and a growing municipal autonomy reflected, from the eleventh through the fourteenth centuries, that growing interdependence between lords and peasants. For such reasons, monarchs like Sancho Ramírez and James I in Levante and Sancho the Wise and Sancho the Strong in Navarra, as well as the feudal lords, encouraged the settlement of the rural population and new urban foundations. The immense majority were in Navarra, Levante, Castille, and the Basque country; very few were set up in Andalusia. The founders of new towns adopted varied designs. Sometimes they were irregular, because of the site chosen and spontaneous growth; but frequently they were regular, because this was the design most adaptable to an easy subdivision of lands (Torres Balbas 1954). Regular town planning was also the mark of some towns which arose along the route of pilgrimages to Santiago de Compostela; the same was true of some new districts of Jaca at the end of the eleventh century, and Pamplona, in the twelfth century (Torres Balbas 1954: 52).

The use of regular designs in the construction of *bastides* was a practice employed with considerable frequency in England, Wales, and English Gascony during the eleventh century, and even during the tenth. Beresford cites 97 new cities founded in those three regions between the year 960 (New Romney, in Kent, England) and 1320 (Durance, Lot, and Garonne in Gascony) in which a clear gridiron design survives (Beresford 1967: 151–153, Table 5). Forty-five of those new cities, or 46.3 percent, were in Gascony. I do not know what percentage the figure signifies in relation to the total number of new *bastides* founded during those centuries, which probably came to a few hundred; but it shows that the gridiron was a generalized form (Beresford 1967: 147). In spite of the preference for a gridiron design, a great variety of forms existed for gathering together small groups of buildings; and a rectilinear design could be adopted to sites of different sizes and topographic features. Furthermore, I would like to point out that the gridiron was apparently used more consistently in Gascony because most of the *bastides* in that region were founded within a short period and, therefore, built rapidly (Beresford 1967: 150). Gascony is linked to Navarre, and the route of pilgrimages to Compostela passed through those provinces of France and Spain. The squares of those settlements were also regular. There was a tendency to locate them near the geometric centers of populations in cities without rivers, like Beaumont du Perigord and Monsegur in the Gironde; at times the squares were eccentric, located along the river, which provided the boundary of one side of the settlement, as in Sainte Foy la Grande (in Gironde). These three foundations, like Montpazier, Libourne, Villeneuve sur Lot, Lalinde, and others, have regular designs and were constructed during the second half of the eighteenth century. The squares of some of them, possibly where the busiest markets were installed, were surrounded on all sides by arcades, which constituted areas for trade activities. The location of churches was usually eccentric with respect to the general plan; the church-square relationship continued medieval principles of perspective and asymmetry.

I do not know the origin of the gridiron form adopted by the *conquistadores*, but the checkerboard was definitely used for these new markets – which were both agricultural and manufacturing cities at least two centuries earlier than in Gascony. The gridiron was definitely employed with frequency on both sides of the Pyrenees in the thirteenth century, as was the use of arcades surrounding the main square and a gradual interrelation between the location of the church and the square.

After Torres Balbas' excellent essay on Spanish cities during the Middle Ages there have been no comparable studies, as far as I know, on the subject. Regrettably, Beresford's detailed work does not concern itself with the new medieval cities to the south of the Pyrenees. If, out of practical considerations, Spain did produce some examples of urban regularity before 1500, this was limited to new foundations (almost none of which attained national importance) or the enlargement of some smaller cities. I do not know of any study concerned specifically with the criteria used in the sixteenth century to control the urban growth of the principal cities. It would appear that Valladolid, Granada, Toledo, Zaragoza, and Barcelona (the cities chosen by Charles V for the temporary residence of his court) as well as Sevilla, Córdoba, and other larger cities grew by the spontaneous addition of new parts. The efforts of Charles V were directed to improving communications between cities, introducing some minor modifications, and constructing palaces in cities selected for the temporary location of the court. For example, in order to construct the palace in the Alhambra of Granada he had part of it destroyed; in Toledo he had the Alcazar rebuilt and the water supply improved.[9] One consequence of these royal initiatives was the straightening out of some streets, which in no way modified the medieval features of those cities.[10]

During his reign, Charles V had hardly any influence on the permanent characteristics of Spanish cities. He concerned himself only with some ornamentation, a few laws limiting the size of balconies and projections, and decoration of same for his court festivals (Cervera 1954: 115–119). All progress was concentrated on the construction of a number of palaces and, in particular, *colegios* [secondary schools] in the university cities of Salamanca and Alcalá de Henares.

Changes only began to occur in Spain at the beginning of the reign of Phillip II, but by 1556 the urban model which was to last for the whole colonial period had already been developed in Spain's American territories.

Urban theory had sporadic exponents in Spain, separated from each other by centuries (Torres Balbas 1954: 50, 51–52, 89–107). Portugal never possessed a theoretical interest in the city which responded, as in the Italy of the fifteenth and sixteenth centuries, to a cultural movement or a practical need. In Italy, the initial development of the theory of the city reflected interest in the classical cultures of antiquity and was based on the perusal of their writers. That was not the situation in Spain. It is true that in 1573 Phillip II signed the "Decrees on Population" which, insofar as they related to town planning, were to serve as the bases (almost a century later) for the corresponding chapters of the "Laws of the Indies." However, all he did was to endorse legally a procedure which was already being carried out. In arrangement and vocabulary some of the articles of the "Decrees" reveal the influence of the Italian Renaissance theory of the ideal city and through it of classical antiquity. The articles selected were the

[9] Cervera (1954: 116); Torres Balbas (1954); Gutkind (1967). Gutkind follows the chapters of Torres Balbas and Cervera in the work quoted; he incorporates some excellent photographs.

[10] An excellent collection of plans and views of Spanish cities in the middle of the sixteenth century appears in Braun and Hogenberg (1594).

most obvious ones. Because of their purely practical nature, they had already been put into use by urban man and by the discoverers and conquerors of America when they decided to make their conquests permanent through the creation of a new city. Both the "Decrees" of 1573 and the "Laws of the Indies" of 1681 reflect the influence of the practical experience already gained in America. In addition, the theoretical inheritance of the Italian Renaissance is seen in the organization and wording of the two bodies of laws.

The only Spanish pre-Renaissance theoretician to attempt a "complete theory of the ideal city" was Eximeniç (Torres Balbas 1954: 89; Guarda 1965). The layout of his city was square with forts at each corner and gates situated in the center of each side. Two principal thoroughfares bisected the city into four areas of identical, square blocks. The square, which was surrounded by arcades and was accessible from the corners, was close to the city's center. The church and archbishop's palace formed another unit, also close to the intersection of the two principal streets; each district was to have its convents and businesses; the prince's palace was to be eccentric. As Torres Balbas has pointed out, the regular geometric design was chosen because of its practicality and defensive advantages, but also because it brought together the requisite conditions of beauty (1954: 91). It is not easy to specify the exact influence of Eximeniç's ideas on the construction of the new cities around the end of the fourteenth century. Torres Balbas suggested, without much conviction, that the Catalan friar's principles might have been applied in Castellón and Villarreal.

The integrated elements which must have formed the model for the Spanish American colonial city had already been used in the new Spanish foundations of the period of the Reconquest and had been synthesized by Eximeniç. These elements included an orderly design and later the gridiron of equal blocks; the square surrounded by arcades, accessible from the corners – not from the center of the sides, as was to occur after the Italian Renaissance; the square formed by one unbuilt block; the extolling of the gridiron pattern because of its practical, defensive and esthetic values; and the basic concept of designing districts. The church still did not face the main square, but this did not occur in the first Spanish urban foundations in America either.

Having dismissed native influence and the practical application of Renaissance theories or practices, I favor the following alternative: the standard Spanish American colonial city was a late medieval model perfected in Spain. When brought to America, it was gradually adapted to the following: the practical necessities of an accelerated founding process of vast scope; institutions developed for colonial life; and the concern of their leaders (conquerors and colonizers) to establish their rights over the new territories by rapidly establishing a new city, with everything that implied, both legally and politically. The city was Spain's great colonizing instrument in America. During the stages of discovery and conquest and, later, during the first stages of the colony, when private initiative was indispensable, the city was the indispensable form of life. It was necessary in order to unite isolated groups of Spaniards. It was also required to exploit (as rapidly and efficiently as possible) the natural and human resources of each territory.

At least until 1540 or 1550, the defensive systems of the first Spanish American cities also corresponded to a medieval model. The first fortifications were simple palisades, designed to keep Indians out of the settlements. Other European countries did not disturb the Spanish during the first decades. In cities constructed by a definite standard (e.g. Santo Domingo and San Juan), isolated fortifications were built to defend access to a river or bay used as a port, or to protect a place of unloading. The need to fortify and surround a city completely was felt some time later and took some time to become a reality. The peripheral fortification of Santo Domingo was only begun in 1543 (Palm 1955; 156). The Homenaje tower in Santo Domingo, completed around 1507, is an isolated construction, with a square layout and medieval features (Palm 1955: 84, 88, 157). The first defensive masonwork tower of San Juan was an isolated construction of circular layout, completed on a platform crowned with merlons. Today it is superimposed by the low bulwarks of the seventeenth-century fortifications.

TOWN-PLANNING THEORY AND PRACTICE IN PORTUGAL BEFORE 1520

Jaime Cortesão has written that Portugal is the region of the Iberian Peninsula with the most direct contact with the ocean (Cortesão 1964: 16–31). Because of its geographic position, its ports, favored by contacts with an ancient maritime route, became necessary stopping places between northern and southern Europe. In the twelfth century, when all of Portugal was reconquered from the Arabs, it was already a densely populated region living on its fishing and agriculture.

The story of how a small kingdom, with scarcely a million inhabitants, in the fifteenth century became the principal factor for the expansion of the maritime routes of the period, and the story of the royal house of Aviz which promoted these routes, have been the object of some excellent studies (Parry 1949, 1964). In the fifteenth century the Portuguese nation possessed sufficient unity, and psychological attitude, and the leadership to change medieval geography. Spain was undertaking the last stage of its war on the Reconquest, while trying to attain national unity. In Italy the Papacy was being confronted by the kingdom of Naples, the republic of Venice, and the dukedom of Milan, with Florence playing the principal role in that peninsula's policy. The Hundred Years' War was developing between France and England, as a result of which England was to be involved in the War of the Roses and France with the succession of weak and treasonous kings. At this time Portugal took the first steps which were to provide this small kingdom with the riches, power, and prestige of the great nations.

Lisbon was the center of all that activity. It was the principal port, the place of residence of the royal family, the capital of the kingdom, and the site of a university; at the same time it was the principal port of Western Europe in the fourteenth and fifteenth centuries, the meeting place of Genoese and Venetian, French and Flemish, English and Scandinavian traders. Lisbon was also one of the most active centers in the preparation of navigation charts and the application of the latest innovations of maritime technology.

"Lisbon was enterprising, opulent and optimistic" (Morison 1942: 32). A city of almost 80,000 inhabitants at the end of the fifteenth century; constructed, like Rome, on hills and the intermediate valleys; hemmed in by Arab ramparts – the Cerca Máxima – and later by the new line of ramparts – la Cerca Nuova, or Cerca de D. Fernando, constructed by order of King Fernando after the attack by the armies of Henry II of Castile, in 1373 (Vieira da Silva 1950).

At the end of the fourteenth century, Lisbon had 103.6 hectares of area, 6.6. times larger than the Moorish city. Its perimeter reached 5,350 meters: its longest side, as would tend to occur in subsequent centuries, was parallel to the Tajo River and reached 1,750 meters (Vieira da Silva 1950: 10). Not all the area within the walls was built up. Its winding streets, its pronounced unevenness, its churches and castles constructed on top of hills, gave it a medieval appearance and contour. Seen from the Almada, on the opposite shore of the Tajo, it resembled a *"bexuga de peixe"* (de Góis 1937).[11] The principal commercial street was the "rua Nova dos Mercaderes," where merchants from around the world gathered. On the rua Nova were the shops of engravers, jewellers, and goldsmiths, the guild houses and the houses of exchange (de Góis 1937: 48ff.).

The city in the fifteenth and sixteenth centuries lacked planned squares. During the reigns of Juan II (1481–1495) and Manuel I (1495–1521), when Portuguese maritime undertakings were at their

[11]   The author was Director of the Archives of the Kingdom during the first half of the sixteenth century.

height, la Praça do Rossio was an extensive and undefined area to the north of the city. Here fairs, executions, and the *autos de fé* were held. Even older were the Terreiro do Paço, and the Paço da Ribeira, extensive, undefined areas which served as places of disembarkation and open-air workshops for the many activities associated with the port and shipyard.

Medieval Portuguese cities have not been studied to any extent. The *Livro das fortalezas de Duarte Darmas* was possibly prepared between 1520 and 1530 by order of King Manuel I, whom Duarte served as *escudero* (Darmas 1943). It contains drawings of two façades of fifty-seven fortresses – originally there were sixty – located throughout the kingdom. In construction, all the fortresses were medieval and built at the tops of hills or elevations. None reveal modifications incorporating the latest advances in military engineering which came into use in Italy after 1500. Some were isolated fortresses, others had nearby towns which were not protected by the ramparts; frequently the walls extend from the fortresses and surround the towns constructed on the slopes, as in Monforte, Arronches, Elvas, and Monforte de Río Livre. In these cases, the design of the towns when seen in contour was always irregular. The towns partially surround the fortresses by the least abrupt and most accessible part.

Many Portuguese cities originated during the Roman period or on the ruins of an ancient fortified place prior to the Roman occupation, including (among others) Lisbon (Olisipo), Porto (Cale), Coimbra (Eminium), Evora (Ebora), Braganza (Juliobriga), Beja (Pax Julia), Mertola (Myrtilis), Braga (Bracara), Chaves (Aqua Fluvia), and Alcacer do Sol (Salacia). Braga, in the fifteenth and sixteenth centuries, when Portugal reached its golden age, had a quite orderly design surrounded by a circular wall, like Bragança. But Lisbon, Porto and Coimbra were cities on a hill, with irregular designs.

The plans of Evora, Elbas, Beja, Viseu, and Salingas approximate the characteristic radial model of some medieval cities, in spite of the prior Roman occupation. The orderly design of Viana do Castelo (in spite of its medieval form) and its adaptation to a hilltop site, as in Monsaraz, are quite exceptional. Perhaps the only orderly example is Tomar, the city of the Knights of the Order of Christ, constructed on the shores of the Nabão River. The regular layout of its houses, at the foot of the castle of the Order, might have been decreed by Prince Henry the Navigator, who was the Grand Master of the Order (Gutkind 1967: 48–53; and especially Santos Simões (1943). However, it is an isolated example.

During the seventeenth century various systems of urban fortifications were constructed – or planned – in Portugal, following the principle of polygonal, peripheral forms surrounded by triangular bulwarks, or variations of this form. The fortifications of Elvas, with seven bulwarks and two forts, are among the most elaborate. The same is true of Lisbon's defenses, with its 32 bulwarks designed in 1650, as well as those designed and only partially constructed for Beja. These were the first town plans which derived from the Italian Renaissance, which, however, influenced only the outer appearance of some cities, not their design or esthetics.

As far as town planning is concerned, when Portugal became a world power with colonies and territories in Africa, Asia, and Latin America, it was still a medieval country. As Lavedan says, one cannot speak of town planning (in Lisbon) before the time of the Marquis de Pombal (Lavedan 1959: 408).

Portugal's first establishments in America, like her first on the west coast of Africa, in India, and in the Far East, were intended to serve the trade of goods. They were not established with the sense of permanence associated with an intention to colonize. They were simple *factorías* (*feitorías*) suitable for a wharf and a site for gathering products to be traded, and defended by a simple palisade and fort-house surrounded by a moat. That kind of commercial-military establishment was the only type Portugal established in Brazil until 1530. Only two of the *factorías* established during those first decades can have given rise to later permanent groupings: Cabo Frio, 120 kilometers to the northeast of Rio de Janeiro, and Igaraçu, to the north of Pernambuco (de Azevedo 1956: 11). This first period of "spontaneous" colonization of Brazil ended in 1530, when Portugal decided to adopt a firmer position with her American possessions. The solution was to introduce the system of *capitanías*, granting the governors broad civil and military powers, such as the power to found *vilas* [chartered towns]. In 1532 São Vicente, in the present state of São Paulo, was the first of a group of six *vilas* founded along the coast between that date and 1549. The other five were Igaraçu (1536) and Olinda (1537) in Pernambuco and Porto Seguro (1535), San Jorge dos Ilheus (1536), and Santa Cruz (1536) in Bahia (de Azevedo 1956: 11ff.).

São Vicente and Olinda were the most important settlements of those decades. Very little is known of the first. It was surrounded by a palisade and in the middle of the sixteenth century was made up of simple houses arranged without any order (de Azevedo 1956: 75 quoting Torre de Souza). Possibly it was never more than a *feitoría*, although of greater size than its contemporaries. The plan of São Vicente by Vingboons, at the beginning of the seventeenth century, shows a town with very few houses, whose port was surrounded by a series of square forts with bulwarks at the corners. Olinda, on the other hand, founded by Duarte Coelho, possessed a medieval design which can still be seen.

Defensive factors spurred Coelho, a veteran of the wars of India (where he fought under the orders of Albuquerque), to choose a hill instead of a level site – one close to the excellent natural port where later Recife (Mauricia) was to be developed. A defensive motive "led grantee Duarte Coelho to climb the slopes of Marim hill and to build, at the top, the medieval town with its convent, its square facing the church, and its castle in the form of a tower" (de Castro 1954: 60). There are various plans and views of Olinda from the first half of the seventeenth century, Kaspar van Baerle's plan of 1647 being perhaps the most accurate. One sees in it the above-mentioned features, in spite of the fact that the plan does not have topographical markings. The irregular squares facing or surrounding the principal churches of the city and the winding nature of the streets are worthy of note.

The fact is, as Goulart says, "the Portuguese policy for Brazil, in the middle of the sixteenth century, sought to use to the maximum the resources of private citizens (colonists and grantees) without damaging their programs in India, which at the time used most of their resources" (Goulart Reis Filho 1968). The Crown left in the hands of the grantees the responsibility for building the towns they needed for their operations. They did not attempt to dictate, as did the Spanish Crown, the characteristics of the settlements. The result was that of the thirty-seven populated areas – *vilas* and cities – founded between 1532 and 1650, scarcely seven were on behalf of the Portuguese Crown (Goular Reis Filho 1968). Two other settlements of the second half of the sixteenth century also reveal medieval features, owing undoubtedly to the features of the sites, which were chosen for defensive reasons: São Paulo, a religious settlement of 1558, and Rio de Janeiro. Both conformed to the name of "acropolis-cities" which was given to them by Aroldo de Azevedo, especially Rio de Janeiro, limited as it was during the sixteenth century, to the bluff of São Januário (or Castillo), a natural bulwark which rose very close to the sea and was surrounded by flooded lands, lagoons, etc." (de Azeveda 1956: 67).

The decision of the Portuguese Crown to intervene directly in Brazil's affairs took form with the setting up of the *Capitanía General* with its capital in Salvador. Some facts are important: Salvador, and later Rio de Janeiro and in the seventeenth century São Luis and Belem, were to be regional centers (Goulart Reis Filho 1968: 68); second, an architect was appointed, under the direct orders of the King, to direct the construction of Salvador (Sampaio 1949).[12]

I do not know the details of the instructions the King of Portugal may have given Tomé de Souza, the *Capitán-General*, or Luiz Díaz, the architect, but undoubtedly they were not as precise as those of the future decrees of Phillip II. They may possibly have been an

[12] Chapters 6, 11, and 12 include a detailed résumé of the first decades of the city.

example of *laissez faire*, like the instructions Ovando and Diego Colón received when they went to Santo Domingo. But the fact of sending a professional man, as Portugal did to her other territories in the East, is significant.

The nature of the site where Salvador was built necessitated the use of a triangular outer form fortified with six bulwarks and a wall. Within the walls, four longitudinal and three transverse streets were designed. The principal street, rua Direita dos Mercaderes,was the largest and ran from north to south, connecting the city's two gates (Sampaio 1949: 188). The other longitudinal streets, known today by the names of rua da Ajuda, do Päo de Lot, and dos Capitaes, were parallel to the earlier one and ended at the bulwarks. The three transverse roads were also parallel: vía de Assemblea, vía das Vassouras, and vía do Berquo, as they are known today. Limited by the topographic features of the site, Salvador's design displayed, within a few years of the founding, features of regularity, though without the rigid layout of the Spanish American model. A plan of Bahia of 1638 found in the Royal Archives at The Hague (Inv. No. 2166) shows those features clearly. São Luis and Belem were also designed in an ordered fashion, as can be verified in plans of the seventeenth and eighteenth centuries respectively.[13] As to Rio de Janeiro, when in the seventeenth century it began to expand by way of the level areas surrounding the original site, a design of very orderly features was also used. The fact is that already in the sixteenth century, as Goulart pointed out (following the studies of Mario Tavares Chicó), orderly designs were frequently adopted by the Portuguese in their overseas colonies (Goulart Reis Filho 1968: 71ff.). Nevertheless, the formal inspiration and defense system of some Portuguese cities in India appear to deviate from Renaissance theories. These theories do not appear to have influenced the Portuguese foundations in Brazil.

TOWN-PLANNING THEORY AND PRACTICE IN HOLLAND BEFORE 1600

In 1602 and 1621 were founded the East India and West India Companies respectively. Similar in their objectives and organization, they nevertheless had profound differences in their orientation, development, and practical results. The first did not operate in America. The second operated in Africa and essentially in three American regions:

[13]   A plan of Belem of 1791 shows the features indicated. On the other hand, on a plan of Belem and its environs of the seventeenth century, the original of which is found in the Royal Archives at The Hague (Inv. No. 2155), the city is still in a very embryonic state, although relatively ordered.

the present maritime states of the eastern United States, where they founded New Amsterdam in 1625: on the north and northeastern coast of Brazil, where they built Pernambuco or Mauricia at the beginning of 1637; and in the Islands of the Caribbëan, where they occupied the islands of Tobago, San Eustaquio, San Martín and Curaçao in the 1630's, and Saba and the British Virgin Islands in the 1640's (West and Augelli 1966: 72–73, Table 3.1).

The seventeenth century was the Dutch golden age. From the first decades of that century, Holland became the principal maritime nation of Europe, and its merchant fleet the principal one of the world. Thus, in the first decades of the seventeenth century, a political and commercial process reached its culmination. Since the fourteenth century Dutch merchants had entered into competition with the powerful cities of the Hanseatic League. As Holland lacked the natural resources of the countries with whom she was competing, her artisans devoted themselves to the processing of raw materials and the finishing of imported products – as well as to a commerce which gradually expanded in products and markets. Dutch maritime technology of the sixteenth and seventeenth centuries had no rivals: their type of ship (the *fluit*), because of its great storage capacity and low operating cost, revolutionized the transport of cargoes.

The truce of 1609 marked the final break of the Dutch provinces with Spain. The result of almost half a century of wars was twofold: on the one hand, an independent and Protestant Dutch Republic emerged. Equally significant was the policy of religious tolerance which, initiated by the leader of the revolt against Spain, William Prince of Orange, and continued by his successors, attracted political and religious refugees from all Europe. The immigrants' contribution of capital commercial ability, and artisan expertise spurred Dutch cities to a period of glory unlike any they had ever known.

Holland's consolidation as the principal trade power of the seventeenth century reflected the importance acquired by North Sea and Atlantic ports in world maritime trade. It also reflected the decline experienced by the ports of the Hanseatic League and the Mediterranean. The commercial dynamism of the Hanseatic League had been very much linked to the use of Europe's internal rivers and canals. In the seventeenth century Amsterdam occupied the rôle of continental financial and trade center, which had been held by Antwerp a century before, Lisbon in the fifteenth century, and Venice between the twelfth and fourteenth centuries. It was "the reign of a city – the last where a true empire based on trade and credit was able to become an actual fact, without the support of the forces of a unified modern state" (Barbour 1966: 13). During the sixteenth and seventeenth centuries, various European states were also formed which were unified and increasingly centralized in their administration and with significant advances in transport and communications systems and agricultural and mining production.

At the end of the sixteenth century, Europe experienced a rapid demographic growth which favored merchants prepared for the purchase and sale of goods. No one in Europe possessed the organization of the Dutch merchants. Only the London merchants appeared as their potential rivals. This rivalry was not to shift in London's favor until the end of the seventeenth century.

The West India Company was controlled by merchants and investors from Amsterdam who were interested in the importing of cotton, sugar (sugar refining was an important activity in Amsterdam), and tobacco coming from the tropical regions of America, and in the exporting of wool textiles and metals. From the beginning it comprised a belligerent mixture of trade and religion. "The majority of their directors were dedicated Calvinists from the south whose idea was to combine business with a religious crusade againt the Papacy" (Wilson 1968: 210). This strategy signified a tactical error, since it departed from the traditional Dutch trade line of not mixing politics with business.[14] Furthermore, the Company depended much on the trade of one product, sugar, whose price fluctuated on the market and allowed little profit. For years the shareholders received no profits and the Company ended up involved in the slave trade. The Company's objective was trade, for which it had to compete in distant lands with an expanding England and a Portugal in decline. To fulfill this objective it was endowed with very broad civil and military powers, as is indicated by the procedure used in the conquest of northeastern Brazil and the capture of Bahia and Olinda. The Company was able to undertake diplomatic negotiations and assume responsibilities of government in accordance with its own interests.

At the beginning of the seventeenth century, Holland and Belgium were the two most densely populated and urbanized countries of Europe. In fact, owing to its limited area, Holland was a country with a small population. This constituted a limitation to Dutch trade expansionist policy. Amsterdam was its principal city. In 1622 it had more than 100,000 inhabitants, a third of them immigrants or children of immigrants (Wilson 1968: 26). In 1650 it had 170,000 inhabitants (Burke 1956). In 1660 Leiden had 70,000 persons (Barbour 1966: 17). Haarlem had 40,000 inhabitants in 1600. Together with Rotterdam, Alkmaar, and Hoorn (commercial centers), Utrecht (a religious and university center), Delft and Groningen (university centers), and Brielle, the principal commercial center of Zeeland, they were the ten

[14]   On the activities of the West India Company, see Wilson (1968, especially Chapters 12 and 13) and Boxer (1957, especially Chapter 1, and 1966).

most important cities of Holland. Their origin, like that of the majority of Dutch cities, was medieval. Some, like Utrecht and Maastricht, had a Roman origin.

It is possible that around the twelfth or thirteenth century the distribution of Dutch urban centers was the same as in the fifteenth and sixteenth centuries, based on a selection of the best physical conditions of the soil, navigable ways, suitable topography, mining resources, and a location with defensive and political-administrative qualities. But Holland is a territory without high topographical features. In any event, because of flooding and land reclamation programs, the selection of comparatively high and permanent sites was of great importance. Moreover, since medieval times and even before, many Dutch cities were interconnected by networks of canals linking them with the great commercial rivers of Europe's interior and the maritime estuaries. Thus a city's future depended on its location. This meant that the value of land was very high. Due to the great need to construct canals for commerce, to drain lands and build containing dikes, and to carry out costly filling in and consolidation, it was necessary from a very early date to control unrestricted growth of cities and to impose certain regulatory measures (Burke 1956: 33).

Dutch cities were compact and orderly because of practical necessity. They were built in an orderly fashion because this was required by the design of the canals, the movement of transport barges, and the need to obtain maximum benefit from the land. The commercial advantages of a site were fundmental in the locating and growth of a city. The Dutch accepted the challenge of a coast with few natural refuges and a topography which had to be constantly improved and cared for. A lack of natural advantages did not restrict their choice. By means of dikes, canals and ports, roads and bridges, drainage and refilling programs, numerous sites were conditioned to permit the expansion of a city or the construction of a new one; that is, if the site favored commercial communications by land, river, or sea.

Almost all the town-planning principles – both theoretical and practical – accepted in Europe between the thirteenth and seventeenth centuries were represented in some manner in Holland. None had a very marked influence. The Dutch, an energetic people with a strong sense of cooperation, developed an original type of city, that which was best adapted to their technical possibilities, topography, and construction materials, as well as to the commercial, financial, and industrial role it was to play. At the end of the thirteenth century, for example, two *bastides* were built in Zeeland for purposes similar to those constructed in England, Wales, and the southwest of France. Neither the esthetic principles of the urban architecture of the Renaissance, nor the theories of ideal cities, nor the radial-concentric plan (with the exception of Coevorden, built in 1597), nor the total plan of the baroque period left their mark in Holland. Some exceptions exist: Willemstad, a small fortified city in 1583, had a system of ramparts with seven bulwarks which surrounded a heptagonal urban arrangement: it also had a principal avenue which culminated at a church located in the center of the square. These two basic principles of military engineering and Renaissance civil architecture were incorporated into a plan with zoning principles similar to those proposed by Renaissance theoreticians. The sense of general symmetry and layout of component parts was that favored by Renaissance architects. In Klundert the same principles were followed, except that a canal replaced the central avenue of Willemstad.[15]

Anyone who has spent some days in Leiden or Haarlem or has visited Alkmaar or Amsterdam, and has gone over them slowly, looking on a map for the process of their growth in time, will have noticed the following: near the original central nucleus (corresponding to a quite early period of their evolution), there are districts which are well ordered and without pretensions, displaying great architectural unity.

Just like other medieval European cities of the end of the fifteenth century, the Dutch added new districts when the pressure of population required it. Contrary to what happened in other regions, however, they did so in a well-ordered manner and sought to improve the integration of new districts with old ones. The decision to adopt a new expansion was carefully evaluated. It was not generally a matter of expansion over solid lands, but over lands which had to be prepared, drained, refilled, and then maintained. As part of those new districts served commercial purposes, they, like the old districts, also had to be provided with canals of an adequate depth. This type of city, where streets alternate with canals, or, more frequently, canals were bordered on each side by wide cobblestone streets, is called *grachtenstad*, literally, "canal city."

This principle had been used since the medieval period as, for example, in the center of Leiden; but its design was still irregular. During the fifteenth century and possibly even before, some cities designed extensions following the standard mentioned above; in addition, they were characterized by the lack of a principal center and by the absence of large unbuilt spaces, whether squares or streets. Land was very expensive and its use was maximized. Similarly, practical criteria were adopted for the use of the ground: commercial districts, according to the products they stored and their origin, were located near the port or along the principal or secondary canals; the hospital, arsenal, gunpowder store, and gallows in suitable sites;

[15]   See the plans in Burke's work (1956).

a broad esplanade near the port allowed the unloading of products, for which hoists were used. As Burke says, rarely did any of those extensions contain anything other than canals, streets, houses, warehouses, and workshops, and they lacked squares, unbuilt spaces, and main buildings.

Haarlem's expansion was planned in 1426, when the city had between 5,000 and 10,000 inhabitants; and again in 1576, in accordance with the principles which have been explained. In 1610 and again in 1659, regular expansions were designed in Leiden. This type of expansion was also used in Alkmaar, Gouda, and Amsterdam, "whose development in the beginning of the seventeenth century represents, in conception and implementation, the most audacious, extensive, and successful town planning design ever attempted in the country and undoubtedly, for that period, in the world" (Burke 1956: 141).

While the kingdoms and dukedoms of Europe built palaces which were out of proportion to the limited size of their capitals, the bourgeoisie of Amsterdam devoted themselves to creating "not an attractive palace but an attractive city" (Rasmussen 1951: 80). In Amsterdam the majority of the town-planning principles and architectural techniques in vogue in Holland during the sixteenth and seventeenth centuries were overturned.

The problem of the expansion of a city which broadly tripled its population between 1600 and 1650 raised formidable technical problems as well as problems of financial and human resources. The problem was faced by the city council in the sixteenth century. At the end of the century a program was initiated which permitted expansion from 200 to 805 hectares, through the construction of a number of radial canals interconnecting with three concentric canals surrounding the old part of the city, the latter formed by two blocks of constructions on either side of the canal of the Amstel River. The expansion, begun around 1610, included a defensive rampart with twenty-six bulwarks along the part unprotected by the river. Unlike the medieval section, the seventeenth-century expansion was carried out on the basis of parallel rows of streets and canals bordered by tree-lined streets. It provided the maximum regularity permitted by a radial-concentric scheme which had as its center the original shell. The residential districts of the bourgeoisie of Amsterdam can still be seen today. They are large, solid, comfortable houses without pretensions: "tall houses, narrow, and with narrow brick fronts; the doors are marked by ornamental architraves, with well-spaced windows decorated with motifs in the form of shells and the like. Only the upper half of the window openings were glazed; the rest were protected by means of shutters. The corners, keystones, and links between the walls were marked by natural stone..." (Burke 1956).

The Dutch builders carried that model of a city to other regions of Europe and to the territories they conquered in Asia and America, where they established cities as a base of operations. In Europe, "Gothenburg was planned and designed by Dutch engineers with canals and locks in the Dutch style" (Wilson 1968). In southeast Asia, they founded Batavia in 1619. Its construction, in spite of the thousands of kilometers separating it from Brazil and the Caribbean, was undertaken in accordance with the same principles, organization, and military discipline which characterized all operations of both the East and West India Companies.

Recife was the principal city constructed by the Dutch in what is today Latin America, although its control over the northeast region of Brazil was relatively brief. In Recife, as in Batavia and in the cities of Holland, there was an apparent indifference for the constructive qualities of the site: as long as the site had good access by land and sea and was easy to defend. By means of canals they ensured the draining of lands and transport of cargoes in Batavia and Recife.

Recife's urban design is orderly and exact, with streets alternating with canals and intersecting with each other at right angles. The city was bisected by a principal canal several times wider than the secondary canals. The site required the construction of piles to support the houses, which following Dutch tradition were of bricks, two and later three storeys high, with sloping roofs and narrow fronts, decorated with stepped gables. In short, cities without pretensions, but functional on the whole and in their separate elements, created for effective use. Those were the elements of Recife as well as of Batavia.

The difference of standards between the Dutch and Portuguese is observed from the beginning. A few kilometers to the north of the site of Pernambuco was Olinda; together with Salvador and Rio de Janeiro it was one of the three principal cities of Brazil in 1630. I have already referred to the location and urban features of Olinda. Here I wish to stress that Olinda was soon rejected by the Dutch because of different defensive criteria and its distance from the port. The natural port of Olinda was five kilometers to the south of the city, at the point where the Capibaribi and Biberibi come together at the end of a narrow sandbar. There the mill owners and merchants of Olinda had built warehouses for their products, and there were also some houses for their staff, customs officials, and fishermen. From the east a reef protected the mouth of the rivers, forming a good, natural, defendable port. The original nucleus of Recife grew rapidly and without any plan. It was a point for the loading and unloading of products which, by means of barges, were carried to the foot of the hill where Olinda was built.

Olinda was captured by the Dutch in 1630. A year later they burned Olinda and made the decision to establish a new city on Antonio Vaz, the island which faces the town of Recife in the west, protected by the reef and sandbar. With the influx of population from Olinda and the activity of the Dutch, Recife grew rapidly, to the point where the narrow features of the original site were insufficient to absorb the growth. Although the Dutch tried to remodel and defend Recife – by straightening some streets and surrounding it by a palisade – a more radical decision was necessary.

In 1636 Johan Maurits was appointed governor and captain-general. Within a short time of arriving, in January 1637, he settled on Antonio Vaz Island, where there were already some residents. He planned a new city in an area which, though swampy, had the triple advantage of closeness to the port, links with the mainland, and better defensive conditions. A plan of 1648 shows the three groupings: the irregular (almost radial) design of Olinda: the narrow, well-ordered development of Recife, hemmed in by the shape of the peninsula; and the new, orderly, strongly fortified plan of Mauritsstad, to which the city's civic center was moved.

But Mauritsstad was not a simple colonial station, just as Johan Maurits was not an ordinary colonial governor.[16] A member of the family of William of Orange, educated in Herborn, Basel, and Geneva, successful as a soldier in the Thirty Years' War, he displayed a tireless activity during the seven years of his governing. "During his stay in Brazil Johan Maurits gathered around him a carefully selected group of forty-six investigators, scientists, artists and artisans from Holland, each with his special functions and responsibilities" (Boxer 1957: 112). In Mauricia he had built an astronomical observatory (where Marcgraf carried out meteorological and astronomical observations), a zoo, and a botanical garden. In the north of Antonio Vaz Island he built his palace, the Castle of Vrijburg, the largest and most sumptuous building of Brazil at that time, which he surrounded carefully with gardens and terraces. In the west he built the palace of Boa Vista.

This was the city the Dutch endeavored to use for the conquest of the rich provinces of the south. It was a gigantic trade center, from which a humanist *gran señor* governed who combined the rare qualities of soldier, administrator and promoter of the arts and sciences. It was the city of merchants and soldiers which did not succeed in taking root in the land, in spite of Maurits's personal concern and affection for Brazil. It never became a center for colonization with long-term regional expansion.

[16] See the excellent chapter which Boxer devotes to Johan Maurits: (1957: 67–111, 112–158).

The interest of the Dutch in Curaçao was purely commercial. The small island without any raised parts was not suitable for agriculture. On the other hand, it was unsurpassably located for purposes of trading with the Spanish possessions of northern South America. The founding of Fort Amsterdam, today called Willemstad, dates from the 1630's. It was initially (and continued to be during the colonial period) a trade center, frequently for illicit trade. The site chosen was to the east of a narrow canal which permitted access to a natural port, Santa Ana Bay. The Dutch built an ordered city on a high piece of land. The design is rectilinear although, because of the requirements of the contours of the coast, it was necessary to adapt it to a trapezoidal shape. The city was strongly defended and surrounded, on the land side, by ramparts and bulwarks.

Although from the town-planning point of view Fort Amsterdam did not offer anything noteworthy, its constructors repeated the narrow, three-storey houses, with sloping roofs, strongly colored and decorated with baroque parapets which could be seen in Amsterdam or Haarlem. Following Dutch custom, merchants lived in the same building where they had their shop or warehouse. Even today one can see, facing the canal which gives access to the port, a row of eighteenth-century houses on which the above features are preserved.

In Paramaribo we again find the Dutch architecture, incorporating canals in the city's plan and using a simple rectilinear design modified by a bend of the Surinam River.

During the 1590's many signs appeared which indicated that Castile's economy was beginning to break up in the face of the imperial adventures of Phillip II (Elliot 1966: 281); but Philip II was a bureaucrat with good advisors and good credit, and Phillip III was not. Starting from the end of the sixteenth century, Spain's power began to decline. The first significant areas of the Spanish empire to become independent were, in fact, the Dutch provinces. The fundamental military defeats were against the French. The strongest religious rivalry was experienced from the English. Between 1625 and 1635, those three countries penetrated openly into the Caribbean.

Spain then concentrated on her principal islands. Fortifying Havana, San Juan, Santo Domingo, and the principal ports of the coast of Tierra Firme (Cartagena, Portobelo, and Veracruz), she sought to keep open the shipping lines between her colonies and the mother country. The fortification of those ports was part of a continental defense plan worked out and initiated in the time of Phillip II. At the same time, although without ceasing to recognize her rights over them, she abandoned the smaller islands and the western section of Hispaniola, which were less important than her other possessions.

By the middle of the seventeenth century, the English and French set up a plantation economy on those islands; while not achieving a great degree of efficiency, this did permit the prosperity of their diminished number of owners. They did not found any important cities. On the one hand, the rural economy did not justify them; on the other hand, none of the islands had the population and resources to maintain them. The absenteeism of planters was high and their interests took them away to live in their possessions (West and Augelli 1966: 95ff.).

Jamaica was the principal English colony in the Caribbean. In May 1655, when the army of Penn and Venables occupied the island, only one Spanish city (the present-day Spanish Town) and some scattered smaller groupings existed there. Nothing but the outline remains of the Spanish foundation. The English used it in their turn but, simultaneously, encouraged the development of a disordered group of houses at the end of the Palisadoes, a narrow sandbar which encircles Kingston Bay. Port Royal was the place where the bucca-neers sold the fruit of their assaults. It had the appearance of a camp, despite the fortifications built by the English between approximately 1675 and 1690. Its shape conformed to the land. It was formed of three wide radial streets which started from the dockyards, to the northeast of the populated center, cut by secondary lanes basically in the same layout shown by a plan of 1692 after the earthquake. After its destruction that year by the earthquake, and with piracy having declined in the Caribbean, it never recovered, although it continued to be inhabited. The English founded Kingston in 1692 or 1693. From the beginning it was a city planned in accordance with a design of parallel streets which formed rectangular blocks in a proportion of roughly 1:4 and 1:2, alternating in a north–south direction; the width of the blocks going east-west is the same. The plan which Jacques Bellin included in his *Atlas* shows the city in the 1750's (Bellin 1764: Plate 59 [Plate 58 represents Port Royal]). It is possibly the oldest plan known of Kingston and should reflect the city as it was originally designed.[17] In Bellin's time, the location of the Plaza de Armas appears eccentic; it is possible that a series of block rows were added to the east of the colony's center in the eighteenth century. The only *plaza* was square in shape and very large. In the center there was an enclosed fountain at the crossway of the two main axes of the city: Calle del Rey (N-S) and Calle de la Reina (E-W). But other streets opened into the square: two, not as wide, at each of its corners, and others, still narrower, at the north and south sides. These three differing street widths, suggesting their relative importance, are one of the few interesting features of the design. The only church faced

[17] It is the only plan of Kingston included in the collection of Kapp (1968).

the square on its south side and its front jutted out somewhat over the building lines on either side.

Kingston's plan is not of great originality and lacks esthetic interest. It is a functional design, easy to subdivide, and one which permitted movement. Only two elements deserve to be pointed out: the intentional adoption of streets of different widths, according to their importance, in accordance with a rectilinear design; and the proportions of the square and the central means of access. Both elements were new in America at that time and had not been used by the Spanish and Portuguese. What, then, could have been the origin of that plan?

The fire which almost completely destroyed London in 1666 gave rise to various proposals to reconstruct a commercial city of some 400,000 inhabitants. Until that time it had been characterized by its congestion and medieval design (Rasmussen 1937: 99–112). Three weeks after the fire, the King already had in his possession at least four proposals to reconstruct the city. They all had in common a rectilinear design, a checkerboard. Wren's and the various proposals of Evelyn included several diagonals cutting the gridiron. Evelyn's first two proposals included squares with means of access through the middle of the sides; moreover, in the memorandum Evelyn enclosed with his first proposal, he recommended giving different widths to the streets according to their importance. Hooke's proposal was possibly a gridiron with variants in the form of large squares accessible through the middle of the sides. The same distinction between the widths of the streets and the use of long and narrow blocks (ratio of 1:7) was included in Knight's proposal. This system of extended rectangular blocks had already been used in suburbs of London for speculative reasons.

None of these proposals was implemented, but they had their influence on London's building codes and in regulations concerned with the width of streets, the height of buldings, and construction systems.

Evelyn was well acquainted with the cities of Holland and Wren with those of France. It is interesting to speculate on the influence which the Dutch functionalism of the seventeenth century and the baroque ideas and gardening technique of the court of Louis XIV may have had on them. The ideas of both, as well as those of Hooke and Knight, were undoubtedly reported, though the municipal council of London must have decided against them. They reflected, in synthesis, a number of the town-planning ideas in vogue on the continent in the middle of the seventeenth century.

Kingston's plan, as far as I know, was not repeated in any other English foundation in America.

The colonization of Martinique and Guadelupe was started in 1635 by la Compagnie des Iles d'Amérique, created on Richelieu's initiative to replace the San Cristóbal Company. The two islands were the principal French colonies in America in the seventeenth century, as France's direct intervention in Haiti only began in 1697, as a consequence of the Treaty of Ryswick with Spain.

Martinique was the more important of the two and its economy, initially concentrated on the growing of cotton and tobacco, inclined toward sugar, starting in the mid-seventeenth century. Under Louis XIV and his Minister Colbert, France pursued a dubious policy; it aspired to the self-sufficiency of her colonies while restricting their trade with other American territories. Trade with France and the development of the French merchant marine spurred trade to the point where around 1680 some 300 ships were trading with the islands. The islands had an economy based on the plantation system and developed no cities of importance in the seventeenth century. At the end of the seventeenth century, Fort de France, founded in 1638, was the principal town of Martinique and its capital.[18] For thirty years it was a disordered group of houses, until Colbert ordered that it should be built in accordance with a special plan around 1668. A plan of the period even surpasses the size and elaboration of the fortifications of Port Royal, for a town of only eleven rectangular blocks of houses. Nine of the blocks, forming a gridiron pattern parallel to the line of the coast, appear to have constituted the original nucleus; the central block was left unbuilt, and in its center a church was built; two squares parallel to the previous northwest-southeast arrangement are slightly trapezoidal and may have been added later.[19]

CONCLUSIONS

A more detailed comparative analysis of town-planning theories and practices existing in each of the European countries which had colonies and founded cities in America would permit better understanding of the reasons why the types of cities finally constructed were adopted. This preliminary essay permits one to draw the following conclusions.:

1. Practical experiences count for more than theoretical ones in the adoption of the urban forms used by the Spanish, Portuguese, and

[18]   Saint Pierre was founded three years earlier in 1635. Lavedan attributes the plan of Fort de France to Nicolás-François de Blondel (Lavedan 1959: II, 480–482). Lavedan believes that the design of Fort de France resembles Rochefort's, which was designed by Blondel or Le Vau around 1667.
[19]   This concerns J. van Keulen's plan, of about 1700. Lavedan's description has some discrepancies *vis-à-vis* van Keulen's plan, the accuracy of which I have not been able to verify.

Dutch in the sixteenth and seventeenth centuries. English and French colonies preferred a more rural form of life and, except for Kingston, they did not attempt important urban settlements before 1700. The cities founded by the French in Haiti in the eighteenth century were adjusted to their experience in France.

2. In each case the experience brought by Europeans was only partially modified by local conditions. Therefore, the Spanish American, Portuguese Brazilian, Dutch, English, and French cities are easily distinguishable from each other. The Spanish were the only ones to attempt a model type. In the other cases, although adapted to principles and town-planning experience recognized in their countries, they faced problems with greater flexibility.

3. The civil architecture of those cities also reflected experience in the countries of origin: the Andalusian house in Spanish American cities, the bourgeois residence in Dutch cities, the "Georgian" country style in the rural regions of Jamaica, and so on for each country.

REFERENCES

ARGAN, GIULIO
   1969   *The renaissance city.* New York: George Braziller.
BARBOUR, VIOLET
   1966   *Capitalism in Amsterdam in the 17th century.* Ann Arbor, Mich.: University of Michigan Press.
BELLIN, JACQUES
   1764   *Petit atlas maritime,* volume one, Paris.
BERESFORD, MAURICE
   1967   *New towns of the middle ages.* London: Butterworth Press.
BOXER, C. R.
   1957   *The Dutch in Brazil.* Oxford: Clarendon Press.
   1966   *The Dutch seaborne empire.* New York: Alfred Knopf.
BRANDI, KARL
   1967   *The emperor Charles V.* London: Jonathan Cape.
BRAUN, GEORGIUS, FRANCISCO HOGENBERG
   1594   *Civitatis orbis terrarum.*
BURKE, GERALD L.
   1956   *The making of Dutch towns: a study of urban towns from the tenth to the seventeenth centuries.* London: Cleaver House.
CARR-SAUNDERS, M.
   1939   *Población mundial.* Mexico City.
CATANEO, PIETRO
   1572   *L'architettura de Pietro Cataneo.* Venice.
CERVERA, LUÍS
   1954   "La época de los austrias," in *Resumen del urbanismo en España.* Edited by L. Torres Balbas, et al. Madrid: Instituto de Estudios de Administración Local.
CORTESÃO, JAIME
   1964   "Teoria geográfica de formação dum estado no ocidente da penin-

sula," in *Os factores democráticos na formação de Portugal*. Lisbon: Portugalia.

DARMAS, DUARTE
1943   *Reprodução anotada do livro das fortalezas*. Edited by Jõao de Almeida. Lisbon: Imperio.

DE AZEVEDO, AROLDO
1956   *Vilas e cidades do Brasil colonial*. Boletín 28, Facultad de Filosofía, Ciencias y Letras. Universidad de São Paulo.

DE CASTRO, JOSUE
1954   *A cidade do Recife. Ensaio de geografía urbana*. Rio de Janeiro: Casa do Estudiante do Brasil.

DE GÓIS, DAMIÃO
1937   *Lisboa de quinhentos. Descrição de Lisboa*. Lisbon: Livraria Avelar Machado.

DE LA CROIX, HORST
1960   Military architecture and the radial city plan in sixteenth-century Italy. *Art Bulletin* 42 (4): 263–290.

ELLIOT, J. H.
1966   *Imperial Spain; 1469–1716*. New York: New American Library.

GIAVONNI, GUSTAVO
1931   *L'urbanistica dall'antichità ad oggi*. Milan.

GÓNGORA, MARIO
1962   *Los grupos de conquistadores en Tierra Firme (1509–1530). Fisonomía histórico-social de un tipo de conquista*. Santiago: Centro de Historia Colonial, Universidad de Chile.

GOULART REIS FILHO, NESTOR
1968   *Contribução ao estudo da evolução urbana do Brasil*. São Paulo: Livreira Pioneria.

GUARDA, GABRIEL
1965   Santo Tomás de Aquinas y las fuentes del urbanismo indiano. *Boletín de la Academia Chilena de la Historia* 33 (5–29).

GUTKIND, E. A.
1967   *Urban development in southern Europe: Spain and Portugal*. New York: The Free Press.

HARDOY, JORGE E.
1968   El modelo clásico de la ciudad colonial hispánoamericano. Un ensayo sobre la legislación urbana y la política urbana de España en América durante las primeras décadas del período colonial. *Instituto Di Tella Publicaciones*. Buenos Aires. Also published in *Actas y Memorias del 38° Congreso Internacional de Americanistas* 3, Stuttgart, 1968.

JARA, ÁLVARO, *editor*
1969   *Tierras nuevas*. Mexico City: El Colegio de México.

KAPP, KIT S.
1968   *The printed maps of Jamaica*. Jamaica: Bolivar Press.

LAVEDAN, HENRI
1959   *Histoire de l'urbanisme. Renaissance et temps modernes*. Edited by Henri Laurens. Paris.

MORISON, SAMUEL ELIOT
1942   *Admiral of the ocean sea. A life of Christopher Columbus*, volume one. Boston: Little, Brown.

PALM, ERWIN
1955   *Los monumentos arquitectónicos de La Española*, volume one. Universidad Autónoma de Santo Domingo.

PARRY, J. H.
  1949   *Europe and a wider world.* London.
  1964   *The age of reconnaissance.* New York: New American Library.
RASMUSSEN, STEEN EILER
  1937   "Two planning schemes in 1966," in *London: the unique city.*
         London: Jonathan Cape.
  1951   *Towns and buildings.* Cambridge, Mass.: Harvard University Press.
RICARD, ROBERT
  1950   La plaza mayor en España y en América española. *Estudios Geográficos* 11. Madrid.
SAMPAIO, THEODORO
  1949   *Historia da fundação da cidade da Salvador.* Bahia: Benedivita.
SANTOS SIMÕES, J. M.
  1943   *Tomar e a sua Judiaria.* Tomar.
TORRES BALBAS, L.
  1954   "La edad media," in *Resumen histórico del urbanismo en España.*
         Madrid: Instituto de Estudios de Administración Local.
VIEIRA DA SILVA, AUGUSTO
  1950   *Plantas topográficas de Lisboa.* Lisbon.
WEST, R. C., J. P. AUGELLI
  1966   *Middle America, its lands and people.* Englewood Cliffs, N.J.:
         Prentice-Hall.
WILSON, CHARLES
  1968   *The Dutch republic.* New York: McGraw-Hill.
ZEVI, BRUNO
  1960   *Biagio Rosetti, architetto ferrarese. Il primo urbanista moderno europeo.* Edited by Giulio Einaudi. Turin.

COLONIAL

Urban Preeminence and the Urban System in Colonial America

FRÉDÉRIC MAURO

It has been a long time since the historian Jaime Cortesão (1953) contrasted the Portuguese colonist – seaman and navigator but also sedentary farmer – with the Spanish colonist – jurist, soldier, horse-man, and stockbreeder, who ranged hundreds and thousands of kilometers inland but detested a sedentary life. The Portuguese was a colonist, the Spaniard a conquistador. The former sought the benefits of trade, the latter the prestige of power. The Portuguese settler was thus closer to the Anglo-Saxon, the Dutchman, and even the Frenchman than to the Spaniard. The originality of Spanish coloni-zation lay in the prime importance which was attached to the town in colonial Spain.

SPANISH AMERICA

I use the word "preeminence" with regard to the town or city in Spanish America to translate the Castilian *primacía*. This word implies both the primacy and the precedence of the town in the newly forming civilization. Why? How? These are questions that spring to mind before we can examine the consequences and effects of this primacy and precedence on the colonial urban system.

Origins and Aspects of Urban Preeminence

THE PENINSULAR HERITAGE. Over twenty years ago J. Bishko (1952) in his study of stockbreeding in America showed the importance of what he called the *peninsular background*. What applies to stockbreeding also applies to other aspects of Spanish civilization. In particular, the importance of towns in the Indies derived from the importance they had developed in the mother country. It is the paradox of the Mediterranean countries that these essentially rural economies, societies, and civilizations should have regarded the town as Paradise. These societies did, in fact, develop urban commerce and industry, but they suffered at the turn of the sixteenth century and again at the turn of the seventeenth century, and by the beginning of the eighteenth century they had become more rural than their Dutch or English counterparts. Their towns were the centers of rural regions, dominated by a rural aristocracy which maintained a residence and spent its money in them. This rural aristocracy encouraged baroque art, which has been contrasted with the classical art of the Northern urban civilizations (Mauro 1966: part three, ch. 3, and the works of Tapie and Francastel referred to therein).

The ideal life was considered to be that of the nobleman who lived off the land but was able to spend the winter in town, ensuring his prestige there and putting on a proud and generous front. This was especially easy if he owned herds of cattle and was not burdened with a more sedentary kind of farming. The "bourgeois betrayal" discussed by Fernand Braudel (1967) was not so much a return to the land or an abandonment of the town; it was rather a case of the bourgeois wanting to become a country squire while retaining his *pied à terre* or private house in town and with it his political influence. The preference for the town was so great that it even permeated rural life itself: Mediterranean peoples do not appreciate living in scattered dwellings. To see this, one has only to look at the countryside of southern Italy where the villages are more like towns with an already developed "urban" character. There are probably economic reasons for this clustering and it doubtless explains the Mediterranean man's fear of isolation, his love of the "street," and his legendary passion for talking and conversation.

THE CRUSADING SPIRIT. To this aspect of the *peninsular background* must be added another, linked to Spain's military and political history. For Spain, the Conquest of the New World was another Crusade, the continuation of the Reconquest of the Peninsula. It was therefore not unexpected that the forms of the two campaigns should become fused in the minds of Spaniards. By following Cortés and Pizarro they could remain faithful to the great ancestors, to Cid Campeador. Now what were the methods of the Reconquest? To capture enemy towns, to Hispanicize them, to set up military command posts and administration, and to make them the centers from which to Christianize the surrounding region. The interview between the Catholic monarchs and Christopher Columbus during the siege of Granada was prophetic from this point of view. Without realizing it, the discoverer of America was asking for the right to pursue throughout the world the task that Ferdinand and Isabella were completing in the Peninsula. Southern Spain had already had time to become a happy and remarkable blend of two urban Mediterranean civilizations – the Western and the Eastern – one of Greco-Roman origin and the other Eastern and Hellenistic, and therefore in its own way of Greek origin. The ancient idea that civilizing and colonizing mean building appears here more strongly than ever: why should it not have crossed the Atlantic?

But the American Conquest was, above all, the conquest of two great empires of the plateaus: the Aztec and the Inca. Now these were urban empires for rather different reasons than those underlying the "urban" nature of Spanish civilization. They both came about through conquests of peoples living in highly concentrated communities. Here the rugged terrain and the lack of wheels and draught animals meant that distances between the group members had to be as short as possible. Settlements developed in the midst of narrow fertile areas which were cultivated as much as possible. Urban craftsmanship provided the rest. Only messages and objects of great value were transported over long distances. As in a primitive society, community ties were very strong and further increased the intensity of urban life. Both the Northern and Southern empires were able to impose their rule only by constructing powerful capitals to head urban hierarchies linked to strong administrative hierarchies. Jorge Hardoy (1964) clearly illustrated the importance of this pre-Spanish urban system. Tenochtitlán and Cuzco were impressive capital cities in relation to the technology available at the time. Even in their construction these cities had some Roman or Egyptian features – whether one thinks of the pyramids or of those massive blocks used to build the Indian walls of Cuzco and the citadel towering above it.

Spanish urban civilization, after meeting and incorporating Arab urban civilization, then met and incorporated Indian urban civilization. In some cases it settled on its ruins, as in Mexico City and Cuzco and in others it built its own cities beside the ruins, as in Lima – a Spanish city surrounded by pre-Spanish cities. Everywhere it went it took over the system of interurban relations created by the Indians.

This accounts for the primacy and precedence of the town in the Spanish system in America. What the Spaniards did first during the Conquest was to go from one town to another – even if the towns they were heading for were sometimes imaginary – subduing them, setting up administrative and legal authorities, and providing links with the outside. It was also in the town that the major religious institutions (cathedrals, churches, and convents) were set up. The towns also quickly became rallying points for merchants and craftsmen who had come over from the Peninsula. A *modus vivendi* was established with the Indian population of the towns; some kind of segregation generally occurred, the Spanish town being set up adjacent to the Indian one but separate from it. In the case of Mexico City the Spanish town was laid out in the center of Tenochtitlán and depended on the surrounding Indian quarters for a whole range of services (domestics, provisions, craftsmen, retail trade, upkeep of the roads). The Spanish found it difficult to entirely prevent the Indians from settling in the Spanish quarter. This quarter had been built on the razed part of the Aztec capital and, in any case, the Spanish town was always referred to by the conquistador as the heir and the continuator of the Indian city. (For further information on this and the following paragraphs see Gibson [1968], Chevalier [1952], Hardoy [1968], and Guarda [this volume; also 1968].)

AGRARIAN INSTITUTION. The land tenure system of Spanish America also illustrates the primacy and precedence of the town. The *caballerías* (of about 105 acres) were distributed to civil servants or soldiers, town dwellers who very quickly slipped into habits of absenteeism. The same situation occurred with the *estancias* [farms or ranches], whether they were devoted primarily to cultivation or to livestock. Under the *encomienda* system, a whole village was generally entrusted to a Spaniard. The village's workers were placed at his disposal and he was expected in exchange to protect and evangelize the village, thus (ideally) "identifying his own interest with the preservation of that village." The village included what the Spaniards called a *cabecera* [principal settlement of a district] and dependencies known as *barrios, estancias,* or *sujetos.* Thus, on the lowest rung of the urban ladder a certain hierarchy of Indian origin was preserved and crystallized.

Just as the *encomienda* reinforced the trend towards absenteeism among the holders of *caballerías* or *estancias* the same applied to those who reaped the benefits of the *repartimiento forzoso* [forced distribution] after the suppression of the *encomienda.* Provided with free agricultural labor which they entrusted to overseers, the owners could lead a life of pleasure in the city similar to that which they had enjoyed in their native Castile or Aragon. In fact, it was due to this supply of labor that they were able to build their luxury town houses, particularly in Mexico City and Puebla. (Examples of these in Mexico City were the *casas viejas* and the *casas nuevas* of Cortés on the Zócalo and the private residences described in the dialogues of Cervantes de Salazar.)

While *encomiendas* were always given to private individuals, *repartimientos forzosos* could be bestowed on corporations, municipalities, religious orders, and craft guilds. This made possible and encouraged the building in the cities of churches and cathedrals, convents and monasteries, hospitals, almshouses and asylums, mints, and town halls. It further strengthened urban dominance and increased the share of investments channeled toward the cities. In Mexico City construction was carried out by workers subject to the *repartimiento* in both halves of the city – Tenochtitlán and Tlatelolco – and by people belonging to their *sujetos* or to other neighboring *cabeceras* such as Ixtapalapa. Similarly, in Puebla the Indians of Tlaxcala and Cholula were used. Vast roadworks were carried out under the *repartimiento:* for instance, the upkeep of the avenues, the construction of new ones, the conversion of the canals into streets, the paving of the streets, and the construction of bridges, aqueducts, and dams in Mexico City.

The replacement of the *encomienda* by the *repartimiento forzoso* took place at a time when the *caballerías* were being consolidated as *estancias de labor* [farms devoted to agriculture]. These two institutions – the *repartimiento* and the *estancia* – dominated the Mexican agrarian system from the middle of the sixteenth to the middle of the seventeenth century. They made it possible to supply large and expanding Spanish cities with wheat. These cities established *pósitos* or *alhóndigas* [storehouses and official grain markets].

In the seventeenth century, contemporary with the transformation of the *repartimiento* into free work and then into bond service for debts, the development of the *hacienda*, or large enclosed estate, was greatly influenced by the existence of the cities. As Charles Gibson explains, the town had a positive influence on the *hacienda* because it provided a market for the *hacienda's* produce; it also had a negative influence since the scarcity of capital and of possibilities to invest in the towns forced the population to invest in land which became increasingly expensive. The *hacenderos* [hacienda owners] tried, in spite of existing legislation, to seize the property of Indian communities and to take over Indian villages. Each time the *hacenderos* were successful they dealt a blow to native urbanism.

THE CHURCH. The Church played an important part in the development of the towns, not only because of the existence of its religious institutions or its large-scale ownership of property, but also because it was often responsible for altering the layout of the city and the customs of the native community by destroying Indian religious buildings and building new ones. It was often the Church that introduced Spanish municipal institutions to the Indian village or market town.

The Church achieved this mainly by grouping two or three Indian villages into a *congregación*, thereby setting an example for the *encomenderos* and for the government. It was in this way that the Church fulfilled its civilizing and evangelizing mission to primitive Californian communities in the eighteenth century. It gave Indian and other towns the names of saints in the Christian calendar. To console the Indians for not having many administrative or sacerdotal responsibilities, it created for them the duties of *mayordomo* and *sacristán* in the parishes. In the Spanish towns the building of churches and convents played a major role in the town plan. The festivals were based on the Christian calendar, and even the *cofradías* [brotherhoods grouping men of the same trade] had a religious orientation. As time went by the regular clergy tended to desert the countryside to join the laity in the towns.

The birth and evolution, or development, of urban centers in Spanish America during the colonial period can be largely explained, therefore, in terms of administrative, social, and religious factors. Economic factors played only a secondary part. This had important consequences for the development of the urban system.

The Effects of Urban Preeminence on the Urban System

The preeminence of the town which made it an instrument of conquest, of colonization, of prestige and social life, and even of evangelization and cultural development left a well-known mark on the urban tissue: the gridiron layout surrounding the *plaza mayor*. This grid, which was imported from Spain, gave the Spanish American cities a uniformity which was only rarely modified, as in Guanajuato, by features of the landscape. An effort was made, as far as possible, to choose large, flat sites. But the preeminence of the towns gave the urban network a special character which influenced both the position of the towns and the hierarchy among them. We must now distinguish between the different levels: local, regional and national.

LOCAL LEVEL. At this level, it was the Indian urban system which finally dominated, crystalized by the *encomienda*, though sometimes altered through the action of the Church which did not hesitate to regroup populations, or even to set up *reducciones* [settlements of Christianized Indians]. At the head of a group was the *cabecera* or chief town of the parish (*doctrina*), and dependent on it, the *sujetos*. Roads linked the *sujetos* to the *cabecera*, where the *padre* or *cura* [priest] was to be found and also a municipal organization which was based on the Spanish model imposed by the conquistadores, and consisted of a *cabildo* with an *alcalde* and *regidores*. These Indian magistrates, who were dependent on the provincial government, were elected by the Indians on a rota basis, a system which enabled each *sujeto* to take part in the life of the *cabecera*. The *congregaciones*, the groups organized by the Church, only served to reinforce this system, sometimes going so far as to suppress the *sujetos* for the benefit of the *cabecera*.

REGIONAL LEVEL. Here the main link was the chief town of the province where the governor lived. The governor was known as the *corregidor* or the *alcalde mayor*, depending on the size of this chief town (Haring 1947). In general, a traditional Indian market town was chosen, the capital of a pre-Aztec or pre-Inca people (Cholula, Tlaxcala, Chiclayo, Huancayo), or a crossroads, or some other point from which it would be easy to dominate and control the region administratively and militarily. From this center a number of roads, which were at least suitable for mules, led to each of the *cabeceras* in the district. Today these places are chief towns of provinces, departments, or states.

THE "NATIONAL" LEVEL. In territories which were later to become national states, there was generally a capital, the seat of an *audiencia* (Guadalajara, Quito, or Chuquisaca). Such cities quickly became important because of their administrative and judicial functions. The president of the *audiencia* acted as a governor-general and represented the viceroy. The district was called a *presidencia* and its capital was linked by pack roads to all the provincial chief towns which were subordinate to it. It was also frequently linked to the sea and communicated by sea or land with the next higher level – the capital of the viceroyalty or of the captaincy-general.

A very definite urban hierarchy beyond the *presidencia* is difficult to imagine. What more could a captaincy-general have than direct links with Seville and Madrid? And what more could a viceroyalty have than the advantages of a captaincy-general plus an impressive viceregal court, a larger population, and (generally) a university? However, a distinction must be made between the two great original viceroyalties and those created in the eighteenth century.

The original viceroyalties (Mexico City and Lima) did have an impressive viceregal court, a university, and even an Inquisition tribunal. They also played a vital role in the domination of Spanish America. They represented the two major directions of Spanish expansion from the American Mediterranean, their creation marking Spain's total triumph over the American continent. The Madrid government had made them the centers of two great independent empires which, if not rivals, were at least driven by a certain desire to outshine each other. Did the viceroyalty of Lima not finally acquire greater prestige than the viceroyalty of Mexico City and did it not become a promotion for the viceroy of Mexico City to be appointed to Lima? The quantity of silver supplied by each empire varied over time. It was a question of which was the richest. Economic life was governed by their joint monopoly. All of Mexico's trade was controlled by the great merchants of Mexico City, its foreign trade passing through the ports of Vera Cruz on the Atlantic and Acapulco on the Pacific, ports also controlled by these merchants. The silver produced by the Potosí mines had to pass through Lima and was loaded by the Indies fleet at Porto Bello. In practice, this trade "monopoly" gave both Mexico City and Lima privileged positions. The merchants of Lima effectively dominated the Chilean economy – as Gunder Frank (1967) has shown – and the economy of Upper Peru.

But the two empires broke up, for they were unable to maintain their monopoly for long. The setting up of captaincies-general and the appointment in Chile of a governor with the added powers of military captain-general demonstrate that the original hierarchy was difficult to maintain. The conversion of captaincy-general and of a mere *audiencia* into viceroyalties in the eighteenth century modified the urban hierarchy even further by linking a number of centers directly with Seville and by making official what had until then been only clandestine, such as the silver traffic from the Potosí to Buenos Aires. The creation of the system of intendants or administrators had little effect on this hierarchy and hence scarcely affected the urban system.

This general description of the urban system in the Indies must be modified to take into account a number of special factors which made it, in reality, more complex.

MINES. These led to the creation of an anarchic scattering of towns, generally in frontier areas: Chile, Potosí, northwestern Mexico. In Mexico, with the single exception of Taxco, the mining towns were strung along the limits of the wet and the dry regions, or, in other words, between the habitable parts and Chichimec country (and therefore along a frontier in the "Turnerian" sense of the word): San Luis Potosí, Guanajuato, Zacatecas, Durango, to mention only the largest towns. As advance posts they had a military aspect; journeys to Aztec country were made in convoys continually threatened by the *indios bravos* (Chaunu 1960). A certain amount of clustering took place around the larger towns which eventually became chief towns of provinces or intendancies. Their arrangement both in a line along an isohyetal curve and an important route enhanced their political and administrative role. Cerro Potosí, in Upper Peru, turned out after a few attempts to be the richest in ore. With the mercury mine at Huancavelica, which depended on Potosí, the following network was established: Huancavelica-Potosí-Lima-Porto Bello-Seville, with the clandestine variant: Huancavelica-Potosí-Buenos Aires-Lisbon. In Chile it was gold that was sought and found, in the south, on the Araucanian "frontier" of the Bío-Bío. Pedro de Valdivia set up towns in some places and forts in others but his successors had to abandon some of them. The northwestern Mexican system of advance posts was repeated again in southern Chile. At the local level the mine created a fairly anarchic and undefined urban habitat. Towns grew quickly because the men, entirely occupied with mining, had to rely on the outside for all their supplies. This further increased the importance of trade.

PORTS. While their location was primarily governed by the site (cf. Cortés's hesitation over the placing of Vera Cruz), they were also selected for their position on the routes between the Peninsula and the Spanish American capitals. First came the ports of the "American Mediterranean," especially those of the islands on which the nonrural population was concentrated. The market towns and communities in the interior organized themselves in relation to the ports. These ports were scattered along the outward and inward routes used by the Indies fleet. A definite hierarchy prevailed: after assembling off Dominica, the fleet waited till it reached Santo Domingo before dividing into two squadrons. The first sailed up the north coast of Venezuela and New Granada via Cartagena, and as far as Nombre de Dios; the second, the northern squadron, headed for Vera Cruz and supplied Mexico. On the return journey, the fleet reassembled at Santo Domingo before setting off in convoy for Seville. When Nombre de Dios became Porto Bello, the fleet divided into two at Dominica, and Santo Domingo was replaced by Havana as an assembly point (Chaunu 1960). A definite hierarchy therefore existed among the ports: first came Santo Domingo and Havana, followed by Nombre de Dios-Porto Bello and Vera Cruz as bridgeheads to the two Spanish empires. Then came the great ports of the captaincies-general, the largest being Cartagena which shared with the viceregal capitals, the privilege of having an Inquisition tribunal. Finally, there were the small provincial trading ports, the ports of the little islands or of the various areas of the coast. There was a similar hierarchy on the Pacific: Panama (commanding Callao-Lima and to a lesser extent Acapulco) and the Pacific ports commanded by Callao-Lima: Guayaquil, Trujillo, Pisco, Arica (where the ore arrived from Potosí), Valparaiso (which supplied Chile's wheat, tallow, and gold to Callao); finally, still further below, were the small local trading ports.

The Spaniards' first objective, therefore, was to conquer, build or rebuild towns. The network which these towns formed was essentially governed by political, administrative, and military considerations, modified somewhat by the necessity to mine gold and silver and to organize the sea traffic. With these exceptions, the Spanish American urban system was founded on choices that were politically but not economically rational.

PORTUGUESE AMERICA

Brazil never experienced the preeminence of the towns which characterized Spanish America. This was in the first place because of the latter's *peninsular background*. The Portuguese, like the Castilians, experienced the Reconquest over the Moors, but the land recovered from the Moslems was marginal land in which urban civilization was much less advanced. In fact, farming was more developed. Heirs to an essentially agricultural tradition, the Portuguese were also the inheritors of a tradition profoundly influenced by the ocean. Fish helped to provide a balanced diet for part of the population, and because of fishing the Portuguese produced the skillful and stubborn seamen who were to be found at the end of the Middle Ages in the Canary Islands, on the Guinea coast, in the Baltic, and on the coast of Newfoundland. They were the first to fish for cod in these areas and their influence can be seen in the toponymy.

The Portuguese nobles, although great landowners, did not have a real feudal system. Their first colonial empire was essentially maritime, centered on the Portuguese fleets and therefore on the sea or, where necessary, on the islands off the continents. Their Moroccan strongholds were a means of keeping the Arabs away from the coasts of Portugal. Situated on the coast, these fortresses depended entirely on food from the ocean and supplies brought to them from Lisbon or from the islands (Madeira, the Azores). These islands were primarily devoted to cultivation and trade. Once its forests had gone, Madeira was used for the cultivation, in succession, of wheat, sugarcane, and vines. Similar situations existed at Cape Verde and in the Gulf of Guinea (São Tomé and Principe), with the islands on one side and the continent (where one could only land cautiously) on the other. In the Indian Ocean, where the Portuguese East Indies Empire consisted of a string of trading stations – often on islands – which were linked together only by the fleet, the case was similar. It was therefore to be expected that the Portuguese territory in Brazil should initially have consisted of an archipelago where Portuguese seamen became farmers and where the alliance between a newly Christianized bourgeoisie and the younger sons of noble families had led to capitalist exploitation rather than to feudal occupation. Brazilwood, sugarcane, tobacco, and gold were exploited on a speculative and commercial basis (Mauro 1960: especially part one).

The Sixteenth Century

There is no question of the towns in colonial Brazil having played a dominant or a precedent role. At the beginning of the sixteenth century it was not a matter of conquering the country but of setting up modest *factorías* [commercial settlements] to exploit wood for making dyes. The *factorías* acted both as bridgeheads for exploring the interior and as fortresses from which to police the coast, which was infested with smugglers, pirates, and French corsairs. They were also used as depots for storing the wood felled with the help of tractable natives. Products arriving from Portugal for barter were also stored there. More like fortified camps than villages surrounded by palisades, they were supervised by *capitãos de vigia;* in fact, there were probably never more than half a dozen. Only two became urban centers – small ones in fact – which have survived until today: Igaraçu, on the coast of Pernambuco, which is today an historical relic, and Cabo Frio, which became a *cidade* [city] in the first quarter of the seventeenth century and is today a fashionable beach resort (de Azevedo 1956).

After the wood phase came the sugar phase. Santa Cruz was divided into great captaincies entrusted to donatory captains who distributed *sesmarias* or concessions. The new captaincies had trouble organizing themselves: soon the Portuguese government appointed a governor-general in Bahia, and set up an administration based on that of the mother country. However, urban settlement remained on a modest level for the following reasons:

1. When they arrived in Brazil, the Portuguese did not find a strong Indian civilization similar to that of the Aztec, the Maya, the Inca, or even the Chibcha: only primitive peoples, divided into more or less nomadic tribes which had, on the whole, remained in the Neolithic Age and were incapable of building monuments. The Portuguese therefore did not find urban centers to conquer, the subjugation of which would have given them immediate control.

2. The initial preoccupation of the Portuguese was to clear the forest and till the earth for cultivating sugarcane. The patriarchal organization of the sugar mill created a concentrated habitat with the clustering of executive personnel, slaves and their *senzalas* [slave quarters] around the *engenho de açucar* [sugar mill], and the *casa grande.* This was counter-balanced by the scattered farms of the

colonists working for the *senhor de engenho* [sugar plantation owner]. It is difficult to speak in terms of anything more than small *aldeamentos* [settlements] or *povoados* [villages], which the chapel of the *casa grande* nevertheless imbued with a parochial style of life. This was certainly a rural habitat, far more extensive than the urban habitat and prior to it.

3. The Indian *aldeas* created by the Jesuits or the Franciscans were large villages which were set apart from Portuguese settlements to avoid exploitation by the Portuguese. But, unlike the Jesuit *reducciones* of Paraguay, they were never very far from the coast. They were self-sufficient and took little part in urban commercial, administrative, or cultural networks.

The only urban settlements were thus the outlet ports of the *engenhos de açucar* and the points at which sugar was loaded for shipment to Europe. The donatory captains were probably entitled to set up *vilas* [towns], having "termo, juridição, liberdades e insignias de Vilas, segundo a forma e costime de meus Reinos." The first *vila* thus created was the *vila* of São Vicente in 1532 on the Paulista coast. The donatory Martin Alfonso de Sousa had the territory of the *vila* marked off and divided into lots, that is, distributed into *sesmarias*. He had a fort built, together with a town hall, a prison, a church, and a customs house; he appointed judges and gathered *homens bons* [men of standing] to conduct the election of the first municipal magistrates. This example was followed elsewhere and at the end of the sixteenth century there were fourteen *vilas* in Brazil. It was, in fact, often difficult to differentiate them from *povoados* or simple villages. As for the *cidades*, the cities or towns proper, only three are known to have existed in the sixteenth century and none of them was a *vila* or a *povoado* before. They were: (a) São Salvador da Bahia de Todos os Santos, founded by Tomé de Sousa in 1549; (b) São Sebastiao do Rio de Janeiro, founded in 1565 and formally established in 1567; and (c) Filipéia de Nossa Senhora das Neves, later called Paraíba and today João Pessoa, founded in 1585.

In fact, the donatories could not found cities because cities were considered to be heirs to the ancient Roman tradition of independent *municipia*, which could only be set up on allodial land. That is why, when Bahia was founded, the lands of the captaincy, which still belonged to the heirs of its donatory, had to be given back to the Crown. In any case, the three cities, like most of the *vilas*, were sea towns. The only exception was São Paulo de Piratininga, and this *vila* was only a few dozen kilometers from the sea. It was founded in 1554 and designated a *vila* in 1558; a road from São Paulo to the coast already existed before the arrival of the Portuguese.

Is it therefore even justified to speak of an urban system and of an

urban hierarchy? In any case, we can make a distinction between two
levels of organization:

REGIONAL LEVEL. The mills sent their sugar to storage warehouses (called *trapiches* in Bahia and *passos* in Recife) in a few big
ports. From there the sugar was shipped to Europe. These ports were
vilas or *cidades* and corresponded to the seats of the former
captaincies.

NATIONAL LEVEL. Here there were four great centers: São Salvador and Rio de Janeiro were important because of their political and
administrative functions; they both acted as seats of government, the
latter for a short period but the former up until the eighteenth century
when Rio again became the sole seat of government. However, this
political and administrative role was not very important during the
sixteenth century. The prestige of the other two large centers was
based on their economic role, Olinda-Recife, the town of Pernambuco,
and São Paulo, the capital of the south. These were the chief towns
of the two wealthiest captaincies in Brazil. All these centers were
linked together only by the sea. The hierarchy among them is difficult
to establish on the basis of available facts. At many points it has to
rest on purely theoretical considerations.

The Seventeenth Century

Sugar triumphed and with it the power of the *senhores de engenhos*.
But their profits were limited. The principal beneficiaries were the
merchants, the intermediaries with Europe. The towns were ruled by
alliances between the two groups, which were sometimes family
alliances. Religious institutions – convents, churches, schools, *mise-
ricordias* [charitable brotherhoods] – became more numerous. The
municipalities provided sumptuous religious festivals during which
myriads of candles were burned in chapels and in processions. Already
Bahia and Rio had a few baroque churches. Even before the arrival
of the Dutch in 1630, Olinda and its port Recife formed a regional urban
entity: Olinda was the residential quarter of the planters, while in the
port of Recife, sailors, prostitutes, and large- and small-scale trading
thrived.

As sugarcane cultivation penetrated into the interior, the urban
network grew. Small centers developed around the Bahia de Todos
os Santos, or within the Baixada Fluminense coastal plain. Similarly,
in Pernambuco the Capiberibe and Beriberibe Rivers were used to
penetrate the coastal plain. In the São Paulo region stockbreeding,

bandeiras [expeditions of exploration], pack roads, and cattle markets (at Sorocaba for example, which was equivalent to the Feira de Santana in the Bahia region) contributed to the development of a communications system; muledrivers' inns formed the nuclei of population centers.

After 1650 Bahia reached the summit of the Brazilian urban hierarchy. It had 8,000 white inhabitants as well as several thousand Negroes, Indians, mestizos, and mulattos. It had 2,000 houses and twelve churches. It benefited from an influx of immigrants, some of whom came from Portugal (before 1640 they had been fleeing from the authority of the King of Spain) and some from Dutch Brazil. The Dutch exported the sugar from Pernambuco directly to Holland, and the Portuguese, to make up for this loss and to meet the increasing demand from their merchants, set up new *engenhos* in the more southern captaincies.

Mauricia, the new and very modern Dutch quarter of Recife, was a masterpiece of town planning (Watjen 1921; Boxer 1957; Rodrigues and Ribeiro 1940; Gonsalves de Mello 1947) but did not contribute much to improving the urban system in the interior, which was constantly being eroded by dissidents faithful to the Portuguese government. Reorganization of the municipal administration began in 1638. In theory each municipal council was to include both Dutch and Portuguese members. The president of the municipality or *schout* headed a council consisting of five municipal magistrates in Olinda, Itamaraco, Parahyba, and of three in Igaraçu, Serinhaém, and Rio Grande. In each municipality three curators were appointed – two Portuguese and one Dutchman – to take care of the property of orphans. In the capital Mauricia, the municipal council included five Dutchmen and four Portuguese. It tended to encroach upon the prerogatives of the political council and even of the higher council of the colony. Although this organization did not have time to mature, the experiment is of interest to our examination of the urban system in colonial America: an essentially urban civilization such as that of the Dutch tried in vain to create an urban order in a basically rural colony. It failed, although it left some very deep traces behind.

It is also worth noting the difference between the Spanish and the Dutch urban mentalities. According to the Spanish the city was a social and political center in which large landowners congregated to compete with one another and which they tried to master in various ways. For the Dutch the city was a coalition of merchants wanting to make money by buying and selling the agricultural produce from the surrounding countryside and manufactured goods from the outside.

The Eighteenth Century

In the sixteenth and seventeenth centuries the Brazilian urban system resembled those parts of the Spanish American system based on ports and sea traffic. In the eighteenth century the exploitation of the mines added new features which were similar to certain characteristics of the urban systems in southern Chile, Potosí, and northwestern Mexico and, to a certain extent, to the combined characteristics of all three systems. According to Yves Leloup (1969), in Minas as elsewhere

...gold mining in its first stage, that is, the extraction of gold from river deposits by a multitude of goldpanners (*faiscadores*), could not lead to the creation of large, stable settlements but only to simple camps of miserable huts, covered in thatch or palm leaves. These were readily abandoned by an anarchic population to follow the miners in their migration as the river deposits were exhausted or as new, more promising discoveries were announced...There were probably a few craftsmen, one or two shops, and from time to time a priest [who] would come to celebrate Mass in a hut.... In Brazilian history this is what was called the *arraial* "*bandeirante*," taking over from the *pouso* or *rancharia*, a group of a few huts close to the maize, bean, or manioc fields which the *bandeirantes* [explorers and frontier adventurers] had sown during their exploration of the *sertão* [backlands] as a means of ensuring their subsistence; in general, they spent the rainy season there and went on their way during the dry season. The word *arraial* has a number of meanings in Portuguese: camp, country festival...and in today's Brazil, it is also applied to the humblest hamlet, a synonym of *lugarejo* (Leloup 1969: vol. 1, p. 109).

The presence of gold fixed the position of the *arraial*. In most cases this was at the bottom of a slope above the confluence of two rivers, but sheltered from the summer floods. If the alluvial gold was rapidly exhausted, the *arraial* disappeared as quickly as it was created. If it was not, the *arraial* stabilized itself and became a one-street village, with the chapel and the village square sited in a dominant position on a flat piece of ground and the houses built along a street which followed the slope of the river valley away from the chapel square.

Gradually individual exploitation by the *faiscadores* was replaced by large-scale prospecting organized by the major slave owners in order to better capitalize on the gold-bearing veins. The work had to be concentrated; this produced the mining *latifundium*, the equivalent of the rural *latifundium*. The *arraial*, where the bigger miners settled to be near their work, soon became a real town. The Portuguese trade and administration, in particular the tax authorities, "followed them there like leeches" (Leloup 1969: vol. 1, part three). In this way an administrative hierarchy developed. At its head was the *governador* or *capitão geral*, first in Mariana and then in Ouro Preto. (This office was created in 1720.) The level immediately subordinate was that of the *comarca*, a judicial district in which the *ouvidor-corregedor* was the representative of the governor and responsible for the smelting works. In each *vila* forming a district or *termo*, the "good men " – the notables – elected the *senado da câmara* [municipal council] which included a president, three *vereadores* [aldermen], and a prosecutor. The *vila* was also divided into several parishes or *freguesias*.

The division between the four *comarcas* was a simple one: the northwestern quarter (São Francisco basin) formed the Sabará *comarca*; the southwestern quarter, that is, the basin of the Rio Grande, formed the Rio das Mortes *comarca*, with its seat in the Vila de São João del Rei; the northeastern quarter formed the Serro *comarca* and finally, the southeastern quarter formed the *comarca* of the Vila Rica do Ouro Preto.

The *vilas* were nine in number: their creation, staggered in time, was related to their population, the wealth of their trade, the amount of income paid to the Crown, and the status of their inhabitants. The latter undertook to buld a church, a *câmara*, and a prison. In the seventeenth century the title of *cidade* was granted purely as an honor. Apart from the nine *vilas*, the rest of the captaincy was left to the great *sesmarias* owners.

It is difficult to establish a hierarchy among these towns with any certainty, because we do not know their population figures, except for Vila Rica which probably had 30,000 inhabitants. But one can use the number of their churches as a guide. Ouro Preto had thirteen churches; São João del Rei, Sabará, Serro, and Ribeirão do Carmo had at least five each and received the title of *cidade* in 1745; Mariana became the seat of the first bishopric; Minas Novas, Caeté, and Pitangui had three or four churches; São João del Rei was the last of the *vilas* from this point of view. The ghetto town of Diamantina should also be added. Until 1831 it remained administratively a mere *arraial* (Tejuco), so that the intendant could rule there as a master, but after 1750 it became the second largest town of Minas after Ouro Preto, having seven churches.

The Minas urban system, the first major system in the interior before São Paulo, can be entirely explained in terms of mining geography. The Minas urban system was very ill-defined, unlike the urban system of northwestern Mexico (stretched out along a southeast/northwest axis), and the Potosí urban system (concentrated around Potosí itself), with a few poor appendages including the distant mercury mining settlement at Huancavelica. The towns forming it were linked to one another by mule tracks. But these also linked the entire system with the outside world: Bahia, Rio, São Paulo and, through São Paulo, Sorocaba, the great cattle and mule market. Through Sorocaba the whole of southern Brazil as far as the Rio de la Plata converged on

Minas. Thus there existed an urban hierarchy with Rio at the top and on the next level the mining area system, with its lack of internal differentiation. The only hierarchy was political or religious and the religious center (Mariana) was distinct from the political center (Ouro Preto). In economic terms, all the towns of the mining area were more or less directly linked to the coastal centers and in particular to Rio. In the Brazilian urban hierarchy Bahia was on the same level as the mining area and Rio, but like Rio (although to a lesser extent) it controlled part of its supplies. Similarly, São Paulo, the mother of Minas, retained some power over her daughter. However, from the economic point of view it is possible that the real summit of the urban hierarchy was in fact the mining area system. Was it not the development "pole" for the whole of Brazil? The gold market is a sellers' market, unlike the sugar and coffee markets which are buyers' markets. He who produces the precious metal controls the others. The economic hierarchy in descending order was thus Minas, São Paulo, Rio, Bahia, perhaps Recife next, and then less important regional, economic centers. Here the preeminence was economic and the precedence (the great *fazendas de gado* [cattle ranches] developed later) was related to economic factors.[1]

We can see here what it is that separates the urban system of colonial Brazil from that of the nation state of Brazil with its emphasis on coffee and from that of the colonial and postcolonial Spanish American urban systems (one has only to think of the overwhelming role of Buenos Aires since the end of the nineteenth century) and also from those of French or English America.

If we look for parallels in North America, New England, like Virginia or Carolina, was first of all a farming colony in which the towns played only a secondary role – as ports or minor administrative or religious centers – and therefore much more like Brazil than Spanish America. The situation in French Canada was initially one in which pioneers settled along the banks of a river and cleared the land. Quebec and Montreal were administrative centers and also controlled access to the river. The spirit of the French colonization was doubtless more seigneurial than capitalist, but the people who emigrated to Canada were not Mediterraneans; they were Norman, Picard, or Breton peasants and they did not have the town and the street in their blood. Finally, as seamen and farmers they too were more like the Portuguese than like the Spanish.

---

[1] The urban hierarchy outlined above, of course, does not take into account the external dominant capitals such as Lisbon, Amsterdam, London, Seville, and Madrid. As the Potosí mining works very rapidly fell into the hands of the Lima *aviadores* [the outfitters], the situation there was different from that of Minas and probably from that of Mexico.

REFERENCES

BISHKO, C. J.
1952   The peninsular background of Latin American cattle ranching. *Hispanic American Historical Review* (November): 491–515.
BOXER, C. R.
1957   *The Dutch in Brazil.* Oxford: Clarendon Press.
BRAUDEL, FERNAND
1967   *La Méditerranée et le monde méditerranéen à l'époque de Philippe II,* part three (second edition). Paris: Colin.
CHAUNU, P.
1960   *Séville et l'Atlantique. Les structures.* Paris: Institut des Hautes Etudes de l'Amérique Latine.
CHEVALIER, FRANÇOIS
1952   *La formation du grand domaine au Mexique.* Paris: Travaux et Mémoires de l'Institut d'Ethnologie, volume fifty-six.
CORTESÃO, JAIME
1953   Articles published in *O Estado de São Paulo;* especially "O conquistador español o piloto cosmopolita de Portugal," *O Estado de São Paulo,* August 16.
DE AZEVEDO, AROLDO
1956   *Vilas e cidades do Brasil colonial, ensaio de geografia urbana retrospectiva.* São Paulo.
FRANK, ANDRÉ GUNDER
1967   *Capitalism and underdevelopment in Latin America.* New York: Monthly Review Press.
GIBSON, CHARLES
1968   "Spanish Indian institutions and colonial urbanism in New Spain," in *Actas y Memorias del 37° Congreso Internacional de Americanistas* 1: 225–260, Argentina, 1966. Buenos Aires.
GONSALVES DE MELLO, J. A.
1947   *Tempo dos Flamengos.* Rio de Janeiro.
GUARDA, GABRIEL
1968   "Influencia militar en las ciudades del reino de Chile," in *Actas y Memorias del 37° Congresso Internacional de Americanistas* 1, Argentina, 1966. Buenos Aires.
HARDOY, JORGE E.
1964   Centros ceremoniales y ciudades planeadas de la América precolombina. *Ciencia e Investigación* 20 (9): 287–404. September.
1968   "Escales y funciones urbanas en América Hispánica hacia el año 1600," in *Actas y Memorias del 37° Congresso Internacional de Americanistas* 1, Argentina, 1966. Buenos Aires.
HARING, C. H.
1947   *The Spanish empire in America.* New York: Oxford University Press.
LELOUP, YVES
1969   "Les villes du Minas," two volumes. Doctoral dissertation. Paris: Sorbonne.
MAURO, F.
1960   *Le Portugal et l'Atlantique 1570–1670. Etude économique* (especially part one). Paris.
1969   *Le XVIe siècle européen: aspects économiques.* Second edition. Paris. (Originally published in 1966.)

RODRIGUES, J. H., J. RIBEIRO
    1940 *Civilisação holandesa no Brasil.* São Paulo: Biblioteca pedagogica
          brasileira.
WATJEN, H.
    1921 *Das holländische Kolonialreich in Brasilien.* Berlin. (Portuguese
          translation in the Brasiliana Collection 123.)

The Colonial City as a Center for the Spread of Architectural and Pictorial Schools

GRAZIANO GASPARINI

Before coming to the substance of this article, I should give an explanation concerning its title. The organizers of the third symposium on "The urbanization process in Latin America from its origins to the present day," for which this article was originally prepared, considered it necessary to limit participation to a number of researchers who would agree to present papers only on the subjects requested of them. The purpose was to avoid the lack of cohesion and the superficiality noted in some papers of earlier symposiums (Mar del Plata 1966 and Stuttgart 1968). Consequently, the Symposium program was divided into eight sessions, each devoted to a defined subject. At the same time, each session was linked to the general theme. I was requested to write an article under the above title, presented at the session whose theme was "The cultural role of cities."

These introductory remarks are intended to demonstrate that I am not the author of the above title and that furthermore I do not underwrite the hypothesis which regards colonial cities as centers for the spread of schools of painting and architecture. It is an unquestionable fact that some colonial cities were indeed centers which attained a certain artistic level. In addition, they were responsible for the normative and imitative spread of standards. Nevertheless, this was a matter of a second-hand artistic level, one characteristic of cities receiving imported cultural patterns which are adapted for colonial use.

I disagree with the premise that only cities where free creative impulses and standards have been given and are being given may be considered as centers for the spread of culture. For example, Rome and Florence in the past and Paris, London, and New York in the present were and are the true centers for the spread of culture. On the other hand, American cities of the colonial period, because of the very fact that they were "colonial" and governed by a system which was inevitably one of dependence, had no opportunity to produce independent and native artistic expression. Even in colonial cities of considerable importance, such as Mexico City and Lima, artistic activities always derived from European models. Therefore what emanated from these colonial cities had a provincial artistic level which was to undergo subsequent changes whenever it was directed towards places on the periphery.

The colonial city, because it lacked the necessary cultural level, was consequently not a center of expansion which promoted the formation of artistic "schools." Instead, it was a center for the spread of selected forms and concepts which passed through strict controls before being considered suitable for diffusion. To my way of thinking, the definition of "school" may be applied to the collective artistic activity which is distinguished by acknowledging the influence of an exceptional artist, or where one can distinguish selected preferences of form and concept which have been accepted and shared within a selected area and period. In both cases the "school" derives its expression from a series of experiences and inquiries. In the case of colonial artistic expressions, I consider it more appropriate to use that of "regional expressions" rather than that of "schools." For when artistic activity is controlled by rules and principles which curb the development of individual and collective experiences, the awakening of critical processes and the search for direct experience are not possible.

It is true that in the pictorial production of some American regions a unifying and characteristic stamp has been achieved in the sum total of the works (for example, in the so-called "Cuzcan school"); but that peculiar regional similarity, rather than deriving from any principles of experience, derives from the acceptance – without any options – of the principles of authority. The development of individual and collective experiences implies a seeking, a rejection of the culture representing the system, and rebellion against the passive acceptance of designs which represent the principles of authority. It is clear that such conditions do not exist at the cultural level of the colony, because the authoritarian system imposes a structure of the world as revealed by the supreme spiritual authority – in this case the Church. This structure impedes any attempt to discover reality and truth in the development of experiences. Colonial thought, in fact, was controlled for the span of three centuries by the structure which was accepted *a priori* as the unchangeable structure of truth.

Moreover, the difference between social structures of colonial America and those of Europe helps one to understand the differences between the artistic expressions of both continents. It is not only because of its provincial nature that American art achieves a different specific character, but also because of the manner in which the ideas which are permitted to enter the New World are applied and how they act. In spite of possessing common ties, these ideas produce different attitudes. The simple reason is that the manner of channeling them is different, and consequently they also have a different effect on the man living in the colonial world. Hence the importance of the study of ideas which invest all artistic thought and the varying consequences they have on artistic production, when conditions appear which alter the apparently unified nature of these ideas.

In order to understand the cultural role of colonial cities more fully, it is indispensable to know the cultural level of the "colonizer." One must agree that the level of Spanish thought of the seventeenth century was not the most desirable for providing progressive influences for the colonies. Spain lived in its separate world where

...neither the values of intellectual logic and careful analysis which stood out in the French in their seventeenth century nor the earthly and concrete empiricism of the English replace in this world a magic wand which raises to heaven the extremely complex construction of its theology. The "kingdom of man" has started for the other nations of Europe; Spain still wants to maintain itself as the "kingdom of God" (Picón Salas 1965: 106).

Without being aware of the significance of the rise of European capitalism and possessing an economic structure dedicated to maintaining parasitic social categories, Spain, spurred on by religious fanaticism and

...convinced of her redeeming mission, presided over the cultural transformation of Latin America. In the process she made a deep impression on its outlines and also condemned it to backwardness. However, it is possible that without the prudent catechists who were responsible for it, Spain's expansion would not have had the assimilating force which allowed them to live together with others and confront very different peoples, on whom they imposed their cultural and religious stamp (Ribeyro 1969: 4).

"Salvationist" action may explain the justification Spain gives for her presence in America: the evangelistic mission directed to winning the Indians to the Catholic faith. This is no more than a simple rationalization for her activities in exploiting raw materials and manpower: actions which have not attracted the attention of historians of colonial art, and which scarcely have been taken into consideration when analyzing the profound impression they made on colonial society (and consequently on its cultural manifestations). It has an unreal ring to assert that "Christianity, Language, and Architecture are the three great legacies which Spain has left on that vast continent" (Chueca Goítia 1966: 242), when there is not even a mention of that other great legacy: that is, the situation of economic, social, and cultural backwardness which in the long run has caused the underdeveloped condition of Latin America. Socioanthropological studies have uncovered the component relationships of that society and have not hesitated to unveil the contrasting conditions of comfort and misery, of arbitrariness and subjection which constituted the way of life in those three centuries.

Interpretations of the art and architecture of that period, on the other hand, give the impression that "colonial art" was produced in a climate of serenity and well-being permitting the development of an artistic activity which was free, creative, autonomous, and almost unconnected with European influences. This position employs a traditional and self-serving historical methodology based on scholarship without content. It impedes a lasting and true understanding of cultural facts because it uses colonial art as a means of sublimation of that period. It is disturbing to note that this tendency also appears among some American historians who regard colonial art as an artistic expression independent of Spain, where this very same art is considered as an extension of Spanish artistic feeling and consequently is analyzed in terms of "Spanishness" and "invariables." Spanish historians have always tried to prove that Spanish architecture has a "unique nature," apart from the rest of Europe, because they consider that such "differences are constituted by the pure invariables which have appeared through the whole span of the history of Spanish architecture" (Bonet Correa and Villegas 1967: 36). In the same manner, colonial architecture has been interpreted as Spanish American or as a Spanish provincial extension. Angulo finds that Mexican baroque architecture is only "one manifestation more, albeit an important one, of Spanish baroque" (Fernández 1959: 263). The self-sufficient thesis of the stylistic and expressive autonomy of Spain suffers the same faults as that of Mexico when it tries to demonstrate "the Mexican nature" of its colonial art. In both cases the motivation of such theses is a pedantic nationalism which disfigures the truth.

Nor is it appropriate to analyze colonial architecture in terms of "invariables." The theory of invariants seeks to emphasize the elements of permanency rather than critically evaluating the elements of change. It analyzes the work of art which in its occurrence always remains the same and never the same thing. It has recourse to that "sameness" to prove that Latin American architecture is the same as that of Spain, and when it refers specifically to Spain, it is used to prove the persistence, self-sufficiency, and indifference of the Hispanic in the face of European architectural movements (Chueca Goítia 1968: 44 ff.). The thesis of the "insular condition" of Spain also serves to support the permanence of invariables (and quickly to skirt the more risky thesis of a retarded state and intellectual staticism which has its roots in the difficulty of eliminating acknowledgments to the traditional).

Invariables may be associated with the concept of the absence of a definition or typological grouping; they are not based on the creation of form but rather they derive from a series of models. The invariable concept is conditioned by an existing analogy of form and function; it is a plan deduced from a sum of formal variants – functional to a form – a common, basic function. Consequently, even when invariables proceed from experiences of forms which have been realized as artistic forms, they cancel the primary creative value because of the passive repetition. They have a limited interest for esthetics because they deal with a negative and deliberate phase which is linked to popular and traditional components. Moreover, with invariables there are associated affinities, repetitions, and common, visually identifiable features; these are nonproblematic matters which bring together more general features instead of revealing unique and differential features.

The capital cities of colonial America, as Kubler has shown (1964: 81), belong more to the rank of regional capitals than to the rank of capitals in which power is concentrated, since they were subject to orders from Europe. Although "internal organization and functions became American and colonial rather than European " (Kubler 1964: 81) and " in practical aspects they acted as true metropolitan centers, with concentrations of power which were almost autonomous and with powers of decision" (Kubler 1964: 81), nonetheless, in the cultural field, they never departed from European influences and antecedents. The fact that colonial capital cities were subject to foreign political orders and cultural patterns permits one to assert that the American colonies, by their very condition of being colonies, did not have true capitals. When it is said that Mexico City and Lima were capitals of the viceroyalty, that qualification must be interpreted in a symbolic sense, limited to a merely administrative territorial division. For if by capital one understands the seat of power, it is clear that the capital of the Spanish possessions in America was Madrid. Architecture has always reflected the supremacy and possibilities of authority through its monuments. Now, the size of the principal square of Mexico, Zócalo, is what produces the greatest feeling of the presence and strength of authority; nevertheless, comparison with the European palaces of the seventeenth century permits a glimpse of the fact that, besides being the capital of Mexico, the seat of the *controlling power* is at the same time the seat of the *power controlled* from the European capital. The palaces of America are built on a *human scale*, constituted by administrators, never by kings and princes. Viceroys and governors occupy very important positions in the colonial bureaucracy; nevertheless, they continue to belong to the category of those who are "in the King's service" and remain in this position as long as the king considers them suitable. To spend large sums on the building of palaces on American territory would imply in the end a reduction of revenue in the royal coffers. The palace of the viceroy in Mexico is a remarkable construction which, however, remains modest alongside the residences of any elector prince of southern Germany.

Religious architecture, on the other hand, enjoys special privileges because its buildings (1) must demonstrate the authority reconquered by the Counter-Reformation Church; (2) visualize the triumph of the Catholic religion over pre-Columbian idolatrous religions; and (3) actively maintain the evangelizing and teaching work among the native population, while illuminating it with the exuberant opulence of gilded altarpieces. In addition, the fortunes accumulated by the Church allow the carrying out of a prodigious constructive activity which is easily justified by spiritual requirements and the "dignity of worship."

The design of the colonial capital cities has nothing to do with local traditions or with the persistence of pre-Columbian town-planning concepts. Leaving aside exceptional cases of adaptation, as in Cuzco and Cholula, the monotonous form of the gridiron plan, imported from Europe, acquires American characteristics, owing to the persistent repetition of the design in almost all foundations. The gridiron plan appears in American cities from the first foundations and progresses with the regulating norms which Spanish legists dictate for urban design. The laws of the Indies sum up the principles of an experience which has already been carried out, and they are expressed in a language which has its origins in theoretical sources (for example, the treatise of Vegecio, the *De regimine principum* of Saint Thomas, the *Crestia* of the Catalan Eximenic, treatises by Alberti and Vitrubio, etc.).

I believe that no essential difference exists between the opinions of those who interpret the gridiron plan as a classical inheritance and those who see in it the application of *modern* norms, because the two concepts have a relationship of continuity and persistence between them which, while becoming rather lethargic at times, has never completely disappeared from Western culture. This involves a concept, affirmed in the Classical Period, which is maintained alive in the sleepy ideas of the Middle Ages, in spite of very few experiences of it. The Renaissance culture brings this concept back to life and modernizes it, because it finds embodied in it that desire for order and control of reason which is identified with Renaissance culture. This modernism, therefore, rather than representing the putting into practice of new and original ideas, derives rather from ideas which once again are in force. The acceptance of the design and its invariable repetition on American soil contribute to its improvement.

The definition of "school" customarily has been more related to pictorial activities than to architectural ones. In the concrete case of colonial America, this definition has been used to identify the collective pictorial production of some regional centers, but I have not found any effort to point out the regional similarity of architectural works. Thus, while a "Cuzcan school" of painting is accepted, the term "Cuzcan style" has been applied to architectural expressions of the same region which acknowledge an evident influence of Cuzcan models. The so-called "schools" of colonial painting should not be interpreted as creative centers which are differentiated from other routine pictorial production. Differences exist, but they are not significant differences. Pictures painted in Mexico in the eighteenth century have a stamp which distinguishes them from those painted in Cuzco in the same period. But they are only different because they involve two picture-producing centers with few contacts with each other, each one very active, and which in addition to themes which received preference in the region also repeat the manner of representing them.

This similarity in production permits the formation of a regional or local expression which undoubtedly has a family air about it when it belongs to the same "school" and which is therefore different if compared with the production of the other. In the workshops of Cuzco and Quito, painted fabrics are traded by linear length (in amounts exceeding a hundred lengths) and in accordance with the promise to deliver them in a few months. In Cuzco "a Father Nolasco and a Mauricio García, in 1754, arrived at an understanding by public deed to deliver 435 large strips of cloth within a period of seven months" (Guarda n.d.). Such facts allow us to understand today the quantitative rather than qualitative level of those works and the instrumental nature of the propaganda function achieved by painting in the service of the Church. Naturally, all that frantic production of little artistic value maintains a "Cuzcan" regional character when it is made in Cuzco or Quitan if it is produced in Quito.

When one is dealing with the "Cuzcan school," therefore, it should be seen under that name "without any distinction as to the number of paintings which have been produced in the Inca city from the arrival of the Spanish to the years of Independence" (de Mesa and Guisbert 1962). It should not be regarded as the expression of a local sentiment developing in a free manner and based on principles of experience and inquiry. The same standard may be applied to other schools which, although invested with that regional difference, have in common the subject, directors, controls, mass production, and, above all, the artisanal rather than artistic level of everything which is produced. The name of "Cuzcan school" is only justified to locate geographically, in any part of America, a production which is more quantitative than qualitative. At no time was it given that creative impulse which would have managed to link it to reality and have allowed it to withdraw from the norms which were imposed.

Diego Quispe Tito, an Indian by race, must be ignorant of reality, and he stands out according to de Mesa "for having a talent for producing perfect Flemish paintings" (de Mesa and Guisbert 1962: 94). Strictly speaking, this assertion demonstrates the divorced situation existing between the artist and the world surrounding him. He leads a life of activities which appear to be indifferent not only to the problems of his time, but remote from the atmosphere and countryside in which he moves and the society of which he forms a part. As Sebastián Salazar Bondy has very well pointed out, "in colonial art were lacking the creative will and the social cast which this imparts to great works; and lacking that desire or that stamp, there was, in fact, no creation. All was – at times beautifully, it must be added – conformity, repetition, and movement, into which occasionally the candor of a native blew an exceptional breath of personality" (Salazar Bondy 1964).

The cultural activities of colonial America have a clearly directed orientation. In painting, these controls impose the representation of religious scenes because insistence on the religious theme constitutes a valid instrument of evangelization. In fact, Spain takes as her own the mission of converting unbelievers, for which purpose she uses all manifestations and expressions as means of winning them over. For that matter, where are her actions any more than a rationalization tending to justify a colonization process which considers all means valid for the purpose of imposing Catholicism? As a nation which for centuries has had "nonbelievers" on her own soil and which has managed to expel them by the sword and by faith and has established her strength through fervent religious unity, it is understandable that she should feel herself called to undertake new evangelizing missions of a salvationist nature. The conquest of America, which coincides with the expulsion of the Muslims from Spain, is the pretext which ratifies the vocation, and Spain takes on the obligation, according to Unamuno, of "coercing Christians." That is the reason why

...from the first moment, colonial art is surrounded by prohibitions. Both access to truth and escape by the road of phantasy are forbidden; or, to put it better: the role of art as producing a verisimilitude which exceeds reality is replaced by the obligation to represent a truth considered as absolute: even more, its role is reduced to copying or varying such obligatory representations . . . Abroad, colonial authority has used art to organize perception of the world, diverting the eye from reality by every means open to it. Not only are the themes of cultic art, mythology, and mythological nudity excluded, for pedagogical reasons, but obstacles are also placed in the way (until very late in the eighteenth century) of the representation of immediate reality: the landscape and the Indian. They are subjects which lie in the shadow of an official taboo, and, even worse, an unofficial one. All critical observation, all discussion of reality, all penetration of the eye under the surface is undesired (Palm 1966: 37).

One should not be surprised that these opinions of Palm are not shared by some Latin American historians and art critics who, pointing out the existence of the few paintings of landscapes, battles, and views of cities, try to refute the predominant religious theme of colonial painting. Gabriel Guarda has verified the existence of a nude pagan in the painting of Doña Teresa de Sotomayor, painted in 1662 in Concepción. He suggests that "although even today it is an isolated testimony, it would contribute to giving the lie to that too dogmatic opinion on the exclusively religious limitation of the pictorial catalog of the period" (Guarda n.d.). Attempts to refute the essentially religious theme of colonial painting by pointing out the (extremely) limited existence of other subjects remind one in this case of the well-known exceptions which prove the rule.

Another argument which explains the lack of creativity in colonial painting, in addition to the imposition of the religious theme, is the fact that a large part of the representation of that subject is copied from European prints. That is why "reference prints" played a preponderant role in colonial painting. Today many of those which served as models are known, and the number which are unknown must be even greater. The print arrives with the Conquest and in its first years of American life it preserves its black and white character when it is reproduced. Then it passes from the wall to cloth, color is introduced, and production of epidemic proportions commences in order to meet the great demand for religious subjects, from prints by Rubens to those by anonymous artists: everything serves as a model and is transformed in the "American schools." Even Dürer's rhinoceros makes its unexpected appearance in Tunja.

One must point out, in addition, that not only are the subjects controlled but moreover the expressive resources used by religious art are directed to acting on the masses. In the long run, art is a technique of persuasion, and the religious theme utilizes a repertoire which is basically directed to act, with persuasive intent, on the sensibility of the believer. The practical need for visual proof is intended to become a part of the psychology of the faithful through images; so it is that religious painting lends itself to publication and repetition in order to become one of the most persuasive inducements to devotion.

The cultural level of subordination which is characteristic of colonial America imprints the inevitable condition of provincial manifestations on its architecture. The phenomenon of provincialization arises from the derivation, submission, imitation, and differentiation of the activities issuing from the centers of primary creative development. In America the same aspects of provincialization are produced which – leaving aside local variants which are at times rich in their originality – have appeared and do appear in all peripheral cultural expressions. The concept of colonial art is inevitably linked with provincialism; in the case of America, this provincialization is established by its condition as a recipient region in relation to great centers of religious and cultural influence. Although colonial architecture is an essentially repetitive activity, the sum of the various regional expressions and the contributions of distinct origin establish an expressive totality which attains a specific and unitary character. The profusion of distinct contributions is not integrated into a chronological, geographical, or sociological order. It involves a variability which has facilitated divided analyses instead of capturing the unitary significance of that variability. Differences on the level of regional expressions are unquestionable, but the provincial character is unitary. Consequently, the "unity of diversities" permits the formulating of a theoretical model which allows an understanding of the phenomenon.

Among the various cultural areas of colonial America, it is possible to point to the presence of similar elements for all of them and, in turn, to the presence of exclusive elements for specified regions. For example, while Solomon's column appears throughout Hispanic America, the pyramidal pilaster is an epidemic peculiarity in New Spain and a rarity in South America. Cupolas on tambours or octagonal bases are also persistently repeated in New Spain, while the circular form predominates in South America. Decorated façades generally attain a more pronounced exuberance in Mexico and a very different character from those of South America, where one finds greater parsimony in decorative enthusiasm and greater inclination for classical forms. It is in peripheral examples where one notes a greater similarity and a more unitary level of expression: the popular type of monument of the Arequipa-Collao region does not differ substantially from that of Cajamarca, Guatemala, or various places in Mexico. In all those manifestations, in spite of distances and differences, one breathes the same family air: the same language, primitive and characteristic of places which are far removed from the most notable artistic centers.

The reasons for the differences between New Spain and South America have their origins in cultural contacts with sources of different origins and in the gradual degree of reelaborating the forms which have been received. South America receives non-Iberian contributions to a larger degree than New Spain. The latter, on the contrary, retain more intense contacts with the mother country, and the presence of Spanish artists such as Gerónimo de Balbás and Lorenzo Rodríguez facilitates, in the eighteenth century, the spread and reworking of the forms introduced by them.

Foster has pointed out how preference in the acceptance of some forms can exclude the acceptance of others, to such an extent that the origin of an imported and accepted form may be decisive in the formal character of subsequent activities (Foster 1960). As a result, the regional expression of an area acknowledges differences when it is compared with another, because in each the preferential acceptance of characteristics considered as standard is revealed. The repetition and spread of that model in the region of its influence, although it may undergo inevitable changes derived from reinterpretation and local contributions, never loses its relation to the original formal idea: it makes its presence felt in the region and establishes the formal similarities which contribute to connoting common features of regional expression. The towers of the cathedral of Cuzco become a regional model for more than a century, even beyond Lake Titicaca; the "planiform" decoration allows its influence to be felt from Arequipa to distant Potosí; the classical models of Quito have repercussions as far as Pasto, Popayán, and Cali; village plaster ornaments also invade the region, and the works of Gerónimo de Balbás and Lorenzo Rodríguez are the models which encourage the alteration of altarpieces with pyramidal pilasters and the exuberance of altarpiece-like façades. Decentralization, distance, and the lack of contacts between one zone of influence and another, furthermore, facilitate the formation of regional expressions.

What it comes down to is that American regional expressions are the consequence of a process of internal transmissions within limited areas; they are expressed by derivative formal variants of models which receive priority of acceptance. It is essential to point out that they are produced with the subsequent acceptance of formal elements originally appearing in major urban centers and monuments considered as models which were therefore initiators of the formal sequence.

It is clear that architectural types transmitted receive a greater formal comprehension in the important urban centers, since it is there where the most expert artists and the best qualified labor are found. On the other hand, in their successive spread towards peripheral regions, they pass through dissimilar processes of transformation: simplification, exaggeration, incomprehension of form, addition of

local elements blended with elements disfigured due to deficient interpretation and inexpert, coarse execution, etc. The problem of indigenous labor does not constitute a factor of change in colonial
architecture, and differences which have been attributed to contributions of "indigenous sensibility" are no more than alterations and
deformations of the reelaboration process of imported forms and
concepts. At the artisan's level, indigenous labor is expressed with
unequal degrees of ability: from works of great clumsiness to those
which reveal a mastery of the profession which is in no way inferior
to that of European labor.

This is not the time to come back to a discussion on the depreciated
definition of "mestizo architecture" or the unhappier one of "mestizo
style." The discredit attached to them prevents taking them into
consideration. Nevertheless, I deem it appropriate to express my
opinion concerning the participation of the so-called "indigenous
sensibility" in colonial art, since very often this sensibility is associated with manifestations of "mestizo art" for the purpose of emphasizing the distinctive character of works considered as the product
of that sensibility. It should be explained that in almost every case
one is dealing with a directed contribution which passively carries out,
with greater or lesser ability, systems of construction and concepts
of form which have been imposed by the dominant culture. The great
native contribution which permitted the carrying out of that enormous
construction activity is, when one comes down to it, manpower.

When an Indian reveals artistic aptitude, this is taken advantage of
to increase production; rather than appealing to his sensibility and
freedom of expression, his dexterity and low cost are used. Indigenous
artists who act within colonial society are not recognized as inventors
but as "executors." Their works, rather than expressing sentiments
backed by creative impulses, are limited to reproducing and recom-
bining imported motifs. At times, in areas with a great density of native
population, one achieves a unitary stamp in regional expression and
an esthetic similarity in the sum total of works. It is a group sensibility,
proper to the executors of a specified region, which frequently acknowledges the rudimentary skill of the labor. Nevertheless, what is
most evident in those works is, repeating Palm, the mental distance
which occurs between the model and its reproduction. The low degree
of skill and lack of workmanship manifest in the majority of the works
by "native hands," is rudimentary due to immaturity rather than to
inability. And, in this case, the immaturity must be considered as a
consequence of the cultural patterns of the colonial system.

When a native artist or mestizo masters the profession of artistic
activity, the bond between his native "sensibility" and his artistic
purposefulness is broken. A clear example of this is provided by the

three Cuzcan churches of the end of the seventeenth century: San Sebastián with its altarpiece-like façade; San Pedro, derived from experiments which appeared in the cathedral and in the church of the Jesuits; Belén, whose portal revives (by increasing) the effect of the scarab applied around 1651 on the lateral portal of the San Francisco Convent. These three examples adopt the design of the altarpiece façade which stands out among the unadorned surfaces of the lower parts of the towers; the prototype is the cathedral and its influence is also found in the design of the groupings of bells. The names of the "Indian architects" Manuel de Sahuaraura and Juan Tomás Tuyuru Tupac are linked to the three churches; Tuyuru Tupac designed San Pedro with one eye set on the cathedral, from which he copied the portal, and the other on the church of the Jesuits, from which he repeats the chapels between the interior abutments. The presence not only of manpower but also of native "intellect" is a clear proof that the supposed "native sensibility" is not manifested in these cases; on the other hand, it confirms the utilization of the knowledge and skill of the Indian artist, while the certainty exists that his artistic purposefulness is completely European. Nothing suggests indigenous creation in these works: the race does not alter the European architectural purpose for the Indian artist. Moreover, the more inadequate his skills and rough his execution is, the more "mestizo" will be the result of the work.

The homogeneity of "mestizo architecture" and "popular architecture" is of a character common to all peripheral manifestations. In spite of departures in artistic expressions due to regional variations, these departures do not manage to disengage from the style which is imprinted on all colonial manifestations by contact with the dominant culture. Ultimately, the differences are not essential and always concern manifestations of "minor architecture" which at a later date repeat formal and iconographic designs transmitted from larger centers. They never go beyond the level of local expression.

I share the opinion of my Peruvian friend Silva Santisteban that "to revive the concept of "mestizo" as an ideology in order to attempt to explain the origin and the social and cultural personality of Peru is to cling to the colonial myth. The idea of "mestizoism" has traditionally been racist, full of prejudices and domination; to present it as a saving formula, the key to the integration and development of all that is Peruvian, is not only to "ridicule the dead myth of the races but to disregard truth itself" (Silva Santisteban 1969).

REFERENCES

BONET CORREA, ANTONIO, VÍCTOR MANUEL VILLEGAS
  1967   *El barroco en España y en México.* Guanajuato: Universidad de Guanajuato.
CHUECA GOÍTIA, FERNANDO
  1966   Invariante en la arquitectura hispanoamericana. *Revista de Occidente* 38 (May). Madrid.
  1968   El método de los invariantes. *Boletín del Centro de Investigaciones Históricas y Estéticas* 9 (April). Caracas: Universidad Central de Venezuela.
DE MESA, JOSÉ, TERESA GUISBERT
  1962   *Historia de la pintura cuzqueña.* Instituto de Arte Americano e Investigaciones Estéticas. Buenos Aires.
FERNÁNDEZ, JUSTINO
  1959   *El retablo de los reyes.* Mexico City: Instituto de Investigaciones Estéticas, UNAM.
FOSTER, GEORGE
  1960   *Culture and conquest.* Chicago.
GUARDA, GABRIEL, O.S.B.
  n.d.   *En torno a la pintura "colonial" en Chile.* Supplement of *Boletín de la Academia Chilena de la Historia.*
KUBLER, GEORGE
  1964   Ciudades y cultura en el período colonial de América Latina. *Boletín del Centro de Investigaciones Históricas y Estéticas* 1 (January). Caracas: Universidad Central de Venezuela.
PALM, ERWIN WALTER
  1966   El arte del Nuevo Mundo después de la conquista española. *Boletín del Centro de Investigaciones Históricas y Estéticas* 4 (January). Caracas: Universidad Central de Venezuela.
PICÓN SALAS, MARIANO
  1965   *De la conquista a la Independencia.* Mexico City: Fondo de Cultura Económica.
RIBEYRO, DARCY
  1969   *Las Américas y la civilización.* Buenos Aires: Centro Editor de América Latina.
SALAZAR BONDY, SEBASTIÁN
  1964   *Lima la horrible.* Mexico City: ERA.
SILVA SANTISTEBAN, FERNANDO
  1969   El mito del mestizaje. *Aportes* 14 (October). Paris.

Cities and Society in Nineteenth-Century Latin America: The Illustrative Case of Brazil

RICHARD M. MORSE

COMPARATIVE PERSPECTIVES

The historian who deals comprehensively with Latin America must decide whether to treat Spanish and Portuguese America independently or integrally. Urban history, which has enjoyed little attention as a comparative Latin American topic, seems to invite disjunctive treatment. Buarque de Hollanda (1956: Chapter IV) contrasts the painstaking geometric planning of the Spanish highland towns with the spontaneity and irregularity of the Portuguese coastal settlements, a distinction also developed by Ricard (1947: 438) and Smith (1955) while Boxer (1965: 17, 147–149) notes the "striking contrast" between the *cabildo*, with its hereditary offices and close supervision by the *audiencia*, and the *câmara*, with its tradition of popular participation and local autonomy.

Although important differences obviously derive from the respective cultural legacies and practical objectives of colonizing countries, it is clear that these do not exclusively determine the shape of institutions in new countries. In the following discussion of Brazil's 19th-century urban development, the intention is not so much to characterize a Portuguese–American "variant" as to suggest that the Brazilian experience offers analogies with regions and countries of Spanish America. Unfortunately, these analogies will remain largely implicit. Brazil itself is culturally and economically so diverse that to specify them fully would require extensive research and lengthy presentation. Some broad lines of comparison, however, can be sketched against the colonial background.

Generally speaking, the urban historian may expect to encounter parallels between Brazil and the "frontier" regions of Spanish America, a loose term by which I mean those areas less closely supervised by the viceroys of New Spain and Peru. They are the regions where the European relied less upon Amerindian social organization in making his claims upon the fruits of the soil – regions where either Indian labor had to be made "civilized" and sedentary, or African labor had to be imported and regimented, or the European was himself forced to wrest a living from the land. In such areas, municipal life was less strongly nucleated and more precarious because of a narrower economic base, because of pervasive claims of the land, and because of a meager endowment of metropolitan institutions and appurtenances from the mother country.

The urban historian finds analogies, ecological and sociological, between the plantation-based economy of the Brazilian northeast and Caribbean sugar zones; between the mining regions of central Brazil and those of Spanish America; between the plains culture of southern Brazil and that of the La Plata viceroyalty. Furthermore, the present area of São Paulo, Paraná, Paraguay, northeastern Argentina and southeastern Bolivia was once roughly homogeneous with respect to aboriginal stock and acculturation patterns; an agro-pastoral economic base that did not permit urbanization; accumulation of wealth and importation of African slaves; and a common hostility of Paulistas and Paraguayan settlers to the Jesuit master plan for rationalized, quasi-urban "reduction" of the Indians.

Venezuela offers parallels with Brazil at the national rather than at a regional level. In each case there was a preliminary phase of extractive activity (dyewood, pearls), and it was a half century after the discovery before the settlement process gathered shape and momentum. Early towns were small and precarious, and the capitals, Salvador (1549) and Caracas (1567), were established relatively late. For a long period, urban life clung to the coast and was scourged by foreign attackers; the gradual appropriation of the interior was greatly assisted by cattle raising with its dispersive effects on settlement. In both cases, the rhythm of town foundings accelerated sharply in the 17th century[1] and was influenced throughout the colonial period by so-called "cycles" of agricultural exploitation.

Similarities between Brazil and Chile in the 19th century suggest another set of parallels for urban history. Here a sociopolitical comparison might explain how the urban scene provided a setting within which requirements for political stability were mediated to the claims of seigneurial agrarian societies.

Argentina is, of course, Latin America's archetypical instance of 19-century metropolitan growth, and it vividly illustrates the city's cause-and-effect role in a dispersive, agro-pastoral, patrimonial econ-

---

[1]   According to de Azevedo (1945: 12–14, 22–23), 17 cities and *vilas* were established in Brazil in the 16th century and 41 in the 17th. In Venezuela there were 28 foundings in the 16th century and more than 70 in the 17th (Moreno 1960: 118–121).

omy. The two classics, *Facundo* and *Os sertões*, give grounds for the Argentine–Brazil comparison. Both books are contrapuntally concerned with the worlds of city and country, civilization and barbarism, coast and backlands, modernity and archaism, order and anarchy. Yet the defeat of Antônio Conselheiro by the troops from Rio was less transcendental than the defeat of the Argentine *caudillo*. Conselheiro's charisma was exercised in a vacuum, that is, outside the network of rural municipal structures partly defined by the term *coronelismo*. Another messianic movement contemporary with Conselheiro's, that of Padre Cícero in Ceará, occurred within a region where it could find institutional roots.

It soon attracted landless migrants and rich capitalists; it built a city (Joaseiro), overthrew a state government and ended up twenty years later as the largest electoral bailiwick of *coronelismo* in the history of the Brazilian Northeast. Above all, it survived.
 By 1920, the movement that had opposed the State became the State. And, in recent times, it has even come to terms which the Church, but only in part ...(The) movement remains...a dormant cyst, within a tradition-bound society. At any moment, it could turn down the road of heresy, revolution or reaction.[2]

In other words, backlands charisma drew legitimacy from the substrate of Brazilian agrarian society – and even thrust up its own urban challenge to "order and progress " – long after "civilization " had won a Pyrrhic victory in Argentina. The failure of the Argentine backlands to mobilize, and long delaying action help to account for the special pathological dimensions to Argentine urbanization. Not even the State of São Paulo has such a *"cabeza de Goliat"* as Argentina.[3]
 The following discussion of 19th-century Brazil, then, may offer some basis for selective and variable comparison with those regions of Spanish America which inherited a less developed hierarchy of colonial cities, where claims to urban primacy were more disputed, where political and economic power was more diffused across the land, where the central political challenge was not to seize the capital city (Peru, Guatemala) but to enforce its will upon the country (Colombia, Venezuela). At the threshold of the 19th century, much of this outlying zone (to adopt the Spanish administrative perspective) presents more incipient than achieved urbanization. Metropolitan outlook and accouterments are only beginning to appear.[4] The explanatory value of rural-urban distinctions is limited. The urban his-

[2] From unpublished materials by Ralph Della Cava, who has studied Padre Cícero and made the contrast with Conselheiro.
[3] See Louis Couty's interesting comparison, "S. Paulo et Buenos Ayres " (1884).
[4] George A. Kubler (1964) identifies eight "metropolises " for colonial Latin America. Only three were in what is here termed the "outlying zone " (Buenos Aires, Havana, and Rio), all of them late 18th-century parvenus.

torian must pay special attention to interlacing networks of agrarian social organization: how they control and drain off energy from towns without necessarily being "in opposition" to them; how they generate their own municipal centers; and how, during the course of the century, the larger cities begin to transmit impulses to agrarian networks, bringing them into a new gravitational field.

URBAN BRAZIL IN THE EARLY NINETEENTH CENTURY

An economical way to survey human settlements in Brazil in the early 19th century is to do so through the eyes of a keen observer who roamed widely among them. A good choice is Auguste de Saint-Hilaire, whose journeys of more than 6,000 miles through Rio de Janeiro, Espírito Santo, Minas Gerais, Goiás, São Paulo, Santa Catarina, and Uruguay well equipped him to make contrasts and generalizations.

The dominant impression conveyed by de Saint-Hilaire's dozen or so travel volumes is that of a sparsely settled subcontinent, appreciably but not highly differentiated with respect to processes of circulation, economic pursuits, social patterns, and attitudes toward authority. The reader comes to be haunted by a montage of four constantly shifting scenes: the vast backlands with their isolated, impoverished dirt farmers sunk in lethargy and atony; the *fazendas*, islands of patriarchal authority, with their white-washed, dilapidated, sparsely furnished, big houses and their 17th-century technology; the villages, often too dispersed to be recognized as settlement nuclei, virtually enfeoffed to *fazendeiros*, merchants, priests – and to the raw elements of God's nature; and the towns (or ghost towns in the mining zone) with their clustered dwellings and commerce, their flamboyant and archaic civil–religious pageantry, the monotony of their parochial, incommodious life, and the incongruity of their occasional priest or townsman who hungers for news of French politics. From time to time a tribe or *aldéia* of Indians cuts into the montage, flashing us back to primeval Brazil.[5]

The inland *sertões* of Minas and Goiás struck de Saint-Hilaire as a huge region where "a society is not possible." Each man is his own prisoner. Life is concentrated in the family circle; even filial ties are weak, for everywhere sons can move to fresh lands and find plentiful building materials. "In such isolation man slowly deterior-

[5] Although the aborigines and the scenes of primeval life fascinated him, only once did de Saint-Hilaire indulge in the kind of Chèvecoeurian fantasy which was to color the motivations of middle-class European agricultural emigrants to 19th-century Brazil. See Auguste de Saint-Hilaire (1830: vol. 2, pp. 182–184).

ates, falling into a state of complete apathy and brutishness" (1941: 198–199).

Distinctions between village, town, and city are "infinitely less perceptible" than in Europe, where urban populations are stationary except for wealthy families who maintain country houses for "*la belle saison*" and poorer citizens who spend "a few hours in the country" on Sundays and feast days. In Brazil it was the opposite: one *came to town* to celebrate. At other times "the permanent population of towns and villages is extremely meager. Most of their houses belong to farmers who come there only on Sundays for divine services and keep them closed the rest of the week" (1851: vol. 1, pp. 112–113).

A village, oddly enough, was a sign of more dispersed rather than denser settlement. Near Rio de Janeiro, where the land was well distributed and occupied, there was no need for villages. Few residences sprang up around churches, because the churches were within convenient reach of rural dwellings. There was no need for commercial centers because *vendas* sold staple provisions along all the roads and at the doorstep of each *fazendeiro*. Only farther inland, where landholdings were more widely spaced, did farmers need a house in town where their families might rest after a long trip, receive friends, and do business with their scattered neighbors. Such social centers attracted workmen, merchants, and innkeepers, "and this is generally the reason for the growth of those villages of the interior which do not trace their origin to the presence of gold" (de Saint-Hilaire 1830: vol. 1, pp. 53–54).[6]

De Saint-Hilaire's reports of town and village life help explain the inverse correlation between settlement density and village nucleation. He approved of regular gathering places for farmers, but he felt the villages of Minas Gerais to be a mischievous setting. Their permanent population was composed largely of idlers and prostitutes, and their *ranchos* were the scene of shameless libertinism unmatched in the most corrupt towns of France (1847: 127).

If the small towns were not strong nodules of social energy, neither were they woven into a commercially integrated network of hierarchy. Each town related itself independently to Rio. Even Curitiba, seat of a *comarca*, had a short commercial radius. Its well-stocked shops

---

[6] Richard F. Burton (1869: vol. 1, pp. 101–103) identified five evolutionary stages of the traveler's resting place, each representing a higher concentration of commercial services: the *pouso*, or camping ground, where proprietor allowed mules to be watered and tethered; the *rancho*, an unfurnished "traveler's bungalow"; the *venda*, a shop similar to the Spanish American *pulpería*, still not "thoroughly respectable"; the *estalagem, hospedaria*, or inn, such as Burton found at Mariana; and the hotel, such as he found at Barbecena. Goulart (1961: 146) equates these facilities with successive types of settlement: *povoado (rancho)*, *povoaçao (venda)*, *vila (estalagem)* and *cidade* (*ótel*).

were supplied directly from the capital, and the merchants "sold scarcely more than to the local landowners because the merchants of neighboring towns were also supplied from Rio." Similarly, the first French merchant to establish himself in Vila Rica, capital of Minas, was forced to sell at retail for lack of wholesale customers, "wherein he merely imitated the regional merchants, not one of whom sells exclusively wholesale" (1851: vol. 2, p. 120; 1941, 153–154).[7]

The socioeconomic role of the small Brazilian town in this period seems marginal, almost dysfunctional – especially when compared with its organizational and political energies of the 16th and 17th centuries. As a result the historian concerned with urban change finds his attention drawn in two directions: to the "Court" at Rio and gradually to certain provincial capitals as new radiating centers of metropolitan influence; and to agrarian social organization, especially in prosperous plantation zones, and its dominant–submissive inter-actions with small and large loci of urban power.

The fact that even the larger cities of colonial Brazil had enjoyed few of the amenities and little of the splendor of viceregal rule gave special significance to the transfer of the Portuguese court to Rio in 1808. The royal hegira climaxed a century during which, if Furtado's calculation is accurate (1963: 81), Portugal sent more emigrants to Brazil than Spain had to the Indies in three centuries. The advent of the court legitimized, as it were, this demographic translocation, made cultural and stylistic models available, and provided cultural linkage with the Western world. This occurred at the moment when in Spanish America courtly models were about to be dismantled and the urban scene was in many cases to be invaded by *caudillos* of plain and mountain and their plebeian retinues.

The travelers von Spix and von Martius marveled at the changes, the advances in civilization, which the afflux of 24,000 Portuguese and numbers of English, French, Dutch, Germans, and Italians signified for Rio. As the king began to confer titles and offices, wealthy Brazilian families were attracted to the capital; here they acquired a taste for European luxuries and styles of living which they in turn transmitted to other classes. "Even the more remote provinces of the infant kingdom whose inhabitants, led by curiosity, interest, or private business, visited Rio de Janeiro, soon accustomed themselves to recognize that city as the capital, and to adopt the manners and modes of thinking, which, after the arrival of the court, struck them as European" (von Spix and von Martius 1824: vol. 1, pp. 143–144).

[7]   This picture of settlement patterns drawn from de Saint-Hilaire is in essential agreement with Deffontaines' analysis (1938).

THE PROCESS OF "CITIFICATION"

Gilberto Freyre's *Sobrados e mucambos* (1961; see also de Azevedo 1948: ch. 5 and 1950: part 1, ch. 3; Diégues 1964) remains almost as isolated an attempt at synthesis in the field of 19th-century Brazilian or even Latin American urban history as it was when first published. For many readers, his "Proustian" detail and his *obiter dicta* on race mixing obscure the premises of his historiography, although to all it is clear that he is concerned more with "citification" (social cultural, attitudinal) than with urbanization (sociological, political, economic). Like von Spix and von Martius before him, Freyre perceives the Brazilian city as a vehicle rather than an engine for change. His novelistic fascination with sensory immediacies, with character types and *mise en scène*, disguises the fact that his human beings are actors, not agents. Situation is personalized but change is depersonalized. The city square triumphs; plantation manors become city mansions; social barriers develop; a new distribution of power comes about; antagonisms arise; moments of fraternization emerge; social distance shrinks. Patriarchalism moves from plantation to town house, but does not immediately come to terms with the street; house and street are almost enemies. The house itself is a powerful social force; it determines social distance and proximity, governs the role of women, corrects or emphasizes features of isolation.

Freyre's largely implicit hypotheses prompt conjecture about the special nature of Latin American urbanization. What I have said may suggest a schematic or deterministic view. However, he specifically denies economic or geographic determinism. In what may be his fullest theoretical statement he identifies two interacting processes. One is the "integration, maturation and decay of the patriarchal or tutelary form of the organization of family, economy and culture." The other is the "amalgamation of races and cultures," which acts as "the principal solvent of rigidities in...the more or less feudal system of relations...imposed upon situations that are defined not so much by race as by class, groups, and individuals." These two processes, the aristocratic and the democratic, interpenetrate though rarely conflict. They produce the more individualistic, "semi-patriarchal" urban society of the 19th century (1961: vol. 2, pp. 354–355). What is interesting is that Freyre calls these processes primary causes of change rather than effects or secondary causes.

As his subtitle indicates (*Decadence of the rural patriarchy and rise of the urban*), Freyre conceives of patriarchal society as a self-contained system, almost an organism, that undergoes natural stages of growth and decay. By the first half of the 19th century its golden age has passed. This occurs, however, not because of a conventional clash between city and country, commercialism and agrarianism, sophistication and parochialism. On the contrary, the patriarchal system is reembodied in an urban setting. The setting proves corrosive for it, but even the corrosive action is attributed to a kind of neo-patriarchalism. Ethnic and cultural mixing weaken family organization only to produce a transfer of filial loyalty to the political patriarch, the emperor. Elsewhere, in considering economic factors, Freyre maintains his image of a social system subject to corrosion or assault, in this case by an outside "ethic of imperialism" acting to standardize life for commercial purposes. Under such circumstances the "conquered culture is not always able to prevent the moral devaluation of elements seemingly decorative or external but in reality basic to its life and economy" (1961: vol. 1, p. 324).

What Freyre hints at without making explicit is a field theory of Brazilian patriarchalism. The field envelops both urban and rural society, and field disturbances arise not so much from tensions or contradictions inherent in Brazilian institutions as from the vulnerability of cities to subversion from without. However disappointing Freyre's refusal to analyze the dynamics of change, his tableau has at least the virtues of evocativeness, self-consistency, and regional relevance.

The difficulties of trying to isolate and characterize indigenous sources of urban innovation are illustrated by two recent, surprisingly similar studies of entrepreneurship in 19th-century São Paulo and Colombia (Dean 1966; Safford 1965: 503, 526). Both studies lend credence to the patriarchal "field theory" by emphasizing the agrarian backgrounds of native industrial entrepreneurs. Yet both of them play down the cultural preconditions for successful enterprise, while stressing the determinant role of geo-economic and, more loosely, historical and political factors. Divested of psychocultural significance, entrepreneurship becomes a generalized reservoir of energy releasable by happy conjunctions of transcultural "factors." In short, these more scientific or at least more antiseptic statements lose heuristic value for the specifically Latin American scene.

THE RURAL DOMAIN

Without for the moment addressing the problem of conceptualizing the modernizing process in urban Brazil, let us turn to the rural scene, where forces of innovation and resistance are more clearly distinguishable. We have already noted the weak magnetic force of the rural municipal center. According to Dauril Alden (1965), the small town suffered politico-administrative decline in the 18th century as electoral supervision, administrative and judicial functions, and tax-farming were relinquished to royal officials. Portuguese resources and Brazilian geography, however, limited the extension of central control. What largely saved outlying or interstitial regions from anarchy was the militia system. Local magnates who served as *capitães-mores* of militia "performed a variety of administrative tasks throughout the countryside where salaried royal officials, like the ouvidores, seldom ventured" (Alden 1965). Beyond serving as liaisons – transmitting commands downward and reporting information upward – militia commanders were an independent source of authority and organization. De Saint-Hilaire marveled at their ubiquity and inventiveness. Wherever he went they lodged him, gave him orderlies, and alerted neighboring jurisdictions when he resumed traveling. A *capitão-mor* along the São Francisco River was so attentive and was so esteemed by his constituents that he "could not leave him without emotion." In Minas, the *capitães-mores* appointed village commandants similar to mayors. The *capitão-mor* of Curitiba determined how much land farmers should plant, required them to improve their preparation of *mate* to compete with the Paraguayan product, and introduced such crops as wheat and peaches. In the absence of a post between São Paulo and Curitiba, the captain general kept up with events in his jurisdiction by militia couriers who made the rounds of the *capitães-mores* carrying pouches to which only they and he possessed the key (1847: vol. 1, pp. 147–148; 1830: vol. 1, pp. 374–376; 1851: vol. 2, pp. 48–49, 136–139, 155–156, 166–167).[8]

Caio Prado Junior (1963) credits the Marquis of Lavradio with being the first to have appreciated the administrative potential of the militia system, and he quotes the 1779 *relatório* in which Lavradio observes that militia officers imparted notions of respect and discipline to the unruly populace. Prado gives several instances of the use of militia for general municipal duties and concludes:

It is no exaggeration to say that [the militias] made possible legal and administrative order in this vast territory, with its dispersed population and scarcity of regular officials. Over that whole territory they spread the network of administration which could never have been knotted together merely by our sparse official bureaucracy, concentrated as it was in the capitals and larger centers (Prado 1963: 322–326).

The militia system has two important implications for Brazilian urban history. One is that it was not exclusively an imposition of the central government but a system mediating between central and local authority. Militia officers were chosen from lists submitted by municipal *câmaras*, so that the extension of the militias had the effect of

---

[8]   Reports from northeastern Brazil found the administrative efficiency of the militia to be less exemplary: Henry Koster (1817: vol. 1, pp. 252–255; Vilhena 1921: 249–270).

vesting with public authority the private or "natural" command structures headed by local *mandões* and *poderosos do sertão*. Increasing centralization was counterpoised by formalized delegation of authority.[9]

Second, one is led to be sceptical of those who idealize the "democratic" potential of Latin American *câmaras* and *cabildos* and who regret that the tradition of municipal autonomy was smothered so soon after its reassertion at the moment of national independence. If it is true that in Latin America municipal government was elitist, that municipalities were not economically linked in networks and hierarchies, that grass-roots, populist concern with political affairs was only intermittently mobilized, and that localist–centralist tensions were excessively polarized, then the militia system had sounder sociological justification as an instrument for responsible government and territorial integration than did constitutional guarantees of municipal autonomy.

The demise of the militia system was signalized by the creation of the National Guard in 1831, which placed local troops unequivocally under municipal control. A regional logic for this change is supplied in Lucila Herrmann's study (1948) of the municipality of Guaretinguetá in the Paraíba Valley between São Paulo and Rio. In the early 19th century, it was passing from an economy based on subsistence agriculture and prospecting to one based on sugar production.

In the earlier cycle the military pyramid was deeply respected, with the families of each member of the Companies being enrolled with their chief in a position corresponding to his in the military hierarchy.

In the sugar cycle that position is year by year less respected, till finally in [the statistics of] 1836 all persons are listed together, distinguished only by occupation, possessions and, principally, production and number of slaves.

The break-up of the formerly large administrative divisions into smaller ones, with a base more economic and demographic than military, weakens central control and facilitates the creation of powers dispersed throughout the rural areas which compete economically and socially with the central one . . .

At the same time the increasing definition of administrative, military and judicial functions means that gradually the *capitães-mores* find themselves deprived of many prerogatives granted them in early times (Herrmann 1948: 86).

At the risk of oversimplification we can say that the heir to the militia system was *coronelismo*, which developed under the second empire and had its golden age during the first republic. In his classic study (1948), Nunes Leal distinguishes *coronelismo* from the earlier

---

[9]   The interplay of private and public power in Brazilian history is examined by Nestor Duarte (1939).

patriarcalismo. The *coronel* was a municipal boss whose power was rooted in the local political agrarian structure and who, in return for political patronage, delivered the rural vote required by the national electoral regime. It was "a compromise relation between decadent private power and strengthened public power." The private power was not a mere survival from colonial times but an adaptation by which "the residue of our former exorbitant private power managed to coexist with a political regime having a broad representative base." The price paid by the *coronel* for local control was submission to central authority and the need to cultivate the elaborate network of contacts which led to it. He had surrendered the right of rebellion. He set himself against the commercial and industrial development of his municipality and against the education and political enlightenment of his constituency. The decadence of the agrarian structure is precisely the key for understanding the tenacity of *coronelismo*, "because the more the 'natural' influence of the landowners is broken up and diluted the more official support becomes necessary to guarantee the continued supremacy of a local political current."

The dynamics of *coronelismo* help to explain the dearth of local support for municipal autonomy in 19th-century Brazil, in spite of the persuasive appeals which such writers as Tavares Bastos made for it on grounds of political philosophy. The lack of legal autonomy was compensated by extralegal prerogatives which a provincial or state government granted to the local party of its preference. "This governmental compensation in the *coronelista* compromise largely explains the support which state legislators, most of whom were from the interior, always gave to laws designed to stifle the municipality" (Nunes Leal 1948: 7–36, 181–190). (For 19th-century literature on the Brazilian *municipio*, see Canabrava [1947].)

The analysis suggests that a system of baffles obstructed the transmission of urban appurtenances, institutions, and attitudes from city to small town in 19th-century Brazil. It also helps to explain why by the end of the century a few cities were starting to exert a magnetic attraction across the countryside that was out of proportion to any structural changes occurring in the urban variant of patrimonial society. The large Brazilian city confronts us with a paradox. Its "urban" concentration of economic and cultural resources increased its direct entanglements with the rural hinterland to make it a more active theater for *coronelista* politics.

One index of big-city centripetalism is the concentration of credit. In his study of the coffee county of Vassouras, Stein describes a transition "from personal to impersonal credit relationships" occurring in about 1860. Thitherto most planters had obtained credit not from banks but from coffee factors (*comissários*), from members of their extended families, or from local residents who had surplus capital. Now, with the emergence of "the planter–factor–bank triangle of debt relations," the importance of local mortgages with respect to funds obtained from Rio banks declined steadily for the rest of the century (Stein 1957: 238–244). In the first decade of the 20th century, Denis found that "a whole generation of small towns" in São Paulo State had been affected by the coffee crisis. "They are not and never have been coffee markets. The only coffee markets are São Paulo and Santos," whose businessmen and factors "are in direct relation with the planters. The interior towns do not serve as depots for the crop, although they distribute imported merchandise in the agricultural zones." Planters obtained local credit from small banks "which are maintained from afar by the more powerful banks located in São Paulo" (Denis 1928: 110–111).

MIGRATIONS AND METROPOLITAN SOCIETY

An understanding of Brazilian or Latin American small-town life at the end of the 19th century is requisite for interpreting the rural migration to primate cities which was then beginning and which is so prominent a feature of the 20th-century scene. We must be clear about qualitative differences between the rural exodus in the 19th-century industrial nations and in modern Latin America. To suggest what these might be, I have skimmed (and perhaps oversimplified) some conclusions from Louis Chevalier's meticulous study (1950) of the growth of Paris in the 19th century, a city whose political, economic, and cultural primacy particularly invites comparison with the most important cities of Latin America.[10]

1. The rhythm of migration to the capital responded to successive phases of the economy of Paris, "a city which develops harmoniously in its various manufactures and whose production responds to ever increasing internal consumption" (1950: 147).

2. Paris was able to recruit trained labor from the departments, sometimes via relays of intermediate towns, so that the Parisian milieu differed little from those which supplied it, "whether with respect to professional distribution or to social distribution within the professions." The Parisian working class was not a proletarian aristocracy into which one was accepted only after extended residence in the capital. Migrants merely continued their careers in Paris, to the extent

[10]   In the 19th century Paris grew from roughly 500,000 to 3,500,000; São Paulo passed these same figures in less than half that time, between roughly 1917 and 1960. Alain Touraine (1961) examines some aspects of the contrast between Brazilian and European migrations in his study "Industrialisation et conscience ouvrière à São Paulo."

that Paris did not need to provide apprentice training (1950: 20, 203–4, 220–21, 236).

3. Recruitment of migrants was not generally to the lowest economic stratum and to menial occupation. Therefore, new workers were absorbed with relative ease into urban society. Class affiliation erased the memory of departmental origin. "The old quarters of Paris show ... very swift integration of new population elements to the old. Just as it did not undermine the professional structures, immigration respected the character of the quarters, and in this apparently unchanged Parisian setting it is hard to distinguish isolated departmental colonies " (1950: 80, 222, 238, 240).

4. Revolutionary political programs and movements that periodically *emanated from* Paris were not strictly *generated by* the city. The French Revolution and those of 1830 and 1848 were instigated by Frenchmen from the east and north, from "regions more profoundly urban than others in France and maintaining traditions of active, turbulent and often bloody municipal life." The political continuity of the capital responds to "a proletarian and often agrarian tradition preserved in distant cantons of ancient guilds " and renewed in Paris by continual migrations (1950: 15–17).

The fact that not one of these four generalizations can be made about migrations to Latin American primate cities in the 20th century is a telling commentary on the evolution of secondary towns during the century after independence. If they are at all applicable, it is not to domestic migrations but to the flows of Europeans to the large cities of southern Brazil and Argentina after 1870. Yet even the case of the Italians in São Paulo or Buenos Aires deviates from that of Parisian migrants. Many of them went overseas contracted, even subsidized, for *agricultural* labor. Once they ended up in the city, there was irony in the fact that they accommodated to it more easily than did national migrants. Finally, the nature of that accommodation – however successful – was governed by special characteristics of Latin American urban society.

Florestan Fernandes (1964: 53, 82) elaborately contrasts the assimilation of national and of European migrants by São Paulo City in the late 19th century. His Brazilian migrants are freed slaves and in some ways a special case; yet because he is more concerned with the ex-slave's psychological conditioning by the patrimonial agrarian system than with "race" or forced servitude, his points are not irrelevant to the general case of the rural Brazilian migrant.[11] Fernandes finds that the migrant ex-slave surrendered the advantages of

---

[11] The studies by Juarez Rubens Brandão Lopez of the adjustment of rural and small-town Brazilian migrants to industrial labor seem to justify my assumption. See his *Sociedade industrial no Brasil* (1964).

the rural Brazilian town (social stability, traditionalism, subsistence economy) without being compensated by social, economic, and cultural possibilities which big cities characteristically afford. They "lived in the city but did not progress with it and by means of it. They formed a social congeries dispersed through the *barrios*, and they shared only an arduous and often unwholesome existence."

What concerns us here is not the special case of the Negro or mulatto migrant but the social structure and processes of the city which had begun to grow, to modernize, and to industrialize more swiftly than any other in Brazil. Fernandes draws two conclusions in this regard. One is that despite the prosperity and commercializing influence of a "bourgeois revolution," São Paulo's transition to a competitive, class-based society was halting. The two social levels which resisted it most strongly and where archaism was not persevering were precisely the two extremes, the elite and the plebeian strata. Second, Fernandes concludes that the aptitude for change or modernization had less to do with the beliefs and cultural outlook of people and groups than with their location in the urban economic and power structure. With the two poles of society in partial quarantine against innovating influence, the "rusticity" of immigrant ethnic groups "underwent highly variable and fluctuating correction" (1964: 221–222).[12]

The urban ethos which these generalizations suggest gave its impress to the processes that one associates with modernization.

1. *Entrepreneurship.* Half a century after São Paulo's industrial growth began in earnest, and at a time when its region was already advertised as South America's largest industrial park, a Belgian observer wondered why local manufacturers neglected "the *direct* study of the needs of the consumers" and relied for distribution upon wholesalers who served several producers at a time and had no stake in pushing the wares of any one of them. He attributed this lag in part to the heterogeneity of the market, to its different "mentalities, degrees of civilization, material needs," which would have required a diversified research strategy and therefore encouraged industrialists to take the line of least resistance (van Deursen 1934: 318).

Thirty years later the phenomenon persists. We are told that the response of contemporary Paulista entrepreneurs to the market situations "is reduced to the indispensable minimum that allows firms to carry on as economic units organized for profit." However, the Brazilian sociologist of 1963 reverses the explanation of the Belgian economist of 1934. He emphasizes the heterogeneity of industrialists rather than of consumers. The former may be scions of traditional

---

[12]   This analysis bears some similarity to that made of Córdoba, Argentina, in a later period by Juan Carlos Argulla (1963).

families or may be descended from immigrants or may themselves be immigrants. They "constitute by their extraction a heterogeneous social stratum and do not react together as a group before the problems confronting them... If we consider each industrialist we see that he locates himself in society in terms of a status other than that of industrial entrepreneur." The industrialist's reference group tends to be the patriarchal family (whether "rustic" or "seigneurial" version), and his bid for leadership is in the interest of a group and not a class of industrialists (Cardoso 1963: 61–64).

The entrepreneurial relation to the market is critical to the study of urban social process. As Cardoso hints, it raises the fundamental question of the extent to which patrimonial psychology permits self-identification with the Weberian "market situation." In analyzing resistances to what Weber called the "formal rationality of economic action," one can stress "objective" factors (heterogeneous consumers, governmental neomercantilism, family-controlled enterprise, lack of economic "education," monopolistic trading areas) or one can give primacy to a "subjective" factor, to an enduring philosophic conception of self and society (see Weber 1964a). Within the traditions of Marxism and North American "positivism" (as distinguished from "empiricism"), the choice is preconditioned, as it need not be for an eclectic cultural historian.

2. *Absorption of immigrants.* A study of Italian immigrants and their descendants in São Paulo concludes that the Brazilian tradition of linking physical labor with depressed racial groups caused the immigrant worker to perceive his situation in ethnic rather than economic terms, to "discover" that he was Italian. The cultural reality worked against the economic to stigmatize physical labor and petty commerce. The new middle class, composed to a large extent of immigrant groups,

...tends initially to contribute to an artificial overcrowding of the traditional professions, which continue to maintain at least social prestige if not economic power; this means that the Brazilian middle class does not see the intellectual as its class representative – whose function would be to articulate its interest and ideals – but as a signore (Castaldi 1960).[13]

The Brazilian urban milieu encouraged the European immigrant to abandon the very ethic of work which had assured his survival and early advancement and to adopt a set of private seigneurial attitudes rather than a generalized "way of life."

3. *Social mobility.* The studies of the Hutchinson group on social structure and mobility in São Paulo are important for determining whether one can feasibly speak of the generalized case of the Latin

[13] Similar attitudes characterized the Chilean middle class as analyzed by Frederick B. Pike (1963).

American city. São Paulo is an extreme instance of innovation and modernization. In less than a century it has grown from a small town of 25,000 to a metropolis of 4,500,000 and absorbed heavy foreign immigration. The colonial economy of its region was oriented to subsistence agriculture and prospecting, and supported no elaborate bureaucratic or seigneurial social structures; its 19th century prosperity derived from a coffee economy which was in many ways capitalistic and antitraditional. Yet the Hutchinson study reveals a curious condition of sociological stasis.

To make this point, the study distinguished between "structural mobility" (mobility resulting from industrial expansion which creates new jobs at certain status levels) and "mobility through change of position" (the movement of a given person from one status level to another). The former type "contributes almost nothing to the social fluidity which might encourage circulation of people among positions in accordance with individual capacities." The latter type depends upon lack of social rigidity and recognition of capacity; logically it demands that for each ascension to higher status there can be a corresponding descent to a lower one.

Compared with Great Britain, considered a model of rigid class structure, São Paulo shows much less movement among social classes. Much of the social mobility observable in the city is attributable to a structural mobility which is irrelevant to the problem of equality of opportunity. It therefore seems that Brazil's traditional class structure was little affected by the economic development undergone by São Paulo in the last fifty years.

Other conclusions are that Italian immigrants have been more mobile than native-born Brazilians; that many immigrants achieved success with little education; that the education received by immigrants' children had a largely symbolic value; that there seems to be little correlation between a person's intelligence and the probability of his improving his social status; that "personality" rather than capacity is the critical motive force for upward mobility; and that both formal education and familial conventions tend to produce "an average individual who gives greater value to preservation of status than to the risks inherent in mobility." In Hutchinson's summary: "First, industrial development did not bring about the dissolution of class boundaries as had been predicted. Second, wider access to the education system did not produce an increase in social mobility."[14]

If these generalizations properly reflect the logic of social structure and process in Brazil's most "urban" and industrialized city, they also offer grounds for supposing that Latin American urban societies might be taken as a general family – however heterogeneous its membership

[14] See Hutchinson's "Introducão" and his "Mudanças de *status* social de uma geração para outra" (1960).

and however closely related it may be to other families. The recent sociological studies certainly suggest that the modalities and hiatuses of social organization in São Paulo at the threshold of this century and in the first bloom of industrial expansion were not unlike those described by Capelo in 1900 for Lima, which then seemed a city prototypically arrested and tradition-bound.

TOWARD A GENERAL LATIN AMERICAN CASE

It is not simply to assuage the classificatory compulsion that one postulates a Latin American family of cities. One does it as an aid to selecting modes of analysis useful for comparative research. However familiar they may seem, a case can be made that the cues which Weber (1964) and Durkheim (1933) supply for the study of Latin American societies have not yet been fully exploited.[15]

From Weber one might take the paradigm of the patrimonial society,[16] imbuing it with the *raison d'être* of a Catholic way of life summarized in *The sociology of religion* (1964b). Hutchinson's conclusions about status determinants in São Paulo correspond closely to Weber's explanation of the community in which grace is institutionally dispensed. In such a society, the personal qualifications of those seeking "salvation" are a matter of indifference to the institution distributing grace. Salvation is universal and therefore accessible to other than "virtuosi"; in fact, the virtuoso is regarded with suspicion if he seeks to attain grace by his unaided power. The level of expected ethical accomplishment is set low, and the virtuoso's good works are properly accrued for the credit of his institution as well as for himself so that the overage can be distributed to those in need.

Against this paradigm which helps to align historico-cultural factors, one can project Durkheim's requirements for organic solidarity as engendered by the division of labor (1933). Attention must be paid to subtleties of analysis not found in simpler sociological polarities. One must be mindful of Durkheim's "abnormal forms" of division of labor which fail to produce solidarity,[17] and of his "corporative regime" proposed in the preface to the second edition of *Division of labor* as an alternative to competitive "anarchy."

Juxtaposing the Catholic–patrimonial paradigm and the require-

[15]   More modern and better sterilized tools have been assembled in the energetically researched *Study of urbanization* (Hauser and Schnore 1965); however, they seem more suitable for scraping than for cutting.
[16]   An attempt to adapt the patrimonial model to Latin America will be found in my essay "The heritage of Latin America" (Hartz 1964). See also Magali Sarfatti (1966).
[17]   Durkheim's second abnormal form, "forced division of labor," is relevant to the Hutchinson studies (1933: 374–388).

ments for organic solidarity has several advantages for the study of Latin American cities. (1) It draws attention to morphology, process, and mind-set rather than to artificial historical "stages" and dynamisms. (2) It neither establishes nor requires observance of rural–urban dichotomies. (3) It leads us to construe urban change in Latin America as the transactions between a preexisting social ethic and the flexible, transcultural requirements, both moral and organizational, of industrial society – and not an extraneous ethic impinging upon an "archaic" social system, or as the collision of two closed and self-consistent systems. (4) It requires cultural sympathy of the social scientist and points him toward Durkheim's conviction that the primary need of modern society is for "moral rearmament rather than economic reconstruction."[18]

REFERENCES

ALDEN, DAURIL
 1965   "The Colonial elite and the expanded bureaucracy of Brazil during the golden age." Paper presented at the annual meeting of the American Historical Association, December.
ARGULLA, JUAN CARLOS
 1963   Aspectos sociales del proceso de industrialización en una comunidad urbana. *Revista Mexicana de Sociología* 25 (2): 747–772.
BOXER, C. R.
 1965   *Portuguese society in the tropics, the municipal councils of Goa, Macao, Bahia, and Luanda 1510–1800.* Madison and Milwaukee: University of Wisconsin Press.
BRANDÃO LOPEZ, JUAREZ RUBENS
 1964   *Sociedade industrial no Brasil.* São Paulo.
BUARQUE DE HOLLANDA, SERGIO
 1956   *Raízes do Brasil* (third edition). Rio de Janeiro.
BURTON, RICHARD F.
 1869   *Explorations of the highlands of the Brazil,* two volumes. London.
CANABRAVA, A. P.
 1947   Tendências da bibliografia sobre a história administrativa do município. *Revista de Administração* 1 (1): 80–87.
CAPELO, JOAQUIN
 1895–1902   *Sociología de Lima,* four volumes. Lima.
CARDOSO, FERNANDO H.
 1963   " El empresario industrial en América Latina. 2. Brasil." Comisión Económica para América E/CN. 12/642/Add. 2 (February): 61–64.
CASTALDI, CARLOS
 1960   "Õ ajustamento do imigrante à comunidade paulistana," in *Mobilidade e trabalho, un estudo na cidade de São Paulo.* Edited by Bertram Hutchinson, 281–359.
CHEVALIER, LOUIS
 1950   *La formation de la population parisienne au XIX siècle.* Paris.

[18]   The phrase is Alvin W. Gouldner's in his introduction to Emile Durkheim, *Socialism* (1962: 23).

COUTY, LOUIS
1884 "S. Paulo et Buenos Ayres," in *Le Brésil en 1884*. Rio de Janeiro.
DEAN, WARREN
1966 The planter as entrepreneur: the case of São Paulo. *Hispanic American Historical Review* 46 (2): 138–152.
DE AZEVEDO, AROLDO
1945 *Vilas cidades do Brasil colonial*. São Paulo.
1948 *Canaviais e engenhos na vida política do Brasil*. Rio de Janeiro.
1950 *Brazilian culture*. New York.
DEFFONTAINES, PIERRE
1938 "Rapports fonctionnels entre les agglomérations urbains et rurales: un exemple en pays de colonisation, le Brésil," in *Comptes Rendus* 2: 139–144 (Travaux de la Section 3a). Congrès International de Géographie. Leiden.
DENIS, PIERRE
1928 *Le Brésil au XXe siècle* (seventh edition). Paris.
DE SAINT-HILAIRE, AUGUSTE
1830 *Voyage dans les provinces de Rio de Janeiro et de Minas Geraes*, two volumes. Paris.
1847 *Voyages aux sources du Rio S. Francisco et dans la province de Goyaz*, two volumes. Paris.
1851 *Voyage dans les provinces de Saint-Paul et de Sainte Cathérine*, two volumes. Paris.
1941 *Viagem pelo distrito dos diamantes e litoral do São Paulo*. São Paulo.
DIÉGUES, MANUEL, JR.
1964 *Imigração, urbanização, industrialização*. Rio de Janeiro.
DUARTE, NESTOR
1939 *A ordem privada e a organização politica nacional*. São Paulo.
DURKHEIM, EMILE
1933 *The division of labor in society*. New York.
FERNANDES, FLORESTAN
1964 *A integração do negro à sociedades de classes*. São Paulo.
FREYRE, GILBERTO
1961 *Sobrados e mucambos* (third edition), two volumes. Rio de Janeiro.
FURTADO, CELSO
1963 *The economic growth of Brazil*. Berkeley and Los Angeles: University of California Press.
GOULART, JOSÉ ALIPIO
1961 *Tropas e tropieros na formação do Brasil*. Rio de Janeiro.
GOULDNER, ALVIN W.
1962 "Introduction," in *Socialism*. By Emile Durkheim. New York.
HARTZ, LOUIS, *editor*
1964 *Founding of new societies*. New York: Harcourt Brace Jovanovich.
HAUSER, PHILIP M., LEO F. SCHNORE, *editors*
1965 *Study of urbanization*. New York.
HERRMANN, LUCILA
1948 Evolucao da estructura social de Guarantinguetá num período de trezentos anos. *Revista de Administração* 2 (5–6): 86.
HUTCHINSON, BERTRAM
1960 "Introdução" and "Mudanças de *status* social de uma geração para outra," in *Mobilidade e trabalho, un estudo na cidade de São Paulo*. São Paulo.

KOSTER, HENRY
1817 *Travels in Brazil in the years from 1809 to 1815*, two volumes. Philadelphia.

KUBLER, GEORGE A.
1964 Cities and culture in the colonial period in Latin America. *Diogenes* 47: 53–62.

MORENO, ARELLANO
1960 *Orígenes de la economía venezolana* (second edition). Caracas and Madrid.

MORSE, RICHARD M.
1964 "The heritage of Latin America," in *Founding of new societies*. Edited by Louis Hartz. New York: Harcourt Brace Jovanovich.

NUNES LEAL, VICTOR
1948 *Coronelismo, enxada e voto, o município e o regime representativo no Brasil*. Rio de Janeiro.

PIKE, FREDERICK B.
1963 Aspects of class relations in Chile, 1850–1960. *Hispanic American Historical Review* 43 (1): 14–33.

PRADO, CAIO, JR.
1963 *Formação do Brasil contemporáneo, colonia* (seventh edition). São Paulo.

RICARD, ROBERT
1947 *La plaza mayor* en Espagne et en Amérique. *Annales, Economies, Sociétés-Civilisations* 2 (4): 438.

SAFFORD, FRANK
1965 Foreign and national enterprise in nineteenth-century Colombia. *Business History Review* 39 (4).

SARFATTI, MAGALI
1966 *Spanish bureaucratic patrimonialism in America*. Berkeley: University of California Press.

SMITH, ROBERT C.
1955 Colonial towns of Spanish and Portuguese America. *Journal of the Society of Architectural Historians* 14 (4): 1–12.

STEIN, STANLEY
1957 *Vassouras, a Brazilian coffee county, 1850–1900*. Cambridge.

TOURAINE, ALAIN
1961 Industrialisation et conscience ouvrière à São Paulo. *Sociologie du Travail* 3 (4): 77–95.

VAN DEURSEN, HENRY
1934 L'émancipation industrielle du Brésil. Caractères et développement de l'industrie dans l'état de São Paulo. *Revue Economique Internationale* 3 (2).

VILHENA, LUÍZ DOS SANTOS
1921 *Recopilação de noticias soteropolitanas e brasilicas*. Bahia: Imprensa Oficial do Estado.

VON SPIX, J. B., C. F. P. VON MARTIUS
1824 *Travels in Brazil, in the years 1817–1820*, two volumes. London.

WEBER, MAX
1964a *The theory of social and economic organization*, part two. New York.
1964b *The sociology of religion*. Boston.

INDEPENDENCE AND MODERN

Services in the Contemporary Latin American City: The Case of Chile

MARKOS MAMALAKIS

The size and role of services in rural, urban, and overall growth depends on the variety of needs they satisfy and their efficiency. In satisfying needs, services perform the functions of time, location, and quantity transformation; of quality maintenance and improvement; and of information transmission, money, and cultural and religious enrichment. The absolute value added and relative importance of the various service subsectors in performing these functions have been estimated for 1969 and are presented in Table 1.

The time-transformation function is defined as the set of actions changing the time dimension of goods or service stocks and flows in a manner filling the time gap between production and use. The time dimension was changed by trade and banking generating 6.0 percent of GDP and employing 3.1 percent of the labor force in 1969. The services performing this function were heavily concentrated in the Santiago-Valparaíso urban agglomeration, which became the dominant commercial entity.

There exists ample evidence that the commerce[1] sector's performance of the time-transformation function for mining, agriculture, industry, and other urban services has been inadequate and discriminatory in spite of the high "productivity" and relative income share in trade and banking. Furthermore, banking services deteriorated significantly between 1940 and 1958, recovering only partially during 1968–1972 (Fuenzalida and Undurraga 1968: 27–31, 36–46, 66–70,

Portions of this research were financed by funds provided by the Agency for International Development under contract CSD/2492. However the views expressed in this paper do not necessarily reflect those of AID. This paper was first presented at the Rome, September 3–9, 1972, Urbanization Symposium of the 40th International Congress of Americanists.
[1]   Commerce is always defined as the combined trade and banking sectors.

Table 1. Developmental functions and income and employment created in performing, by service sectors: total and urban, 1969 (in millions of escudos, 1965 prices, and thousands of persons)

Sector performing functions	Transformation of Time Absolute (1)	% (2)	Location Absolute (3)	% (4)	Quantity Absolute (5)	% (6)	Quality Maintenance Absolute (7)	% (8)	Improvement Absolute (9)	% (10)	Transmission of information Absolute (11)	% (12)	Money function Absolute (13)	% (14)	Cultural and religious enrichment functions Absolute (15)	% (16)	Total Absolute (17)	% (18)
Trade																		
Total																		
Income	1,000.7	5.93	796.7	4.72	962.5	5.70	318.7	1.89					108.4	0.64			3,187.0	18.88
Labor	83.9	3.01	95.4	3.42	148.7	5.34	38.1	1.36					15.3	0.54			381.4	13.67
Urban																		
Income	950.7	5.63	770.0	4.56	950.0	5.63	290.0	1.72					104.0	0.62			3,064.7	18.16
Labor	80.0	2.87	92.0	3.30	140.0	5.03	36.0	1.29					15.0	0.54			363.0	13.03
Transport																		
Total																		
Income			770.4	4.57							85.6	0.51					856.0	5.08
Labor			150.4	5.40							17.0	0.61					167.4	6.01
Urban																		
Income			740.0	4.39							82.0	0.49					822.0	4.88
Labor			140.0	5.03							16.0	0.57					156.0	5.60
Gas, water, and electricity																		
Total																		
Income			54.7	0.32													54.7	0.32
Labor			2.9	0.10													2.9	0.10
Urban																		
Income			50.0	0.30													50.0	0.30
Labor			2.7	0.10													2.7	0.10
Services																		
Total																		
Income			164.5	0.97	164.5	0.97	1,645.0	9.75	987.0	5.85	85.6	0.51			329.0	1.95	3,290.0	19.49
Labor			35.1	1.26	35.1	1.26	351.1	12.61	210.6	7.56	17.0	0.61			70.2	2.52	702.1	25.21
Urban																		
Income			160.0	0.95	160.0	0.95	1,600.0	9.50	987.0	5.85	82.0	0.49			300.0	1.78	3,207.0	19.03
Labor			34.5	1.24	34.5	1.24	340.0	12.22	210.6	7.56	16.0	0.57			63.2	2.27	682.8	24.63
Total services																		
Total																		
Income	1,000.7	5.93	1,786.3	10.58	1,127.0	6.67	1,963.7	11.64	987.0	5.85	85.6	0.51	108.4	0.64	329.0	1.95	7,387.7	43.77
Labor	83.9	3.01	283.8	10.18	183.8	6.60	389.2	13.97	210.6	7.56	17.0	0.61	15.3	0.54	70.2	2.52	1,253.8	44.99
Urban																		
Income	950.7	5.63	1,720.0	10.20	1,110.0	6.58	1,890.0	11.22	987.0	5.85	82.0	0.49	104.0	0.62	300.0	1.78	7,143.7	42.37
Labor	80.0	2.87	269.2	9.67	174.5	6.27	376.0	13.51	210.6	7.56	16.0	0.57	15.0	0.54	63.2	2.27	1,204.5	43.26

Source: The basic data were obtained and calculations were made by using information from the Oficina de Planificación Nacional (1971: Table 1; and 1972: 45–50, Tables 1, 2–4).
Notes: The term "income" is used here as a synonym to product or value added. The term "labor" stands for employment. The estimates for the urban segment were made by the author. Ownership

127–143). The widespread and continuous decay of the rural capital stock and much of the plight of the urban misery belts were directly caused by the inflexible, selective, and often even retrogressing time-transforming performance of the banking system. The high incomes earned in trade and banking are in part explained by efficiency, as measured by the predominance of well-educated, white-collar workers and persons working on their own account, but also to a large extent by gains generated by inflationary and protection induced quasi-rents.

The doubts cast about the ability of Chile's urban services to transform the time dimension in a manner satisfying the rapidly changing modern urban and rural needs may be well justified: the Marxist thesis that this inability is the consequence of oligarchic concentration of private ownership, however, is neither accurate nor revealing (Inostroza 1971). Salvador Allende's almost total nationalization of the banking system, which placated the communist critics and partly redistributed credit in favor of the previously neglected small enterprises and farmers, has hardly improved the banking system's overall ability to perform the time-transformation function efficiently and effectively. On the contrary, the monetary crisis of 1972 suggests that its ability may even have suffered a gross deterioration. The qualitative and quantitative differences between services in modern and colonial cities performing the time-transformation function thus may be less than suspected, and the absolute performance level in Chile's modern cities may be significantly below that of the pre-1930 period and of services in nineteenth-century European urban centers of lesser income – always *mutatis mutandis.*

Transformation of the location dimension in 1969 was performed exclusively by service sectors – trade, 4.7 percent of GDP and 3.4 percent of employment; transport, 4.6 per cent of GDP and 5.4 percent of labor force; gas, water, and electricity, 0.3 percent of GDP and 0.1 percent of labor force; and personal services, 1.0 percent of GDP and 1.3 percent of the labor force – generating 10.6 percent of GDP and absorbing 10 percent of the labor force. Whatever the potential performance of the transport and communications system, it did not succeed in achieving a harmonious correspondence between the spatial distribution of persons, income, and consumption. The other services performing the location-changing function also maintained or even strengthened the status quo of vast urban-rural inequalities of the spatial distribution of income and capital instead of acting as catalysts in the lowering of the existing barriers.

In performing the quantity-changing function, which alongside the location-changing was almost exclusively urban, the trade and personal services gave rise to a total of 6.7 percent of GDP and absorbed 6.6 percent of the labor force in 1969. Once more, in performing these functions, the respective sectors have not stimulated production.

More important than the time-, location-, and quantity-transforma-
tion functions, which are complementary to production and "subsistence," i.e. always necessary, are the quality-maintenance and
improvement ones. It is these two latter ones which can create the
modernization poles throughout the economy and thus change the
modes and means of production. The income created in maintaining
quality in 1969 was slightly in excess of 10 percent of GDP and in
improving quality 6.0 per cent. Approximately one-fifth of the labor
force was engaged in maintaining and improving the quality of Chile's
production system. The major problem may lie not so much in the
amount of resources (income and employment) used in maintaining
and improving quality – although either category could be augmented
– but in that all these critical services are performed in and for the
urban areas, with minimum modernization linkages among interregional, service-agricultural, and even intraurban rich-poor segments.

URBAN SERVICES IN INCOME DISTRIBUTION

The interactions between urban services and rural commodity sectors
were weak, distorted, and inadequate, with their shape deeply influenced by the income distribution pattern.

There has been a major disparity between the spatial distribution
of population and the spatial distribution of the benefits of produc-
tions. This distorted pattern was heavily influenced by the size and
nature of services. In part, it resulted from the extreme concentration
of income in selected urban services.

Services in Chile's contemporary cities succeeded in transforming
the distribution of income away from a spectrum compatible with the
spatial distribution of population. This was achieved by controlling
the government and by using it to impose rules affecting present as
well as future distribution. Present income distribution was shaped in
part by the strongly monopolistic, monopsonistic trade services which
returned, with government assistance, to the agricultural macrosocietal hinterland, employing 25 percent of the labor force in 1969,
only 7.5 percent of the country's income (Mamalakis 1972b: 5). This
ex-post-agricultural income share failed to provide the minimum
incentives required for continuous, increased production. Furthermore, urban services transferred to the rural population a dispropor-
tionately small share of the massive resource surpluses contributed
to central Chile by mining and from abroad – foreign aid and credits.
Educational services were distributed spatially in a pattern discrim-
inating against the rural population, directly jeopardizing the im-

mediate accumulation of human rural capital and, indirectly, rural physical capital. This discrimination not only reduced the hinterland's capacity to supply the cities and urban services with food and raw materials but also increasingly placed in jeopardy the welfare of the cities, of its service population, and of the hinterland itself.

Equally unproductive socially, and politically explosive, were the enormous disparities of the intracity distribution of service income against the masses concentrated in the *callampas*. The neglected and discriminated-against segments of the contemporary cities were a mere extension of the equally neglected rural poverty areas.

The aggregate quality of the production system and human life has been maintained or even improved, but its distribution has deteriorated. Quality-improving services have catered almost exclusively to the cities and their privileged groups with the rural and marginal population segments not only being neglected but also frequently suffering absolute and relative losses in benefits. The minor improvements in benefit distribution under Salvador Allende affected the intracity rather than the urban-rural distribution pattern.

Even the intraservice distribution of income from service output has been highly unequal, with segments of personal services being grossly neglected. This pattern is a symptom, cause, and effect of the urban-rural and intraurban disequilibria which push surplus labor into such open-entry service sectors as trade and personal services.

It is necessary to recognize that urban services have been the primary determinant of the spatial and sectoral distribution of income: and they have been traditionally utilized to maintain concentrated, inequitable, and discriminatory patterns by any and all leading groups – rural elites, industrialists, foreigners, miners, or middle classes.

URBAN SERVICES AND CAPITAL FORMATION

Capital formation in Chile's urban services had a twofold link to growth. On the one side, some of the service output constituted accumulation of human capital. On the other side, physical investment in services was an indicator of the nation's priorities and the growth potential of services. In the present article, I enter into areas where absolutely no research has been previously attempted, and this is particularly true in the area of capital formation in services by functions. The estimates of urban capital formation should be used with caution because they are tentative.

Capital formation in urban services was 55 percent of the total in 1965. Thus, the share in investment of urban services exceeded their relative contribution to income. One-third of all investment in services

Table 2. Fixed-capital formation in services by functions and type of machinery and equipment: total and urban 1965 (in millions of escudos and in percentages of total fixed-capital formation)

Sector performing functions	Time				Transformation of location				Quantity				Quality maintenance				Quality improvement			
	Absolute		Percent		Absolute		Percent		Absolute		Percent		Absolute		Percent		Absolute		Percent	
	Total (1)	Urban (2)	Total (3)	Urban (4)	Total (5)	Urban (6)	Total (7)	Urban (8)	Total (9)	Urban (10)	Total (11)	Urban (12)	Total (13)	Urban (14)	Total (15)	Urban (16)	Total (17)	Urban (18)	Total (19)	Urban (20)
Trade and banking																				
Gross investment*	15.0	15.0	0.52	0.52	15.0	14.8	0.52	0.52	10.0	9.9	0.35	0.35	10.0	9.9	0.35	0.35	120.0	118.0	4.20	4.13
Machinery and equipment	8.0	8.0	0.28	0.28	8.0	7.9	0.28	0.28	5.0	4.9	0.17	0.17	5.0	4.9	0.17	0.17	45.0	44.0	1.57	1.54
National	4.0	4.0	0.14	0.14	4.0	3.9	0.14	0.14	2.0	1.9	0.07	0.07	2.0	1.9	0.07	0.07	14.0	13.5	0.49	0.47
Imported	4.0	4.0	0.14	0.14	4.0	4.0	0.14	0.14	3.0	3.0	0.10	0.10	3.0	3.0	0.10	0.10	31.0	30.5	1.08	1.07
Transport, storage and communications																				
Gross investment*					400.0	380.0	13.99	13.99												
Machinery and equipment					110.0	110.0	3.85	3.50												
National					15.0	10.0	0.52	0.35												
Imported					95.0	90.0	3.32	3.15												
Gas, water and electricity																				
Gross investment*					120.0	118.0	4.20	4.13					54.0	52.0	1.89	1.82				
Machinery and equipment					16.0	16.0	0.56	0.56					7.0	7.0	0.24	0.24				
National					2.0	2.0	0.07	0.07					0.0	0.0	0.00	0.00				
Imported					14.0	14.0	0.49	0.49					7.0	7.0	0.24	0.24				
Personal services and public administration																				
Gross investment*					20.0	19.8	0.70	0.69	25.0	24.0	0.87	0.84	180.0	175.0	6.30	6.12				
Machinery and equipment					7.0	7.0	0.24	0.24	9.0	9.0	0.31	0.31	67.0	66.0	2.34	2.31				
National					2.0	2.0	0.07	0.07	3.0	3.0	0.10	0.10	21.0	20.0	0.73	0.70				
Imported					5.0	5.0	0.17	0.17	6.0	6.0	0.21	0.21	46.0	46.0	1.61	1.61				
Ownership of dwellings																				
Gross investment*													250.0	250.0	8.74	8.74	262.0	262.0	9.16	9.16
Machinery and equipment													0.0	0.0	0.00	0.00	0.0	0.0	0.00	0.00
National													0.0	0.0	0.00	0.00	0.0	0.0	0.00	0.00
Imported													0.0	0.0	0.00	0.00	0.0	0.0	0.00	0.00
Total in services																				
Gross investment*	15.0	15.0	0.52	0.52	555.0	532.6	19.41	18.63	35.0	33.9	1.22	1.19	494.0	486.9	17.28	17.03	382.0	380.0	13.36	13.29
Machinery and equipment	8.0	8.0	0.28	0.28	141.0	130.9	4.93	4.58	14.0	13.9	0.48	0.48	79.0	77.9	2.74	2.72	45.0	44.0	1.57	1.54
National	4.0	4.0	0.14	0.14	23.0	17.9	0.80	0.63	5.0	4.9	0.17	0.17	23.0	21.9	0.80	0.77	14.0	13.5	0.49	0.47
Imported	3.0	4.0	0.14	0.14	118.0	113.0	4.12	3.95	9.0	9.0	0.31	0.31	56.0	56.0	1.95	1.95	31.0	31.0	1.08	1.07

Sector performing functions	Transmission of information				Money function				Cultural and religious enrichment functions				Total			
	Absolute		Percent		Absolute		Percent		Absolute		Percent		Absolute		Percent	
	Total (21)	Urban (22)	Total (23)	Urban (24)	Total (25)	Urban (26)	Total (27)	Urban (28)	Total (29)	Urban (30)	Total (31)	Urban (32)	Total (33)	Urban (34)	Total (35)	Urban (36)
Trade and banking																
Gross investment*					16.0	16.0	0.56	0.56					66.0	65.6	2.30	2.30
Machinery and equipment					9.0	9.0	0.32	0.32					35.0	34.7	1.22	1.22
National					5.0	5.0	0.17	0.17					17.0	16.7	0.59	0.59
Imported					4.0	4.0	0.14	0.14					18.0	18.0	0.62	0.62
Transport, storage, and communications																
Gross investment*	58.0	57.0	2.03	1.99									458.0	437.0	16.02	15.28
Machinery and equipment	17.0	17.0	0.59	0.59									127.0	117.0	4.44	4.09
National	2.0	2.0	0.7	0.07									17.0	12.0	0.59	0.42
Imported	15.0	15.0	0.52	0.52									110.0	105.0	3.84	3.67
Gas, water, and electricity																
Gross investment*													174.0	170.0	6.09	5.95
Machinery and equipment													23.0	23.0	0.80	0.80
National													2.0	2.0	0.07	0.07
Imported													21.0	21.0	0.73	0.73
Personal services and public administration																
Gross investment*									54.0	53.0	1.89	1.85	399.0	389.8	13.96	13.63
Machinery and equipment									21.0	20.5	0.74	0.72	149.0	146.5	5.20	5.12
National									6.0	6.0	0.21	0.21	46.0	44.5	1.60	1.55
Imported									15.0	14.5	0.53	0.51	103.0	102.0	3.60	3.57
Ownership of dwellings																
Gross investment*													512.0	512.0	17.90	17.90
Machinery and equipment													0.0	0.0	0.00	0.00
National													0.0	0.0	0.00	0.00
Imported													0.0	0.0	0.00	0.00
Total in services																
Gross investment*	58.0	57.0	2.03	1.99	16.0	16.0	0.56	0.56	54.0	53.0	1.89	1.85	1609.0	1574.0	56.27	55.06
Machinery and equipment	17.0	17.0	0.59	0.59	9.0	9.0	0.32	0.32	21.0	20.5	0.74	0.72	334.0	321.2	11.66	11.23
National	2.0	2.0	0.07	0.07	5.0	5.0	0.17	0.17	6.0	6.0	0.21	0.21	82.0	75.2	2.85	2.63
Imported	15.0	15.0	0.52	0.52	4.0	4.0	0.14	0.14	15.0	14.5	0.53	0.51	252.0	246.0	8.79	8.59

Source: Obtained or calculated by using information found in Oficina de Planificación Nacional (n.d.: Tables 1–3).
Note: * Gross investment stands for gross investment in fixed-capital formation. The estimates of urban capital formation were made by the author.

or 19 percent of fixed-capital formation, was allocated in urban sectors performing the location-transformation function (Table 2, Column 8). The most important investment recipients in this group were the transportation and gas, water, and electricity sectors. Much, if not all, of this investment was in response to the demands of the mushrooming urban population, especially in Santiago Province. The contemporary city in Latin America, as exemplified by Chile's urban areas, requires a share of resources to transform the location dimension of persons and products substantially in excess of that used in previous historical periods. The actual size of resources used may be severely under-estimated, since the contribution of private cars in performing this function is not included. The costs of performing this function and the share of investment absorbed by it are likely to increase pro-portionally faster than the urban population, due to diseconomies from rising population densities. Fixed-capital formation in the sectors performing the other two functions, complementary to pro-duction of transforming the time and quantity dimensions, was mini-mal, accounting for only 2.5 percent of total gross fixed-capital formation. It is likely that these functions may have been efficiently performed with equally small amounts of investment in pre-Columbian and colonial cities.

The investment resources actually utilized in maintaining and im-proving the quality of input and output amounted to 30 percent of gross-fixed capital formation (GFCF) and more than half of the investment in services. The largest share – 17 percent of GFCF – was used in performing the quality-maintenance function, with more than half of this share reflecting investment in dwellings (Table 2: Column 16). The unprecedented popular demands for adequate housing faci-lities and the extent to which governments respond to them may raise the share of resources used for housing in contemporary cities to levels far above those experienced previously in Latin America.

The high investment share allocated in the quality-maintenance function occurred in spite of a highly inequitable and discriminatory distribution of housing units. The rural inhabitants and the urban poor, who were grossly and continuously ignored, have emerged as a powerful political force under Salvador Allende, and his desire to meet their demands is likely to maintain or raise housing investment. Because more than half of housing investment improves the quality of life (Table 2: Column 10), the rise in this investment is likely to increase the overall welfare of the Chilean people. Unless, however, rural and urban inhabitants receive equal treatment, adequate housing services will remain as unevenly distributed between urban and rural areas as in the past.

With more than 25 percent of all investment in services used in the quality-improvement function in 1965 (Table 2: Column 20), the aggregate quality of Chilean life improved considerably. What constituted a severe growth bottleneck, however, was the concentration of this improvement among the urban privileged classes with only negligible benefits accruing to the rural and urban poor. Once more, under President Salvador Allende it was the urban lower-middle classes and poor that became major beneficiaries of quality-improving investments. As the amount of investment resources available remained constant or declined, major losses in the quality of life were sustained by the rich, upper-middle classes, and even some previously privileged blue-collar workers. Unfortunately, few statistics are available on these points for the years 1970–1972.

Services improving the quality of Chile's human, physical, and institutional capital were growth-promoting in an aggregative, global sense until 1970 since both their income contribution and investment share were significant, but growth-impeding in that they accentuated existing urban-rural disequilibria in physical and human capital stock endowments, modernization capacity, access to and enjoyment of benefits, and so forth. The spatially and sectorally inequitable accumulation of human capital gave rise to a phenomenon where sectoral clashes penalizing agriculture and favoring urban services coincided with spatial, urban-rural clashes, where major urban population segments emerged as dominant, and rural inhabitants were treated as second-class citizens.

The sociopolitical environment that produced this discrepancy between the spatial distribution of the population and the benefits offered by services did not result from a control of the urban decision-making apparatus by a decadent, oligarchic, power-hungry elite. It resulted, rather, from the coincidence of interests among the urban constituents, namely, the blue- and white-collar workers, parties, consumers, government, employers, the rich and even the inhabitants of the *callampas*.

With the advent of Allende, the distribution of quality-maintaining and -improving service-investment has become growth-making – a radical and unique change in Chile's economic history – but gross investment in performing these functions has suffered, if not fallen, leading to a negligible or zero aggregate gain.

Capital formation in the remaining functions of information transmission, money, and cultural and religious enrichment has been small, and, once more, almost exclusively urban.

CONCLUSION

The high concentration of all services in urban areas and the use of the government apparatus to maintain a production, distribution, and capital-formation system concerning services which favored the city, stand out as the major characteristics of Chile's contemporary urban services and as a major deterrent to economic growth and social peace. This pattern prevailed on subsistence (complementary to production) as well as on autonomous quality-maintaining and -improving services.

REFERENCES

FUENZALIDA, JAVIER, SERGIO UNDURRAGA
  1968   *El crédito y su distribución en Chile.* Santiago: Editorial Lambda.
INOSTROZA, ALFONSO
  1971   "Statement by Mr. Alfonso Inostroza, president of the Central Bank of the Republic of Chile. Monetary Policy," in *CORFO Chile Economic Notes, March 1971, Special Issue, Excerpts from the CIAP Meeting in Chile.*
MAMALAKIS, MARKOS J.
  1970   *Urbanization and sectoral transformation in Latin America, 1950–1965.* University of Wisconsin-Milwaukee, Latin American Center Discussion Paper 24. Milwaukee. (Reprinted 1976 in *El Trimestre Económico 170*).
  1972a *Employment and unemployment dimensions of production, distribution and allocation in Chile.* University of Wisconsin-Milwaukee, Latin American Center Discussion Paper 39. Milwaukee.
  1972b "New Dimensions in national accounting with special reference to Chile." Paper presented at the Conference on National Accounts and Planning of the Development Center of the Organization for Economic Cooperation and Development, November 1972.
  1976   "The service sector: its growth and functions," in *The growth and structure of the Chilean economy: from independence to Allende.* New Haven, Connecticut: Yale University Press.
MORSE, RICHARD M.
  1965   Recent research on Latin American urbanization: a selective survey with commentary. *Latin American Research Review* 1 (1): 35–74.
  1971   Trends and issues in Latin American urban research, 1965–1970. *Latin American Research Review* 6 (1): 3–34, 6 (2): 19–75.
OFICINA DE PLANIFICACIÓN NACIONAL (ODEPLAN)
  1971   *Población ocupado por sectores economicos, 1960–1970.* Santiago: ODEPLAN, Presidencia de la República.
  1972   *Cuentas nacionales de Chile, 1960–1970.* Santiago: ODEPLAN, Presidencia de la República.
  n.d.   *Inversión geográfica bruta en capital fijo por sectores de destino 1962–1966.* Santiago: ODEPLAN, Presidencia de República.

SECTION THREE

Case Studies

The Internal Structure of Cities in America: Pre-Columbian Cities; The Case of Tenochtitlán

EDWARD E. CALNEK

According to the traditional Aztec histories, Tenochtitlán was founded on a small island near the western shore of Lake Texcoco in the Valley of Mexico in 1325 A.D. It achieved independence in about 1427, and commenced a vigorous career of military expansion which continued until the Spanish invasion in 1519. The entire process of urban development, therefore, spanned slightly less than two centuries. At the end of this period Tenochtitlán was unquestionably the largest and most highly urbanized city in the New World, and the political center of an empire that extended from the Gulf Coast to the Pacific, and southward at some points to the modern frontier between Mexico and Guatemala.

Reliable quantitative evidence relating to urban growth rates is entirely unavailable. The Aztec chronicles suggest moderate but continuous increases in the urban population throughout the preimperial period – in part stimulated by state initiatives designed to induce outsiders to settle and marry within the city (Duran 1951: vol. 1, pp. 60–61). When Chimalpopoca assumed the throne in 1415, Tenochtitlán was described as beginning to assume a more *urban* aspect, as the marshy zone which surrounded the city was gradually converted to dry land, and well-built houses of stone and adobe began to replace the nondescript huts (*chozas*) of earlier times (Duran 1951: vol. 1, p. 62). The wealth and prestige that resulted from even early military successes evidently began to attract immigrants in significantly larger numbers. The *Crónica X* (Barlow 1945) – a sixteenth-century Nahuatl history

This paper is based on research supported by a National Science Foundation Research Grant (GS-1287), and by a University of Rochester Summer Faculty Research Grant. I am indebted to René Millon and Barbara J. Price for valuable comments on an earlier version of this paper.

independently translated by Duran (1951) and Tezozomoc (1944) – relates that vigorous state intervention was required to control internal disorders, and to organize a population which had begun to include large numbers of foreigners, as well as an expanding population of Aztec descent, during the reign of Motecuàzoma I, 1440–1468 (Duran 1951: vol. 1, pp. 213–214).

The size and population of the city in 1519 remain somewhat conjectural. A recently completed reconstruction of the urban boundaries of Tenochtitlán, based primarily on the analysis of documentary source materials (Calnek 1969, 1972), indicates that the city occupied at least twelve square kilometers of more or less continuously settled terrain. Archaeological evidence obtained during recent subway excavations in Mexico City indicates that this may be a highly conservative estimate (J. Gussinyer, personal communication), and it is possible that the total area was as large as fifteen to twenty square kilometers – two to three times the area specified in most previous estimates (Toussaint et al. 1938: 72).

Population figures valid for the time of the Conquest or earlier are equally problematic. I am now attempting to estimate the probable population of the city in 1519 by collecting genealogies and census data from early colonial period archival sources in forms that can be linked to the specific types of settlement pattern and household organization. This will provide estimates of the probable population densities of several typical urban residential neighborhoods and, ultimately, the approximate range of magnitude of the urban population as a whole. A very crude set of computations of this type, projected against an assumed area of twelve square kilometers, has resulted in figures falling in the general range of 150,000 to 200,000 inhabitants. It should be emphasized, however, that this phase in a more general investigation of settlement pattern and demography at Tenochtitlán is still at an early stage, and substantial modification of these figures may be required in the light of future research.

The existence of a significant immigrant population within the city has already been noted. This included organized craft groups, such as the lapidaries, who are said to have originated at Xochimilco (de Torquemada 1723: vol. 2, p. 60); rulers, noblemen, or warriors from subject states, who enjoyed special privileges or were required to spend a part of each year at the imperial court (Cortés 1963: 75; Díaz del Castillo 1960: 176); and probably numerous others whose presence can be attributed to the simple attraction of the urban milieu. The city was also a place of refuge for peoples displaced by war. A number of Huexotzincans, for example, were permitted to settle in Tenochtitlán when their homeland was devastated by war (Duran 1951: vol. 1, pp. 476–477; Tezozomoc 1944: 460–470). The existence of houses occupied by people from Cuauhquechollan near the great market of Tlatelolco is mentioned by de Sahagun (1955: 103).

That outsiders were easily accepted and integrated into local populations from comparatively early times is clear from other historical references. The Aztecs had intermarried and mingled with the people of Colhuacan prior to the foundation of Tenochtitlán (Icazbalceta 1941: 225–226; Duran 1951: vol. 1, p. 33). When Colhuacan itself was destroyed some years later, refugees from that town built a small temple and occupied one of the southern districts of Tenochtitlán (Icazbalceta 1941: 228). The possibility that the Aztecs might move en masse to Azcapotzalco, where they might take refuge among friends and acquaintances in the crowded *barrios* of that city, was discussed by the Tenochcan rulers on the eve of their rebellion against the much larger and more powerful city-state in about 1426 or 1427 (Duran 1951: vol. 1, p. 70).

During the period of greatest imperial power at Tenochtitlán, literally tens of thousands of people visited the city on important market days (Conquistador Anónimo 1941: 43; Cortés 1963: 72). Others continuously arrived bearing tributes, or to perform labor services (Duran 1951: 213). Thus, the city, at virtually all times from the mid-fifteenth century until the Spanish conquest, was the focal point for large and continuous movements of men and goods. In some cases, large groups had to be accommodated for periods of several days or even weeks. Visiting dignitaries were traditionally accorded hospitality at the royal court. The king himself was expected to employ a part of the revenues from his personal estates for this purpose (Carrasco 1967: 149; Duran 1951: vol. 1, p. 101). The men from a town named Cuitlatenamic owned a house, or at least maintained a permanent relationship with an Aztec household, where they stayed when they brought tribute or had other business in the city (Archivo General de la Nación [AGN], Ramo de Tierras, volume 34, expediente 4, folios 2, 32, 82). Several early Spanish writers mention stands where cooked foods could be purchased, and houses which functioned as hostels for overnight stays (Díaz del Castillo 1960: 159; MacNutt 1912: vol. 2, p. 109).

There is, in short, substantial evidence for movement between cities and other localities, ranging from permanent immigration, to brief visits for market exchange, to delivery of tribute, and the like. Although the internal organization of cities is necessarily based on the permanently resident population, it is evident that the internal structure of Tenochtitlán had developed sufficient flexibility to integrate a steady flow of outsiders who intended to remain in the city, as well as the large transient population that had become a virtually permanent feature of urban life.

I emphasize this in order to suggest something of the quality of urban life in those aspects which do not emerge with any clarity from analytical studies of internal organization, which are likely to be concerned with the structure and interrelationships of groups whose membership was fixed on the basis of territory, kinship, occupation, or other types of relatively permanent affiliation.

In this paper I attempt to define the principal types of social groupings that can be identified on the basis of historical and ethnographic descriptions of the city on the eve of the Conquest, and linked to at least potentially identifiable architectural *markers* of the kind described below. The most serious difficulty in the organization of sociological data with respect to architectural settings results from the fact that archaeological data are, as yet, extremely limited for Tenochtitlán, while good descriptions are available only for a small number of the more monumental types of public buildings and, because they were the subject of frequent litigation during the early colonial period, a few of the simpler kinds of domestic architecture (Calnek 1972). Thus, it is frequently possible to link social groups or activities to specific structures which are identified by name in the chronicles, but for which no physical characteristics whatever can be objectively described.

It is convenient to begin by examining the principal territorial divisions of the city (Figure 1), because they can be described with considerable precision on the basis of written documents or early maps, although it is unlikely that their sociological correlates will ever be completely known. The largest unit – the city itself – originally consisted of two separately organized political states: Tenochtitlán and Tlatelolco. Both were closely linked by geographic proximity, history, and cultural and ethnic identity, and the two populations maintained an exceptionally close ceremonial and economic relationship both before and after the Conquest and annexation of Tlatelolco by its more powerful sister city in 1473 (see, for example, Duran 1951; Tezozomoc 1944; Berlin 1948). The fact that both cities originated and developed as separate political units is reflected in the duplication of large, walled, ceremonial precincts, associated with a *tecpan* [administrative palace], and a market in both cities. Together, these constituted an extraordinarily monumental and, in principle, easily identifiable complex, which was the focal point of government, religion, and economic life for each city. At Tenochtitlán (and probably at Tlatelolco, although good descriptions of the *tecpan* there are not available) there was, nonetheless, a strict segregation of the architectural components associated with each. The ceremonial precinct included temples dedicated to the most important deities, and residential complexes occupied by members of the temple communities (Duran 1951: 82–83), and was sharply differentiated from the palace,

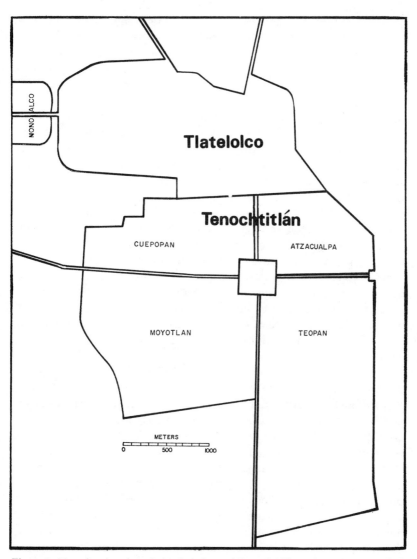

Figure 1. Map showing the relative locations of Tenochtitlán and Tlatelolco, and of the four Great Quarters of Tenochtitlán

which functioned as the focal point of secular authority. The *tecpan* included the personal shrine of the ruler and his household, but otherwise lacked definable architectural characteristics relating to the state religion. It corresponded, therefore, to the predominantly secular character of kingship and civil administration, as described in the Aztec and Spanish chronicles. Although there are repeated references to the personal divinity of the king (Duran 1951: vol. 1, pp. 162, 292,

421), it is notable that he was not the object of organized cult activities of any kind during his lifetime or after his death.

The physical differentiation of sacred and secular localities was partially bridged by the fact that the king and other noblemen were also high priests (Duran 1951: vol. 1, p. 196; de Alva Ixtlilxochitl 1952: vol. 2, pp. 305–306). Explicitly ecclesiastical functions were performed at sacred localities outside the *tecpan*, and marked by the adoption of entirely different personal regalia in each setting (Duran 1951: vol. 1, p. 196). The duality of roles, in short, linked the palace to the temple, but within carefully organized and sharply differentiated social and architectural contexts. The generally higher rank of secular officials over the priesthood is most effectively expressed by Duran (1951: vol. 2, pp. 124–125), who observes that men who demonstrated their personal worth and piety within the priesthood were ultimately *promoted* to offices of the highest honor and authority within the state (*"los sacauan a dignidades y cargos honrosos en las republicas"*). The titles of office which are cited at the end of this section indicate that he is referring to men who were already royal princes of the highest rank. The ceremonial precinct, therefore, was symbolically identified with the Tenochcan state, but was clearly subordinate to the palace insofar as the distribution of political, and even ecclesiastical, authority was concerned.

This type of organization is evidently reflected in the greater architectural prominence and independence of the palace with respect to ceremonial structures, and possibly in the closed-in character of the precinct – its isolation from the day-to-day life of the city – as compared with Teotihuacán. Thus, large, complex, and even luxurious residential quarters adjoin religious structures at Teotihuacán, but they are clearly subordinated to an architectural design that emphasized the mass of the temple pyramid as its dominant component. No palace thus far identified at Teotihuacán approaches the size and independence of the palace of Motecuàzoma II, as described by such early chroniclers as Cortés (1963: 77–79). This structure occupied an estimated area of 2.4 hectares – approximately double the combined areas of three closely related residential complexes that adjoin the Temple of Quetzalcoatl in the Ciudadela at Teotihuacán (R. Millon, personal communication). The secular component of the urban center also included large palaces occupied by Axayacatl (1469–1481), and the Cihuacoatl – a dignitary whose rank was second only to that of the king himself (see Marquina 1960: Lámina 2).

It can also be noted that, while the great temples occupied the highest rank within the inventory of religious structures of the city as a whole, they do not stand at the apex of a hierarchically organized system of temple communities. The individual temples located in the ceremonial precinct *outranked* those associated with the Great Quarters and the *barrios* (see below), but rank order in this case did not correspond to a rigidly organized chain-of-command. The palace occupied by a reigning monarch, in contrast, included numerous functionally differentiated halls and patios – each concerned with clearly defined administrative, military, or judicial functions, which ultimately engaged much wider groups by the delegation of authority through officials of progressively lower rank (de Sahagun 1954: 41–45; Duran 1951: vol. 2, pp. 161–166). The *barrio* headmen, for example, assembled each day at the *calpixcalli*, where they awaited orders from the king or other high officials, and transmitted them to lower officials who supervised their execution (Duran 1951: vol. 1, pp. 323–324, vol. 2, p. 165; de Torquemada 1723: vol. 2, pp. 544–545). Separate courts existed to hear cases brought by noblemen or commoners. The judges controlled a staff of lower officials who maintained order, made arrests, recorded decisions, and carried them out (de Benavente Motolinia 1903: 303–312; de Sahagun 1954: 41–42; de Torquemada 1723: vol. 2, pp. 351–353). The great military councils deliberated at the palace; the army was thereafter mobilized by Great Quarters and then by *barrios*, by officers whose rank was linked to each level of the military chain-of-command (de Sahagun 1954: 51; Tezozomoc 1944: 273, 284, 403, 437, etc.).

Tenochtitlán was divided into four *Great Quarters*, marked off by four avenues that extended in the cardinal directions from the gates of the ceremonial precinct (Figure 1). A large temple or temple complex was located in each of the Great Quarters, but nothing whatever is known of its actual size or architectural character (*Códice Franciscano* 1941: 6). Tezozomoc mentions structures called *huehue-callis* (1944: 399), occupied by officials described as the "absolute lords" (*sefieres absolutes*) or "chiefs" (*caudillos*) of the quarters (1944: 284, 315–316, 399–400, 437, etc.). These may have adjoined the temples and plazas associated with the Great Quarters, to replicate, on a smaller scale, the pattern already described for the urban center. Unfortunately, no other source can be cited in support of this interpretation, and it is possible that the *huehuecalli* had been incorporated into the *tecpan* at some time during the imperial period.

The Great Quarters were subdivided into *barrios* called *tlaxillacallis* in late pre-Hispanic and early colonial texts. The *tlaxillacallis* bear the same names as were employed to identify units called *calpullis*. Examination of the contexts in which each term occurs in the de Sahagun texts suggests that *calpulli* referred to a certain kind of corporate, localized social group; *tlaxillacalli* is most frequently employed as a locational reference. It would appear, consequently, that individuals were conceived as *members* of a named *calpulli*; they *resided* in a *tlaxillacalli* or *barrio* bearing the same name. Although it is impossible to summarize the full range of documentary source materials bearing on this question, it is likely that *calpulli* membership was critical in relation to occupation, and personal membership in certain types of ritual groups (Monzon 1949: 47–51). The territorial framework provided by the *tlaxillacalli* may have been exploited as a primary component for the internal administrative organization of the Aztec state. That the two types of affiliation did not result in entirely coterminous social groups is at least suggested by Duran's reference to the possibility that marriages could occur between members of different *barrios* (1951: vol. 2, pp. 228–229), and the occurrence of several cases of uxorilocal residence in early colonial archival texts. Thus, a *platero* [gold- or silversmith], who resided with his wife's family in the *barrio* named Zacatlan in the Great Quarter of Atzacualpa, acknowledged the authority of the "lords" (*principales*) of the *plateros'* guild, which was centered in the *barrio* of Yopico in Moyotlan, up to the time of his death in 1453. He himself employed an apprentice from Copolco in Cuepopan, who appears as a craftsman in his own right at a later date (AGN, Ramo de Tierras, volume 30, expedient 1, folios 14–16, 64). Although little more than two decades had elapsed since the Conquest, there is no indication that this arrangement was considered unusual.

Much stronger supporting documentation will, of course, be required to establish a significant differentiation in group membership based on the *calpulli* and *tlaxillacalli*. The existing evidence at least suggests that the rules governing membership and residence were considerably more complex than previously supposed.

The *barrios* – conceived as territorial units – were marked by a structure which housed the patron deities of the group (Duran 1951: vol. 2, p. 148; de Sahagun 1951: 16, 39, etc.). This was evidently a part of a larger complex which also included a *telpochcalli* ["young men's house"] (de Sahagun 1954: 58; Duran 1951: vol. 1, pp. 216–217), and, in most or all cases, a plaza or market (Cortés 1963: 72; López de Gomara 1943: vol. 1, p. 236). The architectural characteristics of these units cannot be adequately defined at present, but they should have formed a distinctive type of complex, which could be easily distinguished from those marking the Great Quarters and the city in overall scale. The *calpulli* temple, as illustrated by de Sahagun (1951: Figure 51), does not seem to have been a large pyramid-temple, but is shown as an almost houselike structure, constructed over a low-stepped platform within a small walled enclosure which included other buildings as well. In addition to providing the locus for public and private rituals dedicated to local dieties, it was also the meeting place for *barrio* elders, and the focal point for large ceremonials organized by occupationally specialized groups (de Sahagun 1951, 1959, etc.). They provided, in short, a kind of *civic center*, where a great variety of activities took place, essential to the urban neighborhoods, and in relation to which the social identities of the greater part of the urban population were most immediately expressed.

Although each *barrio* was divided into groups of houses or households for administrative purposes (Duran 1951: vol. 1, pp. 323–324), there are no references to distinctive architectural features occupying an intermediate position between the *calpulli* center and the individual residential sites. Domestic architecture represents an entirely distinct level of organization, directly below the *tlaxillacalli*. Here, I will merely sketch out a few of its salient characteristics, and their relation to the internal organization of household groups – primarily because of the great importance of these data for comparison with, and the interpretation of, settlement patterns at Teotihuacán and other earlier cities. There is, fortunately, a good deal of detailed archival evidence relating to residential sites and to household organization – including genealogies and census data which, in some cases, can be followed out over periods ranging up to five or six generations – that is, over time periods sufficiently long to yield important insights into developmental cycles at the level of the elementary household or domestic group.

A number of typical residential sites at Tenochtitlán have been illustrated in Figure 2. All have been drawn to the same scale from early ground plans or written descriptions which include the dimensions of basic site components. Residential sites characteristically take the form of walled compounds, which enclosed a number of separately entered dwelling units that faced inward on an open patio space. Each compound was normally occupied by a bilateral joint family – most frequently, a group consisting of an elderly couple, their married children (including daughters, although virilocal residence was most common), and grandchildren, or some derivative unit at later stages in the normal cycle of family development.

Each married couple occupied a single one- or two-room dwelling or, in some cases, a single floor within a two-story house. If sufficient space were available, a new dwelling might be constructed to accommodate a child at the time of his or her marriage. There are also cases where childless couples invited a nephew or other close kinsman to occupy a vacant house at their site. Conversely, corporate family organization appears to have been successful only when the joint family was based on parents and children, siblings, or first cousins. There are several cases in which the death of the last male in a generation of siblings or first cousins was followed by a dispute and the physical subdivision of the original site. One of the most interesting

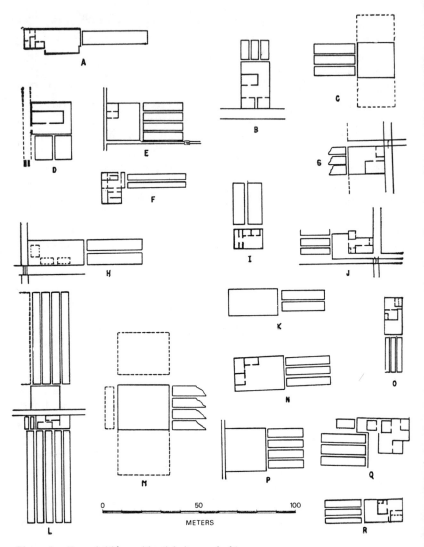

Figure 2.   Tenochtitlán residential sites and *chinampas*

results of this process lies in the fact that the household which occupied each segment of the original site was frequently as large as that prior to division within a single generation or two. Very small sites – which may have resulted from this type of subdivision – appear most frequently toward the center of the city, a datum of considerable demographic interest if we observe that the depth of occupation there is likely to have spanned four to six generations, as against two or three generations in the more peripheral localities.

The Tenochtitlán household compound most closely resembles the individual apartments within the Teotihuacán *apartment compounds* in scale, but it was an architecturally *free* unit, in the sense that each compound at Tenochtitlán enjoyed direct access to streets and canals, and was related to neighboring sites mainly by the fact of physical juxtaposition, rather than assimilation to large unitary structures of the Teotihuacán type. This, in turn, may reflect a greater freedom in the organization of productive activities, interpersonal or interhousehold bonds, and greater possibilities for upward mobility based on wealth or personal achievement than was characteristic of Teotihuacán society. Even commoners could achieve high rank through military service, or the acquisition of great personal wealth (Duran 1951: vol. 1, pp. 239ff., vol. 2, pp. 124, 164–165; de Sahagun 1959). The architectural segregation of relatively small residential compounds permitted the public display of status markers – most commonly architectural ornamentation – to distinguish individual compounds from even their immediate neighbors (Tezozomoc 1944: 144).

In conclusion, it can be observed that we now begin to control sufficient information about Tenochtitlán and Teotihuacán to permit systematic correlations between settlement pattern data and social organization, and to use this information in preliminary comparisons of the internal structure and development of both cities.

REFERENCES

Archivo General de la Nación (AGN)
    n.d.   Unpublished manuscripts, Ramo de Tierras, volumes 30, 34.
BARLOW, ROBERT
    1945   La Crónica X. *Revista Mexicana de Estudios Antropológicos* 7: 65–87.
BERLIN, H., *editor*
    1948   *Anales de Tlatelolco.* Unos annales historicos de la nación mexicana y codice de Tlatelolco. Mexico City: Robredo.
CALNEK, EDWARD
    1969   "Urbanization at Tenochtitlán." Paper delivered at the Sixty-eighth Annual Meeting of the American Anthropological Association, New Orleans.
    1972   Settlement pattern and Chinampa agriculture at Tenochtitlán. *American Antiquity* 37 (1).
CARRASCO, PEDRO
    1967   Relaciones sobre la organización social indígena en el siglo XVI. *Estudios de Cultura Nahuatl* 7: 119–154.
Códice Franciscano
    1941   In *Nueva colección de documentos para la historia de México*, volume two. Edited by J. García Icazbalceta. Mexico City: Hayhoe.
CONQUISTADOR ANÓNIMO
    1941   *Relación de algunas cosas de la Nueva España y de la gran ciudad*

de Temistitan México, escrita por un compañero de Hernán Cortés.
Mexico City: América.

CORTÉS, HERNÁN
1963   *Cartas y documentos.* Mexico City: Porrua.

DE ALVA IXTLILXOCHITL, FERNANDO
1952   *Historia de la nación chichimeca,* two volumes. Mexico City.

DE BENAVENTE MOTOLINIA, FATHER TORIBIO
1903   *Memoriales.* Edited by Luis García Pimentel. Documentos historicos de Méjico, volume one. Mexico City: Casa del Editor.

DE SAHAGUN, FATHER BERNARDINO
1950   *The Florentine codex,* book one: *The gods.* Edited and translated by A. J. O. Anderson and C. E. Dibble. Monographs of the School of American Research. Santa Fe: School of American Research and the University of Utah.
1951   *The Florentine codex,* book two: *The ceremonies.*
1954   *The Florentine codex,* book eight: *Kings and lords.*
1955   *The Florentine codex,* book twelve: *The conquest of Mexico.*
1959   *The Florentine codex,* book nine: *The merchants.*

DE TORQUEMADA, JUAN
1723   *Primera (segunda, tercera) parte de los veinte i un libros rituales i monarchia indiana,* three volumes. Madrid.

DÍAZ DEL CASTILLO, BERNAL
1960   *Historia de la conquista de la Nueva España.* Mexico City: Porrua.

DURAN, DIEGO
1951 [1867–1880]   *Historia de las Indias de Nueva España y Islas de Tierra Firme,* two volumes and atlas. Mexico City.

ICAZBALCETA, JOAQUÍN GARCÍA, *editor*
1941   *Nueva colección de documentos para la historia de México. Pomar – Zurita – Relaciones Antiguas (Siglo XVI).* México City.

MACNUTT, F. A., *editor and translator*
1912   *De orbe novo. The eight decades of Peter Martyr D'Anghera,* two volumes. New York: Putnam.

MARQUINA, IGNACIO
1960   *El templo mayor de México.* Mexico City: Instituto Nacional de Antropología e Historia.

MONZON, ARTURO
1949   *El calpulli en la organización social de los tenochca.* Publicaciones del Instituto de Historia, first series, 14. Mexico City.

TEZOZOMOC, HERNANDO ALVARADO
1944   *Crónica mexicana.* Mexico City.

TOUSSAINT, MANUEL, FEDERICO GÓMEZ DE OROZCO, JUSTINO FERNÁNDEZ
1938   *Planos de la ciudad de México. Siglos XVI y XVII.* Mexico City.

Open-Grid Town Plans in Europe and America

GEORGE KUBLER

During twenty-five years of sporadic discussion, the main questions have remained the same. Was the great Mexican urban campaign (see Plate 1) patterned on pre-Conquest native traditions? Were its solutions transferred to America from Spain and from Spain alone? Or was the pattern derived from a variety of European sources?

Some have stressed native Mesoamerican traditions. John McAndrew, for example, prefers such an interpretation to the idea that "regularly planned towns in Spain or anywhere else in Europe, antique, medieval, or Renaissance" should have been known "to the actual planners of the standardized Mexican towns" (1965: 105). Others prefer to find the model both in the system used by the Catholic Kings on the Peninsula, and in classical sources. Thus Diego Angulo first suggested (1945: vol. 1, p. 81) that Santo Domingo in 1502 (see Plate 2) repeated elements of the reticulated plans of Santa Fe near Granada (see Plate 3) and Puerto Real on the bay of Cádiz. He also noted that the new plan of Mexico City (see Plate 4), begun in 1523–1524 by Alonso García Bravo, was "cuadriculada según el patrón clásico" (Angulo 1945: 81). Still others, like Erwin Walter Palm (1955: vol. 1, pp. 63–75) and George Foster (1960: 46) pointed, like the present writer (Kubler 1942), to numerous medieval examples in Europe and to Renaissance urban theory.[1] The discussion thus divided among Mexican, Hispanic, and European hypotheses.

---

[1] Torres Balbas (1954: 66–67) regards Briviesca as having a reticulated plan of early fourteenth-century date, showing the influence of the bastides of southwestern France. Its housewall related it to Valbonne, but a historical connection is lacking. Another reticulated open grid was Puerto Real, founded in 1483 by charter of the Catholic Kings, for 200 settlers who were to build houses within one year (Foster [1960: 44]; Muro Orejón [1950: 746–757]). Santa Fe outside Granada in 1491 was a *castrum* built for the siege, with walls surrounding its regular blocks. It therefore belonged to another series.

It was originally suggested in 1942 that the Mendicant towns of sixteenth-century Mexico were analogous – in having unwalled or open-grid plans and fortress-churches – to the unfortified open-grid *villes neuves* of southwestern France, as built during the thirteenth century under the supervision of Mendicant friars who worked under the authority of the French crown (Kubler 1948: 68–102). This hypothesis was independently repeated in 1960 when George Foster phrased it as follows: "It seems very likely that Spanish American grid-plan towns are transplanted bastides, of the type of Pau and Carcassonne, or Montpazier (see Plate 5) in the Dordogne (1284)" (Foster 1960: 39, 46). Unfortunately, Foster derived *bastide* from *bastille*, thereby imposing upon the term a military meaning it was never intended to convey. The Latin origin is *terrae bastitae*, or rural landholdings which form built-up properties (de Ribbe 1898: 441).

When the original hypothesis first appeared, Harold Wethey at once expressed complete disagreement (Wethey 1942: 384), stating his belief that the absence of town walls in the French towns corresponded only to "the desire of the French Crown to limit the power and independence of the towns," and in Mexico to a "lack of necessity . . . for the expensive and elaborate circumvallation." He also rejected non-Spanish sources for Mexican architecture in general, thereby aligning himself with Hispanists who prefer to treat America as a colonial peninsular extension unconnected with the rest of Europe.

John McAndrew has also disagreed recently with the hypothesis, saying "it is not easy to concede that any of these European regular towns, whether medieval Dalmatian ports or post-Albigensian 'new towns' in southern France, would have had any direct effect on those in Mexico. . . . There was little tradition and no body of theory to transmit their forms across three thousand miles and three hundred years . . ." (McAndrew 1965: 105).

Notwithstanding these disagreements, all who have worked on the question agree more or less that regular medieval towns in Spain and in southwestern France are acceptable as older parallels, but unconvincing as direct models because of their remoteness in time from the Mexican examples. In addition, the Italian grid towns are later than the American ones. Thus the Mexican sixteenth-century towns seemed to owe no direct debt to immediately contemporary and closely similar European models.[2]

New evidence was needed to break this verbal stalemate, and it is here submitted in the history of the repopulation before 1519 of a devastated countryside between Grasse and Nice where new, unwalled gridiron towns were built on the initiative of the Benedictine

---

[2]   In its general form, this problem was discussed by the author at the Caracas Seminar on Architectural Historiography (Kubler i.p.).

abbey of St. Honorat of Lérins.[3] These towns – Valbonne (1519), Mouans-Sartoux (1504), and Vallauris (1501) – have never before been mentioned in the American connection.

Valbonne (see Plates 6–9) is the nearly intact masterpiece of this colonial enterprise of the High Renaissance. Unlike the older towns of the region, which perch upon hilltops and cliffs, the new settlements were laid out near the rivers on wide valley floors and along the principal roads, as open, undefended towns for trade. There the traffic of the time could move easily to and from market, within the new network of wide, straight streets and tidy blocks, and without the restraint of fortifications and city gates. The settlers benefitted from peaceful conditions and from new entrepreneurial methods of making urban construction possible.

The depopulation of this region between the Saigne and the Var rivers[4] began with the Black Death of 1348–1350, coming from Asia, striking the Mediterranean ports in 1348, and spreading over southern France from Marseille. Provence lost a third of its people in two years. Peasant revolts like the Jacquerie of 1358 aggravated the ruin of the emptied countryside. Jeanne d'Anjou, who had inherited Provence in 1343, ruled from Naples while armed bands pillaged the survivors of the plague who had retreated to walled hilltop citadels. During the Great Schism, Queen Jeanne was loyal to the Pope of Avignon, but the towns around Nice were of divided allegiance, with Vence, for example, staying loyal to Urban VI in Rome. When the Queen died in 1382, civil war began in Provence between Angevin and Unionist factions, between the partisans of Clement VII at Avignon and Urban VI in Rome, between Raimond de Turenne in the west and Duke Amédée of Savoy in the east, when old villages like Mouans, Sartoux, Vallauris, and Valbonne were destroyed and abandoned about 1390. New plagues in 1392–1394, and 1416, and 1451–1470, as well as pirates from Genoa and Spain after 1400, made all resettlement impossible until the end of the century. In 1519, Valbonne and Sartoux were described as "depuis longtemps ruinés, inhabités, incultes, pierreux et couverts de bois" (Aubenas 1943: 94).

Some years before 1500, King René of Anjou, and the feudal lords of Provence, together with the Benedictines of Lérins, began serious efforts to encourage the repopulation of the region by offering attractive exemptions and franchises to persons who would lease holdings from the lords of the land for resettlement and for the building of new

---

[3] Roger Aubenas has published the charters for nine of these towns (Aubenas 1943: 1–131).
[4] A useful account of the history of the region has been made by Robert Jeancard (1952). The little book by Jean-François Palanque (1963) is inaccurate and undocumented. Nothing is said about the plan of the town.

towns. The Genoese accordingly offered to send settlers recruited from among their own crowded valleys along the Ligurian coast. Nearly 500 families emigrated to the empty fields and valleys between Grasse and Nice from 1461 to 1520. Twenty families came to La Napoule in 1461; forty to Mons in 1468; thirty to Agrimont; fifty to Biot in 1470; fifty-two to Cabris and others in 1496; twenty-seven to Auribeau in 1497; seventy persons to Vallauris in 1501.[5] The last place to be resettled was Valbonne in 1519 with over one hundred colonists recruited from nearby towns rather than from Italy. The ruins of the abandoned village stood near the monastery of Valbonne, and its prior was the lord of the land. The abbey had originally been founded in 1199 as a house of the order of Chalais, an order parallel and similar to the Cistercians, spreading to Provence during the twelfth century from the mother-house founded in 1100 at Chalais in Dauphiné. Like the Cistercians, the Chalaisians built austerely with minimal display. At its peak, the order had twelve houses, but it was dissolved during the fourteenth century, and Valbonne was united with Lérins in 1303 (Cottineau 1937: 3270; Brouillard 1949: s.v. Chalais).

The lord-prior of the abbey of Valbonne, Dom Antoine Taxil, was also the friar-supervisor of buildings, or *ouvrier*, at the monastery of Lérins. In 1519 he secured authority both from the cathedral chapter of Grasse and from Pope Leo X to repopulate his ruined and empty domain, long uninhabited and covered with woods, with a new town at Valbonne which would absorb the revived produce of the surrounding country.

An *acte d'habitation* was accordingly drawn and signed on October 13, 1519, by Dom Antoine Taxil and the future inhabitants of Valbonne. This was a contractual treaty binding the lord-prior to concede substantial guarantees and franchises to a number of heads of families who were not previously subjects of the lord, and who agreed in return to settle at a designated place as his subjects. One version of the *acte d'habitation* lists 105 names from nearly eighteen places, and another digest of seventeenth-century date mentions 112 "habitants ou futur habitants dudit Valbonne," who were to compose the founding families of the new town.[6]

The tenants signing this lease of lands in perpetuity agreed to pay 600 florins annually to the lord-prior (article 3) and to submit to

---

[5] Jeancard (1952: 47–59). Aubenas (1943: viii–xi) notes similar *actes d'habitation* in the opposite direction much earlier, as when in 1273 a colony of Provençaux resettled a part of Apulia. Aubenas also gives a list of eighteen other resettlement acts in Provence proper after 1468 and before 1501.

[6] The *capitula* of 1519 (Aubenas 1943: 94) list 105 names, but a digest of the seventeenth century (Moris 1905: 128–131) mentions the figure of 112 "habitants ou futur habitants dudit Valbonne." The eighteen nearby places were Grasse, Vence, Chateauneuf, Saint-Paul, Cagnes, Villeneuve, Lérins, Bar, Fréjus, Antibes, Créolières, Vintimille, Mougins, Castellane, Riez, Cannes, Cipières, and Vallauris (Aubenas, *Chartes*, 1943, 94–95).

certain levies on their crops (article 5). In addition, they agreed to build houses within four months of drawing lots for land, and to build the town according to the "façon, forme et le plan "given by the lord-prior.[7] If their constructions encroached upon the streets more than 1½ palms, the lord-prior reserved the right to destroy the offending portions.[8]

At Valbonne (see Plates 6 and 7) as at Vallauris and Mouans-Sartoux a little earlier, the tenants built regular streets four meters wide intersecting at right angles and forming blocks ca. 25 × 15 meters. At Valbonne no walls other than the houses surround the houses (see Plate 8). In place of fortifications, a wall of houses is all that delimits the boundaries. Within the housewall, there are thirty-six rectangular house blocks, each with the long axis running east and west. A north-south main street is axial, and it runs at a right angle to the bank of the Brague River. The east–west main street divides the town into a northern section of nineteen blocks, and a southern section of fifteen blocks. Two blocks are taken by the public square, surrounded by arcaded walks (see Plate 9) and occupying an area in the southwestern quarter rather than the intersection of the main streets. This off-center position of the square (as in southwestern France three centuries earlier, Plate 5) permits traffic to enter at its corners. Such corner entrances would have required four blocks instead of two, if the square had been evenly centered on the principal or axial intersection.

In 1519 only 112 houses were projected, each with its stable. Produce gardens and meadows were to be taxed separately, and tithes went to the lord-prior, whose animals had rights of passage. The community was also required to mill the lord-prior's grain in its own mills without payment, and press his olives, and bake his bread. The lord-prior reserved to himself the administration of justice and the right to appoint civil and criminal officers. Water rights as well as hunting and fishing rights remained his. The community retained control of pastures. The lord-prior supported a chaplain and a deacon, but the community was free to support another priest (*capellanum populi*) of its own choosing, and it assumed the costs of maintaining the fabric and cult objects of the church. The community also reserved the right to elect syndics and other officers, and to hold assemblies in the presence of the lord-prior or his representatives.

The gradual evolution of the idea of Valbonne can be traced in

---

[7] Aubenas (1943: 109): "Item capitularunt...edificare villam...juxta modum et formam et designationem...datos per dietum dominum priorem."
[8] Aubenas (1943: article 55): "Item capitularunt quod venustas et decor viarum et carreriarum...in villa edificanda conservetur, quod non liceat...alicui...in carrerus publicis ante domos eorumdem vel aliter in dicta villa facere...gradus nec exitus... nec tabulas in carreria intrantes, ultra unum palmum cum dimidio, et si...aliquis contrarium fecerit, liceat domino priori....id destruere....etiamsi ibidem longo tempore stetissent."

earlier *actes d'habitation* where the idea of a town built on a speculative lease by its tenants goes back at least to 1501. At Vallauris,
for example, the lord-prior from Lérins in 1501 was Raynier de
Lascaris, who leased lands to seventy inhabitants for town use (Aubenas 1943: 59–68). The charter obliged them to follow the lord-prior's
plan, consisting of three long, parallel streets (see Plate 10) which
still appear in the plan of Vallauris today.[9] Dom Raynier also exacted
certain services lacking in the charter of Valbonne, such as four days
of service from each inhabitant for 5 years to repair the castle, and
personal attendants on his journeys away from town. The charter of
Valbonne evidently had to be made more attractive than the earlier
ones, by omitting all measures binding the tenants to live in the new
town. Nor did the lord-prior of Valbonne dare to exact any draft labor
beyond milling, pressing, and baking. In 1519 the need for a stable
rural economy had become urgent, with the emergence of the region
upon the world scene of imperial politics.

The physical resemblances of this regional open-city plan to the new
American towns of the sixteenth century in the Spanish colonies (see
Plate 1) are close enough in time and in political connection to require
close attention. The legal forms of the *actes d'habitation* of course
bear no likeness to the conditions of fiduciary *encomienda* under which
colonists and friars enjoyed the usufruct of Indian labor during the
early years of the American colonies (Simpson 1950). Our concern
here is with the physical and geometric similarities, and with possible
governmental links relating Mexico and southeastern France. The
physical resemblances are obvious, but the administrative links
require further study of the relation of Valbonne to Lérins.

The *acte d'habitation* of 1519 makes it clear that Valbonne was
owned by Dom Antoine Taxil.[10] He was the active lord-prior, taking
initiative and collecting rent, services, and levies. At nearby Opio,
however, lands covered in the lease were owned jointly by him and
one other lord. The other lord was the bishop of Grasse, Augustin
Grimaldi, who was in 1519 also the commendatory abbot of Lérins,
and ruling prince of Monaco after 1523. Jeancard has suggested that
Augustin Grimaldi himself drew up the plans for Valbonne.[11] But the

---

[9] Aubenas (1943: 65. article 18): "Item quod dicta universitas et homines particulares
eiusdem teneantur. . . .edifficare in dicto loco villam et domos eorum similiter carrerias
et menia et exitus ville predicte juxta formam et designaciones. . .dandas per dictum
dominum priorem et non alias" (the elisions are those of the Aubenas edition).

[10] Aubenas (1943: 95, article 1): "Et primo reverendus dominus Anthonius Taxillis. . .
dat et concedit. . .habitantibus et qui in futurum habitabunt locum predictum Vallis-
bone. . .videlicet tres ex quatuor partibus territorii predictorum (locorum) de Sartolis
et de content, Clausona, Villabruco et Defensono ac territorium. . .indivisum. . .cum
reverendo in Christo patre et domino Augustino episcopo Grassensi, in territorio castri
inhabitati de Opio. . ."

[11] R. Jeancard (1952: 139) believed Grimaldi took the idea from thirteenth-century
models like Aigues-Mortes, the lower town at Carcassonne and Montpazier, and he

acte d'habitation of 1519 mentions him only as sharing the lordship of Opio, and not as exercising any rights or enjoying revenues at Valbonne. In fact, the *acte d'habitation* makes it clear that Dom Antoine Taxil was not only professionally expert, but administratively responsible in architectural matters. Article 54 specifies that the plan of the town had been established by the lord-prior, that is, by Antoine Taxil.[12] If he was responsible for the urban form, Taxil's silent partner in the lease of 1519, Augustin Grimaldi, was soon to become a most important ally of Charles V, showered with imperial favors as lord-bishop and ruling prince of Monaco.

Born in 1480, Augustin Grimaldi early attained distinction in humanistic studies, becoming the friend of Gregorio Cortese and Cardinal Sadolet, whose correspondences with him are published in their collected works. He soon attracted the favor of Louis XII, no doubt for political reasons, being named bishop-coadjutor of Grasse in 1498 to assist an uncle, Jean-André Grimaldi, who in 1504 relinquished his own title as commendatory abbot of Lérins to his nephew (Saige 1890: Introduction).

This office had been created in 1464 by the Papacy of Avignon to allow any abbot, who thenceforth might be a layman or a cleric, to enjoy the income of an abbey as if it were a fief without residing there. Thus the Avignon Popes could bestow incomes upon persons whom the prohibition of pluralities prevented from holding the benefices themselves; in short, upon persons without actual right to the office (von Scheurl 1909: 169).

When the uncle died in 1505, the new bishop of Grasse and abbot of Lérins at once showed the temper of his generation by dedicating himself to the reform of St. Honorat (Moris 1905: 36–37). He probably experienced the same disgust with loose rules as his Spanish reforming Mendicant contemporaries when he requested and secured from Leo X in 1515 the union of Lérins with S. Giustina of Padua under the rule of Monte Cassino, a step which required of the abbot that he resign the *commende*. This he did in 1513, keeping, however, the abbot's income. In 1516 ten religious arrived at Lérins from Italy, and among them was Gregorio Cortese, later Cardinal.

Grimaldi's friends, Cortese and Cardinal Sadolet, were among the more eminent scholars to take part in the renovation and internal reform of Italian monasticism. They may in this sense be regarded as among the hierarchical representatives of the Catholic Reformation in Europe, and as key figures in a wide movement of which the Mexican Mendicants, recruited from Extremadura, were the missionary frontiersmen (Bataillon 1937).

observes that such plans had never before been used in the region between the Saigne and the Var.

[12]   See note 16 for text.

Gregorio Cortese became Prior of Lérins and abbot in 1524, going later to Perugia and Venice (1538) on his duties as a Benedictine reformer. While at Padua he invited Raphael to paint a *Last Supper* in the refectory of the abbey, but Raphael refused and a lesser painter was employed.[13] In this connection, Cortese describes the new cloister he planned, as having a marble fountain with dragons, dolphins, and sea monsters in a peristyle Doric court, on which he had insisted against the will of an architect named Pannatius, who wanted to build small twinned columns with spiral shafts beneath arches on a high pedestal. It is difficult to identify such a cloister as Cortese wanted at S. Giustina today, and it is likely that the Italian humanist was describing hopeful projects more than works. In any event, this incident characterizes the architectural aims of Cortese, and it points to classical humanist models for such enterprises as Dom Antoine Taxil's design for Valbonne.

Augustin Grimaldi was not only a reforming humanist prelate; he was also in 1513 a younger son of the reigning house of Monaco, which was soon to become a pivot of imperial strategy against France in Italy. His relations with Spain are first documented by a letter from Ferdinand of Aragón in 1508 thanking him for helping to free some Spanish vessels (Saige 1890: doc. eccl., June 25, 1508).

By 1511 his older brother Lucien (*regnavit* 1505–1523) had entered upon a treaty of alliance and navigation with Ferdinand, securing special privileges for Monegasque commerce, and reflecting the league among Rome, Venice, and Spain against Louis XII of France. Fearful of losing Monaco in 1512, Louis XII modified the harsh treaty of 1509, under diplomatic pressure brought to bear by powerful friends of Augustin Grimaldi at the French court.

Lucien's debts became heavy after 1517. When Genoa fell to the lieutenants of Charles V in 1522, following the declaration of war between France and Spain, Lucien offered Monaco to France, to Genoa, and to the Emperor.

A paper of 1523, written probably by Lucien himself, stressed the strategic and maritime importance of the fortress as the key to Genoa and the gate to Provence. The price of it was to be aid and protection to the lord of Monaco as an independent sovereign, as well as the maintenance of its garrison of 200 men and an annual pension of 200 ducats to the lord. In the event of rupture between France and Monaco, Lucien demanded for his brother, the bishop of Grasse, whose French properties would be confiscated, an annual income from the Papacy and lodging suitable to his rank in Rome (Saige 1890: II, cvi).

[13]   Gothein (1912). Gothein mistakenly believed the letter pertained to Lérins, although the correspondence related to S. Giustina in Padua.

In 1523, Lucien was assassinated in the palace at Monaco on August 22 by a dissolute relative from Genoa, who was probably acting for Andrea Doria to prevent Monaco's defection from the French king. Augustin at once devoted every effort to avenging his brother's death, and, when it became clear to him that he would get no redress from France against the murderers in Genoa, he turned to the imperial forces and to the Papacy. In 1524 he was recognized by Clement VII as sovereign lord of Monaco, and on June 7, the Treaty of Burgos placed Monaco under Spanish protection.

Monaco thereupon became the Emperor's port for seaborne rein-forcements to the armies of Milan, and it was from Monaco that intelligence issued concerning French movements on land and sea. After the defeat of Francis I at Pavia, the Emperor wrote warmly to Augustin Grimaldi to thank the lord-bishop, praise him, and reward him for the great risks he had taken (Labande 1910: 11–12).

In 1526–1527, when the Italian league was forming among the Papacy, Venice, Florence, and Francesco Sforza, Charles V turned once again for aid to his tiny ally in Monaco. After destroying the confederation in 1527, the Emperor rewarded Grimaldi with the bishopric of Oristano in Sardinia, to compensate him for being deprived of Grasse, and with revenues from the dioceses of Burgos and Badajoz.

After the sack of Rome, the lord-bishop, revolted by its excesses, and impatient with disorderly Spanish finances and nonpayments, attempted unsuccessfully to renew his alliance with France and to sell Monaco to the Republic of Genoa. By 1528, however, the Emperor had consolidated his hold on the Mediterranean and Grimaldi could no longer escape his service. His importance to Charles V remained great, and in 1529 he was given a marquisate in Naples with an income of 5,000 ducats.

All the Emperor's letters to Augustin reflect the great importance he gave this ally, honoring him by being couched in French, unlike the rest of the imperial correspondence, and addressing him, like Erasmus, as "*très chier et feal conseiller*" (Labande 1910: vii–viii).

When the Emperor visited Augustin at Monaco in 1529 on August 6, 7, and 8, he was lodged in the palace and visited the fortress. Later in Genoa Augustin visited the Emperor daily from August 12–29, and on the occasion of the coronation in Bologna, Charles V granted him revenues from the vacant bishopric of Majorca.

In 1537 Augustin again was restive, having received the offer of a cardinal's hat from the Pope and his own terms from Francis I if he would leave the Emperor's alliance. To these insinuations, his ally

---

[14] "È usato a dir questo: Cesare ha più bisogno de mi che mi de lui."

replied with renewed grants of money for ships, Sicilian grain, and intensified negotiations to secure him the cardinal's hat. Augustin died suddenly on April 14, 1532, perhaps poisoned, but the alliance with Spain of which he was the architect persisted until 1641.

In 1526, seven years after the resettlement of Valbonne, the grand chancellor of Charles V repeated the grid plan at Gattinara (see Plates 11–13) in the Piemonte. This town was a domain of Mercurino Arborio di Gattinara (1465–1529), who was accustomed to say publicly that the Emperor needed him more than Gattinara needed the Emperor, as reported by the Venetian ambassador, Gaspare Contarini, in 1525 (Claretta 1897).[14]

Gattinara had twice been burned and destroyed by French troops, whose fury was aimed directly at the chancellor, once in April 1524 and again in October 1526 (Bornate 1915: 365, note 1). The chancellor's family were impoverished at the time of his birth in 1465, and his legal studies in Turin were paid for him by his wife (Walser 1959: 161). In 1526 Gattinara's salary was 8,000 ducats per annum, plus travel allowances around 3,500, but payment was irregular (Bornate 1915: 483–484). In 1528 Gattinara wrote despairingly to a friend that he was deep in debt on the dowry due his nieces, and for wages to two nephews as well as eight years' wages to his majordomo and other servants (van der Linden 1936: v. 100, 275, 279). Worries over money and status always pursued him, and much of his private correspondence was devoted to securing overdue payments of salary and to validating grants of domains and titles. Soon after the first destruction of Gattinara in 1524, the chancellor commissioned the majordomo of his household and a son-in-law to make an extended tour in Italy designed to consolidate the domains and titles granted by the Emperor and the Duke of Milan, and to make sure that the Duke of Savoy also acknowledged these grants.[15] At Gattinara, the townfolk had for a long time enjoyed ducal support in throwing off the feudal privileges of the chancellor's family, and it was Mercurino's aim to force the Duke and the townsfolk to recognize his lordship over the town of Gattinara. Mercurino was especially concerned to acquire the nearby domain at Romagnano in order to preserve and secure his rights at Gattinara.[16] Thus he wanted to impose upon his new subjects both imperial and ducal privileges for their own benefit. If they wished to be good *subditi*, he would be a good lord, preventing them from being oppressed, and persuading them to live in peace with one another and with

[15]   Claretta (1897: 122–147). Valenza and Sartirana were granted by Francesco II Sforza of Milan in 1522 and nearby Gattinara was granted by the Emperor Maximilian in 1513.
[16]   Claretta (1897: 126): "potria conservare et assecorare le mie cose de Gattinara et tenir quelli villani in subiectione et potria trouar ben mezo de agiustare con queste ragione quello che teneno li gientil homini et signori particulari," and 130, building a fort between the towns "per potere più facilmente signoriare."

the nobles, for the purpose of benefitting Gattinara with benevolent treatment.[17] Like Valbonne before 1419, Gattinara in 1524–1526 was a desolate and empty countryside, surrounded by neglected fields and famished peasants. In 1528 the English ambassadors traveling from Vercelli to Pavia on their way to the coronation at Bologna, noted empty fields, deserted towns, and great numbers of beggars (Claretta 1897: 117).

The treatment proposed by Gattinara resembled modern economic development plans. The chancellor wished to maximize income from Gattinara by buying up all possible tracts as emphyteutic lands under perpetual lease against ground rents not to exceed five percent per annum of value (Claretta 1897: 139).[18] In short, the lord of the town was engaged in unifying ownership and in systematizing its productivity.

The treatment also resembles the rental of lands to new settlers as practiced at Valbonne. The chancellor planned to buy available plots for annual lease at five percent value to the sellers as well as to gentlemen at Gattinara and foreigners and citizens of Vercelli,[19] thereby placing himself in the same position as the joint lords of Valbonne, who leased their feudal acres to settlers in perpetuity on the abbey domain. Like Valbonne, Gattinara had been ruined and abandoned, needing resettlement and renewal. Both share the form of the open, unwalled grid plan (see Plates 6 and 11) occupying flat and accessible land rather than the defensive hilltops of medieval villages and cities. Both were also land ventures, exploring the possibilities of rental income within the limits of feudal vassallage.

Like Valbonne, Gattinara is an open grid surrounded by a wall of houses (see Plate 11). It is smaller, having only twelve blocks within the housewall, and its public square slightly widened at the intersection of the main streets (see Plates 12 and 13). This square lacks the corner streets of Valbonne. As recorded in Blaeu's *Theatrum. . . Sabaudiae* (1682: Plate 53),[20] the main axial street faces the Sesia

---

[17]   Claretta (1897): "tendendo io a bonificar el dicto loco de Gattinara. . . et cosi poco a poco bisogna adocirgli che cognoscano hauer patrone et padre et non lupo rapace."

[18]   "Item perché io desidero oltra di questo augmentare li redditi e intrate desso loco di Gattinara. . . valendo le peze che se comprarano tanto de reddito certo che posseno portare cinco por cento: se potriano anchora concedere poy in emphiteosi a li medesimi venditori con il ficto o censo predicto de cinco por cento." Emphyteusis in Roman civil law is a perpetual lease of real estate upon condition of taking care of and paying the taxes upon the estate, as well as ground rent.

[19]   Claretta (1897: 139): "se portrà anchora practicare con li gentilhomini del loco et con li extrangeri et citadini vercelesi. . . o per venditione o per contracto emphiteotico . . . perhò in tuti li contracti che se farano se habia questo rispecto che li contracti siano liciti et non exedano el dicto reddito de cinco per cento. . . ficti che serano a pagare in vino."

[20]   Moglia (1887: 215) seeks to deny that Mercurino rebuilt the town. Moglia dated the plan as having been built in the mid-thirteenth century. No documents or other proofs are presented.

River east of the town, and a lesser axis runs north towards the mountains from the convent of S. Clara. The north-south streets are widest: less wide are the secondary streets from east to west. The northwest corner of the town still showed in 1682 as a ruined castle surrounded by a moat and containing a chapel: it stands like a disused bastion at the corner of the new town, whose streets cut off one-fourth of its area. At Valbonne, the remains of the original château and the abbey likewise occupy a corner of the new town plan between it and the Brague River on the southeast.

Of the chancellor's interest in architecture we know that the buildings of his house in Gattinara were his own design.[21] The program for the castle of S. Lorenzo, called *l'aquila imperiale*, on the hill above Gattinara, is described in great detail in a *memoriale* he drafted.[22] Thus it is possible that the actual layout of Gattinara is the chancellor's own design, in which he drew both upon precedents like Valbonne, and upon his own situation, although there is no evidence in the *memoriale* (written late in 1524) that he had begun to think about the physical layout of Gattinara beyond designing his own house and garden. The actual town plan probably dates from 1526, and it is likely that the chancellor specified its exact form in as great detail as his other building projects, in papers still unlocated.

That he knew of Valbonne is circumstantially secured. It was Gattinara who drew up the treaty of Burgos and the declaration of Tordesillas defining the terms of the alliance with Monaco in 1524, and Gattinara was at Monaco for twenty days in 1527 as the guest of Augustin Grimaldi when Rome was sacked and Clement VII taken prisoner.[23]

AN AMERICAN CONNECTION?

Following Angulo (1945), E. W. Palm also observed in 1955 that Santo Domingo in the Caribbean, as rebuilt by Nicolás de Ovando in 1502 (see Plate 2), was a town of straight streets laid out upon an imperfect grid, and that Ovando probably patterned it upon Sante Fe near Granada (see Plate 3), as well as other new towns built by the

[21] Claretta (1897: 140) instructing his majordomo, Carlo Gazino, to make sure that "ledifficio de mia case de Gattinara è stato facto conforme a la mia voluntà e disegno."
[22] Claretta (1897: 144): "se ha da initular el dicto castello l'aquila imperiale et conforme a questo mio intento se potra fare il desegno et modello carculando porte solamente a peza per peza tuto quello potra montare et mandarmelo."
[23] Bornate (1915: 346). In the autobiography Gattinara wrote: "Receptus est autem Mercurinus in arce monaci per ipsius arcis Dominum Augustinum grimaldum grassensem episcopum, cum tanto aplausu et honore ut nil supra dici queat. Quievat ibidem Mercurinus XX dierum spacio..."

Catholic Kings, like Puerto Real on the Bay of Cádiz or Foncea in Logroño.

At this point, it is worth noting that various members of the Grimaldi family were active at Seville and in Santo Domingo as bankers to the Spanish Crown and to merchants operating in America. In 1503 Bernardo Grimaldi, of the Genoese family who were bankers to both Ferdinand of Aragon and to Charles V, was privileged to remain in residence when other aliens living there were required to leave (Carande 1949: 318). Girolandi Grimaldi was another Genoese in Santo Domingo, acting as agent for his compatriots in Seville (Gribaudi 1936: 20), Bartolomeo Grimaldi, Nicola, and Giacomo, who are recorded as residing there between 1506 and 1513 (Almagià 1935).

Finally, it is recorded that Augustin Grimaldi was interested in news from America. In 1528 a manuscript history and description of the newly discovered countries in the Spanish and Portuguese Indies was seen by Grimaldi's emissary at court in Toledo. A copy produced for Grimaldi was translated at Seville from Spanish into Italian for his use (Saige 1890: clxxxiv, 409).

CONCLUSION

These new European towns of the type of Valbonne and Gattinara are, of course, resettlements for purposes of development and speculation, contrived by feudal lords who offered various privileges to possible settlers, in order to produce new sources of income. As town layouts they resemble the bastides of twelfth- and thirteenth-century southwestern France. But as investments, they resembled the irregular new towns of southern Germany and Switzerland, which were initiated in the twelfth century by the Dukes of Zähringen, of which Bern, Thun, Fribourg, or Zurich are notable examples (Hofer 1963; Galantay 1967: 86–93). Yet our sixteenth-century towns differ radically from these earlier speculative ventures by being open, unwalled settlements, and by their reticulated grid plans. They differed above all in being composed of leased plots, which were the principal source of income, rather than customs and taxation, as in the earlier period. The connection, finally, of Valbonne and Gattinara with American colonial enterprise via the Spanish Court, is closer, both in date and in influence, than any other dependence that has ever been mentioned for the origins of the unwalled Mexican Mendicant grid town.

REFERENCES

ALMAGIÀ, R.
1935   *Rendiconti della Accademia dei Lincei.* Rome.

ANGULO, DIEGO
1945   *Historia del arte hispanoamericano,* volume one.

AUBENAS, ROGER
1943   Chartes de franchise et actes d'habitation. *Documents, textes, et mémoires pour servir à l'histoire de Cannes et de sa région,* volume one, phase 1, ser. 3a, vol. 17. Cannes.

BATAILLON, MARCEL
1937   *Erasme en Espagne.* Paris.

BLAEU, JOAN
1682   *Theatrum stratuum regiae celsitudinis Sabaudiae ducis.* Amsterdam.

BORNATE, C.
1915   "Historia vitae. . ." *Miscelanea distoria italiana* 48: 365, note 1.

BROUILLARD, R.
1949   *Catholicisme,* volume two.

CARANDE THOBAR, RAMÓN
1949   *Carlos V y sus banqueros.* Madrid.

CLARETTA, G.
1897   Notizie, 70. *Memorie della Accademia della Scienza di Torino,* series two, c. 47, Turin.

Côte d'Azur
1966   *Côte d'Azur, le guide pratique 1966.* Vallauris.

COTTINEAU, L. H.
1937   *Répertoire des abbayes et prieurés,* volume two.

DEL PASO Y TRONCOSO,F.
1905–1906   *Papeles de Nueva España.* Madrid: Gobierno Mexicano.

DE RIBBE, CHARLES
1898   *La societé provençale à la fin du Moyen Âge.* Paris.

FOSTER, GEORGE
1960   *Culture and conquest.* Viking Fund Publications in Anthropology 27. Chicago.

GALANTAY, E.
1967   New towns. *Progressive Architecture* (December).

GOTHEIN, E.
1912   "Rafael und der Abt Gregorio Cortese," in *Sitzungen der Heidelberger Akademie der Wissenschaften, phil./hist. Kl.,* 3 Abh. Heidelberg.

GRIBAUDI, P.
1936   *Bolletino della Società Geografica Italiana.*

GUARDA, GABRIEL
1965   *Santo Tomás de Aquino y las fuentes del urbanismo indiano.* Santiago.

HOFER, PAUL
1963   *Die Städtegründungen des Mittelalters zwischen Genfersee und Rhein.* Bern.

HUYSSER, J.
1962   *Guide touristique.* Valbonne.

JEANCARD, ROBERT
1952   *Les seigneuries d'Outre-Saigne de la reine Jeanne à François Ier.* Cannes.

KUBLER, GEORGE
1942   Mexican urbanism in the sixteenth century. *Art Bulletin* 24: 160–171.
New York: College Art Association of America.
1948   *Mexican architecture of the sixteenth century*, volume one, 68–102.
New Haven, Conn.: Yale University Press.
i.p.   "El problema de los aportes europeos en la arquitectura latinoamericana." Paper presented at the Caracas Seminar on Architectural Historiography. *Boletín del Centro de Investigaciones
Históricas y Estéticas.* Caracas.

LABANDE, L. H.
1910   *Recueil des lettres de l'empereur Charles Quint.* Monaco.

MC ANDREW, JOHN
1965   *The open-air churches of sixteenth-century Mexico.* Cambridge,
Mass.: Harvard University Press.

MOGLIA, G.
1887   *Il Borgo di Gattinara: Memorie storiche.* Vercelli.

MORIS, H.
1905   *Cartulaire de l'abbaye de Lérins.* Paris.

MURO OREJÓN, A.
1950   *Anuario de historia del derecho español* 20.

PALANQUE, JEAN-FRANÇOIS
1963   *Histoire de Valbonne, et ses relations avec les villes d'Antibes et de
Grasse...* Cannes: Robaudy.

PALM, ERWIN WALTER
1955   *Los monumentos arquitectónicos de la Española*,
volume one. Ciudad Trujillo, Santo Domingo.

SAIGE, GUSTAVE
1890   *Documents historiques concernant la principauté de Monaco*,
volume two. Monaco.

SIMPSON, L. B.
1950   *The economienda in New Spain.* Berkeley: University of California
Press.

TORRES BALBAS, LEOPOLDO, *et al.*
1954   *Resumen histórico del urbanismo en España.* Madrid.

VAN DER LINDEN, H.
1936   Articles soumis à Charles Quint. *Bulletin de la commission royale
d'histoire*, volume 100. Brussels.

VON SCHEURL, C. T. G., *editor*
1909   *Schaff-Herzog encyclopaedia of religious knowledge*, volume three.
New York and London: Funk and Wagnalls.

WALSER, F.
1959   *Die spanischen Zentralbehörden und der Staatsrat Karls V.*
Göttingen.

WETHEY, HAROLD
1942   Letter to the Editor. *Art Bulletin* 24. New York: College Art Association of America.

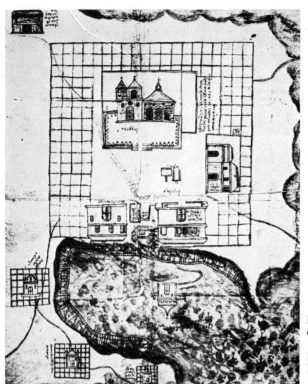

Plate 1. Plan of Tenango del Valle, Mexico, in 1582, as rendered by an Indian draftsman (del Paso y Troncoso 1905–1906)

Plate 2. Plan of Santo Domingo, Dominican Republique after 1502 (Palm 1955: vol. 1, Figure 8)

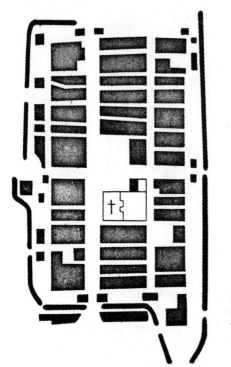

Plate 3. Plan of Santa Fe (Granada), as laid out in 1492 (Foster 1960: 45)

Plate 4. Plan of Mexico City ca. 1570 (García 1929)

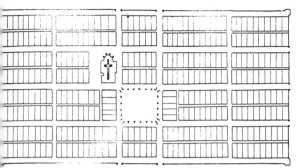

Plate 5. Plan of Montpazier, France (Lavedan 1926: 315)

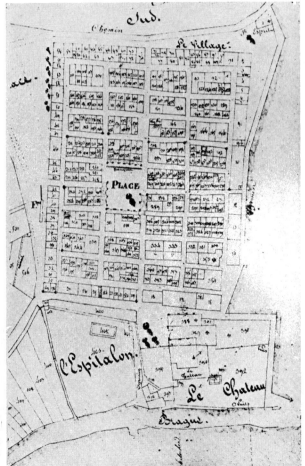

Plate 6. Plan of Valbonne (Alpes-Maritimes), France, in 1857 (Aubenas 1943: 96)

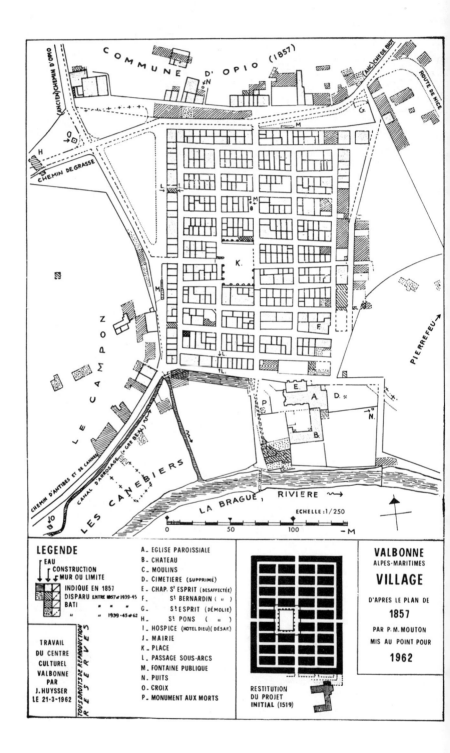

COMMUNE D'OPIO (1857)

(ANC.) CHEMIN D'OPIO

(ANC.) CHE DE BIOT

ROUTE DE NICE

CHEMIN DE GRASSE

LE CAMPON

CHEMIN D'ANTIBES ET DE CANNES

CANAL D'ARROSAGE (C.DE BENI)

LES CANEBIERS

LA BRAGUE, RIVIERE

PIERREFEU

ECHELLE : 1/250

0   50   100   — M

LEGENDE

EAU
CONSTRUCTION
MUR OU LIMITE

INDIQUE EN 1857
DISPARU ENTRE 1857 et 1939-45
BATI
"   "   "   1939-45 et 62

TRAVAIL
DU CENTRE
CULTUREL
VALBONNE
PAR
J. HUYSSER
LE 21-3-1962

TOUS DROITS DE REPRODUCTION
RÉSERVÉS

A _ EGLISE PAROISSIALE
B _ CHATEAU
C _ MOULINS
D _ CIMETIERE (SUPPRIMÉ)
E _ CHAP. St ESPRIT (DESAFFECTÉE)
F _   St BERNARDIN (")
G _   SteESPRIT (DÉMOLIE)
H _   St PONS (")
I _ HOSPICE (HOTEL DIEU)(DÉSAF.)
J _ MAIRIE
K _ PLACE
L _ PASSAGE SOUS-ARCS
M _ FONTAINE PUBLIQUE
N _ PUITS
O _ CROIX
P _ MONUMENT AUX MORTS

VALBONNE
ALPES-MARITIMES

VILLAGE

D'APRES LE PLAN DE

1857

PAR P. M. MOUTON

MIS AU POINT POUR

1962

RESTITUTION
DU PROJET
INITIAL (1519)

Plate 8. Air view of Valbonne from the southwest (courtesy of Photo Combier, Mâcon)

Plate 7. Plan of Valbonne (Alpes-Maritimes), France, in 1962 (Huysser 1962)

Plate 9. Valbonne arcades of 1628 surrounding the Place Nationale (photo courtesy of Photoguy, Nice)

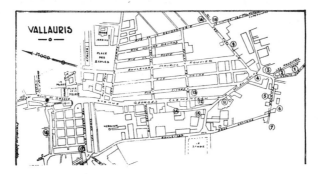

Plate 10. Plan of Vallauris (Côte d'Azur 1966: 123)

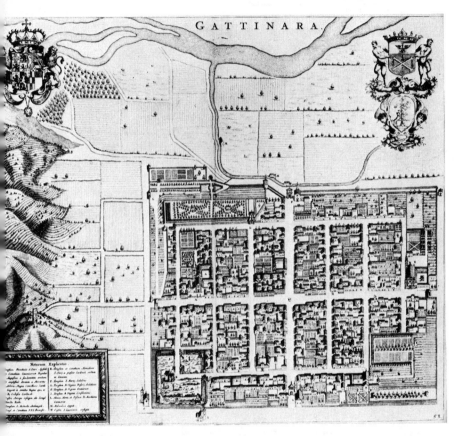

Plate 11. Plan of Gattinara (Blaeu 1682: Plate 53)

Plate 12. View of Gattinara square (photo courtesy of Leonardo Benevolo)

Plate 13. View of portico, main square of Gattinara (photo courtesy of Leonardo Benevolo)

Military Influence in the Cities of the Kingdom of Chile*

GABRIEL GUARDA, O.S.B.

The first impression of Chile experienced by a European enemy rounding the Cape or traversing the Strait of Magellan was the long southwestern flank of the continent. This coast seemed to have a vast number of ports and islands, all vulnerable to assault and occupation. Not just a few points along the coast, but the entire territory was regarded as the key to the Pacific and the bastion of Peru. It was taken for granted that any attack launched against Lima would first require the occupation of Chile. Such a plan had often been discussed in the English, Dutch and French courts. According to an official report presented in 1600 to the War Council of the Indies, "the preservation of Chile is essential for the whole area bordering the South Sea, including the territory of New Spain, Peru, and Tierra Firme. Because this sea stretches from the Strait of Magellan along the coast of Chile as far as the port of Acapulco, serving as garrison and guardian... Chile has become the most jealously guarded territory and the most essential possession of all."[1]

In the interior of Chile colonizers encountered the Araucanians. The fact that the Araucanians were the fiercest of all New World peoples in defending their freedom and resisting civilization gave Chilean colonization an unstable, agitated character. This was particularly so in the southern regions which were at that time the most fertile and populous areas. These factors necessarily had a profound influence on all aspects of the history of Chilean colonization.

Both its geographical position as the gateway to the continent and the Araucanian War greatly influenced the structure of urban centers in Chile. The strategic position of certain ports, for example, resulted

[1] Medina n.d.a: vol. 5, p. 261; n.d.b: 240; n.d.c: 255; n.d.d: 276; n.d.e: 376 Morales Padrón 1962; Medina n.d.f: vol. 3, p. 213.

* Attempts to contact the author in Chile re translation and reference problems were unsuccessful. We apologize for any inconvenience to the reader. – *Publisher.*

in characteristic features. Similarly, the regular presence of fortifications in the interior settlements, at least in some regions, was
another constant feature. Although these particular aspects of Chilean
settlements may not be of transcendental importance to the history
of Latin American urban planning, their presence as constant factors
justifies an evaluative study to determine their relative importance.

I. *Fortified Settlements*

An analysis of 204 Spanish settlements founded in Chile between the
Conquest and Independence reveals that at least half were fortified.[2]
Practically all relate chronologically to the sixteenth and seventeenth
centuries (the period of the Araucanian War) or were located in the
region affected by this war. Of these 204 settlements only 19 were
located in the region affected on the coast, the remaining 185 were
inland. The first conclusion we might draw is that the colonization of
the country was considered more important than its defense against
foreign aggression. Nevertheless, we must not disregard the fact that
eventually the rationale for Chile's costly preservation was that it
played a strategic role as the bastion of Peru.[3]

Thirty of these settlements were destroyed, deserted, or relocated
for military reasons and were rebuilt after each misfortune. They
seemed to possess a defiant determination to survive. Although some
did perish, others were still being restored well into the period of
Independence. (More than a few, in fact, were only restored at the
end of the nineteenth century, after a century and a half of melancholy
slumber in ruins.) If, in addition to the 204 settlements, we consider
the sum total of individual founding ceremonies, often repeated in the
history of a settlement, this figure would be doubled.[4] Moreover, many

[2] Neither figure is definitive. Both relate to my research for a projected publication
on the urban history of the Kingdom of Chile.

[3] In the time of Viceroy Conde de Chincón, the problem of abandoning colonization
for economic reasons was again put forth: "...the Kingom of Chile is the stronghold
of Peru and of all the Indies, the bastion keeping them free from their enemies to the
north, who so covet Chile in order to dominate the South Sea...." Over and above
this strategic argument triumphed the idea of continuing to squander money for
evangelization. Cf. Juan de Jesús (1878: 68ff.), Muzquiz (1945: 170), and Encina (1956:
vol. 3, p. 78).

For the Crown, however, Chile's geopolitical role was often a more important
concern than the domestic Araucanian War. The two largest expeditions sent to the area
during the period of Spanish control were those of Sarmiento de Gamboa (1582, fifteen
ships) and the Marqués de Mancera (1645, seventeen ships). Their common objective
was to fortify the Strait of Magellan and the Valdivia part for use as the key
defensive points of the continent.

[4] Angol is a case in point. It was founded as Los Confines by Pedro de Valdivia in
1553 and abandoned after his death. It was then refounded by García as Los Infantes.
Francisco de Villagra restored it as Los Confines, then Oñez de Loyola restored it as

of the 219 Indian pueblos[5] known to have existed in the same period
were fortified after the Indian fashion,[6] and many suffered similar
catastrophes.[7] This represents a wealth of data substantiating that the
internal war was the most influential factor in determining the
encampment-like nature of Chilean settlements.[8]

A chronological analysis of the development of Spanish settlements
in Chile shows that, from the earliest days, building plans reflected
the classic gridiron arrangement of all New World plans; there was
no concession made to the hostile environment. In fact, to a certain

Angol. Abandoned again in April 1600 by Quiñones, it was refounded eleven years later
by Merlo de la Fuente, with the name of San Luis de Angol, only to be moved in
December of the same year by Governor Jaraquemada. Lazo restored it in January 1637
as San Francisco de la Vega, the name under which it perished by fire the following
year. That same year it was again restored, only to be destroyed again. The Marqués
de Baides refounded it in 1641 as Nuestra Señora de los Remedios, the name it bore
when it again disappeared. Juan Henríquez founded Angolviejo on its ruins, and it was
only restored on 6 December 1862 after native opposition was finally eliminated. This
makes a total of thirteen foundings.

[5] This is a provisional figure. It is difficult to specify the exact number because of
the vague concept of what constituted an Indian pueblo.

[6] The Indians of Buena Esperanza de Rere were divided "into various *reducciones*
[settlements of Christianized Indians] [built] in the form of walled villages, because of
the war (de Olivares 1874: 87). Catentoa in 1755 was "an Indian pueblo with the
designation of fort" (BP [Biblioteca de Palacio] n.d.a). The purpose of the Calbuco
garrison in Chiloé in the seventeenth century was "not so much to wage war against
the enemy...] as to] provide protection for the large number of peaceful Indians
settled on those islands" (Diéz de la Calle 1902: 388).

The fortification of native settlements for defense from attacks by other Indians was
definitely prior to the arrival of the Spanish. Mariño de Lobera (1865: 130) reported
that when the Spaniards reached the Villarrica region they saw "a beautiful meadow
where there were fine houses surrounded by palings, in the form of a fortress."

[7] Most significant was the general revolt of 1769, in which a number of towns, raised
to the rank of *villas* [chartered towns] five years earlier by Governor Guill y Gonzaga,
were set on fire. Among others, they included: S. Carlos de Angol, S. Miguel de
Huequén, S. Julián de Niñinco, Purísima Concepción de Rocalgüé, S. Ignacio de
Marbén, S. Antonio de Buren, S. Javier de Chacaico, S. Juan de Dios de Requén, S.F.
de Borja de Malleco, S. Juan Evangelista de Quechereguas, N. Sra. de los Dolores de
Tucapen, N. Sra. de la Asunción de Lleulleu, N. Sra. de los Remedios de Caramavida,
N. Sra. de Belén de Malguilla, N. Sra. de la Soledad de Pangue, N. Sra del Rosario
de Cuycupil, N. Sra. del Rosario de La Imperial, N. Sra. de la Victoria de Tirúa, N.
Sra. de Monserrate de Tirúa, N. Sra. de la Natividad de Cuinco, N. Sra. de las Nieves
de Tecumávida, N. Sra. del Carmen del Alma, N. Sra. de la Candalaria de Collico,
N. Sra. del Tránsito de Iligue, N. Sra. de la Paz de Rimelhulme, N. Sra. de la
Consolación de Querico, N. Sra. de las Mercedes de Railgue, N. Sra. de Atocha de
Antiguingue, Los Stos. Reyes de Rauco, S. Esteban de Melilpun, S. Blas de Llico, S.
Nicolás de Tolentino de Quiricó, S. Benito de Quiapu, S. Vicente Ferrer de Deunco,
S. Salvador de Lebu, S. Rafael de la Albarrada, N. Sra. del Patrocinio de Maquegua,
la Encarnación de Boroa, N. Sra. de Pastoriza de Imperial Alta, N. Sra. de Copacabana
de Toltén, S. Lucas de Colhué, S. Andrés de Nuñinco, S. Jerónimo de Renaico, S.
Matías de Buren de la Montaña, S. Mateo de Raguel Toro, S. Marcos de Chequenco,
and two other towns in Arauco (cf. ANS [Archivo Nacional de Santiago] n.d.a; also
Carvallo 1875: vol. 9, p. 315ff.).

[8] Because an elaborate techical apparatus was not required for defense against the
natives, the Chilean fortifications are primarily interesting for their influence on urban
development; their architectural value *per se* is secondary.

extent the original first founders appear to have been unaware of native aggressiveness. While they did not completely disregard the defensive factor – virtually inherent in establishing any settlement – the plans they drew up did not expressly acknowledge it.

Santiago del Nuevo Extremo, the first city founded in the territory by Pedro de Valdivia in February 1541, is a case in point. Its grid extended between two river beds which shielded it on the north and south, and it came under the protection of the Huelén Cerro, Santa Lucía, which served as a lookout to the east. However, its longest flank at the opposite end was completely open, and not a single point was designated as a possible defense nucleus.

Seven months after its first founding ceremony, this newly planned city was reduced to ashes by the Mapochino Indians. The colonizers reacted by fortifying one of the *manzanas* [blocks of houses]; this was a practical and quite elementary solution. The area chosen contained the governor's properties on the western side of the plaza. The fortification was adequate for guarding the perimeter and initially could accommodate the entire population.[9] This solution, with minor variations, was applied during the sixteenth century in times of emergencies by other settlements. For example, the Palace of Bishop Cisneros was fortified in 1600 during the great siege of La Imperial (which ended its existence). Similarly, during the siege of Osorno – in the same period and with a similar outcome – the *manzana* facing the plaza and adjoining the main church, including its peculiar extension, was fortified. Villarrica's defense appears to have been similar; in 1602 after three years of heroic siege all its inhabitants perished in the castle, along with the city itself.[10]

Within eight months of its founding by Juan Bohon in December 1543, La Serena was destroyed. This and similar calamities convinced de Valdivia of the true disposition of his ungovernable subjects. Henceforth he was to build a fort before establishing each settlement.[11]

In describing the founding of Concepción in October 1550, de Rosales reports that de Valdivia "decided to build with stone and strong adobe brick because he believed the people whom he fought were fearless and aggressive; all the Spaniards were engaged in laying

[9] Regarding the Santiago fortification, González de Nájera (1889: 209) included a fortress plan for the capital with his original manuscript (Book IV, Discourse I, ch. 5). Regarding subsequent fortifications constructed on Cerro Santa Lucía by Marcó del Pont in 1816 – which did not have the fatal effect intended by their inventors – Rodríguez Ballesteros (1901: Volume VI, 286) reported that they served "neither for defense nor offense, nor was there room for an adequate number of troops, nor would firing arms have sufficient space for operation. After all the money spent, they are only used for firing artillery salutes on holidays, since, upon examination, they cannot serve any other purpose." In fact, this has been their only use up to the present. . . . On the attempt to wall the city in 1657, cf. CHH n.d.: vol. 35, p. 274.)

[10] De Olivares observed its ruins (1864: 137).

the foundations, fetching stones, and making adobe bricks; the work thus proceeded with such admirable speed that in a few days all the houses were completed, as well as the fort with its watchtowers and tall, broad walls, and thus a city was formed" (de Rosales 1877: Volume I, 441; see also Maríno 1865: 115 and de Góngora 1862: 22). A witness of the event described the place as "fortified with towers, where one could be secure, with a guard at its gates night and day" (de Góngora 1862: 22). Similar precautions were taken in establishing La Imperial, Valdivia, Villarrica, and Angol. The governor's successors not only continued this policy, they went even further: increasingly they took into account defensive capabilities and opportunities for mutual assistance when deciding where to locate settlements.

In laying the foundations of Cañete during the summer of 1558, García de Mendoza, after building the fort, "then ordered the laying out of four square plots; he ordered this area to be enclosed by an adobe wall using two sets of molds; this was done with such speed that the work was completed in fifteen days. There were two high mud walls, each bearing a high adobe tower that dominated the countryside and the fort; two artillery pieces were placed on each tower (de Góngora 1862: 86).[12] In Castro de la Nueva Galicia, Marshall Ruiz de Gamboa expressly considered strategic possibilities[13] when building a fort for the defense of its inhabitants. Upon establishing the Chillán fortress, in addition to creating *alcades* [magistrates] and a *cabildo* [municipal council], he appointed an *alcaide* [governor][14] for its castle (ANS n.d.c.).

With the passage of time there was a gradual improvement in defensive measures. For example, in founding Santa Cruz de Oñez, Governor García de Loyola (who, like de Valdivia, was assassinated by Indians) "constructed two fortresses to cover both banks of the river" (Molina 1787). Around 1583 the environs of Villarrica were fortified by a chain of forts (Ruiz de Gamboa [1583]: 149).[15] In

[11] This can be observed in Concepción and Cañete (de Góngora 1862: 22, 86) and in Villarrica and Valdivia (de Herrera 1901: 528).

[12] Cañete was founded specifically for military purposes (cf. de Olivares 1864: 190).

[13] Cf. note 41; Medina n.d.c: vol. 1, p. 252; de Olivares 1864: 366. Defensive needs were considered in the second siting of Angol by García de Mendoza (de Ovalle 1888: vol. 12, p. 333), the siting of Cañete by Quiroga in 1566 (de Góngora 1862: 145, also in Medina n.d.a: vol. 1, p. 59), and of La Imperial (Mariño 1865: 126).

[14] The obsolete knightly institution of the *alcaide* [governor of a fortress] was revived as early as 1550, when Pedro de Valdivia briefed his procurators to the Emperor, who were to request a license to found three or four fortresses in Chile "...inasmuch as this land has a powerful and aggressive people"; de Valdivia reserved for himself the right to appoint the governorships (Medina n.d.a: vol. 9, p. 71). In 1577 Governor Bravo de Saravia was acknowledged as having appointed *alcaides* for Concepción, Cañete, and San Juan de la Frontera (Medina n.d.a: vol. 2, p. 324).

[15] Treutler discovered many remains of fortifications in 1859 around Villarrica (Treutler 1861, 1958: 367ff.).

January 1611 Governor Merlo de la Fuente decided to displace Angol by two blocks from the location designated on its original layout. He enclosed the settlement with high mud walls and erected a fortress in its center "with four square towers at the corners: in this way the town's eight streets were barricaded" (de Rosales 1877: Volume II). A detailed study of the ruins of La Imperial in 1834 reveals that the lower part of the city was walled and that some other areas were fortified (Sanfuentes and Amunátegui 1925: 155).[16]

II. *Fortresses: The Origin of Cities*

In the Middle Ages, European castles and monasteries served as centers for unifying the population, and gradually cities developed around them.[17] Similarly, at the other end of the world, throughout the so-called "colonial centuries" – the American Middle Ages – fortresses, along with convents and missions, gave rise to new settlements.

I have discussed those settlements which were immediately preceded by the building of a fortress. Now I shall briefly analyze the evolutionary development of the castle. Initially conceived as an isolated defensive unit, it later developed into a formal town while retaining the stamp of its original strategic purpose as it developed.

Mariño (1865: 214) reported that García built a new fortress on the ruins of the old Tucapel fortress (*casa fuerte*) erected by Pedro de Valdivia. The fortress "provided the beginnings of a city with the name of Cañete de la Frontera, in honor of the Viceroy, his [García's] father, who was the Marquis of Cañete." The famous Casa de Arauco, also the creation of de Valdivia, was the origin of an important site which – with the various names of *villa* [chartered town] of San Ildefonso and city or *tercio*[18] of San Felipe de Austria – was rebuilt successively by Governors Sotomayor, Oñez de Loyola, and Meneses in 1590, 1596, and 1665. The city of San Francisco de la Selva de Copiapó owed its origin to the *casa fuerte* built by Bohon in 1548[19] (cf.

---

[16] Cf. Sanfuentes and Amunateguí (1925: 154).

[17] Encampments appear at times to have served the same function. Governor Rodrigo de Quiroga, remaining in Arauco with his army in 1577, "settled there, planning a fort and town to provide a place for the soldiers to spend the winter"; the lodging itself "was a whole town..." de Quiroga 1902: 406). The case of Cudico, in Valdivia's jurisdiction, is interesting. Here the old fort of Nuestra Señora del Pilar served as a point of reference for the Franciscan mission of the same name; the mission in turn was the center for the population in the vicinity (cf. ANS n.d.d).

[18] A *tercio* was an infantry regiment; concerning the title of *tercio* for some *presidios* [garrisons], cf. de Olivares (1864: 64).

[19] Mariño (1865: 244) has already alluded to its origin as a *casa fuerte* with high ramparts, governed by García, "with sufficient room inside for many soldiers and large

Benavides 1958: 327ff.). Many other towns and *villas* of the eighteenth century also owed their birth to forts erected in previous centuries: Espíritu Santo de Catirai (1585); Nacimiento de Nuestro Señor, San Antonio de Chacao, and San Antonio de Carelmapu (1604); San Ignacio de la Redención de Boroa (1606); San José de la Mariquina and San Luis de Alba de Cruces (1647); San Miguel de Colcura and Nuestra Señora de Guadalupe de Lota (1662); and Mesamávida and Santo Tomás de Colhuè (1695). Finally, forts gave rise to the following towns of the same name, the majority of which still exist today: San Francisco de Borja de Negrete, Los Angeles, Nuestra Señora de Monserrat de Tirúa, San Carlos de Purén, San Andrés de Nuninco, San Rosendo, Santa Bárbara, Santa Juana, Santa Lucía de Yumbel, San Pedro, Laraquete, Virquén (*sic*), Quepe, Paicaví, and San José de Alcudia de Río Bueno, among others.

The fortress (and consequently the military aspect) was the deciding factor in determining the location of these towns. Indeed, many of them did not undergo any founding ceremony other than the erecting of the fort. In these cases they even lacked the classic gridiron plan; instead they spawned simple, irregular settlements. This purely strategic (and at times circumstantial) priority – as opposed to other considerations which might guarantee the survival of a settlement – was at times the cause of decline or restricted development.

The contemporaries of such experiments were generally conscious of these limitations, which like dense clouds menaced the radiant future they longed for. The attitude of the inhabitants of Valdivia provides a good case in point. In 1761 it had been proposed for purely strategic reasons to move the town to the narrow fortified precinct of Mancera Island. By way of resisting this measure, the threatened inhabitants fended off the sword of Damocles which was hovering like a sceptre over the future of this city. They claimed that "such a settlement cannot endure if we regard it only as a *Presidio*; for it is also an ancient City and the principal Port of this region for the land and kingdoms added to H.M.'s Crown" (ANS [1761]).

III. *Fortified Plazas and* Presidios

According to the strategic requirements of the old settlements of Chile, the idea of creating fortified plazas or garrisoning existing settlements was the logical consequence of pirate attacks and the Araucanian War.

A significant portion of settlements made during the period in question were fortified plazas or *presidios* [garrisons]. They enjoyed a rank midway between the simple settlements "with forts" and the

stables. . . ." The floor appears once again mathematically rectangular on the plan drawn in 1793 by Ojeda y Sasu (see note 31).

large defensive complexes of the coastal cities. Some of the simple settlements cited above took on features of *presidios*, as did the more elaborate complexes which will be discussed below. At this point I shall simply indicate some of the more important ones which exhibit the features of a combined military-urban entity.

I shall begin with the most famous frontier city: Ildefonso de Arauco. Founded by Pedro de Valdivia as a *casa fuerte*, it was moved many times, at times to prevent its devastation and at times as a result of devastation. It was the renowned residence of the Kingdom's field marshals and commissaries-general of the cavalry. The site varied between Lota and Norcún, until it was permanently established by Governor Juan Henríquez on the slopes of the Cerro Colo Colo.

The first in the Carampangue Valley was five-and-a-half kilometers east of the river on almost level terrain, eight *cuadras* [one kilometer] from the sea, at the foot of the ridge which protected it. The original enclosure was in the form of a simple rectangle. After the revolt of 1723, when it was abandoned for a time (cf. de Olivares 1864: 553), it was replaced by a considerably larger enclosure, trapezoidal in form. Its dressed stone wall, 3.89 meters high by 1.94 meters wide, was 312.61 meters long on its shorter (north) side and 347.73 meters on the other sides, one of which overlooked the sea. The largest face, to the south, was a scarp cut into the ridge. Because this ridge provided a point from which enemy attacks could be launched, it was crowned by a triangular redoubt with lateral fortifications.[20] A bulwark was located at each corner and a pair of square towers enclosed the radial curtains where they touched the hill.

The chronicler Carvallo Goyeneche (1875: Volume III, 172 ff.), who fought there, describes this fortified site in detail for us: twenty-four cannons, six on each bulwark or small tower, guard the complex, while the entire wall, in the medieval manner of central Europe, was crowned "with covered ways for building fires in rainy weather." This unusual patrol area could be coursed on horseback.

Three baroque portals[21] interrupted the respective curtains. The

---

[20] Carvallo (1875: vol. 3, p. 172) indicates another fortification on the same hill.

[21] The royal arms of the Crown were engraved on the frieze of the principal (eastern) façade, which was 14.28 meters high; the frieze was topped with five pyramids 1.68 meters high, the pedestals of which were engraved with coats of arms and shields. Over the architrave a large stone bore an inscription with the construction dates; it was topped by a cupola decorated with clusters and a 2.52-meter pyramid. Inside the pyramid there was (of all things) a gunpowder depot, and the royal arms appeared again, "on a shield of elegant design, [as well as] other coats of arms and inscriptions on various shields..."

The other two portals were 11.76 meters high; their pediments were crowned with tree pyramids and shields inscribed "Jesus" and "María." On the inside, elaborate heraldic decoration completed the whole "with ornamentation and elegant designs" (Carvallo 1875: vol. 3, p. 172).

main portal generated an axis which extended from a beautiful chapel[22] located outside the walls of the enclosure, bisected the parade ground on the north and south sides and terminated at the decorated façade of the Jesuit church located on a terrace with eleven steps. An adorned fountain in the middle of the plaza accentuated the axial composition; from a distance this composition reinforced the appearance of the fortress on the hill.

In the mid-eighteenth century, the enclosure contained barracks for two thousand men, pavilions for officers, quarters for the senior military authorities of the kingdom, two churches, and a Jesuit Academy. In addition, there were the houses of forty-eight military families, "on formal streets laid out in parallels; along with those of the soldiers, high officials, officers, and the Jesuit Academy, this makes a fair-sized settlement" (BP n.d.a). In addition, forty families lived in houses outside the enclosed area. An isometric drawing made in 1741 gives us an idea of the whole; the details are significant for their decorative quality (Caravallo 1875: Volume III, 173).[23]

Yumbel, another of the more important fortified frontier sites, was the permanent residence of some of the kingdom's officers, the *sargentos mayores*. Located on level terrain, its rectangular enclosure measured 175.53 by 178.88 meters. Made of stone and adobe, these bulwarked walls enclosed the soldiers' quarters and "houses and cabins with formal streets" for 120 families (BP n.d.a). The church contained a famous image of San Sebastián. This was in fact the main reason the settlement was recorded in history so often, since the weakness of its strategic value meant its stagnation as an urban community.

The original layout of Angol must have had merit, for it was reproduced – its exceptional location already proven – in 1638–1639 by Governor Lazo de la Vega. De Tesillo (1864: 99) described it as "enclosed by four walls with traverses, of 600 *piés* [144 meters] each." A seventeenth-century plan shows its square layout, bisected by two axes that link the gates centered in each wall; each wall was 450 *piés* [126 meters] long. A parade ground faced the main gate; diagonal streets, converging on the center from opposite corners, formed acute

---

[22] The stone cross including pedestal was 5.88 meters high and was covered with inscriptions ("fluted moulding, edging and cornices") (Cavallo 1875: vol. 3, p. 173).
[23] The engraving, sent by President Manso to the King (12 November 1741), belongs to the collection of the Archivo Cartográfico of the Servicio Geográfico del Ejército, in Madrid, where I obtained it thanks to the very kind attention of Colonel Cesáreo Fustel Cadierno. A duplicate, with small differences, is in the Archivo General de Indias (1741b) and has been reproduced by Medina (1953) and Torres Balbas (1951: 99). On the decaying state of the fortified site of Arauco in 1817, cf. CHI [1817]: 331ff.); on its external appearance in 1830, cf. ANS [1830] see Encina (1956: vol. 1, p. 55, Figure 42). The Museo Historico Nacional preserves various ornamental pieces of the enclosure described (n.d.: 40ff.).

and obtuse angles which quite forcibly broke the rigid orthogonal nature of the construction. Compared to other *villas* of the period, Angol as shown on this plan was large enough for a moderate-sized population despite its limited measurements. Its diagonal streets were unique for a seventeenth-century site.

Except for Nacimiento (see below), the other fortified frontier towns, though numerous, do not appear to have been developed or as interesting as those described above. Generally, because of their limited size, their settlements developed outside their walls.

The Purén walls formed a rectangle measuring 84.42 by 145.43 meters. As was customary, Purén was located at the edge of a river gorge, making access difficult. The adjoining *villa*, planned by the engineer Leandro Badarán in 1775, served to open up its grid. This provided more space in the characteristic manner, displacing the regular *manzanas* in order to permit the free action of artillery. As a result, the two fortresses (with the river in the middle) could launch a crossfire, thus creating a coordinated defense nucleus (AGI n.d.a; see also BP 1755).

Santa Juana was located near a large lake which supplied its moats (Rodríguez Ballesteros 1901: Volume V, 303). Opposite, San Juan de Talcamávida was situated on a bluff bordered by the waters of the Bío Bío and another lake (Carvallo 1875; Volume III, 168).

The town of Los Angeles was located at a prudent distance from the fort, which had a moat and bulwarks. The newly formalized settlement "contains parallel streets, and, although the houses are of boards and straw, they are not at all bad (BP n.d.a).[24] The marginal location of the fortress, in the custom of the ancient *alcázar* [castle], was the age-old solution repeated in almost all frontier sites. According to Rodríguez Ballesteros (1901: Volume VI, 120), around 1813 its defensive apparatus had deteriorated and its artillery was gone, though there were "quarters or settlements within its walls."

IV. *Nacimiento*

The strategic fort of Nacimiento de Nuestro Señor was founded at Christmastime 1604 by Governor Ribera "where the Bío Bío and the creek called Vergara meet, [with the aim of] pushing on to Angol and controlling the enemy's land" (de Rosales 1877: Volume II, 409). Núñez de Pineda Bascuñán has provided details of its daily life around

---

[24] The system of small forts located at the edge of settlements or which gave rise to settlements was common in Indian territory throughout the nineteenth century in both Chile and Argentina. On the beginnings of this process in Cuyo, cf. Comadrán Ruíz (1962: 89) and Razori (1945).

1629. At this time it was protected by parapets and countermures and consisted of a church and a settlement. It was dismantled by President Acuña y Cabrera in the general uprising of 1655 (Núñez de Pineda 1948: 426; de Olivares 1874: 105). Later it was restored by Francisco de Meneses who soon enclosed it with a wall with traverses and finished the compound for the troops (de Tesillo 1878: 16). Aided "by nature and by art," the Araucanian chief Butapichón destroyed Nacimiento while it was under the control of Luíz Fernández de Córdoba (de Córdoba 1862: 212, 257). It was attacked again but survived intact until the general uprising of 1723 (de Olivares 1874: 547). Carvallo Goyeneche praised its site, "on an elevation formed by the crest of a low hill, a truly advantageous position " (1875: Volume II, 276).

The advantage of such a location and the historical interest of its exploits was soon complemented by the completion of its definitive town plan, presented on 20 August 1756, when it was formally raised to the rank of *villa* by President Amat. From the description of this ceremony one can infer that the governor himself drew up the plan. Reports of his passion for military and (consequently) engineering matters came to us through the careful studies of Cruces Pozo (1952: 327–345) and Rodríguez Casado and Pérez Embid (1947, 1949).[25]

As to the configuration of the terrain of this villa, "it was an irregular rectangle in the form of a dovetail or hornwork; His Lordship went on to describe the fortification with respect to this Fortified Town as the most developed and the best " (ANS n.d.b).

As I see it, the aggregate with its bulwarks and pinzer-like form belonged to the classification of permanent fortifications. Its unusual construction emphasized the asymmetrical configuration, which became narrower near the town (one might call it "minicephalic ").

Its layout was clearly organized in two parts. The first part, the castle, was formed by a small, irregular citadel in the shape of a quadrangular polygon. It had four similar bulwarks, in corresponding pairs, with dimensions under the norm. The bulwarks on the Río Vergara measured far less than 117 *varas*:[26] the first face was only 30 *varas* and the second was 27 *varas*. And of the 63 *varas* of the flanks only 8 engaged on the first flank and 6 on the second. These were very small measurements indeed. The two bulwarks which provided protection for the inside entranceway were malformed, lacking the first flank on the left-hand bulwark and the second flank on the right-hand bulwark; the curtains of faces 1 and 2 respectively served

---

[25] On the plan of the *villa* ("laid out geometrically "), the name of Salvador Cabrito, general field master, also appears, although it is definitely Amat's drawing.

[26] A *vara* is 835.9 millimeters, or approximately 33 inches.

as the flanks. Such irregularity was unacceptable in European schools of fortification, except in the Spanish. In Spanish America formal precepts were outweighed by geographical and sociopolitical factors.

The second part of the layout consisted of the hornwork, a well-conceived but unsymmetrical work unsuited to its function as the urban conglomerate for a *villa*. It was composed of two bulwarks, a revelin with a parade ground, and drawbridges. The bulwarks were regular but they did not have the usual dimensions: the first face was 107 *varas*, and the second, 105. The flanks of the left bulwark were 30 and 28 *varas* respectively, and 28 and 30 *varas* for the right bulwark. The curtain extended along the castle's moat for 410 *varas*, lacking any salients. The irregular moats became progressively smaller as they approached the castle, dispensing with the minimum 42 *varas* in the line of the salient. There were no counterscarps, covered ways, or esplanades.

According to Colonel Dr. Juan Manuel Zapatero (personal communication), the unusual layout of Nacimiento is a good example of what he considers the "Spanish American school of fortification." It reveals interesting similarities to a distant and significant building, the castle of San Marcos de Apalache in western Florida.

Concerning the *villa* itself,[27] de Olivares (1864: 65) tells us that the president enlarged its jurisdiction by including the dispersed peasant population in the area. Carvallo (1875: Volume III, 168) noted that it was made up of 68 Spanish citizens (*vecinos*), with a total population of 549; from this number two companies of soldiers were recruited. Certainly a reasonable number of Indian servants and friends would have to be added to these figures. In 1762 there were 73 adobe houses and 3 straw huts. Inside the fort the governor had provided a fine church, 27.58 by 12.53 meters, with "an elegant altarpiece"; in addition, there were galleries, ovens, dungeons, and the like (ANS n.d.b),[28]

The extraordinary layout of Nacimiento can be seen in its first two plans, in my possession, dated respectively 1756 and 1757. The first is undoubtedly the original design, the basis for the layout (ANS [1756a]).[29] The second, I believe, is only a copy of the first, and not

[27] I should like to express my appreciation for the interesting technical comments on the Nacimiento fortifications provided by Colonel Dr. Juan Manuel Zapatero.

[28] Since 1628 a famous statue called S. Virgen de Boroa has been kept in the church (cf. *Boletín* 1940: 21). It is on record that a settlement of friendly Indians was under the protection of the fortified town: also, that the fort was garrisoned in 1762 by a company of veteran foot soldiers under the command of a commissioned captain (cf. ANS n.d.e).

[29] Reproduced here (see Plate 3). This authorized copy was made available through the courtesy of the custodian of the Archivo Nacional de Santiago, Juan Eyzaguirre. I wish to express my appreciation to Sr. Eyziguirre for providing research facilities.

a drawing of what had been built by that time.[30] A third plan, of 1793, drawn *in situ* by Captain Juan Bautista de Ojeda y Zassu,[31] shows us only the site of the fort and the springers of the arches adjoining the streets; here we can see the alterations which took place in carrying out the original plans. The four bulwarks of the fortress appear to be complete; the characteristic layout of the half bulwarks of the land side (originally planned) are omitted, and the moats have become paved roads. However, the report accompanying this plan alludes to the defenses anticipated for the *villa* in Amat's original plan, with its scarps and palisades. In addition, its population had increased "because of the fine opportunities it enjoys under the protection of that fortress."

A fourth plan, dated 1860 (BNS [1860]), shows the radial design of the streets quite disfigured. This leads one to presume that either the initial plan was only partially realized, or that use and abuse by the inhabitants slowly distorted it. Nevertheless, this plan shows the same angle indicated in the original plans of 1756 and 1757 on the only remaining radial street. It also confirms the shape of the fort as shown by Ojeda y Zassu in 1793 (an indication that it was made perhaps prior to Amat's plan). On the other hand, it introduces a significant progression in the length of the *manzanas* which, as if following the original conception, grow gradually longer in direct proportion to their distance from the fortress. As it is an incomplete sketch, the traces of the old gorge cannot be seen. On the other hand, it does show the disappearance of the lateral walls, which are broken by the extension of the transverse streets and the consequent overflow of the construction.

A fifth plan, of 1863 (BNS [1863],[32] shows a completely symmetric arrangement; it demonstrates most eloquently the triumph of the

[30] It is found in the third section of the fourfold plan of *villas* founded by Amat, preserved in the Servicio Histórico Militar, Madrid (Maps and Plans C-VI-No. 6,168). I wish to thank my esteemed friend, Dr. Juan Manuel Zapatero, Colonel Jefe del Negociado Ultramar, who helped me obtain a reproduction of this plan in 1954. It has been published by Rodríguez Casado and Pérez Embid (1949: 22) and by Jaime Eyzaguirre (1965: 282).

[31] The original is in the British Museum: I consulted a photocopy in the Archive Nacional, Santiago (ANS [1793]): The text of the report sent to President Higgins is published in Anrique (n.d.).

[32] Although such an excessive variety in only three years is suspicious, both documents offer sufficient evidence of authenticity. Concerning Nacimiento, a letter sent in 1803 by President Muñoz de Guzmán to García Carrasco, Commandante de Ingenieros de la Frontera [Commander of Frontier Engineers], indicates that the latter's services were required at that time "especially for Nacimiento, the plan for which is being drawn up (Muñoz de Guzmán 1913: 89). Around 1748 José Perfecto de Salas proposed that Nacimiento (under whose protection the Indian settlement of Santa Fe was) should be the permanent seat of the *sargentos mayores* [senior officers] of the kingdom because of its advantageous geographical location (cf. Donoso 1963: 86, 125).

traditional gridiron pattern over radial innovations. Undoubtedly the irregular plots assigned by the planner (they were slightly trapezoidal, measuring 1671 meters in the front and 33.43 in the back) must have presented the builders with a real enigma. Several factors conspired to weaken the rigidity of the original design – the outer walls were of poor quality (prematurely decaying after only a few years), and the waning of the Araucanian War made their costly repair unnecessary. The inhabitants were thus freed from all hindrances and returned instinctively to the lines to which they were accustomed. In any case, the interesting layout of Nacimiento is unique in Chile and at that time was exceptional in America.

DEFENSE OF THE PACIFIC

I should now like to discuss the whole group of fortifications sur-rounding the major parts of the kingdom, considering their role as strongholds of the South Sea and outposts of the viceroyalty. These systems can be classified as simple or complex according to their construction and geopolitical role in relation to the sea. The technical capacity of their armaments was generally superior to that of the fortified towns considered above.

Valdivia was outstanding both as a port and as a fortress. Its constellation of fortifications earned it the title of "capital of the South Sea" from the Council of the Indies in 1707 (AGI [1707]).[33]

Next in importance was San Carlos de Ancud. At the end of the eighteenth century it came to challenge the unquestioned primacy of Valdivia. Even though the quality of its castles might not have been superior, the opinion of the municipal and viceregal officials was that it excelled Valdivia.

Valparaíso, though inferior as a port, enjoyed the greatest trade because it served the capital, Santiago. It also served as a nucleus for Concepción, the second market of the kingdom. Its defensive layout was definitely inferior to those discussed above.

La Serena was the most modest of all, though not the least signifi-cant, considering derivation of its town plan. I have reserved La Serena and Valdivia for a more detailed analysis and will begin with a short survey of the others.

---

[33] It is interesting that the ports most needing fortification in 1599 (judging by the number of castles and artillery requested by Governor Oñez de Loyola) were not Valdivia or Concepción. They were, in fact, Valparaíso and La Serena, "with greater capacity and better design for such; in this way they would be able to maintain a strong resistance with [only] a moderate force" (BNS [1599]).

I. *Concepción*

The urban design of Concepción, Chile's military capital, suffered least from the impact of the vast defensive system of which it was the virtual center. It was the official seat of the governors (the captains-general) who went from here to the theater of war, and no other city in the country presented such a martial appearance in its daily life. According to Mariño (1865: 290, 325), "it has been devastated many times and has never been free from great misfortunes. This adversity continues to the present day, for no man dares to venture half a league from the city because of the obvious danger." The royal *audiencia* originally installed in the southern metropolis survived continued surprise attacks: "In the eight months I was there," writes a distressed counselor to the king in 1576 (CDI 1576: 277), "few days passed in which it was not necessary to leave off from writing and take up arms...". Even when the war to the south of the Bío Bío was ended, military exercises continued to provide the basic tenor of daily activities.[34]

Pedro de Valdivia founded the city in 1550, selecting the site for a city "larger than Seville" (de Valdivia [1550]: Volume IX, 66). However, the vicissitudes of war so limited its development that it was mockingly compared to Torrelodones (de Valdivia [1550]: Volume I, 208). The pride of the city, taking precedent over the cathedral, was the guardroom and weapons chamber constructed by Governor Lazo de la Vega in 1633. This was "an excellent architectural design which rivals the best of its kind to be found in Europe" (de Tesillo 1878: 65). The famous Fort Penco was more adorned with artistic shields and heraldic pieces than equipped with defensive apparatus. According to Frezier (1732: 14), in 1712 it was in such a state that its lateral fortifications only defended the anchoring ground; it was only 68.21 meters long by 13.643 wide, and half of this area had no platform.[35] The cannons, cast a century earlier in Lima, had burst vents and were poorly mounted on gun carriages which were themselves in very poor condition.

Each threat of attack by pirates provoked an improvization of defenses. Most of these, due to their makeshift nature, disappeared as soon as the panic produced by the imminent danger was past, leaving no trace in the urban design. In 1615 Alonso de Ribera built "many gabions and redoubts in the harbor, massive parapets and

[34] "The *presidio* and soldiery serving in the defense of this city are splendid: here regiments enter and leave every day, as is the custom and practice of countries at war" (de Ovalle 1888: vol. 1, p. 310).
[35] At the time of Independence it was still in existence with six cannons, brick barracks, and officers' quarters (Rodríguez Ballesteros 1901: vol. 5, p. 310).

trenches with gabions and heavy fascines, platforms, orillons, and other elements" (de Rosales 1877: Volume II, 610). In 1684, in the face of an English threat, a battery platform appeared as if by magic; with its sixteen heavy-caliber pieces, barracks, and underground storerooms, it survived until the following century (Carvallo 1875: Volume II, 182).[36]

The transfer of the city in 1751 to Mocha Valley finally rid it of such elaborate defenses, though the inevitable fortress of lime and brick crowned the hills of its new surroundings (Gómez de Vidaurre (n.d.: Volume XIV, 345).[37] To offset this move, a fortification for the new port of Talcahuano was built; the port, though somewhat distant from the city, was completely dependent on it. The layout of the city, pressed close to the looming hills, was regular; successive fortifications were to flank its prominent points. In 1875 San Agustín castle, on the beach, harbored thirteen artillery pieces along its 50.15-meter front. Soon Gálvez castle displayed an equal number on its brick parapets (AGI [1875]). Around the time of independence Talcahuano was considered by some to be the keystone in the strategy of the kingdom (BNS 1960: 21).

The defenses built during the famous siege of the separatist revolution, however, did not influence its urban development.

Concepción, together with the old Penco site and Talcahuano, formed the nucleus of a vast, flexible defense system not only for the coast but also for the interior towns. Moreover, the southern metropolis and its port also served as an administrative center for the fortifications of Lirquén and the excellent military complex on the Gulf of Arauco (with the fortresses of Colcura, Arauco, Tucapel, and Santa Juana).

II. *Valparaíso*

The irregular layout of Valparaíso was not a result of its well-known fortifications, which were built at a later date. Nevertheless, the presence of these fortifications must have contributed to its military character, so common in most early Chilean settlements. The irregular layout was the direct consequence of the fact that it was never

[36] The plan Frezier published (1732) shows the exact location of the fort in the city center; it is next to the interesting succession of plazas and "plazuelas" [small squares] extending some five blocks and comprising a large official quarter surrounded by public buildings, a hospital, convents, and churches.

[37] Carvallo Goyeneche (1875: vol. 2, p. 314) says that this was a small castle, San Clemente, built by President Guilly Gonzaga.

formally founded (although its ancestry is older than that of Santiago itself; it was named by Juan de Saavedra on the 1536 Almagro expedition).

It received the coveted title of *ciudad* [city] only in 1802, by which time it had been extensively developed (BNS 1802, cf. de Ramón Folch 1953: 177). Its port, such as it was, was very poor, and its existence was only justified by the need for a passage to the capital. "In fact," Carvallo Goyeneche proclaimed "it is not a port; the whole port area is exposed to the north and northeast winds – which in winter are very fierce – providing no safety for the ships."

Valparaíso was fortified by Governor Henríquez in accordance with the royal *cédula* [decree] of 6 July 1674 which ordered the fortifying of all sites in the kingdom threatened with invasion by the English. It would appear that its layout is owed to the engineering enterprises of General Jerónimo Hurtado de Mendoza y Quiroga (Carvallo 1875: Volume II, 81). This grandee built the castle of Concepción (the old castle) with its eight artillery pieces of varying calibres, and the Cabritería battery with its five pieces; the two structures could combine their discharges. The fortification was not completely formalized until the garrisoning of the port under the *cédula* of 4 February 1678.

At this time a military administration was established there. In 1684 President Garro built San José castle; with its ten cannons and numerous buildings, it became the governors' residence (Carvallo 1875: Volume II, 172, cf. also p. 454, note 53 and p. 183: and Volume III, p. 82).[38] De Olivares (1874: 460) praised the excellent condition of this fortress in 1736. Twenty-seven years later it was strengthened when President Guill y Gonzaga built the castle of San Antonio. El Espaldón battery was added in 1793 and El Barón castle in 1796 (AGI [1796]).

All that remains is to emphasize the distinctive nature of Chile's commercial port – unusual for its urban plan rather than for its defenses. "The place where the inhabitants settled," said the Governor to the Viceroy in 1682,

... is a very narrow stretch of land; the lots are so narrow that [the inhabitants] have only managed to build the houses where they live and the warehouses where they store goods for marketing by dint of much effort in leveling the hills and slopes that stretch to the very edge of the water.... There is no suitable place for fortifications, because all existing sites are irregular and unprotected, giving no assurance that one could resist an actual invasion if it should come to pass (AGI [1682]).

"Its layout," said Carvallo (1875: Volume III, 82), "could not be

---

[38] The desecrated ruins of San José castle have finally been declared a National monument by Decree 2372 of 19 February 1963.

worse....By excavations, some [individuals] make small plots on which they build their little, uncomfortable houses." According to Walpole, an English traveler, in 1884

...there are few places which can produce so profound an impression of ugliness on the newcomer as Valparaíso. ... The city appears to have been clustered – to its detriment – around two or three towers; and it appears to have been saved from falling into the bay by an ingenious construction of intercrossed pillars.... Of course, it in no way resembles a Spanish city; except for being divided into blocks [cuadras] wherever space permits, it would pass for a European spa (Walpole: 1935: 321).

Right in the middle of that urban labryinth, the old castles and batteries harbored the dwellings which could not be placed elsewhere due to the lack of level sites. A certain medieval air came to dominate the old walls, crowned by protruding balconies.[39]

III. San Carlos de Ancud

The founding of this city as the new provincial government seat for Chiloé (later raised to the category of *intendencia*) was the result of military considerations. The creation of the new seat came about because of the increasing value of the Archipelago, beginning in the middle of the eighteenth century, and displaced Castro, the former seat of government. (Because of its interior location – to the east of Isla Grande – the port of Castro had been considered to be of difficult access for European ships which might double the Strait to attack the Chilean coast.)

The fortification of Puerto Inglés on the Gulf of Ancud (the site chosen for the new city) was superior in every way, including its layout. Though novel in many aspects, the plan was not particularly exceptional in comparison with those common in Indian country.[40] The one questionable fact is that its layout was entirely determined by the foundations required for the fortresses. The plan expressly stated that the front "would remain two hundred and fifty *varas* away " from the royal fort, "as the Royal laws command" (de Beranguer [1758]). The town, according to another document (BP n.d.b), was to be entirely geometric "because its streets will be laid out in parallels and the people will be gathered together...under the fort's cannon

[39] There is an excellent lithography by Mazin, taken from a drawing in the collection of Juan Agustín Hurtado Zanartu. On the Valparaíso fortifications, cf. Frezier (1732: 66, 68), Rodríguez Ballesteros (1901: vol. 5, p. 255), BNS ([1762]), ANS ([1773]). Cf. also British Museum (1801).

[40] The original is in the Biblioteca Central de Cataluña (BCC n.d.c) and has been published by Rodríguez Casado and Pérez Embid (1949: 219). One notes the diversity of sizes of the blocks, the presence of "plazuelas" and secondary lanes, and the small size of the lots.

in parceled lots; with this arrangement the troops can be positioned close to the fort at a distance of 290 *varas*, so that at the beat of the drum they can immediately take up their duties."

The bulwarked fortress was laid out elegantly, with indented stretches of wall protected by glacis and esplanades. Its sea face was dressed with stone, though much sod and wood was used as fill. It had a guardroom, royal coffers, barracks, a chapel, and a weapons room (BP n.d.b: Folio 10 verso). It supported up to twenty-four high-caliber cannons and was manned by four companies of artillery forces, infantry, dragoons, and militia (de Beranguer [1770]).

The Campo Santo battery (still in existence) was built by the engineer-governor Carlos de Berenguer at a cost close to thirty thousand *pesos*. The wharf battery was located on the site of the present seminary, to the west of the plaza. Its flanks with nine trajectory cannons dominated the picturesque cove (Rodríguez Ballesteros 1901: Volume V, 366–367).

The San Antonio battery, to the north of Punta de Teque, was built by Governor Quintanilla in 1820. The battery of Poquillihue at the other end of the town covered the southern sector of the anchoring ground. On the opposite shore of the bay was Agüi castle with its thirty cannons. Noted for its military glories, its beautiful façade was completely destroyed in 1824 by Quintanilla. On the same shore, the batteries of Barcacura and La Corona completed the tight ring of fortresses defending the city.

The more dispersed defensive system of Ancud was composed of Fort Chacao (which at one time harbored twenty-one cannons), Coronel fort (facing it, on the mainland), and the fort of San Rafael de Calbuco. Around 1826 the Ancud area was garrisoned by some 5,500 troops composed of veteran companies, assembly units, and militia. The whole life of the city revolved around its remarkable armament. Its siting the direct consequence of military factors, produced one of the most beautiful Chilean cities.[41]

---

[41] Santiago de Castro, the old capital of New Galicia, also received new defenses, though they did not have a direct influence on its classic reticulated plan. De Berenguer, in a letter to Arriaga (AGI [1770]), reported that he had commissioned a plan for its port "in order to develop designs for the works necessary for its defense; . . . I regard it as necessary and indispensable to safeguard the province by fortifying the site and protecting it from assault from the direction of Los Guafos (which, in any case, could never serve as a protection)." Rodríguez Ballesteros (1901: vol. 5, p. 374) reported that around the time of Independence the city had "a beautiful weapons hall, a large number of armaments and a storehouse of gunpowder;" that there were comfortable barracks on the parade ground for eight hundred troops; and that Tauco castle, at the port's entrance, required repairs. The city's old fort had a stormy period during the bloody Dutch attack of 1660; according to Díez de la Calle (1902: 388) the fort was large enough for a garrison of 100 men. It had come to such a state of ruin that in 1773 "it does not serve for the defense of the port; made of earth and wood in a ruinous state, it only serves for defense against the Indians" (BP [1773]: folio 9). On the fortifications of Chiloé, cf. de Guiror [1778] and BNS n.d.a.

IV. Walled Cities

As Palm has astutely pointed out (1955: 156), in America the idea of walling cities generally affected only ports and came into practice as a result of pirate activities. In Chile, however, the need for defense against the aggressive Araucanians gave rise to the building of simple walls even in interior settlements. The principal fortified sites discussed above were a mixture of *ciudad* (a title which engendered pride) and fortress, the latter of varying sizes.

There are reports that upon founding Cañete, García de Mendoza "thought it expedient to fortify it with a good palisade, a moat, a platform, and a great deal of artillery" (Molina 1901 [1787]: 236). Padre de Ovalle reported the same arrangement for Santa Cruz de Oñez (de Ovalle 1888: Volume II, 63). In April 1657 the *audiencia* [royal court] examined an official advisory report from the *cabildo* [city council] of Santiago inquiring "whether it would be appropriate to wall this city because of the uprisings which have occurred in the cities of Concepción, Chillán and other areas, and the captives [they] made off with" (CHH n.d.: Volume XXXV, 274). Though the proposal was later rejected, the very fact that it was raised indicates that this idea was latent in the volatile environment of Indian Flanders.

Undoubtedly the most interesting of all the walled cities in the interior must have been the lower part of La Imperial because of its importance, size, and the time of its construction. Salvador Sanfuentes examined and carefully described its ruins in 1834. According to his report (Sanfuentes and Amunátegui 1925: 154), the site, which was eighteen by twenty *cuadras*, (2.25 by 2.51 kilometers) was located in a horseshoe bend in the river, at a navigable point. An adobe rampart and moat separated the town on its land front. There was undoubtedly a quarter for seamen, since stone docking wharfs with large iron rings for mooring ships can still be seen today. It is interesting that the main part of the town – with its cathedral, churches, and convents – was not located here on the river but in the upper city where no major traces of defenses have been discovered. We get some idea of the primitive construction of the wall from Sanfuentes, who described the sole remaining part of the wall as being in ruin after more than two centuries of abandonment.

Lohmann Villena sees a nostalgia for medieval times reflected in the predilection for the archaic system of city walls. Above and beyond the purely defensive considerations, this predilection reflected what he calls the "manorial spirit": a strong sense of honor was associated with the possession of city walls (Lohmann Villena 1964: 7). In fact, the ancient precept that "in spite of all vicissitudes, the concept the good city creates an integral whole" (Palm 1955: 156) could not have been absent in America at a time when medieval forms and concepts, in the fervor of a romantic view of life, were being employed in the most varied plans. In the capital of a convulsed Chile one even spoke of being "inside" and "outside" nonexistent walls. New governors were presented with symbolic keys to make-believe doors (CHH n.d.: Volume XXXVI, 229). And at least two of the capital's oldest settlements permitted themselves the costly luxury of being completely walled and crowned with towers and turrets.

LA SERENA. The sacking and burning of La Serena by the pirate Bartolomé Sharp on 16 December 1680 finally resulted in the walling in of the city. (It had already been afflicted by pirate attacks on a number of occasions.) The oldest plan, showing the result of this initiative, designated it as a "new fortification" (AGI n.d.c; published by Medina 1953). It outlines an oblong, irregular enclosure flanked by eight bulwarks which virtually surround the entire town. Only the outlying district of Tejar remains outside, where there was a solitary "fortress called Las Peñuelas," in the form of a lunette. The earthquake of July 1730 toppled this lofty enclosure, again leaving the city exposed to the outrages of pirate hordes (Carvallo 1875: Volume II, 253).[42]

A 1773 plan shows its growth to the south (AGI n.d.a, 1773; published by Chueca Goitía and Torres Balbas 1951: 110). Its outlying district is now surrounded by an entirely new wall delineating a gentle arc and studded with six rough bulwarks. The old enclosure has disappeared from the other flanks, but it is certain that the deep ravines, undoubtedly with bluffs, in fact serve as walls. Three strategic points are marked out for the placing of another six bulwarks. A third, very detailed plan by the engineer Pedro Rico in August 1789 (Rico 1789) again shows us the Tejar district, now incorporated and encircled by a new wall with three rectangular platforms and three square towers. Two of these towers flank the portal whose neoclassic lines remained intact to the beginning of this century as a testimony to past greatness (Encina 1956: Volume II, page 1083, Figure 890).

To avoid misconceptions, it should be explained that the ostentatious walls of La Serena were of extremely simple construction; its secondary defenses and those of the anchoring ground of Coquimbo constituted a much larger whole. Gómez de Vidaurre (n.d.: Volume II, 332) tells us that the walls were of adobe; the engineer Rico says they were mud walls (*tapias*). Nevertheless, even aside from its extraordinary dimensions, the stretch of wall on the west side (parallel to the sea) provided magnificent vistas over the beautiful expanse of

[42] On 20 August 1691 and 13 May 1692, the *cabildo* considered moving it to a safer site (cf. *Actas*... 1679–1703).

the bay; such effects were not achieved in any other city in Chile. During the last century a myriad of obstructions spoiled the view, but a few years ago they were removed. Padre de Ovalle once said of the city that it overlooked "the most pleasing and beautiful valley known, full of myrtle trees and groves that seemed to have been intentionally planted there...all sloping downhill, so that the view of the sea is completely open (de Ovalle 1888: Volume I, 332).

V. *Valdivia*

There are a number of unresolved questions concerning the features of Valdivia's layout, its evolution, and the role which its complex system of fortifications played in its development. The unique nature of its urban development requires a more detailed analysis. Its evolution appears to have been in six stages:

1. The original layout with its fort at the time it was founded (1552–1599).
2. Fort Santísima Trinidad (1602–1603).
3. Dutch fort (1643).
4. First walled enclosure (1645–1798).
5. First outer defenses (1774).
6. Second walled enclosure (1779–).

Valdivia was the head of the most powerful defense complex in Chile. In 1692 the Council of the Indies pronounced its fortresses to be the best in America (clearly this was an exaggeration) (AGI [1692]).[43] In 1810 the costs had risen to the astronomic sum of 36 million *pesos* (CHH n.d.: Volume XXXIX, 92). The fifteen castles protecting its port around 1820 were armed with 128 cannons, most capable of shooting incendiary balls (CHH n.d.: Volume XXXIX, 100). Leaving aside the study of secondary urban complexes which later gave rise to the main fortresses,[44] I will limit the analysis to the principal settlement which was a government seat, directly under the jurisdiction of the viceroy of Peru (Guarda 1953).

[43] This appraisal is exaggerated, since Cartagena de Indias, Havana, and San Juan (Puerto Rico) were better. More realistic is the opinion of Antoniozini, the general artillery commander of the viceroyalty of Peru. In a report of 15 September 1779, he said that Valdivia is simply "better endowed than Lima, El Callao, and Chiloé;" that is, the large fortified cities of the Pacific (AGI [1779]).

[44] The most interesting settlement originating from these castles was Mancera, built on a small island in the middle of the Valdivia estuary; it was fortified in 1645 by San Pedro de Alcántara Castle and Fort San Francisco de Baides. For two years it sheltered the whole population of the *presidio* with its four convents, a hospital, etc. In 1760 it was the seat of government, at which time the plaza was completely rearranged. Its plan, drawn up by Garland in 1765, shows the existence of 113 buildings distributed irregularly with a germ of methodical arrangement evident around the new parade ground (cf. BNS [1765]; BCC [1765]).

1. THE ORIGINAL LAYOUT. The strategic site selected by Pedro de Valdivia was located in a meander of the fast-flowing river which by 1544 had already been named for the governor. The river was navigable by moderate-sized ships, subject to the tides. The excellent location (scarcely seventeen kilometers from a magnificent sea port) acted as a gravitational force, assuring the prosperity of the settlement independent of its defensive qualities, which could become obsolete as ballistics techniques evolved.

Initially the site rose to little more than fifty *toesas* [97.45 meters] above sea level (Carvallo 1875: Volume III, 179).[45] At the neck of and within the promontory, shallów lagoons (*gualves*)[46] virtually isolated the raised plateau, which was only accessible on its land side at two points.

When Valdivia was founded there was a moderate-size town which Mariño describes as being laid out along a tree-lined street or avenue in the northern sector of the promontory (Mariño 1865: 138). This again verifies Hardoy's observation on the importance of native towns as factors in determining sites of Spanish settlements (Hardoy 1965: 386ff.).[47]

It is very difficult to determine the exact layout of the grid designed by the governor at the time of founding (9 February 1552) or to deduce the location of the original fort. Its complex fortresses and walls were continuously altered as a result of five earthquakes and ten general fires. Lacking documents to determine the exact lines of the original drawing, it is only possible to hypothesize on the basis of later plans, documents, and present remains which might have been part of the original construction.

On another occasion I have ventured an outline based on such

[45] The calculation appears excessive; however, I should add that after the great fire of 1909 it was lowered in order to reduce the gradient of the main road. The 1960 cataclysm caused the whole surrounding area to sink three meters, and it is probable that the earthquakes of 1575, 1737, 1835, and 1937 had similar effects. De Ovalle speaks of five *estados* [9.80 meters] (de Ovalle 1888); this is undoubtedly an error.

[46] De Rosales (1877: vol. 1, p. 563) says that the site of the city is bordered by "swamps which time and workmanship will take care of;" he describes the lagoons of Purén in the same manner (1877: vol. 1, p. 462). Carvallo Goyeneche (1875: vol. 3, p. 179), who was born and grew up in the city, says it was surrounded "to the east and south by an inaccessible lake which has only two narrow strips of land: one to the south and the other to the east." Sanfuentes mentioned that at that time (1846) the "*güalves*," or lagoons, were being drained (Sanfuentes and Amunateguí 1925). In 1858 (Notarial...1858) reference was still made to the lagoon, the "Hualve de San Antonio."

[47] Le Merced Convent was built for looking after the natives: it was situated away from the city center. The entire *barrio* was called Carmenga, the name used for the suburb of Santa Ana del Cuzco, where "the Indian *caciques* [chiefs] and priests from all provinces and tribes of the empire have built their houses and settlements" (Vázquez de Espinosa 1948a). The name of Carmenga was also used for the Indian barrio in Guamanga (present-day Ayacucho) (Vázquez de Espinosa 1948b). Cf. Hardoy, 1965: 401.

supporting evidence (Guarda 1957: 61).[48] Even this, however, raises doubts. If (as in fact it would appear) the original plaza was the same as the present one, its relationship to those found in other settlements of the period would be unique, though still within the general classification of American cities. In fact, the Valdivia plaza only occupied the area of two lots (half a *manzana*), despite the usual four of the period. Furthermore, a street ran east–west across its axis. If this were the original 1552 layout, it would have been an exceptional plan, the only similar ones (to my knowledge) being in Vera Cruz, Mexico City,[49] and in (new) Panama City (Chueca and Torres Balbas 1951: 262, 267). The relative narrowness of the usable construction site and the very topography of the land (closed in by ravines, lagoons, and rivers), fully justified such an original solution; because of its uniqueness, however, I propose it with reservations.

It is equally hazardous to determine precisely where the original fort would have been on such a plan. This fort was the focal point of the urban life of the old city, and its existence is attested to by various authors (cf. Vázquez de Espinosa 1948: Number 1994). Pérez García (1900: 272) tells us that the founder intended the western corner of the plaza for the principal church.[50] Mariño (1865: 140) reported that the governor established his residence in the new city, reserving a lot for himself on the same plaza. It is possible to conjecture that – as in Santiago – this building site may have contained the walls of Valdivia's first fortress.

Its unusual geographical situation and an uninterrupted peace permitted the city almost half a century of mining and commercial prosperity, creating an urban unity which is difficult to imagine. There were seven churches, public buildings, a fortress, workshops and warehouses, and more than 450 stone buildings. However, these all disappeared in the general destruction caused by the natives on 24 November 1599; this was the most serious reverse recorded during the hazardous colonization process in Chile. It is known that the original fort (disgracefully disarmed) was in use at the time and that a San Francisco Convent had been set up as an emergency fortress.

2. FORT SANTÍSIMA TRINIDAD. After the site was abandoned, Governor Ribera undertook restoration in 1602 with the construction of a suitable fortress to secure the port and serve as a base for repopulation. Under the patronage of *la Santísima Trinidad* [the Most

[48] The basis of this sketch is the first two *manzanas* to the east of the parade ground. These are the only ones which have retained their sixteenth-century measurements; on some of plot divisions traces of the original barracks complex can still be seen.

[49] Drawn up by Bautista Antonelli in January 1590 (cf. Calderón Quijano 1953: 12, Figure 2).

[50] Probably the same site later occupied by the Cathedral.

Holy Trinity], the new fort was located near the Franciscan convent; it had a population of 800 and "high and strong" gateways (*Revista Chilena* n.d.: 78).[51] This fortress was located on the riverbank in the manner of some of the medieval *alcázares*; its American precedent was the Santo Domingo fortress built by Diego Colón (Palm 1951: 25).

Scarcely two years after it was established, after suffering the most inhuman assaults and incredible hardships, the garrison was reduced to thirty-six men, following the starvation of sixty-one soldiers. Fort Trinidad was then abandoned and with it went the hope of immediately refounding the city.

3. THE DUCTH FORT. A Dutch expedition sent by Prince Maurits of Nassau occupied the site in 1643 and built a third fortress. We lack the plans which would allow us to determine its exact location and features. However, many official cartographic drawings of the port were made during the second half of the seventeenth and the beginning of the eighteenth centuries (Guarda 1953: 74; de la Guilbardière n.d.; Guedeville 1719: Morales Padrón 1962: 576). These consistently indicate a large fortress in a place other than that occupied by the future walled citadel. This allows us to conjecture that the fort was located outside the urban area – perhaps due to the obstruction created by the sixteenth-century ruins which were already covered by dense jungle after forty years of abandonment. According to these drawings, the fortress was located to the south, near the river; it was bulwarked and rectangular in shape. In 1678, once it was suitably equipped for its new requirements, the city's governor, Diego de Marthos, designated it as a barracks for the mulatto battalion (AGI [1678]).

4. FIRST WALLED ENCLOSURE. The Spanish resettlement was personally directed by the Marquis of Mancera. At this time (1645) the first walled enclosure of the city, known as Plaza de Valdivia, was built. Its design was by Constantino Vasconcelos, senior engineer of the viceroyalty. He was also co-designer of the great Lima wall and architect of the large San Francisco Convent in Lima (Lohmann 1964: 115, note 39).[52] It fell upon Governor Francisco Gil Negrete to carry out this project in 1647. He used "long brushwood faggots, well tied,

---

[51] Andrés López de Gamboa, testifying in Santiago (7 November 1646) in the investigation of Diego de Rojas Cervantes, certified that he assisted in the building of Fort Trinidad in Valdivia; he explained that the fort "was founded close to the Valdivia River in the same town which was there before, opposite where San Francisco Convent used to be" (BNM n.d.b).

[52] The original design of the Valdivia site was drafted by Vasconcelos in 1645; (de Aguirre 1645: 74; de Tamayo y Mendoza n.d.: 453).

mixed with a lot of earth . . . [this method was] used for the first time in 1601 at Ostend in Flanders, and [was] called by those in the know small and large fascines " (de Rosales 1877: III, 280). These were very perishable and soon destroyed by the copious Valdivia showers. Finally in 1653 Governor Montero del Aguila completed the magnificent stone wall, hailed as "a remarkable work, unique in Chile, worthy of admiration and eternal fame " (de Rosales 1877: Volume III, 280).

The concept of this citadel appears to be based on a plan designed for Callao's defense and fortification five years earlier by Viceroy Marquis de Mancera. His son, advised by Vasconcelos, used this plan for the new Valdivia site. According to the Callao plan, the defenses consisted of a citadel "with five cavaliers or towers on a height " from which one could strike the enemy and cover the surrounding territory, protecting the entire settlement (Lohmann 1964: 98). This essentially describes the plaza of Valdivia.

It is easy to imagine the disturbance produced by the imposition of this citadel on the old main plaza area, in the heart of the old grid. There was, in fact, an even greater disruption. In what has been seen as a legacy from the ancient Roman *Pomerium* (La Padula 1963: 368), certain Royal Letters Patent of 22 February 1545 and 6 March 1608 (*Recopilación* 1681, [1545], 1681 [1608]) ordered the clearing of a vast area around the fortifications.[53] The purpose of this was to permit the free firing of artillery. The implementation of this order in Valdivia contributed to erasing the last traces of a considerable number of sites. This area did not regain its jurisdiction until a century later, when the demolition of the old enclosure – by this time completely useless – was decreed.

The general layout of the Valdivia citadel was the same as Fort Trinidad (i.e. that of the Iberian *alcázar*). This idea had been considered as long ago as 1390 by Eximeniç the Spanish treatise writer, in his ideal city, which was similar to the cities of the Indies, such as the old capital of La Española. Fernández del Pulgar tells us that the Spanish "built an *alcázar* at the bend in the river, near San Francisco Convent " (del Pulgar 1902: 56).

Nothing is known of its structures, for it was completely destroyed

---

[53] The first order was that "the level country near castles and fortresses be cleared and depopulated; and any house or building within three hundred steps of the wall or so strong that even farther away it might cause damage, should be demolished . . . "; the second referring to towns, indicates "that near the walls or palisades of new towns, at a distance of thee hundred paces, no houses should be built . . . [just] as it is decreed for castles and fortresses." In military parlance a pace (*paso*) is equivalent to 33 cm. A geometric pace, however, is equivalent to 1.39 meters; The first would give a clear radius of almost 100 meters, while the second would give about 400. In Valdivia the houses on the south side of the wall are situated within 50 meters (cf. Notarial n.d.). In Ancud they are indicated as being 208 meters away from the wall. It is very likely that in the case of Valdivia the vestiges of the original town plan had an influence.

by the earthquake of 1737. Governor Navarro Santaella temporarily replaced it with a stockade of round stakes at a distance of 2.92 meters from the edge of the destroyed area.[54] In 1741 it was a rectangular structure, 178.04 by 125.38 meters, protected by five bulwarks and containing four gateways. The original wall of hewn stone was 2.08 meters thick (AGI [1741c]).

The task of rebuilding the old enclosures in stone fell to Governor Saez de Bustamente (1754) who enlarged it to 292.35 by 244.62 meters (Carvallo 1875: Volume III, 180).[55] The two western bulwarks along the river – San Ignacio and San Francisco – had their profiles to the north and south curtains respectively. The two eastern bulwarks (*en barbette*) – Santiago and San Pedro – had no projection, only interior platforms for the artillery. The fifth bulwark, San Miguel, was a massive square cavalier of three stories topped by a belfry with three bells. It has the aspect of an authentic *torre del homenaje* [tower of obeisance], very similar to the one built in 1505 in the first city of America (Palm 1955: 157).[56]

The principal entrance on the north, the "royal" gate, was protected by a portcullis. It was built between May and September 1767 by the distinguished Irish engineer John Garland White (AGI n.d.e). A matching gate at the south end formed an axis with the royal gate; both gateways served as porticos at the respective ends of the *calle real*, which was the principal avenue of the town. There were two smaller gateways in the middle of the two longer walls: San Miguel or Puerta del Norte (because it was located on the northern side of the bulwark of the same name), and La Piedad. The latter gave access to a narrow, stepped road paved with flagstones descending to the river. Five sentry boxes crowned the walls. In 1767 the walls were reinforced by a square auxiliary stockade 2.94 meters high; this protected the surrounding buildings along the river in the lower part of the city.

[54] The stockade was reinforced on the inside by wooden bands. By 1752 it was completely deteriorated.

[55] In conflict with all other witnesses, Carvallo claimed that it had six bulwarks; de Rosales (1877: 279) had said earlier that it only had four. Birt's plan and Garland's testimony in 1767 (ANS n.d.f) are decisive in this matter. Furthermore, on the two plans of the port of 1764 (BNS [1764]), the area of the town is sketched in the known form; this is repeated on the Valdivia-Chiloé road plan (AS n.d.) and on the plan in the Amat collection (BCC n.d.a). On the latter the enclosures of the old convents of San Francisco and La Merced have been added. Cf. also Garland's plan of 1764 (SHM [1764]), the plan in the Biblioteca Nacional de Madrid (BNM n.d.a), and that of Moreno y Pérez (AGI n.d.d).

[56] In 1792 the engineer Olaguer Feliú called it "a kind of *torreón* [a round fortified tower] like those of old...(ANS [1792]). The date of the triple belfry was given by Governor Quijada y Rojas as 1794 (ANS [1794]). In 1740 the expansion of the enclosure to the north had been planned; according to Governor Navarro Santaella, "the whole complex is respectable, even by Europe [an standards], for it has been rebuilt with full military skill" (BNS n.d.b).

Crowded within the walls, situated along the *calle real* and separated by narrow passages and would-be plazas, there were five churches, convents, a hospital, a sanctuary, academies, a palace, official buildings, royal coffers, storehouses, barracks, guardrooms, a flag room, arsenals, workshops, a jail, and even a cemetery. One can easily imagine the urban chaos that this created. Though schematic, José Antonio Birt's plan (drawn in 1763 when the town was dismantled for removal to Mancera) does accurately show the walls of the kingdom's oldest enclosure of its kind (BCC [1763]. It was remarkably similar, if not identical, to the enclosure which the engineer Joaquín de Meramás designed in 1784 for the new fortified town of San Carlos de Barrancas (in present-day U.S.A. territory) (AGI [1784b]) (published by Chueca and Torres Balbas 1951: 130).[57]

5. FIRST OUTER DEFENSES. The construction of the first citadel and clearance of its environs did not prevent the aligning of the houses in the remnants of the old gridiron pattern. In fact the houses in the vicinity simply could not be fitted inside the walls. Soon two new strategic points were established (Los Canelos in the south and El Barro in the east), giving rise to the two principal streets of this urban area. These points secured the natural obstacle provided by the lagoon, the *Gualve* de San Antonio, so that potential invaders could not approach from the land front.

The threat of attack by rebellious Indians in 1774 made Governor Espinosa Dávalos fear the total loss of the city. "To avoid this fatal consequence," he wrote to the king, "the only expedient is to immediately build two towers [*torreones*] like those in Andalusía used against the Moors..." (AGI [1774]). As Palm points out (1955: 54) with regard to the ruins of Concepción de la Vega, these circular structures continued another military tradition of classic medieval taste in America. We see, for example, that two towers were designed for El Callao in 1579 (Lohmann 1964: 22), and that San Juan de Ulúa in Mexico and Zapara in Venezuela have an old tradition of cylindrical towers (Calderón 1953: 104–105, Figures 24, 26; Gasparini 1965: 309). In Chile the famous Casa de Arauco had these towers at one time. Such towers were also located at various points on the Bío Bío frontier line (de Rosales 1877: Volume II, 642; Gazulla 1918: 206).[58]

[57] A subterranean brick tunnel over 200 meters long linked the inside of the citadel to the lake on the promontory (between the present Calle de Independencia and Calle de Caupolicán). The tunnel was discovered in 1910 when the Palacio de la Intendencia was reconstituted (cf. *Correo de Valdivia* 1931).

[58] In 1618 Governor Ulloa y Lemos built a tower, called San Ignacio, in Cayuhuanu (de Rosales 1877: vol. 2, p. 640). In 1655 another was built on the *estancia* [estate] of Fernández de Rebolledo, field master (de Olivares 1874: 109). Governor Meneses built a very famous tower in Laraquete (de Tesillo (1878: 17; de Olivares 1864).

The two fine Valdivia towers have always been the object of keenest curiosity. They were unique for their time, provoking a wave of criticism as to their defensive efficacy, since in practice their narrowness seemed to limit their function to that of watchtowers. However, when they were later used as guardrooms for the second walled line, their existence was finally justified. In terms of town planning, the towers served to emphasize the importance of the two streets, which remained the principal throughways over the years. And the unusual design of the towers surely contributed to shaping the imposing appearance of the military capital of the South Sea.

6. SECOND WALLED ENCLOSURE. Over the years the defenses underwent alterations to meet the strategic needs of the city. The culmination of this process was the achievement of the defense of the promontory neck, cutting the meander on its land front. The city was finally walled along all its borders and on all its flanks.

A royal decree of 1767 had presented the authorities with a pre-emptory order for the building of this ultimate defense. Such a project had already been carried out in 1689 in Portobelo under the same conditions (Céspedes 1952: 256).[59] As in Portobelo, the plan for Valdivia made use of the existing lagoon. It was planned to drain the lagoon in order to create a large moat which would break the two points, linking the meander at its extreme eastern and southern ends. This would divert the waters of the Río Calle Calle to the Río Valdivia, thereby transforming the promontory with its city into an impregnable island. In April 1779 the engineer Antonio Duce agreed to draft plans for this undertaking.

In scope the work was Pharaonic, at least in relation to the means available. In December 1781 the bluffs had been cut and the moat excavated at one of the two access points (AGI [1781]). One hundred and twenty convicts were set to work on the task; four years later Duce was able to report to President Benavides on the advanced state of the project, accompanying his report with a plan (ANS [1785], published in Guarda 1953: 136–137; AGI [1785], published originally by Chueca and Torres 1951: 116, Number 120, and reproduced here through the auspices of José de la Peña y de la Cámara, Director of the Archivo General de Indias.

The defense line thus created extended for 1,600 meters, following the land contours. The settlement was limited on this side by a steep drop to the San Antonio lagoon below, which created a sharp breach running from the lower part of calle de Henríquez up to the edge of the plaza mayor. The need to reduce this perimeter and circumvent

[59] We have already seen a similar solution in Chile in the lower sector of La Imperial in the sixteenth century.

the breach led to the construction of a wide embankment which cut across the lake like the famous causeways of Mexico City. This created the two broad avenues which still exist today. This solution resulted in a considerable reduction of the patrol area and (consequently) in the garrison required during attack.

Situated along the stretches of wall were six simple, triangular bulwarks and six bulwarks of various other shapes. Two portcullis gates secured their respective drawbridges at the only two points of access.

According to a 1794 report, the work progressed slowly. By that date the moat was still not deep enough for the river waters to pass through (ANS [1784]: Part I). In this same year the portcullis gates were mentioned as functioning, but there are no details given on the wall itself. We have to rely on a number of allusions for knowledge of its existence.[60] We also have the testimony (of uncertain value) of the German traveler Treutler (1861: 287), who in 1859 admired its remains.[61] Its batters were probably lined with stone, like some old fortresses of Mancera;[62] dressed stone or lime and brick were reserved for the faces of the two gates. All in all, one can assume that the strength of the wall could not be compared to that of the impregnable castles at the port. The new fortifications were constructed primarily to withstand the assaults of the Indians and enemy European forces which had previously attacked the castles; yet the castles have better withstood the destructive action of both man and natural elements.

In terms of town planning, the construction of the extensive walls created a patrol area for servicing in case of attack. This was a street called *Redonda* [literally "round"] because of the arch it described, parallel to the contours of the fortifications.[63] It henceforth appeared on plans of the city and for a considerable time marked the urban boundary. These walls gave the crowning touch to the military fortification system of the Pacific. Valdivia had the unique privilege of being conceived as a city in accordance with the classical concept. But upon completion, the first walled enclosure immediately lost its

[60] In the residence of Governor Espinosa Dávalos the following inscription appears: thanks to their efforts "the WALL of that town is crowned with *torreones* [round fortified towers] for its defense and for the protection of its sentinels "[emphasis added]; the plan of the "Post and Entrance of the Baldivia [*sic*] River" (de Ulloa and de Ulloa n.d.) shows the city in schematic form, enclosed on its land side by a bulwarked wall. This system repeated (though with greater stylizing) the plan presented by the Marquis de la Victoria to the Naval Secretariat in July 1764 on the basis of a drawing made in 1763 by the officers of the frigate La Liebre (SGE 1763); it is also the same as several other plans (AS n.d.; BNM n.d.a; BCC n.d.). It should be noted, however, that the projected walls had still not been built when these other plans were drawn up.

[61] The remains of the moat were indicated in April 1908 by the Engineer Juan Antoine in his topographic plan of the city.

[62] The castle of San Pedro de Acátara; cf. AGI ([1767]).

[63] Today called Beaucheff and maintaining the same configuration.

raison d'être. It was technically out-of-date, old-fashioned, and a public hazard. Its sentry boxes, fortified towers, and bulwarks were crumbling; in some sectors it was close to collapse; even minimum maintenance became too costly. The wall so confined the population within the city that the original lots were repeatedly subdivided by narrow lanes; this resulted in a labyrinth of broken streets that disfigured the original plan. A council of high officials meeting in March 1792 proposed "the demolition of the mud-wall enclosure which is called a fort, situated in the center of the Town, as it is useless for defense purposes and [this action is] necessary for the enlargement of the environs." The stones were to be used to build larger public buildings; such projects had formerly been precluded because of the obstruction of the old walls. The defensive function of the old wall would be replaced by the completion of the large enclosure planned by Duce (ANS n.d.g).

The new plan of the city was drawn by the engineer Manuel Olaguer Feliú, later to be director of the Royal Corps of Engineers in Madrid. The mayor, in the name of the king, proceeded to apportion the sites which had been freed or on which construction had been prohibited until then.[64] Nevertheless, it appears that some vestiges of the stately enclosure were preserved undamaged. It is on record that the royal gateway with its portcullis still existed in 1811 (ANS [1811]). And Treutler in his travels managed to see the wall face along the river; this wall in fact did not need to be demolished, as it did not obstruct anything (Treutler 1861: 346).[65]

Valdivia's defensive apparatus had considerable influence on the city's urban development, over and above its significance as an example of military architecture. Its defenses determined the originality of its plan which, together with that of Valparaíso, was unique among the Chilean cities. Its irregular perimeter had already been noted in the sixteenth century when "it extended up-river, to take advantage of its pleasant view." (de Rosales 1877: Volume I, 465).

Valdivia's low point came with the decline of Spanish domination. At this time, restricted by the walls the population became so dense that the classic *manzanas* were seriously deformed. In 1803 the houses adjoined one another; This facilitated the spread of fire, already a hazard because of construction with wood. According to Governor Clarke, the main streets (already sixteen *varas* wide) had to be ex-

[64] Olaguer Feliú (ANS n.d.g.) reported having completed the general plan of the fortified site and city of Valdivia in 1798 and would send it as soon as a copy was ready. Unfortunately, I have not been able to find any of these documents, nor the plan sent by President Manso de Velasco to the King in 1741 (AGI [1741a]) nor that of Benavides, of 1784 (AGI [1784a]; cf. BNS n.d.c).

[65] In 1810 there were still ten artillery pieces in the old enclosure (CHI n.d.: vol. 8, p. 348).

panded to twenty-four *varas* in order to stop the spread of such fatal disasters (AGI n.d.f).[66] The recovery of buildable zones in the areas surrounding the old citadel was carried out with precipitate avidity. The commercial areas adjacent to the wharves and under the shelter of the walls were also gradually disfigured, following the irregular topography. In 1841 the Englishman Allan Gardiner visited the city, commenting that "fortunately for the lover of good taste, neither the founders nor their successors have possessed the funds or ability to adapt their irregular site to their favored rectangular plan." As a consequence, he concluded, it is "the most irregular city that one can find in this part of South America, but it has an exact relationship to the character of the surrounding countryside" (Gardiner 1841: 116).

Once underway, it was impossible to halt the course of the unsystematic construction engendered by the fortifications, even where the fortifications themselves had disappeared. In 1864 the local press called upon the city to face this state of disorder by drawing up an official regulatory plan. Some streets were becoming increasingly sinuous. "In buildings constructed two or three years apart," it was asserted, "varying lines and directions are maintained; thus rather than becoming regularized, [the plan] is becoming even more disordered" (Semanario 1864). As a result of improvement in the quality of the buildings, this unsystematic layout unfortunately survived intact into the present century. The great fire of 1909 razed seventeen blocks in the center of the town. This left an open field for the imagination of contemporary town planners, who made opportune use of the possibilities that had faded to a vague historical memory.[67]

CONCLUSIONS

1. Chile's geographical location determined the need for special defense measures.

2. The presence of the extremely warlike Araucanians frequently made fortification of the cities necessary.

[66] From 1645 until the end of the eighteenth century the city's population apparently did not exceed 3,000. At the end of the period of Spanish domination, there appears to have been a considerable increase, caused in part by agricultural and commercial development in the region, though primarily by the massive royalist migration, especially during the fight for independence. Valdivia and Chiloé became the most loyal bastions of the monarchy. According to Miller (1912: 44), the 1820 population of Valdivia was over fifteen thousand; this figure was corroborated by Torrente (n.d.: 506).

[67] The natural lines of the topography were followed in the straightening and connecting of independent streets. This required costly artificial drainage and refilling. The 1960 earthquake returned the area to its original state, destroying the fills and flooding the sites of the former lagoons. The subterranean sources of the lagoons sprang up at the points marked on the old plans.

3. Fifty percent of the settlements built in Chile under Spanish rule were fortified.

4. Almost all cities founded in the sixteenth century, or later in the region affected by the Araucanian War, were fortified.

5. At least thirty settlements owed their origin to the existence of an earlier fort.

6. The Spanish founding policy was preeminently colonizing in nature. Of 104 recorded foundings, only nineteen were ports; and only in the preservation of two (Ancud and Valdivia) did military reasons prevail over purely commercial and economic ones.

7. Fortifications influenced the siting, layout, and subsequent development of both ports and inland settlements, giving these places their characteristic urban stamp.

8. The survival of medieval concepts, forms, and solutions was constantly manifested in the fortifications and in their effects on urban development.

9. Considering the quality of the fortifications – which were usually removed during later urban development – their interest as an influence in urban development is as great as or greater than their intrinsic value or their value as monuments of military architecture.

10. As outstanding contributions to the history of town planning in the Indies, Chile can claim the original arrangement of Nacimiento and the spatial successes of La Serena, San Carlos de Ancud, and Valdivia. These were all products of military requirements.

11. The extent of the effect of fortifications on urbanization in other Spanish American countries should be determined in order to properly evaluate their role in Chilean urban development. This would be especially interesting for Caribbean countries, and for those located in other strategic areas. Similarly, there is a need for the publication of a large number of maps and testimonies which would permit general conclusions and an analysis of reciprocal influences. At the moment these influences are implied, for example, by accomplishments of the same engineer throughout the continent.

REFERENCES

Abbreviations
CDI   *Colección de documentos inéditos para la historia de Chile*, second series. Lima.
CHH   *Colección de historiadores de Chile y documentos relativos a la historia nacional.* Santiago.
CHI   *Colección de historiadores y de documentos relativos a la independencia de Chile.*

Actas del Cabildo...
1679–1703   *Actas del Cabildo de La Serena.* La Serena.
AGI (ARCHIVO GENERAL DE INDIAS), Seville
n.d.a.   Chile 435.
n.d.b.   Chile 434.
n.d.c.   Chile 97: display case 20.
n.d.d.   Perú y Chile 82.
n.d.e.   Indiferente General 1531.
n.d.f.   Chile 204.
n.d.g   Peru 185.
[1678]   Chile 128.
[1682]   Chile 25.
[1692]   Chile 4.
[1707]   Chile 67.
[1741a]   Chile 97.
[1741b]   Chile 433.
[1741c]   Chile 148, notebook 2, folio 209.
[1767]   "Carta de Garland a Guilly, Gonzaga, Mancera 30–IX–1767." Indiferente General 1531.
[1770]   Lima 1492.
[1774]   Chile 434 and Indiferente General 1531.
[1779]   Lima 659.
[1796]   Chile 199.
[1781]   Chile 192, 435.
[1784a]   Chile 97.
[1784b]   Planos de Santo Domingo. Cuba 1393.
[1785]   Chile 436 (Maps and Plans of Peru 83).
[1875]   Chile 436.
AMILCAR RAZORI
1945   *Historia de la ciudad argentina*, volume two. Buenos Aires.
ANRIQUE, NICOLÁS
n.d.   "Informe al Presidente Higgins, 27-I-1793," in *Biblioteca jeográfica-hidrográfica de Chile*, second series.
ANS (ARCHIVO NACIONAL, SANTIAGO)
n.d.a   Gay Morla 53, folios 152ff.
n.d.b   Gay Morla, 34, folio 39.
n.d.c   Real Audiencia 1206.
n.d.d   Gay Morla 24, folio 246.
n.d.e   Real Audiencia 707, folio 3.
n.d.f   Varios 284.
n.d.g   Contraduría Mayor 3664.
1741   Capitanía General, volume 707.
[1756a]   Gay Morla 34, folio 91.

1756   Gay Morla 34, folio 39.
[1761]   Varios 319.
[1773]   Capitanía General, volume 707.
[1792]   Varios 320.
[1793]   Varios 352, folio 62.
[1785]   Varios 284.
[1794]   Contaduría Mayor 123.
[1811]   Gay Morla 54.

AS (ARCHIVO DE SIMANCAS)
n.d.   Maps and plans IV. 37.

BENAVIDES, ALFREDO
1958   El fuerte del capitán Juan Bohon. *Revista Chilena de Historia y Geografía* 126. Santiago.

BCC (BIBLIOTECA CENTRAL DE CATALUÑA), BARCELONA
1765   Manuscript 400, number 3.
1763a   "Plano esquemático de Valdivia," Manuscript 400, number 3.
1763b   Manuscript 400, number 3.
n.d.   "Plano de Valdivia." Manuscript 179.

BNM (BIBLIOTECA NACIONAL, MADRID
n.d.a   "Plano de Valdivia." Manuscript 3111.
n.d.b   Manuscript 11535, folio 26 verso.

BNS (BIBLIOTECA NACIONAL, SANTIAGO)
n.d.a   Manuscript 218, folios 65 and 66.
n.d.b   Manuscript 291, folio 214.
n.d.c   Manuscript 270, number 7725 and Manuscript 291, number 8705.
[1599]   Manuscritos inéditos, volume five, folio 17. Sala José Toribio Medina.
1764   "Planos del puerto de Valdivia." B. 5–14, page 13.
[1762]   Morla Vicuña volume 18, folios 509ff.
[1765]   Mapoteca, Sala José Toribio Medina.
[1802]   Morla Vicuña, volume 103.
[1860]   "Plano de Nacimiento." B.14, number 71.
[1863]   "Plano de Nacimiento." B.14, number 72.
1960   Archivo O'Higgins, volume twenty-two. Santiago.

BOLETÍN . . .
1940   Article in *Boletín de la Academia Chilena de la Historia* 13.

BP (BIBLIOTECA DEL PALACIO), MADRID
n.d.a   Manuscript 2424. Manuscritos de América.
n.d.b   Manuscript 2840, number 1. Miscelánea de Ayala.
[1773]   Manuscript 2840.

BRITISH MUSEUM, LONDON
1801   "Descriptión y memoria militar sobre la necesidad de fortificar el puerto de Valparaíso." Add. 13976, folios 174–180.

CALDERÓN QUIJANO, JOSÉ
1953   *Historia de las fortificaciones de Nueva España.* Seville.

CARVALLO GOYENECHE, VICENTE
1875   Colección de historiadores de Chile y documentos relativos a la historia nacional. Santiago.

CÉSPEDES DEL CASTILLO, GUILLERMO
1952   "La defensa militar del istmo de Panamá a fines del siglo XVII y comienzos del XVIII," in *Anuario de estudios americanos*, volume nine. Seville.

CHI (COLECCIÓN...)
[1817] *Colección de historiadores y de documentos relativos a la independencia de Chile*, volume six.

CHH (COLECCIÓN...)
n.d. *Colección de historiadores de Chile y documentos relativos a la historia nacional.*

CHUECA GOTÍA, FERNANDO, LEOPOLDO TORRES BALBAS
1951 *Planos de ciudades iberoamericanas y filipinas existentes en el Archivo de Indias*, volume one. Madrid.

COMADRÁN RUÍZ, JORGE
1962 "Nacimiento y desarrollo de los núcleos urbanos y del poblamiento de la compaña del país de Cuyo durante la época hispana (1551–1810)," in *Anaurio de estudios americanos*, volume nineteen. Seville.

CORREO DE VALDIVIA
1931 Article in *El correo de Valdivia*, 4 May 1931.

CRUCES POZO, JOSÉ
1952 "Cualidades militares del Virrey Amat," in *Anuario de estudios americanos*, volume nine. Seville.

DE AGUIRRE, MIGUEL
1645 "Población de Valdivia, motivos y medios para aquella fundación...," in *CHH*, volume forty-five. Santiago.

DE BERANGUER, CARLOS
[1758] "Plano de Sn. Carlos, 6-IX-1758." Biblioteca Central de Cataluña.
[1770] "Plano del Fuerte Real de Sn. Carlos, I-II-1770." (Published in Madrid.) Archivo de Planos, Servicio Geográfico del Ejército, Santiago.

DE GÓNGORA MARMOLEJO, ALONSO
1862 "Historia de Chile desde el descubrimiento hasta el año 1575," in *CHH*, volume two. Santiago. Also in *CDI* volume one, page 131.

DE GUIRIOR, MANUEL
[1778] "Instruccion al injeniero extraordinario de los reales ejércitos de Manuel Zorrilla para cumplir con la comisión a que lo he destinado en la isla de Chiloé..., Lima, 10-IX-1778." Chile 435. Archivo General de Indias. Seville.

DE HERRERA, ANTONIO
1901 "Descripción de las islas y tierra firme del mar océano que llaman Indias Occidentales...," in *CHH*, volume twenty-seven. Santiago.

DE LA GUILBARDIÈRE, JOUHAN
n.d. "Plano del puerto de Valdivia." Manuscript Division. New York Public Library. New York.

DEL PULGAR, FERNANDEZ
1902 "Historia del origen de la América o Indias," in *CHH*, volume twenty-nine. Santiago.

DE OLIVARES, PADRE MIGUEL
1864 "Historia militar civil y sagrada de lo acaecido en la conquista y pacificación del reino de Chile...," in *CHH*, volume four. Santiago.
1874 "Historia de la Compañía de Jesús en Chile 1593–1736," in *CHH*, volume seven. Santiago.

DE OVALLE, ALONSO
1888 "Histórica relación del reino de Chile," in *CHH*. Santiago.

DE PASCUAL Y CÓRDOBA Y FIGUEROA, PEDRO PASCUAL
1862 "Historia de Chile," in *CHH*, volume two. Santiago.

DE QUIROGA, ANTONIO
1902 "Memoria de lo sucedido a don...," in *CHH*, volume twenty-four. Santiago.

DE RAMÓN FOLCH, JOSÉ ARMANDO
1953 Descubrimiento de Chile y compañeros de Almagro. Santiago.

DE ROSALES, DIEGO
1877 *Historia general del reino de Chile, Flandés indiano*, volumes one, two, and three. Valparaíso.

DE SOTOMAYOR, ALONSO
"Memorial del gobernador Alonso de Sotomayor al Consejo de Indias 6-XII-1583," in *CDI*.

DE TAMAYO Y MENDOZA, GARCÍA
n.d. "Copia de tres cartas..., in *Biblioteca Hispano Chilena*, volume one. Edited by José Toribio Medina.

DE TESILLO, SANTIAGO
1864 "Guerra de Chile...," in *CHH*, volume five. Santiago.
1878 "Restauración del estado de Arauco y otros progresos militares conseguidos con las armas de S.M. por mano del Senor Jeneral de Artillería don Francisco Meneses...," in *CHH*. volume eleven. Santiago.

DE ULLOA, JORGE, JUAN DE ULLOA
n.d. "Puesto y entrada del río de Baldivia" [sic]. Servicio Geográfico del Ejército. Madrid.
1762 "Plano de Valdivia," in ??

DÍEZ DE LA CALLE, JUAN
1902 "Noticias sacras y reales de las Indias Occidentales," in *CHH*, volume twenty-four, Santiago.

DONOSO, RICARDO
1963 *Un letrado del siglo XVIII, El Dr. José Perfecto de Salas*, volume one. Buenos Aires.

ENCINA, FRANCISCO ANTONIO
1956 *Resumen de la historia de Chile por Leopoldo Castello*, three volumes, Santiago.

EYZAGUIRRE, JAIME
1965 *Historia de Chile*. Santiago.

FREZIER, M.
1732 *Rélation du voyage de la Mer du Sud aux côtes du Chili et du Pérou fait pendant les années 1712, 1713 et 1714*. Paris. (Spanish translation in 1902 by Nicolás Peña. Santiago.)

GARDINER, ALLAN F., R.N.
1841 *A visit to the Indians of the frontiers of Chile*. London.

GASPARINI, GRAZIANO
1965 *Arquitectura colonial venezolana*. Caracas.

GAZULLA, POLICARPO
1918 *Los primeros mercedarios en Chile, 1535–1600*. Santiago.

GÓMEZ DE VIDAURRE, FELIPE
n.d. "Historia geográfica, natural y civil del reino de Chile," in *CHH*. Santiago.

GONZÁLEZ DE NÁJERA, ALONSO
1864 "Historia militar civil y sagrada de lo acaecido en la conquista y pacificación del reino de Chile...," in *CHH*, volume four. Santiago.
1889 "Desengaño y reparo de la guerra del reino de Chile," in *CHH*, volume sixteen. Santiago.

GUARDA, GABRIEL
1953   *Historia de Valdivia 1552–1952.* Santiago.
1957   El urbanismo imperial y las primitivas ciudades de Chile. Finis Terrae 15. Santiago.
1965   *Santo Tomás de Aquino y las fuentes del urbanismo indiano.* Santiago.
GUEDEVILLE, MR.
1719   Plan of Valdivia port. *Atlas historique,* volume four. Amsterdam.
HARDOY, JORGE E.
1965   La influencia del urbanismo indígeno en la localización y trazado de las ciudades coloniales. *Ciencia e Investigación* 21(9).
JUAN DE JESÚS MARÍA, FRAY
1878   "Memorias del reino de Chile y de don Francisco de Meneses," in *CHH,* volume eleven. Santiago.
LA PADULA, ERNESTO
1963   Origen de la ciudad hispanoamericana. *Revista de la Universidad Nacional de Córdoba,* second series 4(3–4).
LOHMANN VILLENA, GUILLERMO
1964   *Las defensas militares de Lima y Callao.* Seville.
MARIÑO DE LOBERA, PEDRO
1865   "Crónica del reino de Chile," in *CHH,* volume six. Santiago.
MÁRQUEZ DE LA PLATA, FERNANDO
n.d.   *Arqueología del antiguo reino de Chile,* volume one. Santiago.
MEDINA, JOSÉ TORIBIO
n.d.a   *Colección de documentos inéditos para la historia de Chile* (CDI), second series. Lima.
n.d.b   "Memorial de Juan Cortés Monroy," in *Biblioteca Hispano Chilena,* volume two.
n.d.c   "Memorial de Flórez de León," in *Biblioteca Hispano Chilena,* volume two.
n.d.d   "Memorial de Francisco de Avedaño," in *Biblioteca Hispano Chilena,* volume two.
n.d.e   "Memorial de Bernardino Morales de Alborñoz," in *Biblioteca Hispano Chilena,* volume one.
n.d.f.   "Memorial del Gobernador Alonso de Sotomayor al Consejo de Indias 6-II-1583," in *Colección de documentos méditos para la historia de Chile* (CDI), second series.
1953   *Cartografía hispanocolonial chilena.* Santiago.
MORALES PADRÓN, FRANCISCO
1962   *Manual de historia universal,* volume five: *Historia de América.* Madrid.
MILLER, JOHN
1912   *Memorias del General Miller al servicio de la república del Perú,* volume one. Santiago.
MOLINA GONZÁLEZ, JUAN IGNACIO
1901   [1787] *Saggio sulla storia del Chile...* Spanish translation by Cruz y Bahamonde in *CHH,* volume twenty-six, Santiago. (Originally published in Bologna.)
MÚÑOZ DE GUZMÁN, PRESIDENTE
1913   "Carta del Presidente Múñoz de Guzmán al Comandante de Ingenieros de la Frontera D. Francisco Antonio García Carrasco, Sago. 24-I-1803," in *CHI,* Volume twenty-five. Santiago.

MUZQUIZ DE MIGUEL, JOSÉ LUIS
1945   *El conde de Chinchón.* Madrid.
NOTARIAL . . .
n.d.   *Notarial Valdivia,* volume one, folio 95.
1858   *Notarial Valdivia, año 1858,* folio 43.
NÚÑEZ DE PINEDA BASCUNÁN, FRANCISCO
1948   El cautiverio feliz. . . . Santiago: González.
PALM, ERWIN WALTER
1951   *Los orígenes del urbanismo en América.* Mexico City.
1955   *Los monumentos arquitectónicos de La Española,* volume one.
Ciudad Trujillo, Santo Domingo.
PÉREZ GARCÍA, JOSÉ
1900   "Historia natural, militar, civil y sagrada del reino de Chile. . .," in
CHH, volume twenty two (I). Santiago.
RAZORI, AMÍLCAR
1945   *Historia de la ciudad argentina,* volume two. Buenos Aires.
RECOPILACIÓN . . .
1681   [1545]   Valladolid, 22-II-1545. *Recopilación de leyes de los reinos de
las Indias,* book, III, Title VII, I.
1681   [1608]   Madrid, 6-III-1608. *Recopilación de leyes de los reinos de las
Indias,* book IV, title VII, XII.
REVISTA CHILENA
n.d.   Article in *Revista Chilena de Historia y Geografía* 52. Santiago.
RICO, PEDRO
1789   "Plano de La Serena." Servicio Geográfico del Ejército. Archivo de
Planos. Madrid.
RODRÍGUEZ BALLESTEROS, JUAN
1901   "Revista de la guerra de la independencia de Chile," in *Colección
de historiadores y de documentos relativos a la independencia de
Chile,* volume six. Santiago.
RODRÍGUEZ CASADO, VICENTE, FLORENTINO PÉREZ EMBID
1947   *Memoria de gobierno del virrey Amat.* Seville.
1949   *Construcciones militares del virrey Amat.* Seville.
RUIZ DE GAMBOA, MARTÍN
[1583]   "Ruiz de Gamboa al virrey, La Imperial, 2-I-1583," in *CDI,* volume
three. Lima.
SANFUENTES, SALVADOR, MIGUEL LUÍS AMUNÁTEGUI
1925   *Valdivia antes de la inmigración.* Valdivia.
SEMANARIO
1864   Articles in *El Semanario,* 21 May and 2 August. Valdivia.
SGE (SERVICIO GEOGRÁFICO DEL EJÉRCITO, MADRID)
1763   "Plano de Valdivia."
SHM (SERVICIO HISTÓRICO MILITAR, MADRID)
[1764]   "Plano de Valdivia," by John Garland. C-VI-N 6169.
TORRENTE, MARIANO
n.d.   *Historia de la revolución hispanoamericana,* volume two.
TORRES, BALBAS
1951   *Planos de ciudades iberoamericanas y filipinas existentes en el Archivo de Indias,* volume one. Madrid.
TREUTLER, PABLO
1861   *La provincia de Valdivida y los araucanos.* Santiago.
1958   *Andanzas de un alemán en Chile.* Santiago, 1958.

VÁZQUEZ DE ESPINOSA, ANTONIO
　1948　*Compendio y descripción de las Indias Occidentales*, Smithsonian
　　　Institution Bulletin 1497. Washington D.C.

WALPOLE, FEDERICO
　1935　Visión de Valparaíso al finalizar la primera mitad del siglo XIX.
　　　Boletín de la Academia Chilena de la Historia 6.

The Urban Center as a Focus of Migration in the Colonial Period: New Spain

WOODROW BORAH and SHERBURNE F. COOK

Ideally a study of the urban center as a focus of migration in any region and at any period in Latin America should cover at least a minimum number of aspects: it should measure in quantifiable form both inflow and outflow; it should give an idea of the movement from countryside to urban center (or the reverse), the distances involved in such movement, the relative attraction of urban centers for rural migrants as against the attraction of other rural areas, and the nature of movement among urban centers. We may point to two hypotheses that ought to be kept in mind for comparison and testing in any study. First, the theory that urbanization tends to take place through the movement of rural migrants into smaller urban centers and that there is then movement from smaller centers to larger ones when the migrants have become accustomed to urban living or as their children search for yet better opportunity. Second, the hypothesis – well established for some urban centers in Europe such as London – that the larger urban centers, having an excess of deaths over births, maintained and increased their population by a steady absorption of migrants from the countryside and smaller towns.

Study in these terms of urban centers in Latin America during the colonial period has been so little done that there is at this time not much basis for generalizations that might apply to all of the continent and a half. Accordingly, we shall limit our inquiry to Mexico during the colonial period. But even with that limitation, one encounters a number of difficulties that must be looked at in order to determine what is possible as of now and what may not be. In the first place, there is the difficulty of applying to New Spain the term "urban center," as it has been used in the distinctly more homogeneous environment of the United States and Western Europe. The division of the population in New Spain into races with differing cultural characteristics automatically complicates the application of terms, because peasant settlement, which is to a great extent Indian settlement, tended to be in relatively dense, nucleated clusters even though economic activity was primarily agricultural, and secondary or tertiary activities relatively unimportant. The Spaniards and mixed-bloods, it is true, tended to settle in aggregations that corresponded far more closely to European terms: that is, in a network of towns functioning as market towns, administrative centers, transportation nodes, commercial and financial foci, manufacturing concentrations, mining camps, or various combinations of these possiblities. In the north of New Spain, essentially a frontier region, the resemblance to Europe became more marked.

In the second place, there is the massive series of problems clustering around sources for migration in the colonial period of Mexico.[1] One of the most useful kinds of sources, direct recording of the movement of persons as it occurred, such as is available through police registration in some countries, existed in New Spain only in two forms. Europeans entering the colony were supposed to have licenses issued in Spain and were supposed to be registered on leaving Spain and upon entering the colony. Similarly, slaves entering the colony were supposed to be recorded as merchandise for levy of royal customs and sales tax, and indeed were supposed further to be recorded in licenses to move merchandise within the colony. Such records, unfortunately, cover very small groups of persons and moreover are tainted by large-scale evasion of the regulations. Furthermore, large masses of the records kept either have been lost or have not yet come to light.

Accordingly, any study of migration for New Spain must rely upon other kinds of documents that both state the place of domicile and place of origin and thus give data on migration – although at varying periods of time, even long after the migration, and with no indication when it occurred. Essentially, there are two classes of such documents. One consists of counts or censuses sufficiently detailed to record place of origin. Throughout the colonial period, such counts were taken for a number of purposes, usually locally and at irregular intervals, but toward the end of the colonial period on a colony-wide basis. Of the earlier kind, the most common is the count of *forasteros* living within an urban center or an Indian community. The purpose of the count might have been to register non-Indians supposed not to be living within an Indian community but nevertheless resident there, or it might have been to locate Indians who had escaped payment of

[1] Our discussion of sources is based on Cook and Borah (1971); on parish registers, see further Borah and Cook (1966: 954–957 *et passim*); and Morin (1972: 389–418).

tribute by moving from their native villages or towns to an urban center. One of the documents we shall use in this essay is a count taken in 1661 in Antequera, present-day Oaxaca, for the purpose of locating fugitive and non-tribute-paying Indians. The later kind of count is best exemplified in the censuses of the second half of the eighteenth century: colony-wide registrations carried out in an attempt to determine the number and nature of the population. The census of 1777, organized by bishoprics and using the parish priests as reporting agents, for many localities gives the place of origin for at least the head of the family or household. We have, unfortunately, only fragments of this census for the bishoprics of Oaxaca, Puebla, and Durango. Even more potentially useful is the so-called military census of 1791–1794, which was organized by civil district (*partido*) and listed the population of which the adult males were subject to military duty. The returns of this registration are a remarkably detailed listing of all ages and both sexes, usually by family or household, with detailed information on place of origin. A substantial proportion of the returns survive in the hundred-odd volumes of the *Ramo de Padrones* in the Mexican national archive. Half of these volumes constitute a registration of Mexico City. Unfortunately, since Indians were not subject to military duty, the count ignored Indians as a category and registered in general only those married to non-Indians. Later counts made in the last years of the colonial period or the first decades of independence tend to be local, but many contain detailed information on place of origin. We shall use the remnants of the *padrón* of Guadalajara made in 1822.

The second class of documents that may give information on place of origin is the parish registers, recording baptisms, marriages, and burials. Such registers became regular practice in New Spain by the second half of the sixteenth century. They were kept within each parish by the local priest under the supervision of the bishop and in accordance with regulations stemming from the Council of Trent but recodified for each archdiocese or diocese. The manner of keeping such records, as well as the diligence of the parish priest, varied widely until the second half of the eighteenth century, when a series of reorganizations and inspections by a remarkable generation of enlightened and zealous prelates brought the keeping of such records to considerable regularity and diligence. Of the three sets of records, those recording baptisms are the least likely to be useful in tracing migration, since they may but more often do not give the place of origin of the parents. Much more useful are the marriage records, particularly if they contain all the documentation of the investigations carried out before the marriage, for they then list the place of origin of the bride and groom and even of their parents and witnesses. The data on migration in the marriage records have the advantage that the age span for the contracting parties is limited to essentially 14–35 years. Unfortunately, archival losses have been especially severe for such detailed marriage records. Most useful in terms of survival of records are the burial registers, which may list the place of origin of the deceased. The age span is, of course, much longer than it is for the marriages. Study of the parish registers is made difficult by the fact that they are kept in each parish and so are widely scattered over Mexico. Their use is further complicated by the highly erratic extent of survival, although one can state a general rule, namely, that the more recent the records the greater the chance of survival. Thus there are few surviving registers from the sixteenth century, a fair number from the seventeenth century, and in most parishes at some point in the eighteenth century there begins a regular series which is still extant. In recent years, a number of projects for filming parish registers and creating substantial collections of film copies have begun to make quantitative analysis possible.

Clearly, the parish registers ultimately will yield substantial information on migration in New Spain, as well as much other data on vital characteristics; equally clearly, the dispersion of the records and the amount of effort required for tabulation and analysis mean that their usefulness at this time remains potential. Furthermore, for the purposes of a paper prepared now and within a short time limit, the extent of effort required for tabulation and analysis in order to make use of the data in the censuses and other colonial counts is beyond possibility. The fifty-odd volumes on Mexico City in the *Ramo de Padrones*, embodying the military census of Revillagigedo, probably contain answers to our questions on the nature of migration to the viceregal capital (although not on migration from it), but processing would require a substantial budget, a staff of research assistants, and furthermore at least two years for completion.

We are thus faced with the problem of the possible, and the possible appears to be examination of a number of documents of far smaller compass, plus the use of tabulations of the military census of 1791–1794 and others for the towns for which they may already have been made. Accordingly, we shall examine material on Antequera, a Spanish urban center placed among the Zapotec peasant population of the central valleys of Oaxaca; a tabulation of the *padrón* of Guadalajara in 1822, which gives information on a major urban center of the west-central area; and tabulations for Guanajuato and Querétaro in 1793, which cover a mining center and a manufacturing and commercial center in the Bajío. Regrettably, the two major urban centers of Mexico City and Puebla cannot be examined for lack of tabulations already made. We shall, however, examine one instance of rural migration, in the last decades of the colonial period, into the coastal zone of west-central Mexico for comparison of patterns of urban and rural migration; and further, we shall examine material from some of the later eighteenth-century censuses for clues as to the role of births in maintaining population in colonial Mexican cities. We can then determine to what extent it is possible to detect patterns in the material examined.

For the city of Antequera, we have available two counts of different coverage, separated by an interval of more than a century. They are a listing of Indian immigrants made in December 1661 and the returns of the census of 1777 for the entire city. The *padrón* of *indios forasteros* of 23 December 1661 is one of the results of the inspection of the regions of Oaxaca, Tehuantepec, and the Mixteca by Lic. Montemayor y Córdova de Cuenca, *oidor* of the Audiencia of Mexico and later famous for a volume of compilation of local ordinances and *autos acordados*. Lic. Montemayor was sent out as special judge to deal with a reported Indian insurrection in the Isthmus of Tehuantepec. In the course of his journey, he examined the accuracy of registration of Indian tributaries and was responsible for much new registration, later contested as including many persons who should have been exempt. The *padrón* for the city of Antequera and the immediately adjacent settlements was part of Montemayor's effort for increasing the royal revenue by stricter application of registration for tribute (Archivo General de Indias 1661).[2] For our purposes it is useful because it constitutes both a list of recent Indian migrants to Antequera and a statement of place of origin and type of employment or residence. The data are summarized in Table 1. The *padrón* lists 189 Indians, male and female, of varied marital status. Presumably it did not include infants and children below the age of puberty. For purposes of comparison, it should be noted that Antequera at this time had a Spanish population of upwards of 500 *vecinos*, or 3,000 persons (Vásquez de Espinoza 1948: Section 504), so that the adult *forasteros* were about 6 percent of the total. The city formed part of a larger urban aggregation, since the Indian town of Oaxaca, tributary to the Marquesado del Valle, bordered directly on it, the central squares of the two being only a few blocks apart. (Today the central square of the Indian town is the main municipal market of the now united urban community.)

Of the total of 189 persons listed, we could not locate the places of origin of four, although they probably lay within the central valleys of Oaxaca. The places of origin of 36 persons are not given in the *padrón*. Of the 149 Indians for whom place of origin is both given and

[2]   For a fuller discussion of the *visita* of Montemayor y Córdova de Cuenca, see Cook and Borah (1968: 33–36).

Table 1. *Indios forasteros* in Antequera, 1661

Region of origin		Married		Unmarried		Widowed		Total
		M	F	M	F	M	F	
Central Valley	– a	6	5		5			
	– b	17	14	11	10			68
	– c							
Zapotecas (Villa Alta)	– a	4	3		2			
	– b	10	7	10	1		1	41
	– c	1	1	1				
Mixteca Alta	– a	1	2	1	1			
	– b	1		1	3		1	13
	– c	1	1					
Coastal Zapotec	b only			2				2
Chinantlá	b only				1			1
Chontales-Choapán	– a				1			
	– b	1		3				5
	– c							
Isthmus of Tehuantepec	– b only	1	1	7	1			10
Chiapa	– b only			2	1			3
Puebla	– b only				1			1
Mexico City	– b only		2	1	1			4
Querétaro	– b only			1				1
Not located	– a							
	– b			1	2			4
	– c				1			
Not indicated	– a	1	2					
	– b	3	9	8	8			36
	– c		1	2	2			
Totals		47	48	51	41		2	189

Total – a	34
Total – b	144
Total – c	11
Grand total	189

Source: Archivo General de Indias (1661).
Notes: a = living by themselves
b = in domestic service
c = in *obraje* or *tienda*

could be located, 68 (or nearly half) came from the central valleys, and 41 from the Mount Zapotec region around Villa Alta; that is, approximately two-thirds came from towns within short distances of Antequera, ranging from a walking time of hours to perhaps a week at most. Far smaller numbers (30 in all) came from the more distant towns of the Mixteca Alta, the Isthmus of Tehuantepec, the Chontales, and the Chinanteca. A few Indians (9) came from truly distant points, such as Chiapa, Puebla, Mexico City, and even from Querétaro. Clearly Indian migration to Antequera came from nearby towns and countryside; the governing factor was difficulty to travel on foot for distances that might require more than a week's walk. Another concomitant factor was probably the difficulty of transmission of news in such conditions of travel.

The *padrón* also gives evidence on type of employment or residence. Of the 189 *indios forasteros* listed, 34 lived by themselves, with no indication in the document of their employment, although most of them probably were in some forms of common labor; 144 were in domestic service; and 11 worked in *obrajes* or shops (*tiendas*). The major form of employment, then, was domestic service, which may even have included some of the Indians listed as living apart. All of the Indians who came from points outside the present state of Oaxaca were in domestic service. One surmises that they moved to Antequera with their Spanish employers. Contrary to what one would expect, the *padrón* lists slightly more men than women.

Our second count for the city of Antequera is the very careful series of returns by parish priests that constitute the census of 1777 for that city. We had tabulated the returns for other purposes (Cook and Borah 1971: 203–212), which unfortunately did not include taking information

Table 2. Population by five-year age groups for Antequera and rural parishes of the bishopric of Oaxaca, 1777

Age group	Antequera			Rural Oaxaca		
	Male	Female	Total	Male	Female	Total
0–4	1,252	1,313	2,565	15,589	15,053	30,642
5–9	884	920	1,804	14,608	13,614	28,222
10–14	947	1,022	1,969	10,744	9,448	20,192
15–19	879	1,012	1,891	7,874	8,323	16,197
20–24	902	1,240	2,142	7,391	8,299	15,690
25–29	858	1,062	1,920	7,413	7,827	15,240
30–34	678	895	1,573	6,266	5,902	12,168
35–39	522	629	1,151	4,996	4,929	9,925
40–44	653	781	1,434	4,590	4,372	8,962
45–49	320	389	709	3,190	2,878	6,068
50–54	461	591	1,052	2,972	2,829	5,801
55–59	185	213	398	1,675	1,538	3,213
60–64	268	340	608	1,923	1,786	3,709
65–69	81	69	150	685	636	1,321
70–74	65	67	132	557	517	1,074
75–79	23	25	48	199	156	355
80–84	20	21	41	260	241	501
85–89	5	2	7	59	38	97
90–	9	7	16	91	39	181
Total	9,012	10,598	19,610	91,082	88,476	179,558

Source: Census of 1777 as analyzed in Cook and Borah (1971: 203, et seq.).

on place of origin, but we can use here the tabulation by five-year age groups (see Table 2). The interesting feature of our tabulation is the rise in number from the age group 5–9 to a new peak in the age group 20–24, and the general clustering of numbers in age groups 10–34. In contrast, the rural areas of the bishopric show the broad-based pyramid with regular attrition from infancy onward that one would associate with an old-regime population. Equally interesting are the distinctly larger numbers of females in the age groups 10–34. The conclusion must be that the unusual features of distribution of age groups in Antequera result from immigration of young adults to the city from the countryside, and that more women came than men – what one would normally expect if the largest opportunity lay in domestic service in what in 1777 was a city of nearly 20,000 persons with only a weak development in manufacturing and commerce relative to such centers as Puebla and San Miguel el Grande. We cannot tell from our tabulation the distances from which migrants came to Oaxaca in the middle of the eighteenth century, but it is likely that the same rule of distance applied.

Our second set of data refers to Guadalajara, a major administrative and commercial center in west-central Mexico. In 1822, the government of Guadalajara prepared a *padrón* or census of the city's inhabitants. Although Mexico had just become independent, the conceptions and methods of listing were those of the later colonial period, and included instructions to give place of origin. The city archive of Guadalajara contains the census sheets for 18 of the 24 *cuarteles* of 1822, but 11 either omit place of origin or give it so carelessly as to be useless. Of the reports of 7 *cuarteles* that are usable, those for *cuarteles* numbers 11, 12, and 23 contain meticulous and full reporting, that for number 1 is complete for only five blocks, number 20 is complete except for a few of the last sheets, that for number 6 gives place of origin for heads of family only, and that for number 17 gives place of origin for whole families but probably omits many single persons. The surviving, usable sheets cover over 3,000 persons, comprising approximately one-third of the population of the city. The number of migrants within the *cuarteles* falls within 25 to 40 percent of total population for each ward, with an average of 35 percent. Accordingly, the surviving, usable sheets of the count of 1822 constitute an adequate and, for our purposes, unbiased sample.

The census of 1822 for Guadalajara has already been analyzed by Professor Cook (1970: 282–283, 291–292). We have reproduced his tabulation in our Table 3. The tabulation distinguishes among residents born in Guadalajara itself; those born in what is now the state of Jalisco; those coming from what today are contiguous states, including Nayarit; those coming from the rest of Mexico, which for convenience

Table 3. Origin of adults in 7 *cuarteles* of Guadalajara, according to the 1822 census

Place of origin	Number of persons	Percent of total	Percent of Immigrants
Guadalajara	5,552	66.2	
Jalisco	1,454	17.3	51.1
Zacatecas	388	4.6	13.6
Aguascalientes	148	1.8	5.2
San Luís Potosí	25	0.3	0.9
Guanajuato	294	3.5	10.3
Michoacán	175	2.1	6.2
Colima	33	0.4	1.2
Nayarit (Tepic)	65	0.8	2.3
Total adjacent states	1,128	13.5	39.7
Federal District	69	0.8	2.4
Northern states[a]	24	0.3	0.8
Central and southern states[b]	62	0.7	2.2
Total balance of Mexico	155	1.8	5.4
Latin America	18	0.2	0.6
Europe	70	0.8	2.5
Undetermined[c]	19	0.2	0.7
All others	107	1.2	3.8
Total immigrants	2,844	33.8	100.0
Total persons	8,396	100.0	

[a] In this table the north and west of Mexico is considered to consist of the following states, when any of such states *is not the home of the population tabulated, nor is adjacent, or contiguous to* that state: Colima, Nayarit, Jalisco, Aguascalientes, Guanajuato, Sinaloa, Zacatecas, San Luís Potosí, Durango, Tamaulipas, Nuevo León, Coahuila, Chihuahua, Sonora, Baja California.
[b] The south and east in an analogous manner consists of the following states (excluding the Federal District): Michoacán, Querétaro, Hidalgo, México, Morelos, Guerrero, Tlaxcala, Puebla, Veracruz, Oaxaca, Chiapas, Tabasco, Campeche, Yucatán, Quintana Roo.
[c] A few names on the census sheets are illegible, or unrecognizable. They are probably minor localities in Jalisco.

is divided into northern and western states, southern and eastern states, and the present Federal District; and finally residents born outside of Mexico, almost all of them immigrants from Europe. The tabulation makes it clear that two-thirds of the residents of Guadalajara in 1822 had been born in the city and one-third had moved to it. Of the migrants, slightly over half had been born in Jalisco, approximately 40 percent were from adjacent states, and 10 percent from all other regions. European migration contributed 2.5 percent. Clearly the inverse principle of distance already noted for the city of

Antequera operated for Guadalajara. One further point to be noted is that most of the migration from adjacent areas of Guadalajara came from the plateau in 1822 and not from the coast. The coast at that time was itself a focus of immigration and resettlement, whereas the plateau was relatively saturated with population.

Our third set of data are on the city of Guanajuato, a major center of mining, commerce, and administration in the last century of the colonial period. We have for it a series of counts made in 1791–1794 which have been preserved in part in the Mexican national archive. They have been tabulated and analyzed by David Brading in a recently published study (Brading 1972: 460–480, especially 464). Professor Brading has tabulated the places of origin of the adult male labor force of the city. There is no reason to suppose that inclusion of women would markedly change the general features of his tabulation. The tabulation indicates that the male work force in Guanajuato was multiracial. The overwhelming proportion had been born in Guanajuato itself (78 percent). The surrounding regions contributed 12 percent of the male work force, more distant regions in New Spain contributed 7 percent. Unfortunately, Professor Brading's tabulation does not break down this category further. Approximately 3 percent of the adult male work force came from Europe. The census for Guanajuato, then, shows the operation of the same principle of inverse distance since 90 percent of the work force either had been born in the city or came from immediately adjacent regions. On the other hand, the attractions of a highly prosperous mining and commercial center drew somewhat larger proportions of migrants from longer distances if one may judge by the slightly larger proportion of European-born residents and the percentage of migrants from beyond the immediate province. The basic aspects remain the very high percentage of residents born in the city or coming from short distances.

Our last set of data for an urban center in New Spain is for the city of Querétaro in 1791–1794, the returns of the military census for the urban core (Archivo General de la Nación 1791–1794) (see Table 4). Querétaro was a prosperous manufacturing center, famous for its *obrajes* producing woolens that were exported as far as Peru, and an important commercial center in the eastern Bajío. Von Humboldt (1966 [1882]: 156, 467, 485) reported that the city as of 1803 had approximately 35,000 inhabitants, of whom 11,500 were Indians. If one adjusts these estimates downward to arrive at a reasonable calculation for 1793, one would estimate the non-Indian population to have been approximately 20,000. Our data then cover perhaps 12 percent of the urban population, but are probably an unbiased sample except to the extent that the people born in Europe would be more

Table 4. Querétaro: place of origin of people reported in military census of 1791–1794 (urban center only)

City	2,150
Present states of Querétaro and Guanajuato	203
Surrounding states – Jalisco, Michoacán, México, Hidalgo, San Luís Potosí, Zacatecas, Aguascalientes	92
Rest of Mexico	8
Europe	128
Could not be located	5
	2,586

Source: Archivo General de la Nación (1791–1794).

Table 5a. Place of origin of adults, 1793 census

Area	Local-born	Immigrants			Total immigrants	Total persons
		Contiguous provinces	Other parts of Mexico	Europe		
Colima[a]						
Number of persons	2857	714	83	22	819	3,676
Percent of persons	77.7	19.4	2.3	0.6	22.3	100.0
Percent of immigrants	—	87.2	10.1	2.7	100.0	—
Ahuacatlán[b]						
Number of persons	921	51	11	3	65	986
Percent of persons	93.4	5.2	1.1	0.3	6.6	100.0
Percent of immigrants	—	78.5	11.9	4.6	100.0	—
Motines[c]						
Number of persons	103	237	13	3	253	356
Percent of persons	28.9	66.6	3.6	0.9	71.1	100.0
Percent of immigrants	—	93.7	5.1	1.2	100.0	—

Notes to Tables 5a and 5b:

[a] Archivo General de la Nación, volume 11, *passim*. The adjacent or contiguous provinces are Jalisco (including Tepic) and Michoacán. Other Mexican provinces include principally Guanajuato and Zacatecas. The local born are from the *villa* of Colima and closely surrounding towns, all within the northeastern half of the present state of Colima.

[b] Archivo General de la Nación, volume 14, *passim*. This tabulation is based upon adult *españoles* and *mestizos*, the negroes and mulattos not appearing in the census. Since the *partido* of Ahuacatlán forms the eastern corner of Nayarit, the contiguous provinces will be Jalisco and the remainder of Nayarit itself. Other Mexican areas include all else.

[c] Archivo General de la Nación, volume 21, *passim*. Tabulation based upon adult *españoles* and *mestizos*. The contiguous provinces are Michaocán, Colima and Jalisco.

Table 5b. Place of origin of adults, 1793; extended detail of place of origin of migrants (Europeans omitted)

| Living in Colima[a] | | | Living in Ahuacatlán[b] | | | Living in Motines[c] | | |
From:	Percent	Number	From:	Percent	Number	From:	Percent	Number
Jalisco: coast and escarpment	46.6	371	Nayarit (Tepic)	16.1	10	Colima	31.7	80
Jalisco: Lake Chapala, north and east	19.0	151	Jalisco: coast and escarpment	50.0	31	Michoacán: west	22.1	56
Michoacán Valladolid and west	22.8	182	Jalisco: Lake Chapala, north and east	16.1	10	Jalisco: coast and escarpment	36.5	92
Nayarit (Tepic)	0.1	1	Michoacán	4.8	3	Jalisco: Lake Chapala, north and east	5.1	13
Aguascalientes	0.2	2	Aguascalientes	3.2	2	Aguascalientes, Guanajuato, Zacatecas	2.3	6
Guanajuato: south and west	4.9	39	Guanajuato	0.0	0	Central Mexico	2.3	6
Zacatecas	4.8	38	Zacatecas	6.5	4			
Central Mexico	1.6	13	Central Mexico	3.2	2			
Total	100.0	797	Total	100.0	62	Total	100.0	253

likely to be counted. Of the 2,586 persons in our sample, the overwhelming majority (2,150) were born in the city itself. The regions adjacent to the city, here defined as the present-day states of Querétaro and Guanajuato, contributed by far the largest proportion of immigrants (203). The present-day states surrounding these two states contributed a smaller number of immigrants (92), and the rest of Mexico very few (8). The proportion of European-born immigrants (128 or 5 percent of the sample) is higher than one would expect but not excessively so. We surmise that the larger and economically more active urban centers attracted higher proportions of the immigrant Europeans. The most surprising feature of the sample is the number of residents born in the city (83 percent), a proportion that is higher than Professor Brading's tabulation shows for Guanajuato. The explanation may lie in the prosperity of the two urban economies, but we are unable to explain why that prosperity did not attract more immigrants.

We turn now to consideration of a tabulation of rural migration to the coastal areas of west-central Mexico in order to determine whether urban and rural migration show the same general pattern or not. Such a comparison is useful because in the colonial period the bulk of internal movement within New Spain took the form of rural migration, the urban centers being too small a proportion of total population to absorb truly significant numbers of people. Our data refer to the three *partidos* of Colima, Ahuacatlán, and Motines, which in the sixteenth century had lost most of their population and in the eighteenth century were rapidly filling up with settlers. Our data are from the military census of 1791–1794 (see Table 5a). For purposes of tabulation, the table, prepared by Professor Cook (1970: 280–282, 288–290) segregates those residents born within the three *partidos*: those born in contiguous provinces, or roughly the territory of the present state of Jalisco; those born elsewhere in Mexico; and those born in Europe. In a further tabulation, Professor Cook has broken down the place of origin of all migrants to the area except Europeans (see Table 5b). For two of the *partidos*, Colima and Ahuacatlán, the overwhelming proportion of the residents were born in the area; Motines differs in that the overwhelming bulk of its residents came from contiguous provinces. In general, the same rule of inverse distance that we have found for urban centers applies to this sample of rural population.

Let us take up one other question we raised at the beginning of this essay, the extent to which colonial Mexican cities had a surplus or deficit of births over deaths. We may find a partial answer in two different kinds of evidence, namely, the reporting of Alexander von Humboldt and our own tabulations of eighteenth-century counts. With the aid of the Archbishop of Mexico, von Humboldt was able to collect baptismal and burial data from the parishes of the archdiocese for terms of years from 1752 to 1802. He presented the following sample data for Mexican towns giving the ratio of births to deaths, the deaths being taken as 100 (1966: 39–40):

Dolores Hidalgo	100:253	Querétaro	100:188
Singuilucan	100:234	Ajapuzco	100:157
Calimaya	100:202	Iguala	100:140
Guanajuato	100:201	Malacatepec	100:134
Santa Ana	100:195	Pánuco	100:123
Márfil	100:194		

Unfortunately, his data suffer from the usual Mexican ambiguity in the definition of town, which includes much rural territory. Only Guanajuato and Querétaro in the above data were largely or entirely urban. Nevertheless, the data do suggest a substantial excess of births over deaths on the plateau, a lesser one in the intermediate zones, and a fairly small one on the coast.

Von Humboldt also gives one datum on Mexico City in a statement that in 1802 there were 5,166 deaths (really births) and 6,155 births (really baptisms) (1966: 131). This is a much smaller excess of births over deaths, the ratio expressed as above being 100: 119. It suggests that in a truly large urban aggregation European conditions might prevail. However, von Humboldt himself warned that the total of deaths was much swollen by the fact that sick and dying Indians came to Mexico City for treatment in its hospitals.

Our own tabulations of the 1777 and 1791–1794 census (Cook and Borah 1966: 251–258) permit another approach by examining the relative proportions of persons within the age group 0–15 in rural and urban areas. For the census of 1777, our tabulations give the age group 0–15 as constituting 44.9 percent in the bishopric of Oaxaca, 45.3 in the bishopric of Puebla, and 45.3 in the bishopric of Durango. For the census of 1793, our tabulations show this age group as constituting from 42.0 to 42.4 percent of total population. Total population within each bishopric and within the colony as a whole was, of course, overwhelmingly rural. Corresponding values for urban entities are: Antequera in 1777, clergy included, 34.3 percent; Antequera in 1793, clergy omitted, 38.6 percent; and Mexico City in 1793, clergy omitted, 33.9 percent. The proportion of the age group 0–15 in the urban centers was somewhat lower than in the countryside. The difference may result in part from the presence of numbers of clergy in the cities and, in part, from the migration of adults to the cities, with a swelling of the age groups 15–35. Nevertheless, a population which was one-third infants and children was maintaining itself and even increasing. The pattern of some of the larger European cities, then, did not apply in New Spain.

Our conclusions from the limited samples of data we have adduced must be as follows: (1) We have no adequate evidence on outflow from cities or movement from city to city. For that we should need tabulations of data for Puebla and Mexico City. Our samples suggest rather little such movement. (2) Colonial Mexican cities did not differ much from the country as a whole in their proportions of young, although the tabulations for Antequera and Mexico City show some-what lower proportions of the age group 0–15 in the population. Accordingly, Mexican cities maintained themselves through their own births and even gained some increase. Migration gave additional increase. Altitude, however, markedly affected the numbers of births and deaths, and the surplus of births over deaths. (3) Migration to urban centers followed a rule of inverse distance, i.e. most migrants came from immediately adjacent areas and the inflow tended to diminish sharply with distance. The only exception was the small inflow of immigrants from Europe, who came to Mexico by ship. This pattern, we may surmise, held as long as colonial conditions of travel and communication obtained. It changed only when the construction of railroads made land travel far easier and erased the factor of distance wherever steel rails reached. In this sense, the colonial period in Mexico lasted until the 1880's and 1890's; for some regions beyond the reach of railroad and motor road, it may still be continuing.

The extent to which our findings for colonial Mexico apply to colonial Latin America as a whole can only be established by much further research.

REFERENCES

ARCHIVO GENERAL DE INDIAS
  1661   "Padrón de indios forasteros en la ciudad de Oaxaca y alrededores (23 December 1661)." Patronato, legato 230A, ramo 8, 2a parte. Unpublished manuscripts. Seville: Archivo General de Indias.
ARCHIVO GENERAL DE LA NACIÓN
  1791–1794   *Ramo de Padrones*, volumes 11, 14, 21, 39. Mexico City: Archivo General de la Nación.
BRADING, DAVID
  1972   Grupos étnicos; clases y estructura ocupacional en Guanajuato (1792). *Historia Mexicana* 21 (3): 460–480.
COOK, SHERBURNE F.
  1970   "Migration as a factor in the history of Mexican population: sample data from west-central Mexico, 1793–1950," in *Population and economics*. Edited by Paul Deprez. Proceedings of Section 5 (Historical Demography) of the 4th Congress of the International Economic Association, Indiana University, Winnipeg.
COOK. SHERBURNE F., WOODROW BORAH
  1966   Marriage and legitimacy in Mexican culture: Mexico and California. *California Law Review* 54 (2): 954–957 *et passim*.
  1968   *The population of the Mixteca Alta, 1520–1960*. Ibero-Americana 50. Berkeley and Los Angeles: University of California Press.
  1971   *Essays in population history: Mexico and the Caribbean*, volume one. Berkeley and Los Angeles: University of California Press.
MORIN, CLAUDE
  1972   Los libros parroquiales como fuente para la historia demográfica y social novohispana. *Historia Mexicana* 21 (3): 389–418.
VÁZQUEZ DE ESPINOSA, ANTONIO
  1948   *Compendio y descripción universal de las Indias Occidentales*. Smithsonian Publication 3898. Washington, D.C.: Smithsonian Institution.
VON HUMBOLDT, ALEXANDER
  1966 [1882]   *Ensayo político sobre el reino de la Nueva España*. Edited and revised version by Juan Ortega y Medina, from the translation by Vicente González Arnao (1882). Mexico City: Porrua.

Regional Economy and Urbanization: Three Examples of the Relationship Between Cities and Regions in New Spain at the End of the Eighteenth Century

ALEJANDRA MORENO TOSCANO

A First View of the Whole

If we were to locate on a map the principal cities of New Spain at the end of the eighteenth century, our first impression would be the importance of the external factor in the economy of New Spain (see Map 1). The cities are situated on the traditional route of colonial

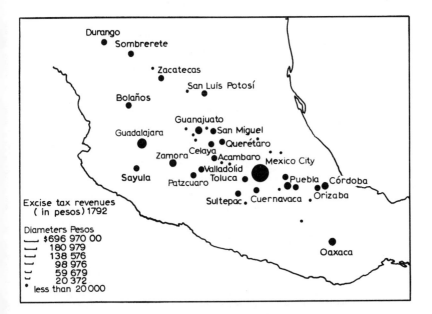

Map 1.   Principal cities of New Spain at the end of the eighteenth century
Source: AGNM (1793). See Appendix for comments on sources.

economic activities: Veracruz–Puebla–Mexico City–Bajío–northern regions. There is in fact nothing new in this distribution, nor in the continued activity of the traditional urban centers, such as Guadalajara and Oaxaca, that are considerably removed from that main axis. Oaxaca, moreover, had been the connecting link between Mexico City and the southern provinces since ancient times. Another important urban area far from the center was the city of Mérida,[1] in Yucatán, whose development should be carefully analyzed. This first view of the overall picture confirms what is already known: the Spanish preference for settling on the tableland, the urban development of mining centers, and the definitive linking – via Veracruz – of New Spain's economy with the Spanish cities.

This distribution, however, exhibits differences which need to be pointed out. For example, one notes varying relationships between cities and regions which indicate marked contrasts and originality among themselves.

A more careful inspection of our map would reveal the presence of cities which act as absolute centers of their respective regions. There were no smaller cities within these regions of influence which might counter-balance their predominant positions. Guadelajara and Oaxaca are classic examples. Puebla itself typifies such a position of predominance.

One – apparently unique – exception of two cities of parallel importance comes immediately into mind. Orizaba and Córdoba, on the Veracruz road, experienced parallel growth even though they were located in the same region and exercised considerable influence over it. These two cities were to act as poles of attraction to a single region without their growth being hindered.

A third type of relationship between cities and regions appears in the Bajío region. Here we find a series of cities of evident importance surrounded by medium-sized and smaller centers. This nucleus of moderate-sized cities in a single region presents an example of a different regional equilibrium of great importance.

Nevertheless, Mexico City stands over and above this regional urban distribution. While acting as a great metropolis, it extended its domination beyond regional frontiers. For this reason, its role should be analyzed separately: this subject is so complex that it goes beyond the limits of the present limited study. Here I shall only analyze the three types of relationships between the cities and regions mentioned above, describing the original features and development of each.

---

[1]   It does not appear on the map included here because there was no information available concerning the excise duties paid by the city.

I. PUEBLA: AN EXAMPLE OF A CITY WHICH ABSORBS ITS REGION

Puebla was founded halfway between Mexico City and Veracruz, in a fertile region with an abundant supply of native manpower. The site soon became the strategic point chosen by travelers to rest from the distressing trip over the hot and unhealthy coastal lands. It was also the place for changing beasts of burden and the center for merchants traversing the road from Mexico City to Veracruz. Puebla was conceived as a center for settling the poorer Spanish who did not receive grants. These immigrants were given facilities to engage in agriculture on moderate-sized haciendas (see Chevalier 1957). In fact, the original idea of making Puebla a city of small farmers was not carried out. It was soon necessary to make limited assignments of Indians in service to ensure the manpower needed by the new farmers (Chevalier 1957). Soon, too, the new city was to become the center of attraction for many of the region's local governors, who established residences there.

That original social function of Puebla undoubtedly promoted its rapid growth during its first years. The 50 founding inhabitants of 1531 were 300 in 1547, 800 in 1570, and 1,500 in 1600 (Chevalier 1957). Moreover, because of its particularly favorable location, it always received an influx of people from Mexico City in times of crisis, as during the flood of 1629.

Puebla had irregular periods of development during the colonial period but always had in its favor the fact that it was a Spanish city and that it was the administrative, ecclesiastical, and commercial capital of a large region containing important centers of native population (Cholula, Tepeaca, Tecamachalco).

Puebla's first period of urban growth occurred in the sixteenth century, during which time its development was encouraged by the authorities. At its founding, all residents were granted exemptions from excise duties and taxes for thirty years (Chevalier 1957: 12) as a means of attracting population. During this century, Puebla and its dependent regions (Atlixco, Cholula, Huejotzingo, Tepeaca) came to constitute the most important agricultural center of the viceroyalty. The first vineyards and orchards of fruit trees appeared in Atlixco at a very early date. The wheat gathered in that valley and in other regions dependent on Puebla reached the Mexico City market regularly. On occasion this wheat also met the requirements of the newly founded mining centers. Puebla and its dependent agricultural region supplied bread and biscuits to markets as far away as Havana and Maracaibo. This was why, during the sixteenth century, the first mills and plows started to operate in this region, which was the first to develop commercial agriculture in New Spain.

To this agricultural development, a definitely urban development of the textile industry was soon added. The first silk weavers were established in Puebla in 1548. Soon they were competing on the American market with fabrics imported from Castile or Venice.[2] This industry helped to extend the economic region dependent on the city of Puebla to Tepeji and the highlands of Oaxaca.

Nevertheless, this first development of the village textile industry was slowed down at the beginning of the seventeenth century, due to the entrance on the market of silks from China and the prohibition against exporting fabrics from New Spain to Peru (Borah 1943: 35).

In the following years, Puebla exchanged silk fabrics for wool fabrics, an activity which developed very slowly. It has even been considered that the setting up of guild statutes for wool weavers (1598) was an indication that the city's market had reached its saturation point. The statutes apparently sought to eliminate many independent weavers and protect the larger factories which were making better quality products (Bazant 1964: 63). Whether or not this is true, the important point is that the wool industry continued to hold its own during the century of depression. However, at the beginning of the eighteenth century its decline was evident in Puebla (Bazant 1964). Development was restrained by several factors: (1) the appearance of manufacturing centers in other places (Cholula, the Bajío region, Toluca); (2) increased possibilities for acquiring imported fabrics; and (3) the increasing restriction of the workers, which further immobilized a manpower which was already tied down by its dependence on traditional guilds.

The development of cotton fabrics initiated another period of industrial expansion in Puebla. The eighteenth century saw the importing of European machines which permitted the manufacture of cloth lengths of thirty yards (Bazant 1964: 66). This, coupled with the advantage of a native manpower which had traditional mastery of the technique of cotton fibers and fabrics, favored the growth of an industry which first had appeared in Puebla in the seventeenth century.

It is possible that, as Bazant has written, the sudden curtailing of development possibilities in the silk industry caused many silk weavers to become cotton weavers. Similarly, years later wool weavers were to exchange their fabrics for cotton fabrics – as occurred in Tlaxcala (Bazant 1964: 67).

[2]   On this industry one may consult Borah (1943) and Bazant (1964: 56–69).

On the other hand, the cotton industry was supplied from the beginning with hand-made thread from the natives in surrounding areas. In turn, the commissioners of Puebla wholesalers bought the entire native production of cotton fabrics and thread from Heujotzingo and Cholula.[3] Later on, however, Puebla factories had to buy cotton containing seeds from more distant areas (Tlalixcoyan, Cotaxtla, Tuxtla, and Cosamaloapan, Veracruz) (Chávez Orozco and Florescano 1965: 24).

Apparently it was the large merchants of Puebla who profited most from the development of this industry. The independent artisans of the city sold their entire production to two or three wholesalers, who took care of its marketing. Thus, at the end of the eighteenth century we find an unusual situation in the development of the Puebla textile industry: a growing tendency towards the development of a capitalist textile industry which is continually restricted through the maintenance of a guild/trade-union organization of the workers.

At the end of the eighteenth century, the textile industry – which gained new impetus with the establishment of the militia – began to attract workers and artisans to Puebla from small, surrounding towns (AGNM 1790). Around that time the city's growth accelerated, as revealed by a résumé of the population census of 1793. This attributed 57,168 inhabitants to the city of Puebla (AGNM n.d.c.). Besides the development of the cotton industry at the end of the century, another element encouraged migration to the big city. Contemporary descriptions and chronicles carried repeated complaints that agriculture was in decline.

The truth is that Puebla and its dependent region had ceased to be the main producing center for cereals. By this time, producing centers had been formed in each of the important regions of the country. Thus, Puebla cereals could not compete with the interior (principally the Bajío, Toluca, and Chalco). Not only did the Puebla region cease to supply Mexico City (whose consumption was now safeguarded by the considerable cereal production of Chalco and Toluca) (Florescano 1969), but neither could it any longer export its wheat to Havana. On top of this, wheat from the Bajío managed to invade Puebla's own village market, causing a fall in local prices: in 1770 wheat for which 12 to 8 pesos per *carga* [about 6 bushels] had been paid was worth no more than 7 or 5 pesos; maize went down

---

[3] A report from Puebla's Intendant, concerning the province of Cholula at the end of the eighteenth century, reveals the situation in which these natives worked, controlled by the warehouses of Puebla: "The spinners of these goods (cotton fabrics) earn so little that they cannot feed themselves: they use three-fourths of an *arroba* [about 25 pounds] in cotton and afterwards spend the whole day in preparing and spinning it; they need another three to bring any profit" (AGNM [Archivo General de la Nación, México] 1790).

from 20 reales per *fanega* [about 1.5 bushels] to 14 reales (Fabián y Fuero 1770: 170).

It appears, then, that about this time a change in the regional development of New Spain became evident; a change which would of necessity adversely affect some regions and favor others.

In the case of Puebla with the reduction in profits for the region's farmers and landholders, the latter did not – or did not wish to – continue investing in their farms. Many complained that they were not even able to recover their farming costs. Some farmers dared to say that the administration of their haciendas was "intolerable." The result was that, perhaps owing to the loss of markets and former profits, there was a large increase in the number of leases and mortgages imposed on agricultural properties.[4] About the same time there was apparently a reduction in the value of rural properties (Fabián y Fuero 1770: 166–177; AGNM 1790). In addition, "fantastic" sales were made, covering only the documentation costs for the transferring of property ownership. In this way they deferred payment of the *censo* [ground rent] or mortgage interest. They resorted to "moratoria," "delays" (*demores*), and payment of the interest. Finally, an attachment was accepted when the value of the land itself did not even cover the interest payments in arrears of the mortgage encumbering it. As a consequence many agricultural properties were abandoned.[5]

This situation indirectly favored the urban merchants. They were the ones who paid in advance for entire harvests, but at a price very much under the one they later fixed for resale. The region's agriculture

[4]   One of the methods the Church used to exercise its influence over the territorial property of New Spain was to allow a church "benefactor" without liquid assets to encumber the income from one or several of his farms with an annual tax in favor of a church or convent. The name of *censo* was given to this encumbrance, which was generally perpetual. It was equivalent to 5 percent interest on uninvested capital which was not demandable, and which depended on the beneficiary. The *censo* developed in such a manner that in fact it came to be a loan protected by a mortgage. This transformation of the territorial *censo* into a mortgage loan was encouraged by the landowners who because they were owners of family estates which could not be sold, or because they needed cash in order to "finance" their farms, applied to a convent for the loan of a certain amount of money in cash. This was in exchange for a *censo* or mortgage on their properties and the obligation to pay an interest of 5 percent per annum on the money lent. (See Florescano and Meyer 1971.)

[5]   Let us quote fragments of the "Carta de Flon a Revillagigedo" (AGNM 1790) which illustrate this situation: "Exorbitant contributions to the Church (both by these wretched Indians and by others possessing farms because of owing practically the whole price to 'dead hands,' as is shown by the enclosed Reports and Notes) held these inhabitants, by the sterile nature of these contributions, in that inertia which is the lot of any man who regards himself as a slave....Farm owners are no more than administrators for those obliged to pay the *censo*. . . and the increased interest they have to pay does not allow them to prosper nor even to live. They sow a great deal but costs are exorbitant and their crops are very bad; but they are satisfied if in their fields they see a hundred oxen with their corresponding Indians and an overseer on horseback who is watching them scratch the earth."

appeared to be in the hands of middlemen. Perhaps this may explain the concentration in the city of former farmers or owners of haciendas whose only control over their property was their old title of ownership.

It is true that agricultural development of the Puebla region appears to have halted and even declined at the end of the eighteenth century due to the development of other centers of production in the area of its former markets (Chalco and Toluca in Mexico City, the Bajío, etc.). On the other hand, trade in the region increased and Puebla was still the great commercial center. In spite of the establishment of the market in Jalapa, it continued to be one of the first cities to receive imported products each year, benefiting from "first prices." We do not know how Puebla merchants operated in the purchase of goods from the Jalapa market, but surely they competed with the merchants of Mexico City in the acquisition of goods. For this reason it is natural to assume that they began their struggle to obtain an independent trade consulate for their city at this time, though it was not obtained until much later (1824).

Possibly it was this commercial importance, besides the development of an urban industry (porcelain, textiles), which continued to maintain Puebla as one of the principal cities of the viceroyalty. The intensity of Puebla trade is obvious from the following list of establishments which were functioning at the beginning of the nineteenth century (Secretaría de Hacienda y Crédito 1944: 53):

45 woolen goods shops	3 warehouses
39 bakeries	286 wine shops
102 grocery shops	12 hardware shops
137 dry goods shops	

Let us see now how Puebla's position was reflected in two urban centers which are under its influence. The first, Atlixco, was founded by the Spanish; the second, Cholula, was an old, native population center.

Atlixco

Atlixco was founded as an extension of Puebla. Puebla's original settlers received numerous land grants in Atlixco because the land was exposed to frost there (Chevalier 1957). By the end of the sixteenth century, Atlixco had already become an important agricultural center. Traditionally, wheat from Atlixco was sold in any market at one peso above the agreed price, since it was considered to be superior in quality. Therefore the marketing crisis which affected the Puebla region at the end of the eighteenth century was a hard blow for Atlixco. In spite of everything, Atlixco continued producing cereals. In 1791, only 34 farms in the valley paid from 35,000 to 37,000 *cargas* of wheat, a similar amount of maize from 5,000 to 6,000 measures of kidney beans and 7,000 to 8,000 *arrobas* of red peppers in accordance with the one-tenth duty required (AGNM 1792a). Nevertheless, the richness of the Atlixco valley accentuated its dependence on Puebla, the commercial and distribution center for the region's products. Commercially it can be said that Atlixco was maintained simply as an extension of the large city. The road linking the two cities, according to the remark of an observer of the period, "is as traveled as a public street." Atlixco's agricultural products were transported along it, to be marketed in Puebla, "without profit for its native soil" (AGNM 1792a).

Atlixco, as an urban center, suffered more strongly than the large city from the loss of agricultural markets. At the end of the eighteenth century, Atlixco seemed like a city in the process of deterioration. A careful observer points out that the city had "many worthless buildings, originally chaplaincies and holy places whose appearance had deteriorated" (AGNM 1792a). The city, like many of the farms and rural properties of the region, was mortgaged.

This observation by a contemporary is not the only indication we have concerning the city's deterioration. When examining the census of Revillagigedo (AGNM 1792c), I took a sample of 200 houses: 27 percent were reported as "walled up," "empty," or "uninhabited."[6]

Moreover, the census of Atlixco shows that a considerable number of single women lived in the small city as heads of families: widows, unmarried women, and women who had been deserted (12 percent of the 200 individuals analyzed). It is likely that as a work force these women could barely have risen above subsistence level with the few occupations open to them: sale of chickens and eggs, manual work, etc.[7] Furthermore, the various services the city retained spoke more of a past vitality than of a present one (inns, post office, excise tax office, tobacco office, the snow-collection stand, convents, one secondary school, one hospital).

[6] This percentage might be much greater if one were to make a complete analysis of the information of the census, since my sample only covered houses on streets adjoining the central plaza.

[7] In reference to this situation we should not fail to consider some observations made by Alzate regarding the Revillagigedo censuses. One of the arguments Alzate adduces to prove that the population of New Spain is much higher than indicated by the census is the following: because of their fear of induction into the militia, many men hid while the census was being taken and their wives declared themselves deserted. This being the case, it would be a matter of absences more fictional than real (AGNM 1791–1792).

Founded as a dependency and extension of Puebla city, Atlixco does not appear to have developed any degree of autonomy. In the 1792 census, of the 200 individuals analyzed not a single landowner or important agricultural official was registered as living in Atlixco. Only a number of overseers, subordinate officials, and farm tenants lived in the small city. The farm owners of the valley, when these farms were not in the hands of religious orders, did not reside in the small town of Atlixco; they established their residence in the city of Puebla. The proximity of the large city thus curbed any possible development. To describe it in the parlance of the period, "The immediacy of Puebla offends it."

In spite of the city's generally known deterioration, Atlixco inhabitants preserved their pride in an old city of Spaniards, though Spaniards residing in the city were few, or were often married to mestizos. The pride of the old Spanish city clashed with a description of the actual situation. One informant says: "the commerce of this town does not correspond to the merits of its population" (AGNM 1792a).

The few Spanish families who settled in Atlixco, along with those who were not Spanish but were concerned with "normal decency in their style of dress," regularly went to Puebla to do their shopping: "families of distinction do not consider even shoes or other articles suitable if they do not come from the city of Puebla" (AGNM 1792a). Naturally, local trade was significantly affected by such attitudes. The dominating presence of Puebla kept Atlixco as a dependent town and an extension of the Puebla market, thereby restricting its opportunities for development.

Cholula

Cholula, another town near Puebla, experienced a more critical situation. At the end of the eighteenth century Governor Manuel Flon described the situation in the district of Cholula as follows: "I consider the proximity of this town to Puebla one of the reasons for its decline and that said decline has been greater to the extent that Puebla has encouraged it" (AGNM 1790).

The fact that Cholula was a town with a non-Spanish majority population appears to have intensified some problems. It was the small artisans, workers, and cotton spinners and weavers who abandoned the town at the end of the eighteenth century in order to seek to set themselves up in Puebla. Of the one hundred wool looms in Cholula in the middle of the eighteenth century, no more than two remained at the close of that century (AGNM 1790). And no one wished to use them. As to the manufacturing of cotton goods, it is reported that there were two hundred individuals "skilled in the trade of spinning cotton who remain unemployed because of a lack of support [for the industry]" (AGNM 1790).

Under such circumstances, it was understandable that many workers should seek to establish themselves in Puebla, with the result – as one informant writes – that "with this emigration houses remain empty, resulting in leaks and collapsing roofs," and the process of the town's deterioration accelerated. Agave cactus began to appear on sites where houses were built.[8]

These developments are a new indication of the difficulties being experienced by agriculture throughout the region. Many of the old day laborers maintained their existence through the sale of the small amount of juice which they extracted from the agave found on the sites, fermented, and sold retail in their own homes.[9]

Cholula had recovered a certain degree of prestige in the middle of the eighteenth century; at the close of that century it was no more than a heap of ruins everywhere: houses had fallen down and the countryside (agave and pasturelands) invaded what in former times was the urban environment. To sum up, Cholula typifies a case of the growing ruralization of an old urban center which had been slowly absorbed by the large city in its proximity.

II. ORIZABA AND CÓRDOBA: A CASE OF PARALLEL GROWTH OF TWO CITIES

Let us now examine another type of regional urban development. In Puebla we found an example of an urban center which gradually absorbed the smaller towns on its periphery. In the case of Orizaba and Córdoba, we find an example of parallel development of two moderate-sized towns.

The traditional route linking the city of Veracruz with the tableland passed through Jalapa. This was the route followed by Hernán Cortés and after him the viceroys. But from a very early date (1535), another route began to be developed which, although longer in distance, turned

[8]   The text says: "Depopulation has resulted in the decline of factories and of the majority of the town's houses, whose lots are now covered with agave" (AGNM 1790).
[9]   "[One ought to] banish all the agave that the Indians have, for it only contributes to increasing their drunkenness. The misuse which is made of this plant does much harm to places where it is grown, and it consumes the small amount of labor required to bring profit to those who have property. The fondness of these natives for their drink has an unequaled attraction for the lazy, greedy, and corrupt" (AGNM 1790: 56). See also Secretaría de Hacienda y Crédito (1944).

out to be shorter in time.[10] This second route was to be the one which muleteers and merchants would gradually prefer, resulting in the appearance of a series of inhabited areas which benefited from the route. Orizaba and Córdoba, in their origins, were post-settlements.

There was a prior circumstance which explained the economic development of these towns. Orizaba and Córdoba, like Jalapa further to the north, represented the geographical boundary of the Spanish settlement of New Spain. They were all located exactly on the boundary of the *tierra caliente* [hot country]. Beyond this only Veracruz, supported from abroad as a necessary linking port with the mother country, dared to defy "the dark vomit," "the diseases and fevers," the mosquitoes and unhealthy climate of the coast. This location on the geographical frontier – the frontier for tropical illnesses – permitted an early development of these sites as places of rest for travelers and for changing animals on the difficult trip along the coastal lands. But, at the same time, this siting permitted the control and marketing of agricultural products from the *tierra caliente* (tobacco, sugarcane, rice, cotton, etc.).

The case of Orizaba appears to be of particular interest. In fact, it is one of the few cases of spontaneous growth of cities which acquired significance during the eighteenth century.

From 1535 and for the whole of the seventeenth century, muleteers and merchants settled on the site of Orizaba. They rested their beasts of burden and took on necessary supplies for continuing the journey to Puebla. It was a stopover for travelers; it had no town plan, no designated *ejidos* [public lands], nor municipal rights before the eighteenth century. It grew as any town grows which is only a stopping place for travelers: along the road, with houses and businesses built by the hands of the travelers themselves. Its *calle real* [main street] was the road for carriages and wagons. As building sites were not subdivided, anyone settling on it did so as best he could. De Villaseñor y Sánchez writes in the middle of the eighteenth century:

The town is one of the best in the Bishopric because of its opulence, comfort, abundance of supplies, and the arrangement of its houses, which form straight streets, of which the main one, the *calle real*, is more than a quarter of a league long (de Villaseñor 1746: 258).

In the middle of the eighteenth century Orizaba had extended along the carriage and wagon road. The parish – center of every planned Spanish settlement – was only to be established very much later,

[10] This route appears originally to have run as follows: Veracruz–Medellín–Paso de los Carros–Cotaxtla–San Juan de la Punta–Córdoba–Orizaba–El Ingenio–Maltrata–Ahuatlán–Nopalucan–El Pinar–Puebla. In 1792 the short road through Acultzingo was opened. (See Florescano 1968.)

around 1720, on one side of the *calle real*, scarcely leaving room for a small plaza, which was, in fact, never built.[11]

The irregular growth of Orizaba is also explained by other special circumstances. It was compressed between properties owned by the counts of the valley, and neither the first count, Don Antonio de Mendoza, first viceroy of New Spain (1545), nor his descendants looked favorably upon the granting of the title of *villa* [chartered town] or city to the settlement. A city would have required a plan, designated *ejidos*, and its own municipal rights; partitions, in short, which would have affected the count's properties. This dispute between the settlers of Orizaba and the counts of the valley lasted many years, continuing until 1756 when Orizaba took possession of lands affecting the properties of the Hurtado de Mendoza family. As a result, it was not until 1764 that Orizaba had its own municipal council and not until 1774 when the title of *villa* was finally granted to it.[12]

These concessions of rank – the commons, the *cabildo* [municipal council], the title deed – were late in coming, a result of pressure which signified the real importance of the town. That importance originated a long time before. Let us recall that in 1724 (with neither *cabildo* nor city hall) Orizaba was the seat, on a single occasion, of the merchants' fair held in Jalapa. This was because it offered better resources and larger warehouses. It should also be pointed out that since 1724 Orizaba had possessed a fair number of looms. In the middle of the eighteenth century, with the creation of the tobacco monopoly, Orizaba became the site of one of the largest cigar factories of New Spain.

At the end of the eighteenth century, its importance as one of the main cities of the region was indisputable. By that time it had acquired specific functions. In the 1792 census (AGNM 1791b), of the 200 individuals analyzed, 16 percent were identified as "cigar and cigarette vendors" and workers or administrators of the cigar factory. Furthermore, its position as a stopover town is shown clearly by the large number of muleteers (8 percent of 300 individuals) registered in it. The appearance of a large number of persons occupied in activities related to the driving of mules, such as mule farriers, also attests to this.

---

[11]   "The Church of Sorrows (Iglesia de los Dolores) was begun in 1720. The site then chosen was completely deserted, bounded to the south by some houses of the old Real Vieja street and to the north by houses of Indians. It was a serious error to locate the church at this point and was unquestionably in large part the origin of the irregularity of the main street. It appears that the intention was to form a small plaza. This would explain the excessive width of the street in front of the chapel. Later on, carelessness and a lack of efficient supervision resulted in houses being built along the road without any irregularity being noticed" (Arroniz 1867: 347).

[12]   For all of the above, see Arroniz (1867: ch. 10–14).

Córdoba

Córdoba, less than 30 kilometers from Orizaba, underwent parallel development. It was founded and designed after Negro insurrections at the beginning of the seventeenth century. For many years it received its provisions from the Orizaba market. This continued until it acquired an independent importance as trade center and warehousing city for the agricultural products of the surrounding region. From then on Córdoba maintained its growth as a center for middlemen merchants (the "traders"), the owners of tobacco, rice, and sugarcane. Its geographic location, closer to the large cotton-producing centers (Tlalixcoyan and Cotaxtla), made it inevitable that this city become an obligatory site for the marketing of this fiber. In addition, many distilleries were established in Córdoba and succeeded in controlling the regional market for cane brandy.

It is interesting to point out that in spite of the fact that Córdoba always had a somewhat smaller population than Orizaba, both cities maintained a parallel growth rate. This parallel growth, which undoubtedly is the cause of rivalries still obvious today, was never hampered by the preponderance of either. This could be explained

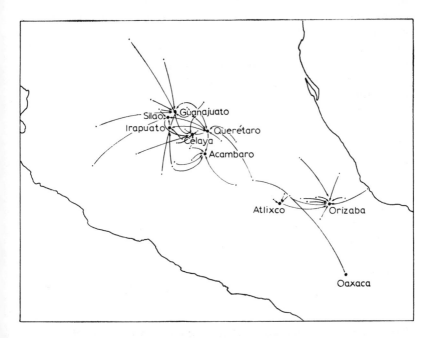

Map 2.   Origins of outsiders residing in a number of cities (1792)
Source: AGNM (1778, 1791a, 1791b, 1791c, 1792b, 1792c, 1792d, 1792e, 1792f, 1792g, 1792h, 1792i).

because both cities fulfilled specific and complementary functions in their domination of the region (activities which were to be defined more clearly with the passage of time: Córdoba, warehouse for agricultural products, and Orizaba, factory center for processing these products).

Orizaba's development as a trade and manufacturing center attracted people from very different parts. None of the cities analyzed in the Bajío or central regions was host to so many strangers as Orizaba (19 percent of 200 individuals); nor do their origins cover so wide a geographical range (see Map 2). I am not familiar with Córdoba's development in the colonial period and for the present cannot add to what has already been said, but I am able to sum up some characteristics of the regional urban development. There was a slow, parallel, and balanced growth of these two cities separated by less than thirty kilometers. This was a growth which for the moment we can attribute only to a possible diversity of complementary functions. Orizaba and Córdoba acted as poles of attraction over the whole agricultural region surrounding them without interfering with one another.

It is interesting to point out that this parallel growth continued to be maintained for many more years. The result is that today the geographic boundaries of these two cities tend to become confused as they extend along the Veracruz road. In spite of this confusion of boundaries, their differentiation today is still very clear. While the region of Nogales-Santa Rosa-Río Blanco-Orizaba is devoted to manufacturing (beer, textile, and paper factories), the Córdoba region is a center for agricultural warehouses, commercial enterprises, and sugar mills.

III. THE BAJÍO: AN EXAMPLE OF AN URBAN NETWORK

At the end of the eighteenth century the Bajío was the only economic complex for capitalist mining operations, commercial agriculture, and industry for the wide markets which had been developed in New Spain.[13] As a result, this region was dotted with numerous smaller towns, moderate-sized urban centers, and larger cities with specific functions.

The larger cities of the Bajío[14] (Guanajuato, Querétaro, Zamora)

[13] Other mining centers developed agriculture but not industry. In 1794 San Luís Potosí had only one factory and Zacatecas none (see Wolf 1955: 177–200).
[14] Traditionally the Bajío is regarded as the extensive area of good land along the rivers linking Lerma de Querétaro and Guadalajara. Nevertheless, in recent geographic studies the name has been extended to all the plains adjoining the Lerma River, both

are located just on the periphery of the agricultural region. At the end of the eighteenth century, the city of Guanajuato (the mining center), and its satellite towns (Márfil, Santa Rosa, Santa Ana), constituted the most important urban center of the region and had a population of 55,000 inhabitants.

Guanajuato was the fourth city of the viceroyalty from the point of view of its trade activity, after Mexico City, Puebla, and Guadalajara.

Querétaro and Zamora, the other large cities of the Bajío, are located at the two geographic entries of the region, serving as "gates of commerce." Querétaro provides the link between Mexico City and trade with the interior (Zacatecas and the mining centers of the north); Zamora, at the other end, is the gateway to trade with the Michoacán lowlands.

After Guanajuato, Querétaro is the next most important urban center of this region. At the end of the eighteenth century, even when less prosperous than Guanajuato, it was undoubtedly a more urbanized city. This situation appears to have various explanations. Guanajuato grew, with a certain lack of order, on a site determined by the existence of mines. For this reason, the city had many deficiencies in its urban services. It often lacked drinking water and was subject to continual floods due to its location in a ravine.[15]

Querétaro, in contrast, was founded and designed as the first point of Spanish expansion to the north. It always enjoyed a privileged location from a trade point of view. In the second half of the eighteenth century, a very important textile industry developed in the city, and it also began to grow as a rest and recreation center. Querétaro and La Cañada were frequented by the wealthy of Mexico City, who found there one of the "most beautiful walks and the most lovely regions which nature can create" thanks to the abundance of the waters, the refreshing forests, the pleasant orchards, the healthful nature of the baths, and the beauty of the view (AGNM n.d.b.).

Furthermore, Querétaro was the religious and artistic center which Guanajuato never became. In Querétaro, for example, we find a good number of students registered. In addition, this is the only region which had such professions as sculptors, musicians, and painters (AGNM n.d.c.).

As a matter of fact, Querétaro was not the only city which played that role in the Bajío region. Zamora and Valladolid also served as

to the north and to the south. This includes essentially all the plains which display a "fractionation between hills or small, relatively recent volcanic massifs which have a common drainage level allowing changes of course for irrigation purposes" (Bataillon 1968: 167). This broad definition suits the Bajío more as a historical region.

[15] A very dramatic account of the consequences of the lack of drinking water and a description of the flood of 1790 may be seen in AGNM (n.d.a.).

centers of religion and education, though (at least to the end of the eighteenth century) in more modest proportions.

Medium-sized and smaller towns were scattered throughout the agricultural region, permitting the development of a complex network of roads. There were also some differences among the activities of towns; for example, manufacturing in San Miguel, Acámbaro, Celaya, and León, and distribution of local agricultural production in Silao, Irapuato, Salamanca, and Salvatierra. This urban complex may be explained by the degree of economic development achieved in this region in the eighteenth century.

In the beginning, the Guanajuato mines were the great spur to the region. Commercial agricultural centers developed around the mines, the production of which increased in proportion to the intensity of mining exploitation. These centers also produced cereals, which were needed to feed the workers and to cover requirements for the maintenance of draft animals. One must remember that the amalgamation process in the Guanajuato mines alone required 14,000 mules by the end of the eighteenth century (Wolf 1955: 183).

The land was very fertile[16] and there was exceptional potential for integrating regional irrigation systems using permanent waters (the Lerma River, freshwater lakes, and springs), old dam structures (Yuriria), and temporary waters (marshes, small lagoons, reservoirs, and bordering areas). This permitted the development of commercial agriculture and consolidation of the original small agricultural settlements. These small agricultural settlements had been founded to insure the provisioning of the Guanajuato mines, but at the end of the eighteenth century it may be said that they had already gone beyond that original market. In fact, the cereals produced in the region of Celaya and Salvatierra satisfied the regular demands of Mexico City. San Miguel el Grande was the principal supplier of meat, fats, and skins for markets as far away and specialized as the ports of Veracruz and Acapulco (Wolf 1955: 184).

Parallel with agriculture, sheep breeding developed in this region, finding a sure market in the numerous local wool workshops in operation. In 1793, in Querétaro alone, 1,500 textile workers were recorded as employed in 215 workshops (Wolf 1955: 183). Textile manufactures were soon augmented by cotton fabrics, using fiber transported from the Michoacán lowlands.

The cities of the Bajío appear to have achieved a significant degree of specialization in textile artisan activities, as is shown by the 1791

[16] Eric Wolf (1955), comparing figures gathered by H. G. Ward (1828), asserts that the Bajío's productivity exceeded that of the Valley of Mexico and the region of Cholula. Nevertheless, we lack precise analyses concerning this point.

censuses.[17] There are numerous recordings of *sarape* [blanket] weavers in San Miguel; shawlmakers, embroiderers, and cotton spinners and weavers in Querétaro; and carders and blanket makers in Celaya. In San Miguel, at the end of the eighteenth century, eighteen textile workshops were registered as Spanish-owned and 348 as native-owned.

Other more specialized manufacturing activities also developed in these cities. Belt making was to have a great success in San Miguel, Acámbaro, and Léon. The chamois skin industry of Celaya and the tanning industry of Querétaro were acknowledged everywhere. In relation to these activities, it should be noted that Mexico City alone paid 250,000 pesos annually in excise tax duties to cover its requirements for cordovans, sheepskins, tanned skins, and hair needed for the manufacture of coaches and saddles "for which an unlimited amount is spent by the many people traveling on horseback" (AGNM c.1790). This demand was met mainly by trade from Querétaro.

But there was a market for these manufactures in the region itself, constituted by the militia corps and by the hacienda peasants, who bought local textiles through the hacienda stores; these groups ensured the consumption of a significant part of Querétaro's textiles (Wolf 1955).

Furthermore, the various products of the region and the security of their local and extraregional markets opened great possibilities for the development of trade activities. Two principal groups operated in the region: the large merchants linked to the monopolists of Mexico City, who concentrated on imported products (mine implements, clothing, fabrics, Spanish brandy), and the lesser dealers, the so-called *tratantes* [traders] who, like the muleteers, apparently worked without any fixed abode. Nor must one forget, within the framework of trade operations, the groups of smugglers who controlled the trade of the Michoacán lowlands.

The development of these groups was to encourage mobility between regional frontiers; their principal outlets to the outside world were the large markets of San Juan de los Lagos and Saltillo (the open market of the north) and Mexico City.

The Bajío, as an economic region, thus operated in two ways. In relation to the north, it functioned as the monopolists of the center, i.e. buying raw materials and returning manufactured products. In

[17] I consulted the censuses (*padrones*) preserved in the Archivo General de la Nación, México, *Ramo de Padrones*, for the following localities: Querétaro (1778 and 1791a), Acámbaro (AGNM 1792i), Dolores (AGNM 1792j), Celaya (AGNM 1791c), San Miguel (AGNM 1792d), Irapuato (1792f), and Silao (1792h).

relation to the center (the capital of the viceroyalty), favored by its geographic location, it acted as the supplier of agricultural products and other raw materials while preserving a certain regional independence (Wolf 1955: 185ff.). In any case, what is important is that wealth returned to the region without being absorbed by Mexico City. At the end of the eighteenth century, the region was able to finance its own numerous sumptuous constructions; these have remained as testaments of the region's prosperity.

Inhabitants of the Bajío were much more creole and mestizo than the settlers of the center. The type of settlers in the Bajío therefore seemed to be much more individualistic and independent than those of other regions. The Guanajuato miners not only were the best-paid workers of New Spain, but until a very late date they benefited from a status of copartners in mining exploitation – at least as long as the system of *buscones* ["searchers"] lasted (see Branding i.p., third essay, "Guanajuato"). In agriculture that same attitude of independence was shown in the continued appearance of small, independent ranches on the large *haciendas*.

In order to emphasize the importance of this more urban type of settler, freer in his movement and employment, it is interesting to recall the comparison Eric Wolf made concerning the number of natives who were not established in towns, i.e. who were free of any link with traditional communities (laborers and vagabonds). These figures were registered in the various provinces of New Spain in the first years of the nineteenth century.[18] In the province of Guanajuato 76,852 "town" Indians were registered as against 164,879 "laborer and vagabond" Indians, while in the province of Puebla there were 459,360 "town" Indians and only 3,095 "laborers and vagabonds." This contrast explains many of the inequalities in the urban development of these regions.

Let me now attempt to point out some of the general characteristics of Bajío's urban development. My conclusions here, as in other parts of this work, are based on a sampling which I took from the Revillagigedo censuses (1791a, 1791b, 1791c). For this reason I do not regard these conclusions as definitive; they are subject to corrections which might arise from a complete analysis of the censuses.

An Example of Population Movement Within Regional Frontiers

The regional integration of the Bajío region, which may be explained by the numerous local markets and the manufacturing development

[18]   Wolf 1955: 191, Table entitled "Total number of individuals in the tax-paying class (1806)."

of the small towns, was revealed by the analysis of the Revillagigedo censuses. Included in this analysis were the local origins of outsiders who had settled in the cities of Querétaro, Celaya, San Miguel, Irapuato, Silao, and Dolores. The proportion of outsiders settling in those cities is small. The numerical impression indicates a relative immobility of population.[19]

But unquestionably the analysis of those origins turns out to be much more significant when translated to visual data (see Map 2). One should note, first, that movements of individuals occurred equally from smaller town to larger and vice versa. It was movement within a region. There was no preference for settling in larger towns. In this sense, the hierarchical ranking of the towns of this region was very much diluted. There is no similarity here to the tendency that I indicated for the city of Puebla in relation to its neighboring towns. In the Bajío, individuals from Querétaro settled in much smaller towns, like Celaya, and those coming from Guanajuato settled in Silao or Irapuato.

Movements, nevertheless, remained confined within the boundaries of the Bajío region. The population movement was expressed here by a kind of "network" which does not appear in any other region analyzed. The regional extensions of this zone also appear emphasized by analysis of origins: extensions in the direction of Guadelajara, in the direction of Zacatecas, and the traditional link of the Acámbaro region with the Toluca Valley were the only ones to cross regional boundaries.

A Region Which Creates and Accumulates Wealth

The development of the mining center of Guanajuato was a typical case of development caused by external demand. The European need for precious metals was the origin of most of the discovery, conquest, and colonization ventures of the mining centers of New Spain. These mining centers fulfilled the economic function of extracting precious metals, coining them, and sending them to Europe. Nevertheless, though a large part of the wealth extracted from the mining centers went abroad, it is also true that the mining regions received considerable investment which stimulated their general economic development.

[19] According to the sample (200 individuals per locality) the proportion of outsiders in the towns of the Bajío was as follows: Celaya, 8%; Querétaro, 5%; Guanajuato, 9%; Silao, 8%; Irapuato, 9%.

Let us remember that in the special case of Orizaba the same sample indicated 18 percent as outsiders.

In the case of Guanajuato, a considerable and constant investment was required at all times to open and deepen tunnels, drain the mines of water, build shafts, and install foundries and metal forges. Such capital investments required the creation of labor sources, assured a market for agricultural products, gave rise to the creation of local road networks, etc. That is to say they promoted the creation of an economic infrastructure which spurred the development of activities other than mining. In this sense, foreign demand stimulated regional development through the return of capital.

From the point of view of agricultural activities, we find a parallel phenomenon of accumulation and local reinvestment of wealth. This also promoted regional development and appears to have been one of the original and distinctive features of the Bajío's development.

The Bajío was a region with large agricultural properties interspersed or surrounded by small, independent ranches. Undoubtedly there were large landowners who absented themselves from their properties, leaving them in charge of overseers, and who established residence in Mexico City. These are well known. But there were even more landowners with not inconsiderable fortunes who, as owners of one or several haciendas in the region, settled in the provincial city of their jurisdiction. There they shared with the merchants the role of leaders of a local élite. The family connections between the hacienda owners of each jurisdiction and public and ecclesiastical administrators are evident from the first superficial examination of the censuses of those provincial cities. Let us quote just a few examples.

In the *villa* [chartered town] of Celaya, Joaquín Márquez appears as the owner of the haciendas of Plancarte and Dongui (AGNM 1791c).[20]

More indicative is the case of José Joaquín Laris, of Silao, who owned the following haciendas and ranches in the jurisdiction of that *villa*: Hacienda del Cubilete, Hacienda de Aguas Buenas, Hacienda de los Aguilares, Rancho de San Juan, Rancho de Charco Largo, Hacienda de Franco, Rancho del Muerto, Hacienda de Nápoles, Hacienda de Chichimequillas (AGNM 1791h).[21]

---

[20]   As there is no indication of the extent of the haciendas registered in the censuses, I thought their permanence in time would be a mark of their importance. In the *Diccionario geográfico, histórico y biográfico* of García Cubas (1891), that is to say, a century later than the information of the Revillagigedo censuses, the Hacienda de Plancarte was registered in the jurisdiction of Celaya with 245 inhabitants. The Dongui hacienda was registered as Hacienda de Dongú, with 109 inhabitants.

[21]   In 1891 the following are registered: Hacienda de Aguas Buenas with 440 inhabitants, Hacienda de los Aguilares with 207 inhabitants, Rancho de Charco Largo with 153 inhabitants, Hacienda de Franco with 373 inhabitants, Hacienda de Chichimequillas with 714 inhabitants; Rancho de San Juan (which appears as Hacienda de San Juan), number of inhabitants not indicated, and the Hacienda de Nápoles (Registered as Rancho de Nápoles) with 458 inhabitants.

In Irapuato one could cite the case of the family of Manuel Lanusa, administrator of the Royal Customs and his brother Ignacio, magistrate (*alcalde ordinario*) of Irapuato. Married to the sisters Josefa and Juana Caballero, they united in their name and as heirs of nobility the haciendas of Guadalupe, el Cuisillo, and San Juan (AGNM 1792h).[22]

In San Miguel el Grande, the Countess of Loxa lived near her hacienda, Alcocer (AGNM 1792f).

The large mining and merchant families – Lanzagorta, Septién, Obregón – had multiple properties in the Bajío region and chose the city of Guanajuato to establish their principal residence.[23]

The absenteeism of the agricultural landowners would have had, in the case of the Bajío, a regional significance. Agricultural capital does not appear to have left the region, in spite of the fact that (as in the case of the Guanajuato miners and merchants) the landowners maintained strong links of interest with Mexico City. The presence of rural landowners in the provincial cities promoted their urban growth. There are many cases known of personal financing of sumptuary constructions by rich landowners domiciled in provincial cities. The activities and wealth of these local landholders would merit deeper study.

The Bajío was, at the end of the eighteenth century, a region in which the creation and accumulation of wealth stimulated an urban development with characteristics which were peculiar to it and different from the other regions of New Spain.

GENERAL CONSIDERATIONS

The survey of the three examples of regional urban development I have presented here shows the integration of some of the regions which comprised the complex structure of New Spain at the end of the eighteenth century.

The roles played by the city in those regions are very diverse. The case of Puebla exemplifies a city which economically dominated its region. Administrative, religious, and educational functions, as well as industrial production and marketing, were centralized in Puebla. This centralization continued progressively to absorb the smaller urban centers surrounding it. The smaller urban centers deteriorated and gradually lost their autonomy. The case of Puebla contrasts with the situation of the cities of the Bajío. No single city in the Bajío played

[22] In 1891 only Hacienda de Guadalupe, with 818 inhabitants, is registered.
[23] See the excellent study *Three essays on Bourbon Mexico* (Branding i.p.) (particularly the second essay on merchants and miners).

a role to such a dominant point. Guanajuato was the region's richest city, the mining center; but the centers of religious and educational functions were Querétaro, Zamora, and Valladolid. Nor did any commercial centralization appear in the Bajío comparable to the situation in Puebla. Though Querétaro may have had a privileged position in the trade activity of the whole region, the roles played by the other cities (such as Guanajuato and Zamora) were no less important.

One fact appears to be definitive in the regional situation we are analyzing here. Puebla had lost the domination of its traditional agricultural markets. Within the respective regions, cereal-producing centers which were closer to their markets have been consolidated.

During the eighteenth century the Bajío was to serve as the "granary of New Spain," a role which Puebla retained for many years. Various situations result from this fact. In the Bajío the security of the agricultural market encouraged landholders to work their lands, to invest in irrigation works, and to watch over their possessions from near at hand. They lived in the small provincial towns of each juris-diction, promoting, in passing, the urban development of those small towns. In Puebla, on the contrary, farmers abandoned the running of their properties to third parties. Consequently, commercial agriculture was consolidated in the Bajío, whereas Puebla saw a revival of the traditional attitude of the landholder who contented himself with owning the land for the sake of ownership alone, establishing his residence in the large city, absenting himself from his haciendas.

Finally, I wish to point out how a position of urban predominance generally evoked a response from the small dependent towns. In order to defend itself, the small town sought to emphasize its deficiencies and to define them as a position of privilege. It converted its lack of development into an idyllic situation – a negative image of the large city – so as to attract the population which would help it arise from its stagnation. This is the eternal propaganda the small town makes for itself, in order to resist the effects of the large city:

. . . needing no recommendation for purposes of convincing one to settle there; for without stumbling upon the dangers of luxury, or begging for courteous behavior, its inhabitants manage to breathe air which is less polluted and which possesses higher qualities; in a country of beautiful vistas, beneficial to the health, temperate in its seasons, fertile in its fields, fair in its prices, comfortable in its lodgings, easy-going in its behavior, provided with all the necessities, resplendent in its shrines, pious in its thoughts, gentle in its people, moderate in its customs, and favored by a large attendance of other motives for providing oneself with a happy life and a successful end (AGNM 1792a).

APPENDIX: COMMENTS ON MAP 1 SOURCES

The methodological requirement demanding the use of a homogeneous source in the preparation of maps did not allow us to prepare a map based on population data of the cities of New Spain. The population censuses commissioned by the second Count of Revillagigedo, which are preserved in the Archivo Nacional de la Nación, unfortunately cover only a small part of the territory of New Spain. Other unpublished sources reviewed provided only isolated facts; consequently I could not use these either.

As I was not able to rely on population data of cities, I determined that the valuation of the economic flows received by a city could be taken as an index of its urban development. And the sources capable of providing that valuation were the registers of revenue from excise taxes.

Registers of excise taxes, however, are a difficult source to handle and subject to a good number of possible criticisms. Nevertheless, I found that this source expressed well on a map the problems I was dealing with concerning relationships between cities, so I decided to include it in this work. This note serves only to indicate some of the limitations presented by this source, so that they may be taken into consideration when reading the map.

The excise tax was the duty levied on every purchase and sales transaction carried out by Spaniards. An excise tax was paid for purchases of agricultural products, real estate, slaves, etc. In this sense, excise tax registers do not provide us with information on the municipal excise duties of each city. The source refers rather to the trade activities of the Spanish group, the most urbanized class of the colonial period.

There were many exceptions made in the payment of the excise tax duty. This must always be taken into account, especially since it was common for exemption from excise duty to be requested for agricultural products intended to supply the mining centers.

The most important limitation of this source is based on the fact that collection of the excise tax was generally made in a global manner. That is to say, by carrying out an *a priori* estimate of the amount of cereal, meat, manufactured goods, and other products to enter each city. Furthermore, this estimate was always made on the "normal prices" of each product in the various cities. On this estimate a (variable) percentage was calculated for the payment of excise duty. It is precisely this last figure which we are dealing with. Thus, we are not working on information of precise entries or actual purchase and sale activities which have taken place in each city. In this sense, the source only provides us with an approximate estimate of differences in rank between each of the cities.

For a large part of the colonial period, the collection of the excise duty was delegated to individuals who "leased" it; i.e. without receiving any salary, they reserved for themselves a certain part of the amounts collected. In exchange, they paid a "fixed rent," which was established in advance for each city. Around the second half of the eighteenth century this procedure was replaced by a system of appointing salaried tax collectors, dependent on the Royal Treasury. This novelty in the procedure of tax collection was reflected immediately by an increase in the amounts collected. Therefore, by the end of the century we can rely on registers which follow a uniform criterion, in addition to the fact that they report on a larger number of towns.

In spite of objections which may be made to using this source, the register I am dealing with provides a view of the whole: an estimate of proportion, of the probable relation which existed between the larger and smaller urban centers of New Spain. With this view of the whole I am able to attempt regional comparisons.

REFERENCES

AGNM (ARCHIVO GENERAL DE LA NACIÓN, MÉXICO)

n.d.a. "Compendiosa descripción de los particulares sucesos que muy amargamente ha llorado la muy opulenta ciudad de Guanajuato," by Francisco Xavier de Gastaneda, in *Historia*, volume 31, folios 162–165.

n.d.b. "Noticias de la ciudad de Querétaro," in *Historia*, volume 31, folios 157–159.

n.d.c. *Historia*, volume 73.

1778 "Padrón general de todas las personas de ambos sexos y de todos los estados, castas y edades empadronadas en la ciudad de Querétaro," in *Padrones*, volume 12.

1790 "Carta de Manuel Flon al Conde de Revillagigedo que acompaña una descripción del estado de las haciendas, ranchos, molinos y batanes del partido de Cholula, 1790," in *Ramo de intendentes*, volume 48.

c.1790 "Relación de los efectos y frutos sobre los cuales recae en México la contribución del derecho de Alcabala," in *Real Aduana*, volume 7, folios 69–84.

1791a "Padrón general de la ciudad de Santiago de Querétaro, pueblo y haciendas de su jurisdicción," in *Padrones*, volume 39.

1791b "Padrón general de la villa de Orizaba," in *Padrones*, volume 19.

1791c "Padrón militar de la ciudad de Celaya, pueblos, haciendas y ranchos de su jurisdicción," in *Padrones*, volume 26.

1791–1792 "Contestaciones habidas entre el virrey Revillagigedo y don Antonio Alzate sobre población y consumos 1691–1792," in *Historia*, volume 74, exp. 1.

1792a "Descripción de la villa de Carrión en el valle de Atlixco para la inteligencia de su padrón, 7 de febrero de 1792," by Ignacio Mayneiro, in *Padrones*, volume 25, folio 7.

1792b Padrón de familias españolas, castizas y mestizas de Oaxaca," in *Padrones*, volume 13.

1792c "Padrón general de españoles, castizos y mestizos perteneniente a la jurisdicción de la villa de Atlixco," in *Padrones*, volume 25.

1792d "Padrón militar de españoles, castizos y mestizos de la villa de San Miguel el Grande," in *Padrones*, volume 36.

1792e "Padrón militar de la ciudad de Lerma mandado formar por el Exmo. Sor. Conde de Revillagigedo," in *Padrones*, volume 12.

1792f "Padrón militar de la congregación de Irapuato," in *Padrones*, volume 37.

1792g "Padrón militar de españoles, castizos y mestizos de la ciudad de Santa Fe de Guanajuato," in *Padrones*, volumes 30–31.

1792h "Padrón militar de españoles, castizos y mestizos de la congregación de Silao, haciendas y ranchos de su jurisdicción," in *Padrones*, volume 42.

1792i   "Padrón militar del pueblo de Acámbaro, haciendas y ranchos de su jurisdicción," in *Padrones*, volume 23.
1792j   "Padrón militar del pueblo de Dolores, haciendas y ranchos de su jurisdicción," in *Padrones*, volume 24.
1792k   "Padrón. . .ciudad de Querétaro," in *Padrones*, volume 39.
1793   "Estado que a consecuencia de superior orden del Exmo. Sor. Virrey . . .se ha formado por la contaduría general de mi cargo. Direccíon de las reales rentas de alcabalas y pulques foráneos. México, 2 de agosto de 1793," in *Historia*, volume 76, exp. 20.

ARRONIZ, JOAQUÍN
1867   *Ensayo de una historia de Orizaba.* Mexico City: Imprenta de Aburto.

BATAILLON, CLAUDE
1968   *Las regiones geográficas en México.* Mexico City: Siglo XXI.

BAZANT, JAN
1964   Evolution of the textile industry of Puebla 1544–1845. *Comparative Studies in Society and History* 7 (1): 56–69. The Hague.

BORAH, WOODROW
1943   *Silk raising in colonial Mexico.* Berkeley: University of California Press.

BRANDING, DAVID A.
i.p.   *Miners and merchants, three essays on Bourbon Mexico 1763–1810.*

CHÁVEZ OROZCO, LUÍS, ENRIQUE FLORESCANO
1965   *Agricultura e industria textil de Veracruz siglo XIX.* Xalapa: Universidad Veracruzana.

CHEVALIER, FRANÇOIS
1957   *Significación social de la fundación de la Puebla de los Angeles.* Mexico City: Centro de Estudios Históricos de Puebla.

DE VILLASEÑOR Y SÁNCHEZ, JOSÉ ANTONIO
1746   *Teatro americano.* Mexico City.

FABIÁN Y FUERO, FRANCISCO
1770   *Colección de providencias diocesanas del obispado de la Puebla de los Angeles.* Puebla: Real Seminario Palafoxiano.

FLORESCANO, ENRIQUE
1968   "El camino México-Veracruz en la época colonial." Unpublished doctoral dissertation. Mexico City: El Colegio de México.
1969   *Precios del maíz y crisis agrícolas en México (1708–1810).* Mexico City: El Colegio de México.

FLORESCANO, ENRIQUE, JEAN MEYER
1971   *Estructuras y problemas agrarios de México, 1500–1821.* Mexico City: Sepsetentas.

GARCÍA CUBAS, ANTONIO
1888–1891   *Diccionario geográfico, histórico y biográfico de los Estados Unidos Mexicanos,* five volumes. Mexico City: Murguía and Señoría de Fomento.

MEYER, JEAN
1973   *Problemas campesionos y revueltas agrarias, 1821–1910.* Mexico City: Sepsetentas.

SECRETARÍA DE HACIENDA Y CRÉDITO
1944   "Noticias estadísticas de la intendencia de Puebla," in *Relaciones estadísticas de Nueva España de principios del siglo XIX.* Archivos

Históricos de Hacienda, volume three. Mexico City: Secretaría de Hacienda y Crédito Publico.

WARD, HENRY GEORGE
1828   *Mexico in 1827*, two volumes. London: H. Colburn.

WOLF, ERIC R.
1955   *The Mexico Bajío in the eighteenth century. An analysis of cultural integration.* Middle American Research Institute Publications 17. New Orleans: Tulane University.

Changing Urban Patterns: The Porteño *Case (1880–1910)*

JAMES R. SCOBIE

This paper provides a preliminary survey based on census data of changes occurring in the city of Buenos Aires from 1880 to 1910, with particular reference to settlement patterns, absorption and impact of immigration, and class composition. The demographic and physical growth of the city in the late nineteenth century raised land values and increased nonresidential uses of land in the downtown center, but these developments were not necessarily the result of change from a preindustrial to an industrial city. Immigrants contributed enormously to the city's commercial and early industrial expansion and underwrote the emergence of Argentina as a major power in Latin America. At the same time, these immigrants remained clustered in nationality groups far more than usually assumed in the *porteño* [of the port, hence Buenos Aires] case. The results of change were also felt on the political scene where the emergence of an urban, working, or lower-middle class can be identified and related to political changes in twentieth-century Argentina.

The municipal censuses of 1887, 1904, and 1909, and occasional references to the national censuses of 1869, 1895, and 1914, constitute the principal sources for this study (see *Censo* 1872, 1889, 1898, 1906, 1910, 1916–1917). In addition to the caution which must be exercised with such census data, considerable interpolation has been required because of changes in the boundaries of census districts between 1887 and 1904. Furthermore, the various groups and classifications, especially of industry and commerce, were also changed between the first and second municipal censuses, and the national censuses added still new categories. For general concepts and bibliography, I am particularly indebted to the recent work by Philip Hauser and Leo Schnore, *The study of urbanization* (1965).[1]

The outline of *porteño* development is well known to those familiar with the dramatic expansion of Latin American economies in the late nineteenth century. In Mexico, Brazil, Argentina, Venezuela, Peru, and Colombia, revolutions of varying magnitudes were brought about by capital, technology, and immigration. Nowhere was the impact more apparent or the change more extensive than in Argentina. In large measure, the prosperity and wealth for such change in Argentina came from the land and from the development of a cereal and livestock production which increased export from 58 million gold pesos in 1880 to 389 million by 1910. But this expansion in no way turned Argentina toward its rural areas. Instead, agricultural wealth was invested in urban development (in this connection see Scobie [1964]).

The city of Buenos Aires and the changes that took place within that sprawling metropolis created the base for an Argentine nation. In the thirty years from 1880 to 1910, the city grew from 300,000 to 1,200,000. The colonial, traditional *gran aldea* or large village, so well described by Lucio V. López (1960), disappeared with the new era. Some of the narrow streets and many of the low Spanish-style dwellings in the downtown area gave way to broad boulevards and granite and marble edifices. The modest, almost Spartan elite which had presided over the early formation of a nation surrendered its power to a new aristocracy characterized by wealth and Parisian customs. The Spanish and mestizo stock disappeared under an avalanche of south Europeans; 2,400,000 made their homes in Argentina in these thirty years, many in the city of Buenos Aires. What was behind these apparent changes? It may well be that the social scientist cannot replace the pictures of a changing society so eloquently painted by Florencio Sánchez (1906a, 1906b, 1907, 1952, 1966) or José Miró [Julián Martel] (1891). But he can give them further meaning and perhaps a new dimension by examining the statistics and the historical detail of those crucial years.

Settlement patterns in Buenos Aires from 1880 to 1910 supply a physical framework for an analysis of the city's development and provide some suggestive contrasts and similarities to models created by the sociologists. Ernest Burgess in 1923 advanced the hypothesis of concentric zones, with the central business district at the core surrounded in order by deteriorating residential, workingman–residential, and suburban–residential or commuter zones. In 1939 Homer Hoyt developed the so-called "sector" or "wedge" theory based on rent patterns, demonstrating considerable heterogeneity and

[1] Also helpful in this same context have been Morse (1965), Breese (1966), McKelvey (1963), Green (1962), Chombart de Lauwe (1952).

numerous subdivisions within each of the zones. About the same time Milla A. Alihan advanced a radial thesis – the spread of settlement along transport lines which radiate from the core. More recently, Leo Schnore has attempted to apply these hypotheses to the Latin American scene and develop therefrom general theories of urbanization (Hauser and Schnore 1965: 347–398). He accepts the *plaza-*centered pattern as basic to the Latin American experience and concludes that this is highly characteristic of the preindustrial city analyzed by Gideon Sjoberg (1960). Only in the contemporary period, with advances in transport technology and the development of industry, does he see a trend for higher socioeconomic classes to move from the core or *plaza* to the periphery of the city. Hypothesizing from the case of small towns in the United States, he suggests that such may be the general experience of the preindustrial city as it emerges into the industrial age.

How does the "traditional Latin American pattern" fit Buenos Aires during these thirty years when the *porteño* city had already shed its title of *gran aldea* and was beginning to experience limited industrialization along with enormous physical and commercial growth? Changes in population density give clear evidence of the spread of the city to outlying districts (see Table 1 and Figures 1 and 2). Comparison of the twelve census districts which formed the populated zone of the federal capital in 1904 and 1909 with the roughly equivalent

Table 1. City of Buenos Aires: population density per hectare

	1869	1887	Census district	1904	1909	Census district
South	3	9	(12)	43	151	(2)
	8	20	(19)	139	156	(3)
	19	88	(20)	157	168	(4)
West	80	221	(7)	291	302	(11)
	73	172	(9)			
	104	269	(8)	319	391	(10)
	23	73	(11)	227	252	(9)
	50	99	(10)	273	315	(8)
Core	143	213	(14)	232	249	(12)
	28	194	(16)			
	177	250	(2)	193	196	(13)
	225	297	(4)			
	165	327	(6)			
	215	258	(1)	227	208	(14)
	273	315	(3)			
	210	311	(5)			
	102	183	(13)	173	162	(20)
North	57	140	(15)	161	168	(19)
	2	16	(17)			

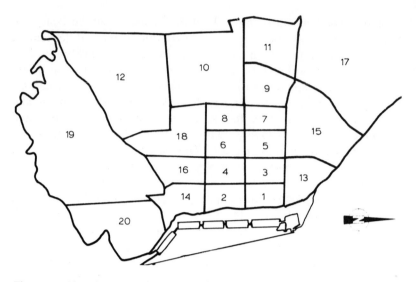

Figure 1.   City of Buenos Aires: census districts, 1887

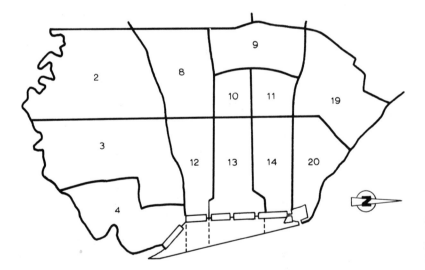

Figure 2.   City of Buenos Aires: census districts, 1904

areas from the 1869 and 1887 censuses shows a sharp increase in densities beyond the downtown core (defined as the four census districts of 1904, 12, 13, 14, and 20, which lay along the river front, bounded on the south by Garay and on the west and north by Entre Ríos and Callao and covering nearly five hundred blocks). Interestingly enough, in the same time span the very center of the downtown core, districts 13 and 14, lost inhabitants, suggesting that homes gradually gave way to commerce, government bureaucracy, and even industry.

Unfortunately, a study of how nonresidential uses of land displaced homes from the downtown core cannot be made solely on census data, because only the census of 1887 located commerce and industry by districts. Some suggestions can be made, however, based on the situation in 1887, which already evidenced considerable concentration of commerce, and from changes in property values between 1887 and 1909.

In 1887 all banks, money exchanges, auction houses, hotels, and virtually all export and import houses were located in districts 12, 13, 14, and 20 (1904 census districts will be used as the basis of comparison here throughout). Even more significantly, the center of the core, districts 13 and 14, contained 93 of the 98 commercial houses, with a declared capital of over 100,000 pesos and 80 percent by declared capital value, of the commercial establishments in the city. Each *barrio* or neighborhood had its own groceries, bakeries, and shops; but the large houses needed to locate themselves at the center of commercial activity. The pattern was thus established by 1887. In subsequent years, such concentration of commerce along the riverfront or in the downtown core undoubtedly continued and increased as the imports and exports of a booming agricultural economy expanded. Less clear was the tendency of Argentina's infant industries to seek a central location. In 1887, 54 percent of industry, by declared capital value, was situated in districts 13 and 14, and small household factories were fairly evenly distributed across the city. The building of several large flour mills on the riverfront certainly increased the industrial capital invested in the downtown area during the first years of the twentieth century. At the same time, however, space and public nuisance considerations encouraged other large industrial enterprises such as tanneries, breweries, and meat-packing plants to locate in the southern part of the city and to establish the first extension of Greater Buenos Aires, across the Riachuelo and beyond the southern boundary of the federal capital. Government administration, like commerce, was firmly situated in the downtown core in 1887 and subsequent developments merely accentuated this concentration. The Casa Rosada (executive office building), located at the east end of

the city's main *plaza*, the Plaza de Mayo, symbolized this centralization. The final acceptance of Buenos Aires as the national capital
in 1880, and the conscious efforts by the national and municipal
governments in the early years of the twentieth century to provide
increased services and supervision for their citizens, stimulated the
growth of a large bureaucracy. The geographical axis of government
power was completed within the downtown core in 1910 when the new
congress building was opened, one mile west of the Casa Rosada, and
linked to the executive by the broad and recently completed Avenida
de Mayo.

The pressures of such nonresidential use of land in the downtown
core receive confirmation in changing land values between 1887 and
1909. Land sales, reported by parish districts in 1887 and by census
districts in 1909, showed that values decreased in proportion to the
distance from the riverfront or the core. Significant in terms of the
direction of growth was the shift in value from south to north – from
the colonial and early national center of the city south of the Plaza
de Mayo, districts 12 and 13, to the locations north of the plaza in
districts 14 and 20. By 1909, land in district 14 sold for twice as much
a square meter as in district 13. By contrast, in 1887 the cost of land
in the two districts was roughly equal and, in the area closest to the
river, land was actually more expensive in section 13. Beyond the
downtown core, the same trend was taking place. As shown in the
figures, there was a marked difference between the jump in land values
in the 1909 districts, 9, 10, 11, and 19 (comparable to the Balvanera
and Pílar parishes of 1887), and the more modest advance of several
of the southern districts, e.g. 2, 3, 4, and 8 (which are comparable
to the San Cristóbal, Santa Lucía, and San Juan Evangelista parishes
of 1887).

Further evidence of the pressure of nonresidential uses in the core
was the development of slums. By the 1880's, the *conventillo* has
become a *porteño* institution. Enterprising landlords honeycombed old
buildings with tiny rooms, confident that the combination of high
density and high rents would pay handsome returns on even the most
expensive land. Although there was some decline between 1887 and
1904 in the percentage of population living in such slums, the four
downtown districts significantly contributed the highest percentages
in 1904; between 24 and 30 percent of each district's population lived
in *conventillos*, again underlining the pressure against normal
residential use of land in this area (Table 2).

As the city grew in these thirty years, therefore, population moved
north and west and in some degree abandoned the downtown core
(Figure 3). The tendency of wealthy families in the 1880's to move
out of the formerly prestigious locations along San Martín and Florida

Table 2. City of Buenos Aires: location of foreign population, 1909

	Census district	Italians	Spaniards	French-men	Germans Austrians	Russian Jews	Syrians
South	(2)	11,114	8,080	581	235	234	126
	(3)	18,333	**18,203**	**2,012**	873	378	**117**
	(4)	20,311	5,384	426	918	421	242
West	(11)	7,496	4,428	**919**	**470**	**4,275**	**234**
	(10)	13,352	5,400	695	202	604	8
	(9)	18,661	9,734	1,356	395	**2,182**	**93**
	(8)	21,202	8,263	970	326	328	75
Core	(12)	12,434	**16,448**	1,153	443	197	**70**
	(13)	6,539	**22,103**	2,118	630	191	**43**
	(14)	10,963	**13,469**	3,588	1,346	**1,833**	**376**
	(20)	8,394	**8,910**	2,234	556	206	**1,396**
North	(19)	17,506	8,450	1,615	768	513	33

(Concentrations above national average indicated in bold figures.)

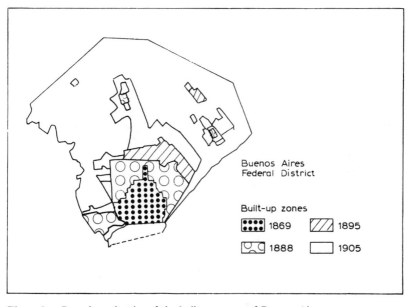

Figure 3.   Growth tendencies of the built-up zones of Buenos Aires
Source: Censo de la capital federal. . . de 1904 (n.d.: 465).

in the downtown core to new mansions on Santa Fe and Avenida Alvear perhaps gave an initial stimulus to the northward move. More significant, however, was the rapid expansion of the streetcar system, from 156 miles in 1890 to 403 miles by 1909. Its pattern of extension was west and north to the suburbs of Flores and Belgrano (incorporated in the federal capital in 1887), and its flow of passengers reflected the new-found facility for the shopkeeper, office worker, clerk, and even the artisan to live beyond the downtown core. The number of passengers rose from an annual total of 56 million in 1890 to 106 million in 1898 – the year electricity began to replace horses, making trips still faster and cheaper – to 282 million by 1909. Other public services had a similar effect advancing settlement and changing land values. Buenos Aires shifted from household wells and cisterns to a municipal water system in these thirty years. At the very start of service in 1887, 50 to 70 percent of the houses in the downtown core received running water. By 1904 almost every house in districts 12, 13, 14, and 20 was connected to the municipal system. Five years later, all houses in the western districts 9, 10, and 11 as well as in the downtown core and in the southern port area (districts 3 and 4) had running water, and facilities were being extended farther west and north. Telephones, gas lines, street paving, and lighting likewise expanded west and north. Although these technological improvements tended to follow rather than lead population, they nevertheless encouraged continued migration from the downtown core and rising land values, which in turn pushed the built-up areas of the federal district toward its northern and western boundaries.

Examination of the census data for these thirty years also provides interesting material on the vital question of absorption of the immigrant. Aside from the well-known concentration of Italians in the southern port area of La Boca and some localized settlements of Jews and Syrians, the literature on immigration has presented the foreigner in Buenos Aires – particularly the south European – as blending readily into his new environment and not isolating himself in nationality groups. Location of nationalities by census districts, however, tends to cast doubts on such generalizations.

The immigrant mass in the case of Buenos Aires was remarkable enough in size alone. In 1887, of a total city population of 433,375, 47 percent were Argentines and 53 percent were foreigners. Forty-five percent (or 92.5 percent of the Argentines) came from the city or province of Buenos Aires, demonstrating the relative absence of internal migration from the provinces. Of the total population, Italians accounted for 31 percent, Spaniards 9 percent, and Frenchmen 5 percent. By 1909, with a total population of 1,231,698, 54 percent were Argentines, 50 percent (once again 92.5 percent of the Argentines) came from the city or province of Buenos Aires, while Italians constituted 22 percent, Spaniards 14 percent, and French 2 percent of the total. Between 1887 and 1909, therefore, there had been a slight increase in the native-born population of the city, but foreigners still constituted nearly half of the total.

An analysis of the origins of population by census districts demonstrates that the highest concentrations of foreign-born population occurred in the downtown core. In district 13, 56 percent of the population in 1887 were foreigners, 53 percent in 1904, 52 percent in 1909 (in contrast with the city average of 46 percent in 1909). In district 14, the foreign-born percentage was 62 in 1887, 56 in 1904, and 62 in 1909. There were also several concentrations of national groups beyond the obvious Italian settlement in La Boca, numbering 20,000 in 1909, or 31 percent of that district's population. As shown in Table 2, the downtown core contributed particularly large concentrations of Spaniards and Frenchmen while relatively large settlements of Russian Jews appeared in districts 9, 11, and 14, and a nucleus of *turcos*, or Syrians, existed in district 20. Such fragmentary statistics suggest that the newest arrivals settled in the "deteriorating" (from a residential viewpoint) downtown core, many of them undoubtedly in *conventillos*, which accords with models and studies of United States immigration.[2] The fact, however, that 26 percent of the houses in district 13 and 16 percent in district 14 were owned by Spaniards (6 and 10 percent respectively for Frenchmen) indicates that all were not poverty-stricken.

Beyond the question of the immigrant's absorption lies another vast field for research and study – the impact of immigration on Argentine development. Although space precludes any adequate exploration of this theme, fragmentary data from the municipal censuses suggests some lines for exploration.

Argentina's great fortune lay in the age distribution of its immigrants, and a substantial part of that country's rapid economic advance in the late nineteenth century can be credited to the fact that other nations had paid for the unproductive early years of its new residents.[3] The Argentine population formed a normal demographic pyramid, heavily oriented toward the nonproductive years (under 15) in 1887. The foreign element, on the other hand, accounted for the great bulk of the male and female population over 20 and thus provided the largest share of the economically active members of society in Buenos Aires.

The impact of the new arrivals made itself most evident in commerce and industry. As indicated in Table 3, commercial and industrial development in the city was almost entirely dependent on foreign owners and heavily dependent on foreign labor. The industrial development in the city was almost entirely dependent between 1887 and

[2]   Hauser and Schnore (1965: 21) draw their conclusions from data in Hauser (1960); Handlin (1951, 1959); and Duncan and Duncan (1957). Also see McKelvey (1963: 66–67).
[3]   Thomas C. Cochran (1964: 44, 85) points out the value of this economic advantage in the U.S. experience.

Table 3.City of Buenos Aires: role of Argentines and foreigners in commerce and industry (percentage of total)

		Industrial establishments		Commercial establishments	
	Nationality	Ownership (%)	Labor force (%)	Ownership (%)	Labor force (%)
1887	Argentines	8	15		22
	Foreigners	92	85	not given	78
	Italians	58	53		39
	Spaniards	12	14		22
	Frenchmen	15	9		8
1909	Argentines	17	36	16	36
	Mixed	13			
	Foreigners	70	64	84	64
	Italians			38	
	Spaniards	Not divided by nationalities		22	
	Frenchmen			9	

1909; but in 1909, 84 percent of the commercial establishments and over 70 percent of the industrial concerns were still owned by foreign entrepreneurs, and foreigners composed 64 percent of the labor force in both commerce and industry.

Statistics suggest that immigration also contributed to developments in the related fields of fertility and education. By the end of the nineteenth century, Argentina no longer attracted a predominantly male inflow as had been the case earlier. Important for Argentine growth was the fact that the fertility of foreign women, particularly Italian women who constituted the largest group, was somewhat higher than that of Argentine women. The shift to larger families between 1887 and 1909, evident in Table 4, was due in part to aging of a population which at least on the Argentine side was comprised largely of children in 1887. At the same time, it should be noted that in 1887 marriages between Argentines had produced 3.2 births per marriage; between foreigners, 5.1 births. And in 1909, married Argentine women had an average of 3.9 children apiece while Italian women averaged 4.9 children.

Along with such obvious benefits from immigration, it was the foreign element which contributed the highest illiteracy rates within the city. Although comparative analysis is difficult because data is presented according to school districts which not only change from census to census but also differ substantially from census districts, some observations can be made. In 1887, 17 percent of Argentines in the city were illiterate as contrasted with 25 percent of foreigners. In 1909 the percentage of illiterates among Argentines had declined

Table 4. City of Buenos Aires: size of families, 1887 and 1909

Number of children in family	Families this size in 1887	Percent	Families this size in 1909	Percent
0	12,722	23.0	19,235	10.1
1	11,930	21.6	22,764	11.9
2	9,960	18.0	21,956	11.5
3	7,537	13.6	20,554	10.8
4	5,362	9.7	18,708	9.8
5	3,493	6.3	16,699	8.8
6	2,124	3.8	14,617	7.7
7	1,140	2.1	10,982	5.8
8	571	1.0	9,012	4.7
9	247	0.4	7,250	3.8
10 or more	165	0.3	14,174	7.4
Total number of married women	55,251		190,186	

to 13 but that for foreigners had risen to 29. Yet from both the 1887 and 1909 censuses, the fact emerges that the highest illiteracy among foreign groups did not occur in the downtown core, again raising a doubt as to whether it was the poorest and least educated foreigners who gathered in the downtown area. In 1887 illiteracy among foreigners in district 13 was 18 percent, while in district 14 it was 14 percent; these percentages were lower than the city average for foreigners and they sharply contrasted with the 34 percent in southwest district 2, 46 percent in southern district 4, or 38 percent in western district 9. In 1909 statistics were given only for the 6–14 age group. Illiteracy in this group in district 13 amounted to 15 percent, and in district 14 it was 19 percent; in the outlying districts 2, 4, and 10, the percentages were 34, 25, and 25 respectively. Although the evidence is far from conclusive, especially in view of superior school facilities and better attendance in the core, there seemed to be some tendency for the poorest-educated foreign elements to appear in the outlying areas of the city.

The city's class structure, as seen through census data and related to potential political power and interests, provides a final area for exploration in this article. Here it is particularly necessary to interpolate from various sections of the appropriate censuses (1887, 1904, 1909, and 1914) and to establish clear if arbitrary definitions. The objective is a statement of class composition for the city as a basis for suggesting possible socioeconomic interests and changes in political power. Because of an environment which placed women in a secondary role and provided them with no political power, the analysis

is restricted to men over fourteen years of age. The three class
groupings, although they have only marginal relation to the United
States experience, reflect contemporary Argentine values on class and
society: a "professional-administrative-owner class" which might
equal the upper and upper-middle category in the United States; a
"working class" which approximates the lower-middle class in the
United States; and a "day-laborer and servant class" which clearly
would be the lower class. Included in the first class are all professional
men, secondary and university students, landowners (*estancieros* and
hacendados), owners of industrial and commercial establishments,
and an arbitrary 10 percent of military and government personnel and
50 percent of those living on annuities. The "working class" is composed of farmers (*quinteros* and *agricultores*), employees in industry,
commerce, and transport, the remaining 90 percent of military and
government personnel, and the balance of pensioners. The "day-
laborer and servant class" includes cartmen, coachmen, and sailors
(the lowest laborers in the transport system), day laborers (*jornaleros*),
domestic servants, peddlers, and miscellaneous and unspecified
laborers.

As might be expected from the previous discussion, the foreign
element predominated in every class grouping, although the margin
declined in most categories as the period advanced (see Table 5).
The socioeconomic level represented by combined Argentine and
foreign totals indicated a moderate growth of the "professional-
administrative-owner class" from 27,000 in 1887 to 52,000 in 1904,
68,000 in 1909, and 82,000 in 1914 – but a slight decline in the relationship of this class to the total, from 15.5 percent in 1887 to 13
percent in 1914. The most striking fact which emerges from Argentine-
foreign totals is the large percentage of population which might be
considered as belonging to the "white-collar" and "blue-collar"
classes. Many worked with their hands, but they no longer could be
labeled in nineteenth-century Latin American terms as the "masses."
This "working class" already comprised half of the economically
active male population of the city in 1887 and rose through successive
booms to 60 percent in 1909. While extensive research on attitudes,
aspirations, and status of this "working class" will be required, it is
suggested that the size and possibly different values of such a
substantial portion of the urban population had enormous impact on
social and economic institutions in the city and eventually on political
structure. The lower class or "day-laborer and servant class," while
growing in absolute numbers, declined from 35 percent of the population in 1887 to 25 percent by 1909. The overall Argentine–foreign class
composition during these thirty years thus remained heavily oriented
toward a middle, albeit lower-middle, group.

Once again, only tentative suggestions can be made at this stage

Table 5. City of Buenos Aires: class composition, 1889 and 1914. Men over fourteen

		1887		1914	
		Argentine	*Foreign*	*Argentine*	*Foreign*
I.	Professional-Administrative-Owner Class	8,900	18,100	38,000	43,700
	Professionals	1,900	2,850	11,750	8,050
	Students	3,300	400	12,700	1,100
	Landowners	800	250	1,750	500
	Military	250	20	3,350	10
	Administrative – Government	550	380	3,650	1,140
	Owners – Industry	600	6,700	2,050	7,850
	Owners – Commerce	1,500	7,500	4,550	22,750
	Pensioners	—	—	1,200	2,300
II.	Working Class	20,400	66,400	121,200	203,900
	Medical – Assistants	—	—	650	850
	Military	2,050	200	3,300	100
	Employees – Government	4,750	3,400	32,900	10,200
	Agriculturists	150	1,700	1,400	4,900
	Employees – Industry	7,150	44,050	53,150	141,550
	Employees – Commerce	6,300	17,050	21,650	36,000
	Employees – Transport	—	—	6,950	8,000
	Pensioners	—	—	1,200	2,300
III.	Servant – day laborer class	11,600	49,300	37,600	178,600
	Transport laborers	2,100	5,150	6,200	23,150
	Day laborers	3,250	23,950	21,800	108,400
	Servants	2,350	6,800	250	2,200
	Peddlers	—	—	350	8,250
	Miscellaneous laborers	50	300	1,050	14,650
	Unspecified labor	3,850	13,100	7,950	21,950

concerning potential class interests and political power, and extended research into voting patterns, party loyalties, and political behavior will be needed to explore any such hypotheses. It appears that this class composition, adjusted to show Argentine men over the voting age of eighteen (see Table 6), may have strongly influenced the development of the Radical Party in the 1890's and the election of that party's candidate to the presidency in 1916. Until the Saenz Peña Law introduced the compulsory secret ballot in 1912, only a portion of the potential electorate even appeared on voter registration lists. The change which occurred in 1912 was dramatic, as shown in the differences between registration lists for the two presidential elections of 1910 and 1916. In 1909 the potential male electorate in the city numbered 149,000; yet only 70,000 appeared on the registration lists for 1910. In 1914 the potential electorate amounted to 156,000, and the registration lists for 1916 showed 165,000 voters.[4] It was undoubt-

[4] *Censo...Buenos Aires...1909* (1910: vol. 2, 380); *Censo nacional de 1914* (1916–1917: vol. 4, 479).

Table 6. City of Buenos Aires: class composition 1887, 1904, 1909, and 1914. Argentine men over eighteen (in thousands)

		1887		1904		1909		1914	
I.	Professional-Administrative-								
	Owner Class	8.0	25%	18.3	23%	24.7	16.5%	35.0	22.5%
	Students	2.4		5.0		5.9		9.7	
	Others	5.6		13.3		18.8		25.3	
II.	Working class	15.0	48%	47.2	58%	92.1	61.5%	92.4	59%
III.	Servant – day laborer class	8.5	27%	15.4	19%	32.6	22%	28.7	18.5%

The "Professional-Administrative-Owner Class," except for students, has been kept with the same figures as "Men over fourteen" classifications, on the assumption that this group was almost entirely older than eighteen. The "student," "working class," and "servant – day laborer class," groupings have each been reduced by the percentage, *14–18 age group, male.* Men over fourteen minus "professional."

edly the build-up in potential voters and finally in registered voters, particularly within the "working class," that strengthened and then brought to power a political movement oriented toward different values from those of the traditional conservative parties. An enfranchised body of which voters constituted 60 percent of the electorate (58 percent in 1904, 61.5 percent in 1909, and 59 percent in 1914), wage earners with aspirations to raise their socioeconomic status, provides interesting implications for further speculation. While there may not be indications that this class operated with defined or common interests, the successes and failures of the Radical Party must be weighed in view of the hopes and aspirations of these lower-middle groups. Substantial research will be needed before it can more than be suggested that the weakness of the Radical Party and the subsequent appeals by Perón may have had roots in a political movement which failed to consider effectively the desires and needs of its largest constituency – the "working class" of the cities.

The rapidity and extent of change in Buenos Aires in these thirty years from 1880 to 1910 provide a particularly appropriate laboratory for the social scientist who wishes to examine urbanization in an historical setting. This paper, based on an early stage of research, can only suggest some directions for further study and some hypotheses related to urbanization patterns in general and to Argentine development in particular.

The rise in land values and the invasion of the core area by non-residential users, the growth of the downtown slum and its occupancy by the newest arrivals to the city, and the outward spread from the center stimulated by technological advances in transportation – all experiences of other urban centers moving from the preindustrial into the industrial age – seem to be repeated also in Buenos Aires. What is not so clear in the Argentine case is the dependence on or relation of such phenomena of urbanization with pre- or postindustrialization. The process appears to be well underway by the census of 1887 when industry still played a minor role and when industrial establishments, rather than being centralized, were widely scattered throughout the city. Undoubtedly the subsequent growth of industry accelerated the process, but what the present article suggests is that the growth of commerce and bureaucracy were the most significant forces in establishing the *porteño* pattern of urbanization and that this pattern was remarkably similar to that of industrializing cities. This may also hold true for other cities in Latin America and in other areas in a preindustrial stage which nevertheless experience many of the same phenomena of urbanization as their counterparts in Western Europe and the United States. Commercial and bureaucratic expansion, therefore, may stimulate the same development as industrialization and result in similar patterns of urban growth.

Considerable research must be done on the absorption and impact of immigration in Buenos Aires. That the immigrant virtually built the city in a socioeconomic sense is undeniable. Certainly Argentina could not have made its forward leap from a second-rate Latin American nation in the 1870's to a significant power by 1910 had it not been for the contribution of immigrants, ages 15 to 50, throughout those thirty years. Commerce and Argentina's infant industries, almost all located in the city of Buenos Aires, depended on foreigners for 80 to 90 percent of their managerial and entrepreneurial abilities and to only a slightly lesser degree for their labor forces. Less easy to document are factors of absorption. The census data suggests, however, that there was far more grouping by nationalities than usually supposed.

Finally, the city of Buenos Aires in these years of change provides a significant departure from the nineteenth-century Latin American stereotype of a small elite class dependent solely on agriculture, mining, or commerce, and a mass of urban and rural poor. The largest *porteño* class is clearly that of the working man whose aspirations lie in the direction of socioeconomic improvement, education, and political power. The rest of Argentina may have more closely approximated the Latin American stereotype, but in Buenos Aires and other emerging, though far smaller, urban centers there existed sufficient lower-middle class elements to dominate the electorate. How much of twentieth-century Argentine political development can be explained on the basis of urban voter interests and groups will depend on further research, but the census material on class composition offers new possibilities for fruitful exploration.

REFERENCES

BREESE, GERALD
1966   *Urbanization in newly developing countries.* Englewood Cliffs, N.J.: Prentice-Hall.

Censo
1872   *Censo nacional de 1869.* Buenos Aires.
1889   *Censo general. . . de la ciudad de Buenos Aires. . . de 1887,* two volumes. Buenos Aires.
1898   *Censo nacional de 1895,* three volumes. Buenos Aires.
1906   *Censo general. . . de la ciudad de Buenos Aires. . . de 1904.* Buenos Aires.
1910   *Censo general. . . de la ciudad de Buenos Aires. . . de 1909,* three volumes. Buenos Aires.
1916–1917   *Censo nacional de 1914,* ten volumes. Buenos Aires.
n.d.   *Censo de la capital federal. . . de 1904.*

CHOMBART DE LAUWE, P. H.
1952   *Paris et l'agglomeration parisienne,* two volumes. Paris: Presses Universitaires de France.

COCHRAN, THOMAS C.
1964   *The inner revolution.* New York: Harper and Row.

DUNCAN, BEVERLY, OTIS D. DUNCAN
1957   *The Negro population of Chicago.* Chicago: University of Chicago Press.

GREEN, CONSTANCE M.
1962   *Washington, village and capital, 1800–1878.* Princeton: Princeton University Press.

HANDLIN, OSCAR
1951   *The uprooted.* Boston: Little, Brown.
1959   *The newcomers.* Cambridge, Mass.: Harvard University Press.

HAUSER, PHILIP
1960   *Population perspectives.* New Brunswick, N.J.: Rutgers University Press.

HAUSER, PHILIP, LEO SCHNORE
1965   "On the spatial structure of cities in the two Americas," in *The study of urbanization.* New York: John Wiley and Sons.

LÓPEZ, LUCIO V.
1960   *La gran aldea.* Buenos Aires.

MC KELVEY, BLAKE
1963   *The urbanization of America, 1860–1915.* New Brunswick, N.J.: Rutgers University Press.

MORSE, RICHARD M.
1965   Recent research on Latin American urbanization: a selective survey with commentary. *Latin American Research Review* (Fall): 35–74.

MIRÓ, JOSÉ [JULIÁN MARTEL]
1891   *La bolsa.* Buenos Aires.

PIERCE, BESSIE L.
1960   *A history of Chicago,* volume two: *From town to city, 1848–1871.* New York: Alfred Knopf.

SÁNCHEZ, FLORENCIO
1906a   *El conventillo.* Buenos Aires.
1906b   *El desalojo.* Buenos Aires.

1907 *Moneda falsa.* Buenos Aires.
1952 *Teatro completo.* Buenos Aires.
1966 *Los huertos, nuestros hijos.*
SCOBIE, JAMES R.
1964 *Revolution on the pampas: a social history of Argentine wheat, 1860–1910.* Austin: University of Texas Press.
SJOBERG, GIDEON
1960 *The preindustrial city: past and present.* Glencoe, Ill.: The Free Press.

Agricultural Development in the Process of Urbanization: Functions of Production, Population Patterns, and Urbanization

ROBERTO CORTÉS CONDE and
NANCY LÓPEZ DE NISNOVICH

The subject of the present study is the evolution of urban formations in Argentina and the way in which they were affected at different historical periods by the changes that took place in economic activity and exploitation of resources.[1]

It is important that the technological nature of production, i.e. the proportions in which resources were utilized in different cases, should be seen to have affected to a considerable degree – quite apart from geographical and natural conditions – the location of population and hence the formation of urban nuclei.

If we were to mark historical periods as bases of dominant economic activities, we could say that in general terms, up to 1930, there were at least three. The first is the colonial period up to the middle or end of the eighteenth century, in which the dominant industry was silver mining, centered on Potosí, the entire economic activity of the time being subordinated to it – agriculture and textiles in the northwest as well as livestock raising, in the coastal region. The second is the period of extensive livestock raising, beginning in the eighteenth century and reaching its peak during the first half of the nineteenth century. It originated way back on the cattle farms and was established definitively under the Buenos Aires regime. The ovine cycle that follows the Confederation and lasts up to the 1880's is a continuation of this period, although with different characteristics. The third and last period is that of the tremendous expansion in agriculture and in the production of purebred stocks, coinciding with the period of mass immigration and lasting till approximately 1930. The nature of the

---

[1] This appears paradoxical in a country like Argentina where production of old was substantially agro-pastoral, and orientated towards exportation. Although it was not always so, differences for other reasons were important.

technology of production and the location of resources in each case produced quite distinct effects on the patterns of population and urbanization. Although these effects have been put forward in another study (Cortés Conde 1968), we will briefly recall them here:

Silver mining, which at that time was intensive, required that everything connected with it should be localized in the place where the metal was found. The value of the mineral justified the high cost of transport, not only of the mineral but also of the labor force and the chattels and provisions necessary to its activity and sustenance. Thus an in-depth penetration of the country occurred (very different from agro-pastoral penetration which tends to cling to the coast); a cluster of villages lined the routes along which the transport of minerals, merchandise, and labor force was effected.

The silver crisis in the eighteenth century, and the break with Upper Peru which resulted from independence in the nineteenth century and cut off the commercial circuits of the north, brought about a profound disorientation of the oldest urban formation. A society ever more isolated, ruralized and sometimes self-sufficient, replaced – though not entirely – the ancient colonial urban splendor in what was now a recessive northwest Argentina. Peace and the hatred of disorder, Sarmiento's lamentations over barbarism, are expressions – with notorious political consequences – of a culture drawn from colonialism, *an urban culture not of the seaport but of the interior*, which Independence reduced to depression.

From the end of the eighteenth century, the development of extensive livestock raising in the coastal region successfully replaced the silver trade but did not contribute in any great measure to the peopling of the rural areas. And this not because of any perversity of the land proprietors, but because livestock raising for leather is not an intensive industry; it requires a very limited personnel at the place of origin of the material, and only a seasonal (and therefore itinerant) work force for a given type of skills (hence the legend of the gaucho). As a result, a predominantly masculine society was created which contributed to a low rate of material growth and to a demographic debilitation lasting for decades. The dearth of population, which was also the dearth of markets, limited urban development which was often represented by small, unstable military forts.[2]

Nevertheless this production which was in great measure self-transporting required, no doubt with a view to a market external to the region, logical outlets along the navigable rivers. There, in the anchorages, a work force began to gather for the tasks of storing,

[2]   On the other hand, neither was it a question of a large population living in subsistence conditions. Even the natives living on the other side of the frontier who made frequent incursions into the interior led a very precarious social existence.

distribution, and shipping, thus forming new nuclei with the characteristics of ports. The banks of the Parana, of the northern Rio de la Plata, and of the navigable sector of the Uruguay witnessed a fairly active interregional economic life. A network of city ports grew up which characterized Argentina in the first half of the nineteenth century.

During the period of agro-pastoral expansion (which is also that of mass immigration), production continued to be based on the exploitation of primary resources and to be orientated towards export. However, what did change was its technological nature. Agriculture, like the raising of purebred stock for beef, needed more labor. It also required that the labor force should reside near the source of supply (the land); otherwise it would be an uneconomical venture. This change in the proportion in which resources were used, and the demand for permanent settlers, had a variety of effects on the patterns of population and urbanization. While the settlement of population in extensive stock raising was orientated toward its markets, in the case of agriculture settlement tended to be orientated not only toward its markets but also towards its sources of supply (Perloff et al. 1960: 75, 111). This affected the urbanization pattern: in the first case, city ports predominated, and in the second, urban centers in the agricultural areas.

Our hypothesis is therefore that in the period of agricultural expansion (including purebred livestock raising), the outstanding characteristic is a *marked urban development in noncoastal agricultural areas*. This situation is in contrast to the previous period in which urban formations were predominantly coastal.

This contradicts the prevailing hypothesis that Argentina presents the paradox of a basically agrarian country with a predominantly seaport urbanism. We are not ignoring the urban development of the coastal region, which was considerable, nor that of Buenos Aires and Rosario, which was even more striking. But from a relative point of view, the area that exhibits the most impressive urban development in the period under consideration, 1870–1914, is the *noncoastal area*. The chief feature of urban development therefore, in our judgment, is the formation in rural areas of a constellation of populated centers employed in processing, distribution, commercialization, and transport of agricultural production, as well as in providing funds for agrarian enterprises, and goods and services to the people employed therein.

The urban growth was obscured by that of Buenos Aires, which in absolute terms never lost its first place. But in relative terms, it was still greater than that of Buenos Aires, at least in the period under consideration. This we shall shortly demonstrate (see Table 4). Urban development was in every way more considerable in the agricultural areas of the interior pampas than in the older coastal areas. This results from the simple fact that, independent of tenancy patterns, agricultural activity demands a higher proportion of labor at the place of origin of resources than does pastoral activity. An internal market was thus created, and various activities of an auxiliary nature connected with sustenance made their appearance. This led to the establishment of agricultural railway stations in places not far distant from where production occurred. On the one hand, transport facilities (the railway was an essential element) and, on the other, the distribution of income (better balanced in agriculture than in extensive livestock raising [Cortés Conde 1969] were factors which diminished transfer costs and produced new demands that tended to encourage the urban development of the area.

We might therefore reformulate the hypothesis as follows: A city-port pattern corresponds to extensive livestock raising, which dominated the first half of the nineteenth century, while agricultural development, without entirely abandoning the pattern of the city-port, acquires its characteristic features in urban development of the agricultural areas of the interior pampas. We agree that the old city-port pattern was not abandoned entirely, but even though it persisted it underwent change. The gravitational pull of the export trade meant that the difference between the ports of internal and external trade became steadily greater. In general, trade was more and more concentrated in a few ports, a process that favored the railway and gave preeminence to Buenos Aires.

To verify this hypothesis, we have undertaken to quantify certain indicators of urban development in a sample taken from two regions of the province of Buenos Aires: Coastal and Central. We believe that these two regions correspond internally to the conditions we are measuring. The first is very old and at every stage in its existence has had river ports, i.e. its economic life has always been linked to the river trade. This region which we call Coastal, North, or Littoral comprises the *partidos* [counties] of Ramallo, San Pedro, Zárate, San Nicolás, Baradero, San Antonio de Areco, and Exaltación de la Cruz (subdivided into Exaltación de la Cruz and Campana in 1895).

The *partidos* belonging to the second region have in common an absence of access to river navigation and to markets other than by land; we call this the Central Region, comprising the *partidos* of Bragado (from which was created General Viamonte in 1908), Las Flores, Azul (subdivided in 1881 into Azul and Olavarría, where General Lamadrid was created in 1890), 9 de Julio (subdivided into 9 de Julio and Pehuajó in 1895, and into 9 de Julio, Pehuajó, and Carlos Casares in 1914) and 25 de Mayo (subdivided into 25 de Mayo and Bolívar in 1881).

As we are concerned with growth tendencies, rather than with growth rate in absolute terms, we have translated the information in each case into index numbers, taking as a base the year in which the comparison begins. We wish to measure the evolution of the two regions from a given situation – that around 1870–1880. We take as the independent variable the modification in the structure of production, of which patterns of population and location are a dependent variable.

Urban development, to be measured by various indicators such as number of villages, population in the villages, and secondary and tertiary activities, is a dependent variable of these activities and of others that manifest themselves in the growth of trade, transport, and income, all of which are factors in the formation of urban nuclei.

Any definition of urban population according to the criteria in force today would seem to us to be totally irrelevant for the period under consideration. Therefore we have deliberately avoided the term "urban population" and speak of population in villages; a village we define as any agglomeration above the minimal level required for a certain interaction and discharging one of the following functions:

1. Distribution
2. Commercialization
3. Transport
4. Administration
5. Education

This definition is adopted, not because we consider these centers as truly urban, but because they are the nuclei that sooner or later with the passage of the years will constitute urban centers. What interests us is the way in which the pattern of urbanization characterizing the pampas today first came into being.

The tables indicate some of the results of our investigation and in large measure confirm our hypothesis.

Table 1, on agricultural-livestock production, shows the changes in the structure of production which have been taken as the independent variable in the process under study. A change in favor of agriculture and cattle and away from sheep was common to both regions, but the marked increase in wheat and in "new" cattle (purebred for meat production) was more pronounced in the Central Region. Furthermore, especially in regard to wheat, relative growth was greater in the Central Region (which previously was entirely pastoral) than on the coast.

As for the population of the *partidos* (a dependent variable), Table 2 shows a greater relative growth in the Central Region; after 1895 it became very much greater.

The increase in population of the rural areas took the form of a

Table 1. Production of wheat and maize, in thousands of tons, and of cattle and sheep, in thousands of heads and in index numbers, in the North and Central Regions (base 1881 = 100)

Region	Maize (tons)	Wheat (tons)	Sheep (head)	Cattle (head)
1881				
North	13	7	4,639	193
Central	125	18	6,333.5	645
	Index	Index	Index	Index
North	100	100	100	100
Central	100	100	100	100
1895				
North	119	30	1,566	162
Central	160	81.5	9,294	1,992
	Index	Index	Index	
North	915	428	34	83
Central	128	453	147	309
1914				
North	68	19	214	157
Central	291*	283	2,720	1,758
North	2,061	271	5	81
Central	233	1,572	43	272

Sources: Censo general de la provincia de Buenos Aires, octubre de 1881 (1883); *Segundo censo de la república de Argentina, mayo de 1895* (1898: vol. 3); and *Tercer censo nacional. . .junio de 1914* (1916–1917: vol. 5, 6).

* Only half of the 1914 production of the *partido* of General Viamonte is incorporated in the Central Region because we are not counting the production of that part which was formed from the *partido* of Lincoln, which is outside our sample. (See the *partidos* constituting each region in Table 2.)

considerable increase in the number of villages (Table 3). While in 1869 the *partidos* of our sample showed only 6 in the North Region and 5 in the Central, in 1881 there were 8 and 7 respectively, and in 1895 the Central had the greater number, 25 to the 16 of the North. By 1914 the Central had 42 as against 23 in the North, and the difference was accentuated still more at the peak of the agricultural expansion. While in the North the number of villages for 1924 had scarcely doubled that for 1914, in the Central it had trebled (48 in the North, 138 in the Central).

The increase of population living in villages (the second indicator we have selected for urban development) was even greater in the Central Region, not merely in relative but in absolute terms as well (Table 4). In 1869 the sample for the North showed 13,400 inhabitants and 7,900 for the Central. In 1914 there were 77,200 in the North and 123,500 in the Central, the latter achieving a still greater development by 1924, with 295,900 inhabitants as against 134,500 in the North. Both regions supported a population living in more or less similar villages

Table 2. Increase of population in the Littoral and Central *partidos*, in thousands of inhabitants (*N*) and in index numbers (base 1869 = 100)

	1869		1881		1895		1914		1924	
	N	Index	N	Index	N	Index	N	Index	N	Index
1. North Region										
Partidos	33.9	100	50.5	149	87.1	257	144	425	165.4	488
2. Central Region										
Partidos	33.6	100	68.3	203	129.7	386	254.5	757	336.3	1,001

1. The *partidos* of the North Region are:

1869, 1881	1895, 1914, 1924
Ramallo	Ramallo
San Pedro	San Pedro
Zárate	Zárate
San Nicolás	San Nicolás
Baradero	Baradero
San Antonio de Areco	San Antonio de Areco
Exaltación de la Cruz	Exaltación de la Cruz Campana

2. The *partidos* of the Central Region are:

1869	1881	1895	1914	1924
Bragado	Bragado	Bragado	Bragado	Bragado
			General	General
			Viamonte[a]	Viamonte
Las Flores	Las Flores	Las Flores	Las Flores	Las Flores
Azul	Azul	Azul	Azul	Azul
	Olavarría	Olavarría	Olavarría	Olavarría
		General	General	General
		Lamadrid[b]	Lamadrid	Lamadrid
9 de Julio	9 de Julio	9 de Julio	9 de Julio	9 de Julio
		Pehuajó	Pehuajó	Pehuajó
			Carlos Casares	Carlos Casares
25 de Mayo	25 de Mayo	25 de Mayo	25 de Mayo	25 de Mayo
	Bolívar	Bolívar	Bolívar	Bolívar

Sources: Primer censo de la república Argentina, septiembre de 1869 (1872); *Segundo censo. . . 1895* (1898: vol. 2); *Tercer censo. . . 1914* (1916–1917: vol 2); *Censo general . . . Buenos Aires. . . 1881* (1883); *Anuario estadístico de la provincia de Buenos Aires, 1924* (1926).

[a] The *partido* of General Viamonte was created in 1908 from part of the *partido* of Bragado (¼), 9 de Julio (¼), and Lincoln (½). Since the most important town, Los Toldos, is in great part situated in Bragado, we include in the region and add to Bragado the population of Los Toldos and half its rural population.

[b] The *partido* of General Lamadrid was created in 1890 from part of Olavarría, the part of Laprida (created in 1889) which was in Olavarría, and a very small part of Suárez. We consider the *partido* within the region as part of Azul.

Table 3. Increase in the number of villages in quantity and in index numbers (base 1969 = 100)

Region	1869		1881		1895[a]		1914[b]		1924	
	N	Index	N	Index	N	Index	N	Index	N	Index
North	6[1]	100	8[3]	133	16[5]	266	23[7]	383	48[9]	800
Central	5[2]	100	7[4]	140	25[6]	500	42[8]	820	138[10]	2,760

[1] The towns of the North Region in 1869, are: San Pedro, Zárate, San Nicolás, San Antonio de Areco, Baradero, and Capilla del Senor.

[2] The towns of the Central Region in 1869 are: Bragado, Las Flores, Azul, 9 de Julio, and 25 de Mayo.

[3] The towns of the North Region in 1881 are the six of 1869 plus Ramallo and Campana.

[4] The towns of the Central Region in 1881 are the five of 1869 plus Olavarría and Bolívar.

[5] The towns of the North Region in 1895 are, in addition to the eight of 1881: Gobernador Castro, Río Tala, Lima, General Rojo, Conesa, Pavón, Sánchez, and El Paraíso.

[6] The towns in the Central Region in 1895 are, in addition to the previous seven: Hinojo, Múñoz, Pourtalé, Rocha, Rosas, Chas, Pehuajó, Dennehy, French, Cambaceres, Carlos Casares, Passo, Chiclana, Castelli, Guanaco, Larrea, Olascoaga, and General Lamadrid.

[7] The towns of the North Region in 1914 are, in addition to the sixteen of 1895: Las Palmas, Alsina, Otamendi, Río Luján, Duggan, Vázquez, and Los Cardales.

[8] The towns of the Central Region in 1914 are, in addition to the previous twenty-five: Francisco Madero, Henderson, San Emilio, Los Toldos or General Viamonte, La Limpia, Máximo Fernández, Shaw, Parish, Cacharí, Pardo, Sierras Bayas, Sierra Chica, Ernestina, Islas, Mosconi, Del Valle, Norberto de la Reistra, and Colonia Nueva Plata. The village of Larrea no longer appears.

[9] The North Region towns in 1924 are, in addition to the previous twenty-three: Santa Lucía, Desvío Kilómetro 168, Desvío Kilómetro 180, Ingeniero Monetta, Oliveira César, Pérez Millan, Campos Salles, Erescano, Desvío Kilómetro 222, Atucha, El Tatú, Escalada, Villa Angus, Villa Fox, Villa Massone, Desvío Kilómetro 128, Ireneo Portela, Vagues, Villa Lia, Chenaut, Desvío Kilómetro 102, Diego Gaynor, Etchegoyen, Parada La Lata, and Parada Orlando.

[10] The towns of the Central Region in 1924 are, in addition to the previous forty-two: Warnes, General O'Brien, Irala, Asamblea, Mechita, Comodoro Py, Nieves, Miramonte, Chillar, Blancagrande, Santo Tomé, Oraogui, Moctezuma, Cerro Sotuyo, Durañona, (Olavarría) Espigas, Yturregui, Mapis, Recalde, Santa Luisa, Villa Mónica, Coronel Boerr, Villela, Plaza Monteor, La Naranja, Napp, Hale, J. F. Ibarra, La Torrecita or Urdampilleta, Paula, Pirovano, Unzué (Bolívar), Vallimanca, Araujo, Desvío Garbarini, Gob, Ugarte, Huetel, Lucas Monteverdi, Mamaguita, Durañona (25 de Mayo), Martín Berraondo, Ortiz de Rosas, Pedernales, Pueblitos, San Enrique, Valdés, Amelia, Bacacay, Corbett, Carlos Naón, Desvio Macoco, Dudignac, 12 de Octubre, El Jabalí, El Tejar, Fauzón, Gallo Llorente, La Niña or Aurora, Morea, Mulcchy, Neild, Norumbega, Patricios, Quiroga, Santos Unzué (9 de Julio), Albariño, Asturias, Capitán Castro, Coraceros, El Recado, Girondo, Herrera Vegas, Inocencio Sosa, La Cotorra, Larromendi, Magdala, María Lucila, Mones Cazón, Bellocq, Cadret, Centenario, Colonia Mauricio, Gobernador Arias, Hortensia, La Dorita, La Sofía, Mauricio Hiersch, Smith, Chancay, La Colina, Rulet, Las Martinetas, Lastra, Líbano, Pontaud, and Quilcó.

Sources: Primer censo...Argentina...1869 (1872); Segundo censo...Argentina.. .1895 (1898: vol. 2); Tercer censo...Argentina. ..1914 (1916–1917): vol. 4); Censo general de la provincia de Buenos Aires...1881 (1883); Anuario estadístico de la provincia de Buenos Aires, 1924 (1926); Salas (1907); Latzina (1891).

Table 4. Population growth in the villages of the North and Central Regions, and in the city of Buenos Aires; in thousands of inhabitants (N) and in index numbers (base $1869 = 100$)

	1869		1881		1885[b]		1914[c]		1924	
Regions[a]	N	Index	N	Index	N	Index	N	Index	N	Index
North	13.4	100	23.7	177	41.0	305	77.2	576	134.5	1,004
Central	7.9	100	16.8	213	41.0	506	123.5	1,563	295.9	3,745
Buenos Aires city	187.0	100	433.0	231	664.0	355	1,577.0	843	1,794.0[d]	959

Sources: Primer censo. . . Argentina. . . 1869 (1872); *Segundo censo. . . Argentina. . . 1895* (1898: vol. 2); *Tercer censo nacional. . . 1914* (1916–1917: vol. 4); *Censo general de la provincia de Buenos Aires. . . 1881* (1883); Salas (1907); Latzina (1891); *Anuario estadístico de la ciudad de Buenos Aires, 1915–1923* (1925).

[a] For the names of the villages in question see Table 3, notes.
[b] See note 1 of Table 3.
[c] See note 2 of Table 3.
[d] This figure is for 1923.

up to 1895, but from then on urbanization in the Central Region is much more marked. A surprising fact – one that emerges from the table of population in villages – is that increase of urban population in the Central Region is relatively still greater than in the city of Buenos Aires, especially after 1914.

The correlation of the increasing number of settlements with that of railway stations is fairly high. It is a well-known fact that railway stations were strategically placed for the distribution of production, men, and merchandise, and were therefore the bases of future urban settlements. For this reason, railway stations are the harbingers of *pueblos* in the nonfluvial region as well (see Table 5).

Urban development in the hitherto empty Central Region was closely linked to the commercialization and transport of the area's production, whereby also, towards the end of the century, it completely outclasses the more ancient and traditional North Region (see Table 6).

We have no data for a comparison with the period before 1885, i.e. before the railway, but such data would necessarily disclose a situation relatively unfavorable to the Central Region, and therefore a growth relatively still more considerable than that indicated by the table. Already in 1885 the volume of freight carried by the railway is much

[a] The data for 1895 are from the *Tercer censo nacional. . . 1914* (1916–1917) for the capitals of *partidos*, and from Latzina (1891), for the other villages.
[b] The *Tercer censo nacional. . . 1914* (1916–1917) covers only the population of the urban centers with 2,000 or more inhabitants. We have made an estimate of that of the other villages from the data of the *Anuario estadístico de la provincia de Buenos Aires, 1924* (1924).

Table 5. Increase in number of railway stations; number of stations (N) and index numbers (base 1885 = 100)

Regions	1885		1896		1914	
	N	Index	N	Index	N	Index
Coastal	5	100	22	440	35	700
Central	5	100	33	660	123	2,460

Sources: Memoria de la Dirección de Ferrocarriles... Buenos Aires, 1885 (1886); Estadística de los ferrocarriles en explotación, 1895 (1897); Estadística de los ferrocarriles en explotación 1914 (1920).

Table 6. Freight sent by rail and boat in the North Region and by rail in the Central Region, in thousands of tons and in index numbers (base 1896 = 100)

Region	1885		1896		1914	
	Tons	Index	Tons	Index	Tons	Index
North						
Rail	13.8		205.0		448.0	
Port[a]	45.6[b]		372.5[c]		663.5	
Total	—	10	577.5	100	1,111.5	193
Central	21.5	5	405.0	100	901.0	219

Sources: Memoria de la Dirección de Ferrocarriles de Buenos Aires, 1885 (1886); Estadística de los ferrocarriles en explotación, 1895 (1897), Estadística de los ferrocarriles en explotación 1914 (1920), Estadística del comercio... navegación... Argentina, 1881 (1882); Anuario de la Dirección General de Estadística, 1895 (1895: volume one); Anuario de la Dirección General de Estadística, 1914 (1915).

[a] These figures stand for tons loaded on sail and steam vessels sailing from the ports of Baradero, Campana, San Nicolás, San Pedro, and Zárate.
[b] This figure is for 1881.
[c] This figure is for 1895.

greater for the Central Region. However, if river transport is added, the Coastal Region in 1885 was still more important and had busier ports: 59.4 (thousands of tons) in the North against 21.5 (thousands of tons) in the Central Region. The total volume carried greatly increased towards 1896, though the part played by railway transport was more important, which shows that there is less difference in absolute volume. The North, however, was still ahead. It maintained its preeminence in absolute terms principally through being a terminal zone for despatch to a port,[3] and through receiving provisions from the other region. However, the relative growth in volume of transport, which gives us an idea of the interregional trade, was greater in the Central Region.

[3] Nevertheless, except for San Nicolás, in general there is no question of overseas ports.

Table 7. Freight dispatched in relation to freight received in 1914 (in thousands of tons)

Region	Freight dispatched	Freight received	Difference FD–FR
North	448	870	−432
Central	901	321	580

Source: Estadística de los ferrocarriles en explotación, 1914 (1920).

Table 8. Commerce: capital in circulation in the principal trades, in thousands of gold pesos and in index numbers (*N*) (base 1881 = 100)

Region	1881		1910	
	Gold pesos	Index	Gold pesos	Index
Coastal	2,519	100	20,510	814
Central	2,386	100	41,869	1,755

Commerce: Number of firms (N) and index numbers (base 1881 = 100)

	N	Index	N	Index
Coastal	682	100	1,795	263
Central	724	100	3,033	418

Average capital per firm (capital, number of firms) in thousands of gold pesos

Coastal	3.69	11.43
Central	3.30	13.80

Sources: Censo general de la provincia de Buenos Aires 1881 (1883); *Anuario oficial de la república de Argentina, 1912* (1912).

One circumstance should be underlined and can be inferred from Table 7: the balance of regional trade was positive for the Central Region and not for the North or Coastal Region. The latter is a receiving region, and the former a providing one. This is because in the North not all production goes to market outside the region; part is consumed, and that portion is greater than that which is provided to other regions (see Table 7).

Commercial activities in the new region, beginning in 1880 with a somewhat smaller volume of capital in circulation, in time doubled that of the older region. Although the number of businesses also increased, it did not do so to the same extent as the capital. Moreover, the volume of capital per business was greater in the Central Region (Table 8).

The same situation did not occur in industry, which for reasons connected with its dependence on overheads and its concern with preparing goods for export, maintained its preference for the Coastal

Table 9. Industries: capital in circulation in the principal industries, in thousands of gold pesos and in index numbers (base 1881 = 100)

Region	1881		1910	
	Gold pesos	Index	Gold pesos	Index
Coastal	5,131	100	23,085	449
Central	1,274	100	8,231	646

Industries and Number of firms (N) and index numbers (base 1881 = 100)

	N	Index	N	Index
Coastal	682	100	1,795	263
Central	724	100	3,033	418

Average capital per firm (capital, number of firms) in thousands of gold pesos

Coastal	20.04	24.77
Central	5.71	4.90

Sources: Censo general de la provincia de Buenos Aires. . . 1881 (1883); Anuario oficial de la República de Argentina, 1912 (1912).

Region (Table 9). Even if the number of business houses had increased more in the Central Region, capital was much more abundant in the Coastal Region. This is reflected in the capital coefficient per firm. The table also shows that while the principal industries existed in the Coastal Region, a quantity of smaller ones were dotted about the interior.

This is totally different from what occurred in commerce and is explained by the fact that while industry is more directed towards external markets (export, cold storage, milling) or to the luxury trade (refining of products for the internal market), commerce is directed towards the internal market, which in this case is that of the new urban centers in rural areas.

This pattern of industrial localization balanced, to a certain extent (though as we can see not completely), the major shift towards the Central Region.

The substantial increase in production and in trade is also visible in banking. The amount of deposits and the assets of the banks, which register very significant increases, was greater in the Central Region. We also see from Table 10 that, although banking activity in the new departments did not proceed at the vertiginous pace of Buenos Aires, it surpasses that of the provincial capital, La Plata. It is interesting to note that deposits increase more than assets, which reflects not only a major increase in wealth, but also a decrease in the promoting activity of the banks. In Buenos Aires (the federal capital), on the other hand, assets increased more than deposits in 1910.

Table 10. Deposits and bills of exchange, in thousands of gold pesos and in index numbers; and the deposit-asset relationship in the banks of the North and the Central Regions, in 1881 and in 1910 (base 1881 = 100)

| | Deposits | | | | Assets | | | | Deposits/ assets | |
| | 1881 | | 1910 | | 1881 | | 1910 | | | |
Region	Gold pesos	Index	Gold pesos	Index	Gold pesos	Index	Gold pesos	Index	1881	1910
North	1,244	100	6,030	485	1,675	100	5,073	303	74	119
Central	737	100	10,057	1,301	1,571	100	13,817	879	50	73
Buenos Aires City[a]	31,045	100	474,315	1,528	20,329	100	429,523	2,113	—	—
La Plata[b]	2,414	100	18,840	780	4,460	100	8,210	184	—	—

Sources: Memorial del Banco...Buenos Aires, 1881 (1882); *Anuario oficial de la República de Argentina, 1912* (1912); *Censo general ...ciudad de Buenos Aires, 1909* (1910: vol. 1); *Reseña estadística y descriptiva de La Plata* (1885).

[a] Since we lack figures for 1910, we have used those of 1909.
[b] Since we lack figures for 1881, we have used those of 1884.

The proportion of deposits to assets in 1881 favored assets, which betokens the financing of production and trade by the banks. The proportion, however, was much more favorable to the new region, where deposits represented 50 percent of the assets. In 1910 the situation changed and deposits were greater; in the Central Region they represented 73 percent of the assets, while in the established Coastal Region they were far above the assets (119 percent). If we consider that the rate of bank interest in Argentina was lower than the market rate, the producers of the older region must have been financing the development of the younger one.

This fact may have other meanings besides that of regional differences. If the volume of population is greater in one region than in another, if the structure of property and tenancy differs[4] which means a difference in the accessibility of credit, not only is one region financing the other, but one population group is financing another group, and this is important if the social characteristics of the two groups are not the same.[5]

The increase in the number of bank branches is another indicator of a different growth in the Central Region (Table 11): from 3 in 1881 to 20 in 1910 (as compared with the 12 attained by the North Region at this date).

[4] It seems fairly certain that small holdings were more prevalent in the North Region, while in the Central middle-sized and large properties predominated.
[5] That is to say, if in the first region small proprietors and tenants predominate and in the second big landowners. This should be the subject of another study.

Table 11. Branches of banks in the North and Central Regions, in numbers (N) and index numbers (base 1881 = 100)

	1881		1910	
Region	N	Index	N	Index
North	3	100	12	400
Central	3	100	20	667

Sources: *Memoria del Banco...Buenos Aires, 1881* (1882); *Anuario oficial... Argentina, 1912* (1912).

Within the change in the relative weight of the two regions, expressing itself in these indicators (commercial, industrial, and above all banking activities), there appears another phenomenon previously unknown in Argentina, which had been an exporting and agro-pastoral country: settlement of population in the agricultural areas and the widening of the home market, which favored not only the increase of population but also a more egalitarian distribution of income. This situation was the result of the new structure of production and the manpower, capital, and services required by it, as well as the sustenance of the population employed in this new structure. These demands, reinforced by a level of income previously unknown to the rural areas, implied habits and patterns of consumption which called forth new activities rooted in a new type of urban nucleus closely adapted to rural life. In these nuclei, the flow of income and cash, in general while not phenomenal, was considerable. This is one of the new phenomena generated by river-oriented Argentina.

REFERENCES

Anuario de la Dirección General de Estadística
   1895   *Anuario de la Dirección...1895.* Buenos Aires: Compañía Sudamericana de Billetes de Banco.
   1915   *Anuario de la Dirección...1914.* Buenos Aires: Compañía Sudamericana de Billetes de Banco.
Anuario estadístico de la ciudad de Buenos Aires
   1925   *Anuario estadistico de la ciudad...1915-1923.* Buenos Aires: Briozzo Hermanos.
Anuario estadístico de la provincia de Buenos Aires
   1926   *Anuario estadístico de la provincia...1924.* La Plata: Dirección General de Estadísticas de la Provincia de Buenos Aires.
Anuario oficial de la república Argentina
   1912   *Anuario oficial...1912.* Ministerios del Interior, Relaciones Exteriores y Agricultura. Buenos Aires: Centenario.

Censo general de la población, edificación, comercio, e industrias de la ciudad de Buenos Aires
1910 *Censo general de la población... 1909.* Buenos Aires: Compañia Sudamericana de Billetes de Banco.
Censo general de la provincia de Buenos Aires
1883 *Censo general de la provincia... octubre de 1881* (demográfico, agrícola, industrial, comercial, etc.). Buenos Aires: El Diario.

CORTÉS CONDE, ROBERTO
1968 "Tendencia en el crecimiento de la población urbana en la Argentina," in *Actas y Memorias del 37° Congreso de Americanistas.* Stuttgart.
1969 "Economías de exportación, El caso de la agricultura en la Argentina." (Mimeograph.) Buenos Aires: Seminarios CIE, ITDT.

Estadística del comercio exterior y de la navegación interior y exterior de la república Argentina
1882 *Estadística del comercio... 1881.* Buenos Aires: Klinzelfriss.
Estadística de los ferrocarriles en explotación
1897 *Estadística de los ferrocarriles... 1895.* Buenos Aires: Dirección de los Ferrocarriles Nacionales.
1920 *Estadística de los ferrocarriles... 1914.* Buenos Aires: Ministerio de Obras Públicas, Dirección General de Ferrocarriles.

LATZINA, FRANCISCO
1891 *Diccionario geográfico argentino.* Buenos Aires: Ramón Espesa.
Memoria de la Dirección de Ferrocarriles de la Provincia de Buenos Aires
1886 *Memoria de la Dirección... 1885.* Buenos Aires: Peusen.
Memoria del Banco de la Provincia de Buenos Aires
1882 *Memoria del Banco... 1881.* Buenos Aires: El Nacional.

PERLOFF, HARRY S. *et al.*
1960 *Regions, resources and economic growth.* Baltimore: Johns Hopkins Press.
Primer Censo de la república Argentina
1872 *Primer Censo... septiembre de 1869.* Buenos Aires: Del Porvenir.
Reseña estadística y descriptiva de La Plata
1885 *Reseña estadística... La Plata.* Buenos Aires: Oficina de Estadística General.

SALAS, CARLOS
1907 *Apuntes sobre la distribución de la población de la provincia de Buenos Aires.* La Plata: Dirección General Estadística de la Provincia de Buenos Aires.
Segundo censo de la república Argentina
1898 *Segundo censo... mayo de 1895.* Buenos Aires: Penitenciaría Nacional.
Tercer censo nacional
1916–1917 *Tercer censo nacional, junio de 1914.* Buenos Aires.

III. PART TWO

The ICAES Papers

The Selected Papers: An Overview

NORA SCOTT KINZER

The extraordinary sessions of Latin American urbanists held in Oshkosh, Wisconsin, and in Chicago in 1973 reiterated the similarities which preoccupy urbanists no matter what their academic persuasion. Anthropologist, sociologist, art historian, political scientist, or historian – all were struck by the relationship between papers and disciplines. At first glance, the titles seemed to represent an impossible hodge-podge of disparate themes. But, as the seminar progressed, it became quite obvious that "*plus ça change...*" was once more operative. Whether the protagonists be Aztec warriors (Edward Calnek, "The city-state in the Basin of Mexico: late pre-Hispanic period") or feuding Brazilian cattle barons (Spencer Leitman, "A Brazilian urban system in the nineteenth century: Pelotas and Rio de Janeiro"), the subject is still political intrigue and instability. Leitman's paper also deals with changing class structure, as does Sidney Markman's analysis of "The gridiron town plan and the caste system in colonial Central America."

The push and pull of migration and its influence on class structure was found in Markman's analysis of Central American towns and was a central theme of the case-study series presented at the seminar. Jorge Balán's paper, "Migrations and urbanization in Brazil, 1870–1930: a global interpretation," is closely linked to the Leitman paper.

Focusing primarily on contemporary society, Larissa Lomnitz's research on underemployed and incipient middle-class residents of a Mexico City slum ("The survival of the unfittest") is remarkably similar to Angelina Pollak-Eltz's data on rural and urban lower-class residents in different areas of Venezuela ("Household composition and mating patterns among lower-class Venezuelans") and to Margo Smith's analysis of Lima servants ("The female domestic servant and social change: Lima, Peru").

A careful reading of María-Pilar García and Rae Lesser Blumberg's "The unplanned ecology of a planned industrial city: the case of Ciudad Guayana, Venezuela," is essential to understand the frames of reference of the Lomnitz, Smith, and Pollak-Eltz papers. While these three case studies are microlevel, they do have further implication for macrostudy and, indeed, for policy implementation. The García-Blumberg paper shows how microstudies and research are ignored by the large-scale planners to the detriment of such planning.

Alex Stepick's contribution, "Values and migration decision making," is an attempt not only to conceptualize but also to empirically measure values and attitudes. Stepick's work is thus intertwined with the migration studies of Smith, Lomnitz, Pollak-Eltz, and García-Blumberg.

While these papers are valuable contributions in themselves, it is really only as a whole that their significance can be measured. As teachers we exhort our students to look at "the whole picture"; as researchers we often ignore our own advice; and as planners we all too often bow to expediency. We do need to maintain a historical perspective, but we should be ready to hearken to the art historian, the anthropologist working in the field, and the quantitatively oriented sociologist. Not having done so and continuing not to do so, why is it that we are forever bewildered at our failures?

In conferences such as these, the historian speaks to the anthropologist and political scientist. We all nod our heads in agreement and commiserate with each other. The question is now not one of philosophical agreement but rather of practical policy. Who listens to all of us?

The City-State in the Basin of Mexico: Late Pre-Hispanic Period

EDWARD E. CALNEK

The political system which developed in the Basin of Mexico during the Late post-Classic period (c. 1200–1521 A.D.) was based on the city-state as its basic unit of organization. Even the Aztec capital, Tenochtitlán, was still only one among approximately sixty similarly organized city-states, at the same time that it functioned as the capital of a conquest empire which included several hundred thousand square kilometers of territory and populations numbering in the millions (Barlow 1949: Sanders and Price 1968: 151–152). Each city-state was ruled by its own *tlatoani* [king or ruler], who was selected from among the members of a hereditary ruling dynasty. Local governmental systems were largely staffed by other high-ranking members of the dynastic group.

Broader forms of political organization – coalitions and empires – were commonly held together by simple bilateral or multilateral treaty agreements which specified the rights and obligations of each of the parties. The famous Triple Alliance (Tenochtitlán, Texcoco, and Tlacopan) functioned on the basis of consensual agreement among the three monarchs. (A nominal parity between the three rulers was asserted up to the time of the Conquest. By 1519, nonetheless, the rulers of Texcoco and Tlacopán usually *wanted to do* whatever was proposed by Motecuhzoma of Tenochtitlán.) A similar arrangement existed within the Chalcan confederacy, and was fairly common elsewhere in Mesoamerica. Conquest armies, of course, were based on nonsymmetrical agreements. Subject states paid tribute, provided military and labor support, and met other obligations as specified in formal treaties negotiated following their defeat.

From a strictly legalistic standpoint, the full responsibility for carrying out treaty provisions devolved on local kings, who otherwise retained a nearly complete autonomy in the administration of their own states. Indeed, the imperial centers rarely intervened in purely local matters, preferring instead a policy of "indirect rule," as discussed below. The most significant advantage to this system was simply that traditional institutions – most notably, the quasi-sacred bond held to exist between a reigning dynasty (but not individual kings!) and its own lands and people – were not openly attacked or violated. A particular monarch might be executed, exiled, or simply deposed. Even when a military governor (*cuauhtlatoani*) was appointed, however, this was commonly conceived as a holding action, since local dynasties were usually restored in the course of a generation or two.

An important disadvantage of the system – at least as perceived from the imperial centers – was that local sovereigns retained ultimate control over their own manpower and material resources, which could be easily turned against their masters when a favorable situation arose. The negative consequences of "indirect rule," nonetheless, were strongly marked only during the thirteenth and fourteenth centuries, when tiny "conquest empires" followed each other with bewildering rapidity. By the early fifteenth century a single city-state, Azcapotzalco, had secured a dominant position within the Basin as a whole, and was able to extend its conquests for a considerable distance to the north and west (Barlow 1949: 33ff.). The empire of Azcapotzalco succumbed very quickly to a crisis over the dynastic succession, however (de Alva Ixtlilxochitl 1952: vol. 2, pp. 107ff.). Its collapse was quickly followed by the rise of the Triple Alliance, which endured up to the time of the Spanish invasion.

What is chiefly remarkable about this process is that the imperial capitals did not attempt to resolve the problem of control by simply annexing and abolishing petty kingdoms that fell under their control. On the contrary, strenuous efforts were made to protect and even strengthen local monarchies, by arranging interdynastic marriages, and thereafter *protecting* local kings against internal opposition. The Tenochcan monarchy, for example, was founded by the son of an Aztec nobleman and a princess from Colhuacan. His son married a princess from Azcapotzalco. The birth of a male child, Chimalpopoca, was followed almost immediately by a relaxation of tribute obligations and a variety of other benefits (Duran 1951: vol. 1, pp. 47ff.). These and similar strategies did not invariably guarantee the loyalty of subject states, but did greatly facilitate working relationships between superordinate and subordinate dynasties.

The dynamic qualities of the political system were closely linked to the fact that conquered states were expected to support their masters in subsequent military campaigns. Because governmental systems were encapsulated within very small-scale territorial boundaries, the result was that even the most populous capital cities were rapidly outnumbered by their subjects; they could retain internal control and continue external policies of military expansion only insofar as they enjoyed a more or less enthusiastic support from the same communities that would have benefited most immediately from their defeat. This is to say that conquered states found themselves in the anomalous position of policing each other, as well as making up the greater part of the imperial armies.

During the early period, intercity struggles were commonly fought out first through the manipulation of cross-cutting loyalties and interests, long before armies of conquest took to the field. The great Tezozomoc of Azcapotzalco was a master political strategist, who resorted to open warfare only when the outcome was virtually assured. In addition to political marriages, the available strategies included systematic attempts to detach the principal allies or subjects of powerful opponents by what amounted to outright bribery, as well as promises of "better terms" to city-states which defected to the opposing side. The long contest for supremacy between Azcapotzalco and Texcoco began with the latter in a strong military position at the beginning of the fifteenth century. In the space of two decades, nonetheless, the Texcocan ruler, Ixtlilxochitl, found himself stripped of supporters, and was easily defeated by Tezozomoc's armies. The instability of the political system is strikingly illustrated by the very rapid collapse of Azcapotzalco's empire under Tezozomoc's successor, Maxtla, who quickly alienated his chief allies, including the Aztecs, and was forced into exile within two or three years of the beginning of his reign (de Alva Ixtlilxochitl 1952: vol. 2, ch. 14–31).

We are plainly considering a highly unstable balance-of-power mechanism at this point. The most potent imperial centers found themselves the principal targets of countercoalitions and internal rebellions. No attempt was made, as noted earlier, to rationalize this situation either by dissolving local city-states as autonomous governmental systems, or by imposing some form of direct administration on conquered territories. Whether the perpetuation of an "anachronistic" system of this type indicates the "primitive" level of political organization achieved by the ancient Mesoamericans, as supposed by many recent writers, is by no means certain, however. The Aztec empire clearly lacked the well-defined hierarchy of authority reported from the Andean region (Katz 1972: 314–317), but, as Adams (1966: 159ff.) points out, it was relatively stable, and must therefore be regarded as highly successful. Indeed, it is far from clear that the imposition of provincial governors is more effective than indirect rule, as the former can offer an extremely convenient target for communities bent on rebellion. The fact that rebellions occurred almost continuously within the Aztec empire offers no strong counterargument, as individual rebellions were rapidly and often brutally suppressed. In addition, it can be noted that, if the localities actually in rebellion at any specific point in time are plotted on a map of the empire as a whole, it is clear that genuinely large-scale, as opposed to localized, antiimperial coalitions *never* developed. It must be remembered in this context that the empire eventually included more than five hundred towns and cities (*Epistolario de Nueva España* [*ENE*] 1939–1942: vol. 14, pp. 118–122). The fact that a half dozen were likely to make an attempt to regain independence from time to time is less important than the fact that very few of their neighbors were willing to risk the consequences of an unsuccessful uprising.

By the late fifteenth century the Triple Alliance was able to mobilize, equip, and support armies numbering in the tens of thousands for periods of several months at a time. The fact that troops supplied by subject states shared in the spoils of conquest contributed to the high morale, and excellent fighting qualities, of armies recruited mainly from subject peoples.

In considering the evolution of the city-state system within the Basin of Mexico, therefore, it is useful to recognize at least three major phases of development. The first, spanning the late thirteenth and early fourteenth centuries, was devoted largely to the recolonization of an area that had been underdeveloped, underpopulated, and politically marginal, from the time of Teotihuacán's fall in about A.D. 750 until it was reopened to settlement following the collapse of the Toltecs in the late twelfth century A.D. (Parsons 1970). Virtually all of the city-states in existence at the time of the Spanish conquest were founded during this period, and they remained remarkably stable with respect to territorial frontiers thereafter. The second phase was dominated by an intense struggle for hegemony over the Basin as a whole, which culminated first in Azcapotzalco's short-lived empire in the early fifteenth century, and that of the Triple Alliance, ultimately dominated by Tenochtitlán. A relatively firm control over the entire Basin was completed with the fall of Chalco in about 1463. The great importance of this event is reflected in maps of the empire which show it doubling or tripling in extent between that time and about 1500 (see Kelly and Palerm 1952). The third phase, corresponding roughly to the period 1463–1519, included a final consolidation of political control within the Basin, and the creation of a variety of somewhat distinct control mechanisms outside.

It must be emphasized that the three phases outlined here should not be taken entirely literally, as there was a good deal of overlapping of processes which were sometimes initiated during one phase, but reached their culmination in the next. The process of internal consolidation during the last phase was begun with the widespread occurrence of interdynastic marriages in the first and second, which had the long-term effect of linking aristocratic groups throughout the Basin into a complex web of kinship affiliations, which, in turn, laid a basis for their gradual emergence as a single ruling class much later on. When the Tenochcan emperors demanded that subject rulers spend a part of each year residing at the imperial court, they were commonly welcoming close kinsmen, who were members of the royal dynasty of Tenochtitlán, as well as members of local ruling elites. In the late fifteenth and early sixteenth centuries, the links between originally separate royal dynasties had become so close that the rulers of Ixtapalapa, Xochimilco, Azcapotzalco, and several other prominent city-states were legitimate candidates for the Tenochcan throne, and sometimes combined high rank in the Aztec hierarchy with the title of *tlatoani* elsewhere. Cuitlahuac, for example, was king of Iztapalapa, but also a high-ranking commander of the Tenochcan armies, and the main leader of the opposition to the Spanish before he succeeded Motecuhzoma Xocoyotzin to the throne in 1520 (Tezozomoc 1949: 159–160). Among the lower nobility, the right to share in tribute redistributions and other benefits created a vested interest which transcended local boundaries and hinged instead on the perpetuation of the imperialist status quo.

Viewed from this standpoint, the formal survival or the city-state system as the *legal* framework for larger forms of political organization is less significant than the de facto consolidation of dynastic interests, and their expression in the imperial system. The growing importance of the imperial courts as focal points for the gradual coalescence of originally separate dynastic groups should not be underestimated. Although local noblemen were nominally subjects only of their own *tlatoani*, and only through this relationship of the emperors, cross-cutting kinship affiliations tended to override this distinction. In addition, the emperors often distributed their largesse directly to individuals brought into their presence, rather than to local kings, who might then redistribute large quantities of goods to their own followers. The fact is that members of the nobility throughout the Basin of Mexico derived important advantages from *both* affiliations.

That the peoples of Central Mexico did not lack organizational skills, but merely chose not to apply them directly within certain political domains, is demonstrated by the system for collecting tribute. The scale of this enterprise is shown both by the number of politically distinct units (500–600) which had to be managed, and the sheer quantities of food-stuffs and goods to be collected, stored, transported, and disbursed. Initially, the responsibility for meeting tribute obligations appears to have devolved solely on local monarchs. By the mid-fifteenth century, however, the Tenochca began to appoint *calpixque* [stewards] to supervise collections at the capital towns of all major provinces.

By the time of the Spanish conquest, the empire had been divided into approximately thirty-eight large tributary provinces, each of which was under the authority of a *hueilcalpixqui* [great steward], who resided in one of the more important local towns or cities. The *hueicalpixqui* was directly subordinate to the *petlacalcatl* in Tenoch-titlán, and supervised the activities of lower ranking *calpixque* who were assigned to progressively smaller territories on the basis of convenience, rather than in strict accordance with preexisting political boundaries (Calnek 1966). This is to say that, while local sovereigns retained civil authority in most matters, they were almost entirely bypassed by bureaucratic functionaries where the fiscal interests of the imperial centers were involved. While the extent and significance of these developments require further investigation, it would seem that the evolution of the tribute system tended to erode the *actual* powers of local monarchs, without violating the concept of local autonomy in any overt way. At the least, the creation of a hierarchically orga-nized *calpixque* system guaranteed an imperial *presence* in the most remote areas and also established permanent lines of communication between the center and even the most distant provinces.

We must conclude from this that the Aztecs were familiar with the virtues of rational hierarchical organization, but applied their skills only to domains where vital economic interests were involved. Within the strictly political domain, entirely different strategies were preferred.

In the course of this discussion it has been possible to move from the seemingly anarchic constitution of autonomous city-states created during the thirteenth century, to the strongly centralized imperialist systems which developed in the fifteenth and early sixteenth centuries. The latter maintained an appearance of local autonomy, while at the same time creating a community of interests among aristocratic elites within the Basin of Mexico. The tribute system, in its later forms, provided an efficient mechanism for maintaining contact with, if not overtly dominating, literally hundreds of petty monarchies in other regions. Owing to the brevity of this presentation it has not been possible to explore other important and directly relevant develop-ments in the economic sphere – most notably, the growing importance of craft production and long-distance trade, or to consider the political importance of such systems as the Triple Alliance, which were at least in part designed to stabilize the position of each of its members against purely internal threats. The *theoretical* instability of city-state systems unquestionably stimulated the development of political stra-tegies designed to minimize centrifugal tendencies. The internal logic of the system, when viewed over relatively long periods of time, was plainly in the direction of a strong consolidation of interests, which was sufficient to erode, if not overcome, divisive factors inherent in the formal properties of the city-state system.

The intention here has been to emphasize certain features of the political system which are only implicit in the basic historical sources, that quite often present official ideologies rather than the realities of social development. It is one thing to note that subject rulers were *obliged* to participate in the life of the imperial court. This assumes an entirely different meaning once we note that the rulers in question were likely to be sons, grandsons, cousins, nephews, or even brothers of the reigning emperor. The degree of stability achieved by the system must be evaluated in relation to its line of development over time. This was plainly in the direction of greater centralization and increasing stability, with progressively larger types of organization evolving in each phase. A similar line of analysis could be easily applied to economic organization, where the tendency was from simple reliance on relatively self-sufficient agricultural systems, to an extremely complex interdependency between urban centers and their rural support areas. The most highly developed agricultural systems were, by the time of the Conquest, producing for urban markets, with the result that even peasant farmers were occupational *specialists*. It should also be clear that future investigations must be explicitly diachronic rather than synchronic, as social institutions were continuously *becoming* something else, while sometimes retaining the same outward forms. It is impossible to describe the social organization of Tenochtitlán, Texcoco, or the Basin of Mexico as a whole outside this framework, without creating serious distortions of the historical reality. Kingship meant one thing in the early fourteenth century and something entirely different in 1519. Synchronic analysis, if of any value at all, is most useful in establishing arbitrary basepoints from which to measure change, rather than as an objective description of social reality in itself.

REFERENCES

ADAMS, R. MC C
   1966   *The evolution of urban society: early Mesopotamia and preHispanic Mexico.* Chicago: Aldine.
BARLOW, R. F.
   1949   *The extent of the empire of the Culhua Mexica.* Ibero-Americana: 28. Berkeley and Los Angeles: University of California Press.
BERLIN, H., *editor and translator*
   1948   *Anales de Tlatelolco: fuentes para la historia de México.* Mexico City: Antigua Libreria Robredo de José Porrua e Hijoa.

470 EDWARD E. CALNEK

CALNEK, EDWARD E.
  1966 "The Aztec imperial bureaucracy." Paper read at the Sixty-fifth
        Annual Meeting of the American Anthropological Association,
        Pittsburgh.
DE ALVA IXTLILXOCHITL, FERNANDO
  1952 *Obras historicas*, two volumes. Edited by Alfredo Chavero. Mexico
        City: Editorial Nacional.
DURAN, DIEGO
  1951 [1867–1880] *Historia de las Indias de Nueva España y Islas de
        Tierra Firme*, two volumes. Mexico: Atlas.
Epistolario de Nueva España (ENE)
  1939–1942 Sixteen volumes. Edited by F. del Paso y Troncoso. Mexico
        City.
KATZ, F.
  1972 *The ancient American civilizations*. New York: Praeger.
KELLY, I., A. PALERM
  1952 *The Tajin Totonac*, part one. Smithsonian Institution, Institute of
        Social Anthropology, Publication 13. Washington.
PARSONS, J. R.
  1970 An archaeological evaluation of the Codice Xolotl. *American Anti-
        quity* 35 (4): 431–440.
SANDERS, W. T., B. J. PRICE
  1968 *Mesoamerica: the evolution of a civilization*. New York: Random
        House.
TEZOZOMOC, HERNANDO ALVARADO
  1949 *Crónica Mexicayotl*. Publicationes del Instituto de Historia, series
        one, No. 10. Translated and edited by Adrian León. Mexico City:
        Universidad Nacional Autonoma de México.

The Gridiron Town Plan and the Caste System in Colonial Central America

S. D. MARKMAN

Because they have been isolated for centuries and thus conserve many pristine colonial traits, a number of cities and towns of Central America, especially some small villages of present-day highland Chiapas and Guatemala, serve as an assemblage of urban artifacts by means of which the early stages of the history of urbanization in Hispano-America may be reconstructed. And even in those cities of Central America that have been swept into the mainstream of the twentieth century, recent developments are hardly commensurate with the changes, both physical and socioeconomic, that were witnessed in Bogotá, Quito, or Lima, let alone such truly megalopolitan centers as Mexico City or Buenos Aires.[1] For the historian of the urbanization process in the New World, it is a fortunate circumstance, therefore, that in Central America there still exist towns that have preserved in various degrees the physical aspect of their pristine colonial character.

The Spaniards became urbanization experts well before the middle of the sixteenth century in Central America. By 1553 the majority of the colonial urban centers were already in existence, exclusive of the uncounted number of settlements which were later abolished or moved to other sites – and all this barely twenty-five years after the first Spanish permanent settlement at Ciudad Vieja in 1527. This was actually the second site for the city, the first being an abortive attempt at Iximché in 1524 in the vicinity of a pre-Columbian urban grouping.[2]

[1] Morse (1965: 42) observes that only eight "second-echelon" metropolitan centers developed with commanding positions in their own regional spheres, but not on an international scale: Mexico City, Lima, Guatemala City, Bogotá, Quito, Buenos Aires, Havana, and Rio de Janeiro. Only three are truly metropolitan today: Mexico City, Buenos Aires, and Rio de Janeiro.

[2] Vásquez (1944: vol. 1, pp. 128ff.), quoting a communication of the first bishop of Guatemala, Fransisco de Marroquín, says that by 1553 most of the Indians had already

The fervor of urbanization in sixteenth-century Central America
was motivated by a two-fold purpose reflected in the two types of
towns founded hard upon the conquest. Though essentially the same

gathered into towns, especially through the efforts of the Franciscans, of which order
both he and Marroquín were members. The same may be said for Honduras; see
Lunardi (1946: 67ff.), who lists the towns ranking them according to population
together with their founding dates as follows: 68, Trujillo by 1525; 73, Puerto Cortés
(Puerto Caballos) by 1524; 74, San Gil de Buenavista (Nito), 1524; 76, Triumfo de la
Cruz, 1524, which was soon abandoned; 78, Naco in 1524; 80, Toreaba, 1524; 81,
Villa de la Frontera de Cáceres, 1526; 81, Villa de la Buena Esperanza, 1533–1534,
abandoned in 1536; 84, Choluteca, 1535; 84, San Pedro Sula, 1535; 84, Gracia a
Dios, 1536; 84, Comayagua, 1537; 88, Villa de Nueva Salamanca, 1543(?). He derives
these dates from contemporary accounts, which he does not always cite.

Other Central American towns founded in the sixteenth century are: Ciudad Real
(San Cristóbal de las Casas) in April of 1526 and Chiapa or Chiapa de Indios (Chiapa
de Corzo) in March of 1526 (Markman 1963: 7, Note 1); Santiago de los Caballeros
de Guatemala (Ciudad Vieja) in 1527 (Markman 1966a: 11); the same moved in 1541
(Antigua Guatemala) (Markman 1966a); the first Spanish settlement, founded by Pedro
de Alvarado, at the Cakchiquel ceremonial center of Iximché, established in July 1524
and abandoned in August of that same year – see ASGH (1965: vol. 38, p. 79), *Libro
Viejo* (1934: 281), the second letter of Alvarado to Cortés in which he reports that he
founded a town for Spaniards. The letter is actually dated 27 July 1533 and he does
not specify where the site was or the date of its founding. See also Recinos (1949: 57ff.),
also *Libro Viejo* (1934: 5) for the *cabildo*, in fragmentary condition, recording the
establishment of the city under the advocation of Santiago dated July 25, 1524, and
Pérez Valenzuela (1960: 32–33); also Guillemín (1959: 22), identifying Iximché with the
pre-Columbian site where Alvarado established the town referred to as Guatemala as
well as Santiago. See also Szecsy (1953a) for a report of the preliminary excavations
at the site and its identification with Santiago Guatemala.

Other towns in Central America also founded in the sixteenth century may be listed
as follows: Granada in Nicaragua in 1527 (Juarros 1936: vol. 2, p. 132; de Remesal 1932:
vol. 2, p. 310; López de Velasco 1894: 321ff.; Ponce 1873: vol. 1, p. 365); San Miguel
in El Salvador, before 1550, according to López de Velasco (1894: vol. 1, p. 297);
Realejo in Nicaragua in 1534 (Juarros 1936: vol. 1, p. 43); Nueva Segovia (El Ocotal)
in Nicaragua by Pedrarias Dávila early in the century (López de Velasco 1894: 326);
Léon, Nicaragua, first established in 1527 (Juarros 1936: vol. 2, p. 133; López de
Velasco 1894: 318; Diez de la Calle 1646: 129ff.); San Miguel in El Salvador before 1550
(López de Velasco 1894: 297); San Salvador by 1543, when it received its official title
from Charles V, according to Vásquez de Espinosa (1943: 26ff.); Cartago in Costa Rica
in 1573 (AGG: A 1.23 [1573] 1512–334); Tegucigalpa, Honduras, also in 1573, as a *real
de minas* in 1579 (Bonilla 1945: 242).

Hardoy and Aranovich (1967: 354 ff.) give a ranking of the cities of Latin America
reported by López de Velasco (1894) for 1580 and by Vásquez de Espinosa (1943) for
1630, eighteen of which are in the former Reino de Guatemala, out of a total of 260.
The towns are ranked in numerical order according to the number of *vecinos* reported
in 1580 for each as follows: Antigua Guatemala, 6; Sonsonate, 9; Chiapa (probably San
Cristóbal de las Casas), 25; Granada, 25; León, 36; San Salvador, 36; San Miguel (in
El Salvador, 41; Valladolid (Comayagua, Honduras), 45; Trujillo (give its location as
in Veraguas, but there is also a Trujillo in Honduras), 45; Cartago, 70; Gueguetlán
(Huehuetán), 70; Gracia a Dios, 79; San Pedro (not specified where – there are a number
of San Pedros in sixteenth-century Central America), 79; San Jorge de Olano (possibly
Olancho in Honduras, no longer existing), 90; Nueva Segovia (Ocotal), 90; Choluteca,
103; Realejo, 103. Towns are given ranks from 1 to 4. None in Central America is ranked
in the first category, in fact only the capital city, Antigua Guatemala, is ranked 2, the
rest are either in category 3 or 4.

See also Chueca Goitía et al. (1951: vol. 1, pp. vii ff.) for a brief and eulogistic
statement relative to the urban creativity of Spain in the New World.

as regards plan and spatial extension, they were quite different insti-tutionally: *pueblos de españoles* for the conquistadors-turned-settlers and *pueblos de indios* for the recently conquered natives (Markman 1971: *passim*). *Pueblos de españoles* were established primarily as centers for political, ecclesiastical, and economic control of the hinter-land, whereas *pueblos de indios* served as sites for the concentration of the Indian population who were to be controlled the more readily politically, ecclesiastically, and economically. However, many of these sixteenth-century foundations lost their original juridically seg-regated character with the eventual disintegration of the caste system. The historical, economic, and social forces at play during the course of the colonial period also served to transform the pristine physical character of many of the two original types of towns. By the eighteenth century strictly monoracial towns were rare, except in the remote highland areas of Chiapas and Guatemala. The caste system ultimately became a *de jure* vestige or fossil once the physical and spiritual conquests of the natives were consummated by the Spaniards, who in their turn were overwhelmed by a biological conquest. The most visible consequence of the biological conquest was the formation of a vast segment of colonial society that did not fit into the racial categories by means of which the population had originally been divided into castes.[3]

The Spanish cultural institutions brought to America and especially the neomedieval social structure into which the European Spanish population was organized in *pueblos de españoles* are reflected in the location on the grid plan of building plots assigned to the governing bodies, the church authorities, and the settlers themselves, both the leaders and the rank and file. That towns reserved exclusively for Spaniards were primarily centers of control is reflected in the layout on the ground of a physical paradigm in space, a visible table of organization of Spanish society in the New World.

The residents of the *pueblos de indios* were objects of control and were all members of the same caste. Because its residents were forced to live in what for them was a contrived, exotic urban environment, more frequently than not against their will, with social distinctions and ranks of former days proscribed, and to be members of a single class in colonial society as a whole, the physical layout of Indian towns could hardly serve as a paradigm for ranking the inhabitants. The location of the sites assigned for dwellings did not reflect any social distinction. The church and/or *convento* and the government house

---

[3]   For the history of the caste system and the population of colonial Central America see especially Barón Castro (1942: *passim*). For a bibliography on the caste system in colonial Central America and elsewhere in the New World, see Note 25 dealing with mestization.

on the plaza represented external authorities rather than any internal power structure. Because they were mainly engaged in agricultural pursuits, it was extremely difficult to force the Indians to live in the towns founded for them. Some, especially in contemporary highland Chiapas, eventually became no more than places of residence for the "cargo-holders" (officials) who changed periodically, so that the towns became religious and market centers in a manner not too different from what had been common before the conquest.[4]

The earliest intimation that the layout of the *pueblos de españoles* founded in the sixteenth century was conceived of as a physical paradigm for locating the different classes of Spanish society destined to live in these towns comes from Jorge de Alvarado, brother of Pedro de Alvarado, in the act of founding the first permanent settlement in Central America, in the valley of Almolonga, now Ciudad Vieja, Guatemala, on November 21, 1527.[5] The organization of colonial

[4]   See Markman (i.p.a.: *passim*, 1963: 21ff.) for the problems of gathering the Indians into towns in the early sixteenth century. See also Vogt (1969: vol. 7, p. 150, Figure 3) for the "vacant town" type. For Tzotzil settlement patterns, the vacant town, see Laughlin (1969: vol. 7, p. 170). Also see Note 21 below.

[5]   For the text of Alvarado's order see *Libro viejo* (1934: 29), ASGH (1927–1928: 106), and Pérez Valenzuela (1960: 32–33): "Asentá escribano que yo, por virtud de los poderes que tengo de los gobernadores de su magestad, con acuerdo y parecer de los alcaldes y regidores que están presentes, asiento y pueblo aquí en este sitio la ciudad de Santiago, el cual dicho sitio es término de la provincia de Guatemala.

"Primeramente ante todas cosas mando que se haga la traza de la dicha ciudad, poniendo las calles norte-sur, leste-hueste.

"Otro si mando que sean señalados cuatro solares en cuatro calles en ellas incorporados, por plaza de la dicha ciudad.

"Otro si mando que sean señalados dos solares junto á la plaza, en el lugar más conveniente, donde la iglesia sea edificada, la cual sea de la advocación de del Señor Santiago...

"Otro si mando que se señale un sitio para un hospital, á donde los pobres y peregrinos sean acorridos y curados...

"Yten mando que se señale un sitio cual convenga para una capilla y adoratorio...

"Otro si mando que se señale un sitio cual convenga, donde á suplicación desta cibdad, su magestad mande hacer una fortaleza, o su gobernador en su real nombre, para la guarda y seguridad de la dicha ciudad.

"Otro si mando que junto a la plaza sean señalados cuatro solares, el uno para casa de cabildo, y el otro para la cárcel pública, y los otros para propios de la ciudad.

"Señalados los sitios y solares de susocontenidos, mando que los demas solares sean repartidos por los vecinos que son y fueren de la dicha ciudad, como y de la manera que se haya hecho en las ciudades, villas y lugares que en esta Nueva España estan poblados de españoles, no excediendo ni traspasando la orden acostumbrada. Jorge de Alvarado."

It was three years before this permanent site was picked. The first Spanish town was founded July 25, 1524, at Iximché, a small pre-Columbian ceremonial center of post-Classic origin. The hostility of the local Indians forced the Spaniards out the following month. The city then existed on the paper of the *cabildos* held from time to time until the site at Almolonga, after some debate, was finally selected. For Iximché see ASGH (1965: vol. 38, p. 79) and Recinos (1952: 164); also the second letter of Alvarado, dated 27 July 1524, in which he says, "...donde para mejor conquistar y pacificar esta tierra tan grande y tan rezia de gente hize y edifiqué en nombre de su majestad una ciudad de españoles del señor Santiago..." (*Libro viejo* 1934: 281); also Villacorta (1925–1926:

society is clearly indicated by the explicit location, in the very heart of the town, of the plaza which was laid out first, giving it a spatial preeminence in the grid of streets emanating from it north-south and east-west. The civil and ecclesiastical authorities also were located on the plaza.

Jorge Alvarado's pointed remark that the rest of the plots should be distributed according to the manner and customs in which this was done in the rest of New Spain would seem to indicate that the organization of the space of the town, a grid of streets surrounding a plaza, and the placement of the *vecinos* along those streets had already been formulated in fact, if not yet in official regulations or directives from Spain. In other words, the plaza and the town represent the germinal unit, the nucleus or center from which the surrounding countryside may be conquered and brought into the Spanish realm. Pedro de Alvarado had said as much in his second letter to the Crown, regarding the first short-lived Spanish settlement at Iximché in 1524, "donde para mejor conquistar y pacificar. . . hize y edifiqué una ciudad de españoles. . . . ."[6]

This act of Alvarado, bringing into existence a town conceived of as a base from which first to conquer and then to control the country, could hardly have been original with him. Efficacious methods of conquest and settlement seem to have been arrived at almost at once and, though of extremely recent origin, are referred to as if they had been long-standing methods well seasoned by years of experience. For example, only three years later, 1527, and but five or six after the founding of Mexico, and a scant generation since the Spanish settlement at Santo Domingo, his brother Jorge already refers to an established custom to follow as a guide in the distribution of plots to the *vecinos*. To found a town was to create a practical tool for a specific purpose, the extension of the central authority of the Spanish Crown in the New World. The best means of achieving this end was a chain of cities, of power centers spread over the vast American continent, each link being a fixed point in space from which control – economic, political, ecclesiastical – radiated and interconnected with other units as part of an urban hierarchy of *caserios, lugares, pueblos, villas, ciudades*,[7] terms still employed in modern-day Guatemala.

passim). For an excavation report on Iximché see Szecsy (1953a) and Guillemín (1959: *passim*). For some excavations carried out at the first permanent settlement at Almolonga, Ciudad Vieja, see Szecsy (1953b: *passim*). The lesson was well learned and never again were populated indigenous sites picked for Spanish towns because most of these were either well fortified by nature or by man-made works. See Díaz del Castillo (1933–1934: vol. 2, pp. 106ff.) speaking of Utatlán, and Ximénez (1929–1931: vol. 1, p. 122) with regard to Chiapa (Chiapa de Córzo, Chiapas).

[6]   See *Libro viejo* (1934: 281); also references in Note 5 above.
[7]   See Foster (1960: 48) for a discussion of the plaza and the grid plan as the geographical

The plaza of the Spanish town became the locus for the highest ranks or echelons of the power structure of colonial society – the church, the city hall, and the jail. Though Jorge de Alvarado makes no mention of distinction in rank as a basis for assigning plots to the *vecinos* at Almolonga, there is some evidence forthcoming elsewhere that the leaders, the elite of the Spanish forces, were indeed given special consideration in the choice of building sites, sometimes directly on the main plaza. For example, the house of the conquistador Montejo still stands on the main plaza of Mérida, and needs no further documentation. When Villa Real (later Ciudad Real and now San Cristóbal de las Casas, Chiapas) was laid out in 1528, "en forma de pueblo por barrios, cuadras y calles . . . ,"[8] the *vecinos* who had been assigned plots were requested to come to the city council and sign for them in the official *libro de cabildo*.

Diego de Mazariegos, the leader of the conquistadors, asked for four *solares*, three for himself and one for his son, in recognition of his services. Though not identified with certainty, the house he built may be the one still standing on the southwest corner of the plaza of San Cristóbal.[9] De Remesal (1932: vol. 2, p. 386), usually a reliable reporter, goes on to say that for similar reasons of extraordinary service, choice plots were assigned to Pedro de Estrada, Francisco de Lintorne, and others. Once the plots in town had all been distributed the land in the countryside was parceled out ". . . por caballerías y peonerías a los vecinos de la villa." *Caballerías*, each 600 by 300 feet (*piés*), were used to measure out the land allotted those of the conquistadors who brought horses with them, and *peonerías*, each 100 by 50 feet, were the units employed for foot soldiers.

The location of the elite classes of conquest society in the center of the towns, either on, or adjacent to the main plaza, may also have been customary among the indigenes before the advent of the Spaniards, if Bishop de Landa's description of some of the pre-Conquest urban centers of Yucatan may be accepted as reliable, and

and cultural center of the power structure. He rightly considers the plazas in the New World, not so much representing the diffusion of a material trait, as the utilization of an old idea for specific political, religious and economic goals. See also Stanislawski (1946: 108ff.), who recognizes the grid plan as reflective of a centralized power for military and political control.

[8]   De Remesal (1932: vol. 2, pp. 385ff.), writing at the beginning of the seventeenth century.

[9]   This house is traditionally identified as having belonged to Diego de Mazariegos (see Markman 1963: photograph between pages 94–95). It is quite possible, however, that Mazariegos' house no longer exists, and also that its site was on the south side of the plaza across from the cathedral, now occupied by some nondescript temporary structures. The present Casa de la Sirena, on the east half of the south side of the plaza (Markman 1963: 108), may possibly have been built by his son Luís or have belonged to another conquistador, Andrés de la Tobilla.

not a case of his interpreting the facts from the European point of view. He says that before the coming of the Spaniards the Indians lived in very civilized fashion close together in towns, in the middle of which there were the temples on plazas and around which were also the houses of the rulers and the priests; then beyond were the houses of the higher classes and still further away on the outskirts of town, those of the common people.[10]

Whether de Landa's description of the social stratification of post-Classic Yucatec society on the actual ground plan of towns is correct is not as pertinent as the question as to whether or not he was unwittingly describing a tradition already implanted in Spanish cities in Mexico and Central America, whereby the choicest sites were considered to be those on the plazas or at least contiguous to it. For example, in 1541 when Antigua Guatemala, the new capital after the destruction of Ciudad Vieja, was laid out, it is reported that the building plots were distributed "...conforme a la calidad de los vecinos..."[11]

The elitist character of the sixteenth-century *pueblo de españoles* is further attested to by the fact that the plan itself, the *traza*, had a status in law. The very physical shape of the town with its plaza and grid of streets was established verbally by means of a legal instrument before a single foundation trench for any building was dug. And only Spaniards could be inscribed as official residents, that is as *vecinos*. In the course of time, as the population of Spanish towns increased in size, usually because of the growth in the numbers of the members of racially mixed origin, the official physical town plan was extended in special acts of the city council, sanctioned by the Crown; as, for example, in the case of Antigua Guatemala in 1559, and again in 1641, and a number of times again during the eighteenth century.[12]

From the very first, those Indians required to serve as a labor force for the city were established in *barrios* outside the official *traza*, usually referred to as being *extramuros* of the city. By 1686, according to Fuentes y Guzmán, there were ten such wards on the outskirts of the central area of town, the original official *traza*. The plans of some were eventually integrated into the gridiron scheme, the streets of

[10] De Landa (1966: 28). For a good translation and a well-annotated edition see Tozzer (1941: 62).
[11] De Remesal (1932: vol. 2, p. 45). "Primero edificaron la plaza y las cuadras que están cerca de ella y luego se extendieron a todas partes." The *traza* [plan] then was enlarged before the plots were distributed according to the quality of the *vecinos*. This might be interpreted as implying that the highest ranks of the *vecinos* were given plots on the first streets laid out contiguous to the plaza, and only when these were extended were the rest of the *vecinos* in the lower echelons assigned plots.
[12] Markman (1966a: 12–16). For the official status of the *traza*, the grid plan, see Markman (1971: Note 32) and Borah (1973: *passim*) for an extensive bibliography.

which had been extended as the racially mixed non-Spanish population grew.[13] The original intention was to segregate the Indians from the Spaniards. However, in the course of time, as people of neither of the two main original castes, *español* and *indio*, but *mestizos*, *mulatos* and mixtures of all, became more and more numerous, they naturally settled in the new streets opened up as the official *traza* was enlarged by the extension of the town plan. The original official *traza* around the plaza remained the particular preserve of the purely Spanish elements of society.

From the very first, satellite *pueblos de indios* were also established in the vicinity of *pueblos de españoles* in order to ensure the availability of a labor force on the farms of the surrounding countryside or for personal services for the Spaniards or for public works. Sometimes these satellite Indian towns were located on the very outskirts of Spanish towns, as, for example, Jocotenango to the north of Antigua, or Subtiava to the west of León. There were thirty-one such satellite Indian towns around Antigua Guatemala, some at a considerable distance away, most of which had been founded in the sixteenth century, and whose inhabitants had originally been brought together from afar to serve as a labor force on the lands held in *encomienda* by *vecinos* of the city.[14]

Some of these towns were actually held in *encomienda* by religious orders, especially the Franciscans who derived a considerable part of

[13] Fuentes y Guzmám (1932–1933: vol. 1, pp. 136 ff.), and Markman (1966a: 14). The ten *barrios* were as follows: (1) San Francisco, inhabited by Indians, probably one of the first *barrios* for Indians and established at the time the city was founded in 1541; (2) El Tortuguero, along the southern edge of town, about three squares below and to the east of the *plaza mayor*; (3) San Sebastián, to the northeast of the main *traza* and beyond the *convento* of La Merced; (4) El Manchén, further north still; (5) San Jerónimo, west of San Sebastián, inhabited by people of completely mixed and no especially definable racial caste; (6) Santiago, which Fuentes calls an *arrabal*, not identified today and probably a slum area; (7) Espíritu Santo, to the southwest on the edge of town; (8) Santo Domingo, the area near the Dominican *convento* to the northeast of the main *traza*; (9) La Chácara on the eastern edge of town; and (10) La Candelaria, a populous neighborhood to the northeast beyond the *barrio* of Santo Domingo. See Pardo and Zamora Castellanos (1943) for plans of the colonial town.
[14] Juarros (1936: vol. 2, pp. 221ff.), writing at the very end of the eighteenth century. All had been established as far back as the sixteenth as follows: to the east, Santa Inés, Santa Ana, Santa Isabel, San Cristóbal el Alto, San Cristóbal el Bajo, San Bartolomé Carmona (abandoned in his day), and San Juan del Obispo: to the south, Santa Catalina Bobadilla, San Gaspar Vivar, San Pedro (Huertas), San Lucas, San Miguel, and Almolonga (Ciudad Vieja); to the southwest, San Miguel Milpas Dueñas, Santa Catarina, San Andrés, San Antonio Aguascalientes, San Lorenzo (el Cubo), and Santiago; to the west, San Andrés Deán, San Bartolomé; to the northwest, San Dionisio Pastores and San Lucas de las Carretas; to the north, Jocotenango, Utateca, and San Felipe; and to the northeast, Santo Tomás, San Miguel, San Bartolomé Milpas Altas, Santa Lucía, and Magdalena. Most of these towns still exist today and may be located on the map, "Departamento de Sacatepéquez," scale 1: 100,000, as well as in the gazeteer (Dirección General de Estadística 1953: 35ff.).

their income from them.[15] Satellite Indian towns were established around every Spanish town, repeating with but slight variations the case of Antigua Guatemala. For example, San Cristóbal de las Casas (Villa Real or Ciudad Real in colonial times) had five Indian *barrios*. At first these were located a short distance from the main center, but eventually, with the growth of the city, they were incorporated into the grid of streets so that today they are almost indistinguishable, except for the church and plaza in each.[16] This particular type of *pueblo de indios*, the satellite town, was different from those established by the religious orders as part of their missionary activities, which were scattered far and wide in remote areas, frequently far from the major Spanish urban centers.[17]

The Spaniards were never a numerous caste in relation to the Indian and, eventually, to the *mestizo* and other castes, numbering some 2,300 *vecinos* in 1580 and about 2,900 *vecinos* in 1630 in all of Central America.[18] In fact, the total population of the Reino de Guatemala near the end of the colonial period in 1776, by which time the difference between *pueblo de indios* and *pueblos de españoles* no longer had any significance, was estimated to be 805,000 inhabitants, plus 8,000 more for Guatemala City. The number of urban centers at that time totaled twelve *ciudades*, twenty-one *villages*, and 705 *pueblos* (Juarros 1936: vol. 1, pp. 66ff.; AGG: A 1.10 [1773] 18.773–244). By the early nineteenth century, circa 1839, of the twenty-nine cities in all Central America, only eleven were considered important from the point of view of a visitor from the United States (Montgomery 1839).

[15] Fuentes y Guzmán (1932–1933: vol. 1, p. 376), writing circa 1690, gives eight of the towns listed in Note 14 above as *encomiendas* of the Franciscan *convento* in Antigua.

[16] See Markman (1963: 105). The five are El Cerrillo, Cuxtitali, San Antonio, San Diego, and Mexicanos. See Juarros (1936: vol. 1, p. 16); the names of the five *barrios* appear in a report dated 1785 concerning the damage caused by a flood (AGG: A 1. 1 [1785] 17–1); see also Trens (1957: 221), who also gives the names of the Indian *barrios*. Also at some distance from town, all originally held in *encomienda* by *vecinos* of San Cristóbal, are San Felipe Ecatepec, Chamula, Zinacantán, and Iluistán, among others.

[17] See Markman (1971: *passim*) for the type founded by religious orders.

[18] These figures are given by Hardoy and Aranovich (1967). By 1580 or so, according to a geographical report, Archivo de Indias, Sevilla: Audiencia de Guatemala, *Estante* 2, *Cajón* 2, *Legajo* 4, Tomo 1, Folio 57, "Pueblos . . . Audiencia de Guatemala, 1581," and López de Velasco (1894: 284), there were but five *pueblos de españoles* in the province of Guatemala: Santiago (Antigua), San Salvador, Sonsonate, San Miguel, and Choluteca. Ponce (1873: vol. 1, p. 344), says that in all the province of Honduras there were five or six: Comayagua, Trujillo, Gracias a Dios, Olancho, San Pedro in Comayagua, and Agalteca. In all of the Soconusco, the Pacific littoral of Chiapas, there was but one Spanish town, Huehuetán (López de Velasco 1894: 302ff.) Even more scant were the population and the number of Spanish towns in the rest of Central America, i.e. in Nicaragua, Costa Rica, and highland Chiapas, where San Cristóbal de las Casas (Ciudad Real) was the only Spanish town.

Many of the *pueblos de indios* became ghost towns when it was found that their locations were unsuitable for economic reasons or because of bad climatic conditions.[19] Also, in some cases, because of great distances from Spanish towns, control was difficult. The lines of authority and power were overextended in space, so that many of the Indians would run off and go back to their former life, especially in the Petén and in Verapaz, Guatemala (Cevallos 1935–1936; AGG: A 1.18.4 [1650] 38.300–4501). In El Salvador, in the eighteenth century, apparently not only Indians but even the *ladinos* preferred to live in the country rather than in towns.[20]

But unlike *pueblos de españoles*, the population of Indian towns by law lacked social stratification, the Indian having been forcibly settled there, and the class stratification of his former society extinguished.[21] The physical layout of the town, often hastily executed, was not conceived of as a paradigm for the social ranking of the inhabitants because they were all indistinguishably members of one class, *indio*. As long as the Indian town remained solely a *pueblo* for Indians and was not invaded by members of other castes, it consisted of hardly more than a plaza with a church, the street plan remaining ever embryonic. Control of the Indian residents, except in satellite towns, was concentrated in the ecclesiastical authority as represented by the one monumental building on the only urban space in town, the church on the plaza.

If contemporary practice is any clue to colonial customs, the example of so many contemporary towns of highland Chiapas and Guatemala that are still not much more than a church plaza surrounded by corn fields, and are in fact "vacant towns" inhabited by alternating "cargo-holders," as mentioned above, may be accepted as evidence of the original appearance of the *pueblo de indios* of the sixteenth century, both satellite and missionary.[22] The symbolic values associated with the plaza in *pueblos de españoles* were totally foreign to

[19]   In the seventeenth century, many towns near Comitán, Chiapas, were abandoned (Ximénez 1929–31: vol. 2, p. 199); also in the Golfo Dulce area and in the Alcaldía de Amatique, Guatemala (Fuentes y Guzmán 1932–1933: vol. 2, pp. 289ff., 295ff.).

[20]   Cortés y Larraz (n.d.: folio 89), reports that three-quarters of the population of the parish of Chalatenango lived in *despoblados*, and that three-quarters of that population was *ladino*. In folios 112–113, he describes and laments the Indians' custom of living in solitude. To a Spaniard this was incomprehensible.

[21]   For the gathering of Indians into towns see Markman (1963: 21ff., also 1971: *passim*). See also a *cédula* of 1540 ordering that Indians be urbanized (AGG: A 1.23 [1540] 1511–10, also A 1.2.4 [1540] 5752–54 *vuelto*). This *cédula* is cited by de Remesal (1932: vol. 1,p. 220); Vásquez (1944: vol. 1, pp. 66ff.); and Fuentes y Guzmán (1932–1933: vol. 2, p. 446). For gathering of Indians into towns see also de Remesal (1932: vol. 2, pp. 211, 244, 245). A similar *cédula* was emitted for Peru, 22 July 1595, according to de Remesal (1932: vol. 2, pp. 243, 244, 246).

[22]   See Markman (i.p.b. *passim*) for an analysis of this particular urban scheme; see also Note 4, above, for "vacant towns" in contemporary highland Chiapas.

those of the *pueblo de indios*. The *plaza mayor* of Spanish towns was the location and seat of political authority, of the market and of commerce, and was the main religious center. To live in its proximity implied that one was either a member of the power structure or of the elite of local Spanish society. In the *pueblo de indios*, the plaza was just a vaguely defined vacant space dominated by a church,[23] its sole architectural distinction.

The physical conquest of Guatemala and the rest of Central America was effected by a remarkably scant number of determined men and within a remarkably short space of time, most of the country having been pacified and being under control by the end of the sixteenth century. However, in the biological conquest that ensued, the victors turned out to be the vanquished. By the eighteenth century, the elite caste which had populated the Spanish towns had become almost extinct, by mixing not only with the indigenes to form the *mestizo* caste, but also with exotic racial elements from a distant continent, Africa. As a result of the intermixing of the three racial strains, the caste system itself, the juridical instrument by means of which society was organized, lost its meaning and usefulness as the racial qualifications for each social category, or caste, became blurred.[24]

This process of the mestization of the population was dramatically

[23]   Ricard (1950: 325ff.), rightly observes that the Hispano-American town is a plaza surrounded by streets, that the plaza is really a *plaza del estado*, that is a seat of authority. This is quite contrary to the Renaissance conception of the plaza (Zucker 1959: 140), a man-made order to establish definite spatial limits, a space unified by architectural means, space articulated by the buildings around it, in fine, an aesthetic interpretation current in Renaissance Europe. The city plan and the plaza of Antigua Guatemala were designed by an Italian military engineer-architect, Bautista Antonelli (Juarros 1936: vol. 2, p. 178).

The strict orthogonal layout with the open *plaza* as the center and the origin of the grid must not be taken at face value as being based on Renaissance theories of town planning. The question is one of answering whether Antonelli was continuing a practice already in use when Ciudad Vieja was laid out in 1527 and San Cristóbal de las Casas in 1528. Was he primarily concerned with aesthetic considerations expressed in the Italian theories of the "ideal city" of the time (Rosenau 1959), or was he guided by practical considerations? See Markman (1966a: 11, 56) for biographical data on Antonelli; also Angulo Iñiguez (1942), and Calderón Quijano (1953: 12–18) for Antonelli's activities in Mexico before going to Guatemala.

In the New World, however, the plaza becomes a sociopolitical instrument, at least in Spanish towns, which by the seventeenth and eighteenth centuries is embellished with fountains and arcades. But from the very first the architectural elements which define that space are directly reflective of the institutions or authorities they house – church, jail, city hall, government offices, mint, commercial establishments. None of these institutions, except that of the church, is a determinant of the architectural treatment of the plazas in *pueblos de indios*. Government buildings and commercial establishments even today in Indian towns of highland Chiapas and Guatemala are largely nondescript, except for the schools in the last few years. For an excellent synthesis of the literature on the origin of the grid plan in America, see Borah (1973: *passim*).

[24]   For a discussion of the term *casta* see Morse (1965: 40ff.), who believes it is reminiscent of the Thomist-Aristotelian notion of a functional social hierarchy.

reflected in the changes that gradually took place in both Spanish and Indian towns in the Reino de Guatemala during the colonial period, not so much in the external physical aspect of the town plan, as in the symbolic values formerly attached to its various parts.[25]

In time, pure Spaniards were totally outnumbered in Spanish towns, as were Indians also outnumbered in many Indian towns. It would seem that the Indian population of satellite towns and *barrios* was not so much converted to Christianity and other European institutions as it was bred to them. Just as Indian towns were eventually invaded by *ladinos*, i.e. people of mixed racial ancestry, so were Spanish towns which, as a result, ultimately lost their elitist identity in the ever-increasing rise in the numbers of residents of mixed ancestry. The *mise en scène* of the mestization process in colonial Central America was primarily urban. The enormous growth of the racially intermixed and urbanized population was the cause of the repeated need to extend the street plan of Antigua, rather than any numerical increase of the elite caste of Spaniards, which actually decreased during the course of time.[26]

[25]   There has been much interest in the history of race mixture – *mestizaje* – in recent years, particular in colonial Central America. One of the best general works dealing with the caste system as a whole is Barón Castro (1942). See also Adams (1964); Magnus Mörner (1964); Samayoa Guevara (1960, 1962, 1966); de Solano (1969); and Markman (1966b). Other works of a more general nature of interest to the problem of *mestizaje* are: Calderón Quijano (1971); Esteva Fabregat (1964); Konetzke (1946, 1953); Kubler (1966); Lipschutz (1967); Moreno Navarro (1969); Mörner (1960, 1967); Rosenblatt (1954, 1967); Salas (1960); Zavala (1971).

[26]   See Notes 12 and 13 above. By 1810, the majority of the urban population of the Reino de Guatemala were *pardos*, i.e. people of no particularly determined race, but a mixture of all three. See Larrazabal (1953–1954: 87ff.), who gives the following statistics on the population: 646,660 *indios*; 313, 334 *pardos y algunos negros*; 40,000 *blancos*. The term *pardo* was already in use by the end of the seventeenth century in Antigua Guatemala. The residents of the *barrio* of San Jerónimo were termed *pardos* at the time of an uprising or riot, which took place 15 September 1697 (Pardo 1944: 120). The term *ladino* was also commonly employed during the colonial period. For example, Fuentes y Guzmán (1932–1933: vol. 2, p. 242), around 1690, speaking of the town of San Cristóbal Cazabastlán (Acasaguastlán), gives the number of *indios* and *ladinos* resident there saying "...así llamamos en los pueblos de indios los que son españoles, mestizos, mulatos y negros, a diferencia de los indios que solo hablan su materna." *Ladino* may also mean an accultured Indian. Vásquez (1944: vol. 4, p. 37), referring to the population of San Juan del Obispo in 1689 reports a "barrio de indios ladinos" as distinct from one of *indios*; also Fuentes y Guzmán (1932–1933: vol. 3, p. 448), says that those Indians who had been trained and educated were quite "cortesanos y ladinos, como los de Nicaragua, los mejicanos de San Salvador, los de Comayagua, Quetzaltenango, Huehuetenango, Chinautla, Petapa, Amatitlán, Santa Ynés Petapa, Mixco, Almolonga, y de los barrios de la Candelaria, Santiago, San Gerónimo, San Antón, Espíritu Santo, Santa Ynés del Monte Policiano, que son bastante ladinos..." Juarros (1936: vol. 2, p. 87), giving statistics on the population of some towns in El Salvador, uses the term *pardo* for San Miguel and San Vicente, but for Sonsonate, he distinguishes between Spaniards and *indios* with a third classification, *mulato*, who outnumber the other two castes almost five to one. He uses this term also in giving the population figures for León and Granada, Nicaragua (1936: vol. 1, pp. 40ff.). But here he separates the population into four categories, *españoles, mestizos, mulatos,*

As mestization increased, the traditional social hierarchy, which had been based on ethnic or racial origin, could no longer function. The only racially distinguishable castes by the end of the colonial period were still the Spanish, almost extinct by then, and the more numerous Indian. The *mestizo* and *mulato* castes had blended entirely. The five castes – *español, indio, mestizo, mulato, zambo*, the latter a mixture of Indian and Negro – were still employed for legal matters in the mid-eighteenth century.[27]

However, by the end of the eighteenth century the five were reduced to three – *español, indio*, and a racially indeterminate third, sometimes called *pardo*, or *mulato*. *Ladino* began to be employed with greater frequency by the beginning of the nineteenth century, because by 1800 the population was completely mixed, except for the larger nonurbanized Indian population, i.e. nonurbanized in large towns or cities but still living in small villages.[28] From very early in the colonial period, as people of mixed ancestry began to outnumber the Spaniards in Spanish towns and also overflowed into Indian towns, the authorities tried to prohibit this movement by means of special decrees, the idea being to ensure the continued services of Indians for the Spanish

indios. In the case of Realejo, Nicaragua, he says (1936: vol. 1, p. 43) all are *mulatos*, and in El Viejo there are only fifty-nine Spaniards out of a total population of 2,968, the rest being *mulatos*. Even by mid-eighteenth century in the geographical report on the Valley of Guatemala (Antigua) the majority caste in the population was given as *mulato* (AGG: A 1.17 [1740] 5002–210).

[27] Pardo (1944: 216); an ordinance prohibiting the use of firearms in Antigua, Guatemala, with punishment for infractions scaled according to the caste of the delinquent.

[28] In Honduras, Nicaragua, and Costa Rica three main castes are referred to by Juarros (1936: vol. 1, pp. 32ff.): *españoles, mestizos, mulatos*. In some cases, as for example, Quetzaltenango, he is rather vague as to caste denominations (1936: vol. 1, pp. 49ff.), and gives figures only for *indios* and *ladinos*. In the province of Escuintla (1936: vol. 1, pp. 20ff.), he speaks of twenty-three *pueblos de indios* and eleven *pueblos de mulatos*. Cortés y Larraz (n.d.: folio 237), reporting in the third quarter of the eighteenth century on the Valle de las Vacas, where Guatemala City was eventually to be located, says there were 7,139 inhabitants, a mixture of Spaniards, *ladinos*, and Indians and that it was impossible to distinguish the three main castes. In 1765 in Honduras, the population was quite mixed (AGG: A 1. 17 [1765] 13.999–1840), where it is reported there were two *villas de españoles y mulatos*, five *minerales* inhabited by *gente de otra jaez*, seventeen *pueblos de indios* and that in Tegucigalpa there were but seventy *vecinos*, presumably Spaniards. For the disintegration of the caste system in Antigua Guatemala, see Markman (1966a: 14ff., 19, 46ff., 49–50).

[29] Garcia Peláez (1943–1944: vol. 2, 152ff.) summarizes the history of the movement of *ladinos* into Indian towns and the legal measures enacted against this practice, which began as far back as the sixteenth and seventeenth centuries. The towns in the vicinity of Antigua where this had occurred are Mixco, Petapa, Amatitlán, San Andrés Itzapa, Escuintla, all mentioned by Fuentes y Guzmán (1932–1933: vol. 3, p. 448; see Note 26 above), where Spaniards and *mulatos* had appropriated Indian land. See also Juarros (1936: vol. 2, p. 215) and Fuentes y Guzmán (1932–1933: vol. 1, p. 411) for towns with a mixed racial population. See also Larreinaga (1857: 266) for a *cédula*, dated 22 December 1605, prohibiting other castes from living in *pueblos de indios* and another *cédula*, of 26 April 1762, explicitly prohibiting *ladinos* from taking up residence in Indian towns.

elite caste on the one hand, and to control the *ladinos* who wished to be free of restraints imposed on them in Spanish towns.[29]

The rise in the numbers of the *ladino* population brought with it the eventual decimation of the elite Spanish caste, which declined not only in numbers but also in economic power. By the end of the colonial period, the segregated urban centers, reserved exclusively for Spaniards, were overrun by non-Spanish elements of the population who, for them, were social inferiors.[30] Little by little, members of the indeterminate racial caste of *ladinos* began to occupy what had been the choice building sites in the vicinity of the *plaza mayor*. The original distribution of buildings sites according to the quality of the recipient was no longer the factor in determining the ownership of real property which could be, and was sold by members of the Spanish caste, as their fortunes declined, to anyone, including *ladinos*. The location of real property, that is of individual houses on streets near the plaza, was no longer indicative of the caste of the owner, but rather of his position in the new society, now more often than not based on personal wealth instead of family lineage.

The offices of government and the church still dominated the plaza, but the other sides, at least one side and the central open space as well, were given over to commercial enterprises, a custom harking back to the very founding of the Spanish towns in the sixteenth century. But the *portál del comercio* became very valuable real estate and by the eighteenth century had passed through many changes of ownership since it had been first granted to the original *vecinos* when the cities were laid out. The sites on the corners of the streets leading away from the plaza, often occupied by the houses of the conquistadors and other meritorious settlers, also became valuable real property which could be and was sold to members of any caste so long as they had the means to pay.[31] *Mestizos* and *mulatos*, i.e. *ladinos*, eventually rose in social status, beginning with their admission to craft guilds, to the religious orders, and ultimately by intermarriage with members of the Spanish caste.[32]

[30]   García Peláez (1943–1944: vol. 2, p. 217), writing between 1834 and 1841, laments that there were not thirty illustrious families left in Guatemala City He mentions the extinction of certain noble families, and that some girls of good families were reduced to doing work formerly done by their slaves. The plebians are on the ascent "...decaecen las familias ilustres, se abaten los ánimos de los niños á barajarse, y tripularse entre negros y mulatos. Bien lastimoso ejemplo son algunas familias, a que no ha quedado más que el nombre mezclados por su probreza en el plebe."

[31]   For the history of the *plaza mayor* of Guatemala City, laid out after the destruction of Antigua in 1773, and the commercial establishments on the south side, see Markman (1966a: *passim*).

[32]   See Samayoa Guevara (1960) for the admission of people of mixed ancestry to the craft guilds after 1750; also (1962) for an extended treatment of the craft guilds in the Reino de Guatemala. See also, Markman (1966b: *passim*). With regard to the religious orders, all castes, even Spaniards born in America, had been excluded at first. Spaniards

The paradigm for ranking the social classes on the checkerboard plan of the Spanish town had lost its pristine symbolic meaning by the end of the colonial period and no longer reflected the original hierarchy of colonial society in Central America. The plaza remained the center of the religious, political, and commercial affairs of the city, but the location of private houses in its proximity now reflected the material wealth of the owners and not necessarily their position in the dead and fossilized caste system.

REFERENCES

ADAMS, RICHARD N.
  1964   La mestización cultural en Centroamérica. *Revista de Indias* 24 (95–96).
AGG
  Archivo General del Gobierno de Guatemala, Guatemala, C.A. Documents are classified as follows: section, date, *legajo*, *expediente*, e.g. A 1.10 [1565] 33256–210.
ANGULO INIGUEZ, DIEGO
  1942   *Bautista Antonelli, las fortificaciones americanas del siglo XVI*. Madrid: Real Academia de la Historia.
ASGH
  1924– *Anales de la Sociedad de Geografía e Historia de Guatemala*. Guatemala City.
  1927–1928   Fundación de la ciudad de Guatemala, 1527. *Anales de la Sociedad de Geografía e Historia de Guatemala*. Guatemala City.
  1927–1928   Fundación de la ciudad de Guatemala, 1527. *Anales de la Sociedad de Geografía e Historia de Guatemala*. Guatemala City.
  1965   *Anales de la Sociedad di Geografía e Historia de Guatemala*. Guatemala City.
BARÓN CASTRO, RODOLFO
  1942   *La población de El Salvador*. Madrid.
BCIHE
  1964   *Boletín del Centro de Investigaciones Históricas y Estéticas*. Universidad Central de Caracas. Facultad de Arquitectura y Urbanismo.
BONILLA, MARCELINA
  1945   *Diccionario histórico-geográfico de las poblaciones de Honduras*. Tegucigalpa.
BORAH, WOODROW
  1973   La influencia cultural en la formación del primer plano para centros urbanos que perduran hasta nuestros días. *Boletín del Centro de Investigaciones Históricas y Estéticas* 15: 55–76.
CALDERÓN QUIJANO, JOSÉ ANTONIO
  1953   *Fortificaciones en Nueva España*. Seville.

born in Spain but who had arrived in Guatemala before the age of ten were also excluded from religious orders; see de Remesal (1932: vol. 2, pp. 311–315). By the seventeenth century this policy changed and *criollos*, i.e. Spaniards born in the New World, were admitted and eventually *mestizos* were too.

486 S. D. MARKMAN

1971 *Población y raza en Hispanoamérica: discurso de ingreso a la Real Academia Sevillana de Buenas Lettras.* Seville.

CEVALLOS, FR. BERNARDINO (fl. ca. 1750)
1935–1936 Visión de paz; Nueva Yerusalén. *Anales de la Sociedad de Geografía e Historia de Guatemala* 12: 463–485. Guatemala City.

CHUECA GOÍTIA, FERNANDO, LEOPOLDO TORRES BALBAS, JULIO GONZALES Y GONZALES
1951 *Planos de ciudades iberoamericanas y filipinas existentes en el Archivo de Indias,* two volumes. Madrid.

CORTÉS Y LARRAZ, PEDRO (fl. 1711–1786)
n.d. "Descripción geográfico-moral de las diócesis de Goathemala." Unpublished manuscript. Archivo de Indias, Audiencia de Guatemala 948, Seville.
1958 *Descripción geográfico-moral.* Biblioteca Goathemala. Guatemala City: Sociedad de Geografía e Historia de Guatemala.

DE LANDA, FRAY DIEGO (fl. sixteenth century)
1966 *Relación de las cosas de Yucatán* (ninth edition). Notes and introduction by Ángel María Garibay K. Mexico City.

DE REMESAL, FRAY ANTONIO (fl. early seventeenth century)
1932 *Historia general de las Indias Occidentales, y particular de la gobernación de Chiapas y Guatemala* (second edition), two volumes. Biblioteca Goathemala. Guatemala City: Sociedad de Geografía e Historia de Guatemala.

DE SOLANO, FRANCISCO
1969 Aéreas linguísticas y población de habla indígena en Guatemala en 1772. *Revista Española de Antropología Americana* 4: 145–200.

DÍAZ DEL CASTILLO, BERNAL (fl. 1496–1584)
1933–1934 *Verdadera y notable relación del descubrimiento y conquista de la Nueva España y Guatemala,* two volumes. Guatemala City.

DÍAZ DE LA CALLE, JUAN (fl. mid-sixteenth century)
1646 *Memorial y noticias sacras y reales de las Indias Occidentales.* Madrid.

DIRECCIÓN GENERAL DE ESTADÍSTICA: REPÚBLICA DE GUATEMALA
1953 *Departementos, municipios, ciudades, villas, pueblos, aldeas y caseríos de la República de Guatemala.* Guatemala City.

ESTEVA FABREGAT, CLAUDIO
1964 El mestizaje en Iberoamérica. *Revista de Indias* 24 (95–96): 279–354.

FOSTER, GEORGE M.
1960 *Culture and conquest.* New York.

FUENTES Y GUZMÁN, FRANCISCO ANTONIO (fl. seventeenth century)
1932–1933 *Recordación florida,* three volumes. Biblioteca Goathemala. Guatemala City: Sociedad de Geografía e Historia de Guatemala.

GARCÍA PELÁEZ, FRANCISCO DE PAULA (fl. 1785–1867)
1943–1944 *Memorias para la historia del antiguo reyno de Guatemala* (second edition), four volumes. Biblioteca Payo de Rivera. Guatemala City.

GUILLEMÍN, JORGE F.
1959 Iximché. *Antropología e Historia* 11 (2): 22–64. Guatemala City: Instituto de Antropología e Historia de Guatemala.

HARDOY, JORGE, CARMEN ARANOVICH
1967 Cuadro comparativo de los centros de colonización existentes en 1580 y 1630. *Desarrollo Económico* 7 (27): 349–360.

JUARROS, DOMINGO (fl. 1752–1820)
  1936   *Compendio de la historia de la ciudad de Guatemala* (third edition), two volumes. Biblioteca Payo de Rivera. Guatemala City.

KONETZKE, RICHARD
  1946   El mestizaje y su importancia en el desarrollo de la población hispano-americana durante la época colonial. *Revista de Indias* (23–24): 7–14, 215–237.
  1953   *Colección de documentos para la historia de la formación social de Hispanoamérica, 1493–1810*, five volumes. Madrid.

KUBLER, GEORGE
  1966   Indianismo y mestizaje. *Revista de Occidente* 4 (38): 158–167.

LARRAZABAL, ANTONIO (fl. early nineteenth century)
  1953–1954   Apuntamientos sobre agricultura y comercio del reyno de Guatemala. *Anales de la Sociedad de Geografía e Historia de Guatemala* 27: 87–109. Guatemala City.

LARREINAGA, MIGUEL (fl. 1771–1847)
  1857   *Prontuario de las reales cédulas... del antiguo reino de Guatemala desde... 1600 hasta 1818.* Guatemala City.

LAUGHLIN, ROBERT M.
  1969   "The Tzotzil," in *Handbook of Middle American Indians*, volume seven. Edited by Robert Wauchope, 152–194. Austin, Texas: University of Texas Press.

Libro Rotulado
  1534   *Libro rotulado: Cartas barias antiguas.* Contains letters of Pedro de Alvarado, Bishop Francisco Marroquín, Bishop Fray Bartolomé de Las Casas, as well as others, all dating ca. 1534. Archivo General del Gobierno de Guatemala A 1.2.5 [1534] 1576–2202. Guatemala City.

Libro Viejo
  1934   *Libro viejo de la fundación de Guatemala y papeles relativos a D. Pedro de Alvarado.* Biblioteca Goathemala. Guatemala City: Sociedad de Geografía e Historia de Guatemala.

LIPSCHUTZ, ALEJANDRO
  1967   *El problema racial en la conquista de América y el mestizaje*, second edition. Santiago, Chile.

LÓPEZ DE VELASCO, JUAN (fl. sixteenth century)
  1894   *Geografía y descripción universal de las Indias.* Madrid.

LUNARDI, FEDERICO
  1946   *La fundación de la ciudad de Gracias a Dios y de las primeras villas y ciudades de Honduras.* Tegucigalpa.

MARKMAN, S. D.
  1963   *San Cristóbal de las Casas.* Seville: Escuela de Estudios Hispano-americanos.
  1966a   *The colonial architecture of Antigua Guatemala.* Philadelphia: American Philosophical Society.
  1966b   "The non-Spanish labor force in the development of the colonial architecture of Guatemala," in *Actas y Memorias del 36° Congreso Internacional de Americanistas, Seville 1964* 4: 189–194.
  1971   "Pueblos de españoles y pueblos de indios en el reino de Guatemala." *Boletín del Centro de Investigaciones Históricas y Estéticas.* Universidad Central de Guatemala. Facultad de Arquitectura y Urbanismo. Caracas.

i.p.a.   "Pueblos de españoles and pueblos de indios," in *Verhandlungen des XXXVIII. Internationalen Amerikanistenkongresses, Stuttgart, 1968.* Munich.

i.p.b.   El paisaje urbano dominicano de pueblos de indios en Chiapas colonial. *Revista de Indias.* Madrid.

MONTGOMERY, GEORGE W.
1839   *Narrative of a journey to Guatemala in Central America in 1838.* New York.

MORENO NAVARRO, ISIDORO
1969   Un aspecto del mestizaje americano. El problema de terminología. *Revista Española de Antropología Americana* 4: 201–218.

MÖRNER, MAGNUS
1960   *El mestizaje, en la historia de Iberoamérica.* Stockholm.
1964   "La política de segregación y el mestizaje en la audiencia de Guatemala." *Revista de Indias* 24 (95–96): 137–152.
1967   *Race mixture in the history of Latin America.* Boston: Little, Brown.

MÖRNER, MAGNUS, editor
1970   *Race and class in Latin America.* Institute for Latin American Studies Series. New York: Columbia University Press.

MORSE, RICHARD M.
1965   Recent research on Latin American urbanization: a selective survey with commentary. *Latin American Research Review* (1): 35–74.

PARDO, J. JOAQUIN
1944   *Efemérides para escribir la historia de. . . Santiago de los caballeros del reino de Guatemala.* Guatemala City.

PARDO, J. JOAQUIN, PEDRO ZAMORA CASTELLANOS
1943   *Guía turística de las ruinas de la Antigua Guatemala.* Guatemala City.

PÉREZ VALENZUELA, PEDRO
1960   Ciudad Vieja. *Universidad de San Carlos de Guatemala.*

PONCE, ALONSO (fl. ca. 1586)
1873   *Relación y verdadera de algunas cosas de las muchas que sucedieron al Padre Fray Alonso Ponce en las provincias de Nueva España,* two volumes. Madrid.

RECINOS, ADRIAN
1949   La ciudad de Guatemala, 1524–1773. *Antropología e Historia de Guatemala* 1 (1): 57–62. Instituto de Antropología e Historia de Guatemala. Guatemala City.
1952   *Pedro de Alvarado, conquistador de México y Guatemala.* Mexico City.

RICARD, ROBERT
1950   La plaza mayor en España y en América española. *Estudios Geográficos* 11: 321–327. Madrid.

ROSENAU, HELEN
1959   *Ideal city: its architectural evolution.* New York: Harper and Row.

ROSENBLATT, ÁNGEL
1954   *La población indígena y el mestizaje en América.* Buenos Aires: Nova.
1967   La población de América en 1492. Viejos y nuevos cálculos. *El Colegio de México.* Mexico City.

SALAS, ALBERTO M.
1960   *Crónica florida del mestizaje de las Indias. Siglo XVI.* Buenos Aires.

SAMAYOA GUEVARA, HÉCTOR HUMBERTO
1960 "La reorganización gremial guatemaltense en la segunda mitad del siglo XVIII. *Antropología e Historia de Guatemala* 12 (1): 63–106. Instituto de Antropología e Historia de Guatemala. Guatemala City.
1962 *Los gremios de artesanos en la ciudad de Guatemala, 1524–1821.* Guatemala City.
1966 El mestizo en Guatemala en el siglo XVI, a través de la legislación indiana. *Antropología e Historia de Guatemala* 18 (7): 65–74.

STANISLAWSKI, DAN
1946 The origin and spread of the grid pattern town. *Geographical Review* 36: 105–120.

SZECSY, JANOS
1953a *Iximché.* Universidad de San Carlos de Guatemala, Facultad de Humanidades. Guatemala City.
1953b *Santiago de los caballeros de Guatemala en Almolonga. Investigaciones del año 1950.* Guatemala City.

TOZZER, ALFRED M.
1941 *Landa's "Relacion de las cosas de Yucatán," a translation.* Papers of the Peabody Museum 18. Cambridge, Mass.: Harvard University Press.

TRENS, MANUEL
1957 *Bosquejos históricos de San Cristóbal Las Casas.* Mexico City.

VÁSQUEZ, FRANCISCO (fl. 1647–ca. 1714)
1944 [1837] *Crónica de la provincia del santísimo nombre de Jesús de Guatemala de la orden de n. seráfico padre San Francisco en el reino de la Nueva España* (second edition), four volumes. Biblioteca Goathemala. Guatemala City: Sociedad de Geografía e Historia de Guatemala.

VÁSQUEZ DE ESPINOZA, ANTONIO (d. 1630)
1943 *La audiencia de Guatemala. Primera parte. Libro quinto del compendio y descripción de las Indias Occidentales, por A.V.E., año de 1629.* Guatemala City.

VILLACORTA, C., JOSÉ ANTONIO
1925–1926 Las cartas relaciones de don Pedro de Alvarado. *Anales de la Sociedad de Geografía e Historia de Guatemala* 2: 215ff. Guatemala City.

VOGT, EVAN
1969 "Chiapas Highlands," in *Handbook of Middle American Indians,* volume seven. Edited by Robert Wauchope, 133–151. Austin, Texas: University of Texas Press.

XIMÉNEZ, FRANCISCO (fl. 1666–ca. 1722)
1929–1931 *Historia de la provincia de San Vicente de Chiapa y Guatemala de la Orden de Predicadores,* three volumes. Biblioteca Goathemala. Guatemala City: Sociedad de Geografía e Historia de Guatemala.

ZAVALA, SILVIO
1971 *Las instituciones jurídicas en la conquista de América.* Mexico City.

ZUCKER, PAUL
1959 *Town and square: from the agora to the village green.* Cambridge, Mass.: M.I.T. Press.

COMMENT by Selma F. Rubin

One school of modern architecture believes that form should follow function in construction, and the same is true of cities. The form of any city may be considered to be the product of all its institutions, especially its political institutions. When changes occur in a city, it is usually the result of the introduction of new institutions or of old institutions changing. Perhaps, as in the case of the *pueblos de indios*, it may be that there were no previous institutions. In short, cities change to meet reality, rather than to conform to a master plan. Dr. Markman discusses this phenomenon in his study of the gridiron city plan and the caste system in colonial Central America.

The paper stresses the role of conscious planning in the spatial structure of the towns and the fact that the "elite were given special consideration in the choice of building sites." He demonstrates the interaction between the breakup of the traditional hierarchy in society and the symbolic meaning of the gridiron plan of the town in colonial Central America. At the end of the colonial period, although the physical form of the checkerboard city remained intact, it no longer reflected the original intent of the founders regarding caste.

Dr. Markman attributes the changing nature of the residential patterns to an increasingly *mestizo* population as well as the decline in economic power of the original Spanish elite. And yet, in a way, there was no basic change because the best centrally located residential areas were still occupied by an elite at the end of the colonial era. The only difference was that it was an elite based on wealth rather than on birth and was no longer reflective of the "fossilized caste system."

Studies such as Dr. Markham has produced are extremely valuable, not only because they are case histories of particular cities in time and place, but because a localistic approach helps to modify easy generalizations by providing exceptions and differences. They allow us to have significant insights into specific problems and situations and also form a basis for comparative studies of urban areas without respect to time or geographic location.

A Brazilian Urban System
in the Nineteenth Century:
Pelotas and Rio de Janeiro

SPENCER L. LEITMAN

The urban expansion of Brazil in the nineteenth century must be seen within the framework of the country's changing economy, the specialized needs of the slave system, and the continuing concentration of central power functions in Rio de Janeiro. In the eighteenth century, when the Luso-Brazilians[1] extended control into the cattle lands of Rio Grande do Sul, three lagoon port towns developed. During the first half of the nineteenth century, each one emphasized a special function: Rio Grande do Norte served as the province's only point of access to the South Atlantic from the elongated lagoons; Pôrto Alegre, controlling the navigable Jacuí River system at the northern extremity of the Patos Lagoon, was the politico-administrative and military complex; and Pelotas, on the channel connecting the Merim and Patos lagoons, was the province's industrial center.

With a large slave force and a vast cattle resource frontier at its command, Pelotas was able to produce *charque*, that is, salt beef, for the plantation slaves and the coastal urban poor, successfully initiating industrialization on an impressive scale. It was primarily through the commercial monopoly of cattle products such as *charque* that Rio de Janeiro incorporated the southern frontier into the national market.

Having a Brazilian outlet in the Plate Basin for cattle products offered advantages to Rio de Janeiro's export-import elite, but it also brought the possibilities of politically serious consequences if it aroused the economic expectations of Riograndense cattle ranchers and *charque* producers. To exploit the plain's natural resources, Rio de Janeiro had encouraged the establishment of Pelotas as a new growth point. But the slave-based industry failed to attract other diverse enterprises or a larger free population; and the town remained

---
[1] Brazilians of Iberian – either Portuguese or Spanish – origin.

only periodically vital. In effect, Rio de Janeiro had developed a satellite town, hundreds of miles distant, which contributed to its own urban growth while it controlled the pace of Pelotense development.

The roots of the imposing *charque* industry in the southern captaincy of Rio Grande were also attributable to the decline of Brazil's northeastern cattle regions, the availability of large reserves of cattle on the southern plains, and the presence of a growing, accessible market. Before Rio Grande do Sul achieved primacy in the production of salt beef in the first decade of the nineteenth century, Ceará, Rio Grande do Norte, Piauí, and Pernambuco supplied Brazil's meat needs (Goulart 1965: 93–97).

Carne do Ceará, or *carne do sol*, as *charque* was called in the Northeast, was an essential part of the diet of Brazil's poor, including slaves in the cities and on sugar plantations (Mawe 1823: 443). Planters needed to bring in *charque* because the high degree of specialization on the sugar plantations had led at times to the elimination of subsistence agriculture. Over the years the sugar planters had progressively pushed the cattle breeders into the merciless climate of the *sertão*, or backlands. For when these two competitive land systems existed in close proximity, unpleasant political situations resulted (Furtado 1965: 58–66).

But, the further back into the *sertão* the stock breeders went, the more difficult it became for them to raise and market their cattle. The poor reputation of the small and bony Northeast cattle rested on the sterile climate that was unsuitable for grasses. Still, in the eighteenth century, the Northeast had an active pastoral economy, natural salt deposits, and market conditions which made Northeast stock breeding potentially productive.

The objective to increase food production in the Northeast remained the same in the eighteenth and nineteenth centuries, but the climatic situation was chronically unstable. When the rains failed, the *sertão* took on all the appearances of a desert. Man and animal thirsted for the dwindling supplies of water. As the dry season turned into years, out-migration occurred. When possible, cattle were moved to scrub land, which soon became grazed over, and the number of water holes diminished. Supplying cattle on the hoof over the backland cattle trails to coastal urban centers proved irregular, as in the case of Salvador, where "the continued sterility, poor pasture, and worse still the rains in summer. . .in the backlands [were] the real causes of the scarcity of cattle in this city" (Biblioteca Nacional [BN] 1784).

Crown authorities knew that food shortages in the cities sparked lower-class resentments, which convinced them to look for and encourage new sources of supply (Arquivo Histórico [AHRGS] 1798). The Great Drought of 1793–1794 "killed thousands of head of cattle

and depopulated [the Northeast's] innumerable and large fazendas,"
leaving Rio Grande do Sul the only Brazilian region able to provide
significant amounts of *charque* (see Table 1; Vilhena 1921: vol. 2, p.
630). Without adequate foodstuffs, Brazil's export economy, based on
plantation slave labor, would face staggering problems.

With a strong ranching tradition and technological experience from
the salt-beef establishments in the Northeast, the Luso-Brazilians
adapted to their new surroundings in Rio Grande do Sul, which were
far better for ranching than those in Portugal or in any other area of
Brazil at that time. Cattle hunters and muleteers from São Paulo and
Laguna had opened Rio Grande do Sul to Luso-Brazilian penetration
by the middle of the eighteenth century (Cesar 1970: 88–89).

Subsequent imperial wars against the Spanish-Americans, which
lasted into the nineteenth century, added the soldier-rancher to the
population, and a small number of Azorian peasants brought in by the
Portuguese Crown eventually entered the ranching economy (Rüdiger
1965: 67). By the time of the Portuguese court's arrival in Brazil in
1808, Rio Grande do Sul *charqueadas*, or salt-beef processing establishments, were feeding Ceará's slave population (Koster 1817: 228).

The coming of *charque* industry in 1780 had a multiple effect on the
hinterland, forcing cattlemen to hold rodeos, seek better pasture lands,
more clearly divide properties, and push across Riograndense
frontiers into the neutral lands which separated the Luso-Brazilians
from the Spanish-Americans (Saint-Hilaire 1939; Osório 1922;
Machado 1947: 131). Output levels in the period 1811–1820 were high,
owing their success, however, more to market usurpation than to the
slow process of ranch rationalization. Luso-Brazilian military victo-
ries against the Spanish-Americans had resulted in a redirection of the
flow of cattle from Uruguay to Pelotas (Beraza 1964: 103; Humphreys
1940: 77,81). In addition, Riograndense cattlemen attached to guerrilla
and militia units extended their ranch operations into Uruguay, maintaining commercial links with Pelotas.

After Uruguayan independence in 1828, Pelotas' production leveled
off, but Riograndense ranchers remained entrenched inside Uruguay.
Prolonged civil disturbances in the new republican state during the
next four decades allowed Pelotas to supply part of the Brazilian
charque market, while Riograndense ranchers reinforced their hold
on northern Uruguay. In 1850 Riograndenses operated 400 ranches in
Uruguay, with hundreds of thousands of head of cattle in an area of
more than 1,800 square leagues (Brazil 1857). From these well-stocked
natural ranges and from the cattle lands of the province's southwest
Campanha, trail bosses drove their herds to Pelotas.

The *charqueadas* were strung out along the Pelotas, São Gonçalo,
and Santa Barbara rivers, a short distance from the town itself. In

Table 1. Rio Grande do Sul *charque* exports (in kilograms) (From Varela 1897: 462–463)

1808	12,751,080	1858	21,642,140
1812	18,272,704	1859 (first half)	10,896,946
1816	24,378,243	1850–1860	24,905,882
1820	13,939,655	1860–1861	29,335,152
1837–1838	2,292,263	1861–1862	27,753,161
1838–1839	2,310,815	1862–1863	31,231,222
1839–1840	6,362,241	1863–1864	18,389,430
1840–1841	5,835,726	1864–1865	35,192,170
1841–1842	8,818,601	1865–1866	30,864,703
1842–1843	10,845,305	1884–1885	22,644,351
1843–1844	16,345,440	1885–1886	24,221,273
1844–1845	13,969,784	1886–1887	20,108,780
1850	27,079,964	1887 (second half)	6,534,230
1851	28,007,766	1888	27,670,430
1852	21,926,916	1889	25,660,196
1853	25,764,900	1890	26,000,260
1854	20,616,584	1891	33,935,773
1855	17,200,569	1892	35,707,388
1856	18,053,794	1893	32,324,785
1857	21,475,655	1894	28,382,273

Pelotas proper the *charqueadores* had their well-furnished houses. Foreigners were immediately impressed with the town's straight streets, well-kept church, and numerous slave attendants, but most of all by the entrepreneurial behavior of these men who sat on English saddles. One foreign cattle dealer and long-time resident in the province wrote that the elegance and the manners of the Pelotense were those of the most gracious Parisian (Dreys 1927: 112–115). Such men were not only interested in European culture, but in sustaining the growth of their industry. By the 1830's they had placed a steamship on the Patos Lagoon, had interested a North American firm in establishing a steamship line, and had made plans to improve local port and channel facilities (Isabelle 1949: 294, 297).

In contrast, the cattlemen, gauchos, and peons brought the dust and habits of the *Campanha* into Pelotas between the months of December and May. At first glance all the riders, glued to their horses, appeared to dress alike in their calico shirts, the famous pantaloons of the pampas, and the broad-brimmed hats. On closer examination, however, the rancher's garb was of better quality, his side arms up to date, and his spurs of silver (Dreys 1927: 159).

The long drive from roundups in Uruguay could take weeks before the cattle reached the Passo dos Negros, the gateway to the grazed-over flatlands of the cattle fair on the outskirts of the *charqueadas*. As on the trail, the drovers' days were full of movement until the entire herd was sold. Executing tasks with extraordinary speed and apparent ease, they kept the various herds from mixing. The horsemen cut their herds into lots consisting of hundreds of head, while the *charqueadores* went about closing deals, after "calculating [the cattle's] value quickly and with admirable precision" (Smith 1922: 137–138).

In the warm summer months, when the meat and hides dried best, some *charqueadas* could run through 30,000 head (d'Azeredo 1957: 33–34). The entire animal was turned into salable products: *charque*, hides (salted and dried), tallow, grease, hair, and horns. During the production season, rivers ran red with blood, and the entrails choked even the canoe traffic (Dreys 1927: 138). The lean longhorn Rio-grandense cattle accepted the salting process readily.

After being salted, pressed, and dried, *charque* weighed less than an equal quantity of fresh meat, with a preservation period of at least ten months (Couty 1881b: 183–195). Packed on the backs of sure-footed mules, *charque* could reach the most isolated plantations tucked away in mountain valleys. Although predominantly dependent upon slaves, and without machines, the *charqueadas* were industrial enterprises in that a comprehensive coordination of material and the application of different technical skills all pointed toward the common purpose of production (Gilberti 1961: 89–90).

Even with the capitalist impediment, slavery, to industrialization, *charqueadores* were not ready to destroy the slave system. For socio-political reasons, the *charqueadores* had to accept the institution of slavery, which imposed certain handicaps on future development (Cardoso 1962: 186–191). In the face of acute labor shortages and abolition of the international slave traffic, Pelotas continued to absorb slave labor, and barracked more than 5,000 slaves in the *charque* industry alone (AHRGS 1832: 155). Despite the protests of a few municipal council members, the province accepted slaves from other parts of the empire who had individually or collectively challenged white rule (Arquivo da Prefeitura Municipal de Pôrto Alegre [AMPA] 1835).

By 1830, approximately 30 percent of the province's 160,000 inhabitants were slaves, in an area one-half the size of France (Arquivo Nacional [AN] n.d.). Inside their plants, *charqueadores*, within the limits of the slave system, arranged men with an eye toward increasing efficiency and production. In the first half of the nineteenth century, the industrial work force of a *charqueada* consisted mostly of slaves, between eighty and one hundred, who worked closely with whites, mestizos, and Guaraní Indians (Dreys 1927: 138–142; Couty 1881b). Integration was a reflection of severe local labor shortages (AN 1824, 1828). By integrating his work force, a *charqueador* could demand the same standards of performance from all his workers, maintain social order, and protect his investment with the use of salaried laborers in the more dangerous tasks.

Not unexpectedly, in a situation where there were practical socio-political considerations operating along with a high degree of specialization, the *charqueadas* were brutal places. One Brazilian scholar, in referring to these penitentiary-like establishments, concludes that the condition of labor was worse there than in any other work situation in Brazil (Cardoso 1962: 159). The slave mortality rate was almost two and one-half times higher than that of the free population in the entire province (Soares 1860: 170). Undoubtedly, then, it was higher in Pelotas. The harsh discipline which the labor process required forced the slave to become a passive instrument of production. Major outbreaks of violence, although not unknown, nevertheless were infrequent. Managerial efficiency, the presence of a large municipal police force, and the ability to close off each *charqueada* separately, if violence occurred, prevented threats to the social system (Dreys 1927: 193).

As Pelotas' industrial activity maintained its importance within the Brazilian economy, its links with the mercantile functions of Rio de Janeiro became increasingly stronger. Responding to demands created by industrial and commercial activities of local port towns along the coast and the industrial activities of Pelotas, Brazil's capital developed secondary activities, such as shipbuilding. The Riograndenses, too, reacting to increases in the *charque* trade, built their own one- and two-masted *sumacas* and *pataxos*, with carrying capacities of 12,000 *arrobas* (approximately 24 tons). Though perhaps not famous for their speed, shape, and quality, these vessels plied the waters between Rio Grande do Sul and Rio de Janeiro by the hundreds, ranging as far north as Maranhão (*Jornal do Commercio* [*JC*] 1829–1835).

From time to time the Riograndenses attempted to assert some degree of economic independence, but it was of a precarious kind, for the Rio de Janeiro merchants controlled the most important aspects of trade: finance, distribution, and commerce. Rio de Janeiro's export-import elite, together with its political allies, opposed the autonomous economic development of the salt-beef and hide industry in Rio Grande do Sul through commercial monopoly, fiscal measures, and military and political force. The detouring of the hide trade away from the emporium of Rio de Janeiro by dealing directly with foreign captains in Rio Grande do Sul in the 1820's and 1830's, many of whom carried salt, was still a narrow market unable to compete with the established trade (de Saint-Adolphe and Milliet 1845: 430–431; *JC* 1835: IX (129), 2).

Pelotas' production increased only when there were political disruptions in the competitive producing Platine states, European blockades of Montevideo and Buenos Aires, and during one period of internal war in Rio Grande do Sul (Cardoso 1962: 179). Rio de Janerio treated Rio Grande do Sul as a type of large *estancia* to serve the needs of the empire, an appendage of a larger economic system which undermined attempts at political and economic diversification.

A constant source of Pelotense irritation were the fiscal and tariff policies of the empire, which discriminated against home production (AHRGS 1834; Arquivo da Assemblea Legislativa do Rio Grande do Sul [AALRGS] 1835). Besides having lower production costs, Pelotense rivals paid modest amounts to export their cattle products (AALRGS 1835). Moreover, the Riograndenses needed more cattle lands in order to expand their industry. Here, too, Rio de Janeiro neglected this special demand, making it perfectly clear to the Riograndenses that it would not promote the extension of Riograndense cattle-raising activities across the border after Uruguayan independence (AHRGS 1829).

Increasingly subordinate to Rio de Janeiro, Pelotas in turn attempted to strengthen its own economic and political relationships with its hinterland. To shore up a faltering economy, keep alive competition with its neighbors, and comply with the political and economic demands coming from Rio de Janeiro, Pelotense *charqueadores* demanded more from their cattle resource frontier in the form of more cattle, taxes, and recruits. For example, in the 1830's tension increased between the lagoon towns and the cattle lands of the *Campanha*, breaking out into a full-scale rebellion known as the Ragamuffin War (1835–1845). It was an expression of maximum tension between two interdependent economic sectors of Rio Grande do Sul, which were both in a subordinate position to the mercantile interests of Rio de Janeiro (Leitman 1973).

The Ragamuffin War provides one of the best insights into the nature of the Pelotas-Rio de Janeiro urban system. Leadership for the movement came from Pelotas' cattle regions of Bagé, Piratini, and above all the Jaguarão which controlled the productive cattle zone of the Uruguayan department of Serro Largo, where Riograndense ranchers predominated. Opposition to the Ragamuffin rebels in the province of Rio Grande do Sul came from Pelotas and the mercantile port of Rio Grande. There was ambivalent support for the cause in Pôrto Alegre, Triumpho, and Rio Pardo, which had modest *charqueada* establishments. Even though many *charqueadores* were proprietors of ranches which fed their own *charqueadas*, the interests of ranchers and *charqueadores* in relation to profits were distinct. Before 1835, one of the important frontier cattle families, who produced the Ragamuffin's general-president, had established a *charqueada* on the frontier at Jaguarao in an attempt to offset pressure being exerted by Pelotas and Pôrto Alegre, the latter carrying out the military and political will of Rio de Janeiro.

From the outset of the Ragamuffin War the Pelotense *charqueadores* remained loyal to the central government in Rio de Janeiro. Pelotas could not sever its economic ties with the capital, for it was part of a single well-articulated national economic system. Exports of salt beef, after falling off in the first two years of the war, rose sharply after 1838. The Ragamuffin rebels were never able to dominate the lagoon waterways and the port towns, except for a brief period in 1835–1836. However, they did keep up military pressure with three separate sieges on Pôrto Alegre and attacks on Pelotas which were, in part, attempts to impress *charqueada* slaves into the rebel ranks. Warned of impending military maneuvers, *charqueadores* moved their work force to more secure areas, where they would set up temporary operations. After 1840 threats on Pelotas disappeared, and most of the *charqueadores* returned. Militarily hard-pressed, the Ragamuffin rebels controlled only parts of the province's cattle interior. Cattle for the Pelotas *charqueadas* came from the same cattle resource frontier which was in a state of rebellion.

Although the Ragamuffins traded cattle with Montevideo for essential military equipment, the rebels relied on the Pelotas *charqueadas* for a market, too. In drawing the cattle from the interior towards Pelotas, both the cattle lands and Pelotas continued to be an essential part of the Rio de Janeiro mercantile system. *Caudillos* leading the rebel armies carried on a personal trade with Pelotas, sealing the fate of the rebellion. This feature of the Rio Grande do Sul economy, perhaps more than the 12,000 Brazilian soldiers under the Duque de Caxias, finally brought the war to a close; for, when the cattle resources of the interior were removed, the rebels had to come to terms.

Thus, the Ragamuffin War did not destroy the Pelotas and Rio de Janeiro urban system. Opportunities for higher profits and speculative commerce had increased the flow of cattle resources to the lagoon towns, especially Pelotas, which, after the war, was in a far better position in relation to the smaller *charqueada* centers of Pôrto Alegre and Triumpho. Yet, despite the concessions that Rio de Janeiro had made to the Ragamuffin rebels during and after the war, Pelotas was falling behind Montevideo and Buenos Aires in scale of enterprise, entrepreneurship, and the accumulation of capital (Cardoso 1962: 181–186).

But the prospects of assembling capital sufficient to establish more and larger *charqueadas* appeared more certain in the 1850's for a number of reasons. In 1842, Rio de Janeiro had imposed a 25 percent tariff on foreign *charque*. Later, in 1851 and again in 1857, Rio de Janeiro had pressured Uruguay to abolish frontier customs on cattle passing from Uruguay to Rio Grande do Sul and to permit Riograndense ranchers to fatten cattle across the border (Brazil 1929a, 1929b). More importantly, perhaps, was the continuation of Platine internal disturbances, which stimulated the cattle flow to Pelotas. The strongest voices in Pelotas, despite significant production increases in the 1850's, called on Rio de Janeiro to raise the duty on foreign *charque* still higher, for Montevideo and Buenos Aires continued to score impressive successes in the Brazilian market. Rio de Janeiro responded, instead, with criticism of Pelotas' inefficient production methods (Cardoso 1962: 177–178).

According to Cardoso's excellent study (1962), industrial slavery imposed limits on rationalizing production. Intensifying production was extremely difficult, if not impossible, when the *charqueador* was more interested in social control and handicapped by high costs. Cardoso also compares other aspects of Riograndense economy to those of the Plate, such as cattle availability, port facilities, capitalist incentives, and entrepreneurship. He is very correct in that this is not a purely economic question, but one which must be seen within a political and social context.

One point is evident, however: the Pelotense *charqueadas* were profitable, otherwise they would not have persisted. The question is still open as to whether or not their profits were lower in comparison with their competitors, as Cardoso contends. One can argue, though, that Pelotas' precarious position throughout the nineteenth century was a result of its strong market ties to Rio de Janeiro rather than industrial slavery (Cardoso 1962: 174). The Pelotas-Rio de Janeiro urban system obstructed diversified production and restricted urbanization in the lagoon port. Shortages of capital and labor, the state of technology, high intraregional transportation costs, and other simultaneously acting forces served as a brake on Pelotas' economic development.

It was not necessary for the Rio de Janeiro mercantilists to invest capital in Pelotas in order to monopolize *charque* in the national market. Rio de Janeiro monopolists were aware that Rio Grande do Sul alone could not supply all of Brazil's *charque* needs, and therefore employed a policy which encouraged foreign competition (Brazil 1929b: 22–23; Cardoso 1962: 179–180). Further, even if the Rio de Janeiro merchants had wanted to invest, it would have been difficult. Brazil lacked financial institutions and methods whereby potential savings could be mobilized and channeled into the *charqueada* industry. Therefore, the best solution was to retain Pelotas as a complementary producer, which would, in addition, provide Rio de Janeiro with a steady revenue.

The early integration of Pelotas into the national economy during the first two decades of the nineteenth century had determined its dependence, and future developments were henceforth advantageous to Rio de Janeiro and detrimental to Rio Grande do Sul. Rio de Janeiro now had a Brazilian cattle-producing area close to Platine reserves which would assure a supply to the national market in times of crisis. Generally, however, the Rio de Janeiro monopolists preferred to buy cheaper and better quality *charque* from the Spanish-Americans. It is important to note that despite all the political disturbances in the nineteenth century in the Plata Basin, including Rio Grande do Sul, there was always one cattle port open. Interior cattle movements were redirected toward that port, and *charqueadores*, both Luso-Brazilian and Spanish-American, often transferred their operations there.

This theme, like Cardoso's thesis, is subject to a number of criticisms. There are other factors which retarded the economic growth of Pelotas, which need further study: fluctuations in the national and international economy, the competitive advantages of Buenos Aires and Montevideo, the entrepreneurial and commercial roles of the Portuguese in Rio de Janeiro, and the monopolization of the supply of foodstuffs in Brazil. Similarly, the development of Pelotas' *charque* and hide export industry was a function of worldwide economic conditions. Whatever other factors need to be considered, Pelotas' industrial activities did bring the southern frontier that much closer to the national scene, and added to the mercantile and urban growth of Rio de Janeiro.

REFERENCES

ARQUIVO DA ASSEMBLEA LEGISLATIVA DO RIO GRANDE DO SUL (AALRGS)
1835 *Actas da Assemblea Provincial, Pôrto Alegre, May 2, 1835*. Arquivo da Assemblea Legislativa do Rio Grande do Sul, Actas da Assemblea Provincial, 1835–1836. Pôrto Alegre.
ARQUIVO DA PREFEITURA MUNICIPAL DE PÔRTO ALEGRE (AMPA)
1835 *Report of Francisco Xavier Ferreira, Pôrto Algre, April 27, 1835*. Arquivo da Prefeitura Municipal de Pôrto Alegre, Livro de Actas. Pôrto Alegre.
ARQUIVO HISTÓRICO DO RIO GRANDE DO SUL (AHRGS)
1798–1799 *Letters by Souza Coutinho to Cabral da Cámara, Palacio de Queluz, September 22, 1798, and May 10, 1799*. Arquivo Histórico do Rio Grande do Sul, Avisos do Governo. Pôrto Alegre.
1829 *Letter by Manuel Jorge Rodrigues to Salvador Maciel, Pôrto Alegre, July 12, 1829*. Arquivo Histórico do Rio Grande do Sul, Avisos do Governo. Pôrto Alegre.
1832 *Letter by Manuel Antônio Galvão to Joaquim Lopes de Barros, Pôrto Alegre, July 7, 1832*. Arquivo Histórico do Rio Grande do Sul, Caixa 155. Pôrto Alegre.
1834 *Conselho General, Pôrto Alegre, January 11, 1834(sessão extraordin-*

aria). Arquivo Histórico do Rio Grande do Sul, Caixa 82, n. 301. Pôrto Alegre.

ARQUIVO NACIONAL (AN)

1824–1828 *Letters by José Feliciano Fernandes Pinheiro to Francisco Villela Barboza, Pôrto Alegre, September 10, 1824; and by Salvador Maciel to Marques de Maceijo, Pôrto Alegre, January 10, 1828.* Arquivo Nacional, XM 144. Rio de Janeiro.

n.d. *José Pedro Cezar, Mapa estatistica.* Arquivo Nacional, 776.6 5G. Rio de Janeiro.

BERAZA, AGUSTIN

1964 *La economia en la Banda Oriental, 1811–1820.* Montevideo: Impr. Nacional.

BIBLIOTECA NACIONAL (BN)

1784 *Letter by Marques de Angeja to José Cezar de Menezes, September 28, 1784.* Biblioteca Nacional, 1–5–2. Rio de Janeiro.

BRAZIL

1857 "Ministerio das Relações Exteriores. Protocollos das conferencias havidas na corte de Rio de Janeiro entre os plenipotenciarios de Brasil a da Republica Orientel do Uruguay para a revisão do tratado de commercio e navigação de 12 de octubre de 1851," in *Relatorio da reparticão dos negocios estrangeiros, 1857.* Rio de Janeiro: Impr. Nacional.

1929a "Tratado de commercio e navigação entre o Brasil e a Republica Oriental do Uruguay, 1851," in *Uruguay-Brasil, commercio e navigação, 1851–1927.* By Henrique Pinheiro de Vasconcellos, Artigo IV. Rio de Janeiro: Impr. Nacional.

1929b "Tratado de commercio e navigação entre o Brasil e a Republica Oriental de Uruguay, 1857," in *Uruaguy-Brasil, commercio e navigação, 1851–1927.* By Henrique Pinheiro de Vasconcellos, Artigo II. Rio de Janeiro: Impr. Nacional.

CARDOSO, FERNANDO HENRIQUE

1962 *Capitalismo e escravidão no Brasil meridional.* São Paulo: Difusão Europeia do Livro.

CESAR, GUILHERMINO

1970 *História do Rio Grande do Sul: periódo colonial.* Pôrto Alegre: Editora Globo.

COUTY, LOUIS

1881a L'alimentation au Brésil et dans les pays voisins. *Revue d'Hygiène et de Police Sanitaire* 3: 183–195; 279–294; 470–486.

1881b *L'esclavage au Brésil.* Paris: Librairie de Guillaumin.

D'AZEREDO, FRANCISCO DE PAULA

1957 Em transito pelo Rio Grande do Sul em 1816. *Provincia de São Pedro* 21: 2634.

DE SAINT-ADOLPHE, J. C., R. MILLIET

1845 *Diccionario geográfico de imperio do Brazil.* Paris: Typ. de Fain et Thunot.

DREYS, NICOLAU

1927 *Notícia descriptiva da provincia do Rio-Grande de S. Pedro do Sul.* Rio Grande: Biblioteca Riograndense.

FURTADO, CELSO

1965 *The economic growth of Brazil: a survey from colonial to modern times.* Berkeley and Los Angeles: University of California Press.

GILBERTI, HORACIO C. E.
1961   *Historia economica de la ganadería argentina.* Buenos Aires: Ediciones Solar/Hachette.

GOULART, JOSÉ ALÍPIO
1965   *Brasil do boi e do couro.* Rio de Janeiro: GRD.

HUMPHREYS, ROBERT ARTHUR, editor
1940   *British consular reports on the trade and politics of Latin America, 1824–1826.* London: Offices of the Royal Historical Society.

ISABELLE, ARSENE
1949   *Viagem ao Rio da Prata e ao Rio Grande do Sul.* Rio de Janeiro: Editora Zelio Valverde.

Jornal do Commercio (JC)
1829–1835   *Jornal do Commercio,* Rio de Janeiro.

KOSTER, HENRY
1817   *Travels in Brazil,* two volumes. Philadelphia: M. Carey and Son.

LEITMAN, SPENCER
1973   "Cattle and caudillos in the Ragamuffin War." Paper presented at the Southwest Social Science Association, Dallas.

MACHADO, ANTONIO CARVOS
1947   A charqueada. *Provincia São Pedro* 8: 121–136.

MAWE, JOHN
1823   *Travels in the interior of Brazil* (second edition). London: Longman.

OSÓRIO, FERNANDO
1922   *A cidade de Pelotas.* Pelotas: Typ. do Diario Popular.

RÜDIGER, SEBALT
1965   *Colonização e propriedade de terras no Rio Grande do Sul: Seculo 18.* Pôrto Alegre: Instituto Estadual do Livro.

SAINT-HILAIRE, AUGUSTO
1939   *Viagem ao Rio Grande do Sul, 1820–1821.* São Paulo: Companhia Editora Nacional.

SMITH, HERBERT H.
1922   *Do Rio de Janeiro a Cuyaba: notas de um naturalista.* São Paulo: Companhia Melhoramentos.

SOARES, SEBASTIÃO FERREIRA
1860   *Notas estatisticas sobre a producção e carestia dos generos alimenticos no imperio do Brazil.* Rio de Janeiro: J. Villeneuve.

VARELA, ALFREDO
1897   *Riogrande do Sul: descripçao physica, historica, e economica.* Pelotas: Echenique e Irmao.

VILHENA, LUÍZ DOS SANTOS
1921   *Recopilçao de noticia soteropolitanas e brasilicas,* three volumes. Bahia: Imprensa Official do Estado.

COMMENT by Selma F. Rubin

It is always possible to explain *why* one city grew while another with apparently equal or superior advantages languished. In modern times the city must be usable by the new methods of transportation, the railroad, the bus or truck, and the airplane. It must be a place where real decisions are made, perhaps the site of government. In the case of Pelotas, as Professor Leitman points out, the city became a growing urban area because of the meat-salting plants located there and through the stimulus of Rio de Janeiro, which wanted to incorporate "the southern frontier into the national market." When, however, the local economy failed to stimulate the growth or demand for local business services, Pelotas remained dependent upon the "goodwill" of Rio de Janeiro for its economic viability.

When the cattle industry declined in the Northeast due to the encroachments of the sugar culture, the political turmoil, and the weather, it was to the advantage of Rio de Janeiro to support the ranching economy in Rio Grande do Sul. During the first half of the nineteenth century Rio de Janeiro encouraged the development of the existing meat-salting plants in Pelotas. As a consequence, Pelotas prospered. This prosperity was based in part on the fact that there were constant internal disturbances in the Plata region which reduced the flow of cattle from Buenos Aires and Montevideo to Rio de Janeiro. After the middle of the century, however, the internal disturbances declined and Buenos Aires and Montevideo were able "to score impressive success in the Brazilian market." Rio de Janeiro encouraged foreign competition but discouraged economic diversification in Pelotas. This, of course, increased the dependency of Pelotas on Rio de Janeiro, and thus the economic growth of Pelotas was retarded. Nevertheless, as Professor Leitman points out, "Pelotas' industrial activities did bring the southern frontier that much closer to the national scene, and added to the mercantile and urban growth of Rio de Janeiro."

The type of economic urban biography that Professor Leitman has written may be of particular value today. Representatives of multinational corporations, for example, might want to take a close look at studies such as his before they authorize feasibility reports and capital investments in developing areas. The existence, or even the possibility of the existence, of an economic dependency relationship like the one between Pelotas and Rio de Janeiro in the nineteenth century might mean a considerable difference in their projected bottom line results.

Migrations and Urbanization
in Brazil, 1870–1930:
A Global Interpretation

JORGE BALÁN

Toward the middle of the nineteenth century, concern over sparse population in the imperial territory increased in Brazil. Almost all of the annual messages of the provincial presidents contained references to this fact, and the imperial government was faced with adopting policies to regulate population expansion. In spite of the rapid increase in the Brazilian population during the eighteenth century and the first half of the nineteenth century, accelerated by the massive importation of slaves, waves of voluntary Portuguese migrants, and the relocation of the imperial court to Brazil, there was no doubt that Brazil's progress was being held back by the lack of population in the extended territory. The Brazilian population was not at all low for the time, estimated at more than six million inhabitants by 1840 (about the same number as in the United States by 1800), and the rate of increase was probably high compared to those of Western Europe. However, more than total volume, the extremely unequal distribution and composition of the population were of great concern to the upper class of the time.

The concern over regulating the distribution of the population had diverse origins. There was a labor scarcity especially for the cultivation of coffee, a new and dynamic sector of the economy that was expanding in the relatively uninhabited southeast. At the same time, however, an effective distribution of the population throughout the territory was necessary to preserve the borders, diminish isolation, and provide soldiers for politico-military contingencies. These necessities became contradictory. Labor for coffee cultivation had to be slave labor, while the settlers and soldiers had to be free men. Possible solutions appeared to be continuation of the slave trade, the possibility of European colonization, or even the settling of the free indigenous population in certain areas through colonization schemes.

The persistence of slavery and the slave trade clearly made the furthering of European immigration and the employment of indigenous free labor more difficult.

Seen from today's perspective, the process begun in Brazil by the middle of the nineteenth century was the formation of a national security with the characteristics of a capitalist structure: regional units were weakly protected by and linked to the imperial center but not integrated economically, and the more dynamic sectors were based on slavery. The crucial point of the process for several decades was the coffee plantation economy, installed in relatively newly and thinly populated regions, which after a century of transformation became the national hegemonic institution. During this long period, demographic problems were often political problems and the object of more or less conscious policies. The adapted solutions clearly reflect the relative success of a new class (or a new sector of an old class) in constructing a capitalist system, and they reflect the emergence of new national political centers.

One way of tracing the formation of capitalist structures in national societies is through following the vicissitudes of the labor force, especially its geographic movements. These are definitive processes: the history of the formation of a formally free labor force, occupationally and geographically mobile, but by necessity tied to salaried work, is part of the history of the formation of modern capitalism. To the extent that this formation is brought about by new economic activities, by expansion of other activities, or by the disappearance of others, the beginning of capitalism in a national society can be described in terms of population movements.

The object of this work is simultaneously ambitious and modest: I want to describe the history of this process in Brazil as seen through the migratory flows that occurred during the years between 1870 and 1930, looking at how migratory flows reflected the relation between population and social structures in the process of change. This objective is quite ambitious and I only claim to give here the rough outline for such an analysis. On the other hand, the work is modest because I do not claim to bring any new evidence. The material about migratory flows and the interpretations of the historical formation of Brazil will be taken from basic sources covering the topics considered:

1. The Brazilian contraband in slaves, which for two decades was an illegal trade tolerated by the Brazilian authorities, and only partially prevented by the British fleet, ended in 1850, coinciding with the development of coffee as the main export product. Brazil was the principal world producer of coffee, a demand for which had increased notoriously with the expansion of the industrial revolution in Europe

and the United States, as was reflected in its high prices, except for occasional crisis years. The opening of virgin lands to expand coffee plantations along the Paraiba Valley demanded increased inputs of labor, which consisted almost solely of slaves. Free workers were used only for limited assignments – for the opening of new lands, for farming for local consumption, and for controlling the transportation of goods by mules. The colonial export economy and slavery in Brazil were thus linked together. So, just as the distribution of land grants depended on the ownership of slaves, obtaining essential credit for the cultivation of coffee also required the ownership of slaves. The nearer an economic sector was to the export sector, and therefore the higher the returns on capital, the greater the use of slaves (Cardoso 1962).[1]

The end of the slave trade brought a scarcity of labor (given the low or negative natural increase in the slave population coupled with the expansion of the coffee economy) with the consequent increase in the slaves' value and an internal mobilization of slaves toward the coffee plantation region. The transfer of slave labor had begun before 1850, but toward the 1870's it increased and became critical for other export sectors. This concentration in and around the Paraiba Valley was a source of justified concern, principally in the northeast, but also in Rio Grande do Sul and in the mining region of Minas Gerais. Unsuccessful attempts were made to prohibit interstate slave trade and at the same time to increase taxes on this trade (Prado 1960: 197–198). The continued expansion of coffee cultivation and the statistics on exportation attest to the inevitability of the relocation of slaves. But this relocation, aggravating the crisis of the slave regime in the regions of origin, only temporarily resolved the problem of the lack of manual labor in the coffee plantation economy.

From a merely quantitative point of view, slavery could not solve the problem of labor scarcity. It is estimated that from the beginning of the eighteenth century to the middle of the nineteenth century three million slaves entered Brazil (Curtin 1969); but around 1872 there were only a million and a half. Moreover, the slaves' escapes, which occurred throughout Brazilian history, increased in number with the abolitionist movement and urbanization. The spontaneous liberations and partial liberations of slaves which occurred before 1888, brought the total number of slaves by that date to little more than one-third of the number recorded in 1872. Yet the demand for labor, even considering only that generated by the expansion of the coffee trade, was at that moment very great – the concentration of the entire slave

[1] In order not to burden the reader, and given the essayist nature of this work, I will limit the references in the text to a minimum. At the end of this article the reader will find a list of the works cited in the text.

population in plantation regions was hardly sufficient to satisfy the demand generated by their development.

On the other hand, the permanance of slavery practically excluded other possible sources of manual labor. Indigenous manual labor was used in activities subsidiary to the coffee economy: in food production, in training jobs, occasionally as tenants harvesting coffee or as foremen and *camaradas* [comrades] on the coffee plantation, and in transportation. The increase in the price of coffee and the scarcity of slaves gradually eliminated the production of foods on large properties and soon effected the absorption of the small ones by the large ones. The free, displaced population was partially integrated into the large haciendas, especially as *agregados*; some emigrated but only rarely did they accept what was generally considered slave work (Stein 1961). Adhering strictly to the values of a slave society, free workers or freed slaves refused to work as wage workers on the level of slaves (Cardoso 1962). Foreign manual labor, which under several programs of colonization had been attracted to Brazil, also could not be added to the slave labor in the production of coffee: in the south they formed colonies outside the export sector of the economy. When they were used to reinforce slave labor (although they were never mixed in the same jobs), they rarely did so successfully. The landholders preferred slave labor, and at the same time the settlers resented the working conditions and the bonds that tied them to the plantation as if they were slaves (Da Costa 1966: 78–83).

2. Discussions on the advantages of European migration increased during the 1870's. Brazil had been the first Latin American country to propose and begin plans for European colonization. On numerous occasions plans for colonization by the indigenous population were also proposed, but rarely implemented. But these plans only partially responded to the labor needs. Excluding some colonization attempts made by the Portuguese government during the eighteenth century (in the period after independence), repeated experiments in colonization were made, especially in the south of the country; these plans gave preference to northern Europeans, Germans, and Swiss. Through the initiative or with the help of the imperial government, the explicit goal was to populate the country. Although welcome, voluntary immigrants, especially Portuguese, had concentrated themselves in the cities (especially Rio de Janeiro) or were tied in one way or another to the dynamic sector of the economy, that is to say, to export. Colonization, in contrast to voluntary immigration, would fill the unpopulated areas and assure control over the national territory. In Rio Grande do Sul and Santa Catarina important colonies were established along the route toward the north, but in Rio de Janeiro

the expansion of coffee cultivation limited the available land for colonization, and in Minas such lands had not really existed since mining began (Da Costa 1966). Official colonization often failed because of the lack of economic viability for a basically political project: without access to markets, colonies rapidly scattered or regressed to subsistence economies (Tavares et al. 1972).

In the decades after the end of the slave traffic, private colonization increased, intended in great part to provide manual labor for the coffee economy. The most important efforts before abolition were in west São Paulo (Diégues 1964). In the majority of the regional coffee estates, all use of slave labor was not abandoned, but foreign manual labor was added in sharecropping systems. Although jobs were clearly separated, with free men and slaves rarely working side by side, in most cases serious friction between landowners and settlers soon arose (Da Costa 1966). Systematically, landowners complained of a lack of discipline and of the impossibility of meeting the contracted obligations in the sharecropping plan, while settlers complained of all the ways by which their incomes were reduced and payment of their contracted debts (and therefore mobility) were impeded. With the juxtaposition of systems of slave and free labor, the landowners who used slaves on part of their lands gave their worst lands for sharecropping and tended to consider free workers as an alternative labor source which diminished the initial investment and lowered maintenance costs. The system that best supplied manual labor with little investment was one of sharecropping as payment against debts. But such a system contradicted the expectations of improvement on the part of the immigrants and tied them as chattels to the coffee plantations, virtually as if they had been slaves (Hall 1969).

The plans of colonization by the indigenous population, the objectives of which were to settle a wandering population and to fill unpopulated areas in a permanent way, never succeeded on a large scale and little mention is made of them in the literature. The difficulties with foreign colonization provoked enthusiasm in Minas Gerais (where such colonization was less important than in São Paulo or further south) for indigenous colonization: "...to the example of what was done in the Province of Bahia, by the action of 'Sinimbu,'" according to the words of the mining vice-president in 1859 (Da Costa 1966: 113; Iglésias 1958: ch. 4). Likewise, in the same year the São Paulo presidential report contained references to a possible trend toward indigenous colonization. However, the settling or redistribution of indigenous manual labor would do little to increase the total volume of the population, a problem which on the national level was as much of economic as of politico-military importance and which provoked greater political controversy than the slave trade. The sparse

population and the relatively large proportion of slaves was a cause
of concern. For this reason there had always been fear of a possible
rebellion caused by escaped slaves and the subsequent formation of
communities of freed or escaped slaves. This fear returned when for
some reason the adult white population diminished. The War of the
Triple Alliance against Paraguay (1865–1870) stimulated these fears.
For the military elite in political ascension, this war demonstrated the
necessity of populating the border regions in order to strengthen them;
the difficulty of recruiting soldiers from the scanty population and the
impossibility of using slaves to make up an army; and the absence of
protection in slave regions when free men were mobilized for war.
This elite, which grew stronger after the war, saw the need for
increased foreign immigration, and therefore supported abolition
(Prado 1960).

3. During the years immediately preceding abolition, the flow of
European immigrants to Brazil began to increase reaching its highest
levels during the following decade, and continued with some inter-
ruptions (e.g. World War I) until the depression of 1930. Although it
was of some importance later, immigration never reached the levels
it had from 1886 to 1895. In absolute terms, immigration to Brazil was
lower than that to Argentina and much lower than that to the United
States. Nevertheless, its impact was crucial for the development of
capitalism in Brazil.

During the decades before the abolition of slavery, a high percentage
of immigrants went to the southern states, especially Rio Grande do
Sul and Santa Catarina, forming population nuclei based on small rural
ownership outside the region of slavery's predominance. In the 1880's
São Paulo and its coffee plantations attracted most immigrants. In the
following decade of greater migrations to Brazil, three related aspects
converged: the high level of immigration to São Paulo increased;
Italian immigrants predominated; and to a great extent immigration
was subsidized by the state government.

Italy became, after its unification, a country with a heavy rate
of emigration. The prolonged crisis between the mid-1880's and
mid-1890's stimulated emigration (especially from the north). In the
five year period between 1886–1890, the total figure exceeded
1,100,000 emigrants, almost sixty percent of whom crossed the
Atlantic. Argentina was the principal recipient of the emigration
(259,000), followed by Brazil (174,000), and the United States (75,000)
(Vázquez-Presedo 1971: 96–97). During part of the period slavery was
still legal in Brazil – which makes its share of the total even more
surprising. In the following period (1891–1895), Brazil moved to the
front with 330,000 Italian immigrants, while the totals for Argentina

and the United States were 259,000 and 170,000, respectively. The depression that affected those two countries in 1890 and the continual rise of coffee prices undoubtedly affected these figures. In the following decades, the United States became the principal recipient of Italian immigrants in the Americas, while Argentina and Brazil divided the rest. Toward the beginning of the twentieth century, the number of immigrants to Argentina increased, to which was added some Italian emigration from Brazil to Argentina. (Argentina was favored by the economic opportunities there, the first crisis of overproduction of coffee in Brazil, and the limitations imposed by the Italian government due to mistreatment of Italian immigrants in Brazil).

The concentration of immigrants in São Paulo toward the end of the 1880's and during the following decades was thus the result of the coffee expansion in that state and the state government's promotion of European immigration. With the decline of coffee in the Paraiba Valley, new lands opened up to the south and west, still in São Paulo's territory. On the new estates, free work began to replace slavery even before abolition. The increasing scarcity of slaves and the more or less certain prospect of abolition, in addition to the technical changes in and the mechanization of production, influenced the transfer to free labor. The expansion of cultivated areas was vital, but it was possible only by increasing the flow of labor in a drastic and rapid way. The firm initiative of the state government, before the proclamation of the Republic, and even more so after the 1891 constitution which delegated the making of immigration policy to other states, reflected the needs of the São Paulo landowners (Hall 1969). Without an organized campaign and without subsidies, there would not have been such a massive influx of immigrants. Minas Gerais never embarked on an immigration policy; thus it received a very small percentage of the total flow, even though coffee continued to be important in this state.

The strong influx of foreign labor, especially Italian, into São Paulo, allowed the coffee landowners to work without free slaves. With abolition in 1888, the majority of ex-slaves tried to escape wage work on the coffee plantations, where they necessarily still had the social, if not the legal, status of slaves. However, deprived of any other means of subsistence, many were forced to return to the coffee plantations. But as free workers in the most dynamic areas, they competed unsuccessfully with immigrant labor, and were even at a disadvantage against indigenous free laborers, who had never been slaves (Fernandes 1965).

In the crucial decade after abolition, then, the great immigration to São Paulo allowed changes within the system at the same time that the coffee economy increased. These changes were gradual: under the sharecropping system habits which had been formed during centuries of slave labor often surfaced. Nevertheless, a basic change was introduced in the subsidizing of immigration, which allowed settlers to establish residence on the coffee plantations practically without previous debts. These debts, in previous decades, had been the strongest bond which the landowner used to tie down labor; for the free colonists debts operated at the same time as the principal source of frustration and temptation for breaking contracts. Wages continued to be low, partially due to the availability of labor from immigration flows and from the reserves created by ex-slaves and indigenous laborers, but the transition to the system of free work had been made. Moreover, the Italian crisis continued without opportunities in Argentina improving substantially at the end of the century. When the situation did improve, the flow detoured to Argentina. At the beginning of the century the Brazilian situation had changed, and an aggressive policy for attracting immigrants, made more difficult by the Italian government, was no longer necessary. The immigrants who arrived during this period were attracted by established links and by possibilities of urban as well as rural work. The first crisis of overproduction of coffee occurred in this period and indicated clearly the limitation of the absorption of great numbers of immigrants within the export economy. The state government thus lost interest in an aggressive immigration policy.

Expansion of the coffee industry in São Paulo brought about a considerable development of the urban economy. The railroad expansion increased the commercial role of several urban centers, especially São Paulo-Santos. A commercial and financial center, this city began to transform itself into an industrial center toward the end of the century. Even before this, Rio de Janeiro was growing rapidly and developing an industrial base. Opportunities for urban employment, especially for manual labor with some specialization and/or capital, rapidly increased. It is not strange, then, that a significant proportion of the new immigrants moved directly to the cities, or returned to the cities from the coffee plantations. It should be remembered that until 1895, Italian immigrants, with considerable industrial experience, came predominantly from northern Italy (Vázquez-Presedo 1971: 101).

4. In the expanding agricultural economy, as well as in the expanding urban economy which existed during the last years of the past century, the massive European immigration relegated indigenous labor to a second place, and ex-slaves to a third place.

During the decades before abolition, the possibilities for replacing slave labor by indigenous labor were mentioned as frequently in the provinces of the south and southeast as in the northeastern provinces. As we have seen, slave labor was used in the export sectors or those tied to them; e.g. for the coffee industry in Rio de Janeiro, Minas, and São Paulo; for the sugar industry in Rio and the northeast; for cattle raising in the south. The northeastern cotton industry was, apparently, an early exception because of its large-scale use of free labor (Correia de Andrade 1964: 149). With abolition, foreign immigration replaced the slaves on the coffee plantations, the most dynamic sector in São Paulo. For the development of other export products, especially in the northeast and north, European immigrant labor was almost nonexistent and, in addition to ex-slaves, indigenous manual labor was used.

These phenomena were reflected in the migrations of the period – in the settling of foreign immigrants and in the movement of the Brazilian population, both free and ex-slave. But it is pertinent to ask why, with its expansion, coffee cultivation did not make use of ex-slave labor, absorbed relatively little indigenous labor available in the region, and did not generate significant interregional migration, at least until World War I. The answer tends to be circular, however: where export sector expansion led to immigration, it very slowly absorbed white and black nationals; where it did not, the main labor force of indigenous origin was integrated into the capitalist sectors, but capital itself more slowly became available. The advantages of the presence of immigrants were only evident once they had immigrated – so we return to the question of why foreign immigration was promoted instead of mobilizing indigenous and ex-slave labor as wage workers, or in any case why both solutions were not tried.[2]

The answer was briefly outlined earlier, but here it can be spelled out from a different perspective. Indigenous manual labor available in the coffee region was rather scarce, dispersed, and only weakly tied to a market economy. Massive recruitment was subjectively and objectively impossible: there was land available to extend to a semi-itinerant subsistence agriculture, and in the minds of landowners and laborers wage work on the coffee plantations would always be connected with slave labor. Among landowners there was a strong prejudice against indigenous manual labor, which was considered to be undisciplined, idle, and violent. The prejudice was probably rooted in reality. Image and reality both grew out of the identification of disciplined labor with forced (slave) labor and from the tradition and material possibility of a subsistence economy on an open frontier. The *agregados* on the large estates were tolerated, and perhaps even sought

[2] Celso Furtado discussed in detail the problem of labor during the period (Furtado 1962: Chapters 21 to 24), which received recent and rigorous attention by Graham and Buarque de Hollanda (1971).

after, because of the many political and economic services they could provide the landowner (Stein 1961).

Sitiantes, *posseiros*, and *meeiros* were also linked in different ways to the plantation economy and, although increasingly less so, to the growth of large estates and the increase of coffee prices. The creation of a proletariat could result only from the elimination of other means of subsistence (i.e. land) and the rise of sectors without the slave tradition. Manual labor freed by the Italian crisis was abundant and, without other means of subsistence, was objectively as much as subjectively suited to capitalist agriculture, once slavery was eliminated. Its existence and recruitment also made the absorption of indigenous labor into rural as well as urban capitalist sectors slower and more gradual.

The absorption was undoubtedly accelerated when the flow of foreign immigrants diminished. The inverse correlation between foreign and internal migratory currents in São Paulo suggests this clearly (Lopes 1971: 57–59). But even before abolition there were clear indications that indigenous manual labor followed the expansion in the coffee industry. The population of the state of São Paulo more than doubled between 1854 and 1872, the increase being most pronounced in the free population which grew from 294,000 to 680,700. This increase cannot be explained by the influx of foreigners, who in 1872 represented only 3.5 percent of the total population (Fernandes 1971). An important part of this increase must have been the result of internal migration, originating especially in Rio de Janeiro and Minas. In these areas, the population of the old mining regions was displaced toward the south and the *matta* region, and included slaves and free men attracted by expansion in the coffee industry. Urbanization during these decades, first in Rio de Janeiro and later in São Paulo, and the ensuing influx of foreigners was in part the result of internal migration. Later, with the increasing migration toward the cities by European immigrants and their descendants, the process of integration with the salaried indigenous manual laborers was accelerated. Toward the 1920's, a little after the flow from Minas Gerais started, the flow of northeastern migrants into Rio de Janeiro and São Paulo began, reflecting the increasing scarcity of manual labor for expansion and diversification in the southeastern economy.

5. The technique adopted focused on the more dynamic sector of the export economy and on the mobility of labor into the regions in which it was localized. There now remained a large area, the northwest, in which almost half of the Brazilian population was located until the end of the Empire, and where during the period analyzed here the most important flow of internal migrants occurred. (This is significant

because migratory flows no matter how important did not proceed to the southeast and were weakly linked with the development of a capitalist economy in this region.) The northeast, the oldest and most densely populated area in Brazil, had experienced an important loss in population to the mining regions during the eighteenth century. During the nineteenth century, especially up until the last quarter, population increased rather rapidly and advanced into the *sertao* [the arid interior]. After a long period of stagnation the sugar economy began to pick up, due to some technical innovations and improvements, in the beginning of the nineteenth century and continued to expand into the second half of the century. Cotton cultivation, which emerged as a new export product toward the end of the eighteenth century, advanced considerably during the nineteenth century, and reached its highest point during the years of the United States' Civil War. Unlike sugar, cotton was also cultivated outside the coastal area and *zona da matta*. It was cultivated especially in small and medium size properties which produced both cotton and food crops such as corn and beans. Although there were also large plantations, these were more the exception than the rule, since the use of slave labor was limited by low profit margins. With its short vegetative cycle, cotton was not limited like sugar cane by the need for year-round care (Correia de Andrade 1964: 149). Both the cotton and sugar economies were tied in several ways with the subsistence economy of the *sertao*, promoting considerable geographic and demographic growth in the area during a large part of the century.

The northeastern region suffered a slow process of economic and political marginalization, due to (among other reasons) the low rate of technological adaptation to new situations in the international market and the emergence and development of the coffee economy in the southeast. In the second half of the century an important redistribution of political power on the national level occurred, ending the northeastern political hegemony and thus changing the regional political structure (Palmeira 1966). Within the next twenty-five years various elements contributed to an increased marginalization of the region, while at the same time allowing for greater economic and political autonomy.

The transition from slave to other forms of labor was slower and less drastic in the northeast than in the southeast. The so-called rural complex, which included subsistence sectors tied to an export economy, used more free workers than the coffee plantations, although rarely under a wage system and often with servile relationships. In cotton cultivation, as already indicated, slave labor was almost nonexistent. The manifold relations between subsistence and export economy allowed for diverse ties between landowners and independent farmers. With the scarcity of slaves and their increased cost after 1850 due to the sale of many of them to the coffee plantations, there was a rapid increase in wage labor employment, although it seldom was "pure" and it often remained tied to a subsistence agriculture. The beginning industrialization, especially in Recife, and the technical transformation in the sugar industry, which came about with the emergence of industrial mills, stimulated even further the growth of the urban populations which had resulted from the important rural–urban migration (Singer 1968).

The great drought of 1877–1879, after more than two decades of rather regular rains and continuous increases in cotton production, provoked very important demographic changes, especially in the more affected regions in Ceará, Rio Grande do Norte, and Paraiba. During this period, there was a high mortality rate. Although calculations are only approximate, there is no doubt that total population decreased disasterously in some areas, and that infant mortality reached unusual levels. Moreover, cattle, fundamental to the economy of the region, also died in great numbers, implying in itself serious difficulties in reconstructing nuclei of population. At the same time, there was a mass out-migration from the northeast toward less affected regions and urban centers and to the Amazon area.

Rubber production, whose expansion required only increased quantities of unskilled labor, brought about heavy migratory streams. These originated in the northeast during the 1877 drought and continued through the following three decades until the Brazilian domination of the rubber market collapsed (Furtado 1962). An attractive and commercial activity in which important investments were not required, the production of rubber depended heavily upon the recruitment of labor unavailable in the region. The companies recruited heavily in the ports of the northeast, where a floating population had accumulated because of the drought and later because of crises in the cotton and sugar industries. Labor in rubber extraction was difficult to maintain due to the high mortality rates in the isolated and unsanitary regions of the Amazon and to the high rate of return migration. Attracted by the rapid and, for northeastern standards, fabulous gains, workers were retained through their obligations to pay back debts contracted for the trip and for subsistence food while working in isolated areas. Even so, the tendency for return migration was pronounced and became extreme when the international market provoked a crisis in Brazilian rubber production. From the point of view of the workers the return to subsistence agriculture in the northeast was preferable to similar activities in the isolated Amazon regions.

There were flows also within the northeast in the direction of the coast and the south, and undoubtedly many migrants succeeded during these decades (between the drought of 1877–1879 and World War I) in reaching the southeastern states, especially Minas Gerais. All the cities situated along the coast in the northeast rapidly grew; an incipient industrialization absorbed only a small part of the population increase, and the traditional urban sectors expanded rapidly. In southern Bahia the production of cocoa received a large stimulus thanks to the influx of manual labor originating in the states to the north. Finally, there were also smaller migratory flows to the south between 1872 and 1890. The estimates based on census data indicate this rather clearly (Graham and Buarque de Hollanda 1971), and there also exist references indicating that large numbers of workers moved, during the drought and after, toward Rio de Janeiro (Da Costa 1966: 132). In the Minas coffee areas, where the availability of foreign immigrant labor was minimal, landowners were forced to use free laborers in much the same way that landowners in the northeast had to do after abolition. The same thing must have happened to the sugar plantations in the state of Rio de Janeiro. Probably a large part of the migration toward these states was a result of an expansion of the agricultural subsistence economy. But between 1890 and 1920, migration to these southern states was still relatively unimportant.

During these decades the processes which affected the internal migrations from and within the northeast were only indirectly linked to expansion of the coffee economy in the southeast, except for the flow of slaves. The northeastern states, including Bahia and part of Minas Gerais, had the largest concentration of population at that time. Although the data for the first national census cannot be taken at face value, they do give us an idea of relative magnitudes: of a total population of approximately ten million in 1872, a little more than two million lived in Minas, about 1.4 million in Bahia, approximately the same number in the southern states of the northeast (Sergipe, Alagoas, Pernambuco), and some 1.9 million in the more northern states (Maranhao, Piaui, Ceará, Rio Grande do Norte, Paraiba). Migration due to droughts and the move to the rubber and cocoa regions indicate that a mobile labor force existed because of this crisis and/or because of organized recruitment. Important flows left for the Amazonia, the coastal cities, other states within the region, and down to the Bahian south. Minas as well as Bahia, at least during the last decades of the past century, participated to a degree in the export boom, and the population lost to Rio or São Paulo was replaced by the flow of migrants originating in the north. In the first decades of this century, migrations from Minas to the south became important. But only recently, since the 1930's, can we speak properly of massive migration to the southeast.

Why was labor not heavily recruited from these states for the expansion of the coffee culture in the south, instead of or in addition to promoting foreign immigration? Graham and Buarque de Hollanda discussed this problem in detail, and they found that a satisfactory explanation had to include at least some reference to such diverse factors as: the preferences of the landowners for foreign labor; the difficulties experienced by indigenous labor in adapting to wage labor in a disciplined way; the existence of strong pressures in Italy which allowed for importation of cheap labor in reasonable quantities; the relatively low cost of international transport in Brazil; and the objections to the interregional transfer of labor raised by diverse interest groups (1971: 42 ff.). The analysis by these authors seems complete; however, it should be added that, with the exception of the northern *sertaõ* within the northeast and during droughts, the economic system did not really produce a surplus of labor; moreover, labor remained tied to the archaic sector and was only formally free to migrate. Only with difficulty could the coffee planters compete with the cocoa and rubber interests for labor displaced by the droughts, and adaptation to work on coffee plantations would have been more difficult in any case, especially under the new technological conditions which marked the *paulista* phase of coffee expansion.

6. I have left for the end of this study the examination of a migratory stream undoubtedly important during this period but about which we know little – the migration of freed slaves in the period immediately before and immediately after abolition. Several studies on the integration of the blacks into the class society, especially those by Fernandes (1965, 1971), explain why the process was so slow and relate it to the conditions of abolition and to competition with foreign labor. In the less dynamic export sectors slave laborers were sold or absorbed as wage workers under working conditions which changed very slowly; in the more dynamic agricultural sector (e.g. coffee in São Paulo) and in the incipient industrial and related sectors of the urban economy, slave labor was not absorbed for some time. Such an analysis suggests the existence of important migratory flows which have not been studied in detail and which are probably impossible to reconstruct quantitatively. There was undoubtedly migration to urban centers; but, at least in the case of São Paulo city, this was not as large as accounts of the period indicated, nor was it caused by the expansion of the labor market. During the first decades after abolition a majority of the freed men living there concentrated in peripheral quarters, maintained contact with rural occupations, and formed a subproletariat only marginally occupied by the dynamic sectors of the urban economy. On the other hand, there was considerable migration between rural areas, although reports about its quantity or predominant directions are contradictory. There was perhaps return migration

to the northeast, especially of ex-slaves brought in during the last years of slavery, besides considerable mobility between coffee plantations in the southeast, and finally absorption of a considerable contingent into the subsistence agriculture economy of the region.

It is difficult to give a satisfactory noncircular answer to the question of the use of foreign labor versus the use of indigenous labor (regionally or with interregional migration); moreover, the absorption of ex-slaves (and their consequent migration in different directions) also poses a complex problem. Clearly, as Fernandes demonstrates, or as Cardoso indicates in the case of Rio Grande do Sul:

... the free hand wanted the foreign hand, spotless, not that of the freed man or the black degraded by slavery. This, on the contrary, was considered *in itself*, independently of the slavery system, as the cause of idleness, torpor, dissolution. What was the fruit of slavery became confused with its cause and was taken as a factor of immobility and backwardness (Cardoso 1962: 222; our translation, editors).

Under these conditions, the proletarization of the ex-slave would await a generational restructuring and important changes in the job market.

7. To synthesize the above data, during the late nineteenth and early twentieth centuries, international, interregional, and intraregional migrations of great magnitude and diverse natures occurred in Brazil, all of them tied directly or indirectly to the emergence of capitalist structures in the export economy and to important changes in national integration. A recapitulation of the main types of migratory flows then predominant is relevant here:

a. The migration of slaves, which, within the slavery system, meant the transfer of workers as merchandise.

b. Foreign immigration, with its diverse subtypes:

i. Colonization in new areas on small properties;

ii. Contracts of labor under indentured sharecropping;

iii. Subsidized immigration of free manual labor clearly destined for agricultural work but initially rooted in the cities;

iv. Free immigration without intervention by the state or colonization companies.

Although the first two subtypes often met with failure and did not initially constitute a free labor force, taken together the immigrant population and its descendants formed the first important contingent of literally free workers in Brazil, thus constituting the demographic basis of the modern capitalist mode of production.

c. Migration of indigenous labor (which was slow initially but increased during the first decades of this century) into regions where modern capitalism was expanding, filling the gaps left by the rapid flow of foreign laborers and their descendants to the cities.

d. Spontaneous migration of subsistence agriculturists, which, although generally involving short-distance moves, slowly widened the regions occupied by subsistance agriculture economies. These groups were made up of migrants from the southeast (where peasants were expelled by coffee growers and ex-slaves were forced to seek work after abolition); from the northeast before the great drought; and from the north after the decline in rubber production.
e. Migration of labor which was ostensibly free but which was tied by bonds of indenture and recruited in great numbers, deceptively, for the rubber production in Amazonia. This movement was linked to the following one.
f. Massive migrations from disaster areas, such as drought areas, and the flow caused by the disintegration of the rural complex.
g. Migration of freed blacks, displaced by foreign immigrants, who were not assimilated into salaried work.

Undoubtedly (if we take as a definition of "migrant" those whose residence does not coincide with their birthplace), toward the end of the century in Brazil the percentage of migrants was very high, perhaps the highest in all of Brazil's contemporary history. However, even if a great part of these migrations was tied to the emergence of modern capitalism, only a small portion was made up of the movements of free workers responding to the stimuli within a free labor market on which they depended for subsistance. This type of migration, an essential characteristic of capitalistic societies, increased in importance throughout this century to become in recent decades the predominant one.

REFERENCES

CARDOSO, FERNANDO H.
   1962   *Capitalismo e escravidaõ no Brasil meridional.* São Paulo: Difusão Européia do Livro.
CARDOSO, FERNANDO H., ENZO FALETTO
   1969   *Dependencia y desarrol lo en América Latina.* México City: Siglo XXI.
CARONE, EDGAR
   1970   *A República Velha (instituições e classes sociais).* São Paulo: Difusão Européia do Livro.
CORREIA DE ANDRADE, MANUEL
   1964   *A terra e o homem no nordeste* (second edition). São Paulo: Brasiliense.
CURTIN, P.
   1969   *The Atlantic slave trade: a census.* Madison: University of Wisconsin Press.

DA COSTA, EMILIA VIOTTI
1966   *Da senzala à colônia*. São Paulo: Difusão Européia do Livro.

DEAN, WARREN
1971   *A industrialização de São Paulo (1880–1945)*. São Paulo: Difusão Européia do Livro.

DIÉGUES, MANUEL, JR.
1964   *Imigração, urbanização e industriali zação*. Rio de Janeiro: Centro Brasileiro de Pesquisas Educacionais.

FERNANDES, FLORESTAN
1965   *A integração do negro na sociedade de classes*, two volumes. São Paulo: Dominus Editora.
1971   "Do escravo ao cidadão," in *Brancos e negros em São Paulo*, third edition. By Roger Bastide and Florestan Fernandes. São Paulo: Companhia Editora Nacional.

FURTADO, CELSO
1962   *Formación económica del Brasil*. México City: Fondo de Cultura Económica.

GRAHAM, DOUGLAS H.
1971   "Algumas considerações econômicas para política migratória no meio brasileiro," in *Migrações internas no Brasil*. Edited by Manoel Augusto Costa, 13–33. Rio de Janeiro: IPEA/INPES.

GRAHAM, DOUGLAS H., SERGIO BUARQUE DE HOLLANDA
1971   "Migration regional and urban growth and development in Brazil," volume one. São Paulo: Instituto de Pesquisas Económicas, U.S.P. (Mimeographed.)

HALL, MICHAEL M.
1969   "The origins of mass immigration in Brazil." Unpublished doctoral dissertation, Columbia University.

HALPERIN DONGHI, TULIO
1969   *Historia contemporánea de América Latina*. Madrid: Alianza Editorial.

IGLÉSIAS, FRANCISCO
1958   *Política econômica de governo provincial mineiro (1835–1889)*. Rio de Janeiro: Instituto Nacional do Livro.

INSTITUTO BRASILEIRO DE ESTATÍSTICS
n.d.   *Contribuições para o es tudo da demografía do Brasil* (second edition). Rio de Janeiro: Fundaçao IBGE.

LOPES, JUAREZ R. B.
1971   *Desenvolvimento e mudanca social* (second edition). São Paulo: Companhia Editora Nacional.

MORSE, RICHARD M., editor
1971   *The urban development of Latin America, 1750–1920*. Stanford: Center for Latin American Studies, Stanford University.

NICHOLLS, WILLIAM H.
1970   "The agricultural frontier in modern Brazilian history: the case of Paraná, 1920–1965," in *Cultural change in Brazil*. Edited by Merrill Rippy, 36–64. Muncie, Indiana: Ball State University.

PALMEIRA, MOACIR
1966   Nordeste: mudanças políticas no século XX. *Cadernos Brasileiros* 8 (September–October).

PELÁEZ, CARLOS M.
1972   *Historia da industriolização brasileira*. Rio de Janeiro: APEC.

PRADO, CAIO, JR.
1960 *História económica del Brasil.* Buenos Aires: Futuro.

SÁNCHEZ ALBORNOZ, NICOLÁS
1973 *Histórica de la población de América Latina.* Madrid: Alianza Editorial.

SÁNCHEZ ALBORNOZ, NICOLÁS, JOSÉ LUÍS MORENO
n.d. *La población de América Latina: bosque jo histórico.* Buenos Aires: Paidós.

SANTOS, MARÍA JOSÉ et al.
n.d. "Aspectos do crescimento da economia brasileira, 1889–1969," volume two. Rio de Janeiro: Fundação Getúlio Vargas, s/f. (Preliminary mimeographed version.)

SINGER, PAUL
1968 *Desenvolvimento econômico e evolucão urbana.* São Paulo: Companhia Editora Nacional.
1972 "Migraciones internas: consideraciones teóricas sobre su estudio," in *Migración y Desarrollo.* Buenos Aires: CLACSO.

STEIN, STANLEY J.
1961 *Grandeza e decadencia do café no Vale do Paraíba.* São Paulo: Editora Brasiliense.

TAVARES, VANIA PORTO et al.
1972 *Colonização dirigida no Brasil.* Rio de Janeiro: IPEA/INPES.

VÁZQUEZ-PRESEDO, VICENTE
1971 *El caso argentino: migración de factores, comercio exterior y desarrollo, 1875–1914.* Buenos Aires: Eudeba.

WILLEMS, EMILIO
1972 "The rise of a rural middle class in a frontier society," in *Brazil in the sixties.* Edited by Riordan Roett, 325–344. Nashville: Vanderbilt University Press.

COMMENT by Robert Allan White

The title of this paper indicates that the author will be dealing with one of the most popular themes in Brazilian historiography, the changing demographic pattern and growth of cities. The effective occupation of the vast Brazilian subcontinent has fascinated historians since colonial times and served as a point of departure for the work of the father of Brazil's nationalist historical tradition, Capistrano de Abreu. However, Balán's contribution scarcely touches on the theme of population movement as it has been dealt with by other historians. No concrete idea of the numbers of people moving from one place to another emerges nor does the relationship such movement bears to the growth and formation of urban centers. The real concern which motivates Balán's study is the development of a Brazilian working class in response to the implantation of capitalism. Consequently, he devotes most of his attention to discussing the demands placed on the demographic resources of the late Empire and the Old Republic by the growth of the coffee exporting economy geared to satisfy the demands of European and North American markets.

The labor market created by the growing coffee plantations of São Paulo and Minas Gerais could not be satisfied by available manpower for various reasons: Brazilian workers were not free to migrate to the coffee growing regions; the cost of transportation was too great; and the heritage of slavery predisposed plantation owners against Negroes and in favor of foreign labor. Migration which did occur resulted in a shift from the populous northeast to the rubber harvesting areas of the Amazon or the coastal cities, Recife and Rio de Janeiro. Underemployed and unemployed Brazilians were considered unsuitable in comparison with Italian immigrants. Balán emphasizes the failure of Brazilian export agriculture to absorb freed slaves who were left in marginal circumstances as European immigration grew. Recent research by Eulália Maria Lahmeyer Lobo, however, indicates that workers in the factories of Rio de Janeiro's incipient industry were slaves kept on after emancipation. Native-born Brazilians were considered preferable to European workers, they were less demanding and more skilled than Europeans. The obvious racism of Brazil's current labor structure grew more pronounced as industrialization spread and immigrant labor increased.

Balán's essay is based on carefully selected secondary sources, among them works by the best social scientists writing about Latin America today. Although little of what Balán says is new or surprising, he has written a good description of the changing labor patterns of Brazil, calling attention to mobility of workers during the apogee of the neocolonial export economies.

Household Composition and Mating Patterns Among Lower-Class Venezuelans

ANGELINA POLLAK-ELTZ

The subject of this paper is the lower-class Venezuelan family, both in its rural and its urban setting. For the purpose of studying family structure it is necessary to investigate mating patterns and household composition. It is important to look upon the "family" from a dynamic rather than a static point of view and therefore the life cycle of individuals has to be studied carefully.

Field research was undertaken in four rural areas of Venezuela, in which the economic, racial, and historical backgrounds of the people under study differ widely. As space does not permit me to show the statistical material on which the following discussion is based, I want to draw the attention of scholars to my forthcoming book, *The Negro family in Venezuela* (Acta etnografica, Department of Anthropology, University of Vienna, Austria), in which these data will be presented at length. All material was collected only by myself and therefore samples could not be very large, but as they were taken at random in many different small communities (*caserios*) they are fairly representative. Further data were collected in Caracas among immigrant peasants from two of these four areas and among native Caraqueños. Material was gathered by means of questionnaires, lengthy personal interviews, life histories, and participating research in the slums of Caracas. Census figures (1961) were used with great caution.

Before starting the discussion it is necessary to stress the following point: racial discrimination in the North American sense does not exist in Venezuela and racial factors are of minor importance in determining the social position of a person; nevertheless, due to the rigid class system that persisted in the country until a few decades ago, the majority of the darker-skinned people belong to the lower classes, while the upper classes are usually fairer skinned or white. "Pure"

Negroes are rare, due to miscegenation that has taken place ever since the first slaves arrived in this country. "Pure" Indians are likewise rare with the exception of tribal groups that are not considered here. The majority of Venezuelans are therefore of mixed ancestry. However, different racial types dominate in different areas and my studies concentrated on such regions, where these racial variables are noticeable to a high degree.

My research was carried out during the years 1968–1971 in the Barlovento area (Miranda State) among black peasants (Barlovente-ños); in Anzoategui State among mestizo and zambo peasants (Orientales); the ranch laborers of Apure State (Llaneros), small farmers of the Andes region (Andinos); and among urban slum-dwellers in Caracas.

In recent years, lower-class family structure has become a topic of lively discussion among scholars, who usually investigated the Negro family in different parts of the Americas. Certain structural anomalies have come to light that set the Negro family apart from the prevailing pattern of the Euroamerican middle classes, such as, for example, a high incidence of consensual unions, rather than legal marriage, illegitimacy, frequent change of sexual partners, serial polygyny, early extraresidential mating habits and a high frequency of matrifocal consanguineal households. The matrifocal household stands in the center of the debate. Such domestic units have a wide distribution among lower-class Venezuelans too, and therefore I was especially interested in investigating their formation and persistence. These units are formed for the following reasons:

1. Extraresidential mating often associated with polygynous habits. In this case they are permanent and are often carried over to the next generation.

2. Prostitution.

3. Abandonment after a prolonged union (concubinage) or legal union (marriage).

4. Death of a stable partner (widowhood).

5. A stage between consensual unions that is only temporary.

While only a few decades ago scholars blamed the blacks for showing "promiscuous behavior" and rejecting marriage – facts that were either attributed to the insatiable sexual instinct of the Negroes (Elwang 1904) or African heritage (Herskovits 1941: 171–172) or slavery (DuBois 1908: 18; Frazier 1939: 104–106) – modern anthropologists came to realize that these patterns are not restricted to the Negro group alone, but can also be found among other economically marginal and detribalized groups and are rather an indication of the "culture of poverty" (Lewis 1966: 42 ff.). The matrifocal consanguineal household group, which Lewis considers in terms of social disorganization, is taken by González (1969: 16 ff.) to be an alternate type of domestic unit better suited to the precarious economic position of marginal groups in the process of acculturation (neoteric societies). The functional explanations of the above-outlined phenomena are now widely accepted and most of them seem to be of an economic nature. R. T. Smith (1956: 255 ff.) blames the marginal role of the husband/ father in the family on his limited access to economic resources. Rodman (1971: 190 ff.) comes to similar conclusions, but is also aware of cultural and historical factors.

As the Negro family is usually found in the center of the discussion, I have also focused my attention on the Venezuelan blacks. The Barloventeños are the descendants of Negro slaves, who were brought to this area in colonial times. After their liberation (1854) many continued to live in small communities scattered between cocoa plantations and ranches, where they found temporary employment, when not engaged in working on their own small plots for subsistence. Although they are peasants, they despise agricultural work and are not tied to the land by tradition and conviction; they rather stay on because they lack other economic opportunities. These attitudes could not even be changed by the Agrarian Reform.

The following are the points which characterize the "family" among Barloventeños:

1. A high frequency of consensual unions (57 percent in my sample) occur after a period of promiscuous extraresidential mating during adolescence. These unions tend to be stable during the peak of the woman's fertility cycle, when she is in greatest need of a provider/ companion to rear her children, but often break up as soon as one of her sons is able to provide for her.

2. Marriage rarely occurs (18 percent in my sample) and is of little social value. There is no stigma attached to illegitimacy. In the absence of property, inheritance is of no importance. Moreover, people lack the resources to give a lavish wedding party. Often they do not possess the necessary legal documents to enter a legal union. Superstitution also plays a part, as many say that marriage only brings bad luck. Of the few marriages that occur, about half take place before the couple moves together – in this case the girl is supposed to be a virgin – and the other half are performed after a long stable concubinage, either because one of the partners made a vow to get married in return for a miracle performed by a saint or "in extremis" on the deathbed of one of the mates.

3. The Catholic Church has little or no social control and marriage as a sacrament is not recognized by many people. Concubinage is not considered to be sinful. Although many believe that marriage might be "good for the rich," it is beyond their own sphere of ambitions.

Here the term "lower-class value stretch" might be used (Rodman 1963).

4. A girl who has had children by another man will never be legally married by her new companion.

5. Children always stay with their mother, even when she changes partners. In such a case the woman usually owns the house and the man comes to live with her.

6. Children of unattached mothers are often reared by the maternal grandmother, frequently together with the younger siblings of their own mother, while the mother works in the city.

7. Data confirm that each type of domestic unit is associated with a particular type of mating pattern that has its proper place in the life cycle of an individual.

8. The matrifocal, consanguineal household group is found in 22.5 percent of the cases under study. Its formation is due to different circumstances:

(a) Extraresidential mating habits are frequent and women often change their partners, so that in some cases there are as many as five different fathers. Women who have never lived with a permanent mate are often owners of some land that is tilled by their sons. As these young men have to support their mothers and siblings, they cannot set up their own households and find extraresidential mates for their sexual gratification. Daughters of such women may follow the example of their mothers. Some of these women have stable jobs (e.g. cooking on a plantation) and can well afford to raise their children without the aid of a partner. They therefore reject a permanent companion quite consciously.

(b) In some cases the women may be prostitutes.

(c) After a more or less stable concubinage or a series of consensual unions, the woman abandons her mate and is henceforth supported by her own grown-up children. She is then about forty years old and in addition to her younger children may also rear her daughters' offspring. When she gets old she may join the household of one of her daughters. The man may find another woman and start to raise a new family.

9. Early sexual activity leads to early motherhood. Children are desired by men in order to prove their maleness (*machismo*) and by women in order to have a provider for old age. Motherhood is important regardless of marital status. Virginity is not valued. It is rare to find a woman who does not have children, and such a woman is ridiculed or pitied. In this society there is no room for a spinster or "old maid."

10. It is possible that folkways, that have their roots in the plantation economy and slave society of past ages, may be responsible

for the emergence of a polygynous pattern and "promiscuous be-havior" that are reflected in extraresidential mating habits and the emergence of matrifocal consanguineal households. Several factors were responsible for the attenuation of marital ties during slavery days:

(a) Marriage between slaves was not recognized by the Church or by law.

(b) There was no necessity for a couple to stay together in order to rear their children, as the plantation owner cared for his slaves' offspring.

(c) Slave families were often separated by the sale of one partner.

(d) The owner himself set a bad example by siring children with slave girls.

(e) Promiscuity was encouraged, as it was believed that fertility among the female slaves could be increased in this way.

(f) The moral education of the slaves by the Church was neglected.

11. The following factors may be added in order to explain the attenuation of marital ties in modern times:

(a) The marginal economic position of the man in a plantation economy, where he finds work only on a day-to-day basis.

(b) The lack of economic cooperation between a man and his mate in the absence of a well-balanced farm economy.

(c) There is always a possibility for a woman to find employment on her own, and therefore she does not depend on a husband as the sole provider.

(d) Men have stronger obligations towards their mothers and sisters than towards the mother of their own children. She may always turn to her own consanguineal family for help.

(e) Mothers are always supported by their grown children. The father will only be supported if he has contributed to the expenses of rearing his children when they were small.

(f) In the absence of a stable nuclear family, the extended kin-group assumes many responsibilities usually taken by the nuclear group.

(g) There is little or no formality when two people decide to start cohabitation and only gossip comments on this fact. There is no moral issue involved and people do not consider it "sinful" to live in a consensual union.

(h) Romantic love in the modern sense of the word is rare.

(i) There are no common intellectual interests that may draw partners together, as many people are illiterate.

(j) There is little or no social interaction between the man and his spouse, as the world of men is separated from that of women. For recreational purposes he joins his peer group, while she stays home or visits relatives.

I have dwelled on the data collected among Barloventeños at some
length, as they bring to light many structural peculiarities that are
usually associated with the "Negro family" in the Americas. Further
investigations among Orientals have revealed, however, that these
characteristics are by no means found only among blacks with a
history of slavery and plantation work.

The Orientals under study are subsistence farmers (*conuqueros*);
they own and/or operate in small plots of land and use rudimentary
methods of agriculture. Often they supplement their income by occasional work on other people's farms, by fishing or odd jobs. They are
of mixed ancestry, being the descendants of tribal Indians, who were
settled in "misiones" by Spanish monks during colonial times and who
later mixed with white and Negro colonists. Although they were
supervised by the priests, they were always free.

Surveys in this area show that mating pattern and household composition do not differ greatly from those of the Barloventeños. Fifty-
six percent of the people studied lived in consensual unions, 24
percent were married and 20 percent lived in female-centered households. The average number of admitted fathers of children by women
living in such households was 2.1 (Barlovento 2.4), by those living in
consensual unions 1.8 (Barlovento 1.5) and by married women 1.0
(Barlovento 1.0). Women with illegitimate children and no provider
often migrate to the city, leaving their offspring with female relatives.
Again, the economic position of the man is precarious, which seems
to be one of the main reasons for the instability of conjugal ties. The
situation is fairly similar to that found in the Barlovento.

When we turn to the Llaneros of Apure State, the picture is again
similar, although the economic conditions and racial composition of
the people under study differ. The Llaneros are a heterogeneous
group, composed of whites, detribalized Indians, blacks, and mixed-
bloods of all shades. Many work as cowboys on the large ranches or
own a few cows that graze on communal land. This is frontier country
and its inhabitants are highly mobile. The wide-open spaces shelter
adventurers and outcasts. Prostitution is common, and every village
has its brothel. The percentage of matrifocal consanguineal households is very high, in some villages up to 50 percent (about 40 percent
in my study). Women tend their kitchen gardens in order to survive;
others are engaged as housekeepers on outposts of the ranches, where
a woman lives in complete isolation with two or more cowboys for
a year or more, in something like a polyandric household. The offspring of such highly volatile relationships are always raised by the
mother as paternity is uncertain. Extraresidential mating is frequent
due to the fact that men often live on the ranches and only visit their
girlfriends in the villages on weekends. Promiscuity is widespread.

The average number of admitted fathers by women who live alone is 2.8. Stable concubinage (44 percent) or marriage (16 percent) are correlated to homeownership, independant farming or a stable job on the ranch. Again, economic factors are of vital importance in order to determine mating pattern and household structure.

For the purpose of getting a broader view of the rural lower-class family in Venezuela more data were collected among Andean peasants. In the Andes States there is no tradition of slavery, and peasants are the descendants of Spanish homesteaders who gradually mixed with sedentary tribal Indians with a long history of subsistence farming. The Catholic Church is influential in this region. Peasants are usually owners of the land to which they are tied by tradition and their attitudes towards agricultural labor and land ownership are similar to those found among European farmers. Their economy is mixed: coffee is often planted as a cash crop, while they also grow wheat, corn, or potatoes for home consumption. Surpluses are sold on the market and they often raise chickens and a few cows. In order to run such a farm it is necessary that work be divided between the man and his wife; this cooperation automatically leads to more stable marital ties.

According to the 1961 census 66 percent of the women in Tachira State (in the Andes region) who have children are legally married. (This figure also includes urban dwellers.) According to my own studies, 16 percent of the women lived in matrifocal consanguineal household groups, but more than one-third of this group came into being due to the death of a partner for life. Fifty percent of the household heads were legally married and were either small farmers or artisans; 34 percent lived in consensual unions but the majority of these concubinages were of long duration. The extraresidential mating that in the Barlovento leads to the formation of typical matrifocal households is rare in the Andes. As there are no plantations, there are hardly any employment opportunities for single women and therefore when they have to support illegitimate children, they usually leave them with relatives, while they migrate to the city in order to work. The average number of admitted fathers by women in female-centered households is 1.7; for those living in consensual unions 1.2; and for married women 1.1 (due to widowhood and remarriage).

The following conclusion may be drawn from these findings: Race does not seem to be important in determining the household structure and mating pattern of Venezuelan peasants. Economic circumstances seem to be of great importance but the historical background, folkway, and the influence of the Church on the moral attitudes of the people concerned should also be taken into consideration.

To clarify the matter, further research was carried out among Barloventeños and Andinos who migrated to Caracas, and these data

were matched with findings collected among city-born slum-dwellers.
The majority of rural immigrants arrived after 1958 (downfall of the
dictatorship). Research was carried out in slum sections of eastern and
western Caracas, as well as among people who live in public housing
projects. Among the Barloventeños in Caracas 23 percent of the
households under study were of the matrifocal consanguineal type,
43 percent lived in consensual union, and 34 percent were married;
31 percent of the households were composed of nuclear families only
(as compared to 41.5 percent in the rural area). This fact clearly shows
that in the city, due to housing shortage and a constant influx of new
immigrants, household groups tend to be larger, as they absorb
peripheral relatives and friends who move to Caracas until these
people find a place to stay on their own. It seems that consensual
unions are more frequently dissolved due to abandonment, but extraresidential relations of long duration are rarer. Marriage is often
entered into by immigrants upon arrival in order to comply to urban
norms. Mass weddings are sponsored occasionally by the government
in the slums. Many young people get married when they mate for the
first time but these unions are often quite unstable and a divorce is
rarely asked, so that the following union is of the consensual type.
The status of the children of the second union is ambiguous, because,
according to the law, they bear the surname of their mother's legal
husband. As there are employment opportunities for men and women
alike, spinsters often live alone. Ties with relatives in the villages are
not severed. On the contrary, there is a lot of traveling back and
forth and mothers are always supported by their absent children.
Grandmothers in the village may raise their daughters' children, while
the daughters live in Caracas. These ties only become attenuated in
the second generation, when people are completely adapted to city
life. It is not true to say that family ties are disrupted by urbanization;
on the contrary, in the city newcomers always find shelter in the home
of relatives and the economic cooperation of a kin-group may be even
of greater importance here due to economic necessities. In the slums,
members of the same family or the same villages often live next door
to each other.

The following differences between urban and rural Barloventeños
are of importance:

1. Household groups in the city are larger and are composed of a
greater variety of relatives.

2. The number of legal marriages increases due to moral pressure
and the improvement of economic conditions.

3. Matrifocal consanguineal households come about due to abandonment rather than through prolonged extraresidential mating and
can often be considered as a stage between two consensual unions.

Studies carried out among Andinos in Caracas proved again that folkways are carried over to the city. Out of the total, 50 percent were married, 30 percent lived in consensual unions and 20 percent were unattached or lived in matricentered households. The high rate of matrifocal households of Andinos in the city might be due to the fact that – as I mentioned before – many women who have illegitimate children migrate to the city. Most Andinos in Caracas live in large extended family households.

Native Caraqueños studied belonged to the lowest social strata and were descendants of earlier immigrants. In the second generation people from different regions and of different skin color freely intermarry and thus regional differences become blurred. The following findings are of importance:

1. Marriage occurs more frequently than consensual unions (46 percent versus 34 percent); divorce is rare but occurs sometimes.

2. Thirty percent of the households under study were of the matrifocal type, but in some cases were also comprised of the spouses of daughters or sons. In most instances they were formed due to abandonment after the woman passed the childbearing age. Consanguineal groups, due to extraresidential mating, are rare; some are due to prostitution.

3. Early extraresidential mating usually leads to the formation of a consensual union once a child is under way.

4. Girls are usually somewhat older when they start cohabitation, but that does not mean that they do not have very early sexual experiences, only that they know better how to avoid children than girls in the rural areas.

5. Children always remain with their mothers.

6. More households are composed of nuclear families than is the case among immigrants; peripheral relatives are rarely attached.

7. Ties to relatives in the interior are gradually broken.

8. Housing is better and more spacious among Caraqueños than among immigrants.

9. The mother is highly respected and the rallying point of the family even in a home where the father is the actual household head.

When studying the slum culture, one soon becomes aware of the fact that there are at least two social classes living side by side, whose attitudes, aspirations, marital behavior, and economic position are widely different. The lower class consists of marginal people, often first-generation immigrants, who show many general characteristics that Lewis (1966: 42 ff.) considers to be symptomatic of the "culture of poverty": unemployment, poor and overcrowded housing, promiscuity, crime, drugs, malnutrition, poor health, lack of education, female-centered households, unstable marital relations, etc. Among these marginal people there is very little upward mobility and they usually stay away from the other group that can be termed an incipient middle class.

Most members of this class have stable jobs, live in stable consensual unions or are legally married. Their children attend school regularly and want to learn a trade. Their self-built homes in the slums are often quite comfortable and some even rent or own apartments in government-sponsored housing projects. Among this upward mobile group there are Barloventeños, Orientales, Andinos, and Caraqueños. Again, skin color is not important in determining whether a person belongs to this group or not. It rather depends on his own initiative and favorable economic conditions whether he will succeed or not. It may be admitted that many Andinos try hard to move up as soon as they come to the city. This is due to the following facts:

1. Andinos have the reputation of being harder workers and more reliable than natives from the coastal regions. They are therefore employed in preference to Orientales or Barloventeños from the tropical zones, who are often considered to be lazy and unreliable. These assumptions may have something to do with racial stereotypes.

2. Andinos are used to living in a colder climate, where one has to work harder. Moreover, in such a climate, houses are not only used as a shelter to spend the night but as a place to work and live. When Andinos come to the city they try hard to build a nicer home and this desire may often be an incentive to work harder.

3. Many Andinos used to be independent farmers and are thus used to thinking for themselves and are therefore more responsible in their work.

In Caracas I made a special study of this upward mobile group that comprised rural immigrants from the Barlovento, from the Andes and from other areas, as well as native Caraqueños. My research revealed that often migration goes in stages: from a village to a larger community and from there to a more important city. Sometimes this process is spread over two generations. The educational and occupational level of upward mobile groups (regardless of their rural or urban origin) is similar; upward mobility has nothing to do with skin color but rather with educational and economic opportunities, as well as with a personal determination to get on. A prolonged stay in the city blurs regional differences. When employment becomes more stable and better remunerated, the economic position of the male in the family as provider becomes stronger and conjugal ties tend to stabilize too. Matricentered groups that only tolerated a peripheral husband/father figure who never contributed much to the upkeep of the family turn into patripodestal households. Once an incipient middle-class status is reached, marriage as an institution is widely accepted to comply to the prevailing norms. There is an emphasis on the education of the children. A negative aspect of upward mobility is conspicuous consumption. More women work, because they have learned a trade or because their earnings are necessary in order to realize their aspirations. They tend to have fewer children and at a later age. People in the upward mobile group rely less on relatives. Many have severed ties to the extended kin-group altogether in order to avoid being asked to support less successful relatives. As their kin no longer drain them of their savings, these resources can be used to improve the socioeconomic position of their own nuclear family even more. By severing these ties, conjugal relations become stronger. The upward mobile group participates more actively in the political, social, and economic life of the country and takes more advantage of goods and services offered to them. With some luck, their children will become full members of the new middle classes.

To sum up: My studies in different regions of Venezuela and among slum-dwellers in Caracas have shown that:

1. Mating patterns determine household composition and family structure.

2. Mating patterns are determined mostly by economic factors (day labor or work on own farm, the role of the husband/father in the family, related to his position in the social hierarchy, stable jobs or unemployment, housing shortage, migration), but regional differences in folkways (lack of tradition of legal marriage among the descendants of Negro slaves or a long history of stable marital relationships among Andinos), the historical background (slavery and plantation economy or homesteads and independent farming), religious affiliation (influence of the Catholic Church), general attitudes (middle-class respectability associated to marriage, or no stigma attached to illegitimacy, motherhood valued above marriage, superstitions) as well as climatic conditions (tropical lowlands, or the colder Andean region) should be also taken into consideration when studying the lower-class Venezuelan family. It is, however, difficult to determine the relative importance of these factors, although my studies have proved that the strongest weight has to be put on economic conditions.

I am well aware of the shortcomings of my survey, as it is based on relatively few samples due to the fact that I worked completely on my own. I could not afford to hire a staff for screening or a computer. Nevertheless, I believe that the general trends that came to light are correct, although a broader study may yield statistical material of a different quality.

REFERENCES

DU BOIS, W. E. B.
1908 *The Negro American family.* Atlanta University Publication Series.
(Reprinted by M.I.T. Press, Cambridge, Mass., and London 1970.)
ELWANG, W.
1904 *The Negro of Columbia, Miss.* Colombia.
FRAZIER, E. F.
1939 *The Negro family in the United States.* Chicago: University of
Chicago Press.
GONZÁLEZ, NANCIE L.
1969 *Black Carib household structure.* Seattle: University of Washington
Press.
HERSKOVITS, MELVILLE
1941 *The myth of the Negro past.* Boston: Beacon Press.
LEWIS, OSCAR
1966 *La vida.* New York: Random House.
POLLAK-ELTZ, ANGELINA
i.p. *The Negro family in Venezuela.*
RODMAN, HYMAN
1963 The low-class value stretch. *Social Forces* 42: 205 ff.
1971 *Low-class families: the culture of poverty in Negro Trinidad.* New
York: London: Oxford University Press.
SMITH, R. T.
1956 *The Negro family in British Guiana.* London: Routledge and Kegan
Paul.

The Survival of the Unfittest

LARISSA LOMNITZ

This is the story of a shantytown: its formation, its people, and their socioeconomic organization. I shall try to answer a basic question: How do the members of marginal groups, many of them of rural origin, survive in a competitive urban environment?

The reality which underlies this question is familiar to anyone who has observed the outskirts of a Latin American city. Nevertheless, it needs to be analyzed in detail once again. There is an abundant literature on Latin American shantytowns (Leeds 1969; Matos Mar 1968; Nichamin 1968; Bonilla 1961; Safa 1964; Roberts 1968: Peattie 1968; Portes 1972). Yet more social scientists have directed their attention toward the material and cultural deprivation that meets the eye (e.g. Lewis 1959, 1960, 1961, 1969) than toward the sociocultural defense mechanisms which the dwellers have invented – often with considerable success, as witnessed by the proliferation of shantytowns throughout Latin America (Mangin 1967; Mangin and Turner 1968). Millions of illiterate or barely literate people, essentially unprotected by society and largely disowned by organized welfare, have found a way of life and the means of subsistence in the absence of any savings or saleable skills. My fieldwork in Cerrada del Condor has led me to view the shantytown as a new form of social organization, designed to insure the survival of the unfittest members of an urban industrial society: those who, by reason of their socioeconomic back-

I thank Dr. Joaquín Cravioto and Dr. Luís Rangel, under whose direction this work was initiated; Professor Angel Palerm and Professor Richard N. Adams, for their guidance and criticism; Miss Amparo Cervantes, and a group of my students at the Universidad Iberoamericana, for assistance in the field. A large part of this work was done while the author was a staff member of the Universidad Iberoamericana; its completion was made possible by a grant from the Wenner-Gren Foundation and by a scholarship from the Consejo Nacional de Ciencia y Tecnología, México.

ground or because of the pressures of social change, have become the "waste populations of dependent capitalist economies" (Quijano 1970).

This paper is the result of two years of fieldwork, which consisted of a combination of anthropological and sociological methods: participant observation (including field trips to the places of origin of some migrants), unstructured interviews, and quantitative surveys of all households in the shantytown. This combined approach was dictated by the specific conditions of fieldwork in the city, where the homogeneity of the unit of study cannot be taken for granted.

CERRADA DEL CONDOR

The shantytown of Cerrada del Condor sprawls over a ravine in the southern part of Mexico City, facing a cemetery on the opposite slope. The ravine represents the natural boundary between two residential middle-class neighborhoods of fairly recent development. This area comprises the hilly outskirts of the ancient township of Mixcoac, a part of urban Mexico City since about 1940. Prior to that time a few small entrepreneurs raised flowers and tree seedlings on the hills and worked the sand pits in the ravine.

The earliest settler bought a tract of barren land in about 1930, at the very location of the present shantytown. There he settled with his family and began to manufacture adobe bricks. He was later joined by a caretaker of the sand pits. Within ten years there were about a dozen families living in Cerrada del Condor, all of them workers in the adobe industry. Around that time the owner decided to sell fifteen small lots to new settlers, who immediately started to build their homes.

By the end of the 1940's the whole surrounding area was being urbanized. The southward growth of the city had begun to swallow up the towns of Mixcoac and San Angel. The shantytown, however, was unfavorably located on the slopes of the ravine; it was bypassed by the developers. During the 1950's thirty new families arrived; these were workers in the sand pits, the adobe workers, and the housing projects of the neighboring hills, particularly the suburb of Las Aguilas. However a considerable number of relatives of the original settlers, straight from the country, also settled there. After 1960 the shantytown began to grow very rapidly: 111 families joined during this period, plus around 25 families who left during the period of the study (1969–1971) and were not included in the survey.

When both the adobe factory and the sand pits closed down, their owners became the slumlords of the shantytown; yet they did not move away. The settlers pay rent for their house or for the land on which they erect a house of their own. At present the shantytown of Cerrada del Condor includes about 176 households, most of which were surveyed during the study.

Origins of the Settlers

A full 70 percent of the heads of families and their spouses (hereafter referred to as the "settlers") are of rural origin, having migrated to the Mexico City metropolitan area from localities with a population of less than 5,000 (Unikel 1968: 1–18). The remaining 30 percent were born in the Federal District, either as sons or daughters of rural migrants, or of inhabitants of the small towns which are now a part of the southern residential area of the city. The latter might be described as "passive migrants," since they did not have to leave their small towns in order to become urban settlers.

Eighty-six percent of the rural migrants migrated directly to Mexico City without intermediate stops. This high proportion applies to all age groups. In fact, about 70 percent of all the migrants moved in family groups, and only 30 percent were single. The rural migrants came from the most impoverished sectors of the peasantry. Eighteen states are represented in the shantytown, but the states of Guanajuato, Mexico, and San Luís Potosí account for 56.6 percent of all migrants. Veracruz, Zacatecas, and Hidalgo come next, with about 6 to 7 percent each. Nearly all migrants declared that they had been landless field workers or that their landholdings had been too poor for subsistence.

Of migrant heads of families and their spouses, 34.5 percent were illiterate; another 8.7 percent had never been to school but knew rudiments of reading and writing. Another 33.4 percent had had one to three years of schooling. It is probably fair to say that more than half the settlers of rural origin were functionally illiterate at the time that they reached the Federal District. They had neither savings nor skills of any value in the urban labor market.

Among those born in the Federal District the illiteracy rate was significantly lower. Only 16.8 percent had never been to school, and nearly half of those (7.2 percent) taught themselves the rudiments of reading and writing. We shall see later that there is a significant correlation between schooling and economic status, as measured by occupation, income, and material possessions.

When the migrants reach the city, they normally move in with relatives. The presence of a relative in the city is perhaps the most consistent element within the migration process. The role of this relative determines the circumstances of the new life of a migrant family in the city, including its locality of settlement within the metropolitan area, its initial economic status, and its type of work. There is no escaping the economic imperative of living near some set of relatives: the initial term of stay with a given kinship set may be variable, but subsequent moves tend to be made in reference to preexisting groups of relatives elsewhere. Unattached nuclear families soon manage to attract other relatives to the neighborhood.

The Villela Group: An Example of Kinship Migration

Among the thirty-odd households from the State of San Luís Potosí, twenty-five came from the *hacienda-ejido* Villela near Santa María del Río. These families are related through consanguineal and affinal ties. The history of the migration of the Villela group will serve as an example of the process as it can be observed in Cerrada del Condor.

The settlement of migrants from Villela goes back to the early 1950's, when two young men from the village decided to try their luck in Mexico City. They found work in the adobe factory and settled in Cerrada del Condor, and one year later one of them brought a sister and two nieces with their offspring. These nieces later brought their mother and brothers, and other relatives in successive waves. Two other Villela families also migrated to Cerrada del Condor and became related to the first family group by marriage or *compadrazgo*.

After working at various trades, one of the migrants was fortunate to find work as a carpet layer. Later migrants were lodged, fed and counseled by those among their kin already in residence, with the result that practically all the men now work in the carpeting trade. The process can be observed quite generally among family networks and is by no means unique to the Villela network. Thus, all the men in one network polish tombstones; in another, they work as bakers; still others are members of bricklayer gangs, and so on.

Villela settlers in Cerrada del Condor maintain a closely-knit community within the shantytown. They founded the oldest functioning local association: the Villela football club, with three teams in constant training who participate in a league tournament in Mexico City. Social contact among Villela families is intense, and there is a great deal of mutual assistance among them. All migrants express satisfaction about the positive results of their move, and not even the grandmothers show any nostalgia for Villela, where, they say, "we were starving."

Moves Within the City

It has sometimes been assumed that migrants to Mexico City tend initially to gravitate toward the crowded tenements in the old downtown area (Turner and Mangin 1968). Our research in Cerrada del Condor does not confirm this hypothesis. Instead, the place of initial residence is determined by the residence of preexistent cores of relatives in the city. In general, the migrants continue to move within the urban areas, but always in the same general sector of the city. Thus the settlers of Cerrada del Condor were born or migrated initially to the southern part of the metropolitan area, and few of them have more than a very superficial acquaintance with the other parts of the city, including the downtown area. The women and children rarely venture outside the shantytown, and their knowledge of the city is very limited.

The mechanism of moves within the urban area was studied in some detail. In general, a family moved once every five years on the average for the first ten or fifteen years of married life; some families never seemed to settle down. The moves seemed to be caused largely by dislodgment due to the southward growth of the city, coupled with a desire for better work opportunities and more congenial kin. There is an important turnover in Cerrada del Condor: during the period of my study, about twenty-five to thirty families moved away, and some forty new families moved in. Cerrada del Condor has been bypassed by developers and represents an area of refuge for those displaced by urban growth.

However, most of the new settlers in Cerrada del Condor merely follow the pull of relatives who already live in the shantytown. These relatives have told them about cheap available housing and have offered the exchange of mutual help, without which life in a shantytown is extremely difficult. Thus, kinship is also the determining factor in the process of internal migration within the city. When the job opportunities seem sufficiently bright for a nuclear family to move into a new area, they soon bring in other relatives from nearby areas or directly from the country. New migrants may be recruited during trips to the village, as migrant families keep in regular contact with their place of origin. Visits occur normally on festive occasions, such as holidays and celebrations.

In conclusion, it may be said that each migrant helps several new migrants to settle in the city or to move from another part of the city to his shantytown. This he does by providing temporary or permanent lodging, food, information, assistance in job-hunting, moral support and the basis for a more permanent form of exchange to be discussed later.

ECONOMICS OF SHANTYTOWN LIFE

The general economic setting of Cerrada del Condor is one of extreme poverty. A typical room measures ten by twelve feet and contains one or two beds shared among the members of the family. There may also be a table, a chair, a gas or petroleum stove, and sometimes a TV set – 33 percent of all households own one. There are three public water faucets, which are used by most of the population (a few clusters of rooms have a faucet of their own). There is little public or municipal sanitation and drainage; more than four-fifths of the population use the bottom of the gully for a latrine. Sanitary conditions are made more difficult by the presence of a large public garbage dump next to the shantytown.

There is no electric installation; power is obtained by illegal hook-ups to power lines. There are no paved streets, only alleys and gutters left between the residential units.

For purposes of classification the following four economic levels are proposed in Cerrada del Condor:

Level A. Three or more rooms; running water; bathroom or privy; brick construction; cement or tile floor; dining-room furniture; living room; electric appliances such as sewing machine, washer, or refrigerator; gas kitchen.

Level B. Two rooms; cement floor; no running water; some furniture such as a trunk or closet, table and several chairs; some electrical appliance(s); gas kitchen.

Level C. The same as Level B but no electrical appliances (except for radio or TV); lower-quality furniture: petroleum-burner for cooking.

Level D. One room with or without small lean-to for cooking; no furniture (except bed(s) and an occasional rustic table or chair); clothing kept in boxes or under the bed; no appliances (except for radio or TV); petroleum cooking only.

· Statistical testing by means of contingency tables showed that the four criteria used (housing, furniture, type of cooking, and electrical appliances) were highly correlated and consistent. The distribution of economic levels within Cerrada del Condor was found to be as follows: Level A, 7.8 percent; Level B, 8.9 percent; Level C, 23.8 percent; Level D, 59.5 percent. The economic level was also found to be highly correlated with other economic indicators, particularly the type of occupation of the breadwinners. Table 1 shows that the total of unskilled laborers, journeymen, servants, and petty traders corresponds closely to the total of Levels C and D.

Unskilled laborers or apprentices include hod carriers and other construction workers (foremen excepted), house painters, sandpit

Table 1. Occupations of 177 heads of households

	Men		Women	
	Number	Percent	Number	Percent
Unskilled laborers or apprentices	51	32.9	1	4.5
Semiskilled or skilled journeymen or craftsmen	48	31.0	—	—
Industrial workers	16	10.3	—	—
Services	5	3.2	12	54.6
Traders	7	4.5	4	18.2
Employees	8	5.1	1	4.5
Landlords	5	3.3	1	4.5
Unemployed	15	9.7	—	—
Housewives	—	—	3	12.7
	155	100.0	22	100.0

workers, brickmakers, bakers' helpers, truckers' helpers, carpet layers, electricians, gardeners and other unskilled laborers who are paid by the day and earn the minimum legal wage or less. Semiskilled or skilled journeymen or craftsmen are independent or free-lance workers such as bakers, carpet-layer foremen, construction foremen, electrician foremen, truck drivers, tombstone polishers, carpenters, cobblers, blacksmiths, potters and so on. These may earn higher wages, but their job security is usually as low as that of the unskilled workers. Some of them have developed a steady clientele and work with their own assistants, usually relatives.

Industrial workers are those who work in an industrial plant, usually with the lowest wages and bottom qualifications: watchmen, car washers, janitors and unskilled laborers; they do have a weekly or monthly income and some social security. The service occupations include waiters, water carriers, watchmen, icemen and domestic servants. Traders include all kinds of street vendors. None of these have steady incomes or social security.

The employees are unskilled workers who earn fixed salaries: municipal workers (street sweepers, garbagemen) and a few similarly employed with private corporations. These have relatively high job security and other benefits. Finally, there are six households whose income is mainly derived from rentals of property in the shantytown.

About 10 percent of the household heads were out of work at the time of the survey. However, more than 60 percent of those who declared to be working consider intermittent joblessness for variable periods of time to be normal. They have no formal work obligations and may therefore miss one or more days for any or no reason. Thus, the majority of the working population in the shantytown are underemployed (*eventuales*) and have no job security, no social security and no fixed income. They exist from day to day, as urban "hunters and gatherers." Members of economic Level D belong to this group. More than half the settlers in Level D were illiterate. None owned both their home and the lot it was built on; nearly two-thirds paid rent on both counts. All lived in a housing unit consisting of a single room. The average number of people per room was 5.4 if the cooking was done inside, and 6.2 if there was a lean-to for cooking. Of all acknowledged cases of problem drinkers, more than 75 percent belonged to Level D.

In contrast, members of Level A were practically all owners of their homes and lots. Most of them were either born in the Federal District or had lived in town for many years. There was practically no illiteracy, and most settlers had completed third grade. They tended to belong to the upper types of occupations: landlords, employees, traders, and industrial workers; their key distinctive trait is job security. More than half the households in this group included two or more breadwinners. The men were either abstemious or moderate drinkers.

Levels B and C are intermediate, but they can be sharply distinguished. Level B is urban in its type of dwelling, furniture, and life-style, while Level C is still rural in most of these respects. Households of either type can usually be recognized by a glance at their belongings. The transition from Level C to Level B is not determined so much by gross income as by the degree of cultural assimilation to urban life; hence, time of residence in the city is a significant factor. Even the highest income in Cerrada del Condor could easily be used up by a single heavy drinker. Wives receive a weekly allowance and have no direct knowledge of their husband's income. Working wives contribute their total income to household expenses; likewise, sons and daughters hand over their earnings to the mother. The husband's contribution to raising the economic level of the household is largely limited to major appliances, which are purchased on the installment plan. However, if the husband enjoys a steady income and has a tolerant view of a working wife, the economic rise may be rapid by shantytown standards. Nevertheless, the transition from Level C to Level B is rarely accomplished before a household has completed ten years of residence in the city.

SOCIAL ORGANIZATION

The pattern of social organization which prevails in the shantytown can be described as follows. Most nuclear families initially lodge with kin, either in the same residential unit (extended families, 46.7 percent) or in a compound arrangement (27.4 percent). Kinship compounds are groups of neighboring residential units which share a common outdoor area for washing, cooking, playing of children and so on. Each nuclear family in such a cluster forms a separate economic unit. Compound families are related through either consanguinity or affinity; each compound family contains at least two nuclear families.

Extended families, e.g. two brothers with their wives and children, may temporarily share the same residential unit; in the case of newly married couples living with the parents of either husband or wife, the arrangement may be more permanent. Any room or group of rooms having a single private entrance is defined as a residential unit: this excludes tenements of the *vecindad* type, consisting of a series of rooms opening on an alley with a public entrance gate, which may contain several independent family groups. Extended families contain at least two nuclear families; these share the rental expenses or own the property in common. Sometimes they also share living expenses. Televisions are usually shared.

Extended households are more unstable than compound households. Nuclear families in an extended household tend to move into a nearby room of their own or to join a different set of relatives elsewhere. However, those who move away in search of independence and privacy eventually return for security or assistance. In the case of compound households the rate of desertion is much lower. Of forty-four nuclear families who joined a compound arrangement since the beginning of married life, only seven moved away in an attempt to form an independent household.

Thirteen couples began their married life as independent households within the Federal District; these represent the major exception to the proposed pattern of family organization. All these heads of households had been born in Mexico City or had lived there for many years. Yet even these households do not remain independent for long, since they tend to attract other kin who join them in an extended or compound arrangement. The complete data for household types is summarized in Table 2.

The survey included practically all households in the shantytown; subsequent survey data have covered the same sample, but there are occasional small differences in the total number of households because of minor fluctuations in the status of some nuclear families during the fieldwork in progress.

Independent nuclear families are in the minority; those who live within walking distance of relatives are usually waiting for a vacancy to move into a compound-type arrangement. In this case there is much visiting, mutual assistance and other types of interaction, even though

Table 2. Types of households in Cerrada del Condor

Extended families	29
Compound families	68
Independent nuclear families:	
(a) without kin	30
(b) with kin in Cerrada del Condor	28
Other unknown	7
Total households in survey	162

the related nuclear families are not yet fully integrated into a compound household. The term "nuclear family" is used in a broad sense here, as each nuclear family may include one or more individually attached kin. Most of them are older persons, young children or unmarried recent arrivals from the country. Nuclear families may also include the offspring of a previous union of the mother; in two such cases there was no offspring from the present union.

Incomplete nuclear families are those which lack either one of the spouses, or children. There were eight couples living alone in the shantytown: mostly they were older couples whose married children had moved away. The situation in the extended households cannot normally be defined in terms of completeness; extended households aside, 76.8 percent of the remaining nuclear families were complete. The remaining 23.2 percent included largely newly-married couples and older couples. Hence, the overwhelming majority of households are either extended households or complete nuclear families, organized singly or in cluster compounds. A tentative subdivision of the extended households into nuclear families yielded an average of 2.8 nuclear families per household, but it is realized that any attempt to subdivide an extended household is bound to be arbitrary.

In conclusion, the social organization of the shantytown may be described as a collection of family networks which assemble and disband through a dynamic process. There is no official community structure; there are no local authorities or mechanisms of internal control. Cooperation within the family networks is the guiding principle of social organization. The dynamic process includes a pattern of movement from the extended toward the compound household type; this pattern is disclosed by a survey tracing the past moves of each household over the years. The results show that there is an increase of 29 percent in compound household arrangements, against a decrease of 46.7 percent in extended household arrangements, as referred to the initial state of residence. The difference in these figures appears to correspond to those nuclear families who have moved away from extended households but have not yet joined a compound household. Thus, extended households are more characteristic of the initial state of residence, while compound households are typical of the more mature or stable arrangements.

Locality

Table 3 describes the distribution of nuclear families according to locality and household type (a) at time of marriage or initial settlement in the Federal District and (b) at the time of the survey. Note the significantly high figures in the diagonal of the table. This does not contradict the observation of a high mobility from one type of locality or household to another; rather, it indicates that the sample contains a high proportion of young families who have not yet made their first move.

The initial state is frequently patrilocal (45.5 percent). Most migrant families as well as most newly married couples go to live with the husband's relatives, preferably with the husband's parents or brother. Families who start out as patrilocal rarely end up matrilocal, and vice versa. The strongest trend is from patrilocal to neolocal; this simply means that most first residences in the city begin in a patrilocal extended family, and that the first move is usually toward an independent residence within the same neighborhood. Several moves later (including "passive" moves, i.e. receiving a brother or sister, which will change the status of the household to extended or compound) a majority of nuclear families gravitate toward a compound family situation. The final ratio of patrilocality to matrilocality is about three to two.

Table 3. Contingency table for locality of residence (extended or compound) in percentages

Status at time of survey		Initial Status						Neo-locality	ROW TOTALS
		Patrilocality			Matrilocality				
		ext.	comp.	total	ext.	comp.	total		
Patril.	ext.	13.7	0.0	13.7	0.6	0.0	0.6	0.0	14.3
	comp.	5.6	11.8	17.4	0.6	0.0	0.6	3.1	21.1
	total	19.3	11.8	31.1	1.2	0.0	1.2	3.1	35.4
Matril.	ext.	1.9	0.0	1.9	6.9	1.2	8.1	0.6	10.6
	comp.	0.6	0.0	0.6	3.1	10.6	13.7	0.0	14.3
	total	2.5	0.0	2.5	10.0	11.8	21.8	0.6	24.9
Neolocality		10.0	1.9	11.9	3.7	1.9	5.6	20.0	37.5
COLUMN TOTALS		31.8	13.7	45.5	14.9	13.7	28.6	23.7	97.8

It is important to visualize the problem of locality and type of households as a dynamic process, which depends on the economic circumstances, the stage in the life cycle, the availability of vacancies, the personal relationships with relatives, etc. The initial choice of moving in with the family of either spouse is usually an economic one. Since young husbands or wives often do not get along with their in-laws, and conditions in an extended family may be very crowded, the couple tends to move out. However, new circumstances such as the arrival of children, desertion of the husband, loss of employment, and so on, frequently compel the family to return to the shelter of relatives. The preferred arrangement is the compound family, which combines proximity of kin with an adequate amount of independence and privacy.

Kinship Relationships Outside the Shantytown

A dynamic process of physical moves such as we have described, sometimes over large distances, implies a systematic contact between kin beyond the physical boundaries of the shantytown. Such systematic contact has been confirmed through personal observation initially, and later by means of a kinship census covering all households in the shantytown.

Contact with relatives within the Federal District depends on kinship distance and on physical distance. Informants tend to list first their nuclear family of orientation, then other relatives by order of spatial proximity; first those who live in the shantytown, then those who live in nearby shantytowns such as Puente Colorado, and so on. If a relative is not particularly close and lives as much as two hours away by bus from Cerrada del Condor, the contact is unlikely to be significant, and may be lost after a generation. The mother is often the only nexus between such relatives, and contact vanishes after her death. Of course, if there exists a true closeness of relationship, each set of relatives will exert a great deal of "pull" on the other, in order to encourage them to move into as close a neighborhood as possible.

Changes in socioeconomic status become a factor which influences the intensity of contact between kin. A lady informant commented that she hardly ever saw her sisters, who were married to skilled industrial workers: "To tell the truth, I don't like to go and see them because they can dress very nicely and I can't afford to, and so – I feel ashamed." The informant is the daughter of a skilled worker; she married a man who "never finished grade school and is worse off" than her sisters' husbands. Her parents were opposed to the match because her husband had no skills, "not even that of a truck driver, a barber or a carpenter," but she was in love, and they went to live with his parents and they get along very well. At first they lived in the same residential unit (in Cerrada del Condor); now they have a room nearby because "each his own is better."

Contact between migrant families and their relatives in the country has already been discussed in this paper and in related research (Simic 1970; Lomnitz 1969; Kemper 1971; Butterworth 1962; Mangin 1967). Visits to the village occur on festive occasions, such as Mother's Day, All Saints Day, and the festivity of the patron saint of the village. Unmarried migrants often return to the city accompanied by a smaller brother, sister, or cousin, whom they help out until they find a job. Married migrants frequently maintain a share in a small plot of land which they own jointly with a brother, and they time their occasional visits to coincide with harvest time, and so on. Most migrants send money home to their parents or close relatives. Through word of mouth or correspondence they keep up with village gossip; eventually, they are instrumental in promoting the migration of their close kin from the village. For years there is a steady stream of relatives from the country, who are lodged and fed for indeterminate periods of time depending on resources and needs.

Contact with the village gradually wanes over the years. About one-fourth of all informants said they had relatives in the country but had lost all touch: "I haven't seen my folks since I got married and moved to the city eighteen years ago"; "I never went back home since my mother died – my father married again and I don't get along with my stepmother"; "My brothers have moved to the city. I used to visit them and bring them money; now I don't go any more"; "I never went back since my grandparents and parents died." Other migrants, however, said they maintained significant contact through visits to and from the village, through economic interests (land owned in common), through correspondence, through remittances of money, through sentimental pilgrimages (visiting mother's grave on All Saint's Day), and so on.

Local Groups

The shantytown is not organized around central institutions of any kind. Instead, there are several types of groupings, of unequal importance: (a) the family network; (b) the football teams; (c) the medical center; (d) temporary associations.

The family networks will be discussed in greater detail later, as it is our thesis that they represent the effective community for the individual in the shantytown. They are composed of members of an extended or compound family but may include neighbors who are assimilated through fictive kinship. We shall see how these networks have developed into an original system of reciprocal exchange of assistance, which provides a consistent explanation for the fact of survival of large masses of population under the severe economic handicaps of shantytown life.

Other forms of organization at the community level are relatively rudimentary. There are four football teams in Cerrada del Condor. Three of these teams belong in effect to a single large family network, the Villela network described earlier. The fourth is a more recent team whose membership is recruited among young people of the shantytown irrespective of family origins. Significantly, the name of this new team is "Mexico." Football teams represent one of the few vehicles of social contact between men of Cerrada del Condor and men who live in other parts of town. After a game there are drinking sessions which reinforce the team spirit and friendly feelings among members of a team – related through consanguinity or affinity, in the case of the three Villela teams.

The Medical Center deserves a special mention; this center was organized and financed by a group of middle-class ladies from the neighboring residential district, with some assistance from the parish. Later, the National Children's Hospital agreed to staff the Center; but this help has recently been withdrawn. In spite of the modest assistance offered, the Center has become an important part of shantytown life. It is a place where children are welcome during most hours of the day, and where many girls and women can receive guidance from an understanding social worker.

There are no other organizations in Cerrada del Condor at the community level – except for a religious pilgrimage to the Sanctuary of Atotonilco. This pilgrimage is organized four times a year by one of the oldest residents of the shantytown; it is not a permanent organization. The group spends a full week together at the Sanctuary, but the composition of the group changes every time. However, all members of the group are always residents of Cerrada del Condor.

There is no local organization for solving the common problems of shantytown life. Groups of neighbors may band together for specific issues; this has happened three or four times in the existence of Cerrada del Condor. The first time was to request the installation of a public water faucet; previously, people walked about a mile to the nearest water outlet. Another time, a group of women jointly requested an audience with the First Lady, in order to lodge a complaint about some spillage of oil from a refinery that was causing brush fires in the ravine. These exceptional instances of cooperation merely serve to highlight the absence of any organized effort to solve community problems.

A word about membership in urban or national organizations may be relevant here. Contacts with such organizations are minimal. Articulation with Mexican urban culture occurs mainly through work and through mass media such as radio and television. School is, of course, very important among the children's population. Adult reading is limited to sports sheets, comics, and photo-romance magazines.

Only about one-tenth of the men belong to the social security system. About 5 percent are union members. In general, extremely few people belong to any organized group on a national level, such as political parties, religious organizations, and so on.

Networks

Few of the men venture farther into the city than their jobs require; few are acquainted with the center of town and its monuments. Women and children barely know anything of the city beyond a church, a market or the home of some relative. The men's drinking companions are relatives and neighbors; only exceptionally are working companions from outside the shantytown included. In effect, the community of the individual is determined by kinship and residence.

According to Barnes (1954), a network is a social field made up of relations between people. These relations are defined by criteria underlying the field. While Barnes saw a network as essentially unbounded, Meyer (1962) showed how certain types of migrants encapsulate themselves in a bounded network of personal relationships. In the case of Cerrada del Condor, we find networks defined by criteria of neighborhood, social distance, and exchange of goods and services. However, the basic criterion from our standpoint is the existence of continuous flow of reciprocal exchange of goods and services. The criterion of neighborhood is seen primarily as a prerequisite for such a continuous reciprocal exchange, since physical distance can impede it, even between close relatives.

Each network is constituted of nuclear families, not individuals. Initially, we shall use an operational definition of networks as clusters of neighboring nuclear families who practice continuous reciprocal exchange: a total of thirty-nine such networks were identified in Cerrada del Condor. The social relationships which form the basis of these networks are as follows: thirty are networks based on consanguineal and affinal ties, seven are based on kinship but included also one or more families not related by kinship, and eight are formed by families not related by kinship. The number of nuclear families per network is shown in Table 4. The average network contains four nuclear families. Of course, the number of families in a network is not static but changes with time. Initially, the network may consist

Table 4. Number of nuclear families per network

							Total
Number of nuclear families	2	3	4	5	6	uncertain	—
Number of networks	6	12	11	4	4	2	39

of two or three families; it may grow until a part of the network is split off because of lack of room or facilities, and forms a metastasis elsewhere in the shantytown or in a neighboring part of the city, where it initiates a similar process. Table 4 does not include the unattached nuclear families (estimated at less than ten) and those networks that were not identified as such.

Because of the process of network metastasis and growth, several networks can be interrelated through kinship. Thus, the Villela macronetwork includes about twenty-five nuclear families grouped into five networks. Each of these networks internally displays a high intensity of reciprocal exchange of goods and services on a day-to-day basis. The resources of the macronetworks are used more on ritual occasions, in important matters such as job placement, and for the expression of kin solidarity (football teams) and drinking. Reciprocal exchange does occur between families belonging to different networks within a macronetwork system, but the recurrence of such exchanges is less frequent, because no single nuclear family in the shantytown has enough resources to maintain a generalized day-to-day exchange with such a large group of families.

All nuclear families in a network practice reciprocal exchange among each other on an equal footing. In addition, a nuclear family may maintain dyadic relations with families outside the network or belonging to other networks. These dyadic ties are important because they provide the mechanism through which an outside family can be attracted to join the network, or by which a network which has outgrown its optimal size may split.

The types of exchange within networks are reciprocal in all cases. They vary from pooling of resources (in the case of extended families) to dyadic reciprocity in the case of nonkin networks. An intermediate form of exchange, found among compound networks, combines the pooling of certain resources with dyadic exchange among some or all of its members. Hence, the type of reciprocity depends on the social distance between network members. Eight networks were identified as composed entirely of neighbors unrelated through kinship; the prevailing exchange in these networks was dyadic. A member might also maintain a dyadic reciprocity relation with a member of another network, but this relation was one-to-one and did not implicate other network members. Some compound networks were composed of both kin and nonkin members. In these hybrid cases there was both dyadic and polyadic exchange (when each member exchanges with all other members of the network), but the dyadic reciprocity was more pronounced than with pure kinship networks, i.e. compound families, where polyadic exchange and pooling were the dominant type.

Thus, a network constituted as an extended family practices a generalized exchange of goods and services, which includes the informal pooling of resources for rent and entertainment, joint use of cooking facilities, communal child care, etc. Each nuclear family contributes according to its ability and receives according to the availability of resources within the network. There is no accounting of any kind among the members of such a network. In a compound family, on the other hand, each nuclear family has a roof and an economy of its own; yet there is an intense exchange of goods and services in the form of daily borrowings of food, tools, and money. Reciprocity here is not openly acknowledged, but it is definitely expected; each member family is supposed to provide assistance in proportion to its economic ability. Thus, if a nuclear family within a compound network becomes economically more secure than the rest, it may find its resources taxed beyond the actual returns which it can expect from the network; as a result, the more prosperous families may stop asking for and offering services.

One Case History

The network is of the compound type and includes two sisters, A and B, who married two brothers. A nonkin neighbor is also included in the network. A third sister, C, brought in from the village to live with A, soon found employment as a maid living in. On her days off she visited with A. A niece from the country then joined the network with her husband; at first they lived with A, who obtained work for the husband and a room adjoining hers. All men in the network are currently working as tombstone polishers. When C became pregnant she quit her job and went again to live with A. After she had the baby she went to work again and left the baby in A's care during the day.

Meanwhile B's status had been rising steadily. Her husband did not drink and invested in home furnishings. He also found advancement at work and became a skilled worker (in the placement of tombstones). B began to refuse to loan (or ask for favors) within the network, claiming that she had no money. Her sisters, niece, and neighbor gradually stopped requesting assistance, and so did their respective husbands. After a while B found a room just beyond the limits of the shantytown, two blocks away from her former room but endowed with urban utilities. Her economic level is now rated "B."

Sister C found a husband and moved in with him. The husband lived several blocks away from the sisters' compound, outside of Cerrada del Condor. Yet C continues practically to live at A's place whenever her husband is away at work. When she works she leaves her child with A; when she needs money she borrows from A or from her niece. Her interaction with the nonkin member of the network is less intense; yet these neighbors have become double *compadres* in the meantime, and their exchange with both A and the niece and their respective husbands is very active. When a room became available, C began to convince her husband to move in with the network. If this happens, an active exchange between C and the nonkin neighbor is anticipated.

What is Exchanged?

The following items represent the most important objects of exchange in the networks, according to my observation:

1. INFORMATION, including directions for migration, employment and residence; gossip, and orientation about urban life.

2. TRAINING AND JOB ASSISTANCE, including the training and establishing of a relative as a competitor. Thus, a carpet layer or a building constructor would take his newly arrived brother-in-law along as an assistant, teach him the trade, share the salary with him and eventually yield some of his own clientele to set him up as an independent worker.

3. BORROWING money, food, blankets, tools, clothing and every kind of article.

4. SERVICES, including the lodging and care of visiting relatives, widows, orphans and old people; the care and errand running for sick neighbors; and the minding of children for working mothers. Assistance among men includes help in home construction and in carrying materials. Children must lend a hand in carrying water and running all kinds of errands.

5. THE SHARING OF FACILITIES, such as TV set or a latrine (which the men may have built jointly).

6. MORAL AND EMOTIONAL SUPPORT in ritual situations (weddings, baptisms, funerals) as well as in day-to-day interactions (gossip among the women, drinking groups of *cuates* among the men).

It is essential to point out that much of the socializing in the shantytown is based on network affiliation. This constant interaction generates an overriding preoccupation with each other's lives among the members of a network, and a perpetual watching over each other. There is little margin for privacy.

Asymmetrical Exchange

All relations between members of a network are essentially relations among social equals. In general, the component families of the networks have (or lack) the same types of resources. Hence the exchange takes the form of reciprocity, always on a strictly equalitarian basis.

When one nuclear family in a network has access to more economic resources than the others, the equalitarian basis is temporarily or permanently broken. This situation is dealt with according to three entirely different patterns, depending on the degree of urbanization.

1. The traditional rural pattern, exemplified by the Villela networks, is redistribution in the form of alcohol. This pattern appears to be closely associated with the ideology of *cuatismo*, and it effectively insures that no member of the network consolidates a position of economic preeminence, since none can keep surplus earnings for long.

2. An intermediate pattern, represented by two cases in Cerrada del Condor, is the emergence of the *cacique*, even though it is in a rudimentary form. The power of the *cacique* appears to depend primarily on his ability to place migrants in jobs, rather than on his economic position. Such shantytown "big men" may be viewed as mediators between the village and the city, but their function in Cerrada del Condor does not appear to be very important.

3. Finally, there is the pattern described in the preceding case history of a nuclear family that becomes urbanized. Urbanization is denoted by a change in living standards (from Level C to Level B), together with a significant change in the husband's occupation toward a more stable, skilled type of employment. The network ceases to fulfill a useful purpose in the life of the family; rather, it represents an embarrassment and a hindrance. Its multiple obligations are no longer seen as relevant to the economic progress of the family. In all cases, the ties with the network were cut after a period of drastic reduction in the intensity of exchange, and the urbanized family eventually moved out of the shantytown.

The significance of these three patterns, taken together, represents one of the strongest lines of evidence in support of our interpretation of shantytown networks as economic structures which represent a specific response of marginal populations to economic insecurity in the city.

Reinforcing Mechanisms

These economic structures are seen as the underpinning of a social system: the network organization. This social organization in turn is reinforced by ideology and by certain institutions such as *compad-*

razgo and *cuatismo*. The economic basis of networks often is based on the exchange of goods and services among members; when this basis ceases to exist, the network disintegrates. The social structure which is erected on this basis depends on physical and social proximity of network members. Ideally, the networks are composed of neighbors related through kinship.

Actually, many networks contain nonkin members whose allegiance must be reinforced by means of fictive kinship (*compadrazgo*) and other means which will be analyzed presently. Even among kin, relationships are far from secure: economic and personal differences arise frequently under conditions of extreme poverty and crowdedness. The reinforcing mechanisms to be discussed are therefore present in all networks.

Compadrazgo is widely used to reinforce existing or prospective network ties. In Cerrada del Condor the *compadres* have few formal obligations toward each other as such. An informant says: "When choosing a godfather for one's child, one should look for a decent person and a good friend: if it's a couple, they should be properly married. They should be poor so no one can say you picked them out of self-interest." Among 426 *compadres* of baptism (the most important type of *compadrazgo* in the shantytown), 150 were relatives who lived close by, and 200 were nonkin neighbors. Another 92 were relatives who lived elsewhere in the Federal District or in the country, i.e. prospective network affiliates. In all cases of *compadrazgo* the dominant factors were neighborhood and kinship. This equalitarian pattern is at variance with the rural pattern of selecting a *compadre* above one's station in life (Foster 1969; Forbes 1971).

The great importance of *compadrazgo* as a reinforcing mechanism of network structure is also reflected in the variety of types of compadrazgo that continue to be practiced in the shantytown. These types are, in order of decreasing importance: baptism (426 cases), confirmation (291), communion (79), wedding (31), crown or burial (16), Saint's Day (13), fifteenth birthday (10), Divine Child (8), Gospels (8), grade school graduation (4), habit (3), sacrament (2), scapulary (1), cross (1) and St. Martin's (1). All these types of *compadrazgo* mark ritual or life-cycle occasions, including severe illnesses, vows, etc. The obligations among *compadres* are described as follows: "They must treat each other with respect at all times and must exchange greetings whenever they meet." Ideally, some *compadres* should fulfill important economic obligations, such as taking care of a godchild if the father dies; but these obligations are no longer taken very seriously in the shantytown.

The reasons for selecting a *compadre* may be positive or negative. Among the positive reasons is the intention of extending the network:

many cases of *compadrazgo* occur between members of a super-network, i.e. relatives who live in the shantytown but are affiliated with different networks. Other stated reasons are "We know and like them...Our husbands are good friends...We are brothers-in-law and we get along...We are neighbors...We wanted them so as to get to be closer...They helped us...We help each other out." Negative reasons are: "We asked this so as to live in peace with them...It was a way to make up with my sister-in-law...We asked this in order to keep them at a distance."

In one case which was analyzed in depth, the informant had been an old friend of her sister's brother-in-law, who lives in another network in the shantytown. The relationship between the two net-works was marred because of jealousy of the wife of her former boyfriend. In order to mend relations between the in-laws, the infor-mant asked her former boyfriend and his wife to become the god-parents of her child. This placed their relationship above suspicion, since *compadres* have to treat each other with formality and even use the respectful form of address (*Usted*) on all occasions.

Cuatismo is the Mexican form of male friendship. If *compadrazgo* formalizes and legitimizes a relationship between men and women, *cuatismo* provides the emotional content of the relationship. Most groups of *cuates* number four or five men, although there are also smaller and larger groups.

Information on *cuatismo* was largely gathered through wives, since the relationship of *cuatismo* is traditionally exclusive and jealous to the point of secretiveness. *Cuates* (a Nahua term for twins) are close friends who pass the time together, talking, drinking, playing cards or football, watching TV, treating each other in restaurants and having fun together; above all, they are drinking companions. Women are totally excluded from the relationship. A wife "would never dare" to approach a *cuate* of her husband's to request a favor.

Assistance among *cuates* is ruled by social distance. Among rela-tives there will be more unconditional help than among neighbors. In general the *cuates* borrow freely from each other, help each other in looking for work, give each other a hand in fixing their homes, and stand by each other in a fight. Like *compadrazgo*, *cuatismo* is practically universal: the man who has no *cuate* and no *compadre* is lost indeed. Among the total of 106 households headed by men, the circle of *cuates* of the family head was recruited as follows: 86 were groups of *cuates* who live in the immediate vicinity, 9 were mixed groups (some *cuates* living close by and some far away), and 11 were groups who did not live in the immediate neighborhood. Two heads of households had not yet made any *cuates* in the city.

Among the 86 groups of neighborhood *cuates* it was found that 21 were composed exclusively of relatives. Another 20 groups were composed of both relatives and neighbors, and 45 groups included nonkin neighbors only. It is clear that these groups of *cuates* are based on the male sector of the networks described earlier, but they may include their neighbors, work companions, or friends.

The existence of *cuatismo* to reinforce network affiliation is evidence that the networks are not simply built around the wives and mothers, as might be supposed from a superficial analysis. On the contrary, many networks appear to be male-dominated, as reflected by the predominance of patrilocality (Table 2). If networks were based exclusively on the more visible forms of daily exchange of goods and services practiced by women, the strong correlation between networks and groups of *cuates* would be rather puzzling. Actually, however, networks are constituted by nuclear families as entities; all members of each nuclear family participate actively in the relationship.

Drinking relationships among men are exceedingly important and usually take precedence over love relationships. The mere fact of getting drunk together signifies a strong bond between a group. This bond easily extends into all social directions; for example, *compadrazgo* proposals frequently originate in a drinking bout. From a psychological point of view, drinking together is a token of absolute mutual trust which involves a baring of souls to each other (see Lomnitz 1969; Butterworth 1972). From the economic point of view, *cuatismo* implies a mechanism of redistribution through drink which insures that all *cuates* remain economically equal. And from the social point of view, it reinforces existing networks and extends the influence of networks in many directions, since a drinking circle may contain members of several networks.

For example, when M.S. was first interviewed she was in the process of throwing her husband's belongings out of her room. She claimed that her husband was a no-good drunk and that she had had enough of him. In a second interview (one week later), M.S. sheepishly admitted that she was still living with her husband "because he is a *cuate* of my two brothers and they always drink together." The implication was that her brothers might side against her in case of an affront to their *cuate* (and, indirectly, to themselves since drinking was the issue), and thereby threaten the stability of the network.

The *ideology of assistance* is another important factor of network reinforcement. When questioned, most informants are reluctant to describe their own requests for assistance: "Well, I might ask a neighbor for a loan if . . ."; yet they are unanimous in claiming to be always ready to help out their own relatives and neighbors in every possible way.

The duty of assistance is endowed with every positive moral quality;

it is the ethical justification for network relations. Any direct or indirect refusal to help within a network is judged in the harshest possible terms and gives rise to disparaging gossip. People are constantly watching for signs of change in the economic status of all members of the network. Envy and gossip are the twin mechanisms used for keeping the others in line. Any show of selfishness or excessive desire for privacy will set the grapevine buzzing. There will be righteous comments, and eventually someone will find a way to set the errant person straight.

For example, I became friendly with V. and was able to place her as a maid at the home of a visiting professor. I also gave her some used clothes. Once I was seen by neighbors as I handed her a package of clothing. On my next visit she burst out crying. It developed that after my previous visit the neighbors had come to tell her that I had said that the clothing was to be shared by all of them, and they accused her of selfishness. They were concerned that the good job and the presents of clothing would set V. economically above the rest of the network.

Macronetworks

If nuclear families can be compared to the atoms of society, a family network is the molecule of the shantytown social structure. The affinities between atoms within a molecule are strong. but this does not exclude bonds and affinities between different molecules. In particular, several molecules of similar composition may sometimes band together to form macronetworks. An example of such a macronetwork has already been mentioned. Twenty-five households originating from the hacienda Villela live in the shantytown; these households have formed five separate networks. Since all members are mutually related, the affinities between these five Villela networks are high. Though the intensity of economic exchange between members of different Villela networks may not be as high as it is within each network, there is still a regular traffic of reciprocity. One example of this is found in the large number of *compadrazgo* ties between networks; another is the institutionalization of the macronetwork, as found in the Villela football teams, whose members are selected on the basis of belonging to the macronetwork.

Structurally speaking, the members of a macronetwork maintain sets of dyadic reciprocity relations between each other. Where a high intensity of exchange occurs without physical closeness the social distance must be very close, i.e. the parties of the exchange must be related through kinship. When two such parties settle in different parts of the shantytown, and each of them becomes the center of a network of kin, the result is a macronetwork composed of two family networks. On the other hand, if the two parties to the exchange become attached through marriage to nonkin networks, the other network members will not participate in the exchange, and the result will simply be a dyadic relation between two members of different networks.

Reciprocity and Confianza

The types of reciprocity between shantytown members are ruled by a factor which we have called *confianza* (Lomnitz 1971). *Confianza* depends on cultural factors (social distance), physical factors (closeness of residence), and economic factors (the intensity of economic exchange). In some cases social distance may be overruled by physical closeness and intensity of exchange, as when a close friend or *cuate* enjoys a greater *confianza* than a relative who lives elsewhere and is met only occasionally.

The formal categories of social distance are culturally determined. They imply a "series of categories and plans of action" (Bock 1969: 24) which dictate expected behavior between individuals. These categories and plans of action can only be described ethnographically: they represent an essential part of the culture or subculture of a group or subgroup. In Mexico, within the national culture there are subcultures of each social class, each state or region, and so on down to the level of family subculture, which may imply strongly particularized sets of behavior. Two individuals are close in the scale of *confianza* to the extent that they share the same set of behavior expectations, i.e. in proportion to their closeness according to their own formal categories of social distance.

The expectations attached to each formal category include a specific type of reciprocity, which ranges from unconditional sharing to total lack of cooperation and distrust. The scale of *confianza* measures, among other things, the extent to which these expectations are actually fulfilled. Hence the grade of *confianza* is not rigidly determined but may vary during the evolution of the relationship. This scheme differs from the model proposed by Sahlins (1968) where each individual rigidly belonged to a category. On the other hand, the situation in the shantytown is somewhat more rigid than in the urban middle class of Chile (Lomnitz 1971), where the boundaries between categories were more fluid, and individuals tended to change their status of *confianza* depending on the fluctuations of personal friendship.

In order to establish the culturally expected relationship given by the formal categories of social distance, any pair of individuals have to overcome certain resistances. In the case of the shantytown the primary resistance is represented by physical distance, the main obstacle to social contact. The factor of physical nearness thus becomes a major component of *confianza*, both as a positive inducement and as a potential deterrent if absent. Closeness by itself cannot replace social closeness; for example, two neighbors who come from different cultural backgrounds are unlikely to establish a relation of intimate *confianza*. On the other hand, the degree of *confianza* with a given set of relatives is greatly enhanced by the fact of moving physically into their immediate proximity.

In conclusion, *confianza* is variable and flexible while social distance is formal and rigid. *Confianza* is the result of the interaction of physical, economic, and even personal factors (e.g. the fact of getting along or not getting along with someone) with the ideal model of behavior. It measures the difference between real and ideal social distance. When this difference becomes large enough it may be formally acknowledged, for example, by conferring *compadrazgo* on a close neighbor. The scale of *confianza* is also reflected in common speech, as in the term *cuate* which confers the title of "twin brother" on a close friend.

THE ROLE OF NETWORKS IN THE CONTEXT OF MARGINALITY

Urban marginality is not exclusive to underdeveloped societies, as pointed out by Quijano (1970). In a developed society we find marginality as the result of the displacement of certain social strata from the labor market through mechanization and automatization of the means of production. These growing population sectors have no expectancy of absorption into productive occupations and become increasingly dependent on welfare. In effect, they represent *surplus population* (rather than a labor reserve) and therefore an unwanted by-product of the system.

According to Quijano, this situation is considerably aggravated in underdeveloped countries because the rhythm and pattern of industrial development is imposed from abroad. Economic dependence introduces a factor of instability because of the hypertrophic growth of large industrial cities at the expense of the countryside. Accessibility of sources of raw materials and cheap labor attract an overflow of hegemonic capital into formerly preindustrial societies. As a result, (1) there is an increasing gap between "modern" cities, surrounded by huge encampments of slum populations, and "traditional" rural areas on the verge of starvation; (2) new skills required by industrial growth are monopolized by a relatively small labor elite, while the great mass of unskilled peasants and artisans are displaced from their traditional sources of livelihood; and (3) superficial modernization has caused a sudden population explosion, which increases the ranks of urban marginality and rural-urban migrants, thus offsetting any efforts at promoting the gradual absorption of surplus populations into the industrial labor force. On the other hand, there is a further increase in unemployment in the developed countries on account of the competition from cheap labor abroad. Thus the process of marginalization is not transitional but rather intrinsic to the system.

Quijano specifically identifies the capitalistic system in general, and the dependent industrial development observed in Latin America since 1945 in particular, as responsible for the phenomenon of marginality. Adams (1970: 89–94, 1972) generalizes this analysis to apply to any large society which is subject to a process of economic development and technological change. According to Adams, any increment in social organization is achieved at the expense of disorganization among sectors of the same society or of dependent societies. Dialectically speaking, order is the source of disorder: work creates entropy. Starting from an undifferentiated labor force, we may build up an industrial proletariat with highly differentiated skills and a centralized form of organization; but this will generate a marginalization of those populations which can no longer be assimilated or successfully utilized by the more advanced system. Adams likens this evolution to the production of waste materials and contamination of the environment by an industrial process.

In Latin America the urban marginal strata share the following economic characteristics, which are also found among the settlers of Cerrada del Condor: (a) unemployment or underemployment, (b) lack of stable incomes, and (c) generally the lowest level of income within the urban population. Most settlers of Cerrada del Condor are rural migrants, "passive" migrants, or the offspring of migrant parents. Most of them are unskilled workers, such as construction workers, who are hired and fired on a daily basis; journeymen and artisans who are hired for specific jobs and have no fixed income; petty traders; and people who work in menial services. They may be described as urban hunters and gatherers, who live in the interstices of the urban economy where they maintain an undervalued but nevertheless well-defined role. They are both a product of underdevelopment and its wards.

If this vast social group lacks any economic security and has no significant support from organized welfare, how does it survive? This question was asked by Quijano (1970: 97–96), who surmised that there must be some mechanism of reciprocity operating among marginal groups which has not been described. It is the purpose of the present section to analyze this mechanism in some detail as a function of the socioeconomic structure.

The Network as a Reciprocity-Based Survival Mechanism

According to Polanyi (1968: 127–132) and Dalton (1968: 153) there are three forms of exchange of goods and services: (1) market exchange, in which goods and services circulate on the basis of offer and demand, without any long-term social implications attached to the exchange; (2) redistribution of goods and services, which are first concentrated in a single individual or institution whence they flow out toward a community or society; and (3) reciprocity among social equals. Reciprocity defined in this manner is an integral part of a permanent social relationship.

Polanyi (1968a: 43–68) has pointed out that the current supremacy of market exchange is of recent date. Primitive peoples and tribal societies had an economy which was largely based on reciprocity and redistribution. Market exchange was confined to exchange between neighboring tribes or other social groups. The monetary economy which is characteristic of market exchange became dominant towards the end of the Middle Ages in Europe, and its generalization was the result of the capitalist industrial revolution in nineteenth-century Europe. Yet no economic system operates exclusively under a single mode of exchange. One mode, such as market exchange, may be dominant, but other modes exist concurrently and are supported by specific social institutions. The best-known among such institutions are: the monetary and market system in the case of market exchange; taxation and the welfare state in the case of redistribution; and the peer groups in the case of reciprocity.

Why do older modes such as reciprocity persist in modern market-exchange economies? According to Polanyi, a system based exclusively on self-interest would be self-destructive, since all social life is rooted in cooperation. When social expectations rise to a point where they can no longer be satisfied for all members of the society, the system of market exchange enters a period of crisis. Polanyi believes that such a crisis began after the First World War and continued through the Russian Revolution, fascism, and the depression. Social mechanisms of redistribution have become generalized since that time; among the socialist countries they have become the dominant mode of exchange of goods and services.

The role of reciprocity in modern industrial economies is less well defined. Malinowski (1961: 334–350) and Sahlins (1968: 130–177) have described systems of exchange based on reciprocity among primitive tribes. Some authors (Gouldner 1960; Lévi-Strauss 1967: 289; Mauss 1954: 81) speak of the *principle of reciprocity* as a basis of social life; this principle is not to be confused with the specific mode of exchange of goods and services called "reciprocity" by Polanyi and Dalton.

Although reciprocity thus defined seems more characteristic of primitive societies, it does appear in more complex societies as well. For example, the economy of the Inca empire was predominantly redistributive: the state apparatus collected tribute in goods and labor which it utilized in public works and in territorial expansion through warfare. The head of each family was assigned a piece of land according to size of his family. Market exchange was secondary to this system of redistribution; it was limited to barter at community fairs and to major markets controlled by the Inca state. Yet reciprocal exchange played an important role within each community, in the form of mutual assistance among relatives and neighbors, and most importantly in the *minga*, an institution of reciprocal exchange of labor. Under the *minga* system a member of the community may obtain the assistance of the other members for specific tasks such as harvesting or building a house; eventually, each member of the labor pool reciprocates in turn. The *minga* is a characteristic institution of Inca economy, which persists in peasant communities of Peru and Chile.

Economic anthropologists of the formalist school (Firth 1970; Burling 1962: 804, 813–820; Cook 1968: 188–208) have tended to belittle the role of reciprocity and redistribution in modern societies, arguing that more attention ought to be paid to the principle of maximization of resources, which is assumed to operate in market exchange. Anthropologists ought to study the economic structure of a society from the point of view of *which* resources are maximized according to a given system of values, rather than "concocting tortured arguments in defense of a theory which was designed specifically for the analysis of . . . moribund types of economies" (Cook 1968). However, more recent research, including a study of the middle class of Chile (Lomnitz 1971), has shown that reciprocity as a specific mode of exchange among urban societies in the process of industrialization is far from extinct. On the contrary, the role of reciprocity determines the nature and intensity of social relations to such an extent as to make an analysis of the economic history of the Chilean middle class unintelligible without reference to this mode of exchange.

The urban marginal population in Mexico is estimated at four million, a considerable part of the total urban population. While the dominant mode of exchange in the cities is market exchange, no adequate systems of public or private redistribution have been created in response to the needs of a growing mass of marginals left to their own devices. Economic dependence aggravates the problem because capital gains tend to be transferred abroad instead of becoming available for redistribution within the country.

Thus, the marginated individual cannot rely on the social system for his elementary needs of survival. He has nothing to offer the market exchange system: no property, no skills except for his devalued labor. His expectations of absorption into the industrial proletariat are slim, since marginality grows faster than the number of industrial job openings. He has nothing to fall back upon: no savings, no social security of any kind. His chance of survival depends on the creation of a system of exchange entirely distinct from the rules of the marketplace, a system based on his resources in kinship and friendship. This system follows the rules of reciprocity, a mode of exchange between equals, embedded in a fabric of social relations which is persistent in time, rather than casual and momentary as in market exchange. The three basic elements of reciprocity are (a) *confianza*, an ethnographically defined measure of social distance: (b) equivalence of resources (or lack of resources); (c) physical closeness of residence.

Characteristically, reciprocity generates a moral code which is distinct from, and in some ways opposed to, the moral code of market exchange. In a reciprocity relation the emphasis is less on receiving than on giving: the mind of the recipient is preoccupied with reciprocating rather than with extracting a maximum personal benefit from a transaction. Both systems of exchange may be used simultaneously in a different context: a member of a reciprocity network may sell his labor as worker or servant on the urban market. Yet it is the reciprocal exchange among relatives and neighbors in the shantytown which ensures his survival during the frequent and lengthy spells of joblessness. Market exchange represents the ultimate source of livelihood, but it is a livelihood at the subsistence level and without any elements of security. Through sharing these intermittent resources with another six or ten people, the group may successfully survive where as individuals each of them would almost certainly fail.

The networks of reciprocal exchange which we have identified in Cerrada del Condor are functioning economic structures which maximize security, and their success spells survival for large and important sectors of the population. If security can be defined as an objective economic resource, we may bridge the present gulf between substantives and formalists by showing that reciprocity networks maximize security, much in the same manner as market exchange systems maximize other resources. This insight might easily have been overlooked if the shantytown had been studied only with the tools of economic theory rather than through an anthropological approach. Economic structures are an integral part of social relations and cannot be properly understood without a detailed study of social structure.

For example, the role of alcohol consumption in Cerrada del Condor must be analyzed on several levels at once. It is not enough to point out that drinking is negatively correlated with economic status and therefore impedes economic progress. From a sociocultural point of view alcohol consumption is essential to the institution of *cuatismo* which reinforces social cohesion. *Cuatismo* in turn is embedded in the economic structure of shantytown networks, where alcohol consumption has an important role as a mechanism for leveling of income differentials. Inequality would destroy reciprocity relations which are the base of the networks; hence it may be argued that alcohol consumption has a positive role in maximizing economic security among marginal communities. The question is not so much how an individual can be made to stop drinking as whether he can afford not to drink.

This brief example is not intended as an exhaustive discussion of the role of alcohol consumption in Cerrada del Condor; it is mentioned to point out that economic indicators can be subject to erroneous interpretations if considered separately from the sociocultural context in which they occur.

REFERENCES

ADAMS, N. RICHARD
  1970 *Crucifixion by power.* Austin: University of Texas Press.
  1972 "Harnessing technology." Mimeographed preprint.
BARNES, J. A.
  1954 Class committees in a Norwegian island parish. *Human Relations* 7: 39–58.
BOCK, PHILIP
  1969 *Modern cultural anthropology.* New York: Alfred A. Knopf.
BONILLA, F.
  1961 *Rio's Favelas: the rural slum within the city.* Field Staff Report East Coast, South American Series 8(3).
BURLING, R.
  1962 Maximization theories and the study of economic anthropology. *American Anthropologist* 64.
BUTTERWORTH, D.
  1962 A study of the urbanization process among Mixtec migrants from Tilaltongo in Mexico City. *América Indígena* 22: 257–274.
  1972 Two small groups: a comparison of migrants and non-migrants in Mexico City. *Urban Anthropology* 1(1).
COOK, SCOTT
  1968 "The obsolete 'anti-market' mentality: a critique of the substantive

approach to economic anthropology," in *Economic anthropology*. Edited by E. E. LeClair, Jr. and H. K. Schneider, 188–208. New York: Holt, Rinehart and Winston.

DALTON, G.
1968 "The economy as instituted process," in *Economic anthropology*. Edited by E. E. LeClair, Jr. and H. K. Schneider, 143–187. New York: Holt, Rinehart and Winston.

FIRTH, R., *editor*
1970 "Themes in economic anthropology," in *Association of social anthropologists monographs 6*, 1–29. Second edition. Edinburgh: T. A. Constable.

FORBES, JEAN
1971 "El sistema de compadrazgo en Santa María Belén Alzitzinititán, Tlaxcala." Unpublished Master's thesis, Universidad Ibero-americana.

FOSTER, GEORGE
1969 Godparents and social networks in Tzintzuntzan. *Southern Journal of Anthropology* 25: 3.

GOULDNER, ALVIN
1960 The norm of reciprocity: a preliminary statement. *American Sociological Review* 25(2).

KEMPER, R. V.
1971 "Migration and adaptation of Tzintzuntzan peasants in Mexico City." Unpublished doctoral thesis, University of California, Berkeley.

LEEDS, A.
1969 The significant variables determining the character of squatter settlements. *América Latina* 12(3).
1969a "Brazil and the myth of urban rurality," in *City and country of the Third World*. Edited by A. J. Field. Cambridge: Schenkman.

LÉVI-STRAUSS, C.
1967 *Structural anthropology* (second edition). Garden City, New York: Anchor Books, Doubleday and Company.

LEWIS, OSCAR
1959 "The culture of the vecindad in Mexico City: two cases studies," in *Actas del XXXIII Congreso Internacional de Americanistas* I: 387–402. San José, Costa Rica.
1960 The culture of poverty in Mexico City: two case studies. *The Economic Weekly*, special number 12: 965–972.
1961 *The children of Sanchez*. Ne York: Random House.
1969 The material possessions of the poor. *Scientific American* 115–124.

LOMNITZ, LARISSA
1969 Patrones de ingestión de alcohol entre migrantes mapuches en Santiago. *América Indígena* 29(1): 43–71.
1971 "Reciprocity of favors among the urban middle class of Chile," in *Studies in economic anthropology*. Edited by George Dalton. Washington: American Anthropological Association.

MALINOWSKI, B.
1961 *Argonauts of the western Pacific*. New York: E. P. Dutton.

MANGIN, W.
1967 Latin American squatter settlements: a problem and a solution. *Latin America Research Review* 2(3): 65–98.

MANGIN, W., J. TURNER
1968   The barriada movement. *Progressive Architecture* 49(5): 154–162.
MATOS, MAR, J.
1968   *Urbanización y barriadas en América del Sur.* Lima: Instituto de Estudios Peruanos.
MAUSS, M.
1954   *The gift.* London: Cohen and West.
MEYER, P.
1962   Migrancy and the study of Africans in town. *American Anthropologist* 64: 576–592.
NICHAMIN, JULIES
1968   Shantytowns in Latin America: prospects for political change. *Papers of the Michigan Academy of Science, Arts and Letters*, 53(2).
PEATTIE, LISA R.
1968   *The view from the barrio.* Ann Arbor: University of Michigan Press.
POLANYI, K.
1968   "The economy as instituted process," in *Economic anthropology.* Edited by E. E. LeClair, Jr. and H. K. Schneider, 122–142. New York: Holt, Rinehart and Winston.
1968a   *The great transformation.* Boston: Beacon Press.
PORTES, A.
1972   Rationality in the slum: an essay on interpretative sociology. *Comparative Studies in Social History* 14(3); 268–286.
QUIJANO, A.
1970   "Redefinición de la dependencia y proceso de marginalización en Américan Latina." Mimeographed preprint.
ROBERTS, B.
1968   Protestant groups and coping with urban life in Guatemala City. *American Journal of Sociology* 73(6): 735–767.
SAFA, H.
1964   From shantytown to public housing: a comparison of family structure in two urban neighborhoods in Puerto Rico. *Caribbean Studies* 4(1).
SAHLINS, M. D.
1968   "On the sociology of primitive exchange," in *Association of social anthropologists monographs no. 1.* Edited by M. Banton, 13–177. London: Tavistock.
SIMIC, A.
1970   "The peasant urbanites: a study of rural-urban mobility in Serbia." Unpublished doctoral thesis, University of California, Berkeley.
UNIKEL, LUÍS
1968   Ensayo sobre una nueva clasificación de población rural urbana en México. *Demografía y Economía* 1(1): 1–18.

The Female Domestic Servant and Social Change: Lima, Peru

MARGO L. SMITH

In spite of their large numbers and their high degree of visibility, domestic servants in the large urban centers of Latin America generally have been ignored by social scientists and other observers of the urban scene. Servants and the servitude complex in which they live are presented most frequently in a peripheral sense: in supporting roles in novels (Donoso 1965, 1967); as a small part of contemporary urban life (Lewis 1959); as a part of the historical record (Lockhart 1968; Carrio de la Vandera 1966; Prado 1941; von Tschudi 1966); and as a part of either the "Indian problem" or one of the major "social problems" of the urban arena. It is within the context of defining servants as a contemporary "problem" that most of the recent social-science-oriented research on servants in Peru has been framed (Helfer 1966; Pascual Badiola 1968; Flores Guerrero 1961; Vásquez 1969; and numerous journalistic exposés) and that servants have become a main topic for investigation. In these studies, servants also are presented as passive members of a tradition-oriented and essentially static social context.[1]

When the topic of this study was originally suggested to me[2] the

The fieldwork on which this article is based was conducted in Lima, Peru, and the Peruvian provinces, in 1967 and 1968–1970. Financial support was provided by Indiana University, the Alpha Gamma Delta social fraternity, and the Department of Health, Education and Welfare (Fulbright-Hays).

[1]   Nett (1966) depicts the servant system in the Ecuadorean capital city as survival from the colonial period. However, the situation in Quito is not directly comparable to that in Lima. Although both are national capitals, Quito is a highland city whereas Lima is a coastal city. Contrasts between domestic service in the highlands and on the coast are striking and worthy of consideration in another essay.

[2]   Nora S. Kinzer merits the author's appreciation for mentally prodding her along new lines of thinking, but shares none of the responsibility for the ideas expressed here. The author also thanks Richard Schaedel, Robert Myhr, and the other seminar participants for their insightful comments.

opportunity to view the Lima servant from a different perspective was presented. To examine the servant within the context of social change, three general areas of scrutiny come to mind: changes which take place at the individual level between servants and their employers; changes which are taking place within the institution of urban servitude; and changes which can be seen taking place on a broader national scope. An initial view of the Lima servant shows servants to be most visible, in their distinctive uniforms, peering out at the street from the windows or roofs of the houses of their employers, running errands, making purchases in the market, sweeping the sidewalks, walking a few paces behind their employers and carrying all the packages, supervising the out-of-doors play of their employers' children, or chatting with fellow servants on the sidewalk or in the park. Once out of uniform, and on their own time, servants melt into the anonymity of the vast urban lower class. This hardly suggests a social context much different from that of twenty years ago. However, a close scrutiny of the Lima servant and her world reveals factors both stimulating and inhibiting changes on all three of the levels mentioned. But before discussing these factors, it will be useful to provide a profile of the women working as servants in metropolitan Lima and a summary of the urban institution of which they, along with their employers, are the most integral members.[3]

Precise enumeration of the total number of servants in Lima has not been made. Women completely dominate the servant scene; they comprise 88 percent of all Lima servants (Centro Arguideocesano de Pastoral [CAP] 1967). Extrapolating from the fifth and sixth Peruvian national census (Ministerio de Hacienda y Comercio [MHC] 1940, 1961) in which 26,200 and 66,100 women, respectively, were recorded as domestics (representing an increase in the servant segment of economically active females from 25 to 30 percent), a reasonable "estimate" of the number of women employed as servants in 1970 approaches 90,000. If women who have ever worked as servants, but who have managed to extricate themselves from that occupational niche, were to be included in this group as well, the total number of women living in contemporary Lima who have been involved personally in the servitude complex as subordinate members might approach 250,000. There are at least several thousand additional women who have worked as servants in Lima for some time before dropping out and returning to the Peruvian provinces to live.

The servant population is not a homogeneous, monolithic group; rather it reflects the widest spectrum of the lower-class Peruvian population. Yet domestics "typically" represent a relatively narrow band of that spectrum. They are uniformly categorized by their employers as Indians or, at best, *cholas*,[4] categories with both racial

[3]   A detailed view of the Lima servant and urban servitude is presented in Smith (1971).

and ethnic connotations. In actuality, an estimated 95 percent should be lumped, on the basis of their phenotype, into the *mestizo* category. The remainder of the servants are of Negro ancestry (descendants of African slaves brought to work as agricultural laborers on the Peruvian coast).

The majority of servants are older adolescents and young adults; 58 percent range in age from fifteen to twenty-four years (CAP 1967). Most of them are unmarried (some 90 percent according to CAP 1967), not an unexpected finding in light of the young age of the servants and their residence in the homes of their employers. One-quarter of the servants admits to having children: of these, slightly more than half have only one child (MHC 1965: Table 201). Not unexpectedly, as servants become older, they are more likely to have childen, and also more likely to have more children (MHC 1965: Table 201). Although the Lima stereotype of servants as unwed mothers is not supported, the largest percentage of servant mothers are, in fact, unwed (CAP 1967).

Servants have completed very little formal education; a mere 8 percent have continued beyond elementary school (CAP 1967). However, few are illiterate and most have had at least some primary education. *Muchachas*, to employ the derogatory term often used in referring to these female servants, have less formal schooling than either male servants in Lima (CAP 1967), all women migrants to Lima from the provinces 1965: Table 3c), or women born in Lima (MHC 1966: 60). Nearly one-third of the servants are of school age (under nineteen years of age) and literally thousands of them, along with their less educated older counterparts, attend school while they are employed. Additional servants seek employment with this most highly desired fringe benefit.

Servant women are almost exclusively migrants from provincial areas outside of metropolitan Lima (91 percent according to CAP 1967). Nearly 57 percent of them are from the ten highland Andean areas; some 30 percent claim coastal origins; and only about 3 percent are migrants from the jungle areas (CAP 1967). Of these migrants, approximately 40 percent had come from provincial towns with a population of 5,000 or more, and approximately 44 percent had come from towns with a population of 1,000 or more (MHC 1965; Table 11). This certainly does not support another tenet of the servant stereotype: that servants are born and raised in the most remote and isolated corners of the provinces. None of the author's servant informants had been raised in a provincial setting so isolated that some kind of public transportation was not easily accessible.

Nevertheless, the town environment in which the servants were

⁴   The urbanized lower-class woman, a social rank one important step above the lowest rung of Indian.

raised and their family backgrounds are a far cry from the cosmo-politan bustling metropolis of the capital city to which servants have to adjust, often on their first job. They come from predominantly agricultural, poorly educated families. Two-thirds of the servants' fathers are employed as agriculturalists or laborers (Anonymous n.d.: 5). However, servants do not tend to come from the poorest or lowest ranking (in socioeconomic terms) families. Three-quarters of their fathers are landowners, and few of the servants' mothers, if living, are employed outside the home (Escuela Municipal. . .1965–1966). Illiteracy is high among servants' families; half of the fathers are unable to read and write, and, given the generally inferior level of educational achievement of Peruvian women relative to that of men, it can be assumed that an even greater percentage of the servants' mothers also are illiterate. However, the occupational category of the largest percentage of servants' siblings (approximately one-third, according to Escuela Municipal 1965–1966) is that of student. The "typical" servant is one of 5.6 siblings in the family, and has a better then even chance of being either the oldest or the youngest.

Numerous conditions bring about a young woman's move to Lima. The overwhelming majority of them move directly from their home towns to the capital. Most make the move willingly and on their own initiative, some only because they are brought or sent, and a few are brought to the capital very much against their wishes. Specifically, servants mention being motivated to move to the capital by a desire to get ahead (*superación*); the search for a job, or to earn money to buy goods such as clothing or a radio; a desire to see what the capital city is like; a desire to continue their education; or in response to a family situation. Once in Lima, they find that servitude is the only or the best means within their power of supporting themselves and getting what they want out of urban life.[5]

The largest segment of migrant servant women are relatively recent arrivals in the capital, adolescents at the time of their migration, and previously unemployed. Nearly half of them have been in Lima for four and one-half years or less (CAP 1967). Two-thirds of them were between the ages of ten and nineteen years at the time of their migration (CAP 1967). More than half had not been habitually em-ployed in the provinces, but of those who had worked the largest number had been domestics there also (MHC 1965: Table 3a).

The institutionalized social and occupational niche of servant in which nearly two-thirds of employed migrant women find themselves in Lima is a highly structured context which continues to reinforce

---

[5]   Domestic service shelters, in addition to young migrants, some orphans, husbandless young women with a child to support, offspring of the poorest families, and older lower-class widows with numerous children to support.

the rigid socioeconomic hierarchy. Domestics are among those who occupy the lowest rung on the urban socioeconomic scale (Delgado 1968; and Plan Regional 1959). They are completely dominated, exploited, and controlled by groups ranking above them.

Servants are employed almost exclusively on a live-in basis, a pattern preferred by both servants and employers: by the former for the room and board received; and by the latter for the convenience of having the servant on call twenty-four hours a day and for the increased ease of controlling the servant's nonworking activities. Because servants are employed almost exclusively by middle and upper-class families, they are most densely concentrated in the residential neighborhoods of their employers, rather than in the lower-class residential neighborhoods of the servant's relatives. Most servants find that they are the only servants working in the households of their employers and that they are responsible for all general household tasks. However, the more servants are employed by the households the more likely they are to be specialized (the most frequently encountered specialties include two types of nursemaid, cook, and cleaning woman) and also expected to perform any number of strictly personal services for the various members of the employer's family.

A servant's career tends to follow a distinct seven-year pattern. Upon her arrival in Lima, she seeks out relatives or friends from her home town, with whom she spends her first few months. After this initial period of acculturation to the city, these relatives or friends are instrumental in placing her in her first job, usually found by looking for *se necesita muchachá* (servant wanted) placards placed in the windows of houses and apartments in commercial neighborhoods. As the only servant in the household, she receives on-the-job training in a wide variety of household tasks in return for a low salary and few fringe benefits. After six months to a year, the servant moves on to a better job with a higher salary, fringe benefits, and more affluent employers living in a higher-ranking residential neighborhood. This and subsequent jobs are located by means of an employment agency (of which there are thirty in the metropolitan area), want ads in the newspaper, or the recommendation of friends or relatives. She begins to focus on one of the servant specialities and improves her position within the servant hierarchy as she passes from one job to the next. Each job generally lasts from six months to two years.

It is likely that she will have six different jobs during her tenure as a domestic. During this time, her salary and fringe benefits will range from only room and board to an average salary of S/800 per month ($18.25); to a salary perhaps double that plus permission to study, hold a part-time job, or keep a child on the job, in addition to receiving clothing and other gifts. Approaching the age of twenty-four, the servant has a seven-year career behind her and drops out of servitude to concentrate on her legal or common-law husband and her children.

FACTORS STIMULATING OR INHIBITING CHANGES

Looking at domestic service in Lima, we may isolate factors which are stimulating or inhibiting changes at three levels: at the individual level for servant and employer participants; at the level of the urban institution of servitude; and at a national level. Among these, eleven factors appear most prominent.

The Individual Level

The changes at the individual level are the most notable and, in the long run, probably will emerge as the most significant in determining what broader changes will be taking place and how fast these changes will be occurring. Three pertinent elements at this level include the servant as a migrant, the servant's attitudes toward her position and toward change, and the employer's attitudes toward her servants.

THE SERVANT AS MIGRANT.   Most servant women are migrants from other parts of the nation who have come to Lima voluntarily. Whatever are their individual reasons for making the move, they have heard firsthand or via letters from friends and relatives who have visited in or moved to the capital city that life there is very different from that in the home town. They have been alerted, before migrating, to the idea that they will have to make changes in their life upon moving to the capital. Because migrants (soon to become servants) are for the most part self-selected; and because it takes "guts" to migrate, it might be suggested that only those individuals who are willing to make change a part of their lives will be willing to take the first big step of making the move to Lima. It is those people who are seeking change or at least are willing to accept it who will be the migrants.

THE SERVANT'S ATTITUDE TOWARD HER POSITION AND CHANGE. There is no indication that new servants have difficulty adjusting to their occupational status. Long before, they have internalized their subordinate socioeconomic position and learned the appropriate deference-behavior patterns to be used with their employers and other social superiors. They remain easily exploited and intimidated. In most cases, this exploitation takes the form of making the servant work long hours;[6] not permitting a weekly day off (or restricting it to less than a full day); not providing sufficient food; withholding vacation pay or denying the annual vacation altogether; or deducting breakage from the servant's salary – practices which, with the exception of the last one, are prohibited by law but not infrequently encountered. Intimidation is not unknown. Servants may lodge complaints against their employers (in matters pertaining to salary, vacation, and indemnization) with the Division of Women, Children, and Domestics in the Labor Ministry, but then they submit themselves to the challenges of the bureaucrats working there, who automatically assume the servant is not telling the truth (Smith 1971: 300–301).

In addition, servants appear to be perpetuating the status quo by not taking more interest in social change. It is reported, for example, that servants are not caught up in the "revolutionary spirit of change" sought by the Velasco government[7] even though that government has been responsible for significant legislation benefiting the servant segment of the labor force.

However, a recent innovation is being made by servants on the job. Instead of accepting whatever the employer chooses to dole out, servants, particularly the more experienced ones, now ask for raises and fringe benefits, especially permission to attend school. If the request is denied, or the servant has a complaint against her employer which is unresolved, it is not uncommon for the servant simply to quit and seek employment elsewhere.

Servants are not enthusiastic about their occupation. Four different recent studies of Lima servants (Pascual Badiola 1968; Anonymous n.d.; Baldárrago 1970; Stillinger 1966) indicate that, if given their choice of occupation, a maximum of 17 percent would select work as servants (Baldárrago 1970). Instead, they indicated preference, in decreasing order of frequency, for jobs as seamstress, hairdresser, cosmetologist, self-employed (which, for women, usually is taken to mean street or market vending), secretary or office worker, nurse, school teacher, and commercial employee. Although this appears to reflect servants' definite interest in changing their individual situations, these expectations, with the possible exception of self-employment, are unlikely to be realized at the present.

Finally, servants are able to express their interests publicly, but they usually do not do so. Two demonstrations by servants in Lima are

[6] For example, one study indicates that 70 percent of the servants work in excess of eight hours daily (Anonymous n.d.: 67). Supreme Decree #002–70 TR of March 10, 1970, makes mandatory eight hours of rest daily, a recognition of the fact that servants had not been receiving that much time.
[7] Personal communication, Joan de Riviero de Carvalho.

known, and both of these occurred during the first half of 1970. In the first, 200 servants rallied in the small plaza in the affluent San Isidro neighborhood dedicated to Marshall Ramón Castilla (who is remembered for having freed the slaves in Peru). The parading servants carried placards calling for unionization of servants, an eight-hour work day, and a thirty-day annual paid vacation. These servants utilized methods popular with other lower-class groups to court governmental approval of their cause: they all were dressed impeccably, waved Peruvian flags, shouted their support of the government and President Velasco, and elicited sympathetic news coverage in the tabloid *Ojo*. However, two weeks later, a governmental proclamation warned servants against partisan proselytism for social action. Although this demonstration had been organized by Túpac Armando Yupanqui, a radical leftist student group from the National Engineering University, rather than by the servants themselves, the other demonstration was a spontaneous servant effort. On the occasion of the television wedding of María Ramos, the heroine of the rags-to-riches television soap opera *Simplemente María*, 10,000 servants turned out for the ceremony in the church located at the border between a commercial area and a middle-class residential neighborhood. Lima servants are fanatical fans of María, a peasant girl from the provinces who migrates to the capital city, is exploited and eventually befriended in her jobs as a domestic, attends school to become literate and to learn sewing,[8] eventually rises to world fame as a high fashion Paris designer, and marries her former schoolteacher.

What happened to María could, or so some servants believe, happen to others too. This is unlikely, however, because the acquisition of a sewing machine alone is clearly beyond the economic means of most servants. Can future servant activism be anticipated, then, when they realize, as a few already have, that they lack the vocational training, financial resources, and luck of María? So far, María Ramos has left her mark only on a small group of self-identified radical servants called Las Marías which has emerged since 1970.

THE EMPLOYER'S ATTITUDE TOWARD THE SERVANT.   There appears to be some awareness on the part of a minority of employers that the employment situation of their servants should be changed. For example, increasing numbers of employers are permitting, and in some cases insisting, that their servants attend school. In addition, in 1969, a sociologist from the Catholic social science agency (CAP) and a parochial school for servants sponsored a round-table conference

[8]   This is responsible in no small measure for the servants' enthusiasm for education in general, vocational training in sewing (now often included in academic school curriculum as a lure), and their expressed preference for work as a seamstress.

for about twenty-five affluent employers on the improvement of living and working conditions of their servants. A "typical" employer, who considered herself enlightened on the subject of "good treatment" for servants, insisted that she treated her servant "just like a member of her own family." Yet, upon questioning, the same woman consistently referred to her servant as a *muchacha*, acknowledged that her servant wore a uniform (the badge of her status), ate by herself in the kitchen from dishes especially set aside for her after the rest of the family had finished eating, and received hand-me-down clothing as gifts. Other employers would not allow time during the day for their servant-students to study or do other homework. Few are the employers who want to see changes in the servitude complex and support their talk of change with action.

Some employers do tend to acknowledge that changes ARE taking place in the Lima servant world. But these are heralded as detrimental changes marked by a "new servant" who is less obedient and more independent than those of a decade or two ago. Foreigners residing in Lima are also held accountable for this noticeable change because they are said to pay their servants above-average wages and "do not know how to treat servants."

There remain numerous employers who speak of servants generally as half-savage, who consider them invisible objects generally to be ignored (except when needed to do something), or who do not see any need for changes to occur. Education is largely opposed (there is too much work in the household to allow that much time off); classes meet at inconvenient times; servants should not be allowed out of the house without direct supervision; there is no need for servants to be educated (certainly not beyond the basics of reading, writing, and arithmetic); education only would "give the servants ideas" (about changing the status quo); and so on.

At the Institutional Level

An additional five factors can be noted on the institutional level: formal education programs, the government, unionization, employment agencies, and the servant labor market.

FORMAL EDUCATIONAL PROGRAMS. Numerous programs of formal education are available to the Lima servant. The Ministry of Education has established special programs which, although they do not cater exclusively to servants, do list servants in the enrollment records: primary-level night school (*vespertinas*); capacitation (literacy, vocational, and social education) programs; Feminine

Industrial Institutes (a primarily vocational curriculum); and the comprehensive Institute of Special Education (day care for the children of working mothers, adult primary education, and training in household skills).

The Catholic church also sponsors various educational programs directed specifically at the servants in particular parishes. The St. Andrews School and the Sevilla Institute for Domestic Service provide elementary education and vocational training (household skills, sewing, and typing) for migrant girls, who later are placed as domestic servants in "approved" households. Twenty Lima parishes also offer other programs including literacy, primary school, vocational training, medical and dental care, and social (recreation and personal development) clubs for those already working as servants.

In addition, the government of the San Isidro (suburban Lima) district sponsored a short-lived program to teach servants literacy, arithmetic, and the skills requisite to become a competent servant. But servants do not want to go to school to learn to become better servants, so the school folded when it was unsuccessful in recruiting a student body. Small private vocational schools abound, and servant-students are particularly attracted to those offering sewing, hair-dressing, and cosmetology.

In spite of the plethora of opportunities to enroll in some kind of vocational program, these programs do not provide the servant-student with the skills necessary to get a new job related to her training. Sewing courses, for example, prepare the servant to do sewing for herself, but do not prepare her to the level where she could work as a seamstress.

Some of these institutions have a social worker or a teacher assigned to look after the "best interests" of the servant-students in terms of correcting abuses (nonpayment of salary, not allowing the servants sufficient nightly sleep, and sexual exploitation, among others), leading them toward "proper moral standards and attitudes" according to middle-class Peruvian standards, and often acting as informal placement channels by helping servants to find new jobs with "approved" families. Servants are not urged by their teacher or social worker counselors to aspire to any occupation beyond domestic service, nor are they urged to attempt to change the status quo. The goal appears to be to prepare the young women to be good wives and mothers. Any changes to be made should be made by them as individual servants. Any changes in the "system" are the prerogative of the government or of individual employers.

The Young Catholic Working Women, known as the JOC (Juvented de Obreras Católicas), is a program of personal education and consciousness raising, sometimes affiliated with another academic or vocational program. First opened to servants in 1962, it had twenty-one local branches in operation by 1969 in addition to a large house available for members' use. Inasmuch as the purpose of the organization is to "broaden horizons and stimulate thought processes" (Stillinger 1966: 9) of servants via peer group discussion, this organization has been like a bolt of lightning hitting the servant complex. Many employers consider this to be an inflammatory organization because they do not wish their servants "to have their eyes opened" or "to get ideas." They fear the JOC will foment ideas of socioeconomic self-improvement and discontent with the status quo.

So far, according to JOC members, it provides a setting in which servants can feel free to talk to one another about their problems, in which they can have a feeling of self-respect and personal dignity, and in which they can talk about orienting their lives according to their conception of the Christian doctrine. JOC discussions, with perhaps eight to twelve servant-participants plus a servant-moderator, revolve around topics theoretically relevant to young servant women, including: appropriate behavior in a variety of situations, Christian virtues, a work ethic, preparation for motherhood, and the development of friendship. Although this does provide a context in which servant-leaders might emerge, the impact of the JOC on the entire servant community has been small indeed so far; the organization had recruited only 200 members in 1968.

THE GOVERNMENT. Governmental action has the potential for providing significant changes in urban servitude. Legislation providing social benefits for the servant was not forthcoming until two major laws pertaining strictly to domestics came out in 1957. A supplement was effected in 1970, which for the first time included servants as mandatory participants in the national social security program. Servants with complaints against their employers may lodge them with the Labor Ministry's Division of Women and Children and Domestics, or with the police. However, few complaints are lodged: the Labor Ministry office recorded a monthly average of eighty-eight in 1968 and 1969; and less than one percent of the police cases involve servants in any capacity. Servants seeking jobs may, and, with a record 1,879 placements in 1969, increasingly do take advantage of the labor Ministry's employment service, the largest employment agency for servants in the city. The Ministry of Education provides educational programs enumerated above.

However, domestic servants never have occupied a high priority with the government; neither have they had any power or influence to exert leverage to gain additional legal rights, or even to enforce the ones they have. Servant legislation has managed to keep only one step ahead of demands, and has tended to represent final legal recognition of the status quo: benevolent paternalism, employment of minors, and minimal obligations on the part of employers. And to the extent that the laws are observed, it is due solely to the voluntary compliance of the servants and their employers. Legal rights are ignored, abuses of them go unreported, and compensation for reported abuses cannot be enforced.

UNIONIZATION.   Domestic servants have not yet been unionized. Personnel in the Labor Ministry maintain that they recall the registry of a union for servants "many years ago," but they are unable to find documentation of this union. In any event, if such a union did exist at one time, it was ineffectual in bringing changes to the urban servitude complex, and at the present has faded into obscurity.

During 1969, a representative of the Túpac Armando Yupanqui campaigned to organize servants by approaching those who lodged complaints against their employers with the Labor Ministry. This was short-lived because, after a few weeks, the national police, Policía de Investigaciones de Peru (PIP), expelled the organizer from the Ministry offices for making "offensive advances" toward the female servants. Túpac also is responsible for the graffiti demanding social legislation for the benefit of servants, which adorn walls in several locations in the central city and the two middle-class residential suburban districts of Miraflores and San Isidro:

Domestic Social Security.
Social Benefits for Nursemaids, Cooks.
Indemnization for Domestic Employees. We want justice.
We Household Workers demand social benefits. TUPAC.
We Nursemaids, Cooks, Etc., demand social benefits.

There are a substantial number of servants in Lima from which to form a union membership. In addition, there is a feeling of camaraderie among servants, and most servants have many social ties with other servants: former or present servant neighbors or coworkers, fellow students, and friends from the same home town. Servants also are considered to be a social necessity by their urban employers, who cannot imagine how they possibly could survive without their *muchachas*.

Counterbalancing these factors, which might be evaluated as those encouraging unionization and its effective operation, are other factors which effectively are inhibiting the organization of Lima servants. Servants tend to be highly suspicious of outside supervision, such as that exercised by the government or employers. So far, leadership has not emerged from among the servant ranks, out of employment agencies, or the schools run for servants. Servants in multiple-servant households often find themselves in an atmosphere of hostility and competition with their coworkers. Servants are transient and difficult to keep track of; they change jobs frequently, and employers have been known to deny that particular servants are, in fact, working for them. Servants are dispersed in tens of thousands of households throughout the city. Some servants also feel that they are "better off" working as domestics in Lima than they were in the provinces. Finally, servants consider their tenure as domestics to be a brief transition in their lives, and they lack a long-term commitment to their occupation.

EMPLOYMENT AGENCIES. Employment agencies have personal contact with more servants and employers than any other urban institution. But their primary concern is placement rather than fomenting social change among servants. In individual cases, the agencies will try to talk an employer into offering a higher salary: "For that salary, we cannot get you what you are looking for. Good cooks are earning S/—." They also might try to convince the employer to hire a servant-student who will work for a lower salary. Or they might tell a servant that her salary expectations are too high or that she lacks the experience and/or recommendations to get a better job. One chain of agencies has a servant's creed hanging prominently on the wall which advises servants to obey, to seek the love and respect of their employers, to be truthful, not to talk back, etc – certainly in no way a challenge to the status quo.

THE SERVANT LABOR MARKET. The servant market in Lima is a sellers' market. There is no shortage of available jobs. Organized servants could utilize this to get increased salaries and other work benefits. However, there is a constant supply of potential new servants invading the capital. These new migrants have very few occupational opportunities available to them: domestic service, street or market vending, prostitution, and a few factory or workshop jobs. Those who enter domestic service, as the largest number of migrants do, are not attuned to the prevailing conditions in Lima and are less aware of what they could demand from their employers.

At the National Level

Changes which might take place in the broader context of Peruvian society in relation to servants in the capital city can be seen in three areas: stimulation of young provincial girls to migrate to the capital; the introduction of new ideas and material goods to their relatives and friends in the provinces or in the other lower-class neighborhoods of Lima; and the providing of a channel of upward mobility for lower-class provincial girls.

URGE TO MIGRATE.   Servants tend to retain very close ties with their relatives in the provinces. These are maintained via letter, news reports sent with friends from the home town, and, for many, by at least one annual visit to the home town for a vacation. This visit is an opportunity to tell sisters, cousins, and friends what life is like in the capital, usually in very glowing terms. The young women do not miss noticing the servant-visitor's transistor radio, beauty parlor coiffure, makeup, and miniskirt. They hear about having an income and about opportunities to attend school. It is not an unexpected finding that many servants have been prompted to migrate to Lima because an older sister, cousin, or friend was already there. There is no indication that Lima servants will stop encouraging a steady stream of migrants.

INTRODUCTION OF NEW IDEAS AND MATERIAL GOODS. Because of their intimate participation in the households of their middle- and upper-class employers, servants working in the capital are acculturated much more rapidly to the cosmopolitan urban arena, both in terms of new ways of doing things and new material items, than are their migrant sisters who remain in the lower-class residential neighborhoods, such as the squatter settlements ringing the city. Although one might suspect that this would provide the servants with an excellent opportunity for introducing new ideas and new artifacts to their families remaining in the provinces, it appears that the servants' impact is minimal. On the job servants are exposed to new foods, telephones, all kinds of household appliances, new ways of educating and raising children, and new behavior patterns. But on vacations, servants find it easy to slip back into provincial ways. For example, in the house with her family, Navidad M. prefers to wear the midi-length woolen skirts belonging to her mother and sister instead of the miniskirts she wears in public. Most of the servants enjoy living according to provincial patterns for the short vacation period which usually ranges from a week to one month.

At the same time, domestics acknowledge that they would not return to the provinces to live permanently because they feel that they could not easily readjust to provincial life; *ya no me acostumbro* is a frequently heard evaluation. There is no evidence to suggest that servants are introducing new items into the provincial material culture or suggesting new ways of doing things. There is no talk of "why don't you do it this way instead, the way we do it in Lima." And it is impossible superficially to identify the relatively few provincial women who have worked as servants in the capital but who have returned to the provinces to live.

Even in Lima, servants generally do not adopt the artifacts and behavior of their employers beyond a superficial mimicking of fashion or hair style. The households of former servants do not appear modified versions of the houses they once worked, nor are the servants' children raised according to patterns used in dealing with their former employers' children.

From the opposite perspective, it can be noted that the "ruralization" of the city, i.e. the introduction of provincial material culture and behavior patterns, has not been passed from servant to employer, even though it is a prominent feature of contemporary Lima. Employers have not adopted provincial music, dance, or food. Neither do servants appear to practice provincial child-rearing techniques on the offspring of their employers.

PROVIDING A CHANNEL OF UPWARD MOBILITY.   Servitude is most significant in the context of broad social change by providing a channel of upward mobility for the provincial girl (Smith 1973). Migrating to Lima and working as a servant is one of the few opportunities such a girl has. With luck, she will, during her tenure as a servant, meet in Lima a young man (who is more tha likely a migrant to the capital as well) who will marry her and permit her to drop out of the servant world to become an upper lower-class housewife.

When balancing these eleven factors influencing servants, and social change in Lima, one can see that the potential for change is greater than what is being realized. By taking greater advantage of the educational opportunities available, servants would gain the self-confidence and the background knowledge (literacy and arithmetic) which are necessary before effectively competing with the better-educated Lima-born women for jobs outside of the servant sphere. Adequate vocational training, currently unavailable, could prepare servants for new jobs. Unionization and more active government support of servants could bring improvements to those who remain employed as domestics. Servants do continue to stimulate the migration of other young girls to Lima, thus perpetuating part of the wave of rural-urban migration toward the capital and assuring a fresh supply of potential servants for the Lima market, a market which continues to take advantage of their inexperience and naïveté. Domestics also have the opportunity of serving as a channel to convey ideas and material from the city to the provinces, but they do not seem to be doing so effectively. At the present time, the most important contribution servitude is making to the area of social change in Peru is in providing a means of upward mobility for this lowest-ranking urban group. The potential for change is present; the actual changes taking place are small steps, though increasing in frequency. The servant has yet to emerge as the standard bearer for social change in Peru.

REFERENCES

ANONYMOUS
  n.d.   "Encuesta de la Parroquía, 'Santísimo Nombre de Jesús.'" Type-written manuscript of data gathered in 1967. Lima.
BALDÁRRAGO, MARIETTA
  1970   "CIC noticias" (January 8). Mimeographed manuscript. Lima: Centro de Información Católica.
BONILLA, F.
  1968   Manual y leyes del obrero. Lima: Editorial Mercurio.
CARETAS
  1970   Un mito de la vida doméstica. Caretas (February 17–28, 1970): 30–44.
CARRIO DE LA VANDERA
  1966   Reforma del Perú. Lima: Universidad Nacional Mayor de San Marcos.
CENTRO ARGUIDEOCESANO DE PASTORAL (CAP)
  1967   Unpublished census cards, coded and reduced to various tables.
DE LA FLOR CUNEO, MIGUEL
  1966   Beneficios sociales de los trabajadores domesticos. Lima: Escuela Sindical Autónoma de Lima.
DELGADO, CARLOS
  1968   Hacia un nuevo esquema de composición de la sociedad en el Perú. América Latina 2: 3.
DONOSO, JOSÉ
  1965   Coronation. New York: Alfred A. Knopf.
  1967   This Sunday, Translated by Lorraine O'Grady Freeman. New York: Alfred A. Knopf.
DOUGHTY, PAUL L.
  1970   "Behind the back of the city: 'provincial' life in Lima, Peru," in Peasants in cities. Edited by William Mangin. Boston: Houghton Mifflin.
ESCUELA MUNICIPAL DE SERVICIO DOMÉSTICO PAPA JUAN XXIII
  1965–1966   Unpublished data in the Registro de Matrícula (school enrollment records), originally recorded by the school director.
FLORES GUERRERO, TERESA
  1961   "Reglamentación y problemas que conforte el servicio domestico en el Perú." Unpublished thesis, Escuela de Servicio Social del Perú, Lima.
HELFER, RUTH
  1966   El problema social de la empleada doméstica. Lima: Escuela Normal Superior de Mujeres. San Pedro, Monterrico thesis in secondary education).
La Prensa
  1970   "Incorporan a domésticos al seguro social." La Prensa (March 12): 1, 9. Lima.

LEWIS, OSCAR
1959   *Five families.* New York: Random House.

LOCKHART, JAMES
1968   *Spanish Peru 1532–1560.* Madison: University of Wisconsin.

MINISTERIO DE HACIENDA Y COMERCIO (MHC)
1940   *Quinto censo nacional de población 1940,* volume one: *Resúmenes generales.* Lima.
1961   *Sexto censo nacional de población 1961,* volume four: *Características económicas.* Lima.
1965   Unpublished data from computer printout sheets. Lima: Dirección Nacional de Estadística y Censos.
1966   *Encuesta de immigración Lima metropolitana,* volume one (October). Lima: Dirección Nacional de Estadística y Censos.

MORALES ARNAO, ELENA
1969   *Informe anual Agencia Abancay.* Lima: Servicio de Empleos y Recursos Humanos, Ministerio de Trabajo.

NETT, EMILY
1966   The servant class in a developing country: Ecuador. *The Journal of Inter-American Studies* 8:(3) 437–452.

Ojo
1970a   "El mitan de las Mariás." *Ojo* (April 27): 1. Lima.
1970b   "Domésticos se quejan por la jornada de 16 Horas." *Ojo* (April 27): 6. Lima.

PASCUAL BADIOLA, MARÍA PILAR
1968   *"Diagnosis ético-social de las empleadas domésticas."* Unpublished thesis in family education. Pontífica Universidad La Católica, Lima.

PLAN REGIONAL
1959   "La organización social en el Departamento de Puno" and "La cultura: factores institucionales" in *Plan regional para el desarrollo del Sur del Perú 22.* Lima.

PRADO, JAVIER
1941   *Estado social del Perú durante la dominación española,* volume one. Lima: Gil.

SMITH, MARGO L.
1971   "Institutionalized servitude: the female domestic servant in Lima, Peru." Unpublished thesis, Indiana University, Bloomington.
1973   "Domestic service as a channel of upward mobility for the lower-class woman: the Lima case," in *Female and male in Latin America.* Edited by Ann Pescatello. Pittsburgh: University of Pittsburgh.

STILLINGER, MARTHA
1966   "Domestic service in Lima, Peru." Photocopied manuscript.

VÁSQUEZ, JESÚS MARÍA
1969   "Estudio sobre la situación del servicio doméstico en Lima." Mimeographed manuscript. Lima: Misión Conciliar.

Visión
1970   El gran éxito de "Simplemente María." *Visión* (September 11): 87.

VON TSCHUDI, J. J.
1966   *Testimonio del Perú 1838–1842.* Lima: Universidad Nacional Mayor de San Marcos.

The Unplanned Ecology of a Planned Industrial City: The Case of Ciudad Guayana, Venezuela

MARÍA-PILAR GARCÍA and
RAE LESSER BLUMBERG

Since 1961, a planned industrial city has been rising in a remote resource frontier region of Venezuela, hundreds of miles from the nearest large city. While its planners' efforts have been, relatively, highly successful concerning industrial development, in another aspect their plans have gone awry: Ciudad Guayana is growing in precisely the opposite compass direction than planned, and the distribution of its people in physical and social space bears little relationship to the master plan.

We are not attempting an indictment here of what may well be the best example of integrated urban and industrial planning in the Third World, but rather we are trying to understand: why Ciudad Guayana is growing in the opposite compass direction to the one planned, and what are the underlying factors of generalized importance for urban planning anywhere in Latin America.

Basically, we shall argue that the planners did not appear to anticipate or affect the actual distribution of the city's lower income population – its majority – because their models failed adequately to consider salient sociological, legal, and ecological factors – or the implications of their own policies for the spatial distribution of the poor. Based almost exclusively on easily quantifiable physical, industrial, and economic variables, the planners' models did not address such less precise factors as:

1. STRUCTURAL FACTORS AND SOCIAL CLASS. Despite a thriving economic base, less than a third of the population has stable

The authors express their appreciation to William L. Leeds for his constructive and helpful criticisms.

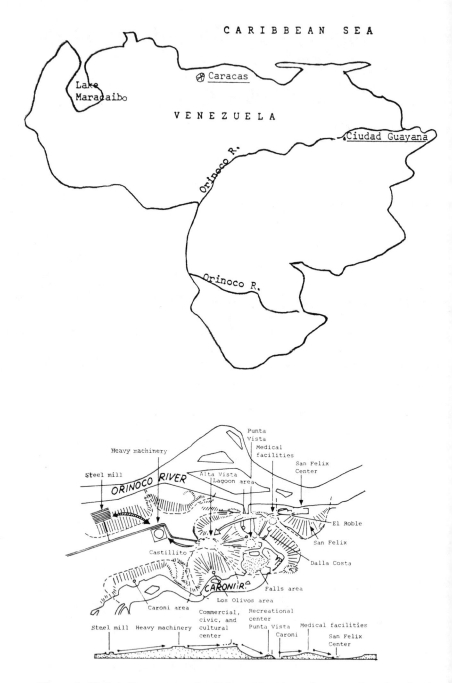

Figure 1. Ciudad Guayana (reprinted from *Planning urban growth and regional development* by Lloyd Rodwin et al., by permission of the M.I.T. Press, Cambridge, Massachusetts)

industrial employment.[1] Moreover, structural unemployment is relatively high: in slack times it may rise to 15 or 20 percent.[2] Not surprisingly, at least half of the population of Ciudad Guayana must be classed as lower income.[3]

2. LIFE-STYLE AND SOCIAL RELATIONS. As a consequence of structural instability and poverty, it would appear that the low-income people need housing without a fixed payment, stores that sell in small quantities and on credit, and access to the people who constitute their major source of economic opportunities – their fellow poor.

The first two factors involving a structurally marginal lower class are common to virtually any Third World city today – planned or unplanned. However, there are additional factors involved in the Ciudad Guayana situation which may be unique – just as there are sure to be in any other example. Nevertheless, these "unique" factors may contain generalizable elements, and are thus no less important to a broad understanding of the process of urban settlement. Here we shall discuss three.

3. LEGAL FACTORS. (a) First and most important is the *Ley del Trabajo* or Work Law for the unionized industrial workers which compensates them for the time and transportation cost of their journey to work if the site of their employment is more than 1.25 miles from a populated center. (The steel mill and other industries providing the main employment are located considerably farther away, we may add.)[4] This law clearly reduces the need for industrial workers to live

[1]   Approximately 26 percent of the total economically active population and 30 percent of the employed economically active population worked in manufacturing in 1970, according to the July *Encuesta de hogares* (Ministerio de Fomento 1970).
[2]   The July 1970 *Encuesta de hogares* shows that 13.9 percent of Ciudad Guayana's economically active population was unemployed. However, this figure oscillated during the previous twelve months between 13.9 and 15.9 percent.
[3]   We follow a frequent usage in Venezuela and consider Bolívares 1,000 ($235) as the upper limit to define lower-income. The study *Mercavi 70* (Banco Nacional 1970) found that 54.2 percent of the families of Ciudad Guayana have a monthly income of Bolívares 1,000 or less. However, we should mention that the low-income groups may be considerably larger because the average figure tends to hide the following facts: (a) that the average family in Ciudad Guayana consisted of 5.5 persons and (b) that the data are for employed persons only. Unemployment in Ciudad Guayana averages around 15 percent of the economically active population but has risen to 20 percent in slack times. By considering these factors, Caminos, Turner, and Steffian (1969) presume that perhaps more than 80 percent of the population of Ciudad Guayana could be considered as lower class.
[4]   The approximate distance from SIDOR-ALCASA (two of the main industries) to the farthest shacktowns on the eastern side is over eighteen miles. The average distance from SIDOR, the steel mill, to downtown San Félix, is approximately fourteen miles.

near their jobs. (b) A second law affecting settlement patterns is the *Ley de Bienhechurías* or Home Improvements Law. This law provides compensation to the owner of an expropriated property for any improvement he or she may have made. It means that if a person's shack is expropriated, one may come out with a large cash settlement. This makes expropriation more expensive and more rare than otherwise would be the case. Below, other legal factors will be discussed as well.

4. ECOLOGY. The climate is so favorable that the most casually constructed shack suffices in the year-round mild, warm weather. Thus, with a minimum of effort and expense, squatters may build a shelter on invaded land. Furthermore, since the terrain is flat and the shape of the city long and narrow, large numbers of these "jerry-built" shacks might be expected to be highly visible. (In contrast, the planners were quite cognizant of ecological factors such as prevalent winds, terrain, and impact of the rivers which are of greater importance for the economic base.)

5. PLANNERS' HOUSING POLICIES. Viewing the shacks (*ranchos*) as social cancers, and unsightly ones as well, Corporación Venezolana de Guayana (CVG), the public agency developing the city, virtually from the beginning *prohibited* their construction in the western half of the city where the *future* planned growth was targeted. In contrast, the small amounts of housing made available by the planners for the poor often proved unsuited to the life-style and housing needs of this structurally marginal group.[5]

The natural result of the above, we propose, has been to facilitate the city's growth to the east, in the direction opposite to its industrial base. In addition to a more detailed description and explanation of this result, we shall attempt also to identify a series of variables that we propose must be taken into account in future theories and policies of urban development wherever a large structurally marginal population may exist.

Correspondingly, this paper will be organized in three sections. The first part answers the questions "What and where is Ciudad Guayana and what are the planners trying to do?" The second part describes and attempts to explain the pattern of urban growth in opposition to the planners' models. The third summarizes the three main recent

[5] Other variables which may be of crucial importance in specific instances include: the local or national political situation, the nature of any local conflicts (e.g. ethnic, interinstitutional, etc.), the kind of planning model being used, and in general the kind of policies of the planning and government institutions and their willingness and ability to make them known to the people.

approaches toward urban development and housing for the poor in Latin America. Then, it focuses on the additional variables that, we propose, must be included if planning models are to influence successfully the pattern of settlement – and the chances of success – of a Third World urban population.

I. WHAT AND WHERE IS CIUDAD GUAYANA AND WHAT ARE THE PLANNERS TRYING TO DO?

A planned industrial city is being created out of the tropical forest and savanna of Venezuela's resource-rich Guayana region.[6] Ciudad Guayana is located at the confluence of the Orinoco and Caroní rivers. The Orinoco serves as the means of transportation of the industrial products to foreign markets, and the Caroní provides the hydroelectric potential necessary for the industrial plants. The city is 698 kilometers – about 420 miles – by road from Caracas, the capital city, and roughly 250 miles south of the metropolitan region of Barcelona-Puerto La Cruz, which is not only the largest urban complex in the eastern part of the country, but also the major port, trade, and service center for the entire area. The site was chosen to maximize the resource base for building an industrial city. The region of Guayana has extraordinary natural resources, such as rich, high-grade iron ore, hydroelectric potential, petroleum, natural gas, and a great variety of other mineral resources. With such abundance of resources and with good roads and the great Orinoco "highway" to the sea, Ciudad Guayana is admirably equipped to be a center for industry. As recently as 1950, the population of the future Ciudad Guayana was only 4,000. However, by the year 1961, when the planning of the city began, the population had reached 42,000 and by 1965 it had risen to 73,000. By 1970, its population was estimated as 142,000 and by 1972 it had risen to an estimated 175,000.[7]

On December 29, 1960, the administration of President Betancourt created a public corporation to develop the region of Guayana and to plan the physical, economic, and social development of the city of

[6]   This largely unexploited region includes all the national area of Venezuela south of the Orinoco River that extends over nearly half the country's land area. The region of Guayana lies within the tropics. The eighth parallel, together with the great Orinoco River, defines its northern boundary; in the south it reaches into the equatorial belt.
[7]   For the years 1950 and 1961 see Ministerio de Fomento (1950, 1965), *Noveno censo general de población, febrero 1961* and *Censo de 1950;* for the year 1965 see *Encuesta sobre características demográficas en Santo Tomé de Guayana, febrero 1965*, published by the Banco Central de Venezuela (1965) for the Corporación Venezolana de Guayana (CVG); and for 1970 and 1972 see the *Inventario de edificaciones* (CVG 1971) and the *CVG informe anual* (1970, 1971); the data for 1972 are from the *CVG informe anual* (1972).

Ciudad Guayana. When the Corporación Venezolana de Guayana (CVG), in collaboration with planners from the Joint Center for Urban Studies of the Massachusetts Institute of Technology and Harvard University, initiated the planning of the city, there was already a series of separate settlements along an eighteen-mile corridor with an approximate population of over 40,000 people. At the western end of the site chosen for the new city there was a steel mill, still under construction, and at the eastern end, an old provincial community called San Félix with about 75 percent of the total population. Between them were a mining company town called Puerto Ordaz with approximately 25 percent of the population, another mining settlement called Palúa, and various smaller developments. The Caroní River, running north-south, cut the area into eastern and western halves. A bridge was already under construction, but, as we shall show, the eastern and western halves have not been fully bridged socially.

One of the objectives of the 1961–1963 plan of urban development was to achieve a balanced physical growth and a unified city (see *CVG informe annual* 1963). Because the planned site for Ciudad Guayana consisted of a set of separate centers, the problem was to tie them all together; in particular, to connect the largest and easternmost existing settlement, San Félix, with the planned new city center to the west. Within this strategy, the goals for Ciudad Guayana, as outlined in the 1963 CVG report, included: (1) the concentration of heavy industries to the west, close to the steel mill, and their future expansion toward the residential areas in the east; (2) the development of residential areas close to the existing ones with their progressive expansion toward the west, or the steel mill. Due to the above-mentioned laws of work regarding transportation, the gradual reduction of the distance between the residential areas in the east and the industrial places of work in the west was considered of primary importance.

In figures, the aim of the CVG was to reverse the 1961 pattern of population distribution, with 25 percent of the people on the west side and 75 percent on the east, to one with 75 percent on the west by 1970.

IIA. URBAN GROWTH TRENDS IN OPPOSITION TO THE PLANNERS' MODELS

After twelve years of planning, as the CVG's annual reports indicate, the planners have not been successful in achieving the projected spatial residential distribution and the urban growth westwards. For example, by 1970, only 29 percent of the population was living in the western sector – versus 25 percent in 1961 – instead of the 75 percent projected in 1963 (see *CVG informe anual* 1963, 1970). The CVG report for 1970 stated its inability to achieve the desired goals of population distribution and projected a revised and less ambitious set of goals for the west.[8] At the same time the CVG's policies did not include opening the west to the kinds of planned squatter developments which could have had a significant impact in turning the tide.

When one analyzes the discrepancies between the goals and what is actually happening it appears that the main problem is that the residents, especially lower-income people and recently arrived migrants, have been constructing their own squatter shacks in the east. They are doing so, at least in part, because of bureaucratic delays and the strict allocation of housing lots or facilities in the "self-help" as well as the more conventional planned housing programs.[9] (Other reasons for this will be discussed below.) This is hardly surprising when we look at CVG policies with respect to lower-income housing. As noted, the problem is that San Félix is spatially farther than Puerto Ordaz from the industrial places of work, and from the planned commercial and business centers of the new (Alta Vista) sector of Ciudad Guayana. These centers remain undeveloped and therefore empty (except for the CVG building and a drive-in movie) while unplanned, small, credit businesses flourish close to the lower-income settlements in and around San Félix.[10]

[8]   On the one hand, Anthony Downs (1969: 212) stated in 1964 the new goals of getting 60 percent of the population to the west side by 1970. On the other hand, the 1970 *CVG informe anual* stated both an optimistic and a pessimistic alternative. Under the pessimistic alternative, only by 1995, when the population approaches 500,000 inhabitants, will the west sector begin to have a larger population than the east. Under the optimistic alternative, by the time the population approaches 500,000, the west sector will have two-thirds of the total. To achieve the optimistic alternative, the policies outlined in the 1970 *CVG informe anual* were: (a) to limit the growth of the east side by postponing investment in services and infrastructure (bridges, highways); (b) to prohibit the invasion of land and the building of shacks in the east; and (c) to build lower-income housing units in the west.

[9]   Quoting Rafael Corrada: "The program of settlement communities for squatters became entangled in bureaucratic procedures. Families were carefully screened to make sure that the poorest or most 'deserving' ones got the available lot first and that no speculation could develop. As a result, it took nearly a year to allocate 434 lots in one settlement community. Even more disappointing was the effective screening of 'antisocial' families by social workers interested in developing 'uncorrupted communities'" (1969: 246).

"Administrative procedures slowed down the settlement program to about half of the rate of incoming squatters. During 1962–1965, squatters built shacks at a rate of about 85 a month. Only 37 of these were built in settlement communities. In the same period the total number of ranchos increased by approximately 2,500. Thus the program allowed around 1,500 ranchos to be located at random outside the settlement communities" (1969: 247).

[10]   The middle class has its shopping center in Puerto Ordaz, also relatively little used by the people of the shacktowns.

IIB. FACTORS THAT EXPLAIN THE DISCREPANCIES BETWEEN THE URBAN GROWTH TRENDS AND THE PLANNERS' MODELS

1. *Structural Factors and Social Class*

At the beginning, the planners of Ciudad Guayana recognized the need for information about the projected rate of population growth, the type of migrants to the city, and the income levels of the population.[11] Even though some of these data were ultimately collected, they seem seldom to have been used by those who should have been doing what we may call the social planning. Instead, the planning concentrated – successfully we may add – on the industrial base and on the provision of services and physical amenities for the middle and upper classes to bring them and keep them in remote Ciudad Guayana. Meanwhile, a great number of people with very low incomes were arriving,[12] and, while the planners were planning their economic models and the location of civic centers and shopping complexes, these people were building their houses.

The planners' concern to eliminate the *ranchos* built by the people, strongly supported by the middle- and upper-class residents of Ciudad Guayana, led the CVG to *prohibit the construction of these ranchos in the western part of the city*. The obvious result was that the city continued to grow towards the east. Given the fact that most of the people of Ciudad Guayana were poor and in general able to live only where they could build their shacks, the result could not have been otherwise; yet the planners did not seem aware of this. Even such a relatively realistic planner as Downs, in 1964, made the unrealistic projection that by 1970, 60 percent of the people would be located on the west side. However, no corresponding plans to permit large-scale shacktown developments or other alternatives on the west were made. More understandably absent from the developers' plans were the unsightly bars and petty-commerce kiosks that form a ubiquitous part of the lower-class life and sources of employment. Nevertheless, the

---

[11]   Among the most relevant studies are: (a) the *Migration survey* (1965) carried out by the CVG and the Banco Central de Venezuela; (b) the *Survey of family living conditions in Santo Tomé de Guayana* carried out by the Banco Central de Venezuela (1962) and the study about *Family income in Santo Tomé de Guayana* also carried out by the Banco Central de Venezuela (1965); (c) *Preliminary studies for the building of low-income housing in Ciudad Guayana* (Banco Obrero n.d.); (d) the Venezuelan censuses of 1950 and 1961 (Ministerio de Fomento 1950, 1965); (e) any of the household surveys (*Encuesta de hogares*) published three times a year (Ministerio de Fomento); (f) studies made by the MIT-Harvard team: Peattie (1968), Porter (1969), Appleyard (1969), Corrada (1966, 1969), and other studies included in Rodwin (1969).

[12]   As we have already mentioned at least 54.2 percent of the incoming population to Ciudad Guayana could be classified as lower-income.

economic and social importance of these bars and petty businesses
has been shown by Morse (1965), Lewis (1960, 1966a, 1966b, 1968),
Mangin (1967), Peattie (1968), and Talton (1969), writing about the
shacktowns of Puerto Rico, Mexico, Peru, and Venezuela.

Another important factor influencing the spatial distribution of
lower-income population is the marginal nature of much of their
employment. In Ciudad Guayana, Peattie (1968) has shown that in the
barrio she studied, La Laja, only one out of six was steadily employed;
the others lived off the sixth. Marginality strikes both sexes. Lower-
income females, largely unskilled, have little choice but casual and
service employment. Typical jobs include laundress, servant, and the
like; and some work as part- or full-time prostitutes. Moreover, over
a fifth of the households are female-headed and cannot count on a male
potential wage-earner in the house.[13] Also, many males have low
potential as wage-earners. Although some males work in industries,[14]
many are unemployed (see Note 2) or work in the service jobs, petty
commerce, or in construction. This last occupation, construction
worker, also has been found to be very important among the lower
classes of Peru, Puerto Rico, Brazil, and Venezuela, as reported by
Turner (1966b, 1967, 1968a), Mangin (1967), Peattie (1968), and Talton
(1969). Since these kinds of jobs, constituting the real economic
prospects of the low-income men and women, are mainly located on
the east side of Ciudad Guayana, it is little wonder that the projections
of even the relatively more realistic planners, such as Downs, were
not met.

2a. *Life-style*

Because the planners apparently did not understand the life-style and
housing needs of the lower classes, imposed by their structural
economic marginality, they constructed a relatively limited number of
housing units, most of them too expensive for such a population.
These units required a down payment plus fixed installments.[15] How-

---

[13]   The studies by Safa (1964) in Puerto Rico; Peattie (1968) in Ciudad Guayana; García
(1971) in Caracas; *Mercavi* study (Banco Nacional 1970) in different cities of Venezuela
have shown that approximately 25 percent of the lower-income households have a
female as the head of the family.

[14]   Approximately 31 percent of economically active males worked in manufacturing,
as against 48 percent in commercial, construction, and service activities, according to
the July 1970 *Encuesta de hogares*. Furthermore, only 14.5 percent of the economically
active women work in manufacturing, as against 62 percent in services and 17 percent
in commerce.

[15]   According to Rafael Corrada (1969: 241) the down payment required for this income
group (less than Bolívares 1,000) was usually 0–10 percent, with an amortization period
of 15–20 years and with an interest rate of 4–6 percent.

ever, had the planners asked for the advice of social scientists at this period (early and mid-1960's), they probably would have followed the same policies. At that time, as we shall see below, the prevailing social science orthodoxy viewed shacktowns as a kind of cancer on the body of the city. Instead of being worked with, they were to be eradicated.[16] In Brasilia, for example, they are completely banned from most of the developed areas, and, as a result, they sprang up so far from town that Brasilia has been experiencing a very strange growth pattern.

In addition to considering the shacks as a form of social pathology, the social science wisdom in those days believed that those fixed monthly installments – the obligation of paying for a home – would stabilize people by providing them with a sense of responsibility. Moreover, the benefits of home ownership were alleged to include holding families together and solving most of the problems of social disorganization. Structural underemployment, and their consequences for life-style and housing needs, were just not considered. Similarly the planners, taking this approach with respect to Ciudad Guayana (Davis and McGinn 1969a, 1969b; MacDonald 1969, among others) did not mention that much of the population of the city did not have steady or regular incomes. Thus, rather than forcing responsibility on them, fixed monthly payments for a home would have forced an impossibility on them because their own incomes were sporadic and their employment opportunities marginal. Furthermore, even though industrial jobs were being created faster in Ciudad Guayana than perhaps in any other comparable planned city, there were not enough to take care of the economic needs of the in-migrants who came. And it must be remembered that they did not come as fast as the planners had originally expected.[17]

The low-income people had to devise their own solutions, but these solutions generally were not viewed as such by the planners. Instead, they were seen as a problem. As we have noted, the plans for Ciudad Guayana called for expansion to the west, but the city was growing to the east – and the planners did not seem to see any relationship between their plans and its logical results, namely, that given the prohibition of *ranchos* in the west, the people continued to build them in the east.

Nevertheless, despite the ban, there was one note of greater realism in Ciudad Guayana that did not exist in many of these other planned cities, particularly Brasilia. The planners faced the fact that squatting

[16]   Some of the proponents of this approach include Coronado (1955), Berckholtz (1963), Patch (1961), Sanabria (1966), Silveira (1963), Schulman (1966), Lleras-Restrepo (1955), and Ospina-Pérez (1948).
[17]   Corrada (1969: 245) notes that in 1965 it became clear that the total population was about 20,000 less than expected.

was inevitable. Therefore, they permitted, and in fact, even encouraged, self-help construction projects, i.e. "planned slums" and
reception areas for newly arrived migrants.[18] This did not come at the
beginning, but a bit later, when the planners realized that the people
not only were building their own shacks, but that they were building
them on land that the planners would have liked to reserve for other
uses. Realizing that it was impossible to build sufficient low-cost
housing fast enough, and wanting to reserve for other purposes the
area where people were squatting, the developers moved to create
model programs for self-help housing in the form of "planned slums"
and of reception areas in the east. Unfortunately, these programs,
according to Corrada (1969: 246) soon bogged down in bureaucracy:
people were rigidly selected and they had to wait for months (see Note
11). Indeed, the planners wanted to wait still longer, until more
socioeconomic and demographic studies could be completed. Meanwhile, the people continued to build.

By the time planners started the self-help housing programs, new
studies started to appear in the literature on housing in Latin America.
These were critical of the view that shacktowns were a cancer to be
eradicated. We shall discuss this further below, but let us mention two
of these "revisionist" authors: Mangin (1963, 1967) and Turner (1963,
1966b, 1967). First of all, they are noteworthy in that they actually
provided data to supersede the myths about the *barrios*. They actually
went into the lower-class areas, lived among the people, observed
them, and found out what their needs were with respect to housing
– rather than attempting to impose a moralistic solution. What they
found out was that people coming to the city for economic opportunities really did not care about off-street play areas for their children
and other such physical amenities. Instead, they learned, many of the
amenities provided in these so-called low-cost housing programs
priced the poor out of the market or caused disasters when – with
depressing frequency – they lost their jobs. Abrams (1964), Peattie
(1968; 1969b), Talton (1969), Wagner et al. (1966), and Caminos,
Turner, and Steffian (1969) make a similar point with respect to
Venezuela, Brazil, Colombia, and Peru.

Turner, writing about the situation in Lima, Peru, posits that housing
needs differ greatly by socioeconomic levels or stages. At the first level
he suggests, when they are newly arrived in the city, what the poor

[18] The CVG considered squatting unavoidable and therefore formulated a settlement
strategy according to which the key to controlling slums in Ciudad Guayana lies in the
ability to control lot sizes and the arrangement pattern for the placement of shacks.
There were designated settlement areas inside the city (in the east) where families could
squat with security of land tenure: the "reception areas" and the "planned " slums.
The self-help construction projects involve assisting lower-income people in building
their own permanent houses as their time and income permit.

need most is easy access to the kind of jobs that they can get –
basically service jobs. Turner, who was peripherally involved in the
planning of Ciudad Guayana (he is also from MIT), saw that at the
first level, the immediate needs of the lowest-income people lay not
in having pretty housing but in having their basic needs provided.
Generally speaking, with their low levels of skills and inadequate
income, such people have to live where they can walk to their work
place. To judge from the experience of Ciudad Guayana, economic
opportunity for most of the people was initially less likely to be in
industry than in marginal service tasks. Therefore, lower-class people
have to be near that part of the population from whom they can gain
income for performing services.

Turner next posits a second level or stage: once people begin to
climb out of the minimum subsistence level and are already earning
money, they can afford to travel to work on public transportation. At
this second stage, what people need most, then, is security in their
housing tenure – particularly freedom from the burden of paying rent.
(Flinn [1968] and Peattie [1968, 1969b] make similar remarks for
Colombia and Venezuela.) At this stage, their employment situation
remains highly unstable. Therefore, if they have to stop paying for
a house when unemployment strikes, they will be forced back to level
one.

2b. *Social Relations*

Another sociological variable that relates to the prevalent distribution
of the low-income people in the east is their pattern of social relations.
It has been found by Bryce-Laporte (1970) and Safa (1964) in Puerto
Rico, and Peattie (1968) and Talton (1969) in Venezuela, that unemployed men tend to spend a great deal of their time socializing in the
neighborhood bars because it is highly functional for them. Studies
on how lower-class people gain employment emphasize the importance of this informal context. As we have noted, for most lower-class
people, the most likely source of income is from providing services
and being involved in petty commercial activities, rather than from
suddenly landing a high-paid industrial job. Thus, the informal setting
provides the equivalent of country club business deals for the middle
and upper middle classes. Also, socializing in bars or in the *barrio* is
a kind of "social investment" that may materialize in economic help
when the person is out of a job for long periods of time. The poor male
worker will need the help of friends, *compadres*, and neighbors, when
unemployed, and those who usually will help him are people of the
same *barrio*. This is one more reason why lower-income people in
Ciudad Guayana tend to live in the east.

Numerous studies in Latin America – Morse (1965), Browning and Feindt (1971), Flinn (1968), Matos Mar (1961), Germani (1961) and Peattie (1968) – have shown the influence of kin on migration. And in Ciudad Guayana, the incoming migrant would be most likely to have a relative or *compadre* already living in the east who could help in finding a place to live and a job. If such a migrant were to go to a CVG planned reception area or lower-income housing development, he or she might be isolated both physically and socially from possible sources of help. This is because, as Stinchcombe (1969), Porter (1969), Corrada (1969), and Peattie (1969c) have emphasized, the unplanned shacktowns are much less segregated by socioeconomic status than the planned housing of the CVG. Similarly, other studies in Latin America – Mangin (1967) in Peru, Lewis (1966a) and Safa (1964) in Puerto Rico, and Flinn (1968) in Colombia – have encountered the same problem of social class segregation in the public housing programs.

Up until now we have discussed the factors stemming from economic marginality, the common fate of vast proportions of the population of any Third World city. Our discussion, we believe, is thus applicable to virtually any Latin American planning effort. In addition, however, each urban development is bound to be affected by certain specific variables. In the case of Ciudad Guayana, we shall consider three sets of factors unique to the situation: several Venezuelan laws, the local climate, and the CVG planners' specific housing programs. In other situations, legal, ecological, and political factors may prove equally important, although in different detail. Conversely, they may not, and factors absent in Ciudad Guayana, such as racial stratification, may loom as crucial. The important point here is that no urban planning effort will reach maximum success if no search is made for the unexpected and unique factors that may enter into the equation.

3. *Legal Factors*

Some peculiar developments related to the legal system in Venezuela ought to be mentioned because we think these laws have had strong influence in the spatial distribution of the shacktowns in Ciudad Guayana. We refer to three laws: (3a) the *Ley del Trabajo* [Law of Work]; (3b) the *Ley de Bienhechurías* [Law of Home Improvements]; and (3c) the *Ley de Despidos, Retiros y Aguinaldos* [Law of Job Dismissals and Bonuses].

a. LEY DEL TRABAJO. As we mentioned above, in Ciudad Guayana there is a work-law that states that companies have to pay for the trip if the distance to work is over 1.25 miles from a center of population.

Also unionized workers receive halftime pay in Ciudad Guayana for the distance travelled over 1.25 miles. This law means that it is more convenient for the low-income people to be located in the east, close to their relatives and friends, than to be located in the west, close to the main industries. We must remember that workers are related by bonds of kinship and/or friendship to the population which is economically dependent on them and which is living on service activities supported by them. Moreover, as the industrial workers have their travel time compensated, and their relatives have to live near the other poor people in order to make a living, it makes great sense for the poor majority to live where the poor people are. Thus, this law contributes to the fact that the shacktowns of Ciudad Guayana tend to be located farther from industrial jobs than might be the case in other cities, such as Lima, the site of Turner's study.

b. LEY DE BIENHECHURÍAS. This Venezuelan Law of Home Improvements means that if expropriated, people who have built shacks must be paid for the improvements put into them. Often, it makes the cost of expropriation too high, leading to a de facto solution of letting the people themselves improve their housing, as the CVG can no longer pay to expropriate the housing of the poor.[19] Also it means that it is a good investment for the low-income people to improve their shacks, because if they are expropriated they will make a profit. The statistics cited by Corrada (1969: 239) show how the squatters' investments in home improvements have skyrocketed the cost of expropriating any but the newest, roughest shacks.

c. LEY DE DESPIDOS, RETIROS Y AGUINALDOS. One other law that should be mentioned dictates that in Venezuela when a longtime worker is discharged he or she is required to receive from fifteen days' to a month's salary for every year worked. If the person works for a big company and has several years of employment, this is a considerable amount of capital. The studies of Peattie (1968) and Talton (1969) show that this capital often is translated into small enterprises. When people receive the money for expropriation from previous shacks, or receive severance pay or some other lump-sum payment (such as the special Christmas bonus, the *aguinaldo*) which Venezuelan law has provided in good number, they are often able to capitalize on this. This is done by opening a small service business,

---

[19]   Corrada states: "Ranchos have been expropriated in Ciudad Guayana at an average cost of $310 in two-year-old sites and $890 in ten-year-old areas. These figures indicate an average appreciation rate of $75 per year, mainly as a result of the squatters' improvements. These expropriation costs are much higher than the $47 for a lot and $324 for a lot with minimum public services (water taps, paved street, and electricity), which were the development costs in the settlement communities" (1969: 239).

or perhaps building a house that they can rent, or maybe adding a room to their present house and getting some income from it by converting it into a small commercial venture, such as a tiny food store or bar.

The three laws described above are certainly, if not unique to Venezuela, very unusual. Nothing comparable is mentioned in the works of Mangin and Turner because the countries where they did their studies are much poorer than Venezuela, with its petroleum-based economy. Indeed, it is unlikely that these governments could have enforced any law compensating workers for travel time to work. Therefore, Venezuela's peculiar position of being one of the richest of the developing Latin American countries may have created legal factors that contributed to the growth of the city of Ciudad Guayana to the east.

4. Ecology

An ecological factor, the year-round mild, warm climate of Ciudad Guayana, also contributes to the fact that despite possible home improvements, the housing of many of the poor remains basically crude shacks. In such a warm climate, almost any material can be used by the poor to build their house: cardboard, zinc, aluminum sheets, etc. Therefore, in Ciudad Guayana the lower-income people would be less concerned with the type of structure and the materials needed to build the house than in other, colder cities. They presumably would be prepared to live in unfinished houses and low-standard shacks if by doing this they could achieve the second-level goals suggested by Turner: residential stability, home ownership, and the economic security of not having to pay a monthly rent or mortgage – and, we might add, of not worrying about paying for the land because it was acquired by invasion.

5. Urban and Housing Policies of the CVG

In contrast to its urban development policies which followed what Peattie (1969c: 461) has termed the "centralized incremental" model of relatively rigid top-down planning, CVG's housing programs for the lower class have been characterized by somewhat greater – albeit still insufficient – proclivities to adapt solutions to the actions of those below. This greater responsiveness to the action of those below she has termed the "evolutionary incremental" model. However, even in housing, the model most frequently used in Ciudad Guayana was the top-down "centralized incremental" one. In this model the values most likely to be implemented are those of the planners and high government officials. These, as we have shown, are very different from the lower class values. The prohibition of shacks in the western part of the city was perhaps largely due to the fact that the middle and upper classes, the planners, and the government officials tend to dislike them. This is undoubtedly one of the principal reasons that lower-class people had to devise their own "evolutionary incremental" model to implement their values and needs in their unplanned housing developments, services, and commercial activities.

A further and more general obstacle to the official policies was that they were not known by the population to whom they were addressed. Appleyard's study of Ciudad Guayana (1969) revealed that half of the people in the sample did not know what the CVG was; and of those who did hear about it half of them did not know what the CVG's proper functions were. Therefore, since the population did not know, much less understand, what was happening in Cuidad Guayana and what the future plans for the city were, they could not possibly act according to the CVG's policy and plans. In fact, they have been acting against those plans as we noted.

It is a truism in the philosophy of science that the variables included in one's research are dictated by one's underlying theory or approach. Therefore, below we shall discuss three social science orientations toward the social reality of the shacktowns, because each one leads to different policy implications with respect to housing. In the case of the first two – those used explicitly or implicitly by the planners of Ciudad Guayana – we argue that important structural variables (e.g. degree of employment, instability) were precluded from consideration by the conceptual bias of the approach. We conclude this section with a preliminary delineation of the factors that we propose must be included.

IIIA.   THREE APPROACHES TOWARD URBAN DEVELOPMENT AND HOUSING

1. *Prevailing Orthodoxy: The Social Cancer Approach*

The first and most popular view about shacktowns in Latin America, from World War II through the mid-1960's, considered them as a "social cancer" in the body of the city that is caused by the "vices" and "pathologies" of lower-income people. Laziness, family disorganization, "voluntary" unemployment, lack of formal education, irresponsibility, and delinquency have been mentioned among the causes for the existence and persistence of the shacktowns (see

Note 16 for the proponents of this approach). This "cancer," say proponents of this view, must be cured by eradication of the shacktown either by sending the people back to the farms – from which they are often incorrectly assumed to have just come – or by moving them into housing projects and planned satellite cities.

At the beginning of the planning of Ciudad Guayana, large and influential sectors of government officials, planners, and middle and upper classes, and even social scientists in both North and South America shared this approach. The prevalent orthodoxy held that transforming the housing of the poor would transform the people from shiftless squatters to solid citizens. [20, 21] Paying a fixed monthly amount for a house, planners believed, would bring social mobility and civic responsibility to the lower class. We think, however, that the planned housing developments of Ciudad Guayana represented mobility only for those who had already begun to rise. These are predominantly the people who either had special skills or had arrived earlier and gotten a toehold in the industrial sector before job and educational qualifications for such employment rose steeply. In contrast, the planned "low-income" housing – characterized by the virtual absence of little credit groceries and bars and the difficulty of access to the marginal service employment opportunities – was clearly unsuited to the needs of the nonindustrially employed and unemployed poor who are more numerous than those in the stable industrial jobs.

2. The Culture of Poverty Approach

In the 1960's a revisionist movement appeared that stressed the positive aspects of the shacktowns, implicitly or explicitly using the concept of the "culture of poverty"[22] (Lewis, 1960, 1966a, 1966b, 1968). In Latin America, a somewhat parallel conceptual orientation emerged, using a concept of "marginality" in which marginality was a characteristic of the poor as individuals, not of their relation to the economic structure (Mattelart and Garretón 1965; Vekemans and

[20] MacDonald believes that: "The persistence of high unemployment among the settled population may be reduced by shifting more of the shanty dwellers into modest housing developments. Presumably voluntary unemployment will decrease as family stability and responsibilities increase. This stability could be promoted by better housing and the longterm responsibilities of paying it off" (1969: 121).

[21] Laun (1973) cites a quote of former Colombian president Lleras-Restrepo (1955) as typical: "What the transformation of housing and of social habits, [as a result], represent [is] an educative and civilizing work [as well as] an effective increase in labor's productivity."

[22] Oscar Lewis (1966b) formulated the concept of "the culture of poverty" as "a label for a specific conceptual model that describes in positive terms a sub-culture of Western society with its own structure and rationale, a way of life handed on from generation to generation along family lines."

Venegas 1966a, 1966b). However, even though this approach stresses the ingenuity of the poor under unfavorable structural conditions, it also seems to imply that the culture of poverty – and the shacktowns – may be permanent and self-perpetuating due to personality and value orientation factors of the people involved.[23]

There is a "laissez-faire" or "self-help equilibrium" approach epitomized by Turner, which may be considered an intermediate case between the second and third (structural) approaches. Turner notes that shacktown dwellers are most in need of rent-free housing close to their sources of employment and that they gradually expand and improve their dwelling as their finances and employment status permit. A viable solution, then, would be not to move the lower-income people to public housing, which required a fixed monthly payment they cannot always meet and which may be located too far from their sources of employment. Instead, Turner argues, one must encourage this natural process of shacktown evolution and let the inhabitants work out their own solutions to their housing problems.

It may be argued that the planners of Ciudad Guayana implicitly followed this approach in the development of reception areas, "planned slums," and self-help housing programs for the people who could not afford to pay for a house. As we have indicated, their success seems quite limited, as great numbers of low-income people built their houses outside of these planned developments. We have already mentioned the strict selection of people who were to live in them and the bureaucratic delays that further constrained the programs. Perhaps a more important reason for this limited success was that planners did not take into account many of the needs of the lowest-income people stemming from their precarious structural position in the economy. Thus, lots, houses, and credit were still more expensive, and the developments more rigidly segregated by social class, than in the unplanned shacktowns favored by the poor. Therefore, these programs of the CVG failed in part to accomplish all their targeted goals because they failed to "bend" far enough to accommodate the structural situation of the lowest-income groups.

3. Structural Approach

The third approach to the shacktowns of Latin America differs from the first two in stressing that the shacktowns owe their existence to external and socioeconomic structural factors. This approach also

[23]   Although the concept of the "culture of poverty" is much more sophisticated than the one of social disorganization or "cancer," Lewis has been severely criticized over the last years for stressing *internal personality and value orientations* which allegedly make the culture of poverty self-perpetuating. According to his critics, Lewis blames the victims while underemphasizing external economic factors.

emerged in the 1960's. All those associated with his view (most importantly, Quijano 1966, 1968, 1971; Cardoso and Faletto 1969; Lessa 1970 and Travieso 1971 in Latin America; and Mangin 1970 in the United States) would agree that: (1) the nature, size, and rate of growth of the economic base of a given Latin American city or country are inadequate to provide the labor force; and (2) as stressed by Turner and the advocates of the second approach, the shacktowns represent an ingenious, adaptive solution to surviving on the unstable economic margins of society.

This third approach seems to be best typified by Mangin, who says that self-help efforts of the shacktown residents within the confines of their shacktown are not enough, since their problems stem from the disequilibria of an economic structure that fails to provide them sufficient economic opportunity. This approach thus denies Turner's notion that the individual, by his or her own labor, can manufacture the resources needed to participate fully in all the advantages society has to offer. Mangin (1970) says that it is not, in most cases, "the fault" of the lower-class people that they do not often attain economic and social progress. Rather, it is the existing socioeconomic structure that denies them opportunities for improvement in such areas as education, employment, and housing.

In our opinion, of the three approaches to the shacktowns, the structural one offers the best explanation of their existence, nature, and continual expansion. In addition, we propose that it helps to explain the pattern of location and growth of the shacktowns of Latin America in general, and of Ciudad Guayana in particular. It does not appear that this approach was ever emphasized by the planners of Ciudad Guayana. However, had they considered the structural variables, they might have predicted, and therefore successfully intervened in, the distribution of shacktowns in the city because it is primarily structural constraints that create and perpetuate them.

IIIB. PRELIMINARY DELINEATION OF STRUCTURAL FACTORS IMPORTANT FOR INTEGRATING LOW-INCOME POPULATION INTO URBAN AND HOUSING DEVELOPMENT PROGRAMS

1. The first structural factor that must be taken into account is: *what* percentage of the urban population may be expected to be *economically marginal*, and *why*.

The "why" is easier to answer: no Latin American urban economy has managed to create stable jobs as fast as the increase in available labor force. In Venezuela, in recent years for example, the creation of jobs of any description has run about 1 percent a year behind the increase in the aspiring labor force.[24]

The question of what percentage of the population may be expected to be economically marginal is more complicated. As we have seen, many service-sector jobs are forms of symbiosis (at best) which permit the otherwise unemployable to live off the earnings of their more fortunate, stably employed counterparts. In fact, a good deal of the petty service-sector activities in Ciudad Guayana – as in Third World cities in general – must be considered as much a form of *involution* as the "agricultural involution" discussed by Geertz (1966) in Java – where, under population pressure, agriculture intensified to the point where people were virtually harvesting single grains of paddy rice with razor blades. Similarly, the subsistence activities of the service sector have involuted to an analogous degree and for roughly the same reasons of population pressure on an insufficiently dynamic and absorptive economy.

The case of Ciudad Guayana shows that such an economy may be very dynamic in some sectors and in total growth figures, while still insufficiently absorptive for the types of people who come. Indeed, Peattie (1969a: 406) cites this as a problem common to Venezuelan growth in general: it is taking place on a capital-intensive, high-technology base, requiring few and relatively highly skilled workers; whereas Venezuelan workers are many and relatively unskilled. The result of this structural disequilibrium is the high rate of unemployment, underemployment, and what we may term "involuted" employment.

2. The next element to be considered in the marginality equation is the *types of people* – as compared to the *types and quantities of jobs*.

With respect to the types of people, we must first consider their *demographic profile*: What percent are in the economically productive years, versus dependents? What is the sex ratio? We learn that in Ciudad Guayana the demographic profile is surprisingly normal for such a young pioneer city;[25] there are many more women with children here than one might expect on the frontier. The children mean a higher dependency ratio – we note that the rate of Ciudad Guayana population growth is so explosive that more than half the population has yet to celebrate its fifteenth birthday (see MacDonald 1969: 110–111). The mothers of these children as we shall point out, face marginality from two sources: familial and economic.

[24]   Victor Childers, in his "Human resource development in Venezuela" (n.d.), uses primarily CORDIPLAN statistics to arrive at the gap between labor force and new jobs.
[25]   See Banco Central de Venezuela (1966: Table 12, page 16). Also reprinted in MacDonald (1969: 110–111).

3. On the one hand, marginality springs from a *prevalent family structure* where unions are impermanent alliances easily broken by the economic instability of the male partner. Studies show that approximately 25 percent of the low-income households have a female as the head of the family. Such findings have been noted by Safa (1964) in Puerto Rico; Peattie (1968) in Ciudad Guayana; García (1971) in Caracas; *Mercavi* study (Banco Nacional 1970) in various cities of Venezuela. On the other hand, the Ciudad Guayana industrial *economic base* has virtually no secure niches for the unskilled females with little education.

4. *The level of education*, then, is perhaps the next salient characteristic of the population. In Venezuela, education was not widely available in rural areas when the present adult population of Ciudad Guayana (mostly migrants from eastern Venezuela) was growing up. Thus for both sexes, the average level is much less than completed primary school. In fact, Davis and McGinn (1969b: 277) note that 80 percent of the population in their Ciudad Guayana study were rural or small-town educated, and that, barring the imported professionals, the average level was under three years of primary school.

Ironically, as Ciudad Guayana has evolved, the larger companies (e.g. the steel and aluminum mills) generally have raised the minimum educational requirements for most stable jobs to a primary school graduation certificate. This illustrates neatly the convenience of "*credendialitis*" as a sorting device for employment in a market of surplus labor. But "blame the victim" theories are hard to sustain here: one cannot be accused of being a lazy, shiftless dropout if there was no primary school offering education beyond the third grade anywhere within miles when one was growing up. In general, the willingness of companies to offer on-the-job training to applicants without "appropriate" credentials varies directly with labor scarcity. And in Ciudad Guayana, this ends the discussion of level of education.

Type of education is another problem. Even when outside agencies give training courses to the unskilled, they might not inculcate a level of skills high enough, or run a placement service active enough, to make their graduates much more attractive to the increasingly selective modern-sector employers. Davis and McGinn (1969b) mention these problems with respect to training programs for construction workers that apparently did not lead to the expected better jobs.

5. And what are the expected better jobs? *Stability* is the next (and perhaps most crucial) factor. If a worker is hired for a good job after months of unemployment only to be laid off after a few months, scarcely a ripple has been made in his or her level of marginality. The

factors associated with stability of employment tend to be tied to both the economic structure and the Venezuelan work law and are complex. For example, in some industries with high technology (e.g. modern textile manufacturing), workers can be trained for their jobs in a negligible amount of time. Venezuelan work laws start giving most employees expensive fringe benefits such as vacation, severance pay, and bonus rights after four to eight months on the job. Accordingly, it is little wonder that one source estimates the average duration of employment for unskilled workers in such industries to be just below the "magic number" (see CEVEPOF-CISOR 1973: 48).

In Ciudad Guayana, the industrial jobs by contrast tend to be stable, highly paid, unionized, and to require a relatively high level of skills. The problems, of course, is landing such a job in the first place. But once employed, the worker is protected by the investment the companies would have to make to train a replacement and the power of the unions. Thus two distinct strata of job stability exist in glaring contrast: an unusually stable industrial sector and a residue of frequently unstable service, commercial, and construction jobs for which the remaining two-thirds of the economically active population competes.

6. In short, *economic indexes for planners* should include the average duration of the job, and the average number of hours of employment it provides on a year-round basis, cross-tabulated by type of industry or economic activity. Even if the planners may not be able radically to change the economic structure, they should be able to formulate more realistic and ameliorative policies if they know to what extent a city's economic base is lopsided with unstable industrial jobs and marginal commercial enterprises.

7. Less obvious but also important information for planners concerns the *work and housing laws*. We have shown how three of these laws affected population distribution in Ciudad Guayana. In addition, we have suggested that the content of a government's work laws may affect the policies of employers concerning duration (and other conditions) of employment.

8. Also stemming from the argument presented in this paper is the suggestion that planners examine the *social implications* of local *ecology*. Thus a warm, benign climate can reduce the need for elaborately constructed shelter. Similarly, a toll bridge or ferry connecting two halves of a river-bisected city can increase the access of the poor to economic opportunities located on the other side. The planner must remain sensitive to possible unanticipated social consequences of ecology.

9. *Labor force entry factors.* What causes the contrast between those who have already found a toehold in the island of stable industrial employment and those still struggling in the vast surrounding sea of marginality? The cause, in Ciudad Guayana, apparently does not lie in superior moral qualities, attitudes toward modernization, or labor force commitment. Instead, Peattie (1969a: 406) indicates (and we agree) that it seems a function of either (a) having arrived or (b) having arrived with a higher level of skills than one's fellow migrants – or both. Moreover, she sees forces at work tending further to separate those with a toehold on stability from the still-marginal: (1) the capital-intensive technology of Ciudad Guayana requiring a relatively small number of workers with relatively high level of skills and (2) the growing need for formal education as part of the entry requirements for many industrial jobs, which correlates with the ending of the first pioneering phase of establishing a labor force and economic base simultaneously.

10. Peattie's notion of a growing gap between those beginning to make it and their still-struggling counterparts leads us to two more factors having ramifications for housing policy: (a) *migration* and (b) *mobility*.

Both the rates and nature of migration and mobility should be studied to determine probable population size and composition, and quality and size of housing needed by the residents. A main advantage of the shack is its easy *expandability*. Under the impetus of added family members, including in-migrating adult kin, or good fortune, people may strive for expanded quarters. A housing policy that freezes people into units that are difficult either to upgrade or expand may be shutting the door on the evolutionary potential of low-income housing as manifested in the shacktowns.

11. Furthermore, aside from instability of income, an obvious problem exists with *level of income* for the economically marginal. The combination of these factors is devastating with respect to any housing program based on middle-class notions of convenient monthly payments.

With respect to income level, we note that the percent of wages needed for food is inversely related to wealth. Thus, even a hypothetical "model" subsidized housing program, aimed at charging only 10 percent of monthly income of the very poor, and provided a moratorium during periods of unemployment, may cause real hardship. Consumer studies of United States working and middle classes may find that 20 percent of net (or 25 percent of gross) income is "reasonable" for rent. But for people facing the option of living rent-free in a squatter's shack or cutting their food budget and living in a tiny planned housing unit, the former seems the "reasonable" choice.

12. Another desirable type of information for planners is a consumption budget study by level, stability, and frequency of receipt of income for the population in question. Among the poor, such a study would probably reveal that, because of their economic situation, expenditures for food – in addition to being a high percentage of income – tend to be made for minute quantities purchased on a daily basis and often for credit (see Lewis 1960, 1966a for typical data supporting this). Accordingly, such information could make it clear that these life-style requirements of the poor are not served by large "cash and carry" supermarkets alone.

Above, we have suggested that planners collect information on the "mix" of jobs available in the *local economy*, emphasizing the percentages which are stable and the percentage of each wage level for each of the major economic activities. Now we are calling for two types of information collected from the *individual household*: (a) economic activities data, and (b) consumption budgets. The combination of these data could provide realistic information as to how much – if anything – different segments of the lower-income groups could pay for housing without great inconvenience.

13. The list of studies we have been proposing requires one crucial addition: a survey in which the planners *ask the poor people* about what they want and need in housing. This could touch on cost, size, expandability, access to kin, primary schools, credit groceries (and even bars), public transportation, desired municipal services, and architectural features – such as adapting the building materials and ventilation to the tropical climate.

14. *Political considerations* – including the relative power of the housing and mortgage lobby – may lead to adoption of plans for low-income housing that effectively freeze out or result in disservice to the overwhelming majority of the intended clientele. The power of the housing and credit groups may mean that "financial" criteria are used to determine the nature and cost of low-income housing units.[26] By these "financial" criteria, housing for the very poor is a bad risk.

[26] Laun (1973), in an unpublished University of Wisconsin paper about low-cost urban housing in Colombia, stresses the extent to which these programs utilized terms and criteria of cost and resident selection parallel to those used by commercial lending institutions. This cut off the really poor and reduced to a "trickle" the truly low-cost housing units constructed. For example, Laun discusses late 1940's lending laws aimed at providing more low-cost housing for the poor which nevertheless requires "a first mortgage collateral and adequate income prospects to assure mortgage payments."

Other political factors are the *power* of the planning institution versus other institutions, and versus organized subgroups of the local population. In the case of Ciudad Guayana, the power potential of the CVG is quite high, although it is not always realized, for reasons having to do with national political policy – an area beyond the scope of this paper.

SUMMARY AND CONCLUSIONS

We have not intended this report as a mere explanation of why the city of Ciudad Guayana is growing in the opposite direction of the planners' models, although we feel that our explanation of the reasons for the city's growth to the east are clear and adequate. Instead, we have sought to highlight the structural conditions that generate the economically marginal people, who have flocked to the east, and the life-style and housing adaptations forced upon them by their structural conditions. Neither the structural marginality nor the resultant life-style and housing needs have entered into much urban development and housing policies – in Ciudad Guayana or anywhere else. Thus, in a final section, we have attempted a preliminary delineation of the factors – primarily structural – that we argue must be taken into account in urban and housing development if a low-income population is involved.

What would be the result in Ciudad Guayana, if none of the factors we have stressed is now taken into account and the city continued to grow under existing conditions? We may speculate about a long list of possible consequences, but let us mention just four points:

1. The city will continue to grow vigorously toward the east.

2. Because of the work law reimbursing commuting time and costs, the expenses to the large industries on the west will continue to rise with increasing average commuting distance and number of workers.

3. It would appear that the eastern and western halves of Ciudad Guayana will grow increasingly segregated by socioeconomic class and economic activity.

4. As a result, political conflict between the eastern and western parts of Ciudad Guayana might be expected to increase (see Stinchcombe 1969, who made a similar prediction) due to the increasingly divergent interests of the two halves.

Our final point must be that even if the real housing needs of the poor become known by means of social science research incorporating the factors outlined in the preceding section, this does not mean that housing policies will automatically begin to reflect the structural conditions and needs of the intended residents. For housing policies generally reflect the power distribution in a society, and power is something which for the poor is usually in short supply.

REFERENCES

ABOUHAMAD, JEANETTE
  1959   *Estudio de El Pedregal.* Caracas: Universidad Central de Venezuela.
ABRAMS, CHARLES
  1964   *Man's struggle for shelter in an urbanizing world.* Cambridge, Massachusetts: M.I.T. Press.
APPLEYARD, DONALD
  1969   "City designers and the pluralistic city," in *Planning urban growth and regional development.* Edited by L. Rodwin et al., 422–452. Cambridge, Massachusetts: M.I.T. Press.
BANCO CENTRAL DE VENEZUELA
  1962   *Survey of family living conditions in Santo Tomé de Guayana.* Caracas: Corporación Venezolana de Guayana (CVG).
  1965   *Family income in Santo Tomé de Guayana.* Caracas: Corporación Venezolana de Guayana (CVG).
  1966   *Encuesta sobre características demográficas, ingresos familiares, características de la vivienda, tipo de transporte utilizado de las familias de Santo Tomé de Guayana, febrero 1965.* Caracas: Corporación Venezolana de Guayana (CVG).
BANCO NACIONAL DE AHORRO Y PRÉSTAMO
  1970   *Mercavi 70.* Caracas.
BANCO OBRERO
  1959   *Proyecto de evaluación de los superbloques.* Caracas: Tipografía Vargas.
  n.d.   *Preliminary studies for the building of low-income housing in Ciudad Guayana.* Internal report of Banco Obrero. Caracas.
BERCKHOLTZ, PABLO
  1963   *Barrios marginales: aberración social.* Lima.
BEYER, GLENN
  1967   *The urban explosion in Latin America.* Ithaca, N.Y.: Cornell University Press.
BONILLA, FRANK
  1970   "Rio's favelas: the rural slums within the city," in *Peasants in cities.* Edited by W. Mangin, 72–84. Boston: Houghton Mifflin.
BROWNING, H., W. FEINDT
  1971   The social and economic context of migration to Monterrey," in *Latin American urban research,* volume one. Edited by F. Rabinowitz and F. Trueblood, 45–70. Beverly Hills: Sage Publications.
BRYCE-LAPORTE, SIMON
  1970   "Urban relocation and family adaptation in Puerto Rico: a case study in urban ethnography," in *Peasants in cities.* Edited by W. Mangin, 85–97. Boston: Houghton Mifflin.
CAMINOS, H., J. U. TURNER, J. A. STEFFIAN
  1969   *Urban dwelling environments: an elementary survey of settlements for the study of design determinants.* M.I.T. Report 16. Cambridge, Massachusetts: M.I.T. Press.

CARDOSO, F. H., E. FALETTO
1969   *Dependencia y desarrollo en América Latina.* Mexico: Siglo XXI.
CEVEPOF-CISOR
1973   *El status ocupacional de los jefes de hogares de bajos ingresos.* Serie Investigación y Planificatión de Recursos Humanos. Caracas: CORDIPLAN.
CHILDERS, VICTOR
n.d.   "Human resource development in Venezuela." Unpublished first draft. (An expansion of the 1967 unpublished doctoral dissertation, "Unemployment in Venezuela," Indiana University.)
CORONADO, JORGE
1955   *Sugestiones para la erradicación del Campamento San Diego (tugurio) en la ciudad de Guatemala.* Guatemala.
CORPORACIÓN VENEZOLANA DE GUAYANA (CVG)
1963–1972   *Informe anual.* Caracas.
1965   *Migration survey.* Caracas.
1967   *Inventario de edificaciones, Ciudad Guayana.* Caracas.
1969–1971   *Inventario de edificaciones y servicios públicos, Ciudad Guayana.* Caracas: Corporación Venezolana de Guayana.
CORRADA, RAFAEL
1966   "The housing development program for Ciudad Guayana," in *Housing policy for a developing Latin economy.* Edited by C. Frankenhoff, 108–130. University of Puerto Rico: Housing Policy Seminar.
1969   "The housing program," in *Planning urban growth and regional development.* Edited by L. Rodwin et al., 236–251. Cambridge, Massachusetts: M.I.T. Press.
DAVIS, R. C., N. F. MC GINN
1969a   *Build a mill, build a house, build a school: industrialization, urbanization and education in Ciudad Guayana.* Cambridge, Massachusetts: Harvard University Press.
1969b   "Education and regional development," in *Planning urban growth and regional development.* Edited by L. Rodwin et al., 270–285. Cambridge, Massachusetts: M.I.T. Press.
DIETZ, H.
1969   Urban squatter settlements in Peru: a case history and analysis. *Journal of Inter-American Studies* 11: 353–370.
DORSELAER, J., A. GREGORY
1962   *La urbanización en América Latina.* Bogota: Oficina Internacional de Investigaciones Sociales de FERES.
DOWNS, ANTHONY
1969   "Creating a land development strategy for Ciudad Guayana," in *Planning urban growth and regional development.* Edited by L. Rodwin et al., 202–218. Cambridge, Massachusetts: M.I.T. Press.
FLINN, W. L.
1968   The process of migration to a shantytown in Bogota, Colombia. *Inter-American Economic Affairs* 22: 77–88.
FRANKENHOFF, CHARLES, *editor*
1966   *Housing policy for a developing Latin economy.* University of Puerto Rico: Housing Policy Seminar.
FRIEDMANN, JOHN
1966   *Regional development policy: a case study of Venezuela.* Cambridge, Massachusetts: M.I.T. Press.

GANS, H. J.
    1967   *People and plans*. New York: Basic Books.
GARCÍA, MARÍA-PILAR
    1971   "Female employment and fertility in one parent (mother) families
            in the lower socio-economic class of the Metropolitan Area of
            Caracas, Venezuela." Bogota: Ford Foundation. (Mimeographed).
GEERTZ, CLIFFORD
    1966   *Agricultural involution*. Englewood Cliffs, N.J.: Prentice-Hall.
GERMANI, GINO
    1961   "Inquiry into the social effects of urbanization in a working-class
            district of Buenos Aires," in *Urbanization in Latin America*. Edited
            by P. M. Hauser, 206–233. New York: UNESCO.
HARDOY, J. E., R. L. SCHAEDEL
    1969   *The urbanization process in America from its origin to the present
            day*. Buenos Aires.
HAUSER, P. M., *editor*
    1961   *Urbanization in Latin America*. New York: UNESCO
HAUSER, P. M., L. F. SCHNORE
    1965   *The study of urbanization*. New York: John Wiley and Sons.
KARST, K., M. SCHWARTZ
    1968   "The internal norms and sanctions in ten barrios in Caracas." Los
            Angeles: University of California. (Mimeographed.)
LAUN, JOHN
    1973   "Low-cost housing in Colombia, 1942–1972: the rhetoric and reality
            of reform." Madison: University of Wisconsin. (Mimeographed.)
LESSA, CARLOS
    1970   De la constitución actual del capitalismo dependiente (industriali-
            zación, marginalización, sociedad opulenta). *Cuadernos de la
            Sociedad Venezolana de Planificación* 94–95: 3–53.
LEWIS, OSCAR
    1960   *The children of Sanchez*. New York: Random House.
    1966a   *La Vida: a Puerto Rican family in the culture of poverty*. New York:
            Random House.
    1966b   The culture of poverty. *Scientific American* 215 (7): 19–25.
    1968   *A study of slum culture: backgrounds for La Vida*. New York:
            Random House.
LLERAS-RESTREPO, CARLOS
    1955   *De la república a la dictadura*. Bogota: Argra.
MACDONALD, JOHN S.
    1969   "Migration and the population of Ciudad Guayana," in *Planning
            urban growth and regional migration*. Edited by L. Rodwin et al.,
            109–125. Cambridge, Massachusetts: M.I.T. Press.
MANGIN, WILLIAM
    1963   Urbanization case in Peru. *Architectural Design* 33: 366–370.
    1967   Latin American squatter settlements: a problem and a solution. *Latin
            American Research Review* 2 (3): 65–98.
    1970   *Peasants in cities*. Boston: Houghton Mifflin.
MANGIN, WILLIAM, JOHN TURNER
    1968   The barriada movement. *Progressive Architecture* 49 (5): 154–162.
MATOS MAR, J.
    1961   "Migration and urbanization," in *Urbanization in Latin America*.
            Edited by P. M. Hauser, 170–190. New York: UNESCO.

1968   *Urbanización y barriadas en América del Sur.* Lima: Instituto de Estudios Peruanos.

MATTELART, A., M. GARRETÓN
1965   *Integración nacional y marginalidad.* Santiago, Chile: Editorial del Pacífico.

MINISTERIO DE FOMENTO
1950   *Censo de 1950.* Caracas: Oficina Central del Censo.
1965   *Noveno censo general de población, febrero 1961.* Caracas: Oficina Central del Censo.
1970   *Encuesta de hogares.* Caracas: Oficina Central del Censo.

MORSE, R. M.
1965   Recent research on Latin American urbanization: a selective survey with commentary. *Latin American Research Review* 1 (1): 35–75.
1971   Trends and issues in urban research. *Latin American Research Review* 6 (1).

OSPINA-PÉREZ, MARIANO
1948   "Le nueva economía colombiana." *XVII Conferencia Agropecuaria de Antioquia.* Medellín.

PATCH, R. W.
1961   *Life in a callejón: a study of urban disorganization.* American Universities Field Staff Reports Service West Coast, South American Series 8 (6). New York.

PEATTIE, LISA
1968   *The view from the barrio.* Ann Arbor: University of Michigan Press.
1969a   "Social mobility and economic development," in *Planning urban growth and regional mobility.* Edited by L. Rodwin et al., 400–410. Cambridge, Massachusetts: M.I.T. Press.
1969b   "Social issues in housing," in *Shaping an urban future.* Edited by B. J. Freiden and W. Nash, 15–34. Cambridge, Massachusetts: M.I.T. Press.
1969c   "Conflicting views of the project: Caracas versus the site," in *Planning urban growth and regional mobility.* Edited by L. Rodwin et al., 453–464. Cambridge, Massachusetts: M.I.T. Press.
1971   "The structural parameters of emerging life styles in Venezuela," in *The culture of poverty: a critique.* Edited by E. B. Leacock, 285–298. New York: Simon and Schuster.

PORTER, WILLIAM
1969   "Changing perspectives on residential area design," in *Planning urban growth and regional mobility.* Edited by L. Rodwin et al., 252–269. Cambridge, Massachusetts: M.I.T. Press.

QUIJANO, ANIBAL
1966   "Notas sobre el concepto de marginalidad social." CEPAL: División de Asuntos sociales. (Mimeographed.)
1968   Dependencia, cambio social y urbanización en América Latina. *Revista Mexicana de Sociología* 30 (3): 525–570.
1971   Re-definición de la dependencia y marginalización en América Latina. *Cuadernos de la Sociedad Venezolana de Planificación* 94–95: 3–53.

RABINOWITZ, F., F. M. FELICITY
1971   *Latin American urban research,* volume one. Beverly Hills: Sage Publications.

RODWIN, LLOYD et al.
1969   Planning urban growth and regional development. Cambridge, Massachusetts: M.I.T. Press.

ROGLER, L. H.
1967   Slum neighborhoods in Latin American. Journal of Inter-American Studies 9 (4): 507–528.

SAFA, HELEN
1964   From shantytown to public housing: a comparison of family structure in the urban neighborhoods in Puerto Rico. Caribbean Studies 4: 3–12.

SALMEN, LAWRENCE
1966   "Report on Vila Kennedy and Vila Esperança." Brazil: Cooperativa Habitacional, COHAB. (Mimeographed.)
1969   A perspective on the resettlement of squatters in Brazil. América Latina 12 (1): 73–93.

SANABRIA, TOMÁS
1966   Los ranchos, afflición urbana. Desarrollo Económico 3 (1).

SCHULMAN, SAM
1966   Latin American shantytowns. New York Times Magazine, January 16.

SILVA, JULIO
1967   "Programa de mejoramiento urbano progresivo," Caracas: Corporación Venezolana de Guayana (CVG). (Mimeographed.)

SILVEIRA, G. P.
1963   Down with shantytowns: Brazilian students lead the way. Community Development Review 8: 2.

SOBERMAN, RICHARD
1967   Transport technology for developing regions: a study of road transportation in Venezuela. Cambridge, Massachusetts: M.I.T. Press.

STINCHCOMBE, ARTHUR
1969   "Social attitudes and planning in The Guayana," in Planning urban growth and regional development. Edited by L. Rodwin et al., 411–421. Cambridge, Massachusetts: M.I.T. Press.

TALTON, RAY
1969   The politics of the barrios of Venezuela. Berkeley: University of California Press.

TRAVIESO, FERNANDO
1971   ¿Ciudad Guayana: Polo de desarrollo? Cuadernos de la Sociedad Venezolana de Planificación 92–93: 77–82.

TURNER, JOHN
1963   Dwelling resources in South America. Architectural Design 33.
1965   Lima's barriadas and corralones: suburbs versus slums. Ekistics 19.
1966a   Assentamientos urbanos no regulados. Cuadernos de la Sociedad Venezolana de Planificación 36.
1966b   "A new view of the housing deficit," in Housing policy for a developing Latin Economy. Edited by Charles Frankenhoff, 35–58. University of Puerto Rico: Housing Policy Seminar.
1967   Barriers and channels for housing development in modernizing countries. Journal of The American Institute of Planners 33 (3): 167–181.
1968a   Housing priorities, settlement patterns, and urban development in modernizing countries. Journal of The American Institute of Planners 34 (6): 354–363.

1968b The squatter settlement: architecture that works. *Architectural Design*, 355–360.
VEKEMANS, R., R. VENEGAS
1966a Marginalidad y promoción popular. *Mensaje 15*. Santiago de Chile.
1966b *Integración nacional y marginalidad*. Santiago de Chile: DESAL.
VIÑALS, ENRICA
1972 "Consideraciones en torno a Ciudad Guayana." Unpublished doctoral dissertation, Universidad Central de Venezuela, Caracas.
WAGNER, B., D. MC VOY, E. GORDON
1966 *Guanabara housing and urban development*. Association for International Development (AID) Housing Report.

COMMENT *by Selma F. Rubin*

The role of the social scientist in city planning cannot be overemphasized. He must work closely with the designers and architects who would be well advised to pay close attention to his suggestions: otherwise, the results may be totally unplanned. The planned city of Ciudad Guayana is an excellent case in point, as Professors García and Blumberg have shown.

Although Ciudad Guayana is not a city like Brasilia that is almost wholly derived from the planners' drafting table, it is nevertheless true that it is a "planned city." The plan, however, has not been entirely successful. The city did not grow as expected. The anticipated residential and industrial patterns did not develop. It was an example once more of a city that adjusted rather than conformed to a master plan.

However, the master plan need not be disregarded entirely. Rather, adjustment under the direction of social scientists is in order, if disorganization, ever-increasing unrest, political and economic alienation, and unrestrained urban sprawl are to be avoided. Ideally, this direction would take several forms, among them a realistic assessment of the types of people involved in the economically marginal population. Professors García and Blumberg have shown that, in a population where marital alliances are highly unstable (chiefly for economic reasons), approximately 25 percent of the low-income families are headed by females, and the level of education is frequently below primary school. Because of the unavailability of further schooling, few jobs are open to unskilled women or those of both sexes lacking a primary diploma. The abundance of more highly educated labor effectively eliminates the unskilled and unschooled from the market in Ciudad Guayana. Further, due to Venezuelan work laws, those fortunate enough to secure adequate employment at unskilled jobs are frequently laid off immediately prior to the point at which the employer would legally be forced to begin giving fringe benefits. Thus, it is argued proper planning must take into account the number of hours of employment a marginal individual may realistically be expected to have during a year, and the duration of such a job.

Another pressing concern, but one which is even more difficult to deal with, is the housing situation. City planners, according to the authors, must take into account both the expandability and mobility of the marginal population when planning low-income housing. Many factors contribute to family size, but one may generalize that very few low-income families do not grow. Placing such a family in a small, rigid unit which makes no allowance for eventual family expansion has the dual effect of making even one additional member an unbearable strain and making the squatter's shack, with its infinite possibilities for expansion, far more attractive than public housing.

Yet another built-in pitfall of subsidized housing is the method of computation used to determine the tenants' rent. Professors García and Blumberg argue that conventional methods of fixing payment inevitably place a devastating strain on the tenants' resources, because the percentage of wages needed for food is inversely related to wealth. Again, when confronted with a choice between living in "good" housing at the cost of cutting an already inadequate food budget and living rent-free in a shack, a person on a marginal income will tend to choose the latter.

Dealing effectively and adequately with the above problems, already beyond the scope of the city planners, requires, as previously stated, a careful survey of economic conditions among the marginal population and a detailed study of available jobs and their expected duration. In addition, the solution to the housing situation must begin with an individualized study of the people themselves and their existing life-styles, as well as their needs and wants.

The prognosis for the implementation of this plan is not good. The political power structure, as well as the traditional method of dealing with public housing and the poor, are likely to come into conflict with the practical solutions of the social scientists, with the outcome predictably inevitable. However, optimism may spring even from the unhappy forecast of the future in Ciudad Guayana, for it has been demonstrated that the skill of the social scientist is now capable of dealing with aberrations in a city plan. Uncontrolled growth and an influx of the economically marginal need not be a disaster if the social scientist and city planner form a working partnership.

Values and Migration Decision Making

ALEX STEPICK

Migration decision making is viewed here from the perspective of people maximizing their value systems. The value systems of the informants are defined by the informants themselves. Maximization of a value system through migration concerns both the values themselves and structural constraints upon them such as economic opportunities. The main thrust of this effort is to establish and analyze the relationship between the values and their constraints.

I shall focus upon the value system and behavior of one individual. First, an ethnography is presented outlining the abstract values and their relationships to the empirical categories, i.e. structural constraints through which values are manifest. This will be done for both the informant's present environment and for potential migration alternatives. Such an approach is equally applicable to those for whom migration would better maximize their value system, those for whom it would not, and those who are recent migrants. The data presented is derived from recent migrants to Oaxaca, Oaxaca, Mexico.

After the ethnography, techniques of data collection and analysis will be summarized. While the statistics are not significant in terms of sample size, they do thoroughly analyze and validate the method and model for one individual. I conclude by outlining methods for applying the model to broader samples.

Support for the fieldwork for this project came from the National Science Foundation (NSF) [gs-30563] and the Institute of Latin American Studies, University of Texas. Principal investigator was Henry Selby. Also, an NSF Traineeship through the University of Texas, Austin, laid the groundwork for the preparation of this paper. I would like to thank Kim Romney, Henry Selby, and Carol Stepick for their criticism and comments on earlier drafts.

MODELING THE VALUE SYSTEM

The value system and its relation to empirical categories were defined through open-ended interviews with a cross-section of informants from the Colonia Benito Juarez, Oaxaca.[1] In the model, the values one tries to maximize are called goals. This is to avoid confusion which may arise when we later speak of how much an individual possesses of a particular goal, i.e. his value on that goal.

Goals in the model presented in Figure 1 and explained in the following ethnography should apply to any *colono* [member of the *colonia*] with the partial exception of liberty, which, as we shall see below, is a special case.

The specifics of the ethnography are from the perspective of one individual, Alejandro. Alejandro is a forty-nine-year-old construction worker, married by the Church, with four children. He has lived in the *colonia* since its inception about ten years ago. His house, with its bright-yellow exterior, is among the better-furnished ones within the *colonia*.

Through the years he has worked in construction, gradually learning carpentry, masonry, electricity, and how to read blueprints. He is now considered a *maestro albanil*, most closely equivalent to a construction foreman.

More important, he has learned to make the necessary job connections to maintain employment and psychological job security in a market flooded with labor. Job security is a principal component of the first goal, "security." Even more important to one's security, according to informant's statements, is the ownership of house and land. Only those who have recently arrived in the city rent a dwelling or live with relatives. As soon as possible a down payment is made on a lot and one begins construction of an adobe house. Alejandro has already completed payments on his lot and the material used in building his house. However, maintenance of these constitutes a small continuing expense.

Although house and lot are considered a part of one's total savings, they are not considered effective, or liquid; rather they are hard savings, for, as is often stated, "Where would one live if he had to sell his house?"

Effective savings, the other component in total savings, consist of

[1]   The research reported here was part of the larger project. I conducted fieldwork in Benito Juarez, while Arthur Murphy, University of Chicago, worked in another *colonia* of Oaxaca, San Juanito. Henry Selby and Jane Granskog worked in the Oaxacan valley village of Santo Tomás Mazaltepec. Nearly all reference to village values and environment comes from that work, although I accept responsibility for any misguided interpretation.

the material valuables one possesses and whatever cash one may have. Alejandro maintains no cash reserve, but his house contains a store-bought bed, a gas stove with oven, a metal dish cabinet, a transistor radio, a guitar, and a clothes closet. These valuables contribute to security because they can be pawned or sold – generally at two-thirds the purchase price. Besides their purchase price, such valuables also constitute a continuing expense in that some of them require maintenance, e.g. batteries for the radio.

The quality of the people in one's environment affects security, too. For if there are thieves and drunks, the security of one's possessions and physical well-being may be greatly threatened. According to those in Benito Juarez, Oaxaca has very good people, while Mexico City contains the largest collection of bad people. The final component of security is one's sex. It is maintained that females are less likely to be attacked by thieves and drunkards.

Effective savings and valuables are also principal components of the second goal, progress. Whereas security appears to reflect material prospects for the future, progress mirrors the same for the present. Thus, not only are valuables and effective savings important, but also significant are the quality of one's dress and food along with the material conditions of the *colonia*, city, or village. Food and dress are a continuing expense – because of the generally low income level within the *colonia*, proportionately a very large expense – although the precise amount varies widely depending upon the strength of one's desires for progress and how many people are in one's family.

The people where one lives are not considered by the informants to influence one's progress, but they do affect the "education in manners and morals of children" – a "pseudo goal," i.e. a subsidiary goal contributing to some more inclusive goals. If children see bad habits, they are more likely to adopt such habits themselves, although this may be partially overcome by the character of the parents them-selves – the second component to this pseudo goal, children's manners.

Alejandro has managed to put his two elder children into secondary school (the younger two have just begun primary school). The daughter has since married, but the son will soon complete a vocational engineering curriculum. This accomplishment pleases Alejandro and is quite significant within the *colonia*, where most children are either still in the primary grades or must quit after these grades because of economic pressures. It pleases Alejandro because his son will be better off than he has been, thus making schooling, a pseudo goal, worthy of expense. Educating his son also provides Alejandro with additional security for the future. Alejandro's son is quite aware of the debt he owes his father, a matter that is becoming very important to Alejandro as he sees that his working days do not stretch too far into the future. Hence, schooling and children's manners combine to form the third goal, "education."

Although the water supply is polluted, sanitary conditions are poor and amoebic dysentery is endemic, Alejandro, informally at least, considers "health" (the fourth goal) to be of little importance. His attitude toward health appears fatalistic.

He admits that the recently provided government free health care should make life better, but he makes little effort in the way of preventive medicine. No savings are set aside for health insurance (the free care is limited in its extent). Despite the fact that government employees have clearly outlined inexpensive and efficient ways to improve the water supply, he has not expended much effort on this. Although some *colonos* are beginning to construct outhouses, they do so generally only at the instigation of the social workers. Alejandro has not yet been pushed sufficiently, and he has no outhouse. Currently, his expenses for his family and work time lost through sickness for himself are very small (less than Mex $100 per year and six days), but only a few years ago he spent nearly Mex $2,000 curing an illness of his younger son. Considering that he earns about Mex $14,000 per year and maintains no cash savings, the illness was a significant strain on his resources. Health is determined, in his mind, more by the immutable aspects of the environment, than by any actions of his.

Alejandro also manages to support a mistress. Although she does not possess any of the valuable amenities of his wife, with the money provided by him and Mex $200 a month from the government for being a widow of a government employee, she does manage to feed herself, her six children and often Alejandro. Alejandro's mistress is his major manifestation of "liberty" (the fifth goal), which, as he says, is "...the freedom to do as one pleases. Being without liberty is like being a bird in a cage. One who is without liberty has to tell his wife wherever he is going. But I am free to divert myself as I please." In contrast to conceptions of the Mexican middle and upper class, Alejandro's conception of liberty (*libertad*) contains no reference to the political sphere.

He diverts himself not only with his mistress, but also through such enjoyments as drinking, attending fiestas, and strolling through the city on Sunday *paseos*. For Alejandro, liberty and "diversions" (the sixth goal) substantially overlap. However, psychologically they are definitely distinct. This becomes evident upon comparing Alejandro's conceptions and manifestations of liberty with those of other *colonos*. Everyone says liberty is a goal and they define it abstractly approximately as Alejandro does. However, they all differ drastically about exactly what constitutes or contributes to this goal. For Alejandro it is diversions and a *casa chica*, but for a woman informant it is precisely the opposite – avoiding fiestas, drinking and, most important, avoiding any sexual relations with men. The relationship of liberty to its environment is thus highly dependent on the individual.

Sunday mornings generally find Alejandro performing community services (*cargos*). Because the *colonia* has only recently been integrated into the city (1972), the labor and materials for all community services, including water, roads, and electricity, have been provided by the *colonos* themselves. The mechanisms through which this is accomplished are called the *cargo* system.

Aside from the material benefits arising from community service there is a certain "respect" (the seventh goal) that accrues to the individual who donates a significant amount of time and, if he possesses them, skills. In the *colonia* participation is truly voluntary, as the provisional committees that organize projects have no sanctions to enforce participation. Gaining respect is particularly important in Alejandro's case, for the current projects are no longer in his section of the *colonia*. Yet, he participates and, in fact, often directs the projects (a position generally avoided because of the jealousy inevitably aroused in some). The fact that he gains respect by this behavior is attested to by the number of fiestas to which he is invited (which are more restricted to invitation in the city than in the villages) and because nearly everyone addresses him by the respectful title of *don*, a title not generally used between *colonos*. "Overall" is reflective of one's overall achievement of the above goals in the value system.

In summary, Alejandro's time is distributed among activities related to working, liberty, community service, diversions, sickness, and wasted time (i.e. time not contributing to any of the goals, e.g. sleeping). As he has completed payments for land and material used in construction of his house and furthermore prefers not to maintain cash savings, his actual expenses are for health, valuables, children's schooling, liberty, diversions, food and dress, and a small amount for maintenance of house and valuables.

ALTERNATIVE ENVIRONMENTS

Migration decision making involves considering alternative environments, i.e. cities or villages other than one's present residence. We can conceptualize values as independent of environments, although as presented in the ethnography they are defined particularly through their substantive manifestations. Examining value systems in alternative environments reveals that the same conceptual value system may assume unique manifestations according to varying environmental constraints.

For example, in Mexico City there is no *cargo* system; therefore,

CITY MODEL

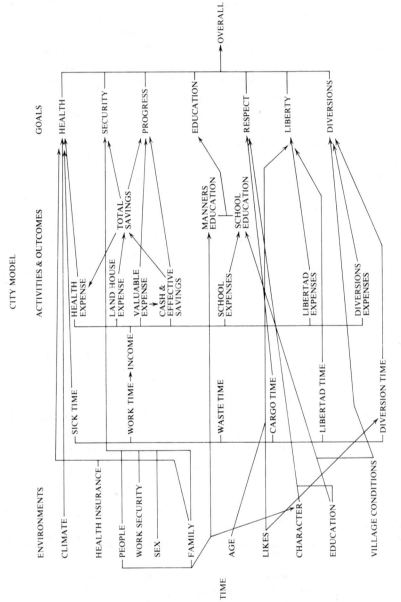

Figure 1.   City model

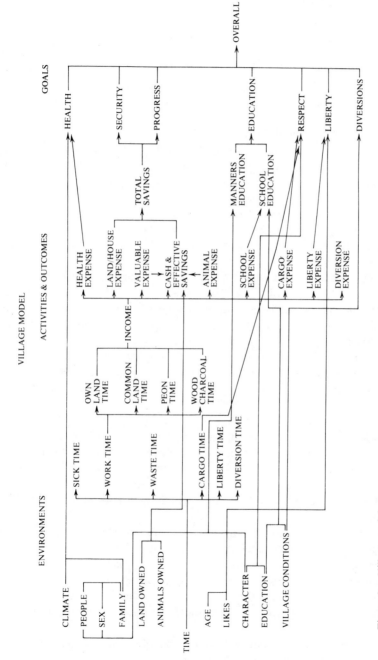

Figure 2. Village model

cargos could no longer be a means for obtaining respect. Nevertheless, respect would still be a goal value: but other means would be employed to achieve respect.

In contrast, all the variables contributing to security in Oaxaca also exist in Mexico City, i.e. people, work security, sex, family, and total savings. Indeed, the lack of a *cargo* system in Mexico City is the only significant difference between Oaxaca and Mexico City.

The implication is not, however, that few differences exist among urban areas with respect to migration. They surely do exist in the number or values of variables in the environments. For example, the people of Mexico City are considered far worse (more likely to corrupt one's children, rob, and deceive) than those of Oaxaca, i.e. Oaxaca sets a higher value on people. Also, Alejandro's family lives in a village close to Oaxaca. If he were in Mexico City he would not be able to visit them often, nor could they easily assist him in an emergency. Thus, Oaxaca has a higher value for the family variable than Mexico City. Such differences would exist for nearly all the model's variables.

The differences between urban areas are not generally ones of kind but rather of quantity. The similarities of the *relationships* between variables in the model are quite substantial. Thus, delineation of the models, as outlined in the above ethnography, for alternative cities is not exceedingly complex.

However, the village differs considerably from the urban areas. Not only do the values of particular variables change, but the environment and activities relating the values and environment also change drastically from the city.

As can be seen from Figure 2, the income possibilities for the village are considerably more diverse than for the urban areas. Working time can be distributed among four categories: working one's own land; working on common land; working as a *peon*, or day laborer, earning about Mex $12.00 per day; and either burning charcoal or shaping wooden house beams for which one earns about Mex $18.00 per day.

The *cargo* system also differs in the village. The social pressure to work on community projects or to assume a civil office is significantly greater than in Benito Juarez where less than 50 percent of the households participate in the *cargo* system. Also, with most *cargos* there is some associated expense, either in direct outlay of money or in time lost which otherwise could have been devoted to producing income.

The final important difference between the expression of values for the rural village and the urban areas is in the importance of owning land and animals. Although in Benito Juarez many people own both, their importance is much less than in the village. Land is insufficient in the city to support income-producing animals or crops. Although ownership of fowl and pigs is quite common, feed is generally specially purchased. However, in the villages both animals and crops are extremely important income producers, important enough to warrant separate listing of them in the model of the village's environment.

Although there are these significant and striking differences between rural and urban areas, a comparison of Figure 1 and Figure 2 reveals more similarities than differences. As was the case when comparing alternative urban environments, delineating the urban and rural environmental differences is not a difficult task.

DATA COLLECTION AND ANALYSIS

To apply the model to actual migration decision making, a means of operationalizing and measuring the value system was derived.[2] However, the direct analysis and measurement of migration decision making is particularly problematical as the observed behavior can be in only one of two categories – migration or nonmigration.

The hypothesis of value maximization was, therefore, tested within a context other than migrations: Is the informant maximizing his distribution of resources, i.e. his time and material goods, within his present environment? We can measure easily how many days the informant spends in activities defined as leisure as compared to working time. The actual distribution of activities and material resources is readily observable. Thus, this observable behavior could be compared with the operationalized model's predictions.

A scaling method was constructed which measured the informant's subjective evaluation or weighting of each variable. These weights formed the basis for a mathematical program designed to maximize one's "overall," given the variables' weightings and the particular environment. The results of the mathematical program indicate the "best" or "rational" distribution of time and money to achieve an overall maximum of the value system. Table 1 compares this "rational" behavior to the informant's observed behavior for one year.

[2] Complete description of data collection and analysis is given in Selby and Hendrix (n.d.) and Stepick and Hendrix (i.p.).

DISCUSSION OF RESULTS AND MIGRATION APPLICATIONS

Although not directly concerned with migration the results shown in Table 1 are relevant as they reveal more clearly the somewhat concealed and complex motivations of migration decision making.

According to the predictions, a "rational" Alejandro would not be entirely motivated materially. He should not spend all his time working and earning money. Clearly he must work, but far less than is possible. He is best off if he works a mere 231 days a year.

Table 1. Observed versus rational distribution of resources

Time	Observed	Rational
Work	242.0	232.0
Sick	12.0	14.0
Community service	52.0	56.0
Liberty	39.0	40.0
Diversions	20.0	22.0
Money (in hundreds of pesos)		
Sickness	12.5	10.0
Food/dress	86.0	73.5
Diversions	12.6	12.7
Valuables	15.0	28.0
School	10.5	10.67
Cash	0.0	0.0
Liberty	36.4	36.2

Rather than earning as much money as possible, a rational Alejandro prefers other activities. Liberty is particularly important. Although he gains no observable benefit, he should still spend one-sixth as much time on liberty as on working. Similarly, despite the fact that his household no longer materially benefits from the community service projects, he should nevertheless contribute a little more than one day a week to these projects.

From this picture of Alejandro's rationality, we can deduce his probable reactions to some situations: as one's marriage type affects one's liberty, being married by civil law is worse than being married by the Church. Being married by civil law provides for redress by the wife against the husband's mistreatment (e.g. adultery). Hence, Alejandro's liberty would be severely curtailed, and we would expect him never to marry by the law.

As he gains from participation in community service, a project within the community which affronts his dignity and does not invite his participation would not be approved or assisted. This is probably why Alejandro still does not have an outhouse, as they have been promoted primarily by the social workers.

As drinking is an important activity, along with the freedom to be drunk in public, Alejandro should not be expected to participate in activities where this would be infringed upon. Thus, most of Alejandro's drinking and social activities occur within the *colonia*, where such an attitude and behavior is condoned.

Finally, although Alejandro might be better off economically in another city, e.g. Mexico City, he may refuse such an alternative for noneconomic reasons, e.g. respect.

Predictions were generated concerning the attractiveness of potential migration sites by supplying the mathematical program with the appropriate variable and value differences within the model. These cities were cited by Alejandro as conceivable migration sites for himself. The scale scores in Table 2 have a possible range of 0–100.

Table 2. Migration predictions

City	Overall scale score
Oaxaca	71.9
Mexico	65.0
Salina Cruz	75.0
Pochutla	76.0
Lagunas Oaxaca	59.0
San Jose Ixtlahuaca	64.0

Interestingly, these predictions do not correspond with observed reality. Two cities, Pochutla and Salina Cruz, are predicted as being preferable to Oaxaca. An inconsistency arises between the results for Alejandro in Oaxaca from Table 1, which appear to confirm the hypothesis of value maximization, and the migration predictions from Table 2 which appear to negate the same hypothesis.

The migration predictions were discussed with the informant and he contended that the mathematical programming predictions were actually more rational than his behavior. Pochutla and Salina Cruz are, overall, better cities for him than Oaxaca. They both are close to the sea, and fishing thus is possible. Alejandro believes that he will not be able to continue in construction work much longer: it is too hazardous and demanding. Thus, he prefers a locality which offers more diverse and secure opportunities for subsistence. In his youth he had worked in both of these cities and was greatly impressed with the ready availability of fish. With the assistance of friends he still has in those cities he could work as a fisherman. Fishing does not pay as well as construction, but he could alternate between the two. He would not have to overwork himself; there would be a constant supply of food and ever-present job security. If his son does not complete his technical training and obtain a job sufficient to support his father, Alejandro claims that he will move to one of these cities.

Thus, the model may have revealed more than was discovered by intensive interviewing. Perhaps the hypothesis of value maximization through migration remains valid. Nevertheless, a problem is raised concerning prediction. A gap appears to exist between being better and being sufficiently better to prompt migration. A hidden factor, relating perhaps to the physical effort involved as opposed to mere intellectual contemplation, has been neglected. For the model to be very applicable to migration prediction this neglected aspect must also be measured. Fortunately, it should not be very difficult to obtain the necessary data. As Alejandro is apparently seriously considering migration, the maximum gap before migration is initiated should be approximately the difference on overall score between Oaxaca and Pochutla. Hence, for him the gap appears to be four or five scale points.

GENERALIZATION OF THE MODEL

Data on a larger sample have been gathered by the author, but analysis is not yet complete. Such data will be used to discern clusters of individuals' value systems. These will then serve as a basis for aggregate predictions.

If people do act according to their value systems, then people who have similar value systems should behave comparably. By "similar value system" I mean not only the relationship between variables but also that the variables' weights are perceived as approximately equal.

For example, although two people may agree on the relationship, they certainly do not necessarily agree upon the "overall" return of the activity, i.e. whether it is worth the effort to obtain respect rather than some other goal. They must weight respect approximately equally if they are expected to act comparably. These weights are derived through analysis of scaling data.

Each individual's weights on the goal values can be used as a basis for defining clusters. Those weights clustering across individuals would imply, if the theory is correct, that those individuals from whom the weights were derived should behave similarly. Well-defined statistical methods exist for determining cluster within data and could easily be employed (see Johnson 1967).

Once these clusters were discerned, one could search for socio-logical correlates. As values are sociocultural products, there should be one or more sociocultural variables which give rise to the clusters of individuals. These variables then could be used to imply a particular weighting within the value system which, in turn, would imply certain tendencies of behavior. To predict, we could then reason directly from observable sociocultural variables to migration decision making.

CONCLUSION

We have looked at the possibilities of viewing migration decision making from the perspective of value maximization. The relationships between values and environmental constraints were analyzed. These relationships demonstrated how values may come to have differing manifestations according to environmental constraints. Migration decision making was conceived as the evaluation of one's overall achievement in terms of his value system subject to the environmental constraints of alternative migration sites.

The hypothesis that behavior is a manifestation of value maximization was examined in the context of distribution of resources within one informant's present environment – Oaxaca. The results appear to confirm the hypothesis while revealing some interesting interactions between values and environment. Applying the hypothesis to migration decision making proved more problematical. Nevertheless, the results and analysis are encouraging as they reveal more of the motivations of migration decision making, besides a deficiency in the model employed.

For those interested in aggregate migration behavior, methods are suggested for extending the model to larger samples. It is suggested that the approach embodied here can incorporate the push/pull effect (in the comparison of migration alternatives) with migration's differential selectivity (in the clusterings of individuals' values).

REFERENCES

JOHNSON, STEPHEN C.
  1967   Hierarchical clustering schemes. *Psychometrika* 32: 241–254.
SELBY, H. A., G. HENDRIX
  n.d.   "Decision making in culture: a Mexican case." Unpublished working paper 1.
STEPICK, A., G. HENDRIX
  i.p.   *Predicting behavior from values.* Paper presented to Mathematical Social Science Board Conference: Data Processing Techniques in Anthropology, Corvallis, Oregon, April 1973.

Biographical Notes

CARMEN ARANOVICH (1937–) received her B.A. in History at the University of Buenos Aires in 1967 and then, following work at the National Council of Scientific and Technical Investigations, received an M.A. from the University of Massachusetts in 1971. Since 1973 she has served as Professor of History at the Universidad Nacional del Sur, Argentina. She has published a great many articles both in the U.S.A. and in Latin America concerning Latin American urban development between the sixteenth and the nineteenth centuries.

JORGE BALÁN (1940–) studied sociology at the University of Buenos Aires and the University of Texas, Austin, where he earned a Ph.D. in 1968. He taught for extended periods of time in Mexico, the United States, and Brazil. Currently he is back in Argentina working at the Instituto Torcuato Di Tella in Buenos Aires. His major interests at the moment are in regional social history and the social organization of labor under varying technological conditions. His publications include *Men in a developing society* (1973), *Centro e periferia no desenvolvimento Brasileiro* (1974), and a number of articles in the major Latin American journals.

RAE LESSER BLUMBERG received her Ph.D. from Northwestern University in 1970. She taught at the University of Wisconsin, Madison, and is presently Acting Associate Professor of Sociology at the University of California, San Diego. Although she has traveled, conducted research, and lived in many countries (principally in Latin America), her main field experience has been in Venezuela. There, she taught and did sociological research for two years at Andrés Bello

University, spent two years as a resident advisor in sociological research for the Ministry of Education, and spent a summer advising in the Ministry of Health and Social Welfare. While at Andrés Bello University, she directed a survey research project on urbanization and development in Ciudad Guayana, Venezuela, and returned there in 1973. Her publications include a book, *Stratification: socio-economic and sexual inequality* (1976), coauthored articles in the *American Journal of Sociology* (on societal complexity and familial complexity), the *American Sociological Review* (on ethnicity and extended familism), and numerous book chapters. Her most recent publications have stemmed from her research on a 1973–1974 Ford Foundation Faculty Fellowship on the role of women in society. Currently, she is working on a book emerging from this fellowship, detailing her theory-testing research (utilizing a 61-society pilot sample) on women's relative economic power as a primary determinant of their status and life options *vis-à-vis* men.

Duccio Bonavía (1935–) obtained his doctorate in Archaeology in 1961 at the Universidad Nacional Mayor de San Marcos in Lima, Peru. He did postgraduate study in the Laboratory of Prehistory and Quaternary Geology of the University of Bordeaux, France. He served as Adjunct Director of the National Museum of Anthropology and Archaeology in Lima, was Director of Antiquities of the Instituto Nacional de Cultura del Perú, and was Professor at the Universidad Nacional Mayor de San Marcos in Lima. At present he is Associate Professor in the Department of Biology of the Universidad Peruana Cayetano Heredia in Lima. His specialty is Andean archaeology, and his interests have been in urbanism, mural art, and the archaeology of the eastern slopes of the Andes. At present he is studying the Lithic Period and ethnobotany. He is author of several monographs and many articles, largely devoted to Andean archaeology. He is the author or coauthor of various books, the most recent of which is *Ricchata Quellccani*, a study of pre-Hispanic mural art.

Woodrow Borah (1912–) was born in Utica, Mississippi, and educated at the University of California, Los Angeles and Berkeley, with a Ph.D. in 1940. Since 1948 he has taught at Berkeley, where he is currently Shepard Professor of History. His studies include monographs on the history of silk raising in Mexico, the trade between Mexico and Peru, the movement of the Indian population, and urban history. Much of his work has been in coauthorship with Sherbourne F. Cole.

HARLEY L. BROWNING (1927–) studied at Columbia and Berkeley where he received his doctorate in 1962. He is Professor of Sociology at the University of Texas at Austin and Director of the Population Research Center at that institution. He is coauthor of *Men in a developing society*, a study of geographic and social mobility in Monterrey, Mexico. His present interest is in understanding the structural transformation of the labor force of countries undergoing economic development.

EDWARD E. CALNEK (1930–) received a Ph.D. in Anthropology at the University of Chicago in 1962 and is currently Associate Professor and Associate Chairman of the Department of Anthropology at the University of Rochester. He has been engaged in archival research relating to the late pre-Hispanic societies of Central Mexico, with emphasis on the urbanization process of Tenochtitlán, based on early-colonial-period archival collections in Spain, Mexico, France, and the United States.

SHERBURNE F. COOK (1896–1974). Born in Springfield, Massachusetts; educated at Harvard in biology (B.A., 1919; M.A., 1923; Ph.D., 1925); a National Research Fellow in the Biological Sciences, 1926–1928, at the Kaiser-Wilhelm Institut in Berlin-Dahlem and the University of Cambridge, Cook spent his academic life at the University of California, Berkeley, where he carried on two distinct scholarly careers, one specializing in physiology with studies of toxic effects of heavy metals, high altitudes, and aging, and one in anthropology and history, with studies of Indians in California and Mexico.

ROBERTO CORTÉS CONDE (1932–) is Chairman of the Board of the Instituto Torcuato Di Tella, Buenos Aires, Argentina, and Visiting Professor at the University of Texas, Austin. He was the recipient of a Guggenheim Fellowship, a Senior Scholar at the universities of Oxford and Cambridge, a Visiting Professor at Yale and Brittingham Professor of the University of Wisconsin, Madison. Between 1974 and 1976 he was Senior Researcher at the Center of Economic Research of the Instituto Torcuato Di Tella. Some of his numerous publications are: "Auge de la economía exportadora y vicissitudes del régimen conservador (1880–1916)," in *Argentina, la república conservadora* (edited by E. Gallo and R. Cortés Conde, 1972), *The first stages of modernization in Spanish America* (1974) and (with Stanley Stein) *Latin America, a guide of its economic history* (forthcoming).

FRANCISCO DE SOLANO (1934–) is Spanish, studied at the universities of Seville, Madrid, and Paris, and received his Ph.D. in American

History. He received fellowships from the Bollingen Foundation, New York (1960–1963) and the Fundação Calouste Gulbenkian, Lisbon (1964–1966). Since 1969 he has been Professor of Spanish American Social and Economic History at the Universidad Complutense, Madrid. He is also a researcher for the CSIC and has been a visiting professor in Lisbon, Guatemala, Paris-Nanterre, and Caracas. Some of his publications are *Urbanización de la población indígena* (1972), *Estudio bibliográfico del proceso urbano iberoamericano* (1973), and *Los mayas del siglo XVIII* (1974). He is Secretary of the Instituto "Fernandez de Oviedo" and Editor of the *Revista de Indias*. In 1974 he received the (Spanish) Premio Nacional de Literatura.

MELVIN L. FOWLER (1924–) was born in Gordon, Nebraska. He studied at Graceland College, Purdue University (B.S.C.E. 1946) and the University of Chicago (M.S., 1949; Ph.D., 1959). He was Curator of Anthropology at the Illinois State Museum (1949–1959), Assistant and Associate Professor of Anthropology and Curator of North American Archaeology at Southern Illinois University (1959–1966), and is now Professor of Anthropology at the University of Wisconsin, Milwaukee (1966–). He held a National Science Foundation Senior Postdoctoral Fellowship (1964–1965) for study at the National Museum of Anthropology of Mexico and Harvard University. His areas of interest are in the prehistory of the Midwestern United States and Central Mexico with special concern with the evolution of complex societies. He is the author of numerous articles and monographs; among his most recent is "Cahokia, ancient capital of the Midwest," Addison-Wesley Module in Anthropology no. 48.

MARÍA-PILAR GARCÍA (1947–) received the *Licenciado* degree in Sociology at the Universidad Andrés Bello in Caracas, Venezuela. In 1970, she received an M.A. in Demography at the University of Chicago. Presently she is finishing her Ph.D. dissertation on a sociological model of urban activities for the population of Ciudad Guayana, Venezuela, for that university and working as director of a major research project at the Corporación Venezolana de Guayana. Her areas of interests are urban planning, demography, human ecology, and urban sociology in Latin America. She is author of several articles about the matrifocal family in Latin America.

GRAZIANO GASPARINI (1926–) is Director of the Centro de Investigaciones Históricas y Estéticas and Professor of History of Architecture at the Universidad Central de Venezuela. He is also founder and editor of the *Boletín del Centro de Investigaciones Históricas y Estéticas*. His professional activities include the restoration of national monuments in Latin America as a consultant for UNESCO and OEA. He is presently involved in Venezuelan restorations as Director of the National Patrimony. Recent publications: *Los retablos del periodo colonial en Venezuela* (1971), *America, Barroco y Arquitectura* (1972), *El arte colonial en Venezuela* (1974), *Significado presente de la arquitectura del pasado* (1975), and (in collaboration with Luise Margolies) *Arquitectura Inka* (1976).

GABRIEL GUARDA GEYWITZ (1928–) is an architect and is Professor of Urban History and of History of the Church at the Catholic University of Santiago, Chile. He is Adjunct Director of the Anthropologic and Historic Museum of the Austral University of Chile, President of the subcommission of architecture of the National Commission for Sacred Arts, member of ICOMOS (UNESCO, Paris), etc. Among his more than seventy published works are *El urbanismo imperial y las primitivas ciudades de Chile* (1957), *La arquitectura rural en al Valle Central de Chile* (1968), *Tres reflexiones en torno a la fundación de la ciudad indiana* (1975), and *Historia urbana del reino de Chile* (1976).

JORGE E. HARDOY (1926–) was born in Buenos Aires and, after becoming an architect, received both his M.A. and Ph.D. in City Planning from Harvard University. He has served as Professor of Urban Planning both at the Universidad del Litoral in Rosario, Argentina, and at Yale University. Since 1966 he has served with the Center of Urban and Regional Studies of the Instituto Torcuato Di Tella in Buenos Aires, acting as Director until 1970 and as chief investigator since 1971. Between 1966 and 1970 he was President of the Interamerican Planning Society and he has published a great many works concerning urbanization in Latin America.

FRIEDRICH KATZ. No biographical data available.

NORA ROSE SCOTT KINZER (1936–) was educated at the University of Toronto (B.A., 1958), Middlebury College (M.A., 1959), and Purdue University (Ph.D., 1971). She served on the faculties of Earlham College and Purdue North Central and has been Senior Research Scientist at the Army Research Institute, Arlington, Virginia, since 1975. Since 1967 she has contributed – sometimes as organizer – many papers to seminars and symposia on the role of women in higher education, Latin American society, politics, the military, etc. Among her latest publications are articles in *Women cross-culturally: change and challenge* (1975) and in *Perspectivas femininas en América Latina* (1976).

GEORGE KUBLER (1912–) is Professor of History of Art at Yale University, where he has taught the history of ancient American art as well as the history of Iberian and Latin American art. His publications include works on the theory of art (*The shape of time*, 1962), on Mexican sixteenth-century architecture (1948), Maya iconography (1969), Portuguese architecture (1972), and art and the architecture in colonial Latin America (1959).

SPENCER LEWIS LEITMAN (1943–) studied at the University of Texas, Austin, where he received his Ph.D. in Latin American History in 1972. His dissertation research under a Fulbright-Hays Doctoral Dissertation Research Fellowship was conducted in southern Brazil in 1969–1970. He has taught at Purdue University and is currently in marketing research in New York City. His publications include studies in Brazilian, Portuguese, and United States history. He is presently working on two complementary studies on southern Brazilian history.

LARISSA LOMNITZ is a social anthropologist specializing in urban problems. A graduate of the University of California at Berkeley and the Universidad Iberoamericana, she lives in Mexico where she is a staff member of the Center for Applied Mathematics and Computer Science (CIMAS) at the University of Mexico. She also teaches at the School of Urban Planning and the Graduate School of Anthropology, both at the University of Mexico. Among her recent publications are "Reciprocity of assistance among the urban middle class of Chile," "The social and economic organization of a Mexican shanty town," and "Power structure and scientific productivity in a research institute." Her current interests include models of social interaction, networks of reciprocity and mutual assistance, and the influence of the power structure on human creativity.

NANCY LÓPEZ DE NISNOVICH (1934–) received her degree in Sociology from the University of Buenos Aires in 1967. She is currently doing research on the comparative development of Tucumán and Mendoza from 1850–1930. One of her papers, "The changes in the economic system and the forces of regionalization and population growth in the province of Buenos Aires," was presented to the IVth Congress of the Argentine Association of Social History and Economics in 1971.

MARKOS MAMALAKIS (1932–) was Visiting Professor at the University of Göttingen in 1976. After teaching at Berkeley, Yale, and the University of Chile, he is now Professor of Economics at the University of Wisconsin, Milwaukee, where he served for five years as Director of the Latin American Center. He has visited, lectured on, and published numerous studies on all Latin American and Caribbean nations, except Cuba. Born in Greece, where he graduated in law, economics, and politics, he studied in Munich, and received his M.A. and Ph.D. at the University of California, Berkeley.

SIDNEY DAVID MARKMAN, Professor of Art History and Archaeology, Duke University, Durham, North Carolina, has devoted the major part of his professional career to the study of the architecture and urbanization of colonial Central America. He is the author of *Colonial architecture of Antigua Guatemala* (1966), a definitive monograph on the architecture and urban history of the former capital of the Reino de Guatemala. He has also published a number of articles in the *Journal of the Society of Architectural Historians* and the *Boletín del Centro de Investigaciones Históricas y Estéticas*, Caracas, Venezuela, as well as a short monograph, *San Cristóbal de las Casas, Chiapas* (1963). Since 1966 he has been a participant in the symposia on urbanization held at the biennial International Congress of Americanists. *Colonial Central America: a bibliography* is to be published by the Arizona State University Press, Tempe, Arizona.

FRÉDÉRIC MAURO (1921–) was born at Valenciennes. He studied history and holds a law degree and a doctorat ès lettres. Between 1957 and 1967 he was Professor of Modern History, and later Professor of Economic History, at the University of Toulouse. He has been a visiting professor at the University of São Paulo and stayed as a UNESCO expert at the University of Nuevo León, Mexico. He received the silver medal of the Centre National de la Recherche Scientifique and is President of the Comité de Coordination des Historiens Latino-Américanistes Européens. Since 1967 he has been a Professor of Latin American History at the University of Paris X-Nanterre and he teaches also at the Institut des Hautes Études de l'Amérique Latine. Between 1960, when *Le Portugal et l'Atlantique au XVIIᵉ siècle* came out, and 1975, when he published *Do Brasil a América: ensaios de historia*, he wrote more than a dozen books.

ALEJANDRA MORENO TOSCANO (1940–) was born in Mexico City, received her Master's degree in History from El Colegio de México (1964) and a doctoral degree in History from the University of Paris (1967). She is Professor at the Colegio de México and is Director of the Seminario de Historia Urbana of the Departamento de Investigaciones Históricas, INAH. Her works include *Geografía económica de México, siglo XVI* (1968) and *El sector externo y la organización espacial y regional de México* (1974). She has also published several articles in *Urban History*.

RICHARD M. MORSE (1922–), Professor of History at Yale, holds a B.A. from Princeton and a Ph.D. from Columbia. He has taught at Columbia, the University of Puerto Rico, and the State University of New York and was Distinguished Lecturer at the University of Guyana (1975). A former fellow of the Guggenheim Foundation and the Center for Advanced Study in the Behavioral Sciences, he chaired the Conference on Latin American History (1969) and was social science adviser to the Ford Foundation in Brazil (1973–1975). His writings include *From community to metropolis: a biography of São Paulo, Brazil* (2nd ed., 1974), *The Bandeirantes* (1965) and several books on Latin American urbanization.

ANGELINA POLLAK-ELTZ (1932–) was born in Vienna, attended American colleges, studied at the universities of Perugia (Italy) and Geneva, and received a Ph.D. in Anthropology from the University of Vienna in 1964. She conducted field research among the Afro-venezuelans, the subject of her Ph.D. thesis. Since 1971 she has been a Professor of Anthropology at the Universidad Catolica Andrés Bello, Caracas. She serves as coeditor of the yearbook *Montalban* (Caracas) and of the *Review of Ethnology* (Vienna). Her writings include *Afrikanische Relikte in der Volkskultur Venezuelas* (1965), *Afroamerikaanse godsdiensten en culten* (1970), *The black family in Venezuela* (1974), and about 150 scientific papers. Her major interests are: syncretistic cults, and acculturation among blacks, migrants, and other minorities in rural and urban areas.

BARBARA J. PRICE obtained a Ph.D. in Anthropology at Columbia University in 1969 and has done fieldwork in Mexico and in Guatemala. Some of her major articles are "Prehispanic irrigation agriculture in nuclear America" (1971), "Commerce and cultural process in Meso-america" (1976), "Shifts in production and organization: a cluster-interaction model" (1977), and "Secondary state formation: an explanatory model" (1977). Her principal research interests are in ecological anthropology, cultural evolution, and sociocultural theory.

ALEJANDRO BORIS ROFMAN (1932–) was born in Rosario, Argentina. He received his B.A. in Economics from the University of Rosario in 1955, his doctorate in Economics from the University of Cordoba, Argentina, and an M.A. in Economics from the University of Penn-sylvania in 1965. He has been Professor of International Economics, Regional Economics, and Social Accounting in Argentine universities and foreign centers of graduate studies. He is a former Director and Researcher of the Center for Urban and Regional Studies in Buenos Aires (1967–1976). In Argentina and elsewhere he has been a member of urban and regional planning teams. Currently he is Visiting Researcher and Professor in CENDES, University of Venezuela, Caracas. His numerous publications include works on regional development in Latin America, the historical configuration of Argentine regional growth, and regional inequalities.

RICHARD P. SCHAEDEL received a Ph.D. in Anthropology from Yale in 1952 and is presently Professor of Anthropology at the University of Texas, Austin. He wrote several articles on prehistoric urbanization in Peru and published *El desarrollo urbano* (1959) and *La demografía y los recursos humanos del sur del Perú* (1967). Together with Jorge E. Hardoy he was coordinator of the symposia on "Urbanization in America from its beginnings to the present day," and editor of *The urbanization process in America from its origins to the present day* (1969) and of *Las ciudades de América Latina y sus areas de influencia a traves de la historia* (1976). From 1965–1970 he was (founding) Editor of the *Latin American Research Review*.

JAMES R. SCOBIE (1929–) was born in Valparaiso, Chile. He received his B.A. from the Woodrow Wilson School for Public and International Affairs at Princeton University in 1950 and his M.A. and Ph.D. in History at Harvard University in 1951 and 1954. A specialist in Argentine and Latin American socioeconomic history, he taught at the University of California, Berkeley (1957–1964) and Indiana University (1964–1977). He has received fellowships from the Social Science Research Council (1959–1960 and 1968–1969), Guggenheim (1967–1968), and National Endowment for the Humanities (1974–1976), and has been a fellow at the Institute for Latin American Studies, Columbia University (1962–1963), and the Institute for Advanced Study, Princeton (1974–1975). His current research explores the comparative urban growth of three Argentine provincial capitals, Corrientes, Salta, and Mendoza; previous major publications include *Revolution on the pampas; a social history of Argentine wheat, 1860–1910* (1964); *Argentina: a city and a nation* (2nd ed., 1971); and *Buenos Aires, plaza to suburb, 1870–1910* (1974).

MARGO L. SMITH (1943–) was educated at Indiana University. Currently she is Associate Professor of Anthropology and Director of the graduate Social Science program at Northeastern Illinois University. She is author of several articles on domestic service in Peru.

ALEX STEPICK, III (1948–) studied at the University of California, Santa Cruz and Irvine, where he received his Ph.D. in Anthropology in 1974. He was on the faculty of the School of Social Sciences, University of California, Irvine, before becoming Assistant Professor at the University of Texas at Dallas in 1975. Since 1974 he has been Research Consultant to the Instituto Nacional para el Desarrollo de la Comunidad Rural y de la Vivienda Popular, State of Oaxaca, Mexico, and lately he served as consultant to development projects in Dallas, Quito, and La Paz. He has contributed papers on migration and the influence of values on behavior to *Demografía y Economia*, *Ethnology*, *International Migration Review*, and *American Ethnologist*, among others. As contributing editor with H. A. Selby he wrote "Ethnography of Middle America: an annotated bibliography," in *Handbook of Latin American Studies* (1971). His research interests are Latin America, development and cultural change, research design and methodology, and urbanization.

Index of Names

Index of Subjects

Abiseo, ruins of, 192
Acámbaro, New Spain, 414, 415
Acapulco, port, Mexico, 256, 257
Acllahuasí weavers, 209
Acta de los cabildos (municipal records of Spanish colonies), 99
Acultzingo, New Spain, 409 n
Adaptation to environment, 52–53
Administrative centers, of colonial Latin America, 142–143, 273; *audiencias*, 83, 84, 225–256, 283; municipalities, 114, 115–116
Administrative function, in Spanish colonial cities, 80–81, 82–85. *See also* Bureaucracy; Centralization; Government
Adobe industry, 538, 540
Aerial photography, and deduction, 186
Africa: labor from, 284; Portuguese in, 232; racial elements from, 481; West India Company, 232
Agave cactus, juice from, 408 and n 9
Agrarian: institution, in Spanish America, 252–253, 284–286; reform, 8–9, 527. *See also* Agriculture
Agriculture: in Andes, 193–195; in Argentina, 443, 445–446, 447–448; Aztec, 469; in Brazil, 19th C., 512–514, 520, 523, of Italy, 15–16th C., 218–222; in Java, involution, 606; in New Spain, 18th C., 401–402, 403–405, 405–406, 408, 412, 414, 416, 418–419, 420; prehistoric potential, 38–39; as primary sector, 155, 156; after Spanish conquest, 67, 103; subsistence farmers, 520, 530; terracing, 194–195; in Venezuela, 527, 530, 531. *See also* Cereals; Maize; Plantations; Wheat

Agua de Onda, 42
Ahuacatlán, Mexico, and migration, 393, 394, 395
Aigues-Mortes, 13th C., 332 n
Alcohol, drinking: in Mexico City shanty town, 550, 551, 552, 555, 558, 566; in Oaxaca, 629; in Venezuela, 598
'Alejandro', of Colonia Benito Juarez, Oaxaca, value system of, 620–623, 626, 628–630
Alimentation. *See* Food
Alkmaar, Holland, 236, 238, 239
Amalucan, Mexico, early town site, 177, 180–183
Amazon Basin, population clustering in, 53
America. *See* Latin America; Mesoamerica; North America; United States of America; *place names*
Amsterdam, Holland: expansion of, 238, 239; houses of, 242; in 17th C., 236; and trade, 235–236
Ancud, Chile, 360, 361, 375
Andean: agriculture, 194–195; archaeology, 185–187; high mountain forests, 194–199; organization of Middle Horizon, 191–193; peasants, family structure of, 531, 533–535; pre-Columbian sites, 185–193. *See also* Andes, the
Andes, the: Inca conquest of, 186, 191–193; on break-up of Inca Empire, 193; hierarchy of authority in, 465; population centers, pre-Columbian, 191–193. *See also* Andean
Angol, Chile (Los Confines): fortification of, 347 and n 13; layout of, 351–352; many refoundings of, 344 n; *1611* displacement of, 348